THE OXFORD HANDBOO

AMERICAN PHILOSOPHY

Cheryl Misak presents the first collective study of the development of philosophy in North America, from the 18th century to the end of the 20th century. Twenty-six leading experts examine distinctive features of American philosophy, trace notable themes, and consider the legacy and influence of leading figures. This will be the first reference point for future work on the subject, and a fascinating resource for anyone interested in modern philosophy or American intellectual history.

Cheryl Misak is Professor of Philosophy and Deputy Provost at the University of Toronto

THE OXFORD HANDBOOK OF

AMERICAN PHILOSOPHY

edited by

CHERYL MISAK

OXFORD

UNIVERSITY PRESS

OXFORD
UNIVERSITY PRESS

Great Clarendon Street, Oxford ox2 6DP

Oxford University Press is a department of the University of Oxford.
It furthers the University's objective of excellence in research, scholarship,
and education by publishing worldwide in

Oxford New York

Auckland Cape Town Dar es Salaam Hong Kong Karachi
Kuala Lumpur Madrid Melbourne Mexico City Nairobi
New Delhi Shanghai Taipei Toronto

With offices in

Argentina Austria Brazil Chile Czech Republic France Greece
Guatemala Hungary Italy Japan Poland Portugal Singapore
South Korea Switzerland Thailand Turkey Ukraine Vietnam

Oxford is a registered trade mark of Oxford University Press
in the UK and in certain other countries

Published in the United States
by Oxford University Press Inc., New York

British Library Cataloguing in Publication Data

Data available

Library of Congress Cataloging-in-Publication Data

The Oxford handbook of American philosophy / edited by Cheryl Misak.
p. cm.—(Oxford handbooks in philosophy)
Includes Index.
ISBN-13: 978–0–19–921931–5 (alk. paper) 1. Philosophy, American,
I. Misak, C.J. (Cheryl J.)
B851.094 2008
191—dc22
2008015965

Typeset by SPI Publisher Services, Pondicherry, India
Printed in Great Britain
on acid-free paper by
Ashford Colour Press Ltd, Gosport, Hampshire

ISBN 978–0–19–921931–5 (hbk)
978–0–19–959247–0 (pbk)

1 3 5 7 9 10 8 6 4 2

PREFACE

'American Philosophy' is of course rather a large topic. While I have tried to have as much of it covered as is possible in a mere few hundred pages, there are no doubt many individual philosophers and topics that deserved more (or indeed some) attention. But perhaps the reader who is alert to the gaps will reflect not only that the aim here was to cover two centuries of philosophical thought, across domains of philosophy as diverse as logic and ethics, but also that a set of challenges was faced due to the geographic nature of the subject matter. What counts as American philosophy? And who counts as an American philosopher?

With respect to the first question, the whole of the Americas are not covered—that would have resulted in a completely unwieldy project and would have destroyed whatever unity there is to be found in the subject matter. There is of course a home-grown philosophy in America—the pragmatism that originated in the mid to late 1800s in Cambridge, Massachusetts. But it would be silly to take pragmatism to be definitive of the spirit of the whole of American philosophy. So I have tried to get across much of pragmatism, from C.S. Peirce to Richard Rorty, without leaving the impression that pragmatism somehow still lingers on every American philosopher's palate.

With respect to the second question, philosophy is an international enterprise, with scholars moving from country to country. I and many of the contributors had to make a set of decisions about who to count as being American. One easy decision was to include the logical empiricists, that impressive set of Germans and Austrians who put what looks like an indelible stamp on philosophy of science and epistemology once they hit the shores of North America. But of course, not all the decisions were that clear-cut. We have tried to speak of those philosophers who spent a significant part of their intellectual life in the United States or had an enormous influence on the way philosophy was practiced there. No doubt this set of decisions will not please everyone.

I thank the contributors for the time and effort they put into their chapters. Those who responded promptly to my initial request have been exceedingly patient and need to be thanked for their good humor as well. Peter Momtchiloff and Nadiah Al-Ammar at Oxford University Press were most helpful, and Mikki Choman went well beyond the call of duty during the final production stages.

Cheryl Misak

Contents

List of Contributors   x

1. Jonathan Edwards and Eighteenth-Century Religious
   Philosophy   1
   ROGER A. WARD

2. Emerson, Romanticism, and Classical American
   Pragmatism   19
   RUSSELL B. GOODMAN

3. Peirce and Pragmatism: American Connections   38
   DOUGLAS ANDERSON

4. William James   60
   HENRY JACKMAN

5. John Dewey: Inquiry, Ethics, and Democracy   87
   MATTHEW FESTENSTEIN

6. Josiah Royce: Idealism, Transcendentalism, Pragmatism   110
   KELLY A. PARKER

7. George Santayana: Ordinary Reflection Systematized   125
   GLENN TILLER

8. A Pragmatist World View: George Herbert Mead's
   Philosophy of the Act   144
   CORNELIS DE WAAL

9. W. E. B. Du Bois: Double-Consciousness, Jamesian
   Sympathy, and the Critical Turn   169
   MITCHELL ABOULAFIA

10. The Pragmatist Family Romance   185
    ROBERT WESTBROOK

11. The Reception of Early American Pragmatism   197
    CHERYL MISAK

12. Whitehead's Metaphysical System   224
    JOHN W. LANGO

13. Thorstein Veblen and American Social Criticism   235
    JOSEPH HEATH

14. Pragmatism and the Cold War   254
    ROBERT TALISSE

15. Pragmatism and the Given: C. I. Lewis, Quine, and Peirce   269
    CHRISTOPHER HOOKWAY

16. W. V. Quine   290
    ARIF AHMED

17. Philosophy of Science in America   339
    ALAN RICHARDSON

18. The Influence of Wittgenstein on American Philosophy   375
    HANS-JOHANN GLOCK

19. Placing in a Space of Norms: Neo-Sellarsian Philosophy
    in the Twenty-first Century   403
    MARK LANCE

20. Rorty, Davidson, and the Future of Metaphysics
    in America   430
    BJØRN RAMBERG

21. Analytic Philosophy in America   449
    SCOTT SOAMES

22. Logic and the Foundations of Mathematics   482
    DANIELLE MACBETH

23. Liberal Equality: What, Where, and Why   515
    KOK-CHOR TAN

24. Legal Philosophy in America   551
    BRIAN H. BIX

25. American Moral Philosophy   578
    BRAD HOOKER

26. Essences, Intersections, and American Feminism   595
    ANN GARRY

Name Index   627

Subject Index   639

LIST OF CONTRIBUTORS

Mitchell Aboulafia is Chair of the Department of Liberal Arts and Professor of Liberal Arts and Philosophy at the Juilliard School. He is the author of *The Cosmopolitan Self: George Herbert Mead and Continental Philosophy* (University of Illinois Press, 2006); *The Mediating Self: Mead, Sartre, and Self-Determination* (Yale University Press, 1986); *The Self-Winding Circle: A Study of Hegel's System* (Warren Green, 1982); and of articles on social theory, as well as on the relationship between American and continental philosophy. He is the editor of *Philosophy, Social Theory, and the Thought of George Herbert Mead* and co-editor of *Habermas and Pragmatism*.

Arif Ahmed is a fellow of Girton College, Cambridge, and a Lecturer in the Faculty of Philosophy.

Douglas Anderson is Professor of Philosophy at Southern Illinois University, Carbondale. His interests are American philosophy and the history of philosophy. He has authored several books on American philosophy and presently writes on the relations between philosophy and other features of American culture.

Brian H. Bix is the Frederick W. Thomas Professor of Law and Philosophy at the University of Minnesota. His publications include *Jurisprudence: Theory and Context* (4th edn., Sweet & Maxwell, 2006); *A Dictionary of Legal Theory* (Oxford University Press, 2004), and *Law, Language, and Legal Determinacy* (Clarendon Press, 1993).

Cornelis de Waal is Associate Professor in Philosophy and Graduate Director at Indiana University/Purdue University, Indianapolis. He is also associate editor of the *Writings of Charles S. Peirce: A Chronological Edition*, which is being published in thirty volumes by Indiana University Press, and of the *Transactions of the Charles S. Peirce Society*. He has published several books, including *On Mead* (Wadsworth, 2002), and *Susan Haack: A Lady of Distinctions. The Philosopher Responds to Her Critics* (Prometheus, 2007).

Matthew Festenstein is Professor of Political Philosophy at the University of York. His books include *Pragmatism and Political Theory: From Dewey to Rorty* (University of Chicago Press, 1997); *Negotiating Diversity: Culture, Deliberation, Trust* (Polity Press, 2005); (co-editor with Richard Rorty) *Critical Dialogues* (Polity Press, 2001); *Political Ideologies* (Oxford University Press, 2005); and *Radicalism in English Political Thought, 1550–1850* (Cambridge University Press, 2007).

Ann Garry is Professor Emerita of Philosophy at California State University, Los Angeles, and Visiting Professor of Philosophy at UCLA. She has written about feminist philosophy since the 1970s and co-edited *Women, Knowledge and Reality* (Routledge, 1996).

Hans-Johann Glock is Professor of Philosophy at the University of Zurich and Visiting Professor at the University of Reading. He is the author of *A Wittgenstein Dictionary* (Blackwell, 1996), *Quine and Davidson on Language, Thought and Reality* (Cambridge University Press, 2003) and *What is Analytic Philosophy?* (Cambridge University Press, 2008). He has edited *The Rise of Analytic Philosophy* (Blackwell, 1997), *Wittgenstein: A Critical Reader* (Blackwell, 2001), and *Strawson and Kant* (Oxford University Press, 2003), and co-edited (with Robert L. Arrington) *Wittgenstein's Philosophical Investigations* (Routledge, 1991), *Wittgenstein and Quine* (Routledge, 1996) and (with John Hyman) *Wittgenstein and Analytic Philosophy* (Oxford University Press, 2008).

Russell B. Goodman is Regents' Professor of Philosophy at the University of New Mexico. He is the author of *American Philosophy and the Romantic Tradition* (Cambridge University Press, 1990) and *Wittgenstein and Willliam James* (Cambridge University Press, 2002), and of papers on Emerson, James, Dewey, Putnam, and Cavell. He is the editor of *Contending with Stanley Cavell* (Oxford University Press, 2005), *Pragmatism: Critical Concepts in Philosophy*, 4 vols. (Routledge, 2005), and *Pragmatism: A Contemporary Reader* (Routledge, 1995). In 2003 and 2005 he directed summer seminars on Emerson for the National Endowment for the Humanities, and in 2007 he directed an NEH summer seminar entitled 'Pragmatism: A Living Tradition'.

Joseph Heath is Associate Professor in the Department of Philosophy at the University of Toronto. He is the author of *Communicative Action and Rational Choice* (MIT Press, 2001), *The Efficient Society* (Penguin, 2001), and, with Andrew Potter, *The Rebel Sell* (HarperCollins, 2004). His research focuses on practical rationality and critical social theory.

Brad Hooker is Professor of Moral Philosophy at the University of Reading. His *Ideal Code, Real World* was published by Oxford University Press in 2000.

Christopher Hookway is Professor of Philosophy at the University of Sheffield.

Henry Jackman is Associate Professor of Philosophy at Toronto's York University. He works primarily in the philosophies of language and mind, and the history of American philosophy, particularly William James. A full CV, and copies of most of this work can be found at <www.jackman.org.>

Mark Lance is Professor of Philosophy and Professor of Justice and Peace at Georgetown University. He has published more than thirty articles primarily in the areas of philosophy of language, philosophical logic, and epistemology. He and Rebecca Kukla recently completed *'Yo!' and 'Lo!': The Pragmatic Topography of the Space of Reasons* (forthcoming from Harvard University Press). He is currently at work on a philosophical exploration of anarchist politics, written for the benefit of activists rather than philosophers.

John W. Lango is Professor of Philosophy at Hunter College of the City University of New York. He is the author of *Whitehead's Ontology* (SUNY Press, 1972), as well as many papers on metaphysics and ethics. He is a co-editor of *Rethinking the Just War Tradition*.

Danielle Macbeth is T. Wistar Brown Professor of Philosophy at Haverford College in Pennsylvania. She is the author of *Frege's Logic* (Harvard University Press, 2005) and has also published on a variety of issues in the philosophy of language, philosophy of mind, history and philosophy of mathematics, and other areas.

Cheryl Misak is Professor of Philosophy at the University of Toronto. She is the author of *Truth and the End of Inquiry: A Peircean Account of Truth* (Clarendon Press, 1991, rev. 2004), *Verificationism: Its History and Prospects* (Routledge, 1995), *Truth, Politics, Morality* (Routledge, 2000), and the editor of *New Pragmatists* (Oxford University Press, 2007) and *The Cambridge Companion to Peirce* (Cambridge University Press, 2004).

Kelly A. Parker is Associate Professor and Chair of the Department of Philosophy at Grand Valley State University in Allendale, Michigan. He was a founding officer of the Josiah Royce Society and served as the Society's President in 2007. His research focuses on American philosophy and environmental philosophy.

Bjørn Ramberg is a professor of philosophy at the University of Oslo, where he is affiliated with the Centre for the Study of Mind in Nature. His publications include essays on Rorty, Davidson, and Dennett.

Alan Richardson is Professor and Distinguished University Scholar in the Department of Philosophy at the University of British Columbia. He is the author of many essays in history of philosophy of science and of the book *Carnap's Construction of the World* (Cambridge University Press, 1997), as well as co-editor of several volumes, including, with Thomas Uebel, *The Cambridge Companion to Logical Empiricism* (Cambridge University Press, 2007).

Scott Soames is Director of the School of Philosophy at the University of Southern California, and author of *Philosophical Analysis in the Twentieth Century* (Princeton University Press, 2003).

Robert Talisse is Associate Professor of Philosophy and Political Science at Vanderbilt University. His work focuses on contemporary political philosophy and pragmatism. His most recent book is *A Pragmatist Philosophy of Democracy* (Routledge, 2007).

Kok-Chor Tan is Associate Professor of Philosophy at the University of Pennsylvania. He works in social and political philosophy, with special interests in topics of global justice. His writings include *Toleration, Diversity and Global Justice* (Penn State Press, 2000) and *Justice without Borders* (Cambridge University Press, 2004).

Glenn Tiller is Assistant Professor of Philosophy at Texas A&M University–Corpus Christi and co-director of the Santayana Society. His work has appeared in the *Journal of the History of Philosophy* and *The Transactions of the Charles S. Peirce Society*.

Roger A. Ward is an associate professor of philosophy at Georgetown College. His publications include *Conversion in American Philosophy* (Fordham University Press, 2004) and articles on Peirce, James, Dewey, and Edwards.

Robert Westbrook is Professor of History at the University of Rochester.

CHAPTER 1

JONATHAN EDWARDS AND EIGHTEENTH-CENTURY RELIGIOUS PHILOSOPHY

ROGER A. WARD

A. INTRODUCTION

JONATHAN EDWARDS (1703–58) is widely considered to be one of North America's most influential theologians and philosophers, but he remains an intensely disputed figure even after nearly three centuries of debate. As a pastor and evangelist, Edwards is credited with sparking the revival that developed into the Great Awakening in New England (1740–4) and redefining the literary form of the Puritan sermon. Some of his best-known works are polemic defenses of Puritan doctrines, *Freedom of the Will* and *Original*

Sin, but his constructive treatises—*The History of the Work of Redemption, Religious Affections, The Nature of True Virtue, The End for Which God Created the World*—and his many sermons and notebooks also reveal a creative philosophical conception that transcended the thought of his day and continues to be fertile ground for scholarship and speculation. Though Edwards speaks in the idiom of eighteenth-century intellectual discourse, his intention is to 'discover' or disclose to his readers the reorienting power of Christian revelation. Edwards's conception of the reality of the divine being, developed from his holistic approach to scripture, his close observation of religious experience in himself and others, and his philosophical analysis, dramatically transformed the Puritan tradition and deeply influenced the development of philosophy in North America. Understanding the origin, content, and coherence of Edwards's philosophy remains a significant task.

Reading Edwards as a philosopher is daunting. Because he quotes few of his sources, and the complexity and volume of his writing is overwhelming, it is easy to discount Edwards's connection to human problems. His human side appears in experiences like his youthful struggle with Calvinism and the 'horrible doctrine' of God's judgment (Edwards 1998: 792) and a conflict with his parents, probably about his status for communion. He did not meet his father's strict standards (Marsden 2003: 57). Later he was confronted by the position of his grandfather Solomon Stoddard, who opened access to communion widely as a 'means of conversion'. In this confused setting Edwards engages his deepest theological and philosophical questions.

Personal spiritual responses are an opening, in Edwards's estimation, for discovering the reality of divine influence. A case in point is Abigail Hutchinson, a quiet unmarried woman not given to enthusiasm. 'She seemed to be astonished', Edwards says, 'at what she read, as what was *real* and very *wonderful*, but quite new to her. ... she wondered within herself that she had never heard of it before; but then immediately recollected herself, and though she had often heard of it and read it, but never till now *saw it as real*' (Edwards 1974: 356). The dynamic response of the divine to the active seeking and perceiving of his congregants deeply influenced Edwards's conception of God's sovereignty. John E. Smith notes that in these events Edwards is 'looking into the heart of the activity of the Spirit in regeneration, not engaged in theological accounts of the manner in which the transformation is supposed to take place, but instead in the description of what *actually* happened' (Smith 1992: 6). In a note to himself, Edwards writes: 'what I need to give a clear and more immediate view of the perfections and glory of God, is a clear knowledge of the manner of God's exerting himself, with respect to spirits and minds, as I have, of his operations concerning matter and bodies' (Marsden 2003: 104). As a young man, Edwards planned a treatise entitled 'A Rational Account of the Main Doctrines of the Christian Religion Attempted', but the works he produced focused instead on interpreting the signs of the work of divine grace and understanding the reality of God who actively transforms souls by 'experimental' means.

Edwards was first and foremost an intellectual for his community, and an account of his place in the philosophical landscape can best be viewed from this perspective. The founding hope of the Puritans was that a faithful religious community, ordered by a covenant with God, would enlighten the whole world. Perry Miller perhaps overemphasizes the self-critical ambition of this 'errand into the wilderness', although New England's identity with Israel led to a New World history that developed into a sacred mythology. This mythology warranted the cultural preservation and continuity of the Puritan community as the prime exemplar of a good human society (Stout 1986: 69). Edwards challenged the confidence common to Puritan practice, but not supported theologically, that meeting external conditions in some way obligated God to preserve the covenant with New England. His use of Locke, Hutcheson, and other modern thinkers is in part a response to Puritanism's failure to describe adequately the transformation of human souls. Philosophy was an opening for productive conceptual inquiry so long as it continued to center on the deliverance of revelation. Edwards exposed the fault line internal to Puritan thinking by affirming that God works through chosen nations and people, but that 'this people'—the current generation—had no guarantee of place. The covenant could be lost by rejecting God's overtures; New England could become a *negative* example in the realization of God's kingdom. Edwards's theology of political history turns on understanding the response of a 'whole person' to the sovereign and gracious God as a microcosm of ultimate reality. This was Edwards's intellectual task for his community.

B. EDUCATION AND IDEALISM

Edwards's collegiate education reflected the tumultuousness of Puritan life. Competing locations and theological orientations that divided students and tutors finally resolved into the institution of Yale College. Records of Edwards's reading are incomplete, but lists from shortly after his time show a range of authors, including standard works of divinity, as well as Descartes, Locke, and Newton. (forthcoming *Works of Jonathan Edwards*, xxvii). In an essay entitled 'Of Being' dating from the 1720s, Edwards states his dual conviction of the 'impossibility that there is nothing', which demonstrates a necessary, infinite, and omnipresent being, and that 'nothing has existence anywhere but in consciousness' (1980: 204). He adopts a phrase of the Cambridge Platonist Henry More in stating that 'space is God', in order to formulate the ultimate character of that which subsists in the absence of any material bodies. He infers that 'beings that have knowledge and consciousness are the only proper and real and substantial beings' (Edwards 1980: 204), setting himself squarely against materialism.

Another early essay, 'The Mind', most likely begun in 1723, contains Edwards's seminal terms 'excellency', 'proportion', 'entity', and 'consent', around which he constructs an ontology of relation. His beginning point is the preference for harmony and beauty in natural and spiritual beings. Excellency, the characteristic agreement of the divine mind with itself, is the basis of moral and aesthetic beauty and all value; hence it is the ultimate principle of all relations. In 'The Mind' Edwards appropriates Locke's idea that 'truth is the agreement of our ideas with existence', but modifies this idea in the sense that 'God and real existence are the same' (1980: 344–5). In a triadic formulation worthy of C. S. Peirce, Edwards says: 'Happiness consists in the perception of these three things: of the consent of being to its own being; of its own consent to being; and of being's consent to being' (1980: 338).

In the section immediately following this sentence Edwards remarks that for Locke a mind or spirit is 'nothing else but consciousness, and what is included in it' (1980: 342). The implied criticism or question is whether Locke's notion of consciousness can support the discovery of excellency. In another place he writes: 'Intelligent beings are the end of creation, that their end must be to behold and admire the doings of God, and to magnify him for them, and to contemplate his glories in them. . . . for we are to remember that the world exists only mentally, so that the very being of the world implies its being perceived or discovered' (Edwards 1980: 79).

Edwards also deviates from Locke's idea of substance. Locke says that 'we have as clear a notion of the substance of spirit as we have of body, the substratum of operations in ourselves within' (Locke 1959: 395). Simple ideas connect directly to 'what is', and abstractions from these ideas constitute general ideas. Edwards disagrees, claiming that general ideas arise from a habit of mind that collects like to like. The constitution of consciousness occurs by experience of orders of relations, not a compounding of simple ideas.

In addition, Edwards argues that the divine consciousness stands in relation to created consciousnesses through rules that reflect the orders of relation. Wallace Anderson points out that Edwards's view 'excludes . . . the very notion of substance as it was entertained during this period. The claim that every real being *must*, as a condition of its reality, stand in some relation to other things, and even to all the other things, implies that the universe is necessarily pluralistic' (Edwards 1980: 85). Consciousnesses are not independent substances, but a 'plurality of items that stand in the same relations as those of the other' (Edwards 1980: 85). Altogether, this real order of ideas comprises what Edwards calls 'the system of the ideal world' (1980: 357). Edwards's realist conception of the order of nature anticipates a pragmatic sense of inquiry, for 'any difference in supposed objects or events implies some difference in the states of affairs that actually are or eventually will be perceived by some mind' (1980: 108).

Edwards is explicitly clear about the potential of intellectual discovery: 'were our thoughts comprehensive and perfect enough, our view of the present state of the world would excite in us a perfect idea of all past changes' (1980: 354). Inquiry into the origin and character of consciousness reveals not an opaque substance, but an intelligible structure that reflects the perfection of the created universe. This is a claim that Edwards later brought to the test in *Religious Affections*, as we will see below. Sang Lee notes that, for Edwards, 'Human beings, as intelligent creatures occupy a unique position in which their laws are singular enough, and their independence from laws of matter great enough, so that they can be said to possess a "secondary and dependent arbitrariness"' (Lee 1998: 73). The arbitrariness of divine action that is the essence of God's sovereignty reflects a habit or pattern of action. So, as Edwards says, 'Man's soul influences the body, continues its nature and powers and constant regular motions and productions, and actuates it as the supreme principle does the universe' (Edwards 1994: 451–2). In this sense intelligent beings act creatively by virtue of an arbitrariness that harmonizes with the arbitrariness of divine action.

Norman Fiering notes that references to harmony were abundant in Edwards's context, for instance in Heereboord, but that Edwards advances a rather scholastic conception where the supreme value is unity (Fiering 1981: 73). Fiering also points out Edwards's similarity to Malebranche's notion that 'though God governs and conserves in accordance with rules and laws determined by perfect wisdom, he does not alter or go against wisdom. Therefore it is appropriate to interpret the world through order, harmony, and beauty' (Fiering 1981: 79). In Edwards's words, 'Truth as to external things, is the consistency of our ideas with those ideas, or that train and series of ideas, that are raised in our minds according to God's stated order and law' (1980: 342).

About the time Edwards wrote these essays or shortly after they were completed, he confesses that he was in a 'low, sunk estate and condition' of religion (Marsden 2003: 111). Whether this spiritual low had direct relation to the comprehensive defense of Christianity that he intended to write, a lack of confidence in his conclusions, or some other specific cause is unclear. About this time, 1727, Edwards began his notes on Scripture, which would grow into one of his major intellectual projects. He also began articles on deism that would inform much of his later writing. Married and settled in Northampton, Edwards wrote his first sermon to be published, 'God Glorified in Man's Dependence', in 1731. 'Man was created holy,' he states, 'for it became God to create holy all his reasonable creatures. It would have been a disparagement to the holiness of God's nature, if he had made an intelligent creature unholy. But now when fallen man is made holy, it is from mere arbitrary grace; God may forever deny holiness to the fallen creature if he pleases, without any disparagement to any of his perfections.' The power of God, though, is sensible in conversion and enriches life with all good. He continues: 'That holy and happy being, and spiritual life, which is produced in the work of conversion, is a far greater and more glorious effect. ... [T]he state from whence the change is made is far more remote from the state attained, than mere death or non-entity' (Edwards 1999b: 204–5). An echo of 'The Mind' is evident in this juxtaposition of non-entity to the glorious state of conversion, which marks a turning of sorts for Edwards from a focus on the philosophical ground of idealism and relational ontology to a theological expression and expansion of these themes.

C. AWAKENING AND AFFECTIONS

The core of Edwards's mature philosophical formulation occurs in the context of religious awakening from 1736 to 1744. The phenomenon of the Awakening challenged Edwards's understanding of the valid responses to the work of grace.

This was a pastoral as well as a theological concern that had long occupied his thought. His pre-revival sermon 'A Divine and Supernatural Light' (1734) explored the peculiar effect of grace by which God 'unites himself with the mind of a saint, takes him for his temple, actuates and influences him as a new, supernatural principle of life and action' in which God 'communicates himself there in his own proper nature' (Edwards 1999*b*: 411). While the light shines only according to God's sovereign action, Edwards urged his congregation to 'earnestly seek' and 'move to it' (1999*b*: 423).

A fuller exploration of the effects of the discovery of God's excellency appears in the *Religious Affections* (1746). In this text Edwards uses and quotes more sources than in any of his other writings. He refers primarily to Puritan divines, and most extensively to Thomas Shepard. An exception is John Smith, a sixteenth-century Cambridge Platonist who, although not a theologian, described 'the excellency and nobleness of true religion' discovered through a spiritual sensation by means of which the truths of religion are apprehended (Edwards 1959: 66). Edwards explores the distinction of this sensation from natural forms of sense, and the alterations within the understanding and active character of individuals that signify its presence.

True religion, Edwards begins, consists primarily in affections, such as love and joy. These are not emotions, but depend on understanding the *object* of love as well as *receiving* the gift of joy. Edwards's original insight, according to John E. Smith, is the uniformity of the gifts of the spirit in true religion with the 'vigorous and sensible exercises of inclination and will' (Smith 1999: 6). 'Affections' refer to the orientation that is discovered within a person's inclinations. A *gracious* affection arises when God 'discovers' himself to the soul sufficient to effect a reorientation of the inclinations. Smith also points out that the gracious affections are not signs indicating the influence of a remote being, 'God'; for Edwards the affections *are* the real presence of the divine Spirit in the soul.

Part 2 of the *Affections* describes twelve signs that give *no clear evidence* of a gracious change in the soul, followed in Part 3 by twelve positive signs of gracious affection. This part of the text has attracted the most scholarly attention. One way of portraying the twelve signs, which are given without an explanation of their number or order, is a fourfold progression of discovery of the excellency of God within the soul's inclinations. Signs 1–3 describe an aesthetic sense of wholeness which Edwards connects to the 'new simple idea' of the metaphysicians, which is a not a new conception but a principle perceived within the understanding that acts as a 'new foundation' in the mind. Sign 3 is that the moral perfection of God becomes an object of the understanding that is loved for its beauty. Next, signs 4–6 follow the individual's reflexive awareness of a new principle in the understanding and will, which Edwards calls the 'sense of the heart'. Sign 5 is the conviction of the truths of the gospel concerning Jesus as the orienting principle of the understanding *and* the will, and sign 6, evangelical humiliation, is the recognition of the extreme state of sin discovered by the absence of the excellency of Christ in the soul. The discovery of the soul's utter helplessness to reorient itself is a work of grace that is answered in signs 7–9. Sign 7, conversion, is an 'alteration in the very nature of the soul' that is 'peculiar to the Spirit of the Lord' which brings a 'new nature' that abides in the soul through the appearance of a Christ-like spirit among the affections. The fourth series of signs, 10–12, describe the beauty, stability, and manifestation in practical living of gracious affections (Ward 2004: 9–19).

Edwards's conception of the soul and the discovery of divine excellency in the *Affections* holds together relational ontology, Puritan theology, and the revival experience in a remarkably coherent description. From this position Edwards was able to perceive the threats to true religion inside and outside his tradition, and to place his thought in relation to the philosophers and theologians of his age. The *Affections* also solidified his conviction that Stoddard's policy of open communion was an error. Extending the rights of membership to men and women who did not exhibit signs of gracious affection truncated their further discovery of God's gracious work. Edwards correctly anticipated that this change of polity would bring 'a separation between me and my people' (1998: 327), and after a drawn-out conflict over the qualification for participating in communion, Edwards was removed from his pulpit. After another year of delay, in 1750 he moved with his family to the small outpost of Stockbridge, where he ministered to a mixed congregation of settlers and Housatanic natives.

D. STOCKBRIDGE TREATISES

One of the reasons for Edwards's forced removal from Northampton was a resistance, even among the faithful, to his doctrinally informed interpretation of religious experience. He discerned a shift in the foundation of Christian thinking toward a dependence on reason as a guide to morality and religion, which manifested itself as a source of anti-conversion pressure and an impulse to seize the false remedy of Arminianism. Edwards responded to this condition by demonstrating the coherence of his philosophical/theological thought formed in close union with his understanding of the coherence of Scripture. In *Freedom of the Will* (1754) Edwards challenges the Arminian understanding of the will, buttressing the doctrinal basis of Calvinism more on philosophical than on theological grounds. Given the absence of theological disputation in this text, Gerald McDermott suggests that exposing Arminianism was a step in Edwards's larger plan to prevent 'the disaster of deism' spreading in New England (McDermott 1992: 47).

Edwards's philosophical defense of Christian orthodoxy had, and continues to have, a monumental influence on American Christianity (Guelzo 1989), through his demonstration of the inconsistency in thinking 'the will itself determines all the free acts of the will'. This is based on the 'great absurdity' that the choice of motive from which free acts follow implies a free act of choice before a free act of choice (Edwards 1957: 189). A self-grounding will violates the stable senses of words and ideas. For instance, 'necessity' in its common sense means 'that one thing supposed, the other certainly follows', while philosophers and divines used the term 'contingent' of an action when 'its connection with its causes is not discerned' (Edwards 1957: 155). Edwards also points out that Arminians, following Locke's lead, consider 'the will' to be something like an independent agent. He strenuously rejects this understanding by emphasizing 'that which has the power is the *soul*' (1957: 163; my emphasis).

The intellectual context of this treatise is significant. There was no official school or spokesperson for Arminianism, so Edwards's choice of interlocutors in a way substantiated this movement, and of the three primary figures he selected, two were more deist than Arminian. Thomas Chubb, a deist, claimed that, in order to be free, the very first in the whole series of actions must be excited by a previous motive (Edwards 1957: 229). Edwards replies that 'when the self-moving power is exerted, it becomes the necessary cause of its effects', reducing his position to 'a heap of absurdities' (1957: 235). This rebuttal is more than a rhetorical flourish. Demonstrating the internal inconsistency of Chubb's position undermines the Arminian claim that Calvinism forced one into irrational corners. At best, Chubb was exchanging one irrational position for another.

Daniel Whitby, an Anglican divine, argued that moral worth depends on the agent's original state of indifference before acting. Only then can a person act freely and earn moral approbation or guilt. Edwards responds to Whitby by showing the impossibility of a state of 'indifference', and pointing out that even Jesus would not meet Whitby's condition of moral worth since he was 'not free to do or refrain' from his actions as Messiah. Again, the rhetorical device draws attention to Whitby's dismissal of the essence of the Christian gospel in order to justify his account of freedom. Finally, Edwards takes up the ideas of Isaac Watts, a former Calvinist and friend who promoted his revival writings in England. Watts says that any 'necessary' action cannot be free. The regularity of God's character and freedom appears in that it is 'impossible [for God] to act otherwise' than in the most fitting way. Edwards shows that this amounts to necessity under a new name, and so according to Watt's own account, 'God exercises no moral excellence, exercising no freedom in these things, because he acts by moral necessity' (Edwards 1957: 382). And if God cannot be morally free according to this understanding, how can this way of thinking support our moral freedom?

Edwards is sensitive to the Arminian goal of locating human responsibility and understanding freedom. But this legitimate inquiry becomes destructive both to human reason and to practice when it vainly challenges God's sovereign choice of those who receive grace and denies the necessity of holiness. He muses, a little sarcastically, whether it would it be better for these thinkers if there were *no* end in view for God's actions (Edwards 1957: 394). Then, in his typical fashion, he runs the opposing position to its logical conclusion: 'Instead of a moral necessity of God's will, arising from or consisting in the infinite perfection and blessedness of the divine Being, we have a fixed unalterable state of things . . . distinct from the nature of the divine mind . . . which God's will is truly subject to . . . so that all is in vain, that is not accommodated to the moral world which depends upon the acts and state of the wills of moral agents' (Edwards 1957: 395–6). The result of the Arminian/deist account of freedom is an absolute determination by fate, which runs directly counter to their desire to secure human freedom (Edwards 1957: 395–6). In other words, human agents are able to discover freedom only in relation to the necessary character of holiness in the divine Being. Otherwise they are condemned to the slavery of determinism. Edwards affirms that in the context of moral necessity 'saints have not their freedom at all diminished, in any respect; and that God himself has the highest possible freedom, according to the true and proper meaning of the term; and that he is in the highest possible respect an agent, and active in the exercise of his infinite holiness though he acts therein in the highest degree necessarily' (1957: 364).

Freedom of the Will is a negative polemic exposing the complete failure of the Arminian and deist line of reason. But in one place Edwards muses that 'means and endeavors to obtain virtue could have an effect . . . through a natural tendency and influence, to prepare and dispose the mind more to virtuous acts . . . by causing the disposition of the heart to be more in favor of such acts' (1957: 368). Exploring this natural tendency toward discovering a supernatural disposition of the heart is his principle aim in *The Nature of True Virtue.* But before completing this work, Edwards met another serious challenge from the rising tide of deism and rationalism. The British divine Dr John Taylor greatly unsettled Christianity with *The Scripture Doctrine of Original Sin* (1738), in which he rejected the universal depravity of mankind and challenged the morality of guilt imputed to Adam's posterity in the Edenic fall. Clyde Holbrook notes that Taylor's ideas found a hold in New England, where traditional doctrines had lost their vigor, citing Jonathan Mayhew's sermonic admonition to 'Exercise your reason, and the liberty you enjoy, in learning the truth, and your deity from it' (Edwards 1970: 11). A debate over the doctrine of original sin in the late 1740s divided New England clergy and churches; but when Edwards responded to this 'paper war', he completely ignored the local fight and took aim at the central ideas of the rational moralists. He attacked their inability to describe the true moral state of mankind's struggle with sin and juxtaposed the hopelessness of their scheme against the redemption offered in Christ. *Original Sin* (1758) not only details the inconsistencies of Taylor's view of Scripture and his 'scheme' of human moral virtue, it also gives Edwards the opportunity to justify this difficult doctrine by Scripture and properly ordered reason.

In *Original Sin* Edwards inquires 'whether we have evidence that the heart of man is naturally of a corrupt and evil disposition' (Edwards 1970: 107). Discovering the reality of the human condition depends on a dispensational understanding of the moral world and the relational nature of human consciousness. In a general sense, Taylor and the thinkers he represents consider the moral world in one dimension. Actions are attributable only to the agents of those actions. As Taylor puts it, there can be no moral guilt 'without having merited the displeasure of the Creator by any personal fault' (Edwards 1970: 111). As we have seen before, Edwards anticipates the cul-de-sac of inquiry in Taylor's moralism; a self-grounding moral character presents an opaque end to inquiry. But to argue otherwise, to argue *for* original sin as an outworking of grace, entails both scriptural ground and philosophical description.

Edwards confronts Taylor's argument by showing that it is inconsistent with experience of human sinfulness, that it destroys the overarching sense of Scripture, and that it fails to provide a satisfactory explanation of human moral conscience under divine influence. Taylor's argument fails to account for the widespread reality of sin, for 'the permanence of effect implies a permanence of cause', which remains submerged in Taylor's 'scheme'. In addition, Taylor cannot explain the absence of positive influence of God's moral government after thousands of years and multiple generations have lived with the 'favor and benefit of death' (Edwards 1970: 212). If it has not worked yet, what is the ground for confidence that it will suddenly begin to have a positive effect now?

Edwards explicitly and in detail destroys Taylor's claims that original sin is not familiar to the biblical writers. Chapter and verse is piled on chapter and verse, demonstrating the breadth of the focus on sin and God's treatment for it. This includes the dispensation of grace to Adam in his original innocence, which, according to Edwards, was that he was given 'superior principles' in addition to natural human virtues. These principles were lost when Adam sinned. Taylor claims that there is no difference between Adam's original condition and that of any other human, to which Edwards quips, 'Paradise must therefore have been a delusion!' (1970: 233). Likewise, Taylor's interpretation of the meaning of 'sin' makes void the large scope of the Epistle to the Romans, particularly the distinction between the two Adams, that 'death comes by one, and life and happiness by the other' (Edwards 1970: 313). Edwards extends Taylor's point to its conclusion that if 'mere justice makes sufficient provision for our being free from all sin and misery by our own power', then 'redemption is needless, and Christ is dead in vain' (Edwards 1970: 357, 356).

The positive justification that original sin is common to humanity drives to its logical conclusion Edwards's conception of personal identity. He argues that a person is not an individual substance, referencing his opposition to Locke on this point, but the function of divine action forming human consciousness into a stable unity. Such a unity is the basis for the reality of human will and understanding sufficient for a reorientation in conversion, 'which Christ says is necessary for everyone, in order to his seeing the kingdom of God, by giving a *new heart and spirit*' (Edwards 1970: 365). The coherence of Scripture, which Taylor's view explodes, is an indication of the divine order surrounding the reality of our condition. 'If we, as we come into the world, are truly sinful and consequently miserable, he acts but a *friendly* part to us who endeavors fully to discover and manifest our disease,' as Christ in his preaching 'tends to search the hearts of men, and to teach them their inbred exceeding depravity, not merely as a matter of speculation, but by a proper conviction of conscience; which is the only knowledge of original sin, that can avail to prepare the mind for receiving Christ's redemption' (Edwards 1970: 424, 429). Just as perceiving divine beauty depends on the disposition of the heart, so the *practical conviction* of sin depends on the disordered character of the affections being discovered in experience. Although the practical conviction of original sin appears to be mitigated by the presence of 'mutual benevolence, tender compassion, etc.', Edwards refers those who 'desire to see them particularly considered' to 'a *Treatise on the Nature of True Virtue* lying by me prepared for the press' (1970: 433). This promissory note should not be seen as a dodge from Edwards's main focus on original sin and the hermeneutical power associated with this doctrine. Human experience of sin is an occasion of inquiry and discovery, and the pervasiveness of sin and the spiritual nature of this struggle provide a stable interpretive connection to Scripture. Scripture is a 'manifold witness' of this interpretive power, and thus the presence of 'sin' as a meaningful and consistent term in a scheme of understanding is an indication of epistemological soundness, not just for theology, but for any attempt to understand the limits of natural reason. Exhibiting the broad reach of his epistemological soundness carries Edwards into the topic of true virtue and natural moral conscience.

Edwards's moral writings, including his 1738 sermon series 'Charity and its Fruits' and the twin dissertations *The End for Which God Created the World* and *The Nature of True Virtue* (1765, published after his death), yield some of the richest ground for theological and philosophical speculation. True religious virtue, Edwards's subject in all these works, is comprehended in love to the divine Being. The presence of this love enables persons to determine whether theirs is a 'real Christian experience' because 'true discoveries excite love in the soul' (Edwards 1989: 145).

Paul Ramsey notices that in the 'Charity' sermons there is a progression of virtues that is due not to a developing rational facility or expanding self-love, but to the expanding and deepening of the immediate perception of divine beauty toward a holistic comprehension of all the saint's habits. In the last sermon, 'Heaven is a World of Love', Edwards states that 'the infinite essential love of God' is 'an infinite and eternal mutual holy energy between Father and the Son, a pure, holy act whereby Deity becomes nothing but an infinite and unchangeable act of love, which proceeds from both the Father and the

Son', and which flows out in 'innumerable streams towards all the created inhabitants of heaven' (1989: 373). This mutuality is reflected in the human response of 'those who have freely chosen that happiness which is to be had in the exercise and enjoyment of such love as is in heaven above all other conceivable happiness', not on the basis of 'rational arguments which may be offered for it', but because 'they have seen that it is so; they know it is so from what they have tasted' (Edwards 1989: 388). This statement does not contradict Edwards's positive consideration in *The End* for the 'attainments of habitual exercise of reason', since it is by reason that 'it might appear by his works what manner of being [God] is, and afford a proper representation of his divine excellencies, and especially his *moral* excellence, consisting in the *disposition of his heart*' (1989: 422). The crucial point is that the ultimate end of inquiry into human morality is the discovery of God's holiness.

Whereas *The End* moves from a scriptural standpoint focusing on God's holiness, *True Virtue* explores the same objective reality from the perspective that God has given 'faculties capable of discovering the immense superiority [of God] to all other beings' (Edwards 1989: 551). Most illuminating is Edwards's appreciation of the 'secondary' beauty of human virtue, whatever its origin. He commends Hutcheson's and Hume's perception of the attraction of a unity of design in virtue, suggesting that 'some image of true spiritual origin of beauty, some image of a higher agreement and consent of spiritual beings' informs his vision (Edwards 1989: 564). 'Natural conscience,' Edwards says, 'if well informed, will approve of true virtue, and will disapprove and condemn the want of it, and opposing to it; and yet without seeing the true beauty of it' (1989: 595).

Edwards reserves his sharpest comments for thinkers who allow for God, but not as the end of all virtue. 'In their ordinary view of things,' he says, '[God's] being is not apt to come into the account, and to have the influence and effect of a real existence,' in comparison with whom 'all the rest are nothing' (Edwards 1989: 611). From this perspective, Edwards evaluates moral philosophy as a search for a replacement of the immediate vision of divine holiness that eludes the reach from 'natural' principles and therefore resolves into something less in terms of generality and power. But even this negative resolution is an opening for divine infusion. 'Every being who has a faculty of will', Edwards says, 'must of necessity have an inclination to happiness', which leads necessarily to the desire for the 'happiness of Being in general' (1989: 621). Finally, Edwards says that natural conscience is not an arbitrarily occurring faculty, or dependent merely on causal circumstances, but is 'ordered by a necessary nature in God' (1989: 623), and so is permanently sustained in moral experience as an image of a higher agreement and consent of spiritual beings.

E. Interpretations and Effects of Edwards

The assessment of the influence of Edwards's thought has engaged many of America's best historians, philosophers, and theologians. His students Joseph Bellamy and Samuel Hopkins sought to clarify his more obscure ideas in the hopes of reigniting a religious awakening. Hopkins, considered by some the 'best representative of Edwardseanism' and the New Divinity movement, focused on defending Edwards's conceptions of sin, virtue, and experimental religion (Boardman 1987: 73, 193). With the object of protecting a system of theology, rather than developing new lines of inquiry, their work has often been criticized as departing from Edwards's spirit and rubbing off the sharp edges of his ideas in order to broaden their appeal (Conforti 1995; Conrad 1981). Allen Guelzo skillfully traces the movement of these thinkers toward a heightened sense of moral ability, reformulating the Fall as an event that did not diminish the power of human understanding, and asserting that there is no natural impossibility to repentance (1989: 104, 136). Joseph Haroutunian (1964 [1932]) famously decried this reformulation of Edwards's thought as a movement from 'piety to moralism'.

Perry Miller (2005) and other admirers of Edwards disconnect his intellectual value from the development of Reformed Christianity, emphasizing his similarities to the transcendentalists' richness of natural inquiry. Morton White highlights the dependence on intuition rather than tradition and the sense of the heart as a 'native antecedent' of Emerson's Reason as grounds that the intention of the transcendentalists was to 'open up for all' the perception of the divine that Edwards described as peculiar to saints (1971: 80).

No thinker of Edwards's power and novelty emerged in America until C. S. Peirce (Smith 1992). Influenced by Plato and Kant, Peirce's semiotic theory of meaning and habit as conceptual discovery provides grounds for comparison to Edwards (Lee 1998; Raposa 1993), as does Peirce's *agapism* as the principle of the universe. The transformation of knowledge in the discovery of the reality of God is another interesting and striking similarity

(Hausman 1987; Ward 2000). William James responds directly to Edwards in *The Varieties of Religious Experience*. James affirms Edwards's focus on the 'fruit not the root' of religious experience, but challenges Edwards's conception of conversion to the character or disposition of God's heart. John Dewey, who was reared in a Calvinist Congregational tradition, makes tangential references to Edwards in his approval of the transcendentalist movement from a divinely infused order to religious naturalism. In *A Common Faith* (1932), Dewey rejects outright the claims of revelation as rationally insupportable, while in other texts he appears to affirm benevolent holism with scriptural allusions such as 'we know that though the universe slay us still we may trust, for our lot is one with whatever is good in existence' (1958: 420). Josiah Royce also does not make direct reference to Edwards, but his metaphysical idealism is similar in spirit, identifying the Absolute with the divine character of Scripture, while his inquiry follows a trajectory toward rational power and interpretation incarnated in the beloved community. For Royce, God is the 'All-knowing Spirit-Interpreter' who opens up inquiry into the immanent/transcendent character of the divine (Oppenheim 2005: 268). But Royce is careful to avoid traditional theological conceptions, and so his thought does not explore the Trinitarian dynamic of holy love in the Godhead *ad intra* as Edwards does.

Jonathan Edwards's life and thought continue to deeply influence American philosophy and theology. The expectation informing American intellectual life that a philosophical reorientation or a spiritual transformation is a potential product of inquiry into experience owes much to Edwards's spirit of discovery.

REFERENCES

Boardman, G. N. (1987). *A History of New England Theology*. New York: Garland Publishing.

Conforti, Joseph A. (1995). *Jonathan Edwards, Religious Tradition and American Culture*. Chapel Hill, NC: University of North Carolina Press.

Conrad, C. (1981). *Samuel Hopkins and the New Divinity Movement: Calvinism, the Congregational Ministry, and Reform in New England between the Great Awakenings*. Grand Rapids, MI: Christian University Press.

——— (1990). *The Theology of Jonathan Edwards: A Reappraisal*. Bloomington, IN: Indiana University Press.

Dewey, J. (1932). *A Common Faith*. New Haven: Yale University Press.

_____ (1958). *Experience and Nature*. New York: Dover Publications.

Edwards, J. (1957). *Works of Jonathan Edwards*, i: *Freedom of the Will*, ed. P. Ramsey. New Haven: Yale University Press.

_____ (1959). *Works of Jonathan Edwards*, ii: *Religious Affections*, ed. J. E. Smith. New Haven: Yale University Press.

_____ (1970). *Works of Jonathan Edwards*, iii: *Original Sin*, ed. C. A. Holbrook. New Haven: Yale University Press.

_____ (1974). *The Works of Jonathan Edwards*, i. Edinburgh: Banner of Truth Trust.

_____ (1980). *Works of Jonathan Edwards*, vi: *Scientific and Philosophical Writings*, ed. W. E. Anderson. New Haven: Yale University Press.

_____ (1989). *Works of Jonathan Edwards*, viii: *Ethical Writings*, ed. P. Ramsey. New Haven: Yale University Press.

_____ (1994). *Works of Jonathan Edwards*, xiii: *The "Miscellanies", Entry Nos. a–z, aa–zz, 1–500*, ed. T. A. Schafer. New Haven: Yale University Press.

_____ (1998). *Works of Jonathan Edwards*, xvi: *Letters and Personal Writings*, ed. G. S. Claghorn. New Haven: Yale University Press.

_____ (1999a). *Works of Jonathan Edwards*, xiv: *Sermons and Discourses 1723–1729*, ed. K. P. Minkema. New Haven: Yale University Press.

_____ (1999b). *Works of Jonathan Edwards*, xvii: *Sermons and Discourses*, ed. Mark Valeri. New Haven: Yale University Press.

Fiering, N. (1981). *Jonathan Edwards, Moral Thought in its British Context*. Chapel Hill, NC: University of North Carolina Press.

Guelzo, A. C. (1989). *Edwards on the Will: A Century of American Theological Debate*. Middletown, CT: Wesleyan University Press.

Haroutanian, J. (1964 [1932]). *Piety Versus Moralism*. Hamden, CT: Archon Books.

Hausman, C. (1987). 'Metaphorical Reference and Peirce's Dynamical Object'. *Transactions of the Charles S. Peirce Society*, 23: 381–409.

Jenson, R. W. (1988). *America's Theologian: A Recommendation of Jonathan Edwards*. New York: Oxford University Press.

Lee, S. H. (1998). *The Philosophical Theology of Jonathan Edwards*. Princeton: Princeton University Press.

Locke, J. (1959). *An Essay Concerning Human Understanding*. New York: Dover Publishing.

McDermott, G. R. (1992). *One Holy and Happy Society: The Public Theology of Jonathan Edwards*. University Park, PA: Pennsylvania State University Press.

_____ (2000). *Jonathan Edwards Confronts the Gods*. New York: Oxford University Press.

Marsden, G. M. (2003). *Jonathan Edwards*. New Haven: Yale University Press.

Mead, S. E. (1942). *Nathanial William Taylor*. Chicago: University of Chicago Press.

Miller, P. (2005). *Jonathan Edwards*. Lincoln, NE: University of Nebraska Press.

Murray, I. H. (1987). *Jonathan Edwards: A New Biography*. Edinburgh and Carlisle, PA: The Banner of Truth Trust.

Noll, M. A. (2002). *America's God: From Jonathan Edwards to Abraham Lincoln*. Oxford: Oxford University Press.

Oppenheim, F. M. (2005). *Reverence for the Relations of Life: Re-imagining Pragmatism via Josiah Royce's Interactions with Peirce, James, and Dewey.* Notre Dame, IN: University of Notre Dame Press.

Raposa, M. (1993). 'Jonathan Edwards' Twelfth Sign'. *International Philosophy Quarterly*, 23/3: 153–62.

Riley, W. (1959). *American Thought: From Puritanism to Pragmatism and Beyond.* Gloucester, MA: Peter Smith.

Savelle, M. (1964). *Colonial Origins of American Thought.* Princeton: Van Nostrand Company.

Smith, J. E. (1976). 'Jonathan Edwards as Philosophical Theologian'. *Review of Metaphysics*, 30/2: 306–24.

——(1992). *Jonathan Edwards: Puritan, Preacher, Philosopher.* Notre Dame, IN: University of Notre Dame Press.

——(1999). 'The Perennial Jonathan Edwards'. In S. H. Lee and A. C. Guelzo (eds.), *Edwards in Our Time: Jonathan Edwards and the Shaping of American Religion*, Grand Rapids, MI: William B. Eerdmans Publishing Co., 1–11.

Stein, S. J. (ed.) (1996). *Jonathan Edward's Writings.* Bloomington, IN: Indiana University Press.

Stout, H. S. (1986). *The New England Soul: Preaching and Religious Culture in Colonial New England.* Oxford: Oxford University Press.

Ward, R. A. (2000). 'Experience as Religious Discovery in Edwards and Peirce'. *Transactions of the Charles S. Peirce Society*, 36/2: 297–309.

——(2004). *Conversion in American Philosophy: Exploring the Practice of Transformation.* New York: Fordham University Press.

Weber, D. (1983). 'The Figure of Jonathan Edwards'. *American Quarterly*, 35/5: 556–64.

White, M. (1971). *Science and Sentiment: Philosophical Thought from Jonathan Edwards to John Dewey.* New York: Oxford University Press.

CHAPTER 2

EMERSON, ROMANTICISM, AND CLASSICAL AMERICAN PRAGMATISM

RUSSELL B. GOODMAN

1. STRANDS OF ROMANTICISM

ON 25 MAY 1903, celebrations of the centenary of Ralph Waldo Emerson's birth took place all over the United States. William James, a professor of philosophy at Harvard, marked the occasion with an address in Concord, Massachusetts, and John Dewey, a professor of philosophy and director of the Laboratory School at the University of Chicago, gave an address at the university. At 61, James was the author of *The Principles of Psychology* (1890), *The Varieties of Religious Experience* (1902), and the first statement of his emerging pragmatism, 'Philosophical Conceptions and Practical Results' (1898). Dewey, at 44, was a leading educational theorist and the editor of

Studies in Logical Theory (1903), the signature document of the 'Chicago School' of pragmatism. The intersection of Emerson's thought with that of these two pragmatists marks a wider affiliation of all of them with romanticism, a tradition in which Emerson plays a major role. As the critic Harold Bloom has written, 'Emerson is to American Romanticism what Wordsworth is to the English or parent version' (1971: 297). This essay considers some romantic themes in the philosophies of James and Dewey, their relations to Emerson, and the appropriation of Emerson by a contemporary American philosopher not in the pragmatist tradition, Stanley Cavell.

Romanticism is too complex a phenomenon to be defined adequately in a few pages, let alone a few paragraphs, but we can think of it as a long process that began in late eighteenth-century Europe and that we are still engaged in: of casting off what Northrop Frye calls 'an encyclopedic myth, derived mainly from the Bible', according to which God is the origin of all creation. In the new romantic myth, human creativity assumes a central place (Frye 1968: 5). Isaiah Berlin puts the contrast as between an older view 'that there is a body of facts to which we must submit', and a newer view that 'there is no copying, there is no adaptation, there is no learning of the rules, there is no external check, there is no structure which you must understand and adapt yourself to before you can proceed. The heart of the entire process is invention, creation, making, out of literally nothing, or out of any materials that may be to hand' (2001 [1999]: 119).

Creating something 'out of literally nothing' is just what some critics accuse the pragmatists of doing, whereas, as we see below, they are better construed as following Berlin's second alternative, creating out of the 'materials that may be to hand'. In any case, the romantic themes that guide the following discussion are: (a) the creative and shaping powers of the human mind; (b) passion and feeling as legitimate responses to and ways of understanding the world; (c) human alienation from the world and recovery from that alienation; and (d) the 'spiritual' potential of ordinary life—what some writers have called 'natural supernaturalism' (Abrams 1971). The romantic allegiances of the pragmatists are sometimes acknowledged, as when John Dewey cites John Keats and Samuel Taylor Coleridge in *Art as Experience*, or William James speaks in favor of 'the personalism and romanticism of the world' in *The Varieties of Religious Experience* (1987: 449); but more often, they are implicit, as in their opposition to 'copy' theories of knowledge or their concern with feeling.

The poetry of Coleridge and William Wordsworth offers us a taste of romantic thought. In 'Dejection: An Ode' (1802) Coleridge finds that the nature we encounter is in some way our creation:

> ... we receive but what we give,
> And in our life alone does nature live:
> Ours is her wedding garment, ours her shroud!

In 'The Recluse' (1814) Wordsworth also speaks of a marriage of self and world:

> ... Paradise and groves
> Elysian, Fortunate Fields—like those of old
> Sought in the Atlantic Main—why should they be
> A history only of departed things,
> Or a mere fiction of what never was?
> For the discerning intellect of Man,
> When wedded to his goodly universe
> In love and holy passion, shall find these
> A simple produce of the common day.

Wordsworth calls for a wedding of self and world that is to be intellectual and emotional at once, and for the recovery of something that he calls 'paradise', but which is not remote or far away. It is a possibility of the here and now, a 'simple produce of the common day'. Notice that God is not in this picture: the responsibility for the wedding that produces paradise rests squarely on the 'intellect of Man ... In love and holy passion'.

There is a direct line from the words of the English romantic poets to Emerson's idea that 'the fountain of all good' is in oneself (CW 1: 79)[1] and to his desire to be shown 'the sublime presence of the highest spiritual cause' not in the 'remote', but in 'the familiar' (CW 1: 67). The line extends beyond Emerson, however, to James's explorations of religious experience and his attempt 'to unite empiricism with spiritualism' (Perry 1935: ii. 443), and to Dewey's call for the cultivation within human experience of what, following John Keats, he calls 'ethereal things'. Coleridge's idea that we both receive and give ourselves the world (an idea that itself derives from Kant and Schelling[2]) is an ancestor both of Emerson's claim in Nature (1836) that we 'conform all

---

[1] References to The Collected Works of Ralph Waldo Emerson are in standard form as follows: CW, volume number followed by page number.

[2] In Biographia Literaria, Coleridge states that Kant's thought took hold of him 'as with a giant's hand' (1965 [1817]: 84).

facts to [our] character' (*CW* 1: 25) and of James's 'humanistic principle' that 'you can't weed out the human contribution' (1987: 598).[3]

2. JAMES AND ROMANTICISM

The background to James's goal of 'uniting empiricism with spiritualism' is his lifelong attempt to set out a 'thicker' concept of experience than in traditional empiricism. Often he attributes to direct, concrete experience what other philosophers have thought of as additions to it. He departs from the British empiricists, for example, in maintaining that we experience relations: 'the relations between things, conjunctive as well as disjunctive, are just as much matters of direct particular experience, neither more nor less so, than the things themselves' (1987: 826). Our experience, James holds, is not a simple set or train of ideas, but a 'stream of thought' that includes 'vague' components. These range from our sense of the world as spreading out behind our backs to the deep sense of the universe that each person has. James calls these senses of the universe our 'consents':

> '*Will you or won't you have it so?*' is the most probing question we are ever asked; we are asked it every hour of the day, and about the largest as well as the smallest, the most theoretical as well as the most practical, things. We answer by *consents or non-consents* and not by words. What wonder that these dumb responses should seem our deepest organs of communication with the nature of things!   (1981 [1890]: 1182)[4]

These dumb responses, James suggests, have epistemological significance—they 'seem' to be 'our deepest organs of communication with the nature of

---

[3] Whether the influence extends to Charles Sanders Peirce is far from clear, but any consideration of the matter would have to take into account the following statement from 'The Law of the Mind' (1892):

I may mention, for the benefit of those who are curious in studying mental biographies, that I was born and reared in the neighborhood of Concord,—I mean in Cambridge,—at the time when Emerson, Hedge, and their friends were disseminating the ideas that they had caught from Schelling, and Schelling from Plotinus, from Boehm, or from God knows what minds stricken with the monstrous mysticism of the East. But the atmosphere of Cambridge held many an antiseptic against Concord transcendentalism; and I am not conscious of having contracted any of that virus. Nevertheless, it is probable that some cultured bacilli, some benignant form of the disease was implanted in my soul, unawares, and that now, after long incubation, it comes to the surface, modified by mathematical conception and by training in physical investigations.   (1992: 312–13)

[4] On romanticism and the inarticulable, see Berlin 2001 [1999]: 121.

things'. If James writes here as a psychologist, reporting on how things seem to us, he writes as a philosopher eight years later in *The Will to Believe* (1897), as he asserts:

The deepest thing in our nature is this *Binnenleben* (as a German doctor lately has called it), this dumb region of the heart in which we dwell alone with our willingnesses and unwillingnesses, our faiths and fears. . . . Here is our deepest organ of communication with the nature of things; and compared with these concrete movements of the soul all abstract statements and scientific arguments . . . sound like mere chatterings of the teeth.   (1979 [1897]: 55)

James works towards 'deep' 'communication' with the world, not only by amplifying the concept of experience but by the way he 'places' experience. Beginning with *The Principles* and culminating in his 'radical empiricism' essays of 1904–5 (published in the posthumous volume entitled *Essays in Radical Empiricism*), James sets out a view of experience as neither mental nor physical.[5] *The Principles of Psychology* contains a memorable early statement of this view:

Certainly a child newly born in Boston, who gets a sensation from the candle flame which lights the bedroom, or from his diaper-pin, does not feel either of these objects to be situated in longitude 71 W. and latitude 42 N. He does not feel them to be in the third story of the house. He does not even feel them in any distinct manner to be to the right or the left of any of the other sensations which he may be getting from other objects in the room at the same time. . . . The flame fills its own place, the pain fills its own place; but as yet these places are neither identified with, nor discriminated from, any other places.   (1981 [1890]: 681–2)

In James's *Essays in Radical Empiricism* these 'places' become the 'primal stuff or material in the world, a stuff of which everything is composed' (1987: 1142). This stuff, James writes, is 'plain unqualified actuality or existence, a simple *that*', undifferentiated into thing and thought, and only 'virtually or potentially either object or subject' (1987: 1151). The child newly born in Boston is neither a disembodied spectator of the world, nor something fundamentally material.

   In *A Pluralistic Universe* James assails materialism for offering no 'intimacy' with the world, for defining 'the world so as to leave man's soul upon it as a sort of outside passenger or alien' (1987: 640). He also condemns absolute idealism for an insufficient appreciation of the otherness of the world, portraying us as wrapped up tightly 'in one vast instantaneous co-implicated completeness

---

[5] Bertrand Russell called the view 'neutral monism' in his *The Analysis of Mind* (1921), the first chapters of which rely heavily on James.

[where] nothing can in any sense ... be really absent from anything else'
(1987: 776). James wants to do justice to both the 'foreignness and intimacy'
(1987: 644) of our position in the world.

In *Pragmatism*, James portrays our intimacy with the world in yet another
way, when he argues that the world we know is shaped by us. 'We carve out
everything,' he states, 'just as we carve out constellations, to suit our human
purposes' (1987: 597). This is a form of the 'invention, creation, making, out
of literally nothing, or out of any materials that may be to hand' identified by
Berlin. James does not hold, however, that we carve 'out of literally nothing'
(how could we?), but instead finds that we have materials at hand, including
our past truths and experience's 'sensible core'. He denies, though, that we
ever get this core 'pure' or undigested; as he puts it, 'the trail of the human
serpent is ... over everything' (1987: 515).

James's imagery in *Pragmatism* sometimes expresses a violent or Promethean creativity:

In our cognitive as well as in our active life we are creative. We add, both to the subject
and to the predicate part of reality. The world stands really malleable, waiting to
receive its final touches at our hands. Like the kingdom of heaven, it suffers violence
willingly. Man engenders truths upon it.   (1987: 599)

James's language echoes the 'Discipline' chapter of *Nature*, where Emerson
writes:

Nature is thoroughly mediate. It is made to serve. It receives the dominion of man as
meekly as the ass on which the Saviour rode. It offers all its kingdoms to man as the
raw material which he may mould into what is useful. Man is never weary of working
it up.   (*CW* 1: 25)

That James recognized the connections between pragmatism and 'Discipline'
is evident from the passages he indexed under the heading 'pragmatism'
in his edition of Emerson's writings (Carpenter 1939; cf. Girel 2004, Bense
2006). However, the relation of these two American philosophers begins well
before James developed pragmatism—in fact, well before the end of James's
first year.

3. JAMES AND EMERSON

Emerson's words literally echoed through the James household in New York
City where William and his brother, Henry Jr., were raised: for their father,

Henry James Sr., was a friend of Emerson's. Early in that friendship Emerson visited the new James home on the east side of Washington Square, and admired the two-month-old William (Allen 1982: 401). Emerson's words echoed in another way, as we learn from a letter that Henry Sr. sent years later, when William was 28 and a recent graduate of the Harvard Medical School:

My dear Emerson,—

Many thanks for Society and Solitude, of which I have read many chapters with hearty liking. But unfortunately just before the new volume arrived, we had got a handsomely bound copy of the new edition of the old essays, and I had been reading them aloud in the evening to Mama and Willy and Alice with such delectation on all sides, that it was vain to attempt renewing the experience.   (Perry 1935: ii. 100)

We do not know when James first read Emerson, although his copies of the first two volumes of Emerson's writings (including *Nature* and his early addresses, and *Essays, First Series*) is inscribed 'William James, 1871', a year after this letter was written. These two volumes are heavily underlined in pencil, pen, and blue pencil, and there are notes in the text, and notes, quotations, and indices on the flyleaves (Carpenter 1939: 42).

Emerson appears in one of James's earliest publications, 'Remarks on Spencer's Definition of Mind as Correspondence' (1878), where James sets out one of his most deeply held beliefs: that all experience is teleological, 'from the vague dawn of discomfort or ease in the polyp to the intellectual joy of Laplace among his formulas'. He accuses Spencer of trying to 'hoodwink teleology out of sight by saying nothing about it', and in support cites Emerson's poem 'Brahma', which says nothing at all about teleology but much about systematically ignoring something:

Well might teleology (had she a voice) exclaim with Emerson's Brahma:

> If the red slayer thinks he slays,
>   Or if the slain think he is slain,
> They know not well the subtle ways
>   I keep, and pass, and turn again.
>
> They reckon ill who leave me out;
>   When me they fly, I am the wings;
> I am the doubter and the doubt, etc.
>
> (James 1978 [1878]: 18)

Emerson's words are in William James's head, part of his normal way of thinking and writing about almost anything.

Emerson appears several times in *The Principles of Psychology* and, in the chapter entitled 'The Perception of Reality', in a manner that presages James's later thought. James is discussing the way moral and religious truths

come 'home' to us far more on some occasions than on others. As Emerson says, 'There is a difference between one and another hour of life, in their authority and subsequent effect. Our faith comes in moments. . . . Yet there is a depth in those brief moments which constrains us to ascribe more reality to them than to all other experiences.   (1981 [1890]: 935)

James is quoting from 'The Over-Soul', and the moments of varying authority and depth that he notes in *The Principles* become the subject of *The Varieties of Religious Experience*, his 'study in human nature' published a decade later in 1902. What Emerson calls the 'depth in those brief moments' becomes in *Varieties* the 'noetic quality' and 'transiency' of mystical experience (1987: 343).

Emerson appears in *Varieties* as an example of a religious writer who, like the Buddhists, does not posit a god: 'Not a deity *in concreto*, not a superhuman person, but the immanent divinity in things, the essentially spiritual structure of the universe, is the object of the transcendentalist cult.' Emerson also appears as a representative of the 'optimistic' 'blue sky' 'religion of healthy-mindedness' with which James contrasts the 'religion of the sick soul'. As such, Emerson is cast as a little naïve, for James plainly favors the more comprehensive view of life of those 'who must be twice-born in order to be happy' (1987: 155). James quotes Emerson's 'Spiritual Laws' to represent the disdain that 'the sky-blue healthy-minded moralist' feels for those who dwell on sin and evil. What appear as sin and evil, Emerson holds, are simply 'the soul's mumps, and measles, and whooping-coughs', things to get over, not to dwell on (1987: 156). This 'self-reliant' attitude will not suffice, James argues, for those who have fully tasted the 'cup of bitterness' that life offers. For these sick souls, surrender, rather than resolute overcoming, is the path to a second birth.

In his centenary address, James is more positive about Emerson, and from his letters of the time he seems to have gained new respect for his thought. He characterizes Emerson as having achieved a blend of the religious and the empirical: 'Emerson held both that "Divinity is everywhere", and that there is just this world: "Other world! There is no other world". All God's life opens into the individual particular, and here and now, or nowhere, is reality' (1987: 1124). Emerson's claim that 'Divinity is everywhere' might have made him,

James states, 'an optimist of the sentimental type', but he achieved a balance: he could 'perceive the full squalor of the individual fact, but he could also see the transfiguration' (1987: 1125). This portrayal of Emerson runs counter to that in *Varieties*, and it was a matter about which James went back and forth (cf. James 1992– : ii. 197).

James praises Emerson for his devotion to his mission of 'spiritual seeing and reporting', and for his opposition 'to borrowing traditions and living at second hand. . . . This faith that in a life at first hand there is something sacred is perhaps the most characteristic note in Emerson's writings' (1987: 1121). The letters James wrote in the months after delivering the address show that he was refocused on his own vocation as a philosopher, his own 'reporting' about the universe. In a long letter to his brother Henry, who by this time had published *The Portrait of a Lady* and *The Wings of the Dove*, he writes:

The reading of the divine Emerson, volume after volume, has done me a lot of good, and, strange to say, has thrown a strong practical light on my own path. The incorruptible way in which he followed his own vocation, of seeing such truths as the Universal Soul vouchsafed to him from day to day and month to month . . . seems to me a moral lesson to all men who have any genius, however small, to foster. I see now with absolute clearness, that greatly as I have been helped and enlarged by my university business hitherto, the time has come when the remnant of my life must be passed in a different manner, contemplatively namely, and with leisure and simplification for the one main thing, which is to report in one book, at least, such impression as my own intellect has received from the Universe.   (1992– : iii. 234)

In *Pragmatism*, the book he published four years later, James argues that making a report of the 'impression' that one's 'own intellect has received from the universe' is just what the great philosophers manage to do. Each of their books, he states, has 'an essential personal flavor', the appreciation of which is 'the finest fruit of our own accomplished philosophical education'. We work over the details of each system, but 'it is on the resultant impression itself that we react. . . . The finally victorious way of looking at things will be the most completely *impressive* way to the normal run of minds' (1987: 502, 503; cf. Girel 2004).

Although James does not mention Emerson in *Pragmatism*, James's indexing of Emerson's writings shows that he was well aware of the connections between them. Under the heading 'Pragmatism' he indexed passages from Emerson's writings that include the words 'action', 'deeds', or 'work'; for example: 'An action is the perfection and publication of thought'; 'Colleges and books only copy the language which the field and work-yard made'; 'Let [the man of letters] endeavor ... to solve the problem of that life which is set before him. And this by punctual action, and not by promises or dreams' (Carpenter 1939: 43). James also indexed two sentences from the 'Prospects' chapter of *Nature* that chime with the robust, Promethean side of his pragmatism: 'Nature is not fixed but fluid. Spirit alters, moulds, makes it. ... Build therefore your own world' (*CW* 1: 44, 45). All these passages as marked by James suggest not so much that Emerson was a pragmatist as that James's pragmatism was Emersonian.

4. DEWEY AND ROMANTICISM

Dewey's version of the marriage of self and world has antecedents in Coleridge's *Aids to Reflection*, which he read when he was an undergraduate at the University of Vermont, and in the philosophy of Hegel, a figure on the fringes of the romantic movement whom Dewey studied as a graduate student at Johns Hopkins. In Coleridge's book Dewey found an experiential notion of faith, as 'a state of the will and the affections, not a merely intellectual assent to doctrinal and historical propositions' (*LW* 5: 182).[6] Hegel, he writes in his autobiography of 1930,

supplied a demand for unification that was doubtless an intense emotional craving, and yet was a hunger that only an intellectualized subject-matter could satisfy. It is more than difficult, it is impossible, to recover that early mood. But the sense of divisions and separations that were, I suppose, borne in upon me as a consequence of a heritage of New England culture, divisions by way of isolation of self from the world, of soul from body, of nature from God, brought a painful oppression. ... Hegel's synthesis of subject and object, matter and spirit, the divine and the human, was, however, no mere intellectual formula; it operated as an immense release, a liberation.   (*LW* 5: 153)

This liberation from 'artificial dividing walls' set Dewey's philosophy on a path of disentanglement from traditional categories of Western thinking, first in a Hegelian version that Dewey called 'absolutism', then in the more experimental versions that he called 'operationalism' and 'pragmatism'. In

---

[6] The quotation is from Dewey's 1929 paper, 'James Marsh and American Philosophy', first published in 1941. Marsh, President of the University of Vermont, wrote an influential introduction to Coleridge's book. According to Dewey, Marsh is a practitioner of 'Romantic philosophy' (*LW* 5: 178). References to the Standard Edition of Dewey's writings published by Southern Illinois University Press are as follows: *EW* = *Early Works*; *MW* = *Middle Works*; *LW* = *Late Works*.

Dewey's great works of the 1920s and 1930s, religious, aesthetic, moral, and in general human phenomena are portrayed not as apart from the rest of the world in a 'subjective' or second-class domain, but as interwoven with and emerging from what Dewey calls 'transactions', 'situations', or 'affairs'. This is a world to which one would like to be connected, as he suggests in a rhetorical question in his early pragmatist essay 'Does Reality Possess Practical Character?' (1908). 'Why', Dewey asks, 'should what gives tragedy, comedy, and poignancy to life be excluded from things?' (*MW* 4: 126).

A prime locus for Dewey's mature approach is *Experience and Nature*, where he sets out a non-dualist metaphysic while being aware that his language is permeated with the very theories he is trying to overcome. In the chapter entitled 'Nature, Life and Body-Mind', Dewey argues that life and mind emerge from the complicated interactions of nature:

Body-mind designates an affair with its own properties. A large part of the diffi-culty in its discussion—perhaps the whole of the difficulty in general apart from detailed questions—is due to vocabulary. Our language is so permeated with con-sequences of theories which have divided the body and mind from each other, making separate existential realms out of them, that we lack words to designate the actual existential facts. Body-mind simply designates what actually takes place when a living body is implicated in situations of discourse, communication and participation.   (*LW* 1: 217)

If we look at things the way Dewey encourages us to do, there is no mind–body problem. We see 'a living body implicated in situations', not an isolated consciousness which may or may not be implicated in anything outside itself (*LW* 1: 202). The 'solution' of the problem of mind–body, then, consists in 'a revision of the preliminary assumptions about existence which generate the problem' (*LW* 1: 202). One of these assumptions is that experience takes place 'below the skin-surface of an organism' (*LW* 1: 215).[7]

Dewey reflects on his quest for a more adequate notion of experience in 'An Empirical Survey of Empiricisms' (1935). For the Greeks, he argues, experience meant the trial-and-error competence of the craftsman, which was inferior to the revolutionary power of thought in the theoretical sciences, especially mathematics. In the seventeenth and eighteenth centuries, experience rather than reason plays the revolutionary and critical role, but there are defects of this second conception of experience: its passive conception of the mind, the

---

[7] Cf. Beiser 2003: 148: 'if we replace the mechanical model of nature with the organic, these mysteries of traditional epistemology disappear. ... There is no dualism between the mental and the physical since both are degrees of organization and development of living force.'

skepticism or distance from the world to which it leads, and its failure to make a place for the features that bring drama, interest, and poignancy to life. He sees the beginnings of a more adequate empiricism in John Stuart Mill, whom he places in a line of English romantic thinkers: 'through the direct influence especially of Coleridge and Wordsworth [Mill] felt the defects of historical empiricism and the need of something that would give a more stable, constructive ground for belief and conduct' (1935: 18). Dewey's more adequate empiricism sees us as biological creatures for whom 'seeing, hearing, loving, imagining' are all ways in which we are 'intrinsically connected with the subject matter of the world' (*MW* 9: 174).

Dewey's philosophy receives its most explicitly romantic formulation in *Art as Experience* (1934), where he turns to the English romantic poets not merely for examples of 'art', but for their assistance in formulating his central claims not only about art as experience but about experience as art. Like Wordsworth and Coleridge, who in the *Lyrical Ballads* sought to 'make the incidents of common life interesting', Dewey seeks the aesthetic in the incidents of ordinary life: in 'the tense grace of the ball-player' and 'the zest of the spectator in poking the wood burning on the hearth and in watching the darting flames and crumbling coals' (*LW* 10: 11). Growing up in Burlington, Vermont, Dewey must have done a lot of poking wood and watching coals, which from his philosophical perspective is a form of inquiry, answering the question, 'What will happen if I do *this*?' Yet this is inquiry not for a particular purpose or goal, but just for the pleasure of it, a point Dewey thoroughly appreciates and uses a passage from Coleridge's *Biographia Literaria* to make:

What Coleridge said of the reader of poetry is true in its way of all who are happily absorbed in their activities of mind and body: 'The reader should be carried forward, not merely or chiefly by the mechanical impulse of curiosity, not by a restless desire to arrive at the final solution, but by the pleasurable activity of the journey itself'.   (*LW* 10: 11)

This pleasurable journey—poking the coals, catching the ball—is a form of the good life. Indeed, this is an old theme of Dewey's, reaching back to some of his earliest writing on education, which, he states, is 'a process of living and not a preparation for future living', composed of 'forms of life . . . that are worth living for their own sake' (*EW* 5: 87).

Dewey is a naturalist, but he does not shy away from the words 'spiritual', 'ideal', and 'ethereal' in talking about the renewed relation to the world for which he calls. The second chapter of *Art as Experience*, entitled 'The Live

Creature and "Ethereal Things"', is indebted to John Keats, who wrote: 'The Sun, the Moon, the Earth and its contents, are material to form greater things, that is ethereal things—greater things than the Creator himself made' (*LW* 10: 26). Dewey adds the biological element to this 'natural supernaturalism' by speaking of 'the live creature'—a phrase that furnishes the title of the first chapter, where Dewey had discussed the ball-player and the poker at the fire. In 'The Live Creature and "Ethereal Things"' Dewey presents an account that gives prominence to both the biological and the 'ethereal', to a 'union of material and ideal': 'The senses are the organs through which the live creature participates directly in the ongoings of the world about him. In this participation the varied wonder and splendor of this world are made actual for him in the qualities he experiences' (*LW* 10: 28). As an example of such experience, he cites a passage from Emerson's *Nature*: 'Crossing a bare common, in snow puddles, at twilight, under a clouded sky, without having in my thought any occurrence of special good fortune, I have enjoyed a perfect exhilaration. I am glad to the brink of fear.' Something of 'the same quality' is found, Dewey holds, 'in every spontaneous and uncoerced esthetic response' (*LW* 10: 35).

5. DEWEY AND EMERSON

Dewey makes use of Emerson's thought not only in *Art as Experience* but in *Democracy and Education* (1916), where he finds Emerson to have struck the proper balance between respect for the child's powers and for the teacher's responsibility for finding the 'direction' in which the child's 'impulses' appropriately point (*MW* 9: 57). Central to Dewey's educational theory is the Emersonian idea that each of us has something original and powerful within us: an 'unattained but attainable self', as Emerson puts it in 'History' (*CW* 2: 5). Deweyan education is the cultivation of this self, a process that is lifelong. Sometimes, as in the chapter entitled 'Education as Growth', Dewey calls this process simply 'growth'.[8]

Dewey's most sustained consideration of Emerson is his 1903 essay for the centenary of Emerson's birth, entitled 'Ralph Waldo Emerson: Philosopher

---

[8] For an account of the relation of Dewey's notion of growth to Emerson's notion of 'the active soul', see Goodman 2007: sect. 3.

of Democracy'. Unlike James, who praises him as a 'real seer' but not as a philosopher, Dewey has no doubts about Emerson's philosophical status, as his title indicates. He begins his argument by criticizing the line often drawn between philosopher and poet, in particular by Plato, and points out that Plato crosses that line, for he is both a philosopher and a poet. Emerson is too, Dewey claims, and indeed he is 'the one citizen of the New World fit to have his name uttered in the same breath with that of Plato' (*MW* 3: 191). Dewey praises Emerson's expanded empiricism and his stress on the power of each individual. Emerson, Dewey states, 'takes the distinctions and classifications which to most philosophers are true in and of and because of their systems, and makes them true of life, of . . . common experience'. In support, he cites a sentence from 'Intellect': 'The Bacon, the Spinoza, the Hume, Schelling, Kant, is only a more or less awkward translator, of things in your consciousness' (*MW* 3: 188).

Emerson's interest in the power of thought or intelligence runs parallel to Dewey's own. His 'idealism', Dewey argues, is in large measure 'a hymn to intelligence, a paean to the all-creating, all-disturbing power of thought'. Dewey cites 'History': 'Beware when the great God lets loose a thinker on this planet. Then all things are at risk. The very hopes of man, the thoughts of his heart, the religion of nations, the manners and morals of mankind are all at the mercy of a new generalization' (*MW* 3: 187). Dewey's reconstructive philosophy aims at no less than such a new set of generalizations. As he put it seventeen years later in his prophetic conclusion to *Reconstruction in Philosophy*:

When philosophy shall have cooperated with the course of events and made clear and coherent the meaning of the daily detail, science and emotion will interpenetrate, practice and imagination will embrace. Poetry and religious feeling will be the unforced flowers of life. To further this articulation and revelation of the meanings of the current course of events is the task and problem of philosophy in days of transition.   (*MW* 12: 201)

6. CAVELL, EMERSON, ROMANTICISM, PRAGMATISM

Stanley Cavell revolutionized the study of the transcendentalists in *The Senses of Walden* (1971) and a series of essays about Emerson collected in

Emerson's Transcendental Etudes (2003). He has also published a book on romanticism, *In Quest of the Ordinary* (1988), that draws out the affinities between Wordsworth's and Coleridge's attention to the common, ordinary, and low, and Wittgenstein's attention to ordinary language, and between Wittgenstein's idea that philosophy arises in a sense of loss or displacement and romanticism's search for a way 'home'.

Cavell claims to 'inherit' the philosophy of Emerson and Thoreau, to bring their words to life in a new way—for example, by understanding *Walden* as being about writing as much as about building, and by finding in Emerson's 'Experience' an 'epistemology of moods'. Cavell resists the suggestion that Emerson is a 'proto-pragmatist', which he sees as one more stage in what he thinks of as the 'repression' of Emerson's and Thoreau's thought—not only by philosophy (which has mostly ignored them in both its analytic and its pragmatist dispensations) but by the culture at large (Cavell 1998). Nevertheless, one can appreciate the ways in which Emerson's thought anticipates and even influences the pragmatists, without neglecting the strong new readings that Cavell provides (cf. Goodman 1990, 2005).

Central to one line of these readings is the idea of reception, an exemplary statement of which appears at the end of Emerson's 'Experience':

I should feel it pitiful to demand a result on this town and country, an overt effect on the instant month and year. The effect is deep and secular as the cause. It works on periods in which mortal lifetime is lost. All I know is reception; I am and I have: but I do not get, and when I have fancied I had gotten anything, I found I did not.   (*CW* 3: 48)

This sounds too long-term for Dewey and other pragmatists, who wish precisely for 'results on this town and country'.[9] Emerson is less confident in our powers, holding that these results are not something we can 'get'—although they may be received. Cavell finds connections between Emersonian reception and Heidegger's ideas of 'letting things be' and thinking as thanking (2003: 144–9), and he argues that, like Heidegger, Emerson engages the philosophy of Kant. Emerson reverses Kant, Cavell argues, in 'picturing the intellectual hemisphere of knowledge as passive or receptive and the intuitive or instinctual hemisphere as active or spontaneous' (2003: 13).

---

[9] I don't mean to suggest that Peirce, or even for the most part James, expected immediate results from their philosophies. Both had 'long-run' conceptions of truth, including the truth of philosophical systems.

James found in Emerson a strong sense of his own vocation, and Dewey praised him for his goal of cultivating the genius in each one of us. Cavell's 'Being Odd, Getting Even' is a study—in far greater detail than anything by James or Dewey—of Emerson's best-known essay, 'Self-Reliance'. The essay is about independence, originality, and 'the authoring of myself' (2003: 89), but also about conformity, fear, and dispiriting routine. At the center of Cavell's interpretation lies this sentence: 'Man is timid and apologetic; he is no longer upright; he dares not say "I think", "I am", but quotes some saint or sage' (*CW* 2: 38). Cavell points out that Emerson is quoting a sage, Descartes. What is his point? Just as Descartes claims that he only knows for certain that he exists when he thinks, Emerson is saying that we only exist—exist in an 'existentialist' sense—when we think for ourselves. Mostly, however, we do not live such a life. Emerson calls our condition 'conformity', and Cavell calls it 'uncreated life' (2003: 89).

Focusing on the words 'timid', 'apologetic', and 'upright' in Emerson's statement, Cavell finds that Emerson diagnoses a customary human life of shame, of apology for our very existence. Emerson's 'proposed therapy is to become ashamed of our shame, to find our ashamed posture more shameful than anything it could be reacting to'. Good posture can be a matter of either standing or sitting, and the idea behind both, Cavell asserts, is 'finding and taking and staying in a place'. Sitting, he continues, is 'the posture of being at home in the world' (2003: 91).

James was a great writer, and Dewey praises Emerson's and Plato's union of philosophy and poetry; but it is Cavell who most intimately integrates the literary and the philosophical in his work—all the while claiming to be a philosopher and that his chosen subjects Emerson and Thoreau are philosophers as well. In doing so, he attempts to reshape what we think of as philosophy. In his essay 'The Philosopher in American Life' he draws a distinction between two forms of 'rigor' in philosophy, one of which proceeds by arguments and the other through 'reading', but reading as described by Emerson and Thoreau. In 'The American Scholar' Emerson calls for 'creative reading as well as creative writing', and in *Walden* Thoreau speaks of 'reading, in a high sense', of books 'that we have to stand on tiptoe to read and devote our most alert and wakeful hours to' (1989 [1854]: 104). For both writers, Cavell argues, reading is a 'process of *being read*' (1988: 16), a process of self-transformation. Emerson's writing speaks to you, intimately, as a friend who by his own example and his pointed questions serves the quest for the better self.

7. CONCLUSION

All the writers considered here think of philosophy as transforming our way of life, and all see a pulse of individuality at the center of such transformations, like a pebble dropped in a pond. Emerson expresses the idea in another way in 'Self-Reliance' when he advises: 'A man should learn to detect and watch that gleam of light which flashes across his mind from within, more than the luster of the firmament of bards and sages' (*CW* 2: 27). Dewey finds this Emersonian spark in each child, in what he calls the child's 'interests': it is these, rather than some subject matter from outside, that are the key to any real education (*EW* 5: 111–50). James holds that our personal points of view, our angles on the universe, are the places where 'we catch reality in the making' and have the deepest insights into its nature. Cavell addresses questions of individual existence in his analyses of Emerson and Thoreau and in his discussions of 'voice' (cf. Cavell 1994 and Gould 1998).

However much they are focused on the self, these romantic philosophers also have much to say about what lies beyond it. Cavell investigates 'the problem of other minds' with the assistance of *King Lear* and *Othello*, and finds that 'acknowledgment' and 'avoidance' play a key role in our knowledge of others. James finds the all-encompassing universe of the absolute idealists suffocating, and wants to do justice to the wildness of the world. Life, he writes, 'feels like a real fight—as if there were something really wild in the universe which we, with all our idealities and faithfulnesses, are needed to redeem' (1979 [1897]: 61). Emerson acknowledges both the power of the individual and the equal power of fate or circumstance. As he writes in 'Fate': 'Once we thought, positive power was all. Now we learn, that negative power, or circumstance, is half' (*CW* 6: 8). Dewey finds the world an 'irresistible mixture of sufficiencies, tight completenesses, order, recurrences which make possible prediction and control, and singularities, ambiguities, uncertain possibilities, processes going on to consequences as yet indeterminate' (*LW* 1: 47).

For all these writers, then, we must negotiate a world that resists but also sustains us, and in which our thought brings us immense power. Perhaps the best advice for conducting ourselves in such a world is Emerson's: 'To finish the moment, to find the journey's end in every step of the road, to live the greatest number of good hours, is wisdom' (*CW* 3: 35).

REFERENCES

Abrams, M. H. (1971). *Natural Supernaturalism: Tradition and Revolution in Romantic Literature*. New York: Norton.

Allen, Gay Wilson (1982). *Waldo Emerson*. New York: Penguin.

Beiser, Frederick C. (2003). *The Romantic Imperative: The Concept of Early German Romanticism*. Cambridge, MA: Harvard University Press.

Bense, James (2006). 'At Odds with "De-transcendentalizing Emerson": The Case of William James'. *New England Quarterly*, 79/3: 355–86.

Berlin, Isaiah (2001 [1999]). *The Roots of Romanticism*. Princeton: Princeton University Press.

Bloom, Harold (1971). *The Ringers in the Tower*. Chicago: University of Chicago Press.

Carpenter, Frederic I. (1939). 'William James and Emerson'. *American Literature*, 11/1: 39–57.

Cavell, Stanley (1971). *The Senses of Walden*. San Francisco: North Point Press.

——— (1988). *In Quest of the Ordinary*. Chicago and London: University of Chicago Press.

——— (1990). *Conditions Handsome and Unhandsome: The Constitution of Emersonian Perfectionism*. Chicago: University of Chicago Press.

——— (1994). *A Pitch of Philosophy: Autobiographical Exercises*. Chicago: University of Chicago Press.

——— (1998). 'What's the Use of Calling Emerson a Pragmatist'. In Morris Dickstein (ed.), *The Revival of Pragmatism: New Essays on Social Thought, Law, and Culture*, Durham, NC, and London: Duke University Press, 72–80.

——— (2003). *Emerson's Transcendental Etudes*. Stanford, CA: Stanford University Press.

Coleridge, Samuel Taylor (1965 [1817]). *Biographia Literaria*. London: J. M. Dent.

——— (1829). *Aids to Reflection*, with a preliminary essay by James Marsh. Burlington, VT: C. Goodrich.

——— (1961). *The Portable Coleridge*, ed. I. A. Richards. New York: Penguin.

Dewey, John (1972). *The Early Works of John Dewey*, v: *Essays, 1882–1898*. Carbondale, IL: Southern Illinois University Press.

——— (1976). *The Middle Works of John Dewey*. Carbondale, IL: Southern Illinois University Press.

——— (1981). *The Later Works of John Dewey*. Carbondale, IL: Southern Illinois University Press.

Emerson, Ralph Waldo (1971–). *The Collected Works of Ralph Waldo Emerson.* Cambridge, MA: Harvard University Press.

Frye, Northrop (1968). *A Study of English Romanticism.* Chicago: University of Chicago Press.

Girel, Mathias (2004). 'Les Angles de l'acte: usages d'Emerson dans la philosophie de William James'. *Cahier Charles V*, 37: 207–45.

Goodman, Russell B. (1990). *American Philosophy and the Romantic Tradition.* Cambridge: Cambridge University Press.

—— (2005). 'Cavell and American Philosophy'. In Russell B. Goodman (ed.), *Contending with Stanley Cavell*, New York: Oxford University Press, 100–17.

—— (2007). 'Two Genealogies of Action in Pragmatism'. *Cognitio*, 8/2: 213–22.

Gould, Timothy (1998). *Hearing Things: Voice and Method in the Writing of Stanley Cavell.* Chicago: University of Chicago Press.

James, William (1978 [1878]). 'Remarks on Spencer's Definition of Mind as Correspondence'. In *Essays in Philosophy*, Cambridge, MA: Harvard University Press, 7–22.

—— (1981 [1890]). *The Principles of Psychology.* Cambridge, MA: Harvard University Press.

—— (1979 [1897]). *The Will to Believe and Other Essays in Popular Philosophy.* Cambridge, MA: Harvard University Press.

—— (1979 [1898]). 'Philosophical Conceptions and Practical Results'. In *Pragmatism*, Cambridge, MA: Harvard University Press, 257–70.

—— (1987). *Writings 1902–1910.* New York: Library of America.

—— (1992–). *The Correspondence of William James*, ed. Ignas K. Skrupskelis and Elizabeth M. Berkeley, 12 vols. Charlottesville, VA, and London: University Press of Virginia.

Peirce, Charles Sanders (1992). *The Essential Peirce*, i, ed. Nathan Houser and Christian Kloesel. Bloomington, IN: Indiana University Press.

Perry, Ralph Barton (1935). *The Thought and Character of William James*, 2 vols. Boston: Little, Brown.

Russell, Bertrand (1921). *The Analysis of Mind.* London: Allen and Unwin.

Thoreau, Henry David (1989 [1854]). *Walden.* Princeton: Princeton University Press.

Wordsworth, William (1982). *The Poetical Works of Wordsworth.* Boston: Houghton Mifflin.

CHAPTER 3

PEIRCE
AND PRAGMATISM:
AMERICAN
CONNECTIONS

DOUGLAS ANDERSON

In 1837 Ralph Waldo Emerson announced his famous search for an American scholar: "Perhaps the time is already come when it ought to be, and will be, something else; when the sluggard intellect of this continent will look from under its iron lids and fill the postponed expectation of the world with something better than the exertions of mechanical skill" (1940: 45). Young Charles Peirce, who recalled Emerson at his family's dinner table and who fondly remembered a carriage ride with Emerson's co-Transcendentalist Margaret Fuller, would by 1871 begin to fill this role of American scholar. Peirce was born to Harvard mathematician Benjamin Peirce and his wife Sarah Mills Peirce in Cambridge, Massachusetts, in 1839. From Cambridge High School Peirce went on to study at Harvard, did a year of graduate study there, and then studied chemistry at the Lawrence Scientific School. His adult public life was constituted by a series of failures; his private life was marked by tireless and financially profitless work in philosophy, logic, and the history of ideas. Peirce worked as an assistant with the Coast Survey beginning in 1872 and then, while continuing to work part-time with the Survey, taught at Johns Hopkins University from 1879 to 1883. Essentially fired by Johns Hopkins in 1883 and by the Coast Survey in 1891, Peirce spent the rest of his life with his second wife Juliette at his home in Milford, Pennsylvania, for the most part impoverished and unrecognized in the academic world. He died there in 1914.

Emerson added that his American scholar "must be an inventor to read well", "must relinquish display and immediate fame", and "worse yet, he must accept—how often!—poverty and solitude" (1940: 51, 55). These additional features well describe Peirce, originator of America's best-known and most widely disseminated philosophical tradition, pragmatism. Peirce seldom championed his own originality. Indeed, he argued repeatedly that pragmatism was incipient in the history of philosophy, and that the novelty of his work was to identify it and develop descriptions of it. "It is my conviction", he argued, "that any philosophical idea that in this age of the world is altogether novel is subject to a *prima facie* presumption of falsity" (1998: 428).

For Peirce, as for Aristotle and Hegel, philosophy was a historical practice. It was not, however, historicist. Each philosopher's task was to engage in a dialogue with the history of philosophy from the perspective of her or his own present doubts and beliefs. This was the basis for Peirce's well-known emphasis on the importance of a community of inquirers who would work together through history to try to advance on the truth. Thus, for Peirce, philosophy was an evolutionary and developmental cultural practice and process.

Richard Rorty famously announced in his *Consequences of Pragmatism* that Peirce's "contribution to pragmatism was merely to have given it a name, and to have stimulated James" (1982: 61). This assessment is much more appropriate to Rorty's rhetorical needs than it is to the history of American thought. Pragmatism was of course first publicly named by William James in a lecture he gave in California in 1898. But the leading ideas of pragmatism grew out of conversations of the so-called "Metaphysical Club" which Peirce and James attended as young men in the 1860s. These ideas were first given articulation in the opening essays of Peirce's 1877 series of essays entitled "Illustrations of the Logic of Science" in the *Popular Science Monthly*. As Peirce recalled,

It appears to have been virtually the philosophy of Socrates. But although it is "an old way of thinking," in the sense that it was practiced by Spinoza, Berkeley, and Kant, I am not aware of it having been formulated, whether as a maxim of logical analysis or otherwise, by anybody before my publication of it in 1878. Naturally, nobody ever heard of pragmatism. . . . So it was not until in 1898—Professor James took hold of the thing, dignified it by calling it by its name in print (which I had never done . . .), furbished it up, and turned it into a philosophical doctrine—that it had any vogue at all.   (CP 6. 490)[1]

Throughout his career Peirce insisted that "pragmatism is, in itself, no doctrine of metaphysics, no attempt to determine any truth of things", but rather "a method of ascertaining the meanings of hard words and of abstract concepts" (1998: 400). This basic method was affirmed by all the pragmatists. The method, as Peirce expressed it in 1878, was to assess the meaning of thoughts by the "habits of action" they entailed—in other words, by way of the "would be" effects we conceive the "object of our conception" to have (1992: 131–2). Moreover, as Peirce admitted, the method, though not a metaphysical doctrine, led to a variety of metaphysical, epistemological, ethical, and political consequences developed variously by himself and by James, Royce, Dewey, and Schiller. This generated the wider philosophical movement that was developed under the name of "pragmatism".

  Peirce's role as the American scholar of the method of pragmatism is clear. He first formulated it, and the other pragmatists drew on this formulation for their own work. Peirce's role in developing the wider philosophical movement is less clear, since as a solitary, impoverished, not widely known scholar, his impact was often obscured. However, Peirce *was* an inventive reader, and the consequences of his own pragmatism served to underwrite and to influence extensively the subsequent work of James, Royce, and Dewey. He acted as a sort of philosophical lens or prism through which the history of Western philosophy took on a uniquely American cast. Pragmatism was, at least in part, the result of his transformative reading of Western thought. He revised the ontological categories; he developed evolutionary theory into a historical and a cosmological theory; he argued for the continuous nature of the real; and he defended a scholastic realism and an objective idealism that entailed the importance of purposes, of natural laws, and of human beliefs and habits. All of these were, for him, upshots of a pragmatic logic that was attuned to the actual practices of scientific inquirers and was what Dewey later called a "theory of inquiry".

---

  [1] Citations of Peirce's *Collected Papers* follow standard practice: *CP* plus volume and paragraph number.

Peirce was clear that his pragmatism, which he later renamed "pragmat-icism", and overall philosophical outlook were a creative development from his reading of the history of philosophy. So, one fruitful way of understanding his work is to outline the basics of his thought by way of its historical connec-tions. To do this, however, it is important to keep in mind the architectonic nature of his work, which was influenced by the history of philosophy; this becomes clear in his explicit imitation of Aristotle, Kant, and Hegel. At various points in his life Peirce wrote essays in which he attempted to sketch his overall outlook; well known among these are his 1868 "On a New List of Categories", his unpublished late 1880s "A Guess at the Riddle", and his 1908 "A Neglected Argument for the Reality of God". Using these and other writings, it is possible to outline, at least in rough fashion, Peirce's pragmatic philosophy and to sketch its influence on the history of American thought.

GREEK CONNECTIONS: MODES OF BEING AND METHOD

The philosophy of Plato, as for all early American philosophy, stood in the background of Peirce's work. His identification of Socrates as a proto-pragmatist was not accidental. Socrates endeavored to treat philosophy as a dialogue among a community of inquirers, and even as some ideas gained clarity, he was willing to live with whatever indeterminacy the conversation yielded. In a rough way, Socrates can be said to be a forerunner of the practice of inductive inquiry (see Ransdell 2000). On the side of metaphysics, Plato's offering of the Ideas or Forms in response to the puzzles generated by Parmenides served as a groundwork for Peirce's own ontological speculations regarding the primary modes of being, of which he believed there were three. Depending on how one interprets Plato, one can see him as a nominalist who made the Forms out to be discrete entities or as an incipient realist who championed the reality of general ideas. Peirce eventually adopted the latter view of Plato, and in 1903 identified Plato's thought as one of the few that squared with his own tripartite ontology: "The metaphysics that recognizes all the categories . . . embraces Kantism,—Reid's philosophy and the Platonic philosophy of which Aristotelianism is a special development" (1998: 180).

To the degree that Plato lurked quietly in the background, Aristotle stood squarely in the foreground as a model of philosophical engagement for Peirce. Peirce often referred to himself as an Aristotelian (especially of the "scholastic" or "realistic" wing) and, in turn, conceived of Aristotle in modern terms: "Aristotle was a thorough-paced scientific man such as we see nowadays except for this, that he ranged over all knowledge" (1998: 28). Peirce, who studied and worked in chemistry, psychology, and astronomy, saw himself in this light: a scientist who was also a logician, a cosmologist, and a metaphysician. In his introduction to "A Guess at the Riddle" Peirce gave voice to his ambitious hope "to make a philosophy like that of Aristotle, that is to say, to outline a theory so comprehensive that, for a long time to come, the entire work of human reason, in mathematics, in psychology, in physical science, in history, in sociology, and in whatever other department there may be, shall appear as the filling up of its detail" (*CP* 1. 1).

Besides the ambition to range widely across the fields of human learning, Peirce drew some more specific lessons from Aristotle. Seeing that philosophy and the special sciences were continuous and not radically separated as some see them today, Peirce sought to link them through the study of logic. In this project, Aristotle served as a mentor. On the one hand, study of formal logic led Aristotle to consider the bases of scientific inquiry in the *Posterior Analytics*. On the other hand, the analysis of the *Categories* led directly to discussions of the metaphysical modes of being. Peirce drew heavily on these foundations.

Logic, for him, came to involve a theory of inquiry and a general theory of signs. How is it that reason takes us from what we do know to the knowing of new things? Peirce early on saw the inadequacy of the deductivist model of the scholastics and the moderns, and he sought to return philosophy to its Aristotelian roots. Deduction—or "demonstration"—was only a link within the larger process of inquiry. This process led from existential doubt to hypotheses (abduction) to predictions (deduction) to testing (induction). The process was also observational and experimental and, as Peirce quickly noted, it was the basis for all learning and education. Logic, as a normative science governing the process of inquiry, also required a discussion of truth as its ideal or regulative hope. The pragmatic conception of truth thus became a central issue in the history of pragmatism, from William James to Richard Rorty. Peirce understood the importance of this conception and worked hard to make clear his own account of truth. Because of the evolutionary nature of scientific inquiry, the ideal of truth was, he suggested, pushed to a "would be" status that characterized the potential outcome of an indefinite history of inquiry carried out by an indefinitely constituted community of inquirers. Truth is thus constituted, as Cheryl Misak has argued, of those beliefs that are indefeasible (2004: 7). This was not a simplistic theory of convergence, as some have suggested, especially since the true and the real are both general and, thus, ultimately unspecifiable. Peirce never expected an *actual* final opinion. As he put it: "I hold that truth's independence of individual opinions is due (so far as there is any 'truth') to its being the predestined result to which sufficient inquiry *would* ultimately lead" (1998: 419).

On the side of metaphysics, Peirce stayed the course of Aristotle's attempt to locate the fundamental categories of being through logical inquiry. "I, for my part," Peirce maintained, "cannot for an instant assent to the proposal to base logic upon metaphysics, inasmuch as I fully agree with Aristotle, Duns Scotus, Kant and all of the profoundest metaphysicians that metaphysics can, on the contrary, have no secure basis except that which the science of logic affords" (1998: 257). Thus, in 1867, following the leads of Aristotle and Kant, Peirce wrote "On a New List of Categories", in which he established his own three fundamental categories: firstness, secondness, and thirdness. "The *list of categories*", he said, "is a table of conceptions drawn from logical analysis of thought and regarded as applicable to being" (*CP* 1. 300). These categories would underwrite his philosophical work for the rest of his career. Peirce notably identified this essay as his "one contribution to philosophy" (*CP* 8. 213), and he returned to it again and again as he developed his systematic work in logic and metaphysics. Though Peirce was quick to say that "nobody will suppose that I wish to claim any originality in reckoning the triad important in philosophy" (*CP* 1. 368), his categories *were* novel, and he spent his career both explicating their meaning and employing them to explicate the other features of his philosophy.

In his "New List" essay Peirce first began this process of explanation and explication. There the categories were identified as Ground, Correlate, and Sign or Interpretant, through an analysis of how a proposition gives articulation to existence and being. Peirce also hinted at the intimate relation between signs and reality, foreshadowing both his semeiotic and his scholastic realism. Furthermore, he made his first specific foray into the categorization of signs, distinguishing among "likenesses, indices, and symbols". Finally, he sketched in Aristotelian fashion a linkage between formal logic with its triad of terms, propositions, and arguments and a logic of inquiry that distinguished three modes of argumentation—hypothesis (later abduction and retroduction), deduction, and induction. Thus, the "New List" set Peirce on the way to achieving his Aristotelian aims, and it manifested in a seminal way both pragmatism and his larger architectonic.

Peirce often emphasized the importance of Aristotle's two modes of being and suggested that, at heart, Aristotle's thought was evolutionary in nature. Looking past Aristotle's conception of substance, Peirce, perhaps inventively, saw in Aristotle's work a foreshadowing of his own categories. Though he occasionally stated that Aristotle addressed all three of his categories, Peirce was insistent that at least two of them were clearly present in Aristotle's work and that this fact set him apart from modern philosophy:

The doctrine of Aristotle is distinguished from substantially all modern philosophy (except perhaps Schelling's or mine) by its recognition of at least two grades of being. That is, besides *actual reactive existence*, Aristotle recognizes a germinal being, an *esse in potentia*, or, as I like to call it, an *esse in futuro*.   (1998: 180; see also *CP* 6. 356)

Modern philosophy, governed, as Peirce thought, by materialism and nominalism, recognized only actual existence (Peirce's secondness), and thus missed the other two categories. Peirce, then, relied on Aristotle as an early authority in defense of spontaneity, possibility, and firstness—the category of the "may be" of the future.

Most importantly, for Peirce, the inclusion of an "embryonic kind of being" suggested that at its heart Aristotle's "system, like all the greatest systems, was evolutionary" (*CP* 1. 22; see also 6. 604). The relation of a tree to its seed was not merely of one discrete entity mechanically causing another; rather, the relationship was constituted by a process of growth in which the outcome was already incipient in the seed. Both the evolutionary process of growth and the continuity of being it implied became key features of Peirce's own metaphysical and cosmological speculations. Impressed as he was with Aristotle's work, Peirce then followed its influence into the late medieval world.

THE MEDIEVAL DIVIDE: SCOTISTIC REALISM

As the Hellenic and Roman worlds were transformed by Christianity, Plato and Aristotle were likewise transformed. Peirce never adhered to medieval deductivism as a philosophical method, and he deplored the medievals' resistance to the scientific study of nature. But he nevertheless appreciated the attitude of medieval philosophers, for whom truth was more important than self-aggrandizement. As Peirce wrote of the scholastic period: "Nothing is more striking in either of the great intellectual products of that age, than the complete absence of self-conceit on the part of the artist or philosopher" (*CP* 8. 11). Peirce took this attitude to be a condition of genuine inquiry.

Still, the Middle Ages provided Peirce's thought with more than an attitude appropriate to inquiry. In tracing the history of logic, he was led to investigate a wide range of medieval thinkers. He was impressed by the closeness of their reasoning, from Augustine to Roscellinus to John of Salisbury to St. Thomas. He was also impressed by the original work in semiotics that was to be found among the medieval logicians. But it was a metaphysical upshot of these logical studies that became the focus of Peirce's medieval study. This upshot was the debate between realism and nominalism. The dispute, driven in part by varying interpretations of Plato and Aristotle, was clearly laid out by Abelard, Salisbury, and others, but reached its zenith in the work of Ockham and Scotus.

The dispute, as Peirce characterized it, was whether generals (signs, concepts, beliefs, and laws) could be real—that is, could be independent of how individual thinkers might regard them. If such generals could be real, then there was reason to defend Peirce's category of thirdness as a true description of the universe. Thus Peirce became an avid defender of scholastic or Scotistic realism, and blamed many of modern philosophy's difficulties on its being premised on a tacit nominalistic ontology. Especially within the history of British philosophy, Peirce laid the blame for this at the feet of Ockham and his followers. He offered as an "unquestionable fact" the belief that "all modern philosophy is built upon Ockhamism, by which I mean that it is all nominalistic" (1998: 156). It was precisely this medieval divide between nominalism and realism that, as Peirce saw it, controlled much of subsequent modern philosophy both in Britain and on the Continent. When we turn to Peirce's legacy in American thought, we will return to this divide and its consequences.

MODERN BRITISH CONNECTIONS: LOGIC, PRAGMATISM, AND COMMON SENSE

Peirce's engagement with the history of modern philosophy was in many ways, though of course not exclusively, a tale of two cultures: the British and the Germanic. I say "not exclusively" because in several essays in the late 1860s Peirce notably attacked Descartes's apriorist intuitionism and dismissed the suggestion that genuine inquiry could effectively begin with a constructed or "fake" doubt. Nevertheless, when working with a broad brush, Peirce persistently drew interesting contrasts between German and British philosophy. The British, so he believed, kept alive the medieval interest in close logical studies and the functions of language, while their metaphysical outlooks seemed haphazardly constructed. "The English", he claimed, tended to pursue "one idea" philosophies that were "interesting and instructive" but "quite unsound" (*CP* 6. 7). At the same time, in reviewing Stanley Jevons's (1874) claim that "dialectic is the art of arts" he wrote:

Jevons adopted the sentence as the motto of his most scientific contribution to logic, and it would express the purpose of my memoirs, which is, upon the ground well prepared by Jevons and his teacher De Morgan, and by the other great English researchers, especially Boole, Whewell, Berkeley, Glanvill, Ockham, and Duns Scotus, to lay a solid foundation upon which may be erected a new logic fit for the life of twentieth century science.   (*CP* 7. 161)

It was on this foundation that Peirce built his initial pragmatism in "The Fixation of Belief" and "How to Make Our Ideas Clear" in the 1870s. And again in the 1880s it served as the basis for his development of his own logic of relatives and, later, for his existential graphs by which this logic of relatives was put to work (see, e.g., 1998: 44–5).

But Peirce's conception of logic was never narrow—never restricted to deductive formalism. Locke, Berkeley, and Hume all pursued philosophy in a way that was partly experimental. Berkeley in particular struck Peirce as a proto-pragmatist in his theory of vision and in his more general explanation of the interpretive and inferential process involved in perception. Berkeley was among those in whose writing Peirce "sometimes came upon strains of thought that recalled the ways of thinking of the laboratory, so that he felt he might trust to them" (*CP* 5. 412; see also 2. 65). Berkeley was also among those who pursued and developed the medieval insight "that every thought is a sign" (*CP* 5. 470) and "that all thinking is performed in Signs" (*CP* 6. 481). Peirce realized that a full logic of inquiry would require not only the technical clarity of a logic of relations but also the breadth and range of a general theory of signs, as he came to describe his semiotic.

Thus, pragmatism, which for Peirce found its home in logic as a theory of meaning, held consequences for the rest of his architectonic. One needed to know something of the nature of inquirers and their practice, of the nature of the truth and reality to which inquiry appealed, and of the nature of the signs by which inquiry took place. Consequently, in his 1903 lectures on pragmatism, Peirce illustrated that pursuing meaning through consequences required a process of inquiry that could relate a concept, a thought, or a sign to its consequences. Following Berkeley's lead, Peirce succinctly stated the relationship in a 1908 letter to Cassius Keyser: "All our thinking takes place in signs of some kind, the premises are signs of the conclusions" (MS L233: 00005).[2] In this way, he came to suggest that pragmatism, broadly understood, is the logic of abduction—that is, of hypothesizing what an abstract concept and its object might mean, of deducing its "would be" consequences, and of testing inductively to see if these consequences are borne out in experience. This is the way he characterized "pragmaticism". A few years later, Peirce offered yet another description of pragmatism. He revised the Scottish common-sense philosophy of Reid and Stewart in light of his own experimentalism, stating that common sensism—when a critical dimension is added—*is* pragmatism. This he called his "critical common sensism". His point was that all thought ultimately comes to rest on instinctive or common-sense beliefs, but that even these most basic and most stable beliefs must be open to criticism and revision whenever a real doubt should arise concerning their import or truth. All beliefs must finally be tested in their living effects.

Despite the extent to which Peirce relied on British logic and even metaphysical theory, he believed, as we noted, that these were systematically undermined by the nominalism inherited from Ockham: "Locke and all his following, Berkeley, Hartley, Hume and even Reid were nominalists" (*CP* 1. 19). He believed that it was a mistake "to suppose that" the doctrine that every thought is a sign "is peculiarly nominalistic" (*CP* 5. 470). His aim, then, was not only to build on the work of the English thinkers but also to couple what he took to be the "truths" of this tradition with his Scotistic-Aristotelian realism to see what the merger would yield. To carry out this task, he turned to the German metaphysicians, especially Kant, Hegel, and Schelling.

---

[2] Citations of *The Charles S. Peirce Papers* follow standard practice: MS number followed by page number.

GERMAN CONNECTIONS: CATEGORIES
AND IDEALISM

Peirce, as much as he respected the intricacy of German idealism, believed that it rested on poor logic. Of Kant, for example, he remarked: "his examination of [the universal categories and the functions of judgment] is most hasty, superficial, trivial, and even trifling, while throughout his works, replete as they are with evidences of logical genius, there is manifest a most astounding ignorance of the traditional logic, even of the very *Summae Logicales*, the elementary schoolbook of the Plantagenet era" (*CP* 1. 560). And in discussing his own development of evolutionary thought, Peirce remarked: "my own method has resulted from a more deliberate examination of the exact theory of logic (in which Hegel's age, and especially his own country, and more especially he himself were decidedly weak)" (*CP* 1. 453). Despite this weakness, the German thinkers offered a strong metaphysical outlook to offset the British nominalistic traditions of materialism and mechanism.

With the exception of Schelling, Peirce did not consider the German idealists to be full-blown realists. Nevertheless, as he put it, Kant and Hegel showed a yearning for realism that was absent among the British and opened avenues by which a contemporary, scientifically minded realism might be achieved. Kant and, even more emphatically, Hegel and Schelling defended several theses that Peirce took to be corollaries of his scholastic realism. Moreover, they tended to resist and to avoid what Peirce referred to as the "daughters of nominalism,—sensationalism, phenomenalism, individualism [which included atomism], and materialism" (*CP* 8. 38).

Kant was decidedly the central figure in Peirce's philosophical development: "Before I came to man's estate, being greatly impressed with Kant's *Critic of the Pure Reason*, my father, who was an eminent mathematician, pointed out to me lacunae in Kant's reasoning" (1998: 423; see also *CP* 1. 300). These lacunae, as we noted, were in part what stimulated Peirce to develop his "new list" of categories. He found persuasive features in Kant's reconstruction of Aristotle's universal categories. As Peirce saw it, Kant was goaded by Leibniz and Hume into seeing the fact that claims to universal and necessary truth went "further than experience can warrant" (*CP* 5. 382). Kant then turned to seek out the conditions of human reasoning. As Peirce put it,

Nature only appears intelligible so far as it appears rational, that is, so far as its processes are seen to be like processes of thought. . . . It follows that if we find three distinct and irreducible forms of rhemata, the ideas of these should be the three elementary conceptions of metaphysics. That there are three elementary forms of categories is the conclusion of Kant, to which Hegel subscribes.   (*CP* 3. 422)

Kant located the three forms in each of his four types of Pure Concepts. Thus Peirce's categories "correspond to the three categories of each of the four triads of Kant's table" (*CP* 8. 329).

What Peirce did was to distill from the Kantian triads and, by way of his own analysis of semiosis, or sign processes, create his own three fundamental categories: "I will only mention here that the ideas which belong to the three forms of rhemata are firstness, secondness, and thirdness; firstness, or spontaneity; secondness, or dependence; thirdness, or mediation" (*CP* 3. 422). Peirce saw in Kant's triads the sort of reciprocal relationship that governed his three forms of being. For example, in establishing causality, Kant maintained the necessity of substance for the possibility of subjective action; then there needed to be the dyadic relation of cause and effect; but finally there needed to be the full *communitas* in which the subject and its other could carry out the causal process. Thus, substance is most necessary, and *communitas* is most sufficient. But the upshot is that while substance and causality can be abstracted from the generality of community, community cannot be obtained merely from the first two. It is precisely the reality of the third—its independence from the first two—that enables all else to be as it is. Peirce believed that Kant had confronted the nominalist/empiricist issue of non-necessary reasoning and worked his way back toward scholastic realism. "Indeed," he claimed, "what Kant called his Copernican step was precisely the passage from the nominalistic to the realistic view of reality. It was the essence of his philosophy to regard the real object as determined by the mind" (*CP* 8. 15).

As a student of Kant, Peirce not surprisingly turned to the work of Hegel. Peirce regarded Hegel as "in some respects the greatest philosopher that ever lived" but also "lamentably deficient in . . . critical severity and sense of fact" (*CP* 1. 524). Peirce believed that Hegel "brought out the three elements much more clearly" than had Kant: "His three stages of thought, although he does not apply the word *category* to them, are what I should call Hegel's Universal Categories... and may I say, at once, that I consider Hegel's three stages as being roughly speaking, the correct list of Universal categories" (*CP* 5. 43). Especially in his *Phenomenology* Hegel developed the variety of ways in which these stages or elements were manifest in experience and nature. The best known of these manifestations is that the categories are put into play organically to provide a picture of the evolution of the stages of history. Hegel understood that "the universe is everywhere permeated with continuous growth" (*CP* 1. 40). Peirce thus saw Hegelian thought as addressing the contemporary need to explore philosophically the facts of evolution in biology, geology, etc. Hegel gave voice to a modern evolutionary philosophy, though in a decidedly seminarian and non-scientific fashion. The Hegelian move to place the categories in a process of growth also led to an affirmation of the continuity of being; organic growth, unlike mechanical causality, featured the relatedness of all that is. Peirce appreciated this turn in Hegel insofar as it helped to make sense of his own synechism. But it arose in part because Hegel focused so exclusively on the dominance of Mind or Spirit, what Peirce thought of as thirdness.

Consequently, Peirce's most consistent critique of Hegel was that, though he brought Kant's triad of forms into clearer focus, he introduced firstness and secondness only to have them be *aufgehoben* (*CP* 5. 79; see also 1. 524, 4. 318, and 8. 41). In doing so, he overlooked the fact that they are as "real and able to stand their ground as the *Begriff* itself" (*CP* 8. 268). Peirce lauded Hegel's recognition of the reality of thirdness—and his "realistic yearnings" (*CP* 1. 19)—since this was precisely the antidote to British nominalism that Peirce wished to develop. But the overlooking of the other two categories was a mistake of Hegel's a priori method. In dismissing secondness, Hegel ignored the "outward clash" and our experiences of the "brute element" (*CP* 8. 272). For Peirce, reason, as thirdness, always remains constrained by the otherness of the brute element. Hegel forgot, Peirce argued, that "I find myself in a world of forces which act upon me, and it is they and not the logical transformations of my thought which determine what I shall ultimately believe" (*CP* 8. 45). The corollary is that because it is a priori, "The Absolute Knowledge of Hegel is nothing but G. W. F. Hegel's idea of himself" (*CP* 8. 118). Likewise, Hegel placed spontaneity at the origin of things only to have it overcome by the orderly march of Reason. In the cosmos, this would mean that possibility, spontaneity, and chance left the realm of nature;

this ran counter to Peirce's acceptance of evolutionary theory and to his statistical understanding of the work of the laws of nature. On the side of intellectual history, it meant that there was little to do except fill out Hegel's Logic. Peirce's fallibilism argued against the implicit hubris of Hegel's apriorist tendencies.

Nevertheless, when all is said and done, Peirce took Hegel's revised Kantianism to be an important development in response to British nominalism, a development that, though itself unscientific, helped to make sense of scientific method and beliefs. As Peirce wrote in 1904:

The truth is that pragmaticism is closely allied to the Hegelian absolute idealism, from which, however, it is sundered by its vigorous denial that the third category . . . suffices to make the world, or is even so much as self-sufficient. Had Hegel, instead of regarding the first two stages with his smile of contempt, held on to them as independent or distinct elements of the triune Reality, pragmatists might have looked up to him as the great vindicator of their truth.   (CP 5. 436)

Like John Dewey after him, Peirce recognized the need to temper Hegel's idealism with his notion of experimental inquiry. He saw his own principles as "what Hegel's might have been had he been educated in a physical laboratory instead of a theological seminary" (CP 8, Bibliography). Peirce turned to the Germans for their sophisticated ontology and their affinity with scholastic realism, but he tempered their absolutist tendencies with the English empirical experimentalism and proto-pragmatism he found in Berkeley and others. In maintaining the tension between the English and the Germans, he transformed both traditions in peculiar ways to form his own "American" philosophy.

American Connections: Peirce as American Scholar

Peirce's later years were filled with solitude and poverty, and if Emerson was right, this probably sealed Peirce's fate as the American scholar. As an inventive reader, he aligned his own thinking with another of the great German idealists, Friedrich Schelling. Though he never gave detailed reasons, he repeatedly identified himself with Schelling. Most likely, Schelling's work approximated the kind of middle ground that Peirce was seeking between

British nominalism and Hegel's absolute idealism. We know at least that Schelling, with his emphasis on freedom, tried to keep firstness categorially independent.

The history of philosophy passed through Peirce's living thought and was transformed into a uniquely American brand of philosophical reasoning. Unfortunately, critics like Paul Carus and the young Royce missed or rejected the novelty of Peirce's transformations and cast him as a relativist and skeptic—a charge that has been leveled at almost every pragmatist. Carus, for example, challenged Peirce's tychism and accused him of being the second coming of David Hume, claiming that "both shake the ultimate ground of scientific research at its root" (1892: 561–2). In response, Peirce quipped: "In the same number of the *Monist* in which Dr. Carus seeks to elevate me to the Satan-throne of a second Hume, I frankly pigeon-hole myself as a modified Schellingian, or New England Transcendentalist" (MS 958. 2). Peirce's attacks on apriorist philosophies were what led to his being likened to Hume. Both men argued that necessary and universal truths were beyond the warrant of human experience. For Carus and other nineteenth-century apriorists, epistemology was a matter of either/or: either you believe in some absolute, a priori truths or, as in the caricature of Hume, you give up on the real possibility of knowledge altogether. The choice is between absolute knowledge and skepticism. But for Peirce, "besides affirmative and negative, there are really probable enunciations, which are intermediate" (1998: 246). Peirce argued that because he was a pragmatist, he was also a probabilist, echoing what he had noted years earlier: "All human affairs rest upon probabilities, and the same thing is true everywhere" (1992: 149).

Pragmatism thus led on the one side to a method of inquiry shared generally by all claiming to be pragmatists in the early years of the twentieth century. If pragmatic meaning was to look at consequences, it would require time and a method of patience—one that could handle human finitude. Such a method, Peirce argued, "is no other than that experimental method by which all the successful sciences . . . have reached the degrees of certainty that are severally proper to them today;—this experimental method being itself nothing but a particular application of an older logical rule, 'By their fruits ye shall know them'" (1998: 400–1). Hegel had been correct to focus on the temporal and the historical development of knowledge; but, Peirce argued, he "overlooked the weakness of individual man, who wants the strength to wield such a weapon as 'the dialectical procedure of knowing'" (*CP* 1. 368).

Human finitude and fallibility require a community of committed inquirers if any move toward truth or what Dewey later called "warranted assertibility" is to be made. This community "must not be limited, but must extend to all races of beings with whom we can come into immediate or mediate intellectual relation" (1992: 149). The self-correction of the Hegelian method was again modified in a somewhat down-to-earth way; for Peirce, unlike Hegel, the self-correction of experimental inquiry was never guaranteed; it required the efforts of human will—only an indefinite community could carry out the ongoing process of criticism and correction. Standing between Hegel and Thomas Kuhn, he maintained that "science does not advance by revolutions, warfare, and cataclysms, but by cooperation, by each researcher's taking advantage of his predecessor's achievements, and by his joining his own work in one continuous piece to that already done" (*CP* 2. 157). The process of learning is human, but it is not chaotic; it is reasonable, but not deductively "rational". Foreshadowing Dewey's transformation from absolutism to experimentalism, Peirce continued his attack on the a priori method: "We must not begin by talking of pure ideas,—vagabond thoughts that tramp the public roads without any human habitation,—but must begin with men and their conversation" (*CP* 8. 112).

Pragmatism as a theory of meaning, and pragmaticism as the method of inquiry underwriting that theory, did not, however, leave one's world view unchanged. The adoption of pragmatic meaning and pragmaticistic epistemology raised metaphysical questions:

There are certain questions commonly reckoned metaphysical, and which certainly are so . . . which as soon as pragmatism is once sincerely accepted, cannot logically resist settlement. These are for example, What is reality? Are necessity and contingency real modes of being? Are the laws of nature real? Can they be assumed to be immutable or are they presumably results of evolution? Is there any real chance, or departure from real law?   (1998: 420)

In exploring Peirce's historical roots, we have already come upon the answers he gave to many of these questions: by way of Kant and Aristotle he arrived at his three universal categories, and by way of the Greeks and Duns Scotus he established his scholastic realism. His architectonic was then developed by bringing his realism and categories to bear on other philosophical questions. We have seen already the categories governing features of logic and semiotic; there are three primary modes of argumentation, and all sign types are divisible into triads. Logic itself Peirce divided into speculative grammar (describing the foundations of representation), critic (considering the truth function of signs and validity of argument forms), and speculative rhetoric (dealing with the dissemination of meaning). Logic itself he then treated as one of three "normative sciences"; the two upon which it relied were aesthetics and ethics. Finally, Peirce placed the normative sciences within his overall outline of philosophical inquiry:

Philosophy has three grand divisions. The first is Phenomenology, which simply contemplates the Universal Phenomenon and discerns its ubiquitous elements, Firstness, Secondness, and Thirdness, together perhaps with other series of categories. The second grand division is Normative Science, which investigates the universal and necessary laws of relation of Phenomena to *Ends*, that is, to Truth, Right, and Beauty. The third grand division is metaphysics, which endeavors to comprehend the Reality of the Phenomena. (*CP* 5. 121)

In Metaphysics itself Peirce placed ontology, religious metaphysics (questions of God, freedom, immortality), and physical metaphysics (questions of nature and cosmology). Though he often wrote on religious themes, his focus was on the first and last of these subdivisions of Metaphysics. His realistic ontology informed every element of his thought. His general synechism meant that no borders were fixed and discrete in the physical world, and that no meanings were without an element of vagueness. By the late nineteenth century, nominalism had become the "default" ontology of the sciences and of culture generally. "The nominalistic *Weltanschauung*", Peirce argued, "has become incorporated into what I will venture to call the very flesh and blood of the average modern mind" (*CP* 5. 61). Peirce fought this trend in part because he believed it ran against the actual practices of scientists. Under his realism, natural laws could be understood as real habits of the universe, not merely as useful constructs of a finite inquirer; natural kinds could likewise be considered real and malleable, thus making sense of evolutionary theory; features of society such as communities and historical "schools" of art and science were to be understood as real and developing; and, finally, statistical inquiry could be considered to reflect the actual state of nature's own development and not be, as it was for Laplace, a poor substitute for a not-yet-realized actual, discrete truth.

Peirce's emphasis on the reality of thirdness led to his identifying his thought with the objective or conditional idealism of Schelling. But Peirce's version of idealism was not intended to be reductive. It argued for possibility, actuality, and generality as modes of reality, but never attempted to reduce one of these to the others. When he turned to cosmology, Peirce aimed to avoid both pure necessity and sheer contingency. Instead, he sought a mediating description in which elements of chance play a role (tychism) and elements of necessity or stability play a role (anancism). For Peirce, the evolutionary story was a story of the dynamic development of natural laws and habits by way of both chance and action.

Although none of the other American pragmatists followed Peirce's intricate development of the consequences of his pragmaticism, each of them developed ideas whose threads are directly traceable to Peircean themes. In both method and metaphysics we find affinities among the early pragmatists. Peirce described pragmatism to Schiller as a developing school. "I would let it grow", he wrote, "and then say it is what a certain group of thinkers who seem to understand one another think, and thus make it the name of a natural class in the Natural History fashion" (MS L390: 2). Peirce was unquestionably, though not always visibly, at the center of the early development of this natural class. He was the intellectual lens, the prism, refracting ideas from the history of philosophy and placing them in an American context. His early essays—especially the "Illustrations of Logic" and the *Monist* "metaphysical" essays—were read widely by other pragmatists. James, Dewey, and Royce refer to them often, and a close reading of each of their works reveals a strong Peircean influence. Furthermore, Peirce corresponded with Royce, James, Dewey, and Schiller, and candidly reflected on their work in relation to his own. As has been remarked by almost every commentator, Peirce renamed his thought "pragmaticism" to distinguish it from what he called "literary pragmatism". However, James and Schiller, as is sometimes argued, were not the only and not the primary pragmatists from whose thought Peirce wanted to distinguish his own. It is a mistake to separate Peirce too radically from the cohort of thinkers who followed his lead in the history of pragmatism. Indeed, in a letter to his friend Francis Russell, he wrote concerning the "pragmaticism" article that has generated so much heat over the years. In the letter Peirce acknowledged important differences among the pragmatists, but then added

that James and Schiller and the Leonardo man whose name just now escapes me, in the first place, have as clear a grasp of the leading ideas of pragmatism and of how they are to be applied as they have of anything in the world, and in my opinion are doing splendid work beneficial extremely to a wider public, and in the second place, they sincerely want to learn, and are learning in truth and actuality certain difficulties under which they labor. In my *Monist* article(s) my purpose has mainly been to insist upon points that other pragmatists do not see, and thus one does not perceive in what I write the warm sympathy I really have with their work.   (MS 387a: 00309)

Peirce and James, as is well known, knew each other as young men and carried on a correspondence until James's death in 1910. James tried unsuccessfully to find work at Harvard for Peirce, and over the years arranged various lecture series for him to disseminate his work. He recognized Peirce's genius, and Peirce, though he chided James for not studying logic, was well aware of James's special gifts. Their work was therefore thoroughly intertwined. Both men were practicing scientists, and both saw the need for a fallibilistic and experimental approach to all inquiry—in this much both were practicing pragmatists.

Interestingly, the two also shared a theory of perception that underwrote their respective theories of inquiry—Peirce's pragmaticism and James's radical empiricism. Both argued that we perceive much more than atomistic entities and events; we also perceive relations in a variety of forms. Peirce wrote to James in 1905 stating that they shared the traditional "doctrine of immediate perception" (*CP* 8. 261).

With respect to pragmatism, the one place where the two seemed to be at odds concerned the nature of truth. In *Pragmatism* James gave a description of truth as that which worked to bring old beliefs and new discoveries into line; he also characterized the inquirer as "making" truth. To the extent that James sounded as if he were relativizing truth, Peirce disagreed. Nevertheless, their differences here are mitigated by the fact that Peirce's conception of the development toward truth as outlined in "The Fixation of Belief" clearly had an impact on James's later writings on truth and pragmatism. There are places in *The Meaning of Truth* where James sounds explicitly Peircean, even though he tended, like Dewey, to focus on the local features of truth.

Peirce chided James for suggesting that pragmatism could work as a simple solvent for metaphysical questions; but they agreed that pragmatism led to and required engagement with metaphysics. And regarding metaphysical issues, their outlooks were much closer than is often recognized.

James did not turn to metaphysics until late in his career. When he did, he showed the influence of Peirce's early writings, especially the 1890s *Monist* essays dealing with cosmology. Just before his death, James wrote to Peirce stating that it was Peirce's "tychism" that most affected his thinking. James's various attempts to describe and defend the existential reality of chance, risk, possibility, and novelty are well known, and in part are traceable to this Peircean influence. The Peircean lens transformed modernism's "box universe" into a continuous but developing and, in part, indefinite cosmos—the kind of cosmos that suited James's own metaphysical commitments to continuity and novelty.

James's colleague Josiah Royce was also affected by Peirce's metaphysics, but in a somewhat different direction. As we noted, Peirce counted Royce among the pragmatists, and Royce identified himself on several occasions as an "absolute pragmatist". Peirce reviewed in print several of Royce's major works, and the two corresponded from the 1890s until the end of Peirce's career. At first, Royce resisted Peirce's attempts to "probabilize" the world and, unlike James, was resistant to Peirce's tychism. The two carried on some correspondence in which Peirce, recognizing Royce's abilities, urged Royce to study logic more extensively. Royce followed Peirce's advice, and in both *The Problem of Christianity* and his later logical and metaphysical work he explicitly refers to Peirce's influence. Perhaps the clearest place to see this influence is in Royce's shift from an "absolute judge" as guarantor of truth to a community of interpreters who work together through time to take us in the direction of truth. Royce also came to include probability theory and the indefiniteness inherent in a logic of relations in his own account of logic and inquiry. His final lectures at Harvard detail Royce's indebtedness to Peirce; indeed, he began one of his early lectures in his 1913–14 seminar on logic by reading at length from a letter Peirce had recently written to him (Costello 1963: 64).

Finally, a careful reading of John Dewey's work at the turn of the twentieth century reveals a Peircean influence both direct and indirect. Dewey read and commented on essays from both "The Ilustrations of the Logic of Science" and the 1890s *Monist* series. And in 1915 he showed himself to be perhaps the clearest and most astute interpreter of Peirce's central ideas. Meanwhile, Peirce read Dewey's works in logical theory, and, though he appreciated Dewey's ability to bring Hegel's sense of historicity down to earth, he worried about what he took to be the lack of formal rigor in Dewey's logic. What stands out, however, is the striking similarity between Dewey's experimentalism and Peirce's theory of inquiry. This was true not only of Dewey's early work but of his last significant work, his *Logic: The Theory of Inquiry*. For Dewey, learning is always experimental, and this led him to argue that, in a practical way, educational theory is the key to cultural development. To ameliorate a culture in its history, it is requisite to adopt an experimental approach to inquiry. This was implicit in Peirce's work as early as "The Fixation of Belief", but never became the overt focus of his thought. Peirce maintained that "the art of thinking must be acknowledged to be the soul of liberal training" (2000: 10), and that therefore "the welfare of the commonwealth depends far less on the assent of all citizens to any definite propositions . . . than it does in the power of recognizing the sort of thought and the sort of methods in which it will be well for the government and public opinion to put their trust" (1992: 51–2). Dewey did not depart from Peircean pragmatism as much as some suggest; rather, he put that pragmatism to work on the short-run issues of American culture, especially in education and democratic practice. In his instrumentalist approach to pragmatism, Dewey argued that "an education based upon the pragmatic conception would inevitably turn out persons who were alive to the necessity of continually testing their ideas and beliefs by putting them into practical application, and of revising their beliefs on the basis of the results of such application" (1977: 188).

Furthermore, we should not be blinded by Dewey's emphasis on the practice of pragmatic method. In a quiet way he appropriated a number of metaphysical ideals key to the idealisms of Hegel and Peirce, and these remained in play even as he adopted a naturalistic stance. Dewey's defense of the efficacy of words, his discourse on the nature of meaning in nature, and his commitment to the power of communication were built around an implicit scholastic realism of the sort Peirce articulated. Dewey agreed, for example, that the habits of persons, communities, and nature were real, and needed to be treated as such. Broadly speaking, for Dewey, habits were real as the ways things behave. Moreover, these habits are malleable and open to revision, as they were for Peirce. Peirce, however, most often left the discussion at the general or theoretical level. Dewey, by contrast, as in *Human Nature and Conduct*, played out the practical effects of taking habits to be modifiable real generals. This belief served as the basis for his ethical meliorism.

On the whole, we might say that Dewey's instrumentalist pragmatism is characterized by a focus on the short run, on ends-in-view, whereas Peirce's pragmaticism focused on the long run, on movement toward truth. Underlying this significant difference in focus, however, lies a core of shared beliefs that came to light in Peirce's early transformations of modern European thought. Thus, the views of James, Royce, and Dewey are not reducible to Peircean pragmaticism, but stand as different ways of developing the initial insights of Peirce's pragmatism. This is the American connection so often overlooked or, in the case of some contemporary commentators, openly resisted. To see pragmatism as a natural history, as Peirce suggested, is itself a pragmatic insight—we see not "thinker A" and her cloned followers, but rather an "American scholar" whose ideas lead in a variety of distinct but related ways to new developments in thought. Thus, for Peirce, and I would say for all the pragmatists, one cannot choose to "do philosophy" or "do history"—one can only do philosophy if one already does history. An American scholar is not an isolated individual but a member of a historical community of inquirers.

REFERENCES

Carus, Paul (1892). 'Mr. Charles S. Peirce's Onslaught on the Doctrine of Necessity'. *The Monist*, 2: 560–82.

Costello, Harry (1963). *Josiah Royce's Seminar, 1913–1914*. Westport, CT: Greenwood Press.

Dewey, John (1977). *John Dewey: The Middle Works*, iv, ed. Jo Ann Boydston. Carbondale, IL: Southern Illinois University Press.

Emerson, Ralph Waldo (1940). *The Complete Essays and Other Writings of Ralph Waldo Emerson*, ed. B. Atkinson. New York: Modern Library.

Jevons, Stanley (1874). *The Principles of Science: A Treatise on Logic and Scientific Method*. London: Macmillan and Co.

Misak, Cheryl (ed.) (2004). *The Cambridge Companion to Peirce*. Cambridge: Cambridge University Press.

Peirce, Charles Sanders (1931–58). *The Collected Papers of Charles Sanders Peirce*, i–vi, ed. C. Hartshorne and P. Weiss; vii, viii, ed. A. Burks. Cambridge, MA: Harvard University Press.

―― (1963–6). *The Charles S. Peirce Papers*. The Houghton Library. Cambridge, MA: Harvard University Library Microreproduction Service.

―― (1992, 1998). *The Essential Peirce*, i, ii, ed. N. Houser and C. Kloesel. Bloomington, IN, and Indianapolis: Indiana University Press.

―― (2000). *Writings of Charles S. Peirce*, ed. N. Houser *et al*. Bloomington, IN, and Indianapolis: Indiana University Press.

Ransdell, Joseph (2000). 'Peirce and the Socratic Tradition'. *Transactions of the Charles S. Peirce Society*, 36/3: 341–56.

Rorty, Richard (1982). *Consequences of Pragmatism*. Minneapolis: University of Minnesota Press.

CHAPTER 4

WILLIAM JAMES

HENRY JACKMAN

INTRODUCTION

WILLIAM JAMES was, by the time of his death in 1910, America's most celebrated psychologist and philosopher. Nevertheless, he is often unfairly portrayed as simply arguing that it is rational for us to believe anything that makes us feel good, since a belief is 'true' whenever believing it promotes our interests. However, James is more justly interpreted as attempting to draw out the consequences of a thoroughgoing naturalism about cognition for our understanding of normative notions like truth, goodness, and rationality. James was almost unique in his time in directly facing the problem of finding a place for value in a world that seemed increasingly to demand a naturalistic understanding, and his doing so without giving up on either the naturalism or the value has made his writings of perennial interest.[1]

I'd like to thank Cheryl Misak, Alex Klein, and Richard Gale for comments on earlier drafts of this piece.

[1] James was an extraordinarily rich thinker, and considerations of space have prevented me both from touching on many topics about which James wrote extensively, and from dealing more substantively with alternative interpretations of those topics upon which I do touch. Nevertheless, I hope that what follows will make it clear why James's thought is as relevant today as it was a century ago.

LIFE AND BACKGROUND

James was born in New York City in 1842. His father, Henry James Sr., was an independently wealthy familiar of Emerson and Thoreau who pursued a nomadic and eccentric life as a free-floating intellectual, self-publishing theologian, and disciple of Swedenborg. William was the elder James's first child, and over the next nineteen years, the growing James family (Henry Sr., his wife Alice, and their children William, Henry Jr. (the novelist), Wilky, Bob, and Alice) moved, on an almost yearly basis, between New York, London, Paris, Geneva, and Newport. After an aborted attempt to become a painter, William James entered Harvard's Lawrence Scientific School in 1861, where he studied chemistry with the university's future president, Charles Eliot, and, before switching to Harvard's medical school in 1864, began lasting and important friendships with Oliver Wendell Holmes Jr. and Charles Sanders Peirce.

When James started at Harvard, the most pressing intellectual questions of the day revolved around Darwin's *On the Origin of Species*, which had been published just five years earlier. The theory divided Harvard's scientific faculty, and while James's own sympathies were clearly on the Darwinian side, he took time off from his medical studies (for which he had a pronounced lack of enthusiasm) to join his Professor Louis Agassiz in his biological expedition up the Amazon, an expedition which was originally intended to find evidence of a 'separate creation' that would tell against Darwin's theory. Darwin's work had a tremendous influence on James in two respects. First of all, it presented a framework for more resolutely naturalistic explanations of human cognition and behavior, explanations that would be radically at odds with the dualist and idealist theories of the mind that were dominant at the time. Secondly, however, this expansion of the range of naturalistic explanation also seemed to support a kind of deterministic materialism that James was never able to reconcile himself with. Responding to both pressures, James gave one of the most thoroughly naturalistic stories of our cognitive life yet seen, while at the same time showing how it need not be the *whole* story, and insisted on keeping a place for faith and free will within the conceptual space framed by his more naturalistic writings in psychology.[2]

James finished his medical degree in 1869, but he never practiced medicine, and in 1870 he suffered a nervous collapse that made him incapable of any work

---

[2] See esp., his "The Dilemma of Determinism" in *WB&OEPP* and the chapters on "Will" and "The Consciousness of Self" in *PP*.

at all.[3] His health had already been 'delicate' for a number of years, and while he was well enough to serve as a lecturer in anatomy at Harvard by 1874, he remained subject to bouts of depression and ill health throughout his life. This affinity with what he later (in *The Varieties of Religious Experience*) referred to as the "sick soul" was an important strain in his thought that contrasted the outwardly "healthy minded" tone of his work. With President Eliot's support, James expanded his teaching duties from physiology to psychology (a field previously covered exclusively by a member of the philosophy faculty, who maintained that the study of the brain could teach us nothing of use about the mind), and James then solidified his position in this area by founding what has generally been taken to be America's first psychology laboratory, in 1875.[4]

In 1878 James published his first substantial philosophical work, "Remarks on Spencer's Definition of Mind as Correspondence" (in *EP*), but the year was also noteworthy for two other reasons. First of all, James married Alice Howe Gibbons, who did much to stabilize his life, and over the next twelve years, they had five children, Henry (1879), William (1882), Herman (1884),[5] Peggy (1887), and Aleck (1890). Secondly, James signed a contract with Henry Holt to produce a textbook on psychology, and while, like his family, the book took him twelve years to complete, the resulting two-volume *Principles of Psychology* (1890) was a tremendous success and established James as the pre-eminent American psychologist of his generation. Psychology and philosophy were less clearly distinguished in those days,[6] and in 1880 James satisfied a long-standing ambition of his by being appointed Assistant Professor of Philosophy at Harvard. He published on philosophical topics throughout his career, but he made his first really big splash outside psychology with the publication of "The Will to Believe" in 1897 and the delivery of "Philosophical Conceptions and Practical Results" in 1898. His philosophical views became a subject of growing intellectual controversy from this time on.

---

[3] His father had had a similar crisis in 1844, and James describes his own experience (while attributing it to a "French correspondent") in *VRE*, 134.

[4] For a discussion of this, see Harper 1949, 1950.

[5] Whose death in 1885 may have helped fuel James's long-standing interest in parapsychology.

[6] *Mind*, for instance, served equally as a journal in philosophy and psychology, and was the main home of most of James's early publications. *The Journal of Philosophy*, founded in 1904 as *The Journal of Philosophy, Psychology, and Scientific Methods* came to play the same dual role in the United States. For a useful discussion of the role played by *Mind* in this period (especially with respect to James's work), see Klein 2007.

After an extended stay in Europe, partially due to lingering ill health, James delivered the Gifford Lectures in Edinburgh in 1901 and 1902, and their subsequent publication in 1902 as *The Varieties of Religious Experience* met with almost universal praise. The same could not be said of the philosophical work that followed, which generated intense discussion on both sides of the Atlantic, but won more critics than converts. In 1907, he both resigned from Harvard and delivered a series of public lectures which appeared later that year as *Pragmatism: A New Name for Some Old Ways of Thinking*. Much of the remaining three years of his life were spent responding to the controversy prompted by this book, and a collection of these responses appeared in 1909 as *The Meaning of Truth*. That same year he published his 1908 Hibbert Lectures from Oxford as *A Pluralistic Universe*, and this was to be his last major publication in his lifetime. James died in 1910 after having abandoned an attempt to write a more systematic and less 'popular' exposition of his philosophical views, the completed material from which appeared as *Some Problems of Philosophy* in 1911.

CONCEPTS AND CONCEPTUALIZATION

The seeds of James's later philosophical views were sown with his earlier psychological work, particularly that on concepts and conceptualization.[7] Starting from the assumption that human conceptualization is a *natural* phenomenon, and that such natural phenomena should be explained in (roughly) Darwinian terms, James concluded that concepts evolved to serve our *practical* rather than *theoretical* interests. Noting that it was far too little recognized "how entirely the intellect is built up of practical interests" (SR 72), James always insisted that conceptions were "teleological instruments" (SR 62) by which we take "a partial aspect of a thing which *for our purposes* we regard as its essential aspect, as the representative of the entire thing".[8] Since the interest of theoretical rationality "is but one of a thousand human purposes" (SR 62), James concluded that our conceptual system evolved to help us *cope with* our environment, not to provide a theoretical account of it. Our conceptual system developed because it was *adaptive*, and

---

[7] Indeed, when he tried to present his philosophical views systematically in *Some Problems of Philosophy*, conceptualization returned as the dominant topic.

[8] "The Sentiment of Rationality" (original version), in *EP*, 34.

while this may be explained by its corresponding to the structure that the world *actually* has, it need not be so.

With this view of concepts comes a particular take on the properties of the world being conceptualized. Rather than thinking that the world had an independent structure that made some properties 'more real' than others,[9] James took the essence of a thing to be whichever of its properties "is so *important for my interests* that in comparison with it I may neglect the rest" (*PP* 961),[10] so that a property "which figures as the essence of a thing on one occasion" may become "a very inessential feature on another" (*PP* 959). The resulting conceptual pluralism in the *Principles of Psychology* is expressed in claims like the following:

The mind, in short, works on the data it receives very much as a sculptor works on his block of stone. In a sense the statue stood there from eternity. But there were a thousand different ones beside it, and the sculptor alone is to thank for having extricated this one from the rest. ... Other sculptors, other statues from the same stone! Other minds, other worlds from the same monotonous and inexpressive chaos!   (*PP* 277)

James develops these themes throughout his career, and they are cashed out most explicitly in *Pragmatism*'s fifth and seventh chapters on common sense and humanism.

One particular problem that James tried to leave out of his *Principles of Psychology* was that of just how an idea (a piece of "flat content" with "no self-transcendency about it" (*ME&N* 17)) could come to be *about* anything external to it. *That* it could was taken as a given, but *how* it could was left unexplained,[11] since, as he put it in 1885, "Although we cannot help believing that our thoughts *do* mean realities and are true or false of them, we cannot for the life of us ascertain how they *can* mean them" (*ECR* 386). His recognition that 'aboutness' couldn't be treated as a *sui generis* property of our mental states is something that distinguishes James, to his credit, from many of his critics. If the aboutness of our thoughts is taken for granted, their truth can seem relatively unproblematic,[12] and much of what James goes on to say about

---

[9] An idea that has recently been rehabilitated in Lewis 1983.

[10] Italics, unless noted otherwise, are James's.

[11] For attempts to avoid this in *PP*, see pp. 212 and 216. James's reluctance to discuss the issue may have been tied to the fact that what he then considered to be the most compelling account of this relation (that presented in Royce 1885) committed one to the sort of absolute idealism that he always found both morally and metaphysically distasteful.

[12] An exemplary combination of these qualities can be found in Pratt 1909, who takes James to task for missing out on the fact that truth simply means "that the object of which one is thinking is as

the truth of our thoughts makes sense only in the context of recognizing that their even having *truth conditions* requires a naturalistic explanation.

James's first attempt to give an explicitly *naturalistic* account of the relation of thought to the world was in 1885's "The Function of Cognition",[13] where he presents a methodological principle that shows up in much of his work:

We are not to ask, "How is self-transcendence possible?" We are only to ask, "How comes it that common sense has assigned a number of cases in which it is assumed not only to be possible but actual? And what are the marks used by common sense to distinguish those cases from the rest?" In short, our inquiry is a chapter in descriptive psychology—hardly anything more.   (*MT* 14)

James took the most basic cases of our thoughts being about the world to be found in perception, where (as he puts it) idea and object "fuse and make an indissoluble marriage" (*ERE* 265), so that to perceive an object "is for mental content and object to be identical" (*MT* 36).[14]

James extends the paradigm of perceptual reference by arguing that one's ideas can know objects outside of one's perceptual field by leading one through a series of experiences that terminate in actual percepts of the objects referred to. For instance, James's "Memorial Hall" idea may just be a dim image in his mind; but if this image allows James to go to the hall and recognize it, then "we may freely say that we had the terminal object 'in mind' from the outset, even altho *at* the outset nothing was there in us but a flat piece of substantive experience like any other, with no self-transcendency about it" (*ERE* 29). Indeed, James argues that "*Such simply and fully verified leadings are certainly the originals and prototypes of the truth-process*", and other cases

one thinks it" (Pratt 2001 [1909], 67), while the fact that one's thoughts do mean things external to them "is merely one of those ultimately simple things which, just because they are ultimate and simple elements of experience, can never be explained further, nor analyzed further, but must be merely recognized and accepted" (ibid. 140). How these issues divide James and his opponents is also clear in James's correspondence with John E. Russell, found in *ERE* 145–53. For a more extended discussion of this issue, see Jackman 1998.

[13]   Many of the themes of this paper were developed in a series of essays he published between 1904 and 1906, and which appeared in 1912 in the posthumously published collection *Essays in Radical Empiricism*. "The Function of Cognition" had originally been intended by James for this collection as well, but since it had already been reprinted in *The Meaning of Truth*, it was not included in the 1912 collection. The goals of this earlier paper are clearly captured by the title of Strong's 1904 essay on it, "A Naturalistic Theory of the Reference of Thought to Reality".

[14]   See also *MT* 35, 61–2. This view was the cornerstone of what later came to be known as his 'doctrine of pure experience', and even if one is not partial to the metaphysical details of James's account of perceptual reference itself, the basic idea that our perceptual contact with the world can serve as a paradigm for how our ideas come to be about it is extremely intuitive. (See Evans 1982, e.g., for a contemporary manifestation of this thought.)

of aboutness "are all conceivable as being verifications arrested, multiplied or substituted one for another" (*PR* 99).

The importance of such "verifications arrested" can be seen in that while James's initial account allows my idea of Memorial Hall to have always referred to the hall once it *actually* leads me to it, common sense suggests that my idea refers to the hall *before* this happens, or even if I *never* track it down at all. Indeed, a large and significant portion of my thoughts seem to lie outside James's initial extension of aboutness to non-perceptual cases. James is aware of this, and he claims that in such cases we 'virtually' refer to the objects of our thoughts.

The key to this difficulty lies in the distinction between knowing as verified and completed, and the same knowing as in transit and on its way. To recur to the Memorial Hall example lately used, it is only when our idea of the hall has actually terminated in the percept that we know 'for certain' that from the beginning it was truly cognitive of *that*. Until established by the end of the process, its quality of knowing that, or indeed of knowing anything, could still be doubted; and yet the knowing really was there, as the result now shows. We were *virtual* knowers of the hall long before we were certified to have been its actual knowers, by the percept's retroactive validating power.   (*ERE* 34)

James goes on to claim that while "the immensely greater part of all our knowing never gets beyond this virtual stage" (*ERE* 34), as long as this 'virtual knowing' can be cashed out whenever it needs to be, there should be no *practical* difference between a theory which says that we are *only virtually* referring in such cases and one that claims that we are *actually* referring in them.[15] The verification processes are still, as James puts it, what truth and intentionality mean "essentially", but this is only to say that we couldn't understand verifiability independently of actual verification.

The importance of "verifications substituted" shows up in two ways. First, it helps account for the *social* character of language and thought. Even if the analysis of the perceptual core of intentionality is individualistic, the extended account of non-perceptual reference makes room for social contributions by stressing that having a thought about an object involves being led to it "through a context which the world provides" (*MT* 35; see also *MT* 21). Consider my ability to identify, say, my own, as opposed to someone else's,

---

[15] "We let our notion pass for true without attempting to verify. If truth means verification-processes essentially, ought we then to call such unverified truths as this abortive? No, for they form the overwhelmingly large number of the truths we live by. Indirect as well as direct verifications pass muster. Where circumstantial is sufficient, we can go without eye-witnessing" (*PR* 99).

copy of *Walden*. This ability is based largely on the fact that it is the only copy of *Walden* sitting on my bookshelf, rather than my knowledge of perceptual features that distinguish it from all other copies of the book, and our being embedded in particular contexts is thus essential to our ability to think about various objects. Furthermore, one's context is a *social* one, and while I couldn't find Memorial Hall on *my own*, given my social context, I would have no trouble locating it if I were placed in Cambridge. I would only need to ask people around me until I found someone who was able to lead me to it. I refer to what I do by many of my (especially technical) terms because the experts I rely on would, if asked, lead me to particular sets of objects. How a term is used in one's social surroundings can thus affect what one's own ideas are about. No one needs to be able to track down the reference for all of their terms, but "beliefs verified concretely by *somebody* are posts of the whole superstructure" (*PR* 100).[16]

The second role for "verifications substituted" regards those things which we could not, perhaps even in principle, have perceptual contact with. (James gives as examples here ether waves, ions, and the contents of other people's minds (*ERE* 34).) Such cases obviously present at least *prima facie* problems for an account of reference that tries to explain it in terms of perceptual contact with the objects referred to. However, if our ideas can lead us to the *environment* of these objects, James argues that such experiences can 'substitute' for actual perceptual contact. Non-actualized cases of virtual knowledge typically "lead to no frustration or contradiction" and to "the *surroundings* of the objects" (*PR* 99–100), and both of these characteristics could be shared by our thought about unobservables. Standard cases of virtual knowledge count as 'knowing' in virtue of having the potential to become like the prototypical cases, and reference to unobservables *counts as* 'knowing' in virtue of sharing the evidential characteristics of the virtual cases.[17] Once we admit the standard cases of virtual reference and allow that "to continue thinking unchallenged is, ninety-nine times out of one hundred, our practical substitute for knowing in the completed sense" (*ERE* 34), reference to unobservables can be admitted as well.

There are two things to note about this account of the relation of thought to the world. First of all, if "the percept's existence as the terminus of the

---

[16] See also *PR* 103, *MT* 91. James's account is thus able to accommodate the type of 'social externalism' associated with Burge 1979, and the "division of linguistic labor" of Putnam 1975.

[17] As James puts it elsewhere: "The untrammeled flowing of the leading-process, its general freedom from clash and contradiction, passes for its indirect verification" (*PR* 103). (Though one should note that for many scientific unobservables James is willing to take an instrumentalist line.)

chain of intermediaries *creates* the function", then *whatever* terminates the chain becomes "what the concept 'had in mind'" (*ERE* 31). This means that what the function is can change over time, and that what our terms *ultimately* refer to is settled only when inquiry reaches its end. "Gold", on such an account, at one point referred to *gold or platinum* since that is what the idea led us to interact with at the time, and only for the last few hundred years has it referred *exclusively* to *gold*.[18] Furthermore, if there is no settled and stable leading relation, then there will be no fact of the matter about what our terms 'ultimately' refer to. Secondly, since what a term leads us to need not be the objects that fit the descriptions originally associated with it, what our terms and concepts refer to need not correspond exactly to the content of the descriptions we associate with them. Consequently, while James's conception of concepts themselves gives them a classically definitional character (see, e.g., *SPP* 47), his view is that their *extension* and truth conditions need not reflect those definitions. This leaves little motivation for any sort of purely a priori analysis of our concepts (even concepts like goodness, rationality, or truth), since that would reveal only their *internal* structure, not the nature of what those concepts were *about*.[19]

Rationality and the Will to Believe

Like his account of aboutness, James's account of rationality and the justification of belief seems to start out as "a chapter in descriptive psychology" (*MT* 14). Beginning with "The Sentiment of Rationality" in 1879,[20] James took an empirical approach to the question of the nature of rationality and, rather than engaging in any a priori analysis, asked what, as a matter of fact, were the signs that determine what we consider "rational" (SR 57). James stressed that we tend to find rational those views that not only pass the canonical tests of rationality (consistency, comprehensiveness, simplicity, etc.), but

[18] Though we can now say that the word *always* referred to gold, since (through its "powers of retroactive legislation" (*PR* 107)) the final identification determines what the function was all along. This aspect of James's view is developed in more detail in Jackman 1998.

[19] In this respect he is like those philosophers (e.g., Devitt (1994) and Kornblith (1994)) who claim to "naturalize" their analysis of philosophical concepts like meaning and knowledge.

[20] This original was combined with material from 1880 when it was reprinted in 1896 under the same title in *The Will to Believe and Other Essays in Popular Philosophy*. Unless stated otherwise, page references will be to this updated version.

also satisfy human cravings that are traditionally viewed as being irrelevant to the question. In particular, he claimed that any view that "disappoints our dearest desires and most cherished powers" (as he thought pessimism and materialistic determinism did (SR 70–1)) would never, ultimately, be considered rational by us (SR 70).[21]

Of course, one could agree with James that our subjective interests contribute to what views fall within the extension of "rational", and still insist that even if such considerations *do* contribute to what we believe, they *shouldn't*. If "rationality" really picks out this sort of 'natural' rationality, it is still an open question whether we should always believe what is "rational" to believe.[22] That we should believe what is rational is a central belief associated with the term, but since James ties the meaning of "rational" to how we actually apply the term, rather than to such general beliefs, we cannot simply assume that the general belief that we ought to believe what is rational to believe is still true. That we shouldn't let our subjective interests contribute to what we believe was the core of the "evidentialist" position, which held, in Clifford's famous terms, that "it is wrong, always, everywhere, and for anyone, to believe anything on insufficient evidence".[23] Unlike the evidentialist, James clearly endorsed the belief-forming practices described in "The Sentiment of Rationality", and his most worked out and important defense of this expansive conception of rationality was found in his infamous essay "The Will to Believe".[24] That essay is commonly portrayed as arguing that we should believe in God because whether or not there is a God, we would be happier believing that there is one; but in addition to misrepresenting the character of James's argument, this misses the fact that while religious belief is the hook by which the audience is drawn into the argument, the essay is about the justification of belief in general. James presents his paper as a "justification of faith" (WB 13), but religious belief was only a particularly vivid and pertinent application of the view. Faith, for James, is "belief in something concerning which doubt is theoretically possible" (SR 76), and since James (like most, if not all, pragmatists)

[21] See also SR 74, 75. For similar remarks on how such factors contribute to what we consider 'real', see *PP* 939–40, 945.

[22] Just as some responded to Strawson's argument that induction was rational because using induction was just part of what we *mean* by being "rational" (Strawson 1952) by saying that this just left us facing the same old problem of induction, but now in the form of the question of whether it was a good thing for us to be "rational".

[23] Clifford 1999 [1877]: 77, quoted in WB 18.

[24] Though many of the same points show up in the expanded version of "The Sentiment of Rationality" that was anthologized in *WB&OEPP*. For a more extended analysis of the argument of WB, see Jackman 1999.

was a fallibilist, he considered doubt to be theoretically possible with respect to *any* belief, so that we cannot "live or think at all without some degree of faith" (SR 79).[25]

The central claim of "The Will to Believe" is that

Our passional nature not only lawfully may, but must, decide an option between propositions, whenever it is a genuine option that cannot by its nature be decided on intellectual grounds; for to say, under such circumstances, "Do not decide, but leave the question open," is itself a passional decision—just like deciding yes or no—and is attended with the same risk of losing truth. (WB 20)

The above passage makes both the *descriptive* claim that, in certain specified circumstances, the contribution of our passional nature can't be avoided and the *normative* claim that this contribution is a good thing, and in both cases our "passional nature" picks out all those 'subjective' factors that James stressed in "The Sentiment of Rationality", including "all those influences, born of the intellectual climate, that makes hypotheses possible or impossible for us, alive or dead" (WB 18). These include not only our natural disinclination to believe views that seem to frustrate our "active tendencies" (SR 70), but also those more contingently 'received ideas' which, while by no means self-evident, are treated as such by everyone in a given cultural context.[26]

The descriptive claim that the contribution of our passional nature is unavoidable is tied to James's understanding of belief in terms of dispositions to action, and to his restricting the claim to "genuine" options between propositions. For James a 'genuine' option must be (1) "live", that is, both choices must actually "make some appeal, however small, to your belief" (WB 14);[27] (2) "forced", that is, the choice presented must be unavoidable, so that it will be more like the choice between staying at a party or leaving it than the choice between going to one party rather than another, which can be avoided by not going to either (WB 14–15); and (3) "momentous" in that "the opportunity is unique, the stake is significant, and the decision is irreversible" (WB 15). If a choice is forced, we can't help but act on it,

---

[25] See also, "the only escape from faith is mental nullity" (SR 78).

[26] James's examples being, e.g., our belief "in molecules and the conservation of energy, in democracy and necessary progress, in Protestant Christianity and the duty of fighting for 'the doctrine of the immortal Monroe'" (WB 18). For a further discussion of the influence of custom on what is considered rational, see SR 67.

[27] The option to believe that the FBI was connected to the Kennedy assassination is live for me, even if I don't actually believe it, while the idea that Martians were so connected is not even live.

and with a momentous option, the forced choice is "irrevocable". However, for James, "belief is measured by action", with the test for belief being "willingness to act", and a "willingness to act irrevocably" constituting full-fledged belief (WB 32, SR 76, WB 14; see also ILWL 50). Consequently, when an option is genuine, *some* belief regarding it must be decided, and since it cannot be, by hypothesis, decided on intellectual grounds, something else must settle the matter. That something is, according to James, our passional nature.

This descriptive claim is, of course, tied to James's conception of belief's constitutive connection to action, but that view of belief is not as essential to the equally important normative claim that the contribution of our passional nature is justified. The evidentialist objects to our ever forming beliefs on the basis of less than conclusive evidence;[28] but James points out that such a position takes epistemic justification to be exclusively governed by the norm that one should try to reason in a fashion that would minimize the number of false beliefs that one forms. While this norm can seem like a reasonable one, there is an equally truth-sensitive epistemic norm that gives the opposite advice about what to do in conditions of uncertainty: that is, we should try to form beliefs in a fashion that would leave us with as many *true* beliefs as possible. As James puts it, "Believe truth! Shun error!—these, we see, are two materially different laws; and by choosing between them we may end by coloring differently our whole intellectual life" (WB 24). Both norms are equally truth-sensitive, and the epistemicist gives no reason to think that the conservative norm of minimizing error should always trump the more liberal norm of maximizing truth. Indeed, James argues that the epistemicists' commitment to the conservative norm is itself just an expression of their own passional nature, in particular, their "private horror of becoming a dupe" (WB 25).

This opens up room for a plurality of epistemic positions, ranging from the extremely conservative one of not believing anything that isn't completely certain to the opposite (and dubiously coherent) extreme of believing everything.[29] However, if the *function* of belief really is to guide action (as it will naturally seem to be within a Darwinian framework), then a conception of

---

[28] Though one should note that James somewhat unfairly implies that Clifford believes that for evidence to be "sufficient", it must be *conclusive*.

[29] Since believing everything would commit one to acting in incompatible ways even on conceptions of the relation of belief and action that are looser than James's, believing *everything* isn't a coherent possibility.

rationality which rules out actually forming any beliefs will seem unsuitable as an account of the rationality of embodied *agents* whose beliefs are required to let them *function within*, rather than just *theorize about*, the world. While there is nothing in James's view that requires that any particular belief formed be one that benefits us, one way in which practical benefits bear on the question of *epistemic* justification relates to just what balance we should have between the conflicting imperatives of maximizing true beliefs and minimizing false ones. For James, the balance between the imperatives that is best will be the one that best serves our interests, and since our interests can change from context to context and person to person,[30] our epistemic norms can vary from context to context as well. For instance, James is quite clear that when forming most of our *scientific* beliefs, our interests dictate that we should try to keep the contribution of our passional nature to a minimum (WB 25–6).[31] Further, determining the right balance for our epistemic norms will be an *empirical*, rather than an a priori, project.[32]

James has two further arguments against evidentialism that are connected to neither his fallibilism nor his conception of the relation between belief and action. First of all, whenever the evidence that would confirm the truth of a particular proposition is available only to those who *already* believe the proposition, evidentialism would frustrate even the inquirer whose interests were *purely* theoretical. James notes that scientists often believe particular theories in advance of finding their confirming evidence, and that in the absence of such 'premature' convictions they may be unable to do the work necessary to find the evidence. *Faith* in both "nature's uniformity" (SR 76) and one's particular theory (WB 26) may occasionally be necessary to sustain certain demanding forms of inquiry (see also WB 19, 27, 28; ILWL 51). The evidentialist may think that this is just a psychological failing on the scientist's part, but if it is true that *humans* have this failing, then it should be rational for them to inquire in a fashion that accommodates it, since any rule "which

[30] James notes that the more purely 'epistemic' demands for simplicity and comprehensiveness often conflict with one another, and that "although all men will insist on being spoken to in the universe in some way, few will insist on being spoken to in the same way" (SR 75). This theme is expanded considerably in the first chapter of *Pragmatism*.

[31] Though, as we shall see, while James advocates a fairly conservative stance when it comes to the *evaluation* of scientific theories, he notes that a more liberal belief-forming procedure is often required for their *discovery* (WB 26).

[32] James could be seen as a precursor of current naturalized epistemologists (such as Stich (1990), Dennett (1987), and Cherniak (1986)) who try to understand our canons of justification in evolutionary terms.

would absolutely prevent [an inquirer] from acknowledging certain kinds of truth if those kinds of truth were really there, would be an irrational rule" (WB 31–2). Furthermore, James points out that in the religious case, the world may simply be set up so that the evidence is not available prior to belief. God may choose to stay hidden from the faithless inquirer, who might thus "cut himself forever from his only opportunity of making the gods' acquaintance" (WB 31).

A second sort of case that causes problems for the evidentialist arises when the facts that we are trying to discover are themselves sensitive to our beliefs, so that purely 'detached' inquiry is impossible. For instance, if I interact with someone while withholding judgment about whether or not they like me, this may result in a lack of warmth on my part that will bring it about that I won't be liked (WB 28). James argues that it is at least *possible* that our belief in the Divine is such a case (ILWL 55), but his most famous illustration is that of an "Alpine climber" who finds himself stuck in a storm and facing a chasm that must be leapt if he is to make it home safely. The climber is (without any *evidence*) confident in his ability to make such a jump, and successfully does so. However, had he been a good evidentialist, and not *believed* that he could jump the chasm in question, his diffidence would have undermined his performance enough for the leap to be fatal (SR 80).

The Alpine climber is an important case for James, but it has led to a number of misunderstandings of his view. First of all, the fact that our beliefs can sometimes contribute to their own truth is occasionally treated as if it was the central point of James's paper, and that such a contribution is a *necessary* condition for the input of our passional nature to be legitimate.[33] However, James's view is not that the contribution of our passional nature is justified only in such cases, but rather that such cases serve as *counterexamples* to the evidentialist suggestion that the passional contribution is *never* justified. Cases like the Alpine climber (and the hidden God) are meant to show that, as a *general* rule, evidentialism is unworkable, and thus to open up a space for the contribution of our passional nature in other cases once global conservatism has been ruled out.

The other way in which the Alpine climber is misleading is that it can suggest that James is arguing that particular beliefs are epistemically justified by their beneficial effects, so that the Alpine climber is justified by the fact that he was better off making the jump than he would have been either making

---

[33] See, e.g., Gale 1980, 1999; Suckiel 1982: 90.

an unsuccessful jump or refusing to attempt a jump or freezing to death. James does note that in such make-true cases it is "the part of wisdom . . . to believe what in the line of your needs" (ILWL 53–4), but one is *epistemically* entitled in such cases to choose *either* option. The diffident Alpine climber would be epistemically justified in believing that he *couldn't* make the jump, even if he had no compelling evidence for this as well. The benefits of a belief may give one reason to prefer one of two epistemically justified options, but they do not, in themselves, provide the epistemic justification. Furthermore, even in these cases, the expected benefits are not supposed to enter explicitly into the agent's *reasoning* about what to believe. The examples James gives, most obviously the Alpine climber, don't involve agents who explicitly engage in any such prudential reasoning when forming their beliefs,[34] which is understandable, since such reasoning would typically *undermine* the relevant 'make-true' effects.

Rather than defending anything like wishful thinking or simply confusing epistemic (truth-directed) and prudential (benefit-directed) justification, James thus defends our natural reasoning processes against the one-sided evidentialist distortion of them that he took to be characteristic of most of the philosophical tradition.

Ethics and Objectivity

Like many naturalists, James found little room for *sui generis* ethical facts in his ontology,[35] and since neither moral relations nor the moral law could "swing *in vacuo*", he took the "only habitat" for goodness, badness, and obligation to be "the mind which feels them" (MPML 145; see also MPML 148). As James puts it, "without a claim actually made by some concrete person there can be no obligation", and "there is some obligation wherever there is a claim" (MPML 148), so that "the essence of good is simply to satisfy demand" (MPML 152–3).[36] James continues here a long tradition

---

[34] Though they are occasionally redescribed in the secondary literature so that the climber explicitly engages in such prudential reasoning. See, e.g., Pojman 1993: 543 and Jordan 1996: 412.

[35] James refers to such a conception as the "superstitious view" of ethical facts (MPML 148).

[36] See also: "every *de facto* claim creates in so far forth an obligation" (MPML 148); "Any desire is imperative to the extent of its amount; it *makes* itself valid by the fact that it exists at all" (MPML 149); and "everything which is demanded is by that fact good" (MPML 155).

of arguing that any facts about values have to be understood in terms of facts about our practice of *valuing*,[37] and this might seem to make goodness, like the valuations that it depends upon, a purely 'subjective' phenomenon. Nevertheless, James still wants our values to be 'objective', since while values are constructed out of our valuations, we intend them to be more than simply expressions of our preferences. Value judgments aspire to be truth-apt, and because of this, any set of valuations can be criticized for being inconsistent, since inconsistent values can no more both be realized than inconsistent beliefs can both be true.

A completely solitary individual could produce objective values simply by reaching an equilibrium among his own demands, and James describes such a moral universe as follows:

Moral relations now have their *status*, in that being's consciousness. So far as he feels anything to be good, he *makes* it good. It *is* good, for him; and being good for him, is absolutely good, for he is the sole creator of values in that universe, and outside of his opinion things have no moral character at all. ... In such a moral solitude it is clear that there can be no outward obligation, and that the only trouble the god-like thinker is liable to have will be over the consistency of his own several ideals with one another. ... Into whatever equilibrium he may settle, though, and however he may straighten out his system, it will be a right system; for beyond the facts of his own subjectivity, there is nothing moral in the world.   (MPML 145–6)

However, such a 'moral solitude' changes radically when another agent appears on the scene. One could have a type of 'twin solitude' if the two agents didn't take any interest in each other (and didn't recognize each other as moral agents at all); but, barring that, recognition and interaction involves trying to bring the combined set of demands into an equilibrium (MPML 146–7). Such an equilibrium need not require that everyone in the group have the *same* desires (any more than the equilibrium of the solitary thinker requires that none of his *prima facie* desires conflict). Rather, just as the equilibrium of the solitary thinker comes from his recognizing and organizing his desires so that his final set is consistent, the social equilibrium requires only that each individual member of a group endorse the same general demands even when these general demands may conflict with their particular desires.

What set of demands could lead to such an equilibrium is an *empirical* rather than an a priori question (MPML 141, 157), but it seems clear that it will be by no means an easy state to achieve, since having a set of enforced social demands

---

[37] For a recent discussion of this tradition in empiricism from Hobbes on, see Putnam 2002.

that simply prevent members of society from *acting* on their conflicting desires is not enough. Because of this, a social equilibrium may *never* be reached, and James's view incorporates a type of meta-ethical fallibilism in which, while we believe that values are objective, we recognize that they could turn out not to be.[38] Indeed, many might, on discovering that objective values require the sort of harmony that James describes, decide that the realization of their values is more important to them than their objectivity, and that no equilibrium is worth reaching if it involves compromise with a set of values significantly different from their own.

Such a stance is not, according to James, an option for the moral philosopher, since for the *moral philosopher* the demand for objectivity is the primary (if not the *only*) value in play (MPML 142). James argues that the philosopher has as his primary ideal "that over all these individual opinions there is a *system of truth* which he can discover if he only takes sufficient pains" (MPML 151; see also MPML 141–2, 146–7). If the moral philosopher's demand is frustrated, and there turns out to be "no one 'objective' truth, but only a multitude of 'subjective' opinions" (MPML 146–7), we have two choices. On the one hand, we can tie the meaning of 'good' to those general beliefs that suggest that it has to be objective, in which case we are committed to a type of 'error theory' in which all our ethical claims are, strictly speaking, false. On the other hand, we can tie the meaning more closely to our actual applications of the term 'good', and recognize that, if all this gets one is a 'subjective' meaning for the term, then that is what we will have to settle for. James doesn't discuss this possibility much in his paper, since, in the role of moral philosopher, he is committed to the sort of objectivity that would obviate such a choice; but questions of this kind will come up again in his discussion of truth, and James is willing to face them more directly there.

Given that others may not prioritize the value of ethical objectivity as James does, is the moral philosopher entitled to believe in objective ethical values? For James, the answer remains "Yes". James thinks that it is at least *possible* that the required conditions could be achieved for two reasons. First, there is the progress he takes us to have made towards that goal so far.[39] Second, there

---

[38] One should note that the "could" here picks out not only *epistemic* possibility, but *metaphysical* possibility as well. Given that their objectivity depends upon how we go on to coordinate our values, there may be no settled fact of the matter as to whether values are objective.

[39] James believes that, as a matter of fact, we are at least moving towards such a harmonious equilibrium, so that "as our present laws and customs have fought and conquered other past ones, so they will in their turn be overthrown by any newly discovered order which will hush up the

is the possibility that some "divine thinker with all enveloping demands" may step in to help us towards that goal (MPML 161). This certainly doesn't give us any *guarantee* that there will ever be an equilibrium among all our values; but the moral philosopher is still entitled to believe that there could be one, and thus in the objectivity of ethical claims, because the question is both evidentially undetermined and arguably "genuine". Further, since it seems certain that we would never reach the kind of consensus required if we *didn't* believe in the possibility of such consensus, it is a case where belief in the fact could help make the fact.[40] The objectivity of value is thus a good candidate to be a "Will to Believe" case, and so the moral philosopher is entitled to believe in such objectivity in spite of his fallibilism.

PRAGMATISM AND TRUTH

James claims that "truth is one species of the good" (*PR* 42), and James's naturalistic approach to truth is similar to, if more controversial than, his approach to the good. Instead of analyzing the concept in purely a priori terms, James asks: "Grant an idea or belief to be true, . . . what concrete difference will its being true make in any one's actual life?" (*PR* 97). His answer is that the true is whatever "proves itself to be good in the way of belief", though it must be good for "definite, assignable reasons" (*PR* 42). In particular, true ideas are "those that we can assimilate, validate, corroborate, and verify" (*PR* 97). Nevertheless, the account of truth in terms of the "expedient in the way of our thinking" (*PR* 106) makes it clear that the 'passional' elements that James took to contribute to rationality are meant to contribute to truth as well.

It seemed to many that James was here simply confusing truth and verification, since, so understood, the truth of a statement could change over time and vary from person to person. James, however, argues that this is precisely what we should say about *subjective* (sometimes "temporary" or "half") truth, since for any individual, to be true "means, *for that individual*, to work satisfactorily for him"; and since such workings and satisfactions

---

complaints that they still give rise to, without producing others louder still" (MPML 156). See also MPML 155–6, 157.

[40] Indeed, James suggests just this in SR 86–7.

"vary from case to case", they "admit of no universal description" (*MT* 132). Nevertheless, James freely admits that there is a *second* sense of truth, *objective* (sometimes "absolute" or "ultimate") truth that is both interpersonally and temporally stable.

The 'absolutely' true, meaning what no farther experience will ever alter, is that ideal vanishing-point towards which we imagine that all our temporary truths will some day converge. ... *Meanwhile we have to live today by what truth we can get today, and be ready to-morrow to call it falsehood.* Ptolemaic astronomy, Euclidean space, Aristotelian logic, scholastic metaphysics, were expedient for centuries, but human experience has boiled over those limits, and we now call these things only relatively true, or true within those borders of experience. 'Absolutely' they are false; for we know that those limits were casual, and might have been transcended by past theorists just as they are by present thinkers. (*PR* 106–7)

However, while James does think that truth "is taken sometimes objectively and sometimes subjectively" (*ERE* 13; see also ML 433), he argues that the pragmatist definition of truth "applies to both" (ML 433), because 'absolute' truth is an idealization of our 'temporary' truths. That is, absolute truth is what we get if we extend the norms that govern our movements from one temporary truth to another to their logical limit. Since absolute truth represents an idealized extension of the application of the norms *already* in play with our temporary truths, there isn't a way for the best application of those temporary norms to lead us away from absolute truth. This leads to a familiar sort of anti-skepticism common to most versions of pragmatism; but what made James's version distinctive was his insistence that, while "the half-true ideas are all along contributing their quota" (*PR* 107), the *subjective* factors that contributed to our temporary truths contribute to absolute truth as well.

James's critics take it for granted that the 'subjective' factors that (justifiably or not) contribute to what is "temporarily true" (i.e., what is believed) will play no role in determining 'objective' truth. This may be true even of those who agree that in cases where the evidence leaves a question undetermined, we can legitimately believe whichever alternative satisfies our more subjective interests. Such critics still insist that, since these subjective interests come into play only when the evidence leaves a question unsettled, and since at the posited ideal terminus of inquiry on a particular question, all the evidence will be in, no subjective factors will be left to contribute to what is 'absolutely' true. For James, by contrast, the subjective factors do not 'wash out' through the idealization process. This is largely because James takes these 'truth processes' to reflect how expressions come to get their *meaning*, not how independently meaningful expressions come to be true, and it is its constitutive contribution to what our expressions mean that allows our 'passional nature' to contribute to even the 'absolute' truth of various claims (see Jackman 1998).

To take a familiar example, the truth conditions of "All Dogs share a common ancestor" may vary depending on whether or not the kind "dog" individuates animals by their genetic makeup or their evolutionary history. The question of which way we should go on this may not be one that can be settled by gathering more evidence, and 'subjective' factors must be brought in to settle the question even under ideal epistemic conditions, since, as James put it in the *Principles*, the essence of a thing is "that one of its properties which is so important for my interests that in comparison with it I may neglect the rest" (*PP* 961). In such cases, the evidence can make it clear that two of our commitments relate to a term conflict, but it is often *subjective* factors that then determine which of the two will be given up. When we discovered what we now call "subatomic" particles, we could have either given up on the truth of "Atoms are indivisible" or "Atoms exist", and our reasons for giving up the first, rather than the second, were as 'subjective' as they were evidentially based.[41]

We can see another instance of this when we consider the truth of religious beliefs. James was unable to accept either "popular Christianity" or "Scholastic Theism" (*VRE* 410), and never had any mystical experiences of his own (*VRE* 301); but defending the legitimacy of religious faith remained a major concern throughout his life. His own religious views were, however, remarkably thin and idiosyncratic. In "The Will to Believe", the "religious hypothesis" that he defends merely involves the affirmations that "the best things are the more eternal things" and that "we are better off even now if we believe [religion's] first affirmation to be true" (WB 29–30), and at the end of the *Varieties of Religious Experience*, he takes the common and generic core or religious belief to be "that the conscious person is continuous with a wider self through which saving experiences come" (*VRE* 405); and he denies that this "wider self" need be infinitely, or even tremendously powerful (*VRE* 413). The resulting conception of religion is so modest that some might fail to recognize it as

---

[41] Similarly, there may seem to be a tension between our general beliefs about freedom and the situations in which we actually call someone "free", and if the two really are incompatible, it won't be a purely non-subjective matter which one should be given up.

religion at all, but this thinned conception has the advantage of making it a lot easier for religious beliefs to be justified, and perhaps even true. Many of the general beliefs associated with "God" or "Religion" were, to James's mind, indefensible, and so he focused on those aspects of religion that were less epistemically problematic. For instance, if holding on to "God exists" required giving up "God is Perfect", or "God created the universe", then James was certainly willing to do so. By contrast, those who worry about the argument from evil typically hold God's omnipotence, benevolence, and omniscience dearer than they do God's existence. The merely "wider self" that James discusses in *Varieties* is certainly not enough to count as divine to many (indeed, his view may be compatible with this wider self being one's own subconscious (*VRE* 403)); but just as with truth and goodness, the question is which part of the conception do we want to hold on to, and that answer will reflect our subjective interests.[42]

Of course, whether or not they accept James's gloss on the nature of absolute truth, most philosophers still insist that such 'objective' truth is the *only* kind of truth, and that James's insistence on referring to our temporary beliefs as *truths* of any sort is just perverse.[43] A *temporary* truth is standardly taken to be no more a *kind* of truth than a *purported* spy is a *kind* of spy.[44] Nevertheless, James's talk of temporary or 'subjective' truths will turn out not to be as unmotivated as it might at first seem, since objective truths don't, for James, exist independently of us, any more than objective values do. His willingness to call certain beliefs of ours "truths" rather than, say, "rational beliefs" stemmed from a suspicion that, at the end of the day, there might not be anything else for the term to pick out.

For James, *reality* is, in a fairly robust sense, independent of us, but "the absolute truth will have to be *made*" (*PR* 107), since it includes both reality being a certain way *and* a claim's managing to pick out precisely that reality

---

[42] Indeed, some of the less charitable readings of James stem from thinking about what James's views would have to be for them to be used to support some of the more robust (and standard) versions of religious belief.

[43] One should note that James's use of "truth" here, seems to be fairly common in other branches of the humanities, where talk of "my truths" or "another culture's truths" is not unusual.

[44] James is quoted by his students as claiming that "It is unfortunate that truth should be used, now for the temporary beliefs of men and now for a purely abstract thing that nobody may, perhaps, ever be in possession of", and wishing that someone "might invent distinct words for *ultimate truth* and *temporary belief*" (ML 433). However, most philosophers think that we *already* have two words that pick out "temporary belief" and "ultimate truth": viz., "belief" and "truth". The "unfortunate" thing, according to such philosophers, is not that "truth" is used in this ambiguous way, but that *James* uses the normally unambiguous word in such an ambiguous fashion.

'absolutely'. Furthermore, while we certainly succeed in making our temporary truths, there will be no guarantee that we *can* make such absolute truths, and thus no way of being certain that any of our claims are (absolutely) true or false. Indeed, James occasionally displays not only fallibilism, but also a good deal of *pessimism* about the existence of absolute truth, which he describes as "a purely abstract thing that nobody may, perhaps, ever be in possession of", and as something that will only be realized with "the perfectly wise man" and "the absolutely complete experience" (*PR* 107), neither of which is an ideal we ever expect to see realized. For a statement to be 'absolutely' true, there must be a verdict that "no farther experience will ever alter" (*PR* 106), and James points out that we have no way of guaranteeing such long-term convergence. Not only might we fail to *actually* get to the end of inquiry, but (even with an *indefinite* prolongation of inquiry) such an end might also not be *possible* to achieve. This may be the case not only globally—that is, there will be no point where *every* question is settled—but also locally—that is, even for *particular* questions we cannot expect to get to a point where their status is definitively settled. Peirce famously tied the truth to an 'end of inquiry' that is sometimes understood as a 'global' position, where *all* questions are settled;[45] but James's formulation of absolute truth has no such commitment, yet his skepticism remains. For many questions, stable convergence might be too demanding, and prolonged inquiry might simply oscillate between a claim and its denial.

Such worries are underwritten by the *instrumentalism* that James endorses in *Pragmatism*. James takes it to be a descriptive fact about the sciences of his day that their practitioners don't take the theories they employ to be *literally* true, since "the enormously rapid multiplication of theories in these latter days has well-nigh upset the notion of any one of them being a more literally objective kind of thing than another", so that we have "become tolerant of symbol instead of reproduction, of approximation instead of exactness, plasticity instead of rigor" (*MT* 40). It is important to note that this instrumentalism is driven not by the fact that we are faced with, say, empirically equivalent but ontologically divergent theories, but rather that we are faced with a plurality of theories none of which we can give up because no subset of them can explain *all* of what the remainder can; they are "each of them good for so much and yet not good for everything" (*MT* 40). Now James *generalizes* this instrumentalism, because he recognizes the phenomena seen

---

[45] For reasons for doubting that this was Peirce's considered position, see Misak 1991.

in competing scientific theories within our conceptual schemes writ large. As he puts it:

There are thus at least three well-characterized levels, stages or types of thought about the world we live in, and the notions of one stage have one kind of merit, those of another stage another kind. It is impossible, however, to say that any stage as yet in sight is absolutely more *true* than any other. . . . There is no *ringing* conclusion possible when we compare these types of thinking, with a view to telling which is the more absolutely true. Their naturalness, their intellectual economy, their fruitfulness for practice, all start up as distinct tests of their veracity, and as a result we get confused. Common sense is *better* for one sphere of life, science for another, philosophic criticism for a third; but whether either be *truer* absolutely, Heaven only knows.   (PR 92–3)

Inquiry into *any* question may never produce a stable answer, since there is no stable framework for inquiry, and when we adopt, say, a scientific framework, many claims that were previously endorsed when using the framework of common sense will be denied because their ontological presuppositions are rejected. This may remain true of even seemingly 'obvious' statements like "There is a table in front of me", which, while stable within the framework of common sense, may not survive in a framework where a term like "table" does not refer.[46]

One might think that this is only a *temporary* state, and that we should eventually expect to find a single explanatory system that could capture all of the truths that we were trying to express with the others. However, James remained pessimistic about the status quo changing, and in his work from 1908 to 1910, he returns to earlier themes that, when developed, can lead one to doubt that any claim that made use of our concepts could ever turn out to be 'absolutely' true. According to James, since concepts emerged to serve our *practical* ends, and our most *fundamental* concepts (such as that of "substance", "causation", or "person") evolved to serve some of our earliest practical ends (PR 83), our conceptual system may be ill suited to "make us theoretically acquainted with the essential nature of reality" (PU 96) in a way that absolute truth requires.[47] James's late claim that logic

[46] For worries about this tension, see Sellars 1963 [1960]; Unger 1979. There will be no fact about which framework will be best for James at least partially because each framework does a particularly good job of satisfying one subset of the demands that, in SR, James argues go into what determines what we consider "rational".

[47] James's infamous rejection of the "logic of identity" in A Pluralistic Universe may thus be best understood as a rejection not so much of logic itself, but of the assumption that the inferential structure of our concepts matches the structure of the world at a 'global' level.

and conceptualization distort our perception of reality, rather than being a retreat from his earlier scientific attitude into a comforting mysticism, is actually a *consequence* of his naturalistic approach to the nature and origin of conceptualization, by which it is "a transformation which the flux of life undergoes at our hands in the interests of practice essentially and only subordinately in the interests of theory" (*PU* 109).

The assumption that, if pushed to their logical limits, our concepts will eventually misrepresent the realities they normally help us cope with is not limited to the concepts of common sense. James seems to suspect that it will be a problem with *any* conceptual system, since *conceptualization itself* misrepresents the 'continuous' nature of reality. Concepts require sharp boundaries, and while the imposition of models of the world where things are sharply defined has tremendous practical value, they inevitably misrepresent the richness of reality, and thus are unable to get to a point of absolute truth. The pinch will always be felt if any concept is extended enough. As James put it, "Conceptual treatment of perceptual reality makes it seem paradoxical and incomprehensible; and when radically and consistently carried out, it leads to the opinion that perceptual experience is not reality at all, but an appearance or illusion" (*SPP* 46).

So what should we say if the 'pessimistic' conclusion that James imagines actually turned out to be the case, and that the regulative ideal of absolute truth that our use aspired to was unsatisfiable? Of course, it would follow that none of our beliefs were 'absolutely' true, but it seems less clear that we should conclude that none of them were *true*. Instead, we should consider the possibility that the unrealizability of absolute truth suggests that the 'absolute' interpretation is not the best account of what we mean by "true". If it turns out that we can't find the grounding for our claims to be 'objectively' true, then we have two choices. We can continue to insist that those factors tying our use to the 'objective' interpretation are essential to the meaning of "truth" and thus adopt an 'error theory' where all of the term's applications are (if not, strictly speaking, false[48]) at least non-denoting, or we can adopt an interpretation of "true" that is a little more subjective, and thus allow at least some of our sentences to be true. Which way we should go with the semantics of "true" is precisely one of those 'subjective' issues discussed above. Our general beliefs

---

[48] One might think that even if nothing turned out to be absolutely true in such a scenario, some could still count as absolutely false if it turned out that they weren't endorsed in any of the alternative frameworks.

about truth (e.g., truth doesn't change) are well entrenched, but so is the belief that some of the things we say are *actually* true, and if the former is incompatible with the latter, then the former may have to go. We prefer, and presuppose, that truth is 'absolute', but if absolute truth is unrealizable, our use of "true" might be best understood as picking out subjective truth[49] rather than nothing at all.[50] Philosophers typically assume that the best way to settle the question of whether "truth" should have a subjective or objective interpretation is to do more *philosophy*; but for James, the question may ultimately be an *empirical* one.

However, while this leads one to a type of *fallibilism* about the existence of objective truth,[51] it doesn't follow that we aren't entitled to believe in it. We can be entitled to such a commitment, because the belief that inquiry could reach the type of stable convergence needed to produce absolute truth is arguably both a genuine option and evidentially undetermined. Consequently, James could argue that we are entitled to believe in objective truth even if we can't be assured that it exists, especially since this is a clear case where believing in something might be necessary for bringing it about. If we didn't believe that anything was true 'absolutely', then we would be less inclined to conduct our inquiries in a fashion that would produce convergence even if it were possible.[52] The epistemologist is entitled to believe in objective truth as another "will to believe" case, but James may be equally entitled to his pessimism; and given that James has reason to think that it is evidentially

---

[49]   As with the ethical case, there is some degree of play as to which type of subjectivism should be endorsed, since even if 'absolute' truth were unattainable, some types of non-absolute truth will be more subjective than others. For instance, tying subjective truth to what my society believes, while still far from absolute truth, might be less subjective than tying it to whatever I believe at any moment.

[50]   In this sense James's account of truth applies to itself. It is, ultimately, subjective factors which would (in the pessimistic scenario) determine whether we give up on the 'absolute' understanding of truth, and just as James claims that the moral philosopher can't accept ethical subjectivism (MPML 142), it may be that philosophers in general are more committed to the objectivity of truth than most. (Indeed, when James talks about the moral philosopher needing a system of truth, he must have such objective truth in mind.) Either way, James's suggestion that there is a 'subjective' sense of truth is far from incoherent.

[51]   James's position here contrasts markedly with that of Royce, who takes a similar connection between convergence and objective truth and, by combining it with what he takes to be an a priori assurance that objective truth and falsity exist, constructs a transcendental argument for the metaphysics required to make convergence inevitable. James is in this respect more like the Peirce who claims: "I do not say that it is infallibly true that there is any belief to which a person would come if he were to carry his inquiries far enough. I only say that that alone is what I call Truth. I cannot infallibly know that there *is* any truth" (Peirce 1966: 398). The difference being, of course, that Peirce takes the fallibilism about absolute truth to be necessarily fallibilism about truth *per se*.

[52]   We would, for instance, feel less pressure to make our belief system consistent.

unsettled whether objective truth is achievable, his talk of 'subjective' truth should not be dismissed as merely confused.

References

Unless otherwise notes, all citations of William James refer to his *Collected Works*, ed. Frederick H. Burkhardt, Fredson Bowers, and Ignas K. Skrupskelis (Cambridge, MA: Harvard University Press). The following abbreviations are used:

ECR	*Essays, Comments, and Reviews*, 1987.
EP	*Essays in Philosophy*, 1978.
ERE	*Essays in Radical Empiricism*, 1912/1976.
ILWL	"Is Life Worth Living", 1895, repr. in *WB&OEPP*.
ME&N	*Manuscript Essays and Notes*, 1988.
ML	Manuscript Lectures, 1988.
MPML	"The Moral Philosopher and the Moral Life", 1891, repr. in *WB&OEPP*.
MT	*The Meaning of Truth*, 1909/1975.
PP	*The Principles of Psychology*, 1890/1981.
PR	*Pragmatism, A New Name for Some Old Ways of Thinking*, 1907/1975.
PU	*A Pluralistic Universe*, 1909/1977.
SPP	*Some Problems of Philosophy*, 1911/1979.
SR	"The Sentiment of Rationality", 1879, 1882, repr. in *WB&OEPP*.
VRE	*The Varieties of Religious Experience*, 1902/1985.
WB	"The Will to Believe", 1896, repr. in *WB&OEPP*.
WB&OEPP	*The Will to Believe, and Other Essays in Popular Philosophy*, 1897/1979.

Burge, T. (1979). "Individualism and the Mental". In *Midwest Studies in Philosophy*, iv: *Studies in Metaphysics*. Minneapolis: University of Minnesota Press, 73–121.

Cherniak, C. (1986). *Minimal Rationality*. Cambridge, MA: MIT Press.

Clifford, W. K. (1999 [1877]). "The Ethics of Belief". In his *The Ethics of Belief and Other Essays*. Amherst, MA: Prometheus Books, 70–96.

Dennett, D. (1987). *The Intentional Stance*. Cambridge, MA: MIT Press.

Devitt, M. (1994). "The Methodology of Naturalistic Semantics", *Journal of Philosophy*, 91/10: 545–72.

Evans, G. (1982). *The Varieties of Reference*. Oxford: Oxford University Press.

Gale, R. (1980). "William James and the Ethics of Belief". *American Philosophical Quarterly*, 17/1: 1–14.

____ (1999). *The Divided Self of William James*. New York: Cambridge University Press.

Harper, R. S. (1949). "The Laboratory of William James". *Harvard Alumni Bulletin*, 52: 169–73.

____ (1950). "The First Psychological Laboratory", *Isis*, 41/2: 158–61.

Jackman, H. (1998). "James' Pragmatic Account of Intentionality and Truth". *Transactions of the Charles S. Peirce Society*, 34/1: 155–81.

⸺(1999). "Prudential Arguments, Naturalized Epistemology, and the Will to Believe". *Transactions of the Charles S. Peirce Society*, 35/1: 1–37.

Jordan, J. (1996). "Pragmatic Arguments and Belief". *American Philosophical Quarterly*, 33/4: 409–20.

Klein, A. (2007). "The Rise of Empiricism: William James, Thomas Hill Green, and the Struggle over Psychology" (Ph.D. thesis, Indiana University).

Kornblith, H. (1994). "What is Naturalistic Epistemology?". In Kornblith (ed.), *Naturalizing Epistemology*. Cambridge, MA: MIT Press, 1–14.

Lewis, D. (1983). "New Work for a Theory of Universals". *Australasian Journal of Philosophy*, 61/4: 343–77.

Misak, C. J. (1991). *Truth and the End of Inquiry*. New York: Oxford University Press.

Peirce, Charles S. (1966). *Charles S. Peirce: Selected Writings*, ed. Philip Weiner. New York: Dover.

Pojman, L. (1993). "Believing, Willing and the Ethics of Belief". In Pojman (ed.), *The Theory of Knowledge*. Belmont, CA: Wadsworth, 525–44.

Pratt, J. B. (2001 [1909]). *What is Pragmatism?* Bristol: Thoemmes Press.

Putnam, H. (1975). "The Meaning of 'Meaning' ". In his *Mind Language and Reality*. Cambridge, MA: Harvard University Press, 215–71.

⸺(2002). *The Collapse of the Fact/Value Dichotomy*. Cambridge, MA: Harvard University Press.

Royce, J. (1885). *The Religious Aspect of Philosophy*. Boston: Houghton, Mifflin & Co.

Sellars, W. (1963 [1960]). "Philosophy and the Scientific Image of Man". In his *Science, Perception and Reality*. London: Routledge, 1–40.

Stich, S. (1990). *The Fragmentation of Reason*. Cambridge, MA: MIT Press.

Strawson, P. F. (1952). *Introduction to Logical Theory*. London: Methuen.

Strong, C. A. (1904). "A Naturalistic Theory of the Reference of Thought to Reality". *Journal of Philosophy*, 1/10 (12 May): 253–360.

Suckiel, E. (1982). *The Pragmatic Philosophy of William James*. Notre Dame, IN: University of Notre Dame Press.

Unger, P. (1979). "Why There Are No People". In *Midwest Studies in Philosophy*, iv: *Studies in Metaphysics*. Minneapolis: University of Minnesota Press, 177–222.

CHAPTER 5

....

JOHN DEWEY: INQUIRY, ETHICS, AND DEMOCRACY

....

MATTHEW FESTENSTEIN

I

....

BOTH JOHN DEWEY's longevity and the scope of his philosophy pose problems
for the commentator. He was born before the American Civil War and died
in the depths of the Cold War. His voluminous output includes work in
epistemology, metaphysics, logic, the philosophy of mind, the philosophy of
science, ethics, political philosophy, aesthetics, and the philosophy of religion.
Across his career, the problems he grappled with, his solutions, and the
philosophical resources that he employed underwent important changes.[1]
The distinctive philosophical vocabulary that he developed was difficult, and
was entwined with the often elusive 'tours, rétours and detours' of his prose
(Schinz 1910: 89). His reputation has endured an unusually sharp roller
coaster ride, from him being designated the 'the guide, the mentor and the

....

[1] For different perspectives on these changes, see White 1964; Coughlan 1975; Boisvert 1988;
Westbrook 1991; Ryan 1995; Welchman 1995.

conscience of the American people' (Commager 1950: 100), via a nadir when he was viewed as at best benign but woolly-minded, to a recent resurgence of interest and respectability.

For all these reasons, Dewey is a tricky but, I think, rewarding challenge. A methodological dilemma that such a lengthy and varied career presents is either to work through a particular text or period, which risks obscuring the range of Dewey's concerns, or to aim at a broader interpretation, which carries with it the danger of textual cherry picking and losing sight of the particular problems and contexts that motivate his particular discussions. With these pitfalls in mind, this chapter takes the second path, albeit with a focus on the later period of Dewey's work. In a late essay, Dewey outlined the project of a philosophical 'movement [...] called in its various aspects by the names of pragmatism, experimentalism, instrumentalism':

It breaks completely with that part of the philosophical tradition which holds that concern with superior reality determines the work to be done by philosophical inquiry. It affirms that the purpose and business of philosophy is wholly with that part of the historic tradition called search for wisdom:—Namely, search for the ends and values that give direction to our collective human activities. It holds that not grasp of eternal and universal Reality but use of the methods and conclusions of our best knowledge, that called scientific, provides the means for conducting this search. It holds that limitations which now exist in this use are to be removed by means of extension of ways of tested knowing that define science from physical and physiological matters to social and distinctly human affairs.   (Dewey 1946: 161)

A few years earlier he offered a similarly resonant claim on behalf of the theory of inquiry:

[F]ailure to institute a logic based inclusively and exclusively on the operations of inquiry has enormous cultural consequences. It encourages obscurantism; it promotes acceptance of beliefs formed before methods of inquiry had reached their present estate; and it tends to relegate scientific (that is, competent) methods of inquiry to a specialized technical field. Since scientific methods simply exhibit free intelligence operating in the best manner available at a given time, the cultural waste, confusion and distortion that results from the failure to use these methods, in all fields in connection with all problems, is incalculable. These considerations reinforce the claim of logical theory, as the theory of inquiry, to assume and to hold a position of primary human importance.   (Dewey 1938b: 527)

There is a rich seam of ambiguity in these claims for the primary human importance of inquiry and for the extension of 'ways of tested knowing' to social affairs. It is true that Dewey believed that there exist identifiable canons of inquiry to be gleaned from the natural sciences, and that there is a broad ethical, cultural, and political need to acknowledge this fact in order to extract social and political life from waste, confusion, and distortion. But it is important to grasp both the precise meaning and the place of this claim in his philosophy, if this is not to lead to a significant misinterpretation. For both many contemporaries and later readers, the key claims were something like the following: that there exists a scientific method, identified, as in the quotation above, with logic; that this should be applied to social inquiry, and that to do so would undermine false factual assumptions on which policies were based; and that therefore public policy needs greater scientific and technical expertise. Policies and proposals for social action should be treated as working hypotheses, open to empirical investigation, rather than as programmes to be rigidly adhered to. The capacity of policy experts to control decisions should be reined in by democratic procedures: this is what distinguishes Dewey from someone like Walter Lippmann, who offered a potent defence of technocracy to which Dewey responded (Lippmann 1965 [1922], 1925; Dewey 1927b; Westbrook 1991: 293–318). In the absence of such constraints, reliance on policy experts will result in an 'oligarchy managed in the interests of the few' (Dewey 1927b: 364–5). However, the force of the call for method, inquiry, and intelligence is in supporting the case for opening up dogmas underlying ethical positions and social policies to empirical scrutiny by those competent to investigate their claims.

Finally, this interpretation of Dewey's conception of inquiry and its significance is wedded to the sense that Deweyan pragmatism is reticent about setting out 'final ends' for the sake of which the exercise of pragmatic intelligence should take place (Richardson 1999: 122). On the one hand, what defines his experimentalism is the use of reflective intelligence to assess and revise judgements in the light of an appraisal of the consequences of acting on them. On the other hand, criteria for judging consequences appear to be undefined in his philosophy, or defined only in notoriously vacuous ways: as what is conducive to 'growth', to the coordination of activities and interests, or to consummatory experience. Rational or 'intelligent' agency, it seems, is viewed as instrumental and goal-directed, but the goals to which it is or should be directed have been left out of the picture of inquiry and practical judgement. From this worry about a hole where an account of the ends of agency should be flows the influential view of Deweyan pragmatism as 'acquiescent' in whatever ethical standards are prevalent, focusing only on the instrumental achievement of pre-given ends and evasive about the moral or practical authority of those ends: as Henry Richardson puts it, 'What had seemed truly liberating [. . .] in Dewey's rhetoric about intelligence has here vanished, and we are left with an uninspiring and uninspired consequentialism' (Richardson 1999: 113). So even such a perceptive and sympathetic commentator as Morton White worries that, lacking a conception of the specific ends or purposes which inquiry or critical intelligence should serve, Dewey's philosophy 'might easily fall into the hands of those willing to cry "science, science" in defence of the most obnoxious ends and means' (White 1957: 201).[2] Whatever Dewey's personal moral or political commitments, this criticism alleges, his experimentalism is vulnerable to appropriation by whatever social forces are most powerful.

The still quite frequent identification of Dewey's pragmatism with Richard Rorty's version of the doctrine has tended to make matters worse here. Rorty celebrates both the groundlessness of his own ethical and political commitments, as a form of 'unjustifiable social hope', and ties this to a call for the recognition of 'the appeal of instrumental rationality' (Rorty 1982: 208; Rorty 1991: 193). And he presents these positions as a revival of the most valuable elements of Dewey's philosophy. Now whatever the merits of Rorty's project or the coherence of his proposals, this association has also tended to increase the sense that Dewey offers a plea for more 'intelligence' while eschewing any philosophical articulation of the purposes to which this is meant to be put.[3]

This interpretation (and the identification with Rortyan pragmatism) is less prevalent than it once was, and its retreat has been a condition for, and a component in, the revival of interest in Dewey's philosophy. However, I think that it is both a live and interesting question, and a useful route into understanding several different elements of Dewey's philosophy, why we should see him as protected from this worry. For, on the face of it, there is a difficulty. It is certainly the case that Dewey explicitly rejects the notion that the exercise of inquiry or pragmatic intelligence should be restricted to the 'truncated and distorted business of finding out means for realizing

[2] See also, e.g., Diggins (1994: 303) on a 'process without a purpose'; Festenstein 1997: 19–23; MacGilvray 2004: ch. 4. For the original charge of the pragmatic acquiescence, see Mumford 1968 [1926]; Dewey 1927a; and the discussion in Westbrook 1990.

[3] On Rorty in relation to the 'acquiescence' worry, see Festenstein 2003. On the accuracy or otherwise of Rorty's view of Dewey, and the significance of this, see, e.g., Brodsky 1982; Edel 1985; Gouinlock 1990; Stuhr 1992; Rorty 1994; Ryan 2001; Hildebrand 2003.

objectives already settled on' (Dewey 1938b: 490).[4] Nevertheless, as we will see, he is sceptical about the notion that we can give any content to the ends of inquiry outside particular situations and contexts. Replying to the charge of moral evasiveness levelled at the first edition of his and James Tufts's textbook on ethics, Dewey writes in a letter to his correspondent Skudder Klyce that 'my only claim is that the objection brought against it is true. I have not given or tried to give any "solutions". But it doesn[']t seem to have occurred to the objectors that to say that moral life is a s[e]ries of problems and that morality *is* their solution as they arise would naturally preclude me from proffering solutions.'[5] And, having encouraged the thought that we should see our ends, not merely our means, as the subject of inquiry and evaluation, he goes on to endorse a conception of scientific inquiry as a matter of relating means and consequences. So there is a question about what resources he can call on in order to move beyond the truncated form of instrumentalism; and it is this that I want to address in this chapter. In doing so, I explore the links between the conceptions of inquiry or pragmatic intelligence in Dewey's work, the meta-ethics of valuation, ethics, and democracy.

In the following section, I outline Dewey's conception of inquiry, drawing principally on his late *Logic*, in order to introduce some key terms and develop a clearer view of the primacy of practical engagement in his understanding of knowledge (II). I go on to look at the notion of valuation, as cognitively on all fours with other forms of inquiry (III). These two sketches set the scene for considering the suspicion that his instrumentalism has nothing determinate to say about the ends to which inquiry is put. One interpretation, put forward by recent sympathetic interpreters of Dewey such as Hilary and Ruth Anna Putnam, is that we should see that certain moral standards are presupposed by the practice of inquiry. I argue that this is compatible with what Dewey says, and can gather some textual support, but is not the whole story (IV). Setting out some key themes from his ethical thought and drawing on the ideas in the theory of valuation, I argue that we can put some ethical flesh on his account of growth as the goal of pragmatic intelligence: the latter is a constitutive part of personal and social growth for Dewey, and this has meaningful ethical and political implications (V).

---

[4] I use the notions of inquiry and pragmatic intelligence interchangeably in this chapter. It should be noted that Dewey's use of his own terminology is slippery and often intriguing.
[5] Letter to Skudder Klyce, 6 May 1915, cited in Edel and Flower 1989: p. xxxiii; on the 1st edn. of Dewey and Tufts's text, Dewey 1908, see Welchman 1995.

II

Dewey's basic move is to see the inquirer as an agent, and inquiry as a way of arriving at what he calls practical judgements. Dewey develops his conception of inquiry against the backcloth of a metaphysical vision of humans as embedded in an objectively precarious world and seeking a mode of activity which will allow them to overcome this precariousness. We engage in inquiry and deploy critical intelligence, he thinks, in response to this challenge. His pragmatism 'starts from [...] functions, both biological and social in character: from organic responses, adjustments. It treats the knowledge standpoint, in all its patterns, structure and purposes, as evolving out of, and operating in the interest of, the guidance and enrichment of these primary human functions' (Dewey 1910a: 88). Inquiry is demanded by what he calls an incomplete situation: that is, one in which something must be done. Dewey follows C. S. Peirce in viewing inquiry as a response to some distress. However, Dewey tends to view this incompleteness in naturalistic terms, as an objective feature of the situation, rather than as a matter of what a particular agent thinks or feels: '*we* are doubtful because the situation is inherently doubtful' (Dewey 1938b: 109).[6] So personal satisfaction is not the *telos* or terminus of inquiry, as critics of pragmatism, notably Russell (1966 [1910]) charged.

While inquiry is prompted by a particular problematic situation, this is not to say that the repertoire of responses is limited to those unreflective ways of adapting to the environment that guide us most of the time. Quite the reverse: 'Instinct and habit express [...] modes of response, but modes inadequate for a progressive being, or for adaptation to an environment presenting novel and unmastered features. Under such conditions, ideas are their surrogates' (Dewey 1910b: 3).[7] So inquiry *qua* reflective thought requires abstraction and conceptualization.

Both the past findings and the rules that govern inquiry are resources for inquiry which are open to correction: the 'attainment of settled beliefs is a progressive matter; there is no belief so settled as not to be exposed to further inquiry' (Dewey 1938b: 16). This is the well-known pragmatist thesis of fallibilism, which Dewey also owes to Peirce: any belief is susceptible to

---

[6] 'The *world* is precarious and perilous' (Dewey 1925a: 44). Compare C. S. Peirce, 'The Fixation of Belief' (*CP* 5. 358–87). On Dewey's logic, see Boisvert 1988; Burke 1994.

[7] Dewey's use of 'habit' here is mildly pejorative, and in later works, notably from *Human Nature and Conduct* onward, it is used in a more evaluatively neutral way.

revision, but only by reference to other beliefs that are held to be 'settled' or 'stable' for the purposes of judging *this* belief.[8] This fallibility extends to include the criteria for success in inquiry, which are only fallible proposals for the resolution of problems not 'cast-iron rules' (Dewey 1910*a*: 241). So, for instance, 'while there is no a priori standard of health with which the actual state of human beings can be compared so as to determine whether they are well or ill, or in what respect they are ill, there have developed, out of past experience, certain criteria which are operatively applicable in new cases as they arise' (Dewey 1939: 233).

In the same way, logical principles are viewed as normative by virtue of their historical success:

Men think in ways they should not when they follow methods of inquiry that experience of past inquiries shows are not competent to reach the intended end of the inquiries in question [...] It does not follow [...] that the 'better' methods are ideally perfect, or that they are regulative or 'normative' because of their conformity to some absolute form. They are the methods which experience up to the present time shows to be the best methods available for achieving certain results, while abstraction of these methods does supply a (relative) norm or standard for further under-takings.   (Dewey 1938*b*: 107–8)

The tools that we use in inquiry are not given a priori and antecedently to inquiry, but have been developed in the course of inquiry, and are used owing to past success. They are 'operative in a manner that tends in the long run, or in continuity of inquiry, to yield results that are either confirmed in further inquiry or that are corrected by use of the same procedures' (Dewey 1938*b*: 345).

Inquiry has as what Dewey calls its end-in-view the formation of a warranted assertion, a term which he seeks to substitute for 'knowledge' in inquiry. What counts as knowledge or warranted assertion, then, is defined in contextualist terms as 'the product of competent inquiries'; beyond this, the meaning of the term 'is so empty that any content or filling may be arbitrarily poured in' (Dewey 1938*b*: 16). As the medical example suggests, it does not follow that what should be taken to fix belief or to provide a satisfactory resolution to a problematic situation boils down to a matter of personal conviction or whim. Rather, the point of the notion of warranted assertion is that we should not imagine that we have knowledge outside the fallible, contextual, and

---

[8] 'That one can be both fallibilistic and anti-skeptical is perhaps *the* unique insight of American pragmatism' (Putnam 1994: 152).

historically developed processes of inquiry that we exercise: so, for example, the data of our senses can be taken to provide infallible knowledge of the world. Similarly, Dewey reserves the term 'object' for 'subject-matter so far as it has been produced and ordered in settled form by means of inquiry' (Dewey 1938b: 122). Dewey resists forms of epistemological realism for which knowledge is a faithful copy of a fixed reality. Such theories commit the 'most pervasive fallacy of philosophic thinking': namely, 'neglect of context' (Dewey 1931: 5).[9] A perception, for example, is not in itself epistemically significant, but only a moment in the organism's response to its environment. Only in the framework of meaningfulness furnished by this wider process of engagement can the mute and inchoate 'undergoings' and 'peripheral stimuli' become what are then misleadingly labelled the 'data' of inquiry. In the course of inquiry, these perceptions may then perform an important functional role in checking our hypotheses; but this should not be confused with epistemological primacy.[10]

Finally, inquiry 'necessarily contains a *practical* factor, an activity of doing and making which reshapes antecedent intellectual material which sets the problem of inquiry' (Dewey 1938b: 162). In keeping with his opposition to 'copy' views of knowledge, Dewey wants to emphasize the ways in which objects of inquiry are created and manipulated through experiment—in Ian Hacking's well-known formulation, inquirers intervene in, rather than merely represent, the world (Hacking 1983). But the end-in-view of inquiry is practical in another way: it is 'evaluated as to its worth on the ground of its ability to resolve the *problem* presented by the conditions under investigation' (Dewey 1939: 232). For Dewey, the conclusion is not simply a change of belief but a re-coordination of dispositions to act that follow (or are entailed by) such a change. Its resolution lies in a 'consummatory' reordering of experience, addressing the problems that prompted inquiry and that have been identified in its course. Dewey's vivid and developed example in the *Logic* is that draining swamps in order to eliminate malaria tested the hypothesis about the disease's cause. Inquiry transfigures our habitual relationships to the environment, opening up new possibilities of action, even if we do not realize those possibilities.

---

[9] For discussion of the significance of this text, see Tiles 1988. In addition to the texts cited, for further consideration of the very interesting question of Dewey's realism, see Hacking 1983; Sleeper 1986; Godfrey-Smith 2002.

[10] As he puts it in *Experience and Nature*, 'the alleged primacy of sensory meanings' embodies 'the fallacy which converts a functional office into an antecedent existence' (1925a: 246). This is an important line of argument in Dewey 1929 (e.g., at p. 91).

III

What Dewey calls 'valuation' is a form of inquiry or exercise of pragmatic intelligence. Dewey does not seek to bolt his conception of inquiry on to a conception of valuing and practical deliberation, understood in independent terms, but to see the latter as itself a form of inquiry—that is, as an exercise of reflective pragmatic intelligence. A value is 'constructed', in his jargon, as a solution to a problem in experience, and can be appraised by assessing the extent to which it solves the problem presented in experience: 'until there is actual or threatened shock and disturbance of a situation [...] there is no need, no desire, no valuation' (Dewey 1939: 239). Where valuation differs from inquiry more generally is in having as its end-in-view not a warranted assertion but specifically a practical judgement.[11] However, this is not meant to downgrade the cognitive status of valuation.

Practical judgements are judgements about what to do, or what should be done: 'He had better consult a physician; it would not be advisable for you to invest in those bonds; the United States should either modify its Monroe Doctrine or else make more efficient military preparations; this is a good time to build a house; if I do that I shall be doing wrong, etc' (Dewey 1915: 15). When we deliberate towards a practical judgement, he argues, we do not apply a standard at which have arrived a priori to the particular case, but aim at the resolution of the specific problematic situation that confronts us. The practical judgement expresses an end-in-view, which is specified by an agent in relation to a specific context of action: 'only by a judgment of means—things having value in the carrying of an indeterminate situation to completion—is the end determinately made out in judgement', and 'the standard of evaluation is formed in the process of practical judgement or valuation. It is not something taken from outside and applied to it' (Dewey 1915: 37, 39). This does not imply the inappropriateness of abstraction or theory in practical judgement any more than it does in inquiry more generally. As Dewey's list of examples suggests, what counts as a practical judgement does not have to be framed in terms that can have no wider application, beyond the particular problem confronting an agent. In order to understand what Dewey means by these last statements, several different kinds of point must be unpacked from them. One is prescriptive, to the effect that

---

[11] There is no space here to discuss another significant dimension of valuation, in Dewey's theory of art: Dewey 1934.

we should not try to impose 'remote' ends on a situation in ignorance of particular local conditions. A general plea for sensitivity to context in practical deliberation, of course, is compatible with the idea that its ends are fixed and knowable a priori, and with the idea that practical reasoning consists purely in working out the most effective means to achieve pre-given ends which are themselves immune from rational appraisal. Beyond this general prescriptive claim, though, are three more distinctive analytical theses, about the cognitive status of values, the reciprocity of the means–end relationship in deliberation, and the problem-solving function of practical judgement.

Dewey distinguishes his view of value from that contained in what he calls empiricism. This is the view that the source of value is preference, and that preferences are insulated from reasoning and criticism: as he puts in *Quest for Certainty*, that 'liking is liking, and one is as good as the other' (Dewey 1929: 210). Dewey distinguishes desires from what he calls 'likings' or 'prizings', which are merely affective responses. For the empiricist, the value of a course of action or object ultimately rests in its being 'prized' or esteemed by the agent. Just as he dismisses the epistemic standing of 'raw' sense data, Dewey, however, distinguishes such primitive and non-cognitive prizings and impulses from desires. Desires in the full sense are complex and cognitive: a desire expresses, more or less explicitly, a practical judgement about what should be done, which itself includes an appraisal of an existing situation, a claim about the causal possibilities of the situation, and a proposal for how to transform it (Dewey 1915: 26, 30–1; 1939: 202). In this sense, desires contain a 'union of prizing and appraising' and 'affective-ideational-motor activity' (Dewey 1939: 218). When we are trying to work out what we should value—that is, what practical judgement will resolve the problematic situation—we do not take desires as given, but as open to critical judgement. What we desire should become a value for us only through the process of practical deliberation or reflection: that is, through 'an investigation of the *claims* of the thing in question to be esteemed, appreciated, prized, cherished. This involves the old and familiar distinction between the apparent and the real good' (Dewey 1925a: 96). Values make a cognitive and practical claim to withstand deliberation or reflection—for reflective endorsement, in Christine Korsgaard's phrase (1996).

If a person, for example, finds after due investigation that an immense amount of effort is required to procure the conditions that are the means required for realization of a desire (including perhaps sacrifice of some other end-values that might be obtained by the same expenditure of effort), does that fact react to modify his original desire and hence, by definition, his valuation? A survey of what takes place in any deliberate activity provides an affirmative answer to this question.   (Dewey 1939: 213)

If I want to drink a cup of coffee, this gives a particular course of action or end-in-view—making coffee—value. This is the value that is 'constructed' in order to deal with the situation. Yet neither the initial desire nor the value is insulated from rational appraisal. The value can be appraised in terms of its effectiveness as a means to the end of drinking coffee: is it better to do this than to go out to a café or prompt someone else to make me a cup? Reflection can also give the value specific content, as one thinks about the various means to *this* end (do I need to buy any equipment or ingredients? Shall I do it now or wait a few minutes?), which in turn allows me to arrive at a judgement about whether the value as an end-in-view satisfies the desire. Reflection on the proposed course of action may also be assessed in terms of other desires and projects (I am too lazy to bother, or too anxious to stop work). The initiating desire may itself be assessed in terms of other values which satisfying it may further or impede: for example, I may reflect on the consequences of caffeine consumption for me. Further, reflection on the desire may lead me to see it as itself an end-in-view initiated by some further desire, such as thirst or a desire to duck out of work for a few minutes, that can itself be appraised, met by other means, etc. The deliberative exercise of pragmatic intelligence towards practical judgement, then, can transform our original desires and generate new ends for action (Dewey 1939: 231).

The second point to pick up here is the famous thesis of the continuum of means and ends, or 'the thoroughly reciprocal character of means and ends in the practical judgment' (Dewey 1915: 37). Deliberate activity is never merely instrumental, according to Dewey, in the sense that it is undertaken solely for the sake of some independent end. Rather, means are constitutively related to the ends-in-view arrived at (Tiles 1988: 158). Examples of this sort of relationship include physical exertion as a part of health, as well as a means to it, or committing particular acts of theft as a part, as well as a means to, becoming a professional thief. This constitutive relationship is usually contrasted with a merely instrumental one: so it makes no difference, as far as the goal of getting to work goes, whether one walks or takes the bus—the latter is not constitutively related to the former, only a more or less efficient means to achieving the desired outcome. The thesis of the continuum of means and ends denies that from the standpoint of practical judgement there can be a purely instrumental relationship of means to end. As noted already, a practical judgement consists in a complex bundle of judgements, which includes an appraisal of an existing situation, a claim about the causal possibilities of the situation, and a proposal for how to transform it. The end-in-view towards which it aims is itself a composite entity: to aim to achieve X by means of Y is to form the end-in-view X-by-way-of-Y. Deliberating in any particular context, what we aim at in deliberation is an end-in-view, in this sense. This may seem like a verbal trick, a way of formulating the relationship of means and ends that obscures the possibility that we can pull out a particular end or goal in practical deliberation (such as getting to work) and consider it in isolation from the particular means one may employ to achieve it. It is not that we cannot distinguish analytically an end from means we may employ to achieve it, or that we cannot judge the effectiveness of those means to achieve a particular end. Rather, Dewey's point is that the view of practical deliberation as consisting only in the appraisal of means with respect to their adequacy in achieving fixed ends, which are themselves viewed as outside the scope of practical deliberation, is massively incomplete and distorting. Part of the point of inquiring into means is to evaluate the end that we are pursuing, not merely to work out how to achieve it. In the process of practical judgement, it would be irrational simply to fix an end, and inquire solely into the means needed to achieve it, and this is not what we do when we deliberate. Instead, the rational agent, exercising pragmatic intelligence, runs through 'dramatic rehearsals' of what is involved in accomplishing different ends-in-view: each 'conflicting habit or impulse takes its turn in projecting itself on the screen of the imagination. It unrolls a picture of its future history' (Dewey 1922: 133; Fesmire 2003). Dewey emphasizes that the reciprocal character of means and ends implies that past values are applicable only in cases where exactly the same means and ends are available. For this reason, 'all judgment, in the degree to which it is critically intelligent, is a transvaluation of prior values', that is, an appraisal of how past values need to be reconstructed in order to deal with current predicaments. Nietzsche, he remarks tartly, would probably have made less of a sensation, but stayed within the limits of wisdom, if he had confined himself to this assertion (Dewey 1915: 47).

Third, practical judgement and the values or ends-in-view at which it arrives should be placed within the framing account of problem solving, of the organism adapting to the shocks and opportunities of its environment.

What constitutes a successful resolution to a problem is accounted for in very formal and minimal terms. For example, from *Theory of Valuation*:

The attained end or consequence is always an organization of activities, where organization is a coordination of all activities which enter as factors. The end-in-view is that particular activity which operates as a coordinating factor of all other subactivities involved. Recognition of the end as a coordination or unified organization of activities, and of the end-in-view as the special activity which is the means of effecting this coordination, does away with any appearance of paradox that seems to be attached to the idea of a temporal continuum of activities in which each successive stage is equally end and means. The *form* of an attained end or consequence is always the same: that of successful coordination.   (Dewey 1939: 234)

The terms in which Dewey describes the outcomes of practical judgement (and inquiry more generally) are highly abstract but suggestive: they include coordination, unification, organization, and (elsewhere) integration and 'consummatory experience'. These seem to be (in Jon Elster's (1983) phrase) states that are necessarily by-products of more concrete activities. We do not aim at coordination or unification when we grapple with a particular problem (we aim at working out what to wear, which political party to support, or whether to declare war—that is, at arriving at an end-in-view with respect to these questions), but a successful resolution achieves them. In one sense, then, we can criticize our ends-in-view with reference to their capacity to solve the problems that confront us. But this is only through raising particular objections to the claims that it makes about the judgements implied about the current situation and the course of action that it proposes. We do not invoke coordination or unified organization as a criterion within practical deliberation.

Even if we accept the constructive conception of intelligence in practical judgement, the continuum of means and ends, and the view of these claims as part of a broader naturalistic intellectual framework of problem resolution, there may still seem to be enough residual empiricism in this account to revive the anxiety with which we started. If the social world inculcates desires and interests that are radically corrupt, then even a more critical and informed conception of how to give expression to those desires and interests may continue to reflect this pathological state of affairs. 'Judgment at some point runs up against the brute act of holding something dear' (Dewey 1915: 46). Understood in this way, the account of valuation may not eliminate the worry that Dewey offers an empty plea for focus on context, intelligence, and the consequences of particular courses of action, while ruling out the thought that we can suggest critical standards by which to appraise various ends-in-view in any systematic fashion: as we have seen, the naturalistic metaphysical account of the situated inquirer does not provide such a standard. This opens up space for the worries about acquiescence and technocracy. If context and situation supply the evaluative yardsticks for action, it is not too great a step to think that the dominant ideas and standards of one's own society are the only ones to deploy in practical judgement. And if the role of critical reflection or pragmatic intelligence is to flesh out the causal possibilities of a situation, rather than to reflect on the ends for which action should be undertaken, then the cadres of instrumental rationality seem well equipped to do the labour of critical reflection for the rest of us.

IV

One part of a response to this worry is epistemological. We should not identify warranted assertions with those we just happen to agree on. Any proposed ends-in-view or knowledge claims are fallible and open to critical reflection, discussion, and possible revision. So we may go on to reflect on the conditions for the exercise of pragmatic intelligence. To investigate our values is to expose them to experiment, reflection, and testing, this line of thought runs, and certain moral, social, and political standards are necessary for the application of intelligence to inquiry, in particular those of openness, revisability, and scepticism about elites (Putnam 1994: 175). In this sense, democracy implies a 'method of organized intelligence' (Dewey 1935: 56).

The virtues of openness to all points of view, and the freedom to offer and criticize claims, are shared by inquiry and democracy. These values provide a framework for discovering worthwhile ways of living: they allow us to test and revise claims, and to seek out better ways of life, protected from putative experts about where our true interests really lie (Dewey 1927b: 293–4). Hypotheses and points of view must be open to scrutiny, challenge, and revision. This requires such fundamental democratic practices as freedom of thought and speech. As Hilary Putnam puts it, the materials to be used in the defence of democracy 'cannot be circumscribed in advance'. Rather, 'we do not know what our needs and interests are and what we are capable of until we engage in politics'. A corollary of this is that 'there can be no final answer to the question "How should we live?", and that we should, therefore, always leave it open to further discussion and experimentation. And that is precisely why we need democracy' (Putnam 1992: 189).[12] To the extent that we are genuinely seeking to deal with practical questions, seeking answers, we should be governed by these standards, and not accept any particular consensus as the truth. Our standards may be corrupt, but democracy provides means to correct them by preserving conditions for future inquiry, scrutiny, and revision.

Finally, a class of putative experts 'is inevitably so removed from common interests as to become a class with private interests and private knowledge, which in social matters is not knowledge at all' (Dewey 1927b: 365; Festenstein 1997: 96–8). Hierarchy, exclusion, and constraint limit the intellectual growth of the oppressed, force the dominant to construct rationalizations to justify their position, and limit the capacity for a society or group to confront and solve problems. In other words, Dewey does not dispute that inquiry should be left in the hands of the competent. But when it came to social and political matters, he believed that most people possessed the relevant capacities and that supporters of technocratic elites overestimated the capacities of the latter and ignored the ways in which their status as elites tended to undermine their own claims to epistemic authority. Democratic social and political arrangements are cognitively superior to Lippmann's trust in expertise through building in mechanisms of public scrutiny and revision of decisions, and subjecting elites to the discipline of periodic election.

The exercise of pragmatic intelligence, then, is not value-neutral. Yet the claim for the democratic presuppositions of inquiry provides only a partial picture of the relationship that Dewey thinks holds between ethics, democracy, and inquiry (Festenstein 1995). For the relationship among fellow citizens (or however we define members of the society) is epistemic, on this view. We are guided by democratic values of openness and inclusion only because we want to guide ourselves intelligently in dealing with problems we encounter. If we take it as the basis of a justificatory account of democracy, the argument for the democratic presuppositions of inquiry seems to offer only an instrumental account of the ethical and political values that it describes. From this perspective, any respect or sympathy that we may feel for others is irrelevant to the justificatory account.

---

[12] See also Anderson 2006; Westbrook 2005: 175–200. For another influential development of this idea, drawing on Peirce, see Misak 2000. For discussion of this line of thought, see Festenstein 2007.

V

To move from an argument for the democratic presuppositions of inquiry to an account of the value of democracy in Dewey's philosophy requires supplementing the argument for the epistemological advantages of democracy—that inquiry rests on certain democratic presuppositions—with an account of the conception of human growth of which the account of pragmatic intelligence is part.

Dewey strikingly defines a moral problem as one which raises a particular question for the selfhood of the agent. There are situations in which an agent confronts a conflict of ends 'so heterogeneous' that they appeal to 'different kinds of disposition' in her (Dewey 1908: 192; cf. Dewey 1932: 165). The question 'finally at stake in any genuinely moral situation' is: 'What shall the agent *be*? What sort of character shall he assume? On its face, the question is, what he shall *do*, shall he act for this or that end. But the incompatibility of the ends forces him back into the question of the kinds of selfhood, of agency, involved in the respective ends' (Dewey 1908: 194–5; 1932: 150). As he puts in the second edition of *Ethics*, 'below the surface' moral deliberation is 'a process of discovering what sort of being a person most wants to become'. Growth is the 'outcome and limit of right action, without being the end-in-*view*' (Dewey 1932: 287, 302). Rather, the claim is that '*the* end is growth itself', and that, if there is a supreme moral principle, it lies in 'the injunction to each self on every possible occasion to identify the self with a new growth that is possible' (Dewey 1932: 308). This injunction seems to epitomize the concern about emptiness, and lack of practical guidance, that critics identify. Like such formulations as consummatory experience or the coordination of interests and activities, this seems to express a merely formal conception of the end of moral inquiry, which needs filling in by more specific criteria, precisely because growth cannot be the end-in-view. Much of the two texts on ethics is devoted to considering how consequentialist, deontological, and virtue-based theories of morality offer different candidates for these criteria.

Yet Dewey does not leave it there, with either the thought that the content that should be given to the notion of growth is purely a matter of what some set of deliberating agents decide or that these agents can flesh out this skeletal notion by plumping for one or other from the three candidate moral theories. For, while as a deliberating agent I cannot simply enjoin myself to 'aim for growth', there are constraints on what can count as a course of action promoting or contributing to growth, in the same way as, in the theory of inquiry, while what counts as knowledge is open to varied contextual specification as the product of competent inquiry, the theory of inquiry itself gives some content to the latter idea. For, first, Dewey avers, growth requires the exercise of pragmatic intelligence, which will lead us to formulate and attach ourselves to new ends, and free us from arbitrariness, coercion, or inertia in our choice of ends (e.g., Dewey 1908: 320, 392; Dewey 1922: 138; and see Richardson 1999: 111). As the account of practical judgement suggested, deliberation opens up even what we may have thought of as fixed ends to scrutiny and appraisal, and involves the creative construction of new values. The exercise of practical intelligence or experimental inquiry is liberating, promoting the 'growth' of those who submit their ends to reflective consideration in this way (Dewey 1932: 302–8; Festenstein 1997: 66–72). As we saw in examining the account of valuation, while both the agent and her environment may have set structures, these do not fix ends about which she must deliberate. The liberating effect of the exercise of pragmatic intelligence in practical deliberation is brought out in this passage from the essay 'The Need for a Recovery of Philosophy', for example:

The pragmatic theory of intelligence means that the function of mind is to project new and more complex ends—to free experience from routine and from caprice. Not the use of thought to accomplish purposes already given either in the mechanism of the body or in that of the existent state of society, but the use of intelligence to liberate and liberalize action, is the pragmatic lesson. Action restricted to given and fixed ends may attain great technical efficiency; but efficiency is the only quality to which it can lay claim. Such action is mechanical (or becomes so), no matter what the scope of the pre-formed end, be it the Will of God or *Kultur*. But the doctrine that intelligence develops within the sphere of action for the sake of possibilities not yet given is the opposite of a doctrine of mechanical efficiency. Intelligence *as* intelligence is inherently forward-looking; only by ignoring its primary function does it become a mere means for an end already given. The latter *is* servile, even when the end is labeled moral, religious or esthetic. But action directed to ends to which the agent has not previously been attached carries with a quickened and enlarged spirit. A pragmatic intelligence is a creative intelligence, not a routine mechanic.   (Dewey 1917: 43)

Growth requires not only that we deliberate in the constructive and 'liberalizing' way set out in the account of practical judgement. Dewey takes the further step of viewing growth as requiring a certain kind of engagement with the needs and interests of others. My exercise of practical intelligence, if it is to be valuable in the sense of contributing to my growth, must be informed by a substantive consideration for the interests of others (Dewey 1927b: 127–8). Human beings are interdependent in multifarious ways, particularly in complex modern societies, and we cannot envisage individual growth outside any social context. Rather, individual 'growth involves becoming responsible, that is, responsive to the needs and claims of others' (Dewey 1932: 304). The core idea is that my own growth is hampered or warped if it takes place at the expense of yours: the '*kind* of self which is formed through action which is faithful to relations with others will be a fuller and broader self than one which is cultivated in isolation from or in opposition to the purposes and needs of others' (Dewey 1932: 299). This is a move with roots in various sorts of social and political philosophy: in idealism, Hegelian theories of recognition, and Rousseauian accounts of liberty and the general will. But is this not an arbitrary stipulation from the point of view of Dewey's pragmatism? It seems to be dogmatic—why should we assume that my growth may not conflict with yours (Festenstein 1997: 58–62)? Why should it be on egalitarian terms?

However, Dewey is not such a simpleton as to imagine that there is no point of view from which we can view my growth as at odds with yours: 'that a man may grow in efficiency as a burglar, as a gangster, or as a corrupt politician, cannot be doubted. But [...] the question is whether growth in this particular direction promotes or retards growth in general' (Dewey 1938a: 19). The point is that, from an ethical perspective, the 'growth' of the corrupt machine politician is a partial and distorted thing, since it sacrifices morally relevant needs and interests of others. It is possible to ignore or override this perspective, although, as we have seen, to do so is to hamper the capacity to identify and address social problems; but then that is what one is doing, stepping outside the space of ethics and the equal consideration of others.

Now this ethical perspective is for Dewey the democratic perspective. If we accept the claim about the mutual interdependence of paths of growth, the argument proceeds as follows. Inquiry as pragmatic intelligence is valued as a constitutive part of a life of growth, not merely as an instrumental means of achieving pre-given ends. Growth for individuals requires the right social and political conditions: my growth or flourishing is mutually interdependent with yours, and requires that you are able to exercise pragmatic intelligence in the making of collective decisions on the same footing as me.

Democracy, in this sense, is a generic 'tendency' of associations, grounded in the personalities of those who compose them, defined by reference to the normative picture of the growth of individual personality through participation in common or shared activities:

From the standpoint of the individual, it consists in having a responsible share according to capacity in forming and directing the activities of the groups to which one belongs and in participating according to need in the values which the groups sustain. From the standpoint of the groups, it demands liberation of the potentialities of members of a group in harmony with the interests and goods which are common.   (Dewey 1927b: 325–6)

Full liberation of an individual's potentialities can be achieved only in a democratic social order, one in which social conflicts are treated as the subject of social inquiry. Dewey's argument that the experimental character of democracy renders it desirable should not merely be interpreted instrumentally, then. He is not saying only that democracy allows a clearer view of social problems and how to address them. His suggestion is also that individuality can be properly expressed only if the individual participates in democratic practices, since social inquiry is a constitutive part of the individual good. The collective exercise of the experimental ethos is an ethical demand of this conception of growth. Exercised properly, this experimental ethos allows individuals to arrive at a common good.

Growth, then, is a matter of realizing developmental potential in a society in which others have the same possibilities of development. Modern societies foster socially useful habits of action and dispositions among their members, and the self-realization of members consists in the expression of these dispositions. In *The Public and Its Problems*, Dewey concedes that 'a member of a robber band may express his powers in a way consonant with belonging to that group and be directed by the interest common to its members'; that is, he can develop in some ways as a member of this gang. Yet the gangster can do so 'only at the cost of repression of those of his potentialities that can be realized only through membership in other groups. The robber band cannot interact flexibly with other groups; it can act only through isolating itself. It must prevent the operation of all interests save those which circumscribe its separateness'. By contrast, 'a good citizen' both enriches and is 'enriched by his participation in family life, industry, scientific and artistic associations. There is a free give-and-take; fullness of integrated personality is therefore possible of achievement, since the pulls and responses of different groups reenforce one another and their values accord' (Dewey 1927b: 327–8).

Severed from wider connections, the members of a robber band will struggle to develop the capacities for practical deliberation that allow for and foster growth ('fullness of integrated personality'), and will find it difficult to grasp the dimensions of their loss; so, for Dewey, we can see that the failure to pursue a form of growth that is responsive to the needs and claims of others is, at least in part, a failure of pragmatic intelligence. A further point to note about Dewey's robber band is the importance that he attaches to the *multiplicity* of forms of membership and association in modern society. Indeed, in this example he identifies the failure to cultivate a variety of forms of association not only as a block on the possibility of growth but with criminality. It is not that Dewey believes that the interests of different individuals and groups cannot conflict. On the contrary, 'there *are* conflicting interests; otherwise there would be no social problems'. The question is 'precisely *how* conflicting claims are to be settled in the interest of all', and 'the method of democracy—inasfar as it is that of organized intelligence—is to bring these conflicts out into the open where their special claims can be seen and appraised, where they can be discussed and judged in the light of more inclusive interests than are represented by either of them separately' (Dewey 1935: 56). If the fullness of integrated personality requires the free and harmonious interaction of different groups, then to block this (through pursuing a career as a robber or a corrupt politician) stifles this possibility—and not just for the delinquent, of course. Dewey's claim is that democracy as communication over the resolution of collective problems opens up this possibility, furnishing a necessary but not sufficient condition of growth, given the reality of social conflicts (Honneth 1998; Festenstein 2001). Just as, as the product of a competent procedure, inquiry is fallible and open to revision, so too is the upshot of a democratic procedure of decision making.

References

Abbreviations:

CP: *Collected Papers of Charles Sanders Peirce*, i–vi, ed. C. Hartshorne and P. Weiss (1931–5); vii and viii, ed. A. Burks (1958). Cambridge, MA: Belknap Press.

LW: *The Later Works of John Dewey, 1925–1953*, ed. Jo Ann Boydston, 17 vols. Carbondale, IL: Southern Illinois University Press, 1981–92.

MW: *The Middle Works of John Dewey, 1899–1924*, ed. Jo Ann Boydston, 15 vols. Carbondale, IL: Southern Illinois University Press, 1976–83.

Anderson, Elizabeth (2006). 'The Epistemology of Democracy'. *Episteme*, 3: 8–22.
Boisvert, Raymond (1988). *Dewey's Metaphysics*. New York: Fordham University Press.

Brodsky, Garry (1982). 'Rorty's Interpretation of Pragmatism'. *Transactions of the Charles S. Peirce Society*, 18: 311–38.

Burke, Thomas (1994). *Dewey's New Logic*. Chicago: University of Chicago Press.

Commager, Henry Steele (1950). *The American Mind*. New Haven: Yale University Press.

Coughlan, Neil (1975). *Young John Dewey*. Chicago: University of Chicago Press.

Dewey, John (1908). *Ethics* (with J. H. Tufts), 1st edn. In *MW* 5: *1908*.

—— (1910*a*). *How We Think*. In *MW* 6: *1910–11*.

—— (1910*b*). 'A Short Catechism Concerning Truth'. In *MW* 6: *1910–11*, 3–11.

—— (1915). 'The Logic of Judgments of Practice'. In *MW* 8: *1915*, 14–82.

—— (1917). 'The Need for a Recovery of Philosophy'. In *MW* 10: *1916–17*, 3–48.

—— (1922). *Human Nature and Conduct*. In *MW* 14: *1922*.

—— (1925*a*). *Experience and Nature*. In *LW* 1: *1925*.

—— (1925*b*). 'Value, Objective Reference and Criticism'. In *LW* 2: *1925–7,7* 8–97.

—— (1927*a*). 'The Pragmatic Acquiescence'. In *LW* 3: *1927–8*, 145–51.

—— (1927*b*). *The Public and Its Problems*. In *LW* 2: *1925–7*.

—— (1929). *Quest for Certainty*. In *LW* 4: *1929*.

—— (1931). 'Context and Thought'. In *LW* 6: *1931–2*, 3–21.

—— (1932). *Ethics* (with J. H. Tufts), 2nd edn. In *LW* 7: *1932*.

—— (1934). *Art as Experience*. In *LW* 10: *1934*.

—— (1935). *Liberalism and Social Action*. In *LW* 11: *1935–7*, 5–65.

—— (1938*a*). *Experience and Education*. In *LW* 13: *1938–9*, 1–62.

—— (1938*b*). *Logic: Theory of Inquiry*. In *LW* 12: *1938*.

—— (1939). *Theory of Valuation*. In *LW* 13: *1938–9*, 189–251.

—— (1946). 'Introduction to *Problems of Men*: Problems of Men and the Present State of Philosophy'. In *LW* 15: *1942–8*, 159–69.

Diggins, John P. (1994). *The Promise of Pragmatism: Modernism and the Crisis of Knowledge and Authority*. Chicago: University of Chicago Press.

Edel, Abraham (1985). 'A Missing Dimension in Rorty's Use of Pragmatism'. *Transactions of the Charles S. Peirce Society*, 21: 21–37.

—— and Flower, Elizabeth (1989). 'Introduction'. In *LW* 7: *1932*.

Elster, Jon (1983). *Sour Grapes: Studies in the Subversion of Rationality*. Cambridge: Cambridge University Press.

Fesmire, Steven (2003). *John Dewey and Moral Imagination: Pragmatism in Ethics*. Bloomington, IN: Indiana University Press.

Festenstein, Matthew (1995). 'Putnam, Pragmatism, and Democratic Theory'. *Review of Politics*, 57: 693–721.

—— (1997). *Pragmatism and Political Theory: From Dewey to Rorty*. Chicago: University of Chicago Press.

—— (2001). 'Inquiry as Critique: On the Legacy of Deweyan Pragmatism for Political Theory'. *Political Studies*, 49: 730–48.

Festenstein, Matthew (2003). 'Politics and Acquiescence in Rortyan Pragmatism'. *Theoria*. 101: 1–24.

Festenstein, Matthew (2007). 'Inquiry and Democracy in Contemporary Pragmatism'. In Patrick Baert and Bryan S. Turner (eds.), *Pragmatism and European Social Theory*, Cambridge: Bardwell Press, 115–36.

Godfrey-Smith, Peter (2002). 'Dewey on Naturalism, Realism and Science'. *Philosophy of Science*, 69 (suppl.): s25–s35.

Gouinlock, James (1990). 'What is the Legacy of Instrumentalism? Rorty's Interpretation of Dewey'. *Journal of the History of Philosophy*, 28: 251–69.

Hacking, Ian (1983). *Representing and Intervening*. Cambridge: Cambridge University Press.

Hildebrand, David L. (2003). *Beyond Realism and Anti-Realism: John Dewey and the Neo-Pragmatists*. Nashville: Vanderbilt University Press.

Honneth, Axel (1998). 'Democracy as Reflexive Cooperation: John Dewey and Democratic Theory Today'. *Political Theory*, 26: 763–83.

Korsgaard, Christine (1996). *The Sources of Normativity*. Cambridge: Cambridge University Press.

Lippmann, Walter (1965 [1922]). *Public Opinion*. New York: Free Press.

—— (1925). *The Phantom Public*. New York: Macmillan.

MacGilvray, Eric (2004). *Reconstructing Public Reason*. Cambridge, MA: Harvard University Press.

Misak, Cheryl (2000). *Truth, Morality and Politics: Pragmatism and Deliberation*. New York: Routledge.

Mumford, Lewis (1968 [1926]). *The Golden Day: A Study in American Experience and Culture*. New York: Dover.

Peirce, Charles Sanders (1931–58). *Collected Papers of Charles Sanders Peirce*, i–vi, ed. C. Hartshorne and P. Weiss (1931–5); vii and viii, ed. A. Burks (1958). Cambridge, MA: Belknap Press.

Putnam, Hilary (1992). *Renewing Philosophy*. Cambridge, MA: Harvard University Press.

—— (1994). *Words and Life*, ed. James Conant. Cambridge, MA: Harvard University Press.

Richardson, Henry (1999). 'Truth and Ends in Dewey's Pragmatism'. In C. Misak (ed.), *Pragmatism*, Alberta: University of Calgary Press, 109–47.

Rorty, Richard (1982). *Consequences of Pragmatism*. Minneapolis: University of Minnesota Press.

—— (1991). *Philosophical Papers*, i: *Objectivity, Relativism, and Truth*. Cambridge: Cambridge University Press.

—— (1994). 'Dewey Between Hegel and Darwin'. In Dorothy Ross (ed.), *Modernist Impulses in the Human Sciences*, Baltimore: Johns Hopkins University Press, 54–68.

Russell, Bertrand (1966 [1910]). *Philosophical Essays*. London: Allen & Unwin.

Ryan, Alan (1995). *John Dewey and the High Tide of American Liberalism*. New York: W. W. Norton.

—— (2001). 'Staunchly Modern, Non-Bourgeois Liberalism'. In Avital Simhony and Daniel Weinstein (eds.), *The New Liberalism: Reconciling Liberty and Community*, Cambridge: Cambridge University Press, 184–204.

Schinz, Albert (1910). *Anti-Pragmatism*. London: T. Fisher Unwin.

Sleeper, Ralph W. (1986). *The Necessity of Pragmatism: John Dewey's Conception of Philosophy*. New Haven: Yale University Press.

Stuhr, John J. (1992). 'Dewey's Reconstruction of Metaphysics'. *Transactions of the Charles S. Peirce Society*, 28: 161–76.

Tiles, J. E. (1988). *Dewey*. London: Routledge.

Welchman, Jennifer (1995). *Dewey's Ethical Theory*. Ithaca, NY: Cornell University Press.

Westbrook, Robert (1990). 'Lewis Mumford, John Dewey and the "Pragmatic Acquiescence"'. In Agatha and Thomas Hughes (eds.), *Lewis Mumford: Public Intellectual*, New York: Oxford University Press, 301–22.

——— (1991). *John Dewey and American Democracy*. Ithaca, NY: Cornell University Press.

——— (2005). *Democratic Hope: Pragmatism and the Politics of Truth*. Ithaca, NY: Cornell University Press.

White, Morton (1957). *Social Thought in America: The Revolt Against Formalism*, rev. edn. Boston: Beacon Press.

——— (1964). *The Origins of Dewey's Instrumentalism*. New York: Octagon Press.

CHAPTER 6

JOSIAH ROYCE: IDEALISM, TRANSCENDENTALISM, PRAGMATISM

KELLY A. PARKER

JOSIAH ROYCE was heavily influenced by post-Kantian German idealists, as were many young American scholars in the late nineteenth century. He was never a mere disciple of this movement, however. His 1878 doctoral dissertation on Kant is in fact surprisingly critical; his response to problems in Kant combines an idealist metaphysics with an explicitly pragmatic epistemology. Royce soon abandoned this early pragmatist line of thought, though, and he maintained a version of Absolute Idealism through the first three decades of his career (Clendenning 1999: 69–70). During this time he was consistently critical of the "instrumentalist" pragmatism promoted by John Dewey and William James.

In 1908, however, Royce described his own position as "Absolute Pragmatism". Pragmatist themes began to appear in his work on ethics and community, most prominently with *The Philosophy of Loyalty* (1908). In *The Problem of Christianity* (1913) he credited Charles S. Peirce's work with enabling him to introduce the infinite community as final guarantor of truth in his system, the place held earlier by the absolute mind. By 1912 Royce had apparently come to regard his position as a variety of Peircean pragmatism, which agreed with Peirce's views in all significant respects, but which extended Peirce's ideas into areas of inquiry (including ethics, social philosophy, and philosophy of religion) that Peirce did not himself develop.

In many respects Royce's late writings obviously extend and develop Peirce's ideas. Royce indeed deserves his reputation as Peirce's first great interpreter; but at the same time, Royce devoted himself to answering questions that Peirce himself scarcely addressed. A central question for current scholars is whether Royce in fact ended his career as a Peircean pragmatist, as he himself seemed to suggest, or whether he transformed and even rejected certain Peircean principles in trying to reconcile pragmatism with his own commitment to idealism and a real transcendental guarantor of truth.

The aim of this essay is to clarify Royce's later "Peircean" pragmatist philosophy. The method of investigation is to lay out a two-pronged comparison. The first compares Royce and Peirce regarding a key concept—the Absolute, in its various manifestations—so as to let their differences and disagreements emerge. The second is to explore some of what Royce and Peirce each had to say about the other's ideas of this key concept, and about their own ideas in comparison with the other. We are quite fortunate in this respect: these are two thinkers who over a period of many years actually communicated with one another, directly and indirectly, personally and publicly, about precisely the issues that concern us.

Part I presents Royce's early notion of the absolute knower, which is supported by his innovative argument from error. Part II presents Royce's later Absolute Pragmatism and Absolute Voluntarism, indicating how Royce extended but retained the argument from error in developing these positions. Part III surveys the later Royce's self-presentation as a Peircean philosopher, and also proposes a speculative account of how he might have identified his own Absolute Pragmatism as a natural extension of Peircean pragmatism. Part IV presents some of Peirce's key statements regarding the Absolute, conceived as a standard of truth and as a metaphysical ultimate. Part V identifies three specific yet significant principles in Royce's late philosophy that Peirce himself would not have endorsed. That these three differences exist indicates that scholars should regard Royce's late work as innovative and not simply as an adoption and extension of Peirce's ideas on logic, inquiry, and metaphysics.

I. Early Royce on Absolute Idealism and Absolute Truth

Royce announced the beginning of his professional career with a novel defense of Absolute Idealism, "the argument from error". Kant had introduced the notion of a "transcendental argument" by asking what the world must be like in order for knowledge of the world to be possible. In *The Religious Aspect of Philosophy* (1885) Royce took the experience of error—a particularly compelling aspect of the phenomenon of knowing—as the starting point for his own transcendental argument. According to Royce's theory of knowledge, an idea (or judgment) is true if it correctly represents its object; error obtains when an idea does not correctly represent its object. It is indisputable that finite minds do sometimes entertain erroneous ideas. Royce pointed out that in such a case the mind must contain an (erroneous) idea and its (false) object, while simultaneously intending, or "pointing toward", the idea's true object. If the mind is able to intend the true object, then that object is somehow available to the mind. How can it be that the true object is in this way available to the mind, but not known? If I think that my keys are on the hall table, but discover that my idea is erroneous, I do not conclude that my keys never existed as the object of my thought. Rather, I focus on an idea that I had all along—that my keys do definitely exist somewhere. They are the true object of an idea, an object which is at the moment available to me only imperfectly. The fact that error does occur indicated to Royce that the true object of any idea must exist, in a fully determinate or absolute state, in some actual mind with which my own mind is or may be connected. From the possibility of error, Royce thus concluded that there is an absolute knower, a mind for which all thoughts correspond correctly and adequately to their true objects: "*Either there is no such thing as error, which statement is a flat self-contradiction, or else there is an infinite unity of conscious thought to which is present all possible truth*" (Royce 2005: 346; emphasis original). Royce explicates the qualities of this infinite unity of thought as follows:

let us overcome all our difficulties by declaring that all the many Beyonds [all moments of time], which single significant judgments seem vaguely and separately to postulate, are present as fully realized intended objects to the unity of an all-inclusive, absolutely clear, universal, and conscious thought, of which all judgments, true or false, are but fragments, the whole being at once Absolute Truth and Absolute Knowledge. Then all our puzzles will disappear at a stroke, and error will be possible, because any one finite thought, viewed in relation to its own intent, may or may not be seen by this higher thought as successful and adequate in this intent.   (Royce 2005: 345–6)

A very late source, from 1915, indicates that Royce held to the implications of this early view for the theory of truth. In his Harvard seminar he said, "If truth belongs to a proposition at all, it belongs to it absolutely and simply. By *absolute truth* you mean exactly the same thing as you mean by *truth*" (Royce 1998: 47). While he recognized that our knowledge is often uncertain, he maintained that the truth status of a proposition is never mutable, never a matter of degree: "the fact that we can get only probability [of knowledge] at any time is not at all inconsistent with the view that the truth in terms of which we can define our probabilities is an absolute relationship" (Royce 1998: 48).

II. THE MIDDLE ROYCE: ABSOLUTE PRAGMATISM/ABSOLUTE VOLUNTARISM

Royce expanded the category of "self-reinstating beliefs" beyond the unity of truth implied in the argument from error. He also explicitly adopted aspects of pragmatism, most notably the notion (explored at length in *The World and the Individual*, First Series) that the meaning of an idea is defined by the possible experiences to which it may lead. Royce returned consistently to the fact that some beliefs are validated analytically, in the sense that they cannot be successfully and consistently denied. To deny these beliefs involves one in a pragmatic or performative contradiction: these beliefs exhibit the trait of pragmatic self-reinstatement. Royce founded his philosophy on the strength of these peculiarly insistent beliefs. He named this form of idealism "Absolute Pragmatism" and "Absolute Voluntarism" (which is an assertion of monism, likely offered against Jamesian pluralism).

Royce identified a number of such self-reinstating beliefs: there is a reality; there is a definite actual truth to any proposition; there are universal logical principles. In each case, to deny the belief is to deny it categorically, and hence to contradict oneself pragmatically. If one asserts "There is no reality", one has just made a claim about the reality whose existence was denied. Likewise, the categorical assertion "There are no universal logical principles", if it were true, would be a very important universal logical principle.

In similar fashion, Royce concluded that there is one right attitude of the will toward the world (and hence one correct metaphysical view, of which this attitude is the expression): namely, loyalty. Loyalty is in the end loyalty to loyalty, truth, and reality itself—the cause of all causes. In 1908 Royce wrote:

> whoever talks of any sort of truth whatever, be that moral or scientific, the truth of common sense or the truth of a philosophy, inevitably implies, in all his assertions about truth, that the world of truth about which he speaks is a world possessing a rational and spiritual unity, is a conscious world of experience, whose type of consciousness is higher in its level than is the type of our human minds, but whose life is such that our life belongs as part to this living whole. This world of truth is the one that you must define, so I insist, if you are to regard any proposition whatever as true, and are then to tell, in a reasonable way, what you mean by the truth of that proposition.   (Royce 1995: 156)

That same year he insisted on the point as a way to preserve truth in the face of pragmatist critiques. In an address entitled "The Problem of Truth in the Light of Recent Discussion" Royce asserted that the absolute truths of pure logic "are truths such that to deny them is simply to reassert them under a new form" (Royce 1951: 91–2). It appears that Royce maintained this argument, also, to the end of his career: it is formally the same as his explanation of Aristotle's argument for the principle of contradiction, which he praised in his 1915–16 Metaphysics lectures.

Having established this point, Royce employed it to reconcile two apparently disparate philosophical views: instrumentalism and voluntarism. First, "In dealing . . . with the concrete objects of experience, we are what the instrumentalists suppose us to be, namely, seekers for successful control over this experience." Second, "and as the voluntarists also correctly emphasize, in all our empirical constructions, scientific and practical, we express our own individual wills and seek such success as we can get". Royce's resolution of these two views is the observation that "there remains the fact that in all these constructions we are expressing a will which, as logic and pure mathematics teach us, has an universal absolute nature,—the same in all of us" (Royce 1951: 95). Following this reconciliation of extant theories, Royce offered the following philosophical prayer to the universal absolute nature, on behalf of his still-vexed colleagues:

Make our deeds logical. Give our thoughts sense and unity. Give our Instrumentalism some serious unity of eternal purpose. Make our Pragmatism more than the mere passing froth of waves that break upon the beach of triviality. In any case, the poet's cry [referencing a quote from Tennyson] is an expression of that Absolute Pragmatism, of that Voluntarism, which recognizes all truth as the essentially eternal creation of the Will.   (Royce 1951: 96)

In *The Problem of Christianity* Royce looked back on his earlier argument from error and reaffirmed it as undergirding his most recent views of truth. Royce named this view of truth "Absolute Pragmatism" and observed that it had "never been pleasing either to rationalists or to empiricists, either to pragmatists or to the ruling type of absolutists" (Royce 2001*b*: 279). Philosophy is more than a theory of truth, of course. Royce insisted that a theory of truth has implications for one's attitude and actions. He followed James in holding that "a philosophy is, in its essence, a resolution to treat the real world as if that world possessed certain characters, and as if our experience enabled us to verify these characters". Royce's "Absolute Voluntarism" goes beyond such mere pragmatism, though, because it points to "one, and but one, general and decisive attitude of the will which is the right attitude, when we stand in the presence of the universe, and when we undertake to choose how we propose to bear ourselves toward the world" (Royce 2001*b*: 349). This attitude is in turn the attitude of loyalty, a positive devotion of the self to a cause. It expresses the metaphysics of interpretation, of the pursuit of truth as a member of an interpreting community. These connections among the individual will, the community, truth, and the constitution of reality define Royce's distinctive philosophical vision.

In *The Problem of Christianity* Royce offered a fascinating variation on his familiar transcendental arguments for a final knower and a final object of knowledge. Under Peirce's influence he recast that knower as an infinite community, and linked his theory of knowledge directly to his metaphysics by identifying that community directly with reality, the final object of knowledge:

Practically I cannot be saved alone; theoretically speaking, I cannot find or even define the truth in terms of my individual experience, without taking account of my relation to the community of those who know. This community, then, is real whatever is real. And in that community my life is interpreted.   (Royce 2001*b*: 357)

Note the novel twist on Descartes's *cogito* here: given Being as a process of interpretation, one cannot successfully doubt the existence of the community of minds and, ultimately, the unity of all minds in a final individual. This renders Royce's Absolute Pragmatism a form of rationalism—a position that Peirce would likely have criticized, just as he had criticized the argument from error in his review of *The World and the Individual*.

Royce reaffirmed his notion of Absolute Pragmatism in the 1914 article "Principles of Logic". Here he linked the objective validity of the laws of logic to the inevitable will to be rational, another statement of his Absolute Voluntarism. The absoluteness of logical principles lies in the fact that "the logical principles define precisely the nature of the 'Will to act in an orderly fashion' or in other words of the 'Will to be Rational'" (Royce 1951: 354). In the same work, he addressed the question of "self-evident" truths. Perhaps influenced by Peirce's critique of direct intuitions, he suggested that elemental concepts of logic are not "self-evident" facts, but rather are yet another instance of self-reinstating truths: "That there are individuals, is too complex to be self-evident, although, upon the other hand, a study of the conception of an individual led us to the assertion, not very fully discussed in this sketch, that this postulate is indeed *at once pragmatic and absolute*" (Royce 1951: 369). In a passage that reveals the basis for Royce's view that the elements of logic are not merely self-evident, Royce discussed Aristotle's "immediate certainties" in his 1915–16 Metaphysics course. Aristotle, Royce explained, presented the principle of contradiction as an immediate certainty. Royce then suggested that this is not actually an immediate intuition, but rather a self-reinstating proposition: "Aristotle himself gives a *reason* for believing it, a very pretty reason"—namely, that to attempt to deny this principle is to affirm it pragmatically (Royce 1998: 46).

A reading of the published record of Royce's 1915–16 Metaphysics course indicates that, for all his Peircean insights about the community and the process of interpretation, and for all his extensions of the argument since he had first discovered it in January 1883, Royce was still attached to his familiar argument from error. He continues to present it, in its original form, until the end of his career.[1]

---

[1] Royce discussed this argument in detail in his lectures during the Fall term of 1915. The second of six questions that Royce posed on the midyear exam for the course asked students to summarize the argument from error; the third question asked them to evaluate and respond to it (Royce 1998: 279). The argument from error was again presented to this class on 11 Jan. 1916, when Royce read it from his original notes, which, he remarked, had been written exactly 33 years previously (Royce 1998: 83).

III. The Later Royce as a Peircean Pragmatist

Royce described his 1912 rediscovery of Peirce's logic and theory of knowledge in Part II of *The Problem of Christianity*, listing the specific works that he had found most significant (Royce 2001b: 275–6). In another, later account of the 1912 Peircean insight, Royce indicated that he saw a considerable affinity between his own prior work and Peirce's:

I often had heard Peirce state, in his own attractive but baffling way, this theory of knowledge. I had supposed it to be fairly well known to me. Yet I had never understood its real force, until I thus saw it in the light of this new review. Then indeed, I observed its close connection with what I had been seeking to formulate in my philosophy of loyalty. I saw also how many aspects of philosophical idealism, when this Peircean theory of knowledge was brought to bear upon them, got a new concreteness, a new significance and a new relation to the methods and to the presuppositions of inductive science. (Royce 2001a: 3–4)

Perhaps Royce's most important specific insight was that Peirce's detailed conception of the ideal community of scientific inquiry provides an excellent model for thinking about other sorts of community. From this basis Royce was able to develop an account of the nature of non-scientific communities of loyal persons:

whatever the methods which are characteristic of the natural sciences, they depend upon and express a very clear and conscious recognition on the part of the scientific inquirer ... that the truth which he seeks when he deals with nature is truth that belongs to the community. And thus the methods of inductive science and the practical attitude of the loyalist have an intimate and close connection. (Royce 2001a: 24)

Such genuine communities may include civil societies, business enterprises, and religious communities whose members are animated by a common purpose and spirit of interpretation.

Royce saw in Peirce's notion of infinite inquiry and his account of the process of interpretation a much-needed balance to the more familiar pragmatism of James:

James, so far as I understand his philosophy, never formed any definite idea of the community, either ethical, or social, or spiritual. [Peirce, on the other hand,] was in ideal, and very sincerely, and in his fragmentary writings, very effectively a loyalist.

The world of the spirit had from the point of view of his philosophy a very genuine unity about it.   (Royce 2001a: 37)

A bit further along in these same lectures, Royce touchingly described Peirce's response to Royce's gift of a copy of *The Problem of Christianity*. Peirce had received the book in the last stages of the illness that ended his life.

He wrote me a very kind letter of acknowledgment which I deeply prize, and which showed that my so belated effort to understand and to expound the side of his opinions which was in question in this book, had received, despite his feebleness and his age, a reasonable and an unexpectedly careful, although necessarily a very summary attention, and that my interpretation of him gained on the whole his approval.   (Royce 2001a: 4)

One must be careful not to read too much into this statement of Royce's, which was certainly given in genuine tribute to Peirce and served to introduce Peirce's name to a distant audience. There is no doubting the deep respect and love that Royce had for his longtime friend. Taking all that into consideration, though, we cannot ignore a distinctive rhetorical purpose that is accomplished by Royce's account of this last communication from Peirce. Royce is concerned that his audience *know* that the neglected maestro of pragmatism had approved Royce's use of his ideas. This description suggests that Royce regarded himself not just as a thinker who used some of Peirce's ideas, but as his loyal and accurate interpreter. This self-description threatens to oversimplify our understanding of the actual relations between these two thinkers' works.

One of the essays that Royce identified as key to his 1911–12 insight was "Some Consequences of Four Incapacities", Peirce's classic frontal assault on rationalism and one of his most cogent early statements of the social-semiotic theory of knowledge. As a way to refine what is involved in Royce's hinted claim to be a loyal and accurate interpreter of Peirce's philosophy, let us construct a Roycean addendum to Peirce's essay. This addendum would extend Peirce's core position by introducing two new items to the four incapacities that Peirce lists (*W* 2. 213). These two items are both self-reinstating or "pragmatically absolute" truths.

Fifth Incapacity: We cannot deny that unity and finality are entailed in any coherent conception of Reality.

Sixth Incapacity: We cannot deny that absolute atemporal immutability and determinacy are entailed in any coherent conception of Truth.

These two speculative Roycean pragmatic "incapacities" will be convenient for reference when we turn briefly to Peirce's views on truth and Reality, in the next section.

As a final piece of evidence that the late Royce sought closer reconciliation between his views and those of other pragmatists, consider his embrace of pluralism. Surviving notes from the 1915–16 seminar record his insistence that "There isn't the least tendency about idealism to make light of the diversities, the conflicts, or the particular unreasonableness of the world. But on the whole, to be is to signify, to express a meaning." He then suggested that he himself had maintained pluralism since at least 1899: "That is the general proposition that in my seventh lecture of *The World and the Individual* I have expressed in the form of the assertion that the real world in its wholeness, its finality, is the complete expression of the meaning of every significant finite idea, so far as that idea has significance. This world is of course monistic and also pluralistic" (Royce 1998: 270). Note Royce's emphasis here on the *finality* and *wholeness* of the real world, the point established in my proposed "Fifth Incapacity", above. Recall Royce's comment regarding Peirce that "The world of the spirit had from the point of view of his philosophy a very genuine unity about it" (Royce 2001a: 37). The second passage also offers a baffling conjunction of *monism* and *pluralism*, which is recorded without further explanation. Frank Oppenheim, editor of the *Metaphysics*, marks this as "A crucial sentence". The statement may indeed be crucial, insofar as it signals Royce's desire to concede ground to those who argue for a pluralistic universe. Royce clearly saw the need to admit pluralism, but apparently could not, or would not, embrace a Peircean universe shot through with objective indeterminacy and the deep fallibilism that Peirce's version of realism entails.

IV. Peirce on Reality and Absolute Truth

We turn now to a brief explication of Peirce's views on Reality and absolute truth, so as to compare these to the later Royce's adaptation and extension of his ideas. We first consider one of the most familiar passages from "Some Consequences of Four Incapacities":

The real, then, is that which, sooner or later, information and reasoning would finally result in, and which is therefore independent of the vagaries of me and you. Thus, the very origin of the conception of reality shows that this conception essentially involves the notion of a COMMUNITY, without definite limits, and capable of an indefinite increase of knowledge.   (*W* 2. 239)

Peirce here endorses two points that Royce accepted. First, there is a reality independent of individuals' ideas about it—a point that Royce had insisted upon since 1883. Second, and more important for understanding Royce's later thought, this passage contains Peirce's claim that this conception of reality entails the supposition of an infinite community which serves as the knowing subject. This passage may well have led Royce to reject his earlier notion of the absolute knower: Peirce had urged Royce to take precisely this turn of thought in his review of Royce's *The World and the Individual*, First Series, in 1900.

Peirce's own notion of the status of the "final opinion" is notoriously complex. Though there is no evidence that Royce ever read it, the following passage provides the account that seems closest to Royce's own notion of the final opinion as Absolute. We will accordingly use this description of the relation between Truth and Reality at the end of infinite inquiry for our comparison of Peirce and Royce:

The purpose of every sign is to express "fact," and by being joined with other signs, to approach as nearly as possible to determining an interpretant which would be the *perfect Truth*, the absolute Truth, and as such (at least, we may use this language) would be the very Universe. Aristotle gropes for a conception of perfection, or *entelechy*, which he never succeeds in making clear. We may adopt the word to mean the very fact, that is, the ideal sign which should be quite perfect, and so identical,—in such identity as a sign may have,—with the very matter denoted united with the very form signified by it. The entelechy of the Universe of being, then, the universe *quâ* fact, will be that Universe in its aspect as a sign, the 'Truth' of being. The 'Truth,' the fact that is not abstracted but complete, is the ultimate interpretant of every sign.   (Peirce 1976: iv. 239–40)

This "entelechy" obviously bears a close connection to Royce's own social theory of metaphysics, where the real world consists in the ultimately unified individual that is the universal community of interpretation.

For all their similarity, however, there is one significant difference between Peirce and Royce concerning the final representation, the community that serves both as knower of "absolute truth" and as the real object of that truth. Royce consistently maintains that this entity is in some sense actual, not merely possible, and not merely (as Peirce sometimes puts it) "fated" to be actual. Consider what Peirce said when he finally came to address the question of whether Reality, understood as described in "Some Consequences" and as the object of the absolute truth in the passage just cited, is actual (or in keeping with Peirce's accustomed terminology, "existent"): "Perhaps there isn't any such thing at all. As I have repeatedly insisted, it is but a retroduction, a working hypothesis which we try, our one desperate forlorn hope of knowing anything" (Peirce 1976: iv. 343).

There is apparently, in Peirce's view, nothing self-contradictory or absurd about supposing there *not* to be an ultimate interpretant that is Reality, or an absolute truth. We indeed must act as if there is, or is fated to be, just such an entity *if we are to function as rational beings with a conception of truth and error*. This is precisely Royce's familiar point. But Peirce does not follow Royce to the conclusion that this final opinion is in any sense metaphysically actual. In "Grounds of Validity of the Laws of Logic: Further Consequences of Four Incapacities", Peirce explicitly denies this conclusion: "this very assumption [that Reality as the object of absolute truth is actual] involves itself a transcendent and supreme interest, and therefore from its very nature is unsusceptible of any support from reasons" (W 2. 271–2). Peirce admits a contingency, a possibility of radical error—in short, a degree of fallibilism—that Royce never accepted, and which he perhaps never quite recognized.

V. Three Significant Points of Difference: Transcendental Argument, Absolute Idealism, Pragmatic Contingency

Based on the comparison of their accounts of the Absolute and the nature of Truth, it appears that Peirce asserts at least three key principles that go against Royce's interpretation and extension of his thought.

First, Peirce held that transcendental arguments, such as the argument from error and its variants, are suspect in metaphysical questions. In fact, Peirce directly criticized Royce's reliance on transcendental argument to establish the notion of the absolute object of knowledge:

where another thinker might speak of a hope, as we have done above, Prof. Royce would substitute a *reductio ad absurdum* of the contrary opinion—a diminution of man's natural sublime attitude to a sorry 'A is A.' Fortunately the logic of those arguments is never impeccable, so that the hopes retain their matter and are not reduced to mere formulae.   (*CP* 8. 105)

In a draft of the same review Peirce identified this fondness for transcendental argument as "Prof. Royce's greatest fault as a philosophical thinker", and continued with the remark that

Such refutations in metaphysics are most frequently downright fallacies due to the loose habits of thinking prevalent in the theological seminaries. ... In the rare instances in which such refutations are really decisive, what happens is, that the refuter, without himself remarking it, slips into his reasoning some experiential fact.   (*CP* 8. 110)

Royce maintained the validity of such transcendental arguments to the end of his career, as ensuring a rational foundation for certainty: "Such, I say, is the principle, at once theoretical and practical, upon which my philosophy must depend. This principle does not itself depend upon the momentary success of any individual idea" (Royce 2001*b* [1913]: 357).

Second, Peirce would not have accepted the Roycean position expressed in my "Fifth Incapacity", that *we cannot deny that unity and finality are entailed in any coherent conception of Truth*. Peirce is more cautious: that we cannot deny this unity and finality, in the sense that we cannot help but believe they obtain, does not guarantee that they do obtain. That things can differ from even our best-established beliefs about them is the principle of Realism upon which Peirce insisted. In the passage quoted previously, Peirce accordingly indicated that he would have spoken of "hope" rather than relying on the apparent power of Royce's rationalist proof that the infinite knower is actual. Peirce emphasized this point elsewhere, when he described Reality as a hypothesis, the result of a compelling abduction based on experience, our "one desperate forlorn hope of knowing anything". In his review of the second volume of *The World and the Individual*, Peirce was even more direct: "Prof. Royce's theory even if it were proved would not afford the slightest rational assurance that there is any thing such as a reality" (*CP* 8. 120).

Third, Royce accepted reality—the object of a perfect representation—as an actuality that enforces the standard of truth on our beliefs. He maintained, as summarized in my "Sixth Incapacity", that *we cannot deny that absolute atemporal immutability and determinacy are entailed in any coherent conception of Truth*. Peirce maintained, however, that during the time process—prior to attaining the hypothetical final representation—there are cases where truth-value is objectively indeterminate. This apparently runs counter to Royce's insistence that truth, where it obtains at all, is "absolute". Peirce insisted on objective indeterminacy in the experienced world, and even developed a three-valued formal logic to accommodate it. Interestingly, Royce hinted at a similar insight at least once, when he suggested the use of "probable" as a predicate in cases where a proposition can be objectively classified as neither "true" nor "false" (Royce 2001a: 32). We cannot of course know whether this insight would have led him to revise his commitment to the unity and finality of the Absolute, had he lived to pursue it.

Disregarding such speculations, we conclude with a few summary observations. Royce stands out among the classical pragmatists as a committed idealist and defender of an unambiguous standard of truth. At the same time, he was fully sensitive to the dynamic and contingent nature of human experience, and to the central importance of communities (whether scientific, civic, or religious) in our individual efforts to make sense of the world. Royce's vision of lives conducted in active loyalty to the highest logical, moral, and religious ideals, so influential during his own lifetime, has certainly fallen out of philosophical fashion during the era of technical analysis and postmodern discourse. His arguments merit serious reconsideration now, however, as we begin to explore the limits and the implications of those more recent modes of thought.

REFERENCES

Clendenning, John (1999). *The Life and Thought of Josiah Royce*, rev. and expanded edn. Nashville: Vanderbilt University Press.

Peirce, Charles S. (1931–58). *Collected Papers of Charles Sanders Peirce*, i–vi, ed. C. Hartshorne and P. Weiss (1931–5); vii and viii, ed. A. Burks (1958). Cambridge, MA: Belknap Press. References to this edition are indicated by *CP* followed by volume and paragraph number.

_____ (1976). *The New Elements of Mathematics*, ed. C. Eisele, 4 vols. The Hague: Mouton Publishers.

_____ (1982–). *Writings of Charles S. Peirce: A Chronological Edition*, ed. E. Moore, C. J. W. Kloesel, *et al.*, 5 vols. to date. Bloomington, IN: Indiana University Press. References to this edition are indicated by *W* followed by volume and page number.

Royce, Josiah (1951). *Royce's Logical Essays: Collected Logical Essays of Josiah Royce*, ed. D. S. Robinson. Dubuque, IA: W. C. Brown Co.

_____ (1965). *The Religious Aspect of Philosophy*. Gloucester, MA: Peter Smith. (References are to selections of this work in Royce 2005.)

_____ (1976). *The World and the Individual*, 2 vols. Gloucester, MA: Peter Smith.

Royce, Josiah (1995). *The Philosophy of Loyalty*. Nashville: Vanderbilt University Press.

_____ (1998). *Metaphysics/Josiah Royce: His Philosophy 9 Course of 1915–1916*, ed. W. E. Hocking, R. Hocking, and F. Oppenheim. Albany, NY: State University of New York Press.

_____ (2001a). *Josiah Royce's Late Writings: A Collection of Unpublished and Scattered Works*, ed. F. Oppenheim, 2 vols. Bristol: Thoemmes Press.

_____ (2001b). *The Problem of Christianity*. Washington: Catholic University of America Press.

_____ (2005). *The Basic Writings of Josiah Royce*, ed. J. J. McDermott, 2 vols. New York: Fordham University Press.

CHAPTER 7

GEORGE SANTAYANA: ORDINARY REFLECTION SYSTEMATIZED

GLENN TILLER

1. LIFE AND REPUTATION

MATERIALIST, atheist, cosmopolitan interpreter of moral and spiritual life, George Santayana (1863–1952) is one of the more enigmatic figures in American philosophy. Once internationally famous, he is today known primarily as the author of a handful of pithy quotations.[1] In addition to writing philosophy, Santayana expressed himself in a variety of forms: autobiography, essays,

---

[1] At the Auschwitz memorial and museum there is a plaque with the following quote attributed to Santayana: 'The one who does not remember history is bound to live through it again.' This is a variation, one of many, on Santayana's original statement: 'Those who cannot remember the past are condemned to repeat it' (*LR1* 284).

poetry, cultural criticism, and a novel.[2] But these literary pursuits, along with his rich, often aphoristic prose style, have produced the common impression that he is best classified as a writer and critic rather than as a philosopher in his own right.[3] Those who have not seriously tested the waters of his philosophical writing often concur; they summarily conclude that his prose is polished, but he is not a serious philosopher. This is a mistake. The driving force behind Santayana's varied writings is a grand system of philosophy based on his ontological categories of essence, matter, truth, and spirit. It is a system that he articulated with increasing clarity through a long life of writing.

Apart from his literary style, why has Santayana remained misunderstood and largely neglected? One explanation is that the American intelligentsia of his time took umbrage at a foreigner who abandoned their country but continued to write pointed commentaries on American culture and derisive critiques of America's leading philosophers.

No doubt there is something to this explanation. Santayana felt little attachment to life in America and the philosophical movements of his day, and this often showed. His origins had much to do with his outsider status. Born in Madrid in 1863 to Spanish parents, he emigrated at the age of 9 to the United States. Although he was to reside in Boston for forty years, he eagerly returned to Europe for extended stays (he crossed the Atlantic almost forty times), and he never gave up his Spanish citizenship. In 1912 he moved to Europe, never to return to America. The commentaries and critiques arriving from Europe were not always warmly welcomed. His critical review of *Experience and Nature* notoriously enraged John Dewey; and his intellectual portrait of Josiah Royce was severe. One angry reviewer was led to ask, 'Who is this dainty, unassimilated man to tell us how to live?'[4]

Another reason for Santayana's neglect is that by retiring early from Harvard and rejecting subsequent offers from other universities, such as Columbia and Oxford, he removed himself from the main philosophical centers of influence

---

[2] Santayana's novel, *The Last Puritan* (1936), was a bestseller. It was translated into several languages and placed him on the cover of *Time* magazine, 3 Feb. 1936.

[3] For example, Santayana is almost never mentioned in contemporary discussions of skepticism and ontology, areas where he made significant contributions. In recent years public perception has slowly started to change, but the notion that he is something less than a full-fledged philosopher has a long history. Donald C. Williams (1954: 31), in a generally appreciative article, put the blame on Santayana. 'George Santayana was a master of solemn showmanship which is to blame for his being taken for a more trivial and alien philosopher than he was, both by those who like the trivial and alien and by those who do not.'

[4] Shorey 1927, quoted in McCormick 1987: 269. For Santayana's review of John Dewey's *Experience and Nature*, see Santayana 1925. For his portrait of Josiah Royce, see Santayana 1920.

and the new generations of graduate students. Had he remained in the USA one can easily imagine that his reputation might have been rather different, for from an early age the life of a Harvard professor was set before him. In 1883, at the age of 19, he entered Harvard. There, under the supervision of Josiah Royce and William James, he completed his Ph.D. in 1889. That same year Harvard offered him an instructorship. In the years that followed, he earned the respect of his former mentors, fascinated his students, and rose, albeit slowly, to the rank of full professor. It was during this time that he published his most influential work, though not his best or his most philosophical—the five-volume *Life of Reason*.[5] From all appearances, he was poised to be a lasting and influential part of the Harvard scene.

However, it was not to be. Santayana was repelled by the business of academia, and he quietly planned his departure from Harvard virtually from the moment he was hired. At the age of 48, when he felt that he had sufficient financial resources, he retired from teaching. For the next forty years he devoted himself to composing his mature system. It was an extremely productive period, during which he produced his greatest works, the epistemological masterpiece *Scepticism and Animal Faith* (1923) and his magnum opus *Realms of Being* (1927–40). But this work was done in isolation in hotels and apartments in England, France, Spain, and Italy—far from the halls of academia. Although his work was discussed in the professional journals, he had no opportunity to expound his views to students, and he acquired no notable disciples.

The above explanations are plausible, but they only go so far. After all, Charles Peirce lived on the margins of society and employment, but he has become a central figure in American philosophy. One might then suppose that Santayana remains in the shadows since no famous contemporary has shone a spotlight on him, as Richard Rorty did for Dewey, and as Hilary Putnam did for James. This is true, but it, too, only goes so far, for we need to ask why this hasn't happened. If we turn to Santayana's writings, and in particular *Scepticism and Animal Faith* and *Realms of Being*, another explanation suggests itself: his standing is a reflection of his unconventional views about the aims and method of philosophy. It is these views that have given rise to misinterpretations and the most virulent criticism.

---

[5] John Dewey, Frederick J. E. Woodbridge of Columbia University, and Morris R. Cohen of City College, New York, among others, gave the *Life of Reason* high praise. Woodbridge and Cohen saw in Santayana a strong ally for philosophical naturalism. As a result, in the early part of the twentieth century, the *Life of Reason* was assigned to philosophy students at Columbia and City College.

Commenting on Santayana's reputation, Hilary Putnam has suggested something like the above diagnosis as well as one or two others. He writes: 'no philosopher since Spinoza (also a materialist, if not an atheist) has been more wholeheartedly devoted to the ideal of pure contemplation than George Santayana.' This kind of contemplation is offputting, he writes, 'because it casts such an unflattering light on the way we mostly live our lives' (Putnam 1984). He also sees in Santayana's language an ironic take on metaphysics, which readers misinterpret to Santayana's detriment. Whatever the merit of these two explanations (they are not elaborated), he puts forward another, which focuses on Santayana's philosophy:

If there has been less attention paid to Santayana's philosophy than to that of Royce or Peirce, this is in large part because his philosophical mood and philosophical intuitions were actually ahead of his time. In many ways he anticipated some of the dominant trends of American philosophy of the present day.[6]

If this is entirely true, it is remarkable, given Santayana's reliance on the history of philosophy. He expressly stated that he took Spinoza as his 'master', and he reached even further back to Lucretius and Democritus as sources of inspiration.[7] 'This philosophy that I have unearthed within me', he wrote, 'is ancient philosophy, very ancient philosophy' (*RB* p. xxxviii). However, Putnam's suggestion that there is *something* about Santayana's metaphilosophical views that accounts for his relative neglect points us in the right direction.

2. REALMS OF BEING

Those who deem Santayana a mere belletrist might be forgiven, since he regularly offered up statements such as 'For good or ill, I am an ignorant man, almost a poet' (*SAF* p. x) and 'I detest disputation and distrust proofs and disproofs' (*PGS* 604). These statements are bound to mislead unless taken in the context of his philosophical aims. For in practice Santayana was not

---

[6] Putnam 1985, quoted in Saatkamp 2004: 136. This statement appears to contradict my earlier claim that Santayana has no famous contemporary advocates. Santayana is occasionally singled out for praise by the likes of Rorty and Putnam, but he has not received the kind of attention that Dewey and James have benefited from.

[7] Santayana did not think that philosophy progresses in the manner of science. 'The progress of philosophy has not been of such a sort that the latest philosophers are always the best: it is quite the other way' (*SE* 208.)

averse to presenting and replying to arguments; and, as we shall see, his system crucially depends on his arguments for radical skepticism. Before discussing these matters, it will be helpful to have before us a summary of the nature and function of Santayana's ontology.

There are four categories in Santayana's ontology. These may be briefly described as follows. The *realm of essence* is the 'infinite multitude of ideal terms (whether ever revealed to anybody or not)' (*RB* p. viii). An essence might be a property, a universal, a mathematical notion, or a qualitative term of thought. A key point is that the being of essences does not depend on either matter or mind; hence their ideal status.[8]

The *realm of matter* is the dynamic universe of physical stuff. Santayana offered a minimal characterization of the realm of matter based on our everyday interactions in the world, but he made no claim to be a scientist (see *RB* 202–35). Rather he held that 'any philosophy is materialistic that, like mine, regards this study, physics, as alone competent to reveal the secret source and method of gross events, or the ways of power' (*PGS* 507–8).[9]

The *realm of truth* follows from the realms of essence and matter. Santayana held that it is axiomatic that matter must embody some essence since '[a] being without any essence is a contradiction in terms. The existence of something without quality would not differ in its absence nor from the existence of anything else' (LSK 116–17; see also *PGS* 25). The realm of truth comprises all the essences embodied by physical things and their relational properties. It is 'that segment of the realm of essence which happens to be illustrated in existence' (*RB* p. xv). Santayana describes the realm of truth as 'impersonal and super-existential' (*RB* 485), since it is not restricted to what currently exists, but also includes what 'has existed, or is destined to exist' (*RB* 485).

---

[8] Santayana regards Leibniz's 'all possible worlds' as a kindred doctrine to his realm of essence. He also finds kindred doctrines in Plato, Spinoza, and Husserl, among others. See *RB* 155–80. The realm of essence also has a family resemblance to Peirce's category of Firstness. Cf. Santayana: 'The principle of essence . . . is identity: the being of each essence is entirely exhausted by its definition: I do not mean its definition in words, but the character which distinguishes it from any other essence' (*RB* 18); Peirce: '[A] First is that whose being is simply in itself, not referring to anything nor lying behind anything'; it is 'the mode of being which consists in its subject being positively such as it is regardless of aught else' (*CP* 1. 356 and 1. 25).

[9] To the objection that a philosopher isn't really a materialist if he accepts other, non-material kinds of being, Santayana replies: 'Materialism by no means implies that nothing exists save matter. Democritus admitted the void to an equal reality, with all the relations and events that motion in that void would involve . . . matter is the only *substance, power,* or *agency* in the universe: and this, not that matter is the only *reality,* is the first principle of materialism' (*PGS* 509).

Finally, the *realm of spirit* is Santayana's term for conscious life. 'Spirit is an awareness natural to animals, revealing the world and themselves in it. Other names for spirit are consciousness, attention, feeling, thought, or any word that marks the total *inner* difference between being awake or asleep, alive or dead' (*RB* 572).[10] Consciousness partakes in all three realms, since its basis is material, it involves an essence, and the fact that a conscious state (generated by the brain) occurs is part of the realm truth.

Turning now to what Santayana intends by his ontology, the following three passages are instructive:

[i] The Realms of Being of which I speak are not parts of a cosmos, nor one great cosmos together: they are only kinds or categories of things which I find conspicuously different and worth distinguishing, at least in my own thoughts. I do not know how many things in the universe at large may fall under each of these classes, nor what other Realms of Being may not exist, to which I have no approach or which I have not happened to distinguish in my personal observation of the world.   (*SAF* p. vi)

From this we may say that Santayana's system is, in the first place, a conceptual scheme of extreme generality. The last sentence about 'personal observation' is important, for it signals a modesty of scope and pretension for this conceptual scheme. Compare, for example, Santayana's position on his four categories to Peirce's position on his three categories. Peirce took his categories to be the omnipresent realities of the universe.[11] In contrast, Santayana thought of his categories as 'partly a free construction' (*SAF*, p. vi). He does not claim to have discovered or even 'guessed at' the universal grammar of thought or being.

The second passage emphasizes the grounding of the categories in common sense. It occurs in the 'General Review' at the end of *Realms of Being*:

[ii] I said in the Preface to *Scepticism and Animal Faith*, 'Here is one more system of philosophy'; and I proceeded to warn the reader that this system would not aspire to be new or personal or metaphysical or a system of the universe. It would be a revision of the categories of common sense, faithful in spirit to orthodox human tradition, and endeavouring only to clarify those categories and disentangle the confusions that inevitably arise when spontaneous fancy comes up against an intricate world.   (*RB* 826)

This passage appears in part to contradict the first passage, for here Santayana states that his categories are *not* personal. But the tension is superficial. While

---

[10] Santayana's account of consciousness is non-reductive and has affinities with the accounts recently defended by Chalmers (1995), Nagel (1986), and McGinn (1991).

[11] See, e.g., Peirce's (1992) 'One, Two, Three: Kantian Categories'.

he does not think the rhetoric he employs (mostly scholastic terminology) is necessary to convey his system, and he does not hold that every possible mind, human or non-human, must appeal to the same categories, he does think that the categories he presents are in fact the rudimentary categories of common sense. 'I think it reasonable to suppose', he writes, 'that the beliefs that prove inevitable for me, after absolutely disinterested criticism, would prove inevitable also to most human beings' (RB p. xxix). Thus while the categories he delineates are likely universal, at least in humans, they are only contingently so. Again, he grants that '[a]nyone who wishes is free to discard these categories and employ others'. But, contrary to appearances, this does not mean that the appeal to categories is without constraints, for he immediately qualifies this statement. 'The only question will be how he will get on; what sort of intellectual dominion and intellectual life he will achieve; also whether he will really be using other categories in his spontaneous and successful contacts with the world, or only a different jargon in his professional philosophy' (RB 453). A major theme running through Realms of Being is the criticism that other systems of philosophy are either partial, or idiosyncratic, or the product of local and passing professional controversies, or ultimately amount to a tacit affirmation of the orthodox categories explicitly denied.[12] Santayana's categories are not Kantian or Peircean, but he has little doubt that they are 'faithful in spirit to orthodox human tradition'.

The third passage sheds some light on why Santayana at times distances himself from professional philosophers and aligns himself with poets:

[iii] [My system] is not an exercise in controversy but in meditation. It addresses itself less to the professional philosophers of the day than to the reflective moments and speculative honesty of any man in any age or country.   (RB p. xxv)

Here Santayana, like James, shows his predilection for connecting philosophy not to technical problems of doubtful relevance but to daily life and thought.[13] Some readers have interpreted Santayana as saying that he has made a clean break from philosophy. Rorty (1982: 41), for example, comments that

---

[12] An extended treatment of this last point is found in 'The Latent Materialism of Idealists', RB 382–98.

[13] Santayana and James certainly shared the idea that philosophy should reach beyond the halls of academia. However, the issue is curiously complicated, partly due to Santayana's categorial approach. For example, Brent (1998: 291) reports that James and Santayana had very different reactions to Peirce's 1903 Harvard lectures. 'Most of [Peirce's] hearers, including James but with the surprising exception of George Santayana (Royce was away), found the lectures obscure, if not unintelligible, because they were so deeply embedded in his largely unpublished theory of categories. James was unable to abstract even a semblance of pragmatism as he knew it from the material Peirce presented.'

Santayana is like Dewey and Heidegger, in that '[he saw] no interesting future for a distinct discipline called "philosophy"', and he held out no hope for 'the successful completion of old "research programs"' and did not suggest new ones. This puts matters a little too strongly. It is true that Santayana rarely hesitated to pillory contemporary philosophy, but this is not because he didn't possess a specific idea of what philosophy is about or see a future for philosophy.[14] Since his views about philosophy and the philosopher's proper vocation are inseparable from his skeptical analysis of knowledge, we shall next consider this analysis. This review will also serve as a general, preemptive reply to a number of typical objections to his system.

3. CRITICISM AND SKEPTICISM

To many critics, Santayana's system seems baroque, and worse still painted with too large, imprecise brush strokes. Several critics charge that it is beset with terminal problems. To some, his realm of essence expands his ontology beyond reasonable limits; for others, it is part of a hopeless search for epistemic certitude. His realm of matter has been attacked on the ground that it is vague and unscientific; some claim that it is simply incoherent, a reversion to a Kantian metaphysical thing-in-itself. Reductivists and other sorts of monists naturally object to his dualistic account of consciousness. And many find his notion of truth far removed from most contemporary discussions, since it is not defined in terms of belief, assertion, or anything else related to human activity.[15]

One senses a common thread running through these objections: a suspicion about the legitimacy of his approach to philosophy. To critics, his approach appears both unmotivated and, given the premium he places on clarified common sense, antithetical to more established methods, such as linguistic analysis, a priori and transcendental arguments, and formal proofs—the

[14] Commenting on the works of his contemporaries, Santayana wrote: 'There is much life in some of them. I like their water-colour sketches of self-consciousness, their rebellious egotism, their fervid reforms of phraseology, their peep-holes through which some very small part of things may be seen very clearly: they have lively wits, but they seem to me like children playing blind-man's-bluff; they are keenly excited at not knowing where they are. They are really here, in the common natural world, where there is nothing in particular to threaten or allure them; and they have only to remove their philosophical bandages in order to perceive it' (SE 210).

[15] Objections of this sort appear in PGS. See also Dewey 1984 [1927]; Lewis 1970; Sprigge 1995 [1974] and 1997; Greenlee 1978; and Stuhr 1997.

methods of 'special schools of philosophy', as Santayana calls them (*SAF* p. v). The underlying complaint is that by eschewing such methods Santayana generates an extravagant system unable to withstand rigorous criticism.

Santayana certainly felt that his critics failed to understand him. His response was typically disinterested. He wrote that he could 'well understand the modern feeling that spirit is nothing, that essence is nothing, and that even matter is nothing' (*PGS* 521). In his view, a highly skeptical attitude was simply part of the spirit of the age, as it had been during the Modern period. He held that such criticism 'must be allowed to go on, it belongs to the ritual of intellectual insurrection' (*PGS* 34). However, for him, the ritual of intellectual insurrection has no special authority, and he regards his philosophy as immune from (broadly understood) rationalist and empiricist criticisms. Somewhat paradoxically, the source of this immunity is derived from his preeminent treatment of skepticism.

In the opening pages of *Scepticism and Animal Faith* Santayana writes:

[I]n the confused state of human speculation . . . a philosopher to-day would be ridiculous and negligible who had not strained his dogmas through the utmost rigours of scepticism. . . . Let me then push scepticism as far as I logically can, and endeavor to clear my mind of illusion, even at the price of intellectual suicide.   (*SAF* 9–10)[16]

Santayana's willingness to engage the skeptic on his own terms sets him apart from his contemporaries, such as Dewey and Peirce. He holds that any claim to factual knowledge might be coherently challenged. The same is true for principles of criticism.[17] No belief is immune from doubt; and he sets forth a sustained line of skeptical argumentation that he describes as a '*reductio ad absurdum* of modern paradoxes' (*RB* p. xxv).

Santayana aims to demonstrate that the logical terminus of the Cartesian skeptical challenge is solipsism of the present moment. A thorough and consistent skeptic is obliged to abandon all claims to memory, expectation, the existence of a self, and even the knowledge that something is 'given' to consciousness. This last point is particularly important. Santayana argues that the skeptic, if awake, must have some essence present to consciousness. However, he is not entitled to assert even something of minimal content like 'this

---

[16] Here it is important to keep in mind that *Scepticism and Animal Faith* is the introduction to *Realms of Being*.

[17] Santayana calls the former 'empirical criticism' and the latter 'transcendental criticism' (*SAF* 3–5).

datum, now' since, in his analysis, the fact of being present to consciousness is not part of the logical content of any given essence. 'In each datum taken separately', he holds, 'there would be no occasion to speak of existence [or presence to consciousness]. It would be an obvious appearance . . . *and the fact that it appeared (which would be the only fact involved) would not appear in it at all*' (*SAF* 44; my emphasis).[18] Thus Cartesian skepticism is not an incoherent exercise, but it concludes with the thought that since '[b]elief in the existence of anything . . . is something radically incapable of proof', the thoroughgoing skeptic must 'abolish . . . that category of thought [existence] altogether' (*SAF* 35). In foundationalist terms, Santayana's position is that there are no *intrinsically credible* beliefs that serve as either an incorrigible or a defeasible foundation for knowledge.[19] The terminus of skepticism is not a state of belief at all; it is a suspension of judgment.

The skeptical analysis of knowledge also shows that there are no first principles of criticism. Santayana maintains that this is something frequently overlooked by the 'special schools'. In their attacks on rival systems, they tacitly make dogmatic assumptions of their own. Thus he chides Descartes for setting 'accidental limits to his scepticism' by not doubting the existence of the self and by assuming the principle of sufficient reason—'a principle for which', Santayana asserts, 'there is no reason at all' (*SAF* 289). And he accuses Hume of 'limping scepticism'. 'Hume seems to have assumed', he writes, 'that every perception perceived itself. He assumed further that these perceptions lay in time and formed certain sequences' (*SAF* 294–6).[20] For Santayana, these principles, mixed as they are with skepticism about other vital assumptions (e.g., induction), are indicative of the 'malicious' psychology of British empiricism, which is founded on a 'halting criticism of immediate experience' (PH 101; *SAF* 200).[21] Kant is similarly faulted for his 'impure' skepticism, for assigning 'conditions to experience', and 'assuming that mind everywhere must have a single grammar' (*SAF* 23, 298–300).[22] Moreover, Santayana rejects various other philosophical 'truths'. For example,

---

[18] Cf. Lewis (1956 [1929]: 53): 'Yet no one but a philosopher could for a moment deny this immediate presence in consciousness of that which no activity of thought can create or alter.'

[19] See M. Williams 1977: 61. See also Hodges and Lachs 2000.

[20] In the *Enquiry*, Hume (1999 [1772]: 108) states: 'It may, therefore, be a subject worthy of curiosity, to enquire what is the nature of that evidence, which assures us of any real existence and matter of fact, beyond the present testimony of our senses, or the records of our memory.'

[21] Santayana had similar things to say about Russell's logical atomism. See, e.g., LGS2 152–3, 161–2, 167–8.

[22] For criticisms of Kant and others in the German tradition see *EGP*.

he calls Ockham's razor 'the weapon of monstrous self-mutilation with which British philosophy, if consistent, would have soon committed suicide' (*RB* 510).

The culmination of Santayana's skeptical analysis of knowledge is that the expression of first principles is not itself critical, but rather a kind of *confession*. Since the critic of knowledge is unable to remain in a state of suspended belief, he will inevitably hold some beliefs and adhere to some principles of criticism. At the limit, the expression of 'first principles cannot be criticism but only confession or propaganda', and thus all criticism must be seen as 'internal to each logical organism or rational mind' (*PGS* 551). It is for this reason that Santayana writes in response to his critics:

As to the contrary principles or preferences that dictate our different views, it would be chimerical and ill-natured to argue. You cannot refute a principle or rebut a preference, you can only indicate its consequences or present alluringly the charms of a rival doctrine.   (*PGS* 604)

Santayana often urges that what is of first importance for the philosopher is not refutation, but rather avoiding misrepresentation and remaining faithful to one's first principles.

One might question Santayana's argument. If there are no beliefs with intrinsic warrant, and no privileged first principles, on what basis can one begin to develop a system of philosophy? His skeptical analysis of knowledge seems to drop us into an intellectual abyss.

Santayana sees things otherwise, and he offers an opposing metaphor. He speaks of the 'apex of scepticism' (*SAF* 108), the 'culminating point of my survey of evidence', and how 'the entanglements I have left behind me and the habitable regions I am looking for lie spread out before me like opposite valleys' (*SAF* 99). On one side, skepticism is 'invincible and complete' (*SAF* 101). But this has the positive effect of liberating the intellect from unnecessary epistemological entanglements. Looking in the other direction, the way is clear for a forthright statement of first principles. Thus, in *Realms of Being* Santayana asserts that '[t]ranscendentalism has two phases or movements—the sceptical one retreating to the immediate, and the assertive one by which objects of belief are defined and marshalled, of such a character and in such an order as intelligent action demands' (*RB* 200).

Although Santayana characterizes the assertive phase as a kind of confession, it is one made unrepentantly. He 'confesses' to a materialism founded on animal faith: 'faith' since from a critical point of view materialism is groundless, and 'animal' since the existence of a dynamic material world is 'the presupposition of all natural investigation and science' (*PGS* 505). Yet he is unrepentant, since he thinks that his confession is no less justified than confessions about other fundamental existential posits. He makes the same point by stating that while his materialism is dogmatic, '[m]y scepticism confirms this dogma' (*PGS* 515). The skeptic can always challenge materialism. But unless the skeptic remains a solipsist of the present moment, challenges to materialism will end with *tu quoque*.[23] With the intellect liberated rather than weighed down by skepticism, Santayana delineates his categories of essence, matter, truth, and spirit. He regards these categories as the ones spontaneously employed, and through reflection distinguished, 'by an animal mind in the presence of nature' (*RB* p. xxxvi). Only an antecedent commitment to contrary first principles can deny the validity of these categories; but any such contrary commitment is only a confession.

4. ORDINARY REFLECTION SYSTEMATIZED

Even if we follow Santayana this far, doubts about his procedure might linger. His position on skepticism leaves open the question of which first principles we should recognize. We've noted his comment that his categories are 'partly a free construction'. But how free? He held that the language and the cultural tradition in which his system is expressed are not essential, and in this sense his system is a free construction. 'English, and the whole Anglo-Saxon tradition in literature and philosophy,' he wrote, 'have always been a medium to me rather than a source' (*PGS* 6). But the medium, for him, is not the message. 'In the past or in the future, my language and my borrowed knowledge would have been different, but under whatever sky I had been born, since it is the same sky, I should have had the same philosophy' (*SAF* p. x). We have also seen that his categorial scheme is not Kantian. Thus he grants that each person is free to 'clean better, if he can, the windows of his soul' (*SAF* p. vi).

In a more fundamental sense Santayana's system is not a free construction. As Sprigge (1969) points out, he was not a voluntarist about belief. The

---

[23] We might see a parallel here with Santayana's claim that genuine ethical disputes terminate in *argumentum ad hominem* (*WD* 147).

doctrine of animal faith is an explicit denial of absolute intellectual freedom. In terms not unlike those Peirce uses to characterize Secondness, Santayana describes the 'shock' of 'brute experience' that 'establishes realism' about the realm of matter (*SAF* 139–46). Materialism is not a doctrine of choice. Still, it is not a *conclusion*. On the contrary, he asserts that it is a presupposition 'I cannot live without making' (*PGS* 505).

The appeal to shock, however, does not fully answer the question of first principles—and for two reasons. First, in its full development the notion of shock is bound up with animal faith, and this in turn appeals to the instinctive commitments of a physical creature in a physical world. Second, shock cannot account for the inclusion of essence, truth, and spirit, since these are not objects of belief. Belief for Santayana is something directed only toward the realm of matter. Commenting on his realms of truth and essence, he writes: 'The smile of the critic who will not be fooled into *believing* in them is entirely justified. They are not proposed as objects of belief. They are proposed as conceptual distinctions and categories of logic; as one of many languages in which the nature of things may be described' (*RB* 453). It follows that these categories are not derived (at least directly) from shock or animal faith.[24]

For Santayana, the question of how first principles and categories are derived is ultimately answered by an appeal to his philosophical aims and what he regards as the chief function of philosophy. A marginal comment at the end of *Realms of Being* perhaps sums it up best: 'This philosophy is ordinary reflection systematized' (*RB* 827).[25] This is both profound and disarming. It is profound, since the task of philosophy is to articulate a comprehensive vision of the world and the human predicament. Yet it is disarming, since philosophy need not appeal to an arcane subject matter. It is with this notion of philosophy in mind that Santayana wrote '*my system is not mine, nor new*', and although 'formed under the fire of contemporary discussions [it] is *no phase of any current movement*' (*SAF* pp. v, viii). He asserted that 'I stand in philosophy exactly where I stand in daily life; I should not be honest otherwise' (*SAF* p. vi). And he added that 'exact science is not necessary to establish my essential doctrine, nor can any of them claim higher warrant than it has in itself: for it rests on public experience' (*SAF* p. x).

---

[24] Lachs (2006: 94) sees this as a problem.

[25] The comment continues 'or lay religion'. This theme is not explored here, though Santayana's terminology (e.g., 'animal faith', 'confession') provide some indication of its meaning.

At this point a pragmatic strain in Santayana's philosophy comes to the fore: it is the function of philosophy that secures its methodology.[26] Since there are no grounded first principles of criticism, we must allow that any method that contributes to clarifying the moral and descriptive aspects of daily life is pertinent.[27]

In Santayana's case, pursuing this goal involves a number of intertwined means that connect to the various aspects of his system. In his treatment of skepticism he employs standard argument forms. Constructively, he draws from past achievements, and his system builds, with qualifications and refinements, on the work of philosophers ranging from the pre-Socratics to Moore and Russell.[28] Apart from his novel terminology, he was not without his own rhetorical strategies for articulating his views. His use of metaphor and other literary devices is not accidental. It is a complementary feature of his position that knowledge and values are relative to our finite physiology and the boundless complexity of the material world. Our thoughts are 'a [human] language,' Santayana held, 'not a mirror' (SAF 179).[29] In a similar vein, he elsewhere wrote that 'all ideas are compatible and supplementary to one another, like the various arts of expression', and 'it is possible to perceive, up to a certain point, the symbolic burden of each of them' (PGS 18). Taking the position that knowledge is non-literal, or symbolic, he employed a literary style that he regarded as a primary instrument for conveying the broad facts of life. With regard to his categories, Kerr-Lawson (2002 and 1987) has helpfully pointed to Santayana's recurrent 'contrastive method' for bringing out logical priorities among the realms and highlighting their *sui*

[26] There are several pragmatic strains in Santayana's philosophy. Recall his statement that in the assertive phase of transcendentalism 'objects of belief are defined and marshalled, of such a character and such an order as intelligent action demands'. Similarly, his doctrine of non-literal knowledge incorporates a pragmatic criterion of warrant. He asks, 'What better criterion have we of truth than pertinence to action and implication in the dynamic order of nature?' (RB 442–3). Santayana called his doctrine of non-literal knowledge 'a sort of pragmatism' (PGS 14). However, there is no easy classification here, for he also declared 'I am no pragmatist' (LGS2 263). For a discussion of Santayana's estranged relationship to the pragmatist movement that focuses on his materialism, see Tiller 2006. For a more wide-ranging discussion see Lachs 2003.

[27] This includes technical methods. On this issue Santayana expressed a note of regret. 'There is one point, indeed, which I am truly sorry not to be able to profit by the guidance of my contemporaries. There is now a great ferment in natural and mathematical philosophy and the times seem ripe for a new system of nature. ... If I were a mathematician I should no doubt regale myself, if not the reader, with [a] ... logistic system of the universe expressed in algebraic symbols' (SAF p. ix).

[28] Santayana remarks that it was his discussions with '[Russell] and Moore that helped me, in 1897, to grind fine and filter Platonic Ideas into my realm of essence' (PGS 587).

[29] Santayana calls the desire for literal knowledge, or human cognition mirroring nature, one of the 'false steps' of philosophy. See 'On the False Steps of Philosophy', in BR 145–74.

generis character. This way of vividly comparing one realm with another is an important feature of his system, since the categories do not lend themselves to reductive definitions.

Given Santayana's aims and his position on skepticism, the guiding principle of philosophy is a resolute commitment to *honesty*. As he puts it, the philosopher 'should substitute the pursuit of sincerity for the pursuit of omniscience' (*PH* 100). That honesty is the central constraint in Santayana's philosophy is a point emphasized by other commentators.[30] By way of conclusion, we might say a little more about this idea and how it is manifested in his life and writings.

The guiding principle of honesty connects with the thesis that the heart of philosophy is confessional. Criticism is first 'invited to do its worst' (*PGS* 18). Once the watershed of criticism is reached, a stabilizing, sincere statement of one's deepest commitments corrects the intellectual nihilism of skepticism (*PGS* 30). Such commitments are rooted in our nature and clarified through reflection and self-examination: the exercise is Socratic. Thus, late in life Santayana observed that 'virtually [my] whole system was latent in me from the beginning' (*PGS* 30). His early letters bear witness to this fact. In his twenties he wrote, after having declared solipsism 'arbitrary' (*LGS*1 48):

There are certain convictions which cannot be exiled from the mind, convictions about everyday practical matters, about history, and about the ordinary passions of men. A system starting from these universal convictions has a foothold in every mind, and can coerce that mind to accept at least some of its content.   (*LGS*1 64)

This early statement neatly summarizes his mature views about how philosophy proceeds. In letters from the same period we find further evidence that his system is about articulating abiding convictions. He expresses his commitment to materialism, to the 'postulate of one eternal and objective truth', and to spirit (see *LGS*1 15, 39, 63). As he matured, the presentation of his system became increasingly subtle, but the core elements were in place at a young age and did not fundamentally alter. While we need not deny that philosophy can be personally transformative, this continuity in Santayana's thought is, as we might expect given his position, that philosophy is an expression of life.

A philosophy of life should also have great synthetic power. In the broadest sense, it should organize the full range of our thought. This is precisely

---

[30] See, e.g., Kerr-Lawson 2004; Lachs 1988: 43 ff. and 2006: 21 ff.; Sprigge 1995 [1974]: 47 ff.

what Santayana's philosophy aspires to do. He wrote that '[t]he intention of my philosophy has certainly been to attain, if possible . . . wide intuitions, and to celebrate the emotions with which they fill the mind' (*PGS* 21). The practical import of this endeavor is found in his sharp commentaries on virtually every major philosophical system; in his close analyses of spiritual life, morals, politics, religion, and art; and in his illuminating reflections on such diverse fields as architecture, friendship, and sports. The wide intuitions that Santayana's philosophy evoke provide him with an exceptionally powerful framework for discussing these and many other subjects. This too is what we should expect from a philosophy of life, from ordinary reflection systematized.

References

The following abbreviations are used for Santayana's works:

BR   *The Birth of Reason and Other Essays*
EGP   *Egotism in German Philosophy*
LGS1   *The Letters of George Santayana*, Book 1: [1868]–1909.
LGS2   *The Letters of George Santayana*, Book 2: 1910–1920.
LR1   *The Life of Reason: Or, The Phases of Human Progress*, i: *Reason and Common Sense*
LSK   'Literal and Symbolic Knowledge'
PGS   *The Philosophy of George Santayana*
PH   'Philosophical Heresy'
RB   *Realms of Being*
SAF   *Scepticism and Animal Faith*
SE   *Soliloquies In England and Later Soliloquies*
WD   *Winds of Doctrine*

References to these works are by the abbreviation followed by the page number.

Brent, Joseph (1998). *Charles Sanders Peirce: A Life*. Bloomington, IN, and Indianapolis: Indiana University Press.

Chalmers, David J. (1995). 'Facing up to the Problem of Consciousness'. *Journal of Consciousness Studies*, 2/3: 200–19.

Dewey, John (1984 [1927]). 'Half-Hearted Naturalism'. In *John Dewey: The Later Works, 1925–1953*, ed. Jo Ann Boydston, iii, Carbondale, IL, and Edwardsville, IL: Southern Illinois University Press, 73–81.

Greenlee, Douglass (1978). 'The Incoherence of Santayana's Scepticism'. *Southern Journal of Philosophy*, 16: 51–60.

Hodges, Michael, and Lachs, John (2000). *Thinking in the Ruins: Wittgenstein and Santayana on Contingency*. Nashville: Vanderbilt University Press.

Hume, David (1999 [1772]). *An Enquiry concerning Human Understanding*. Oxford: Oxford University Press.

Kerr-Lawson, Angus (1987). 'Variations on a Given Theme'. *Overheard in Seville: Bulletin of the Santayana Society*, no. 5: 28–33.

____ (2002). 'The Non-Empiricist Categories of Santayana's Materialism'. *Transactions of the Charles S. Peirce Society*, 38/1–2: 47–77.

____ (2004). 'The Absence of Argument in Santayana'. *Overheard in Seville: Bulletin of the Santayana Society*, no. 24: 29–40.

Lachs, John (1988). *Santayana*. Boston: Twayne Publishers.

____ (2003). *A Community of Individuals*. London: Routledge.

____ (2006). *On Santayana*. Belmont, CA: Thompson Wadsworth.

____ and Hodges, Michael (2000). *Thinking in the Ruins: Wittgenstein and Santayana on Contingency*. Nashville: Vanderbilt University Press.

Lewis, C. I. (1956 [1929]). *Mind and the World Order*. New York: Dover Publications.

____ (1970). *The Collected Papers of Clarence Irving Lewis*, ed. John D. Goheen and John Mothershead, Jr. Stanford, CA: Stanford University Press.

McCormick, John (1987). *George Santayana: A Biography*. New York: Alfred A. Knopf.

McGinn, Colin (1991). *The Problem of Consciousness: Essays Towards Resolution*. Oxford: Blackwell.

Nagel, Thomas (1986). *The View from Nowhere*. New York: Oxford University Press.

Peirce, Charles Sanders (1931–58). *Collected Papers of Charles Sanders Peirce*, i–vi, ed. C. Hartshorne and P. Weiss, vii and viii, ed. A. Burks. Cambridge, MA: Belknap Press of Harvard University Press. References are of the form *CP* followed by volume and paragraph no.

____ (1992). *The Essential Peirce*, i, ed. Nathan Houser and Christian Kloesel. Bloomington, IN, and Indianapolis: Indiana University Press.

Putnam, Hilary (1984). 'Greetings: to the Santayana Society's Anniversary Celebration on Behalf of the Harvard Department of Philosophy'. *Overheard in Seville: Bulletin of the Santayana Society*, no. 2: 24–6.

____ (1985). 'Santayana Restored', brochure for *The Works of George Santayana*. Cambridge, MA: MIT Press.

Rorty, Richard (1982). *Consequences of Pragmatism*. Minneapolis: University of Minnesota Press.

Saatkamp, Herman J. Jr. (2004). 'George Santayana'. In Armen Marsoobian and John Ryder (eds.), The *Blackwell Guide to American Philosophy*, Oxford: Blackwell Publishers, 135–54.

Santayana, George (1967 [1897]). 'Philosophy on the Bleachers'. In James Ballowe (ed.), *George Santayana's America*, Urbana, IL: University of Illinois Press, 121–30.

____ (1905). *The Life of Reason: Or, The Phases of Human Progress*, i: *Reason in Common Sense*. New York: Charles Scribner's Sons.

____ (1915). *Egotism in German Philosophy*. New York: Charles Scribner's Sons.

Santayana, George (1936 [1915]). 'Philosophical Heresy'. In Justus Buchler and Benjamin Schwartz (eds.), *Obiter Scripta*, New York: Charles Scribner's Sons, 94–107.

—— (1936 [1918]). 'Literal and Symbolic Knowledge'. In Justus Buchler and Benjamin Schwartz (eds.), *Obiter Scripta*, New York: Charles Scribner's Sons, 108–50.

—— (1920). *Character and Opinion in the United States: With Reminiscences of William James and Josiah Royce and Academic Life in America*. New York: Charles Scribner's Sons.

—— (1967 [1922]). 'The Progress of Philosophy'. In *Soliloquies In England and Later Soliloquies*, Ann Arbor: University of Michigan Press, 207–16.

—— (1923). *Scepticism and Animal Faith*. New York: Charles Scribner's Sons.

—— (1925). 'Dewey's Naturalistic Metaphysics'. *Journal of Philosophy*, 22/25: 673–8.

—— (1926). *Winds of Doctrine*. London: J. M. Dent & Sons Ltd.

—— (1927). *Platonism and the Spiritual Life*. New York: Charles Scribner's Sons.

—— (1936). *The Last Puritan*. New York: Charles Scribner's Sons.

—— (1991 [1940]). *The Philosophy of George Santayana*, ed. Paul Arthur Schilpp. La Salle, IL: Open Court.

—— (1942). *Realms of Being*, 1-vol. edn., with a new introduction by the author; contains the four books: *The Realm of Essence: Book First* (1927); *The Realm of Matter: Book Second* (1930); *The Realm of Truth: Book Third* (1938); and *The Realm of Spirit: Book Fourth* (1940). New York: Charles Scribner's Sons.

—— (1951). *Dominations and Powers: Reflections on Liberty, Society, and Government*. New York: Charles Scribner's Sons.

—— (1968). *The Birth of Reason and Other Essays*, ed. Daniel Cory. New York: Columbia University Press.

—— (2001). *The Letters of George Santayana*, Book 1: [1868]–1909, *The Works of George Santayana*, v, Book 1, ed. William G. Holzberger. Cambridge, MA: MIT Press.

—— (2001). *The Letters of George Santayana*, Book 2: 1910–1920. *The Works of George Santayana*, v, Book 2, ed. William G. Holzberger. Cambridge, MA: MIT Press.

Shorey, Paul (1927). Review of *Platonism and the Spiritual Life*, *Classsical Philology*, 22/3: 323–4.

Sprigge, T. L. S. (1969). 'Santayana and Verification'. *Inquiry*, 12: 265–86.

—— (1995 [1974]). *Santayana*. London: Routledge.

—— (1997). 'Kerr-Lawson on Truth and Santayana'. *Transactions of the Charles S. Peirce Society*, 33/1: 113–30.

Stuhr, John J. (1997). *Genealogical Pragmatism: Philosophy, Experience, and Community*. Albany, NY: State University of New York Press.

Tiller, Glenn (2006). 'The Unknowable: The Pragmatist Critique of Matter'. *Transactions of the Charles S. Peirce Society*, 42/2: 206–28.

Williams, Donald C. (1954). 'Of Essence and Existence and Santayana'. *Journal of Philosophy*, 51/2: 31–42.

Williams, Michael (1999 [1977]). *Groundless Belief*. Princeton: Princeton University Press.

Internet Resources

Overheard in Seville: Bulletin of the Santayana Society, ed. Angus Kerr-Lawson and Herman J. Saatkamp, Jr. Indianapolis: Indiana University/Purdue University. <http://www.math.uwaterloo.ca/~kerrlaws/Santayana/Bulletin/seville.html>

The Santayana Edition. Indiana University/Purdue University. <http://www.iupui.edu/~santedit/>

CHAPTER 8

A PRAGMATIST WORLD VIEW: GEORGE HERBERT MEAD'S PHILOSOPHY OF THE ACT

CORNELIS DE WAAL

Excuse me, but what do I know about the mountain, the tree, the sea? The mountain is a mountain because I say: 'That is a mountain.' In other words: *'I am the mountain.'* What are we? We are whatever, at any given moment, occupies our attention. I am the mountain, I am the tree, I am the sea. I am also the star, which knows not its own existence!

Luigi Pirandello

IN THE BEGINNING there was neither the word nor the world; in the beginning there was the act. This sums up the basic premise of the pragmatist philosophy of George Herbert Mead (1863–1931). In many ways Mead is the forgotten pragmatist. There is a reason for this. Though he was a brilliant lecturer, he never published a book, and his scattered essays are dense and obscure; they are almost desperate attempts to cram an entire system of thought within the confines of a few pages. Besides being a direct influence on his students—mostly in sociology and social psychology—Mead's main influence is through posthumously published lecture notes made by professional stenographers during the final years of his life.[1] However, with their didactic repetitions and digressions, these lecture notes tend to hide the systematic aspect of Mead's work. Ill at ease with simple solutions, and always aware of the importance of details, Mead always considered his work unfinished, and until the very end he remained very much a searching philosopher. Mead's discomfort with philosophical abstraction and his constant focus on problems rather than theories kept him from writing out a systematic pragmatic position. This leaves the reader who seeks to extract Mead's pragmatist leanings from his work with much surveying to do. This is one such surveying attempt, and it is one that is inspired by the belief that Mead's pragmatism, as it is captured in his philosophy of the act, is the skeleton key to his philosophical system.

LIFE AND INTELLECTUAL CONTEXT

George Herbert Mead was born on 27 February 1863 in South Hadley, Massachusetts. At the age of 7 he moved with his parents and older sister to Oberlin, Ohio, when his father, the Congregationalist minister and pastor Hiram Mead (1827–81), was appointed homiletics professor at Oberlin College. Mead's mother, Elizabeth Storrs Billings (1832–1917), later became president of Mount Holyoke College (1890–1900). In 1883, Mead took his bachelor's degree at Oberlin College, after which he taught briefly in a grade school, before working as a surveyor for Wisconsin Central Railroad

---

[1] *Mind, Self, and Society* (1934) consists of lecture notes taken by professional stenographers during his 1927 course in social psychology. Four other posthumous books appeared, drawn from Mead's notes, stenographic accounts of his courses, and previously published material: *The Philosophy of the Present* (1932), which contains Mead's 1930 Carus Lectures, *Movements of Thought in the Nineteenth Century* (1936), *The Philosophy of the Act* (1938), and *The Individual and the Social Self* (1982). A collection of Mead's published essays can be found in Reck 1964. Mead's papers are held in the Department of Special Collections at the Regenstein Library of the University of Chicago.

Company. In 1887, Mead enrolled at Harvard, where he studied with Josiah Royce. Interestingly, he did not study with William James, though he spent a summer at his vacation home in Chocorua, serving as a tutor for the James children (Mead 1992). Upon receiving his master's degree, Mead went to Germany in the fall of 1888 to work on his Ph.D. He first went to Leipzig, where he studied with Wilhelm Wundt, and then to Berlin, where he studied with Wilhelm Dilthey. Wundt's theory of gestures made a lasting impression on Mead and forms the core of his semiotics. From Dilthey, Mead learned that we can only understand individuals when we study them in their social, cultural, and historic contexts. In addition, Mead was deeply influenced by C. Lloyd Morgan (especially his concept of emergence), Henri Bergson, and the later Alfred North Whitehead.

In the end, Mead did not complete his Ph.D. because in 1891 he was offered a position at the University of Michigan to teach philosophy and psychology. At Michigan, Mead became a close friend of John Dewey. In 1894, Mead followed Dewey to the newly established University of Chicago, where he became one of the central figures in the Chicago school of pragmatism. He was also involved with Jane Addams's Hull House. Among the students Mead influenced at Chicago were the sociologists Herbert Blumer and Ellsworth Faris, the psychologist John B. Watson, and the philosopher-semiotician Charles W. Morris. Though Dewey left in 1904, Mead remained at Chicago until his death on 26 April 1931.

A Philosophy of the Act

As noted, Mead's starting point is neither mind nor matter, but the act. Acts are constrained by the world in which we live, and through interaction with that world—assuming favorable conditions—acting gives rise to awareness, self-awareness, mind, and society. In this process objects, reaching all the way down to subatomic particles, solidify, so to speak, as things that can be acted upon, even if only in principle, or they are derivatives thereof. Mead's approach is behaviorist, in that he explains all mental processes in terms of behavior. His approach differs, however, from that of traditional behaviorists. In contrast to his student, the behaviorist psychologist John B. Watson, and later figures such as B. F. Skinner, Mead insists that behavior cannot be studied in isolation.[2] Advocating a social behaviorism, Mead rejected the laboratory-style approach where subjects are taken from their natural surroundings and studied in tightly controlled situations aimed at isolating very narrowly defined stimulus–response reactions. Following Dewey, Mead rejected the one-dimensional stimulus–response scheme favored by most behaviorists, in which it was presumed that stimulus and response could be neatly separated, as if they were isolable events standing in a one-to-one causal relationship. Instead, Mead maintained, as did Dewey, that stimulus and response belong to a continuous nervous path, a reflex arc. The attitude of the organism—what it thinks is important given its current state and its psycho-physical history—determines what it will react to, what it will ignore, etc. A wildebeest stimulates a lion differently when the lion is hungry than when the lion has just finished a meal. In Mead's view, there is also no sharp separation between the organism and the environment; they are the joint product of a process that shaped them both. This is not to deny that there is a certain asymmetry: the environment is not at the mercy of the organism to the degree that the organism is at the mercy of the environment. Traditional stimulus–response behaviorism makes too sharp a distinction between the individual and its environment, which invites the misconception that you can study people's behavior in a laboratory setting.

Mead's general approach closely resembles that of Charles Peirce in his well-known article "The Fixation of Belief", albeit that Mead, like Dewey, formulated the issue more directly in biological terms. Where Peirce speaks of belief, Mead speaks of homeostatic equilibrium, and where Peirce speaks of doubt, Mead talks about the organism's inhibition to act caused by conflicting tendencies about what to do next. The occurrence of conflicting tendencies to act, Mead terms a *problematic situation* (Dewey prefers to speak of an indeterminate situation).[3] Within the problematic situation, the organism is "out of tune" with its environment. Mead sees the problematic situation as the source of consciousness. A direct or habitual satisfaction of desires goes by unawares; it is only when we are confronted with a problem that inhibits our action that we become aware of the world in which we live. For Mead,

---

[2] John B. Watson's classic paper is "Psychology as the Behaviorist Views It", *Psychological Review*, 20 (1913): 158–77.

[3] In an indeterminate situation the organism doesn't know how to continue; it is a state of discordance. For Dewey, formulating what the problem is puts us already well on our way to the solution. I think this is correct, and that Mead's problematic situation is best understood as an indeterminate situation, not as a situation in which a certain problem has been identified.

consciousness is relational; it is not some ethereal substance. When someone turns off the lights in a room, Mead argues, he is no longer conscious of the objects in the room. Consequently, "the losing of consciousness does not mean the loss of a certain entity, but merely the cutting-off of one's relations with experiences" (Mead 1936: 393).

Mead divides the act into four stages: impulse, perception, manipulation, and consummation. The impulse sets the organism in motion, whereas consummation marks the satisfaction of the desire that initiated the act. Hence, consummation brings the act to a close. This should not be taken as a linear chain of responses to neatly self-contained problematic situations. Organisms often multitask, and problematic situations are typically nested, as when an animal in its search for food is being attacked by a predator.

For the most part, however, impulses are routinely connected with their consummation. What happens in a problematic situation is that the habitual connection between impulse and consummation is thwarted. This gives us the first intermediary phase: perception. In perception the environment opens itself up to the individual. Instead of the traditional distinction between the five senses, Mead distinguishes between contact and distance experience. *Contact experience* is the environment as it appears in immediate unmediated physical opposition, as in a wholly unexpected strike against the back of the head. There is no anticipation, and the experience itself gives no indication as to what happened beyond the direct effect upon the recipient. With *distance experience*, relatively insignificant contact experiences—such as airwaves hitting the eardrum—become signs for possible future contact experiences, allowing the individual to anticipate them. Thus, when I see a ball coming at me, I can modify my behavior so as to seek or avoid the contact experiences associated with the ball.

The third phase is that of manipulation, which is characterized by the interplay of contact and distance experience. In manipulation things are at once seen and felt, which brings together both the promise of contact and its fulfillment. For humans, this is primarily a matter of eye–hand coordination, but for other organisms this may play out differently. For dogs, for instance, "manipulation" is mostly a matter of coordinating nose and mouth. In Mead's view, our conception of physical objects is a product of this manipulation phase. It is hard to ignore the enormous extent to which the hand regulates how we see the world. Distance experiences are invariably understood as past or anticipated manipulatory experiences. When we see a hammer, we see it as something we can grasp. When we see a tree, we see it as something we can climb. Even the moon looks like something we could touch if only our arms were long enough to reach it. Because physical objects represent bundles of manipulatory acts, Mead calls them *collapsed acts*.

On this view, it would be impossible for entirely disembodied spirits to develop the concept of physical object as we know it. For that one needs hands. Our knowledge is an embodied knowledge. In fact, for Mead, the hand, with its juxtaposition of the thumb, is in many respects more characteristic of human intelligence than the brain.

Though Mead makes surprisingly little reference to pragmatism when discussing his philosophy of the act, it is easy to see pragmatism at work in his discussions of the four phases of the act. For instance, the meaning of all distance experiences is determined by the contact experiences we anticipate, given certain courses of action, and (physical) objects are understood in terms of what we can do with them, or by our habitual reactions to them. It is not just that meaning and truth are related to practical consequences, but that action is positioned at the very center of how the world is being comprehended. It is through action that we shape our world. This fits very well with Peirce's pragmatic maxim, which also draws a close connection between thought and action. The pragmatic maxim runs as follows: "Consider what effects, which might conceivably have practical bearings, we conceive the object of our conception to have. Then, our conception of these effects is the whole of our conception of the object" (Peirce 1992: 132). Instead of connecting our conceptions with some type of Platonic world of ideas, Peirce and the pragmatists connect them with the world within which we act. And this is precisely what Mead is doing as well.

THE OBJECTIVE REALITY OF PERSPECTIVES

From his philosophy of the act, and under the influence of the theories of relativity of Einstein and Whitehead, Mead develops a perspectivist theory of reality on which perspectives are not merely subjective mental states of observers, but are objectively there in nature; they are what things are made of. Using Whitehead's terminology, Mead identifies a perspective as a consentient set that is constituted by its relation to a percipient event.[4] A perspective,

---

[4] See Whitehead (1925). In the chapter on scientific relativity, Whitehead writes that "each rigid body defines its own space", adding that "the complete set of bodies, actual or hypothetical, which

then, is an enduring pattern that exhibits a sort of unity. More directly in biological terms, a perspective endures insofar as nature is patient with the organism. The problematic situation discussed above thus occasions a change of the perspective mediated through the two intermediate phases of the act. When analyzing the natural world and our relationship with it, Mead's central notion is not the traditional notion of substance, but that of opposition. For Mead, life is always situated within an environment that at once sustains it and opposes it; or, to put it more exactly, the environment *sustains the organism precisely by opposing it*. Birds can fly because the air resists the push of their wings; the housepainter can climb his ladder because the steps resist his feet; the baseball player can make a strike because the ball resists the swing of her bat. In the end, the individual's relation with its environment runs through contact experiences. Within contact experiences the environment is at once opposed to the individual and united with it. Contact experience shows the two to be of the same kind, at least in some respects, because there are points of contact.

Mead's conception of interaction in terms of perspectives can be broadened to include "any unitary structure, whose nature demands a period within which to be itself"; such structure is both spatial and temporal, and hence should properly be called a process. Because of his focus on opposition rather than substance, Mead moves away from a traditional substance-attribute metaphysics toward a process metaphysics, a move that is accompanied by a shift from a subject–predicate logic to a logic of relations. By taking this approach, Mead also reverses the traditional classification of the sciences wherein physics is thought to be more fundamental than biology, as he extends the model for organic environments to include physics. Inanimate objects have their perspectives too; they are shaped and sustained by their interactions with other perspectives.

In Mead's view, perspectives are objective: they are the objective product of the life history and physical constitution of the organism. The train passenger who looks out of the window sees the landscape differently from someone who is standing close to the tracks: for the passenger, the telephone poles next to the tracks will be seen as flashing by rapidly; for someone not on the train

---

agree in their space-formation will be called a 'consentient' set" (p. 31). Later, having just defined perception as "an awareness of events, or happenings, forming a partially discerned complex within the background of a simultaneous whole of nature", Whitehead characterizes a "percipient event" as the awareness of one event, or group of events, within this discerned complex (p. 68). To my knowledge, Mead never clearly defines the terms.

they appear as a static string reaching from horizon to horizon. Nonetheless, the passenger's perspective is not unique to him; it is one he shares with everyone else on the train who looks out of the window—it is an objective perspective. We could say that, for Mead, there is one reality, which is the open-ended cluster of perspectives, while there are countless actual worlds, as actual worlds are always relative to a perspective.

Mead empathically denies that such perspectives are distortions, subjective or otherwise, of a world that is independent of any particular vantage point. Because of differences in our particular life histories, grass will have a slightly different meaning for you than it has for me. Grass in Holland is much softer (and greener) than the grass in Indiana, which in turn is significantly softer than the grass in South Florida, three places where I have lived. Moreover, due to differences in physical constitution, grass is something quite different for me than for a cow or a beetle. Mead denies that beyond these different perspectives there is such a thing as "the real grass", the grass as it is in and of itself, independently of *any* perspective. Instead, when I say that the cow, the beetle, and I all see the same grass, this is only a confused way of saying that the cow, the beetle, and I, all see *my* grass. For Mead, all we can say is that what we call grass can enter into other perspectives.

Perspectives intersect when elements from one perspective enter into another. For instance, the bee that travels from flower to flower in search of pollen enters the consentient sets of the plants it visits. Mead speaks in this context of the *principle of sociality*; it speaks to the capacity of being multiple things at once. For Mead, the principle of sociality is also the principle of novelty (or *emergence* as he calls it, following C. Lloyd Morgan's terminology), when elements that enter into other perspectives are set into new contexts. As Mead puts it, "there arises something that was not there before . . . we are in a new world" (1938: 641). Hence, for Mead, there is not, first, a fully formed object that subsequently enters different consentient sets where it is distorted, but objects are always themselves constituted by the multiple perspectives through which they are sustained. This happens to the bee, which in its search for food becomes a vehicle for the fertilization and thus the propagation of plants. The act of feeding becomes simultaneously the act of pollination, and the act of pollination endures only as long as the bee continues its search for food. In its search for food, the bee physically enters into other perspectives. As will be shown later, it is characteristic of the human organism that it can position itself not only *physically* in other perspectives, which is what the bee does, but also *mentally*, allowing it to incorporate the standpoints of those perspectives into its own. The human capacity to position itself mentally in other perspectives creates the illusion of the possibility an all-knowing spectator, and of reality as what is perceived by such an all-knowing spectator.

For Mead, a perspective is thus not a subjective distortion of a noumenal reality that lies beyond and is independent of how anyone would see it, and of which each perspective is some sort of distortion; it is an objective and dynamic result of interaction. Recall that, in Mead's philosophy of the act, awareness is a product of problems, of encounters with things that at once obstruct and make possible. This makes the very notion of reality as what would open up to an all-knowing, disinterested spectator a conceptual impossibility, because for such a spectator there would be no problems requiring resolution. Consequently, for Mead, there is no ultimate reality, no independent benchmark to determine the veridicality of any perspective. The universe is, as William James put it, a multiverse (1912: 325). Perspectives are real, they encroach upon one another, they collide, appropriate, etc.; by generating opposition, they both limit one another and allow for the emergence of new things. Like James, Mead believes that we live in an open universe that is still pregnant with real possibility. Though Mead's perspectivist approach applies to all nature, including the inorganic as well as the organic world, I will focus in what follows on human interaction and the perspectives to which this gives rise.

Human Interaction and the Emergence of Self

The consequences of one's acts are seldom limited to one's own perspective. The doe that stirs up and flees from the hunter not only betrays her presence, but also leaves behind the tracks that guide the hunter in his pursuit. For Mead, acts are by nature social. Organisms routinely enter into situations that involve other organisms. The mechanism discussed above equally applies here. Taking the indeterminate situation again as his point of departure, and extrapolating upon Wilhelm Wundt's theory of gestures, Mead distinguishes between two types of interaction: interaction between organisms without selves and interaction between organisms with selves (Mead 1934: 42).[5] The

---

[5] See also Wundt (1900–20), i, or *idem* (1973). See also Darwin (1872).

first he calls the sign situation; the second he calls the symbol situation. Interestingly, Mead seems to have been unaware of Peirce's work in this area.[6] In a way this is not surprising, because Peirce's work in semiotics remained largely unpublished until the *Collected Papers* appeared in the early 1930s, shortly after Mead's death.[7]

In the *sign situation* the overt aspects of the acts of one individual enter into the intermediate phases of the acts of other individuals. For instance, in a dogfight the first overt signs of the behavior of one dog, such as a display of teeth, form the stimulus for the other dog to respond to. Consequently, the acts initiated by the dogs are seldom brought to completion. Because the dogs do not get beyond the first overt phases of their acts, the dogfight reduces to what Mead calls "a conversation of gestures".

It is important to realize, though, what is *not* happening here. Within the sign situation the gestures that control the interaction have no shared meaning. The dogs have no idea how the overt aspects of their behavior are *received* by other dogs. The gnarling dog associates its display of teeth not with the fear it arouses in another dog, but with its own mental states that it has come to associate with the act of gnarling in the presence of other dogs. Especially, when gnarling routinely chases away rival dogs, this sensation is unlikely ever to become that of fear, which is the sensation experienced by the fleeing dogs. Because in the sign situation the individual is unaware of how others experience his gestures, the individual is unable to respond to his own gestures from the standpoint of others. The sign situation functions because within the interaction the various perspectives fit together more or less like the pieces of a jigsaw puzzle. The individuals involved are aware only of their own perspective; they have no concept of the social act (such as the dogfight) in which they are playing their part. Nonetheless, the meaning of such gestures is decidedly pragmatic in nature, as their meaning is couched in terms of their practical consequences, or, in a more Peircean

---

[6] The semiotician Charles W. Morris wrote his 1925 dissertation, "Symbolism and Reality", under Mead's direction. Though there is a cursory discussion of Ogden and Richards (1923), which contains a thirteen-page discussion of Peirce's semiotics in Appendix D, it appears that Morris learned of the book only in a very late stage in his dissertation work (p. 48). Peirce is not mentioned in the dissertation, not even in the chapter on sign theory and formal logic. Instead, Morris writes that his theory of symbolism is heavily indebted to Dewey and his instrumentalism (p. 9). (The page references are to Charles Morris's annotated copy of the dissertation that is part of the Charles W. Morris Collection held at the Institute for American Thought at IUPUI.)

[7] The first volume of *The Collected Papers of Charles Sanders Peirce*, ed. by Charles Hartshorne and Paul Weiss, appeared in the year of Mead's death; a notable exception is Appendix D of Ogden and Richards (1923.).

vein, the habits they elicit.[8] Mead's discussion of animal interaction clearly reveals his semiotic bent, and, like Peirce, he combines pragmatism with semiotics.

Although humans also interact at the level of the sign situation, they are capable of a different type of interaction as well, which Mead calls the *symbol situation*. When I throw a ball to someone else, I adjust my act depending on how I expect the other will react to the approaching ball. This I do by mentally projecting myself into the other person's place. According to Mead, this type of interaction requires that I possess a self. For Mead, the self is formed within the process of interaction. Initially, the individual does not consider itself part of the world it perceives, but sees the latter rather as through a peephole. Mead speaks in this context of a Cyclopean eye. This radical separation between the inner and the outer world developed into a classic paradigm of philosophy in the form of a rigid mind–body dichotomy and a rigid inner–outer dichotomy. For Mead, however, this separation marks only the early phase of our epistemic predicament, one that is soon replaced by another of a very different kind. According to Mead, continued interaction with this so-called outer world causes one object in particular to stand out. This object is different from all the others, in that in my interactions with it I am at once the initiator of the act and the recipient of the act. The crucial difference between me pinching my arm and me pinching, say, a pear, is that when I pinch my arm, I am at once aware of the act of pinching and the sensation it causes in the object, which is not the case when I pinch a pear. It is through a prolonged interaction of the individual with this particular object, as well as the objects that surround it, that the individual begins to realize that it *is* itself this object, and consequently that it is itself an object among objects. For Mead, the moment an organism begins to recognize itself as an object among objects marks the origin of the self. Consequently, the self and physical objects emerge together as each other's correlate; and, like physical objects, the self is in effect a collapsed act, albeit one of a very peculiar kind.

Now Mead very strictly limits the capacity for the development of a self—that is, the capacity to recognize oneself as an object among objects—to human beings; this notwithstanding the fact that there are other organisms that can experience directly the consequences of their acts, as with a dog licking its wounds or hearing itself bark. However, for Mead, the crux to

---

[8] Though phrased more directly in biological terms, Mead's approach is very close to Peirce's in "The Fixation of Belief" and "How to Make Our Ideas Clear". See, e.g., Peirce 1992.

the development of the self is the hand with the juxtaposition of the thumb, because what is required is a conception of objects that gives them (and this includes our own body as one of them) sufficient spatial-temporal solidity for the individual to be able to engage in the mental projection. According to Mead, eye–hand coordination allows this, assuming that the organism has a sufficiently well developed central nervous system, while nose–mouth coordination, or eye–ear coordination falls short of it.[9] The hand can grasp something, completely enclose small objects, delineate the contours of larger things, etc., and allows for an intricate interplay with the eye, thus establishing through manipulation a strong connection between contact and distance experiences.

Assuming we side with Mead in that only hand–eye coordination, or something sufficiently similar to it, can generate a self, two remarks can still be made. First, though Mead himself denies this, there may be other organisms besides humans that can develop selves along these lines. Evidence obtained from primate research suggests that there are (see Gallup 1970, 1975). Second, a strong dichotomy between self-endowed and non-self-endowed organisms seems untenable. There is rather a wide variety of cases, and Mead's approach can prove a viable research paradigm for assessing the behavior, intelligence, awareness, and even world view of a variety of animals by combining his social behaviorism with his notion of the problematic situation and his philosophy of the act.[10]

So what does the world look like for a self-endowed individual? Our own body resists our touch like other objects. The experience of resistance—say, when we push our hand against a heavy door—resembles the experience of pushing that same hand against our forehead. At the same time there is a notable difference. When I push my hand against my forehead, I experience not only the resistance of my head against my hand (as with the heavy door), but I also experience the pressure of my hand against my head. The latter is absent when pushing the door; that is to say, I do not feel how the door is affected by my pushing hand. Mead argues, more generally, that the opposition that the individual experiences from the objects in its environment mirrors

---

[9] Whereas eye–mouth coordination, like eye–hand coordination, connects distance experiences with contact experiences, eye–ear coordination only connects one set of distance experiences with another set of distance experiences.

[10] Other experiments have shown that there is reason to suspect that other animals may have selves as well. See, e.g., Beninger *et al.* (1974). There is also a blossoming field of zoosemiotics. See, e.g., Sebeok (1972).

the force the individual exerts upon those objects. Put briefly, I push against a closed door, and the door, so to speak, *pushes* back. I push harder, and the door pushes harder too, until either of us gives way. More generally, the individual projects his or her own perspective, which is the only frame of reference it has, into the objects with which it interacts. In sum, the individual first recognizes other objects *as things that resemble itself.* That is to say, it ascribes its own inner nature to the objects that surround it, one of which is its own body. The pain experienced when bumping against a table is not just experienced, but also projected into the table: if I am in pain, the table must be in pain too. Like the attribution of (future) contact experiences to distance experiences, this projection is always hypothetical, and is being corrected, or fine-tuned, through prolonged interaction. In the course of interaction the individual learns to differentiate between different kinds of objects based on their response patterns. What sets stones apart from trees, trees from squirrels, squirrels from people, and other people from ourselves, is that they systematically, and persistently, react differently to our advances; hence, they elicit different response patterns.

MEAD'S THEORY OF PLAY AND GAMES

For Mead, the individual's understanding of itself, and of others, is deepened through a process of role-playing, play being the most rudimentary form of conscious activity outside of the problematic situation. It is free, in that the individual is not subjected to the need to solve some pressing problem, like finding food or shelter. Limiting ourselves to self-endowed organisms, play involves the individual projecting itself into other objects, most significantly fellow humans, and playing their roles. In this early stage the child plays consecutively the roles of mother, doctor, babysitter, etc., without integrating them into a social whole in which they all have their part. The individual is wholly immersed in the role it is playing at the moment. It *is* a child, a mother, a doctor, etc. There is not some unified "something" that plays the role of child, mother, doctor, etc., and that can be distinguished from the roles that are being played.

In play the individual plays the roles of others, and responds to them, thus generating "the material out of which he builds up consciousness of others and of self" (Mead 1982: 61); or, as Mead puts it elsewhere (in agreement with his views on the emergence of physical objects and the self), "the individual *is an other before it is a self*" (Mead 1982: 168; emphasis added).

Over time, the roles played by the child become integrated into what Mead terms "games". In a *game*, like soccer, hide-and-seek, baseball, or black jack, different roles are brought together into a common activity that has a structure of its own. The shift from mere play to playing games marks a crucial step for Mead. In a game, roles are brought into unity through rules that determine what counts as a move in the game and what does not. The rules of the game, not the individual actors, determine how each role is to be played. Thus the individual learns to judge its own acts, and those of others, by relating them to the abstract perspective of the rules of the game and the roles that the game allows. Because of this, the unity of the game enables a self that goes beyond a mere aggregate of roles.

Games have their own purpose, which may be different from the aims of any of its players. As Mead puts it, the object of the game resides not in any of the individuals playing the game, but in the life process of the group. Mead terms such objects *social objects*. Individuals can grasp those objects by distancing themselves from their own role and taking the attitude of the group that is playing the game, which is something they can do because they can run mentally through the different roles that constitute the game to see how the different roles hang together. As shown below, this is how in Mead's view social institutions develop. When it comes down to it, all social institutions are in effect games.

According to Mead, one's self is a product of the roles one plays and the games in which one participates. Some of those roles one will be conscious of, while others are acquired unconsciously.[11] The daughter of a dominant mother may play the role of a dominant mother long before she has any children of her own, and without ever realizing she is doing it. It is a role she acquired (and plays) unconsciously. The roles one is conscious of contribute to one's self-image. For instance, someone may understand herself as a spouse, a lover, a mother, a former lawyer, a daughter, a sibling, a long distance runner, a decent cook, an African American, etc. Her self will be unified insofar as these roles (as well as those she plays unconsciously) form a consistent whole, and because all these roles connect to the same physical body.

---

[11] This should not be taken as a stark dichotomy, but rather as a continuum of being more and less aware. The situation is further complicated by the circumstance that roles are related not only to selves, but also to games, each of which comes with its own structure, part of which may escape the player.

The extent to which the self can develop itself is, for Mead, determined in part by the individual's capacity for playing roles—that is, by its capacity to assume the attitudes of others. However, it depends also on the expectations of others. Roles are social objects rather than individual assets. What makes someone a pitcher is that everyone wants him to throw the ball. What makes someone a surgeon is that others allow her to cut into other humans on the assumption that doing so will cure them. Selves are social. Our selves cannot be clearly separated from the selves of others, Mead argues, "since our own selves exist and enter as such into our experience only in so far as the selves of others exist and enter as such into our experience" (Mead 1934: 164).

Some roles one is very conscious of; others one is not even aware of. Some roles are very specific, like being the highest-ranking partner in a Washington DC law firm, whereas others, such as being a Christian, a taxpayer, or a citizen, are more general. One of the most general roles one can play is that of *generalized other*. The generalized other is not the other in this or that specialized role, but solely in the role of human being as such. Just as an individual can interpret himself or his acts from the perspective of his former self, his peers, his parents, the police, or a judge, so he can interpret them from the perspective of the generalized other—that is, from the perspective of the other with all specialized interests removed. When adopting this attitude, the individual takes, as it were, a seat in the audience and looks as a disinterested spectator at the roles it is playing and the games it is involved in. Role-playing and participation in games bring multiple perspectives together, and for Mead it is ultimately the perspective of the generalized other that gives to the individual his unity of self. Incidentally, it was William James who provided Mead with a real-life model of a unified self. In the early 1920s, Mead wrote, reminiscing about his encounters with James: "I have never known another man in whom I have realized that every part of his nature was organized in a consistent self. There seemed to be nothing suppressed. He felt and thought and acted as a whole, so that everything he said and did took on a unique value because he said and did it" (Mead 1992: 590).

For Mead, the perspective of the generalized other is also the perspective of reason. We are not born rational, as if rationality were an instinct or a predisposition instilled in us directly by God; instead, we acquire it when gaining the perspective of the human community. By casting rationality in terms of taking the perspective of generalized other, Mead developed a full-bodied conception of human reason that embraces more than mere calculating intelligence or practical problem-solving ability (what Heidegger calls *das rechnende Denken*). In fact, our intelligence is not what makes us human. It is an aspect of the manipulation phase of the act, and as such it does not require a self. By making human rationality something that is firmly rooted in the process of role-playing, and by thus making empathy and solidarity core components of it, the rationality we associate with ourselves becomes allied more with wisdom than with mere intelligence.

The perspective of the generalized other also lies at the root of morality. Morality, Mead argues, consists in the individual taking the attitude of the generalized other toward his own acts as well as those of others. Morality is thus directly related to the process of role-playing, as role-playing enables the individual to look at himself, as it were, from the vantage point of others. By relating morality to taking the attitude of the generalized other, Mead closely aligned himself with the Golden Rule, which becomes the following: one should always act toward others as one would want others to act toward oneself. Moral judgments are universal, in that they are made from the perspective of the generalized other, meaning that everyone who would take that perspective and is able to sufficiently to appreciate the situation would come to the same judgment. Consequently, the individual's ability to gain a moral consciousness depends on its capacity for entering the perspective of the generalized other. For Mead there is no essential difference between self-criticism and being criticized by others. In both instances certain behavior is viewed from the same perspective: namely, that of the generalized other. Self-criticism is nothing but social criticism internalized, to which the psycho-physical makeup and life history of the individual give a certain flavor. Hence, the social agreement on moral judgments is not a mere external affair in which independent and autonomous individuals surrender their personal beliefs to the opinions of society; rather, it constitutes an integral part of who they are.

In conclusion, in Mead's view, the self reaches its highest grade when the individual comes to understand itself and others in terms of the generalized other. This is not a capability one has received at birth, but is something that is acquired through interaction with others.

LANGUAGE AND MIND

Mead introduced the term "*significant symbol*" to capture the communication specific to self-endowed individuals. Significant symbols are gestures that elicit the same (in the sense of being functionally identical) response in the person making the gesture as in those to whom the gesture is directed. Mead paid particular attention to the *vocal gesture*, as it is a prime example of a gesture that is perceived alike by sign-maker and sign receiver. When I shout to you "Look out!", I am inadvertently also addressing myself, because I too hear what I shout. It evokes the same reaction in the two of us, my own reaction being a suppressed form of what I want you to do (that is to say, it manifests itself in me as a disposition, a tendency, or a readiness).

In solid pragmatic fashion, the tendency to respond to a sign—and this includes significant symbols—constitutes, for Mead, its meaning (recall Peirce's pragmatic maxim quoted above). It is not, however, my *individual* tendency to respond that gives the sign its meaning but how people in my linguistic community tend to respond to it. What we say has meaning only when it is a valid move in a game such as the English language. This is not to deny that such a game is flexible. Take, for instance, James Joyce's *Finnegans Wake*, where the rules of the game are stretched almost to the limit.[12] In Mead's view, linguistic signs have meaning because the speakers of the language position themselves in a general role—which is ultimately that of the generalized other—from which to interpret the sign. You understand my statement "It smells like gas in here", by taking the role of the generalized other. Put briefly, within linguistic conversation, individuals communicate using significant symbols while taking the role of the generalized other. It is the perspective of the generalized other within a certain linguistic community that gives linguistic symbols their meaning.

By invoking the same tendency to act in sign-maker and sign-receiver, significant symbols enable a level of communication that extends far beyond the sign situation. It provides the individual with a high level of control over the responses of others; individuals can even map out whole strategies involving multiple others by mentally running though entire conversations of gestures. Language also brings the process of role-playing described above onto a higher plane. Instead of actually *playing* the roles of her peers, her parents, the school principal, etc., the teenager who is asked by a friend to skip school will merely ask herself, "What will my parents think when they find out?", "What will the principal do?", "Will my friends reject me when I say no?", etc.

---

[12] Theo Lalleman, under the pseudonym of Leon E. Thalma, once began the heroic project of a Dutch translation of *Finnegans Wake*. Parts of this translation appeared in *De Nieuwe Weelde*, 1 (1986): 25; 2 (1986): 17; 3 (1987): 41.

Having interpreted the self as a composite of roles, partially organized in a multiplicity of games and built on the individual's awareness that he is himself an object among objects, Mead developed his view of the mind as a product of the internalization of part of the individual's self-directed interaction, mostly through vocal gestures. Thought, for Mead, is literally the individual talking to himself with the outward signs (such as sound and movement of the lips) suppressed, so that the mind develops as something private.[13] Thinking is nothing but the interaction of the individual with itself through significant symbols, so that there is no difference in kind between thinking and talking to others. This identification of thought with speech is already present in Plato, who explicitly identified thought with silent speech in the *Sophist*. Since mind refers to a conversation of the individual with itself through significant symbols, it is by nature social. All thought comes in the form of a dialogue. In this process, Mead observes, "It is only through taking the role of the other that [the individual] is able to come back on himself and so direct his own process of communication" (Mead 1934: 254).

Mead also discussed this interaction of the individual with himself in terms of the *I* and the *me*. The *I* is the ungraspable dynamic force behind our acts; it is how the impulse presents itself to us. It is ungraspable because it can enter consciousness only *after the act*. For Mead, we always appear to ourselves as a historical figure — as a *me*. The *me* is how we understand ourselves, which is always a reconstruction, a narrative.

The interaction through significant symbols not only enables us consciously to condition others, but through our use of significant symbols we also (and often unconsciously) condition ourselves. In fact, what we generally call "our mind" is largely the internalization of the society within which we live by means of language. In an important sense, language, which is a social medium, dictates our thoughts. Since linguistic symbols, as shown already, ultimately derive their meaning from the perspective of the generalized other, thinking can be described, as does Mead, as "a conversation carried on by the individual between himself and the generalized other" (1934: 254). Put differently, thinking involves a conditioning of the self from the perspective of the generalized other through the medium of language. In short, for Mead, mind is internalized, self-controlled, and self-directed linguistic behavior.

---

[13] This view is also found in John B. Watson's 1913 paper, in Wyczoikowska (1913), and more than a decade before that, in Curtis (1900). It is also found in Charles Peirce's 1868 "Some Questions Concerning Faculties Claimed for Man" (in Peirce 1992: esp. 22 f.)

That thought, for Mead, is nothing but a mode of behavior, makes Mead an ontological behaviorist. Unlike hand gestures, thought is behavior that is almost entirely internalized, thereby making the mind inaccessible to others. However, this inaccessibility is not different in kind from the lack of access a blind person has to another's facial expressions; no special substratum is needed to explain this phenomenon. Another aspect that sets the mind apart from a (linguistic) conversation with others is that when the individual converses with himself, he not only has a high degree of control of the symbols he uses, but also of how he replies to them—even though in both cases the control is far from absolute.

Thus, far from the Cartesian idea of the mind as an autonomous inner realm that comes to the world with its own innate ideas, which it subsequently applies to all it encounters, the mind develops, for Mead, outside-in as the internalization of outward, self-directed behavior. Consequently, Mead did not situate the mind in a particular part of the body, such as the brain, the heart, the lungs, or the pineal gland. Instead, he situated the mind in the conversation the individual has with him or herself. The mind's main alliance is thus not with the individual, but with society. The mind is not so much an intrinsic part of the individual, but rather, the individual partakes in the spirit of the time. In Peirce's words, thought is not in us, but we are in thought (though Mead's inspiration is Dilthey). It is primarily because of our privileged access to mind, or thought, and the amount of control we seem to exercise over it, that we have come to refer to it as "our mind". But both are relative. Sometimes others have a clearer sense of what we think or feel than we do, and our most private thoughts can be utterly beyond our own control, as is the case when we cannot stop mulling something over. In the end, the mind is an imprint of the individual's relations with its environment. It is a conditioning of the individual through the generalized other as it is manifested in the language. For Mead, one only becomes human through the interaction with others, and only insofar as one becomes a member of the human community. To phrase it a bit more paradoxically, one becomes an individual through social control.

Mead's conception of the mind is thoroughly pragmatistic. It is not just that action is the benchmark of our thought, but our thought itself is action. Moreover, since for Mead thought is an internalized conversation with vocal gestures, the pragmatic approach to intelligent behavior as the individual's reaction to problematic situations where habitual reactions fail applies to all thought. In fact, in thought the process of trial and error is internalized, so that the individual gains a much greater control over the problematic situation. Instead of trying out different strategies of action to find one that succeeds, facing in the process the consequences of each error, the individual is now able to sift the different strategies through its mind. In this mental process of trial and error certain habits emerge—so-called habits of thought—just as habits develop for other kinds of behavior (Mead 1934: 90).

SOCIETY

Society precedes the individual self, in that we are typically born into a society that is already there.[14] However, from an evolutionary perspective, self and society emerge together; the general biological principle that organism and environment determine each other applies here too. Mead distinguishes three basic principles through which societies are formed: physiological differentiation (as with colonies of ants, bees, or termites; but it also applies to multicellular organisms as they are in effect societies of differentiated cells), a herding instinct (as with buffalo or wildebeest), and the interaction through significant symbols. Though the first two principles play some role within human society (humans too have some herding instinct, and there is some physical differentiation, most significantly between the sexes), human society is shaped by and large through the exchange of significant symbols.

The ability of each individual mentally to put him or herself in the positions of others allows for complex patterns of interaction that go far beyond what a herding instinct makes possible and that do not require a pre-established physiological differentiation. Take three people who are carrying a tall sideboard up a narrow curved staircase. Putting themselves mentally into each other's positions enables them to coordinate their acts by anticipating what the others can or will do. In addition, they can communicate their views about what the others should do to make the entire enterprise successful. Furthermore, by relating the act to a future state they all agree upon (in this case moving a sideboard to the next floor), the desired outcome is not confined to the perspective of a single individual, as with the sign situation, but becomes a social goal. It is a goal of the group.

[14] There are occasional exceptions. For a discussion of a relatively recent case, see, e.g., Curtiss (1977).

Acts where the participating individuals are guided specifically by the perspective of the group Mead calls *social acts*. The dogfight discussed above is not a social act, as the dogs involved stay trapped in their own perspective: there is no awareness of the dogfight as a self-contained unit that has a purpose and a logic of its own. The situation is different with the small group of people carrying the sideboard up the stairs. What guides their acts is the perspective of the group, and it is this perspective that gives the acts a purpose that goes beyond their individual perspectives. Here the participants comprehend the entire act by positioning themselves in many perspectives (actual ones as well as imagined ones). For Mead, the social act is thus an act the object of which is not confined to the individual perspectives of any of the individuals involved in it, but in what he called the life process of the group itself (Mead 1964: 280). Mead calls the object of a social act a *social object*.

Social acts can develop into the most complex social institutions, such as immigration law, open-heart surgery, or daycare. Consistent with his behaviorism, Mead identifies such institutions as crystallized patterns of interaction; they are "the habits of individuals in their interrelation with each other" (Mead 1936: 366). Institutions are possible, Mead argues, where the community takes participating individuals into account only insofar as they play a particular role, whether it is the role of sales clerk, customer, police officer, surgeon, judge, or teacher. For instance, the institution of debt is possible only when we take certain people specifically in their roles of debtors and creditors—that is, independently of whether they are also diabetics, Latinos, television addicts, or good at telling jokes. This brings Mead's account of institutions fully in line with his philosophy of the act and his discussion of role-playing. In Mead's terms, social institutions can be interpreted as games; that is to say, what they come down to is structured role-playing. Like physical objects and like the self, institutions too are collapsed acts.

Classical liberalists tend to see institutions as external impediments that limit individual freedom and autonomy, leading them to the opinion that fewer institutions *ipso facto* means more freedom. This view is in part the outcome of the Cartesian notion that individuals have their identity already formed before they enter into society, so that the influence of the interaction with others has only a marginal or accidental effect. For Mead, in contrast, the individual self is decidedly a product of its interaction with others: we are the roles we play, and we are shaped by the games in which we participate. As a result, Mead has a very different notion of institutions than the one prevalent in classical liberalism. Institutions should not be looked at as *external* tools or impediments, but they are, in fact, the stuff that selves are made of. We *are* taxpayers, lawyers, homeowners, athletes, etc.; the institutions are within us. Rather than restricting our freedom, institutions enhance our potential, because it is through them that we develop our selves. One can never become a famous opera singer without a multitude of institutions that make that role possible. There is no such thing as a radical divide between individuals and society.

CONCLUSION

The primacy Mead gives to the act, his notion that awareness arises within the problematic situation, and his analysis of the human mind, all clearly situate Mead within the pragmatist camp. Mead did not just argue that thought emerges from action; he went much further by arguing that thought is nothing but action internalized, so that there is no principal difference between a philosophy of the act and a philosophy of mind. What in Mead's view characterizes pragmatism is the "radical position that in immediate experience the percept stands over against the individual, not in a relation of awareness, but simply in that of conduct" (Mead 1964: 271). We grasp what we see in terms of what we can do with it.

Given Mead's account of self and mind, the notion of a disinterested spectator, who, like an omniscient God or the all-knowing narrator of a novel, can see everything "exactly as it is", is untenable. Consequently, such a perspective cannot be taken as a benchmark to distinguish the true from the false. The theory of relativity enables Mead to develop a perspectivist view of reality that circumvents the standard pitfalls of relativism and skepticism, as it allows for perspectives to be objectively there as the basic constituents of the universe. This position allows Mead to maintain that there is something "out there" that confronts us within the problematic situation. However, we do not come to know this "something" by acquiring a sort of mental representation of it that then can be compared, at least ideally, with that of an omniscient, disinterested spectator; we come to know it by learning how to deal with it. For Mead, as for Dewey, we mold our world from what is presented to us through our dealings with what confronts us within the problematic situations we encounter. The furthest we can get in this process is systematically to devise problematic situations, very much like the experimental scientist, and thus extend the scope of our knowledge.

Like Dewey, Mead related truth not to the individual's wishes being satisfied, but to what resolves the problem that is objectively there, and sometimes the desires of the individual are the cause of the problem. Moreover, since we are beings with selves, and because many of our acts are social acts the consummation of which requires the cooperation of others, the majority of those problematic situations are not mere personal affairs of isolated individuals. They are social objects, the meaning of which is constituted not by the idiosyncrasies of the individual and its circumstances, but by the community within which those individuals live and have their being. Mead rejects the atomistic notion of the individual, and the sharp separation of stimulus and response that often accompanies it. His pragmatism, is decidedly a social pragmatism, in which both the object of the act and its completion are not the private business of discrete individuals but are ostensibly social affairs.

To conclude, Mead is clearly a pragmatist, and he is a pragmatist who is definitely worth studying to a much greater extent than is currently done. In his works one finds the groundwork of a comprehensive and systematic philosophy that is both naturalist and pragmatist. His views have deep repercussions for areas ranging from metaphysics and epistemology to ethics, philosophy of mind, philosophy of science, political philosophy, and social philosophy.

REFERENCES

Aboulafia, Mitchell, (1986). *The Mediating Self: Mead, Sartre and Self-Determination.* New Haven: Yale University Press.

_____ (1991). *Philosophy, Social Theory, and the Thought of George Herbert Mead.* Albany, NY: State University of New York Press.

_____ (ed.) (2001). *The Cosmopolitan Self: George Herbert Mead and Continental Philosophy.* Urbana, IL: University of Illinois Press.

Baldwin, John D. (1986). *George Herbert Mead: A Unifying Theory for Sociology.* Beverly Hills, CA: Sage.

Beninger, R. J., *et al.* (1947). "The Ability of Rats to Discriminate their own Behaviors". *Canadian Journal of Psychology*, 28: 79–91.

Cook, Gary A. (1993). *George Herbert Mead: The Making of a Social Pragmatist.* Urbana, IL: University of Illinois Press.

Corti, Walter Robert (ed.) (2002). *The Philosophy of G. H. Mead.* Winterthur, Switzerland: Amriswiler Bucherei.

Curtis, H. S. (1900). "Automatic Movements of the Larynx". *American Journal of Psychology*, 11/2: 237–9.

Curtiss Susan (1977). *Genie: A Psycholinguistic Study of a Modern-Day Wild Child* New York: Academic Press.

Darwin, Charles (1872). *The Expression of the Emotions in Man and Animals*. London: J. Murray.

de Waal, Cornelis (2002). *On Mead*. Belmont, CA: Wadsworth.

Eames, Morris S. (2002). "Mead and the Pragmatic Conception of Truth". In Corti (2002), 135–52.

Gallup, Gordon G. (1970). "Chimpanzees: Self-Recognition". *Science*, 167: 86–7.

____ (1975). "Towards an Operational Definition of Self-Awareness". In R. Tuttle, (ed.), *Socio-ecology and Psychology of Primates*, The Hague: Mouton.

Gunter, P. A. Y. (1990). *Creativity in George Herbert Mead*. Lanham, MD: University Press of America.

Hamilton, Peter (1992). *George Herbert Mead: Critical Assessments*, 4 vols. New York: Routledge.

Hanson, Karen (1987). *The Self Imagined: Philosophical Reflections on the Social Character of Psyche*. New York: Routledge.

James, William (1912). *Essays in Radical Empiricism*. New York: Longmans, Green, and Co.

Joas, Hans (1997). *G. H. Mead: A Contemporary Re-examination of His Thought*. Cambridge, MA: MIT Press.

Kang, Wi Jo (1976). *G. H. Mead's Concept of Rationality: A Study of the Use of Symbols and Other Implements*. The Hague: Mouton.

Mead, George Herbert (1932). *The Philosophy of the Present*, ed. Arthur E. Murphy. Chicago: Open Court.

____ (1934). *Mind, Self, and Society from the Standpoint of a Social Behaviorist*, ed. Charles W. Morris. Chicago: University of Chicago Press.

____ (1936). *Movements of Thought in the Nineteenth Century*, ed. Merritt H. Moore. Chicago: University of Chicago Press.

____ (1938). *The Philosophy of the Act*, ed. Charles W. Morris. Chicago: University of Chicago Press.

____ (1964). *Selected Writings*, ed. Andrew J. Reck. Chicago: University of Chicago Press.

____ (1982). *The Individual and the Social Self: Unpublished Work of George Herbert Mead*, ed. David L. Miller. Chicago: University of Chicago Press.

____ (1992). "George Herbert Mead: An Unpublished Essay on Royce and James", ed. Gary A. Cook, *Transactions of the Charles S. Peirce Society*, 28/3: 583–92.

Miller, David L. (1973). *George Herbert Mead: Self, Language and the World*. Chicago: University of Chicago Press.

Mutaawe Kasozi, Ferdinand (1998). *Self and Social Reality in a Philosophical Anthropology: Inquiring into George Herbert Mead's Socio-philosophical Anthropology*. New York: Peter Lang.

Ogden, C. K., and Richards, I. A. (1923). *The Meaning of Meaning*. New York: Harcourt.

Peirce, C. S. (1992). *The Essential Peirce*, ed. Nathan Houser and Christian Kloesel. Bloomington: Indiana University Press.

Rosenthal, Sandra (1991). *Mead and Merleau-Ponty: Toward a Common Vision*. Albany, NY: State University of New York Press.

Sebeok, Thomas A. (1972). *Perspectives in Zoosemiotics*. The Hague: Mouton.

Shook, John R., and Ryan, Frank X. (2001). *The Chicago School of Pragmatism*, 4 vols. Bristol: Thoemmes Press.

Vaitkus, Steven (1991). *How is Society Possible? Intersubjectivity and the Fiduciary Attitude as Problems of the Social Group in Mead, Gurwitsch, and Schutz*. Dordrecht: Kluwer Academic Publishers.

Watson, John B. (1913). "Psychology as the Behaviorist Views It". *Psychological Review*, 20: 158–77.

Westlund, Olle (2003). *S(t)imulating a Social Psychology: G. H. Mead and the Reality of the Social Object*. Uppsala: Uppsala University Library.

Whitehead, A. N. (1925). *An Enquiry Concerning the Principles of Natural Knowledge*, 2nd edn. Cambridge: Cambridge University Press.

Wundt, Wilhelm (1900–20). *Völkerpsychologie: Eine Untersuchung der Entwicklungsgesetze von Sprache, Mythus und Sitte*, 10 vols. Leipzig: W. Engelmann & A. Kröner.

―― (1973). *The Language of Gestures*. The Hague: Mouton.

Wyczoikowska, Anna (1913). "Theoretical and Experimental Studies in the Mechanism of Speech". *Psychological Review*, 20/6: 448–58.

CHAPTER 9

W. E. B. DU BOIS: DOUBLE-CONSCIOUSNESS, JAMESIAN SYMPATHY, AND THE CRITICAL TURN

MITCHELL ABOULAFIA

The Souls of Black Folk is W. E. B. Du Bois's most famous work. It is a short book, representing a small portion of his *œuvre* (1989 [1903]). It is a relatively early work, composed in large measure of previously published pieces. The famous first chapter, "Of Our Spiritual Strivings", was published originally

I want to thank Professor Catherine Kemp of Brooklyn College for her helpful comments.

as "The Strivings of the Negro People" (1897), some six years before *Souls*.[1]
This was during the period when Du Bois was researching one of his first
major sociological studies, *The Philadelphia Negro* (1899), seven years after he
had graduated from Harvard, and a mere three years after graduate study in
Germany. He was a young man, at the beginning of a turbulent career that
would extend into the 1960s.

The Souls of Black Folk has remained his most influential and widely read
book, although Du Bois appears to have been somewhat ambivalent about it.
In his own review of the book (1904), published a year after *Souls*, he states:

One who is born with a cause is predestined to a certain narrowness of view, and
at the same time to some clearness of vision within his limits with which the world
often finds it well to reckon. My book has many of the defects and some of the
advantages of this situation. Because I am a Negro I lose something of that breadth
of view which the more cosmopolitan races have, and with this goes an intensity of
feeling and conviction which both wins and repels sympathy, and now enlightens,
now puzzles. . . . This is not saying that the style and workmanship of the book make
its meaning altogether clear. . . . Nevertheless, as the feeling is deep the greater the
impelling force to seek to express it. And here the feeling was deep.

In its larger aspects the style is topical—African. This needs no apology. The blood
of my fathers spoke through me and cast off the English restraint of my training and
surroundings. The resulting accomplishment is a matter of taste. Sometimes I think
very well of it and sometimes I do not.

I have quoted this self-review at some length because it not only addresses
Du Bois's feelings about the book, at least in 1904, it also reflects several of
the themes that I will address in this chapter: namely, sympathy, race, and
a Du Boisian notion of cosmopolitanism. As is well known, Du Bois took
a turn toward Marxism later in his career. At the time he wrote *Souls*, his
politics might be described as a progressive conservatism or a conservative
progressivism. Commentators have different views on the extent to which
Du Bois's early work is consistent with his later neo-Marxism. For example,
Adolph L. Reed Jr argues:

[T]hroughout his career Du Bois's writings rested on a conceptual foundation that
is compatible with the collectivist outlook and that this orientation is evident in his

---

[1] "The Strivings of the Negro People" is not identical to the first chapter of *Souls*. For example, in
the article we find the following line, "The freedman has not yet found in freedom his promised land"
(1897: 195); while in the first chapter of *Souls* the line reads, "The Nation has not yet found peace from
its sins; the freedman has not yet found in freedom his promised land" (1989 [1903]: 7). See n. 11
below.

attitudes about the importance of science in social affairs and the proper organization of the Afro-American population as well as in his specific concerns with political positions, such as Pan-Africanism and socialism.   (1977: 22)

Defending or criticizing a claim of this nature is beyond the scope of this chapter. The goal here is more modest. I will argue that the philosophical and conceptual underpinnings of *Souls* can be located in four sources: (1) Williams James's interpretation of the Scottish theories of sympathy and impartiality; (2) notions of cultural or racial differences that can be traced back to Johann Gottfried von Herder; (3) Hegel's concepts of recognition and self-consciousness, and (4) Du Bois's situated experience as an African American. In this chapter I will not be able to supply all of the biographical and historiographical material that would demonstrate that Du Bois was self-consciously drawing on these traditions. But I will supply sufficient textual and circumstantial evidence to defend the plausibility of this claim. Further, my goal here is not simply archeological. I will argue that in *Souls*—specifically in the passages in which he addresses the notion of double-consciousness—Du Bois moves beyond his own very nineteenth-century assumptions about race, and provides a critical edge for rethinking theories of sentiment and sympathy that have informed Anglo-American ethical traditions. In so doing he speaks to current debates regarding whether the sources of ethical life are best understood in terms of reciprocity. *Souls* also remains compelling because Du Bois is seeking to find a path that will allow him to respect and pay homage to cultural differences, while defending the notion of a common humanity that informs this respect.

One of the central goals of *Souls* is to have its readership—in Du Bois's day primarily an educated Anglo audience—appreciate what it means to live behind what Du Bois refers to as "the Veil", where he locates the world of Black experience. Du Bois stresses that he has been on both sides of the Veil, as well as above it. "Leaving, then, the world of the white man, I have stepped within the Veil, raising it that you may view faintly its deeper recesses,—the meaning of its religion, the passion of its human sorrow, and the struggle of its greater souls. ... And, finally, need I add that I who speak here am bone of the bone and flesh of the flesh of them that live within the Veil?" (1989 [1903]: 1–2).[2] Du Bois hopes that if his audience can feel something of what he has felt, of what Blacks in America have experienced, he will invoke

---

[2] Du Bois also states: "Then it dawned upon me with a certain suddenness that I was different from others; or like, mayhap, in heart and life and longing, but shut out from their world by a vast veil.

a natural sympathy. Along with this sympathy, reason will play a vital role in helping us to overcome prejudice. Here are two passages from *Souls*, one of which emphasizes reason, the other sympathy and feeling.

The nineteenth century was the first century of human sympathy,—the age when half wonderingly we began to descry in others that transfigured spark of divinity which we call Myself; when clodhopper and peasants, and tramps and thieves, and millionaires and—sometimes—Negroes, became throbbing souls whose warm pulsing life touched us so nearly that we half gasped with surprise, crying, "Thou too! Hast Thou seen Sorrow and the dull waters of Hopelessness? Hast Thou known Life?" And then all helplessly peered into those Other-worlds, and wailed, "O World of Worlds, how shall man make you one?"   (1989 [1903]: 178)

Again, we may decry the color-prejudice of the South, yet it remains a heavy fact. Such curious kinks of the human mind exist and must be reckoned with soberly. . . . They can be met in but one way,—by the breadth and broadening of human reason, by catholicity of taste and culture.   (1989 [1903]: 76)

Some readers have been perplexed by the appeal to reason and to feeling in *Souls*, as if one had to choose one course over the other. However, if reason is understood as the rationality of the broad-minded and catholic impartial spectator—an understanding that Du Bois would have inherited from James and the Scottish tradition and that is implicit in the passage just cited—then a good deal of the seeming tension evaporates. Du Bois does find himself drawing on this tradition in *Souls*, for example, to discuss self-development. However, he is not only discussing individuals in *Souls*. Du Bois develops an orientation toward race that asks us to sympathize not only with individuals, but with different cultural and racial groups. The challenge is to understand how we can sympathize with those whose cultures are significantly different from our own. The answer for Du Bois entails a notion of humanity that can be found in Herder, as well as in James's appeal to the sympathetic self.

I

Du Bois studied with William James at Harvard for two years, from 1888 to 1890. James's seminal *Principles of Psychology* (1950), which will be addressed

I had thereafter no desire to tear down that veil, to creep through; I held all beyond it in common contempt, and lived above it in a region of blue sky and great wandering shadows" (1989 [1903]: 4).

below, was first published in 1890. In *Dark Voices: W. E. B. Du Bois and American Thought*, Shamoon Zamir argues that in spite of Du Bois's own proclamations regarding his indebtedness to James, the relationship was a complex one from the start. No doubt Du Bois shared many of James's vitalist and volunteerist sensibilities during the period in which he wrote *Souls*, but even when he was James's student, he may have begun to raise questions about James's ahistoricism (Zamir 1995: 51). Zamir also argues that while James certainly appealed to the notion of an impartial spectator and sympathy in his ethics, Du Bois's "own recourse to sympathetic understanding . . . is closer to Boasian attempts at cross-cultural understanding than it is to James's attitudes" (1995: 44). Zamir's position is well-founded, because James's ethical and political attitudes do not develop in the direction of sympathetic attachments to other cultures and their historical trajectories, as they do for Du Bois. Yet James's influence, and through him the Scottish theorists of sentiment, in particular Adam Smith, do play an important role in the psychological assumptions that inform *Souls*. It is because individuals have "Jamesian" souls, selves, that it is possible to motivate them to recognize cultural differences and to move beyond parochialism. James's ideal self, a broad-minded impartial spectator, can help overcome prejudice and inspire African Americans to self-actualize, and it can help Anglos better understand the potentialities of another race. James's orientation also helps account for the manner in which reason or impartiality and feeling are interwoven in Du Bois's text. So before turning to the cultural and racial dimension of Du Bois's thought, and to the notion of double-consciousness, which has Hegelian roots, it is worth exploring in some depth James's account of the self in the *Principles*.

For those attuned to think of the self as a unitary phenomenon, James has a surprise in store in the *Principles*. In "The Consciousness of Self", he begins by speaking of multiple selves, which should be viewed as empirical—the material self, the social self, and the spiritual self—and a metaphysical pure ego. James remains agnostic about the pure ego. He will tell us at the end of the chapter that there may be metaphysical reasons for accepting a pure ego, whether in its spiritualist or transcendental incarnations, but this would carry "us beyond the psychological or naturalistic point of view" (1950 [1890]: 401). The material self is easy enough to understand. In this category we find the body, clothes, family, and home. "All these different things are the objects of instinctive preferences coupled with the most important practical interests of life" (1950 [1890]: 292). Here we should think of the body and its parts as a possession. For James there is "an ... instinctive impulse" that "drives us to collect property" (1950 [1890]: 293), which becomes part of our empirical self.[3] Further, following in John Locke's footsteps, James declares, "The parts of our wealth most intimately ours are those which are saturated with our labor" (1950 [1890]: 293).

Now one might think that some of the things that James includes under the material self—clothing and property, for instance—should fall under the social dimension of the self, especially since James defines "a man's social self" in terms of "the recognition which he gets from his mates" (1950 [1890]: 293). But let us leave aside the question of what should be denominated as material, and turn directly to the social. Generally speaking, the social is the domain of the acknowledgment or recognition of our actions and activities by others. There are in fact multiple social selves. "Properly speaking, *a man has as many social selves as there are individuals who recognize him* and carry an image of him in their mind. To wound any one of these his images is to wound him" (1950 [1890]: 294). This observation is clearly one that Du Bois employs in discussing the damage done to the psyche of African Americans through the lack of appropriate recognition by Anglos. James also claims that the images that others have of an individual fall into classes, so that "we may practically say that he has as many different social selves as there are distinct *groups* of persons about whose opinion he cares. He generally shows a different side of himself to each of these different groups" (1950 [1890]: 294).[4] This insight is utilized by Du Bois in *Souls* when he reflects on the ways in which African Americans have related to different social groups. And as we shall see, it is also an insight that sets the stage for Du Bois's notion of double-consciousness. Finally, the spiritual self should be viewed in terms of psychic dispositions or faculties:[5] for example, "our ability

---

[3] At the beginning of the chapter, James has little problem providing a rather striking definition of the non-transcendental self, which, as Zamir (1995: 157–8) points out, is weighed down with a good deal of ideological baggage. "It is telling that James begins his chapter titled, 'The Consciousness of Self' with a definition of self as a structure of commodity fetishism. '*In its widest possible sense*,' he writes, 'a man's *Self* is the sum total of all that he CAN call his, not only his body and his psychic powers, but his clothes and his house, his wife and his children [! SZ], his ancestors and friends, his reputation and works, his lands and horses, and yacht and bank-account.'"

[4] These insights are developed by George Herbert Mead when he discusses the generalized other (1934: 152–64). It is worth noting that for James the individual who has the greatest power over us in terms of recognition is the person with whom we are in love.

[5] It must be borne in mind that James is speaking of the spiritual self here as an empirical self. As such, it is "a man's inner or subjective being, his psychic faculties or dispositions, taken concretely; not the bare principle of personal Unity, or 'pure' Ego" (1950 [1890]: 296).

to argue and discriminate, . . . our moral sensibility and conscience, . . . our indomitable will" (1950 [1890]: 296).[6]

There is a hierarchy of selves: the merely bodily at the lowest level, the spiritual at the highest, with the extra-corporeal material and social selves ranged similarly in the middle (1950 [1890]: 313; 291–329). According to James, we learn to subordinate our lower to our higher selves. How does this happen? James tells us that there is a kind of moral education of the race, as well as direct ethical judgments whose genealogy is not specified. And there are also judgments "called forth by the acts of others" (1950 [1890]: 314). Here James borrows directly from the Scottish tradition. Our encounters with others lead us to judge ourselves and to develop a higher moral self. "But having constantly to pass judgment on my associates, I come . . . to see . . . my own lusts in the mirror of the lusts of others, and to *think* about them in a very different way from that in which I simply *feel*" (1950 [1890]: 314).

James tells us that for each sort of self (material, social, and spiritual) there is a degree of potentiality for growth, for a widening of the self, that requires us to forgo immediate rewards. "Of all these wider, more potential selves, *the potential social self* is the most interesting . . . by reason of its connection with our moral and religious life " (1950 [1890]: 315). James goes on to declare:

I am always inwardly strengthened in my course and steeled against the loss of my actual social self by the thought of other and better *possible* social judges than those whose verdict goes against me now. The ideal social self which I thus seek in appealing to their decision may be very remote. . . . Yet still the emotion that beckons me on is indubitably the pursuit of an ideal social self, of a self that is at least *worthy* of approving recognition by the highest *possible* judging companion, if such companion there be. This self is the true, the intimate, the ultimate, the permanent Me which I seek. This judge is God, the Absolute Mind, the Great 'Companion.' . . . The impulse to pray is a necessary consequence of the fact that whilst the innermost of the empirical selves of a man is a Self of the *social* sort, it yet can find its only adequate *Socius* in an ideal world.   (1950 [1890]: 315–16)

---

[6] James claims that the common experience of the "spiritual self" is of an "*active* element in all consciousness" (1950 [1890]: 297). We can also address the spiritual self in terms of the stream of consciousness, either as a segment of the stream or in terms of its totality. In so doing, "our considering the spiritual self at all is a reflective process . . . the result of our abandoning the outward-looking point of view, and of our having become able to think of subjectivity as such, *to think of ourselves as thinkers*" (1950 [1890]: 296). James is not suggesting that the spiritual self is always actively reflective: that is, actively thinking about itself as a thinker. The spiritual self may arise due to one's awareness of bodily adjustments, actions and reactions, which generate a form of awareness of self that does not entail active reflection.

Now this is an intriguing turn. Not only do we appear to have left the merely empirical for the ideal, but there is a tension present. On the one hand, the spiritual self, we are told, is the highest self, the most personal aspect of one's self, the sphere of conscience and will. On the other hand, the realm of morality, the realm in which we judge our actions to have moral worth, can be viewed as an extrapolation or development of our social self. And further, there is an inevitable press to the religious from within the social.

All progress in the social Self is the substitution of higher tribunals for lower; this ideal tribunal is the highest; and most men, either continually or occasionally carry a reference to it in their breast. The humblest outcast on this earth can feel himself to be real and valid by pursuit of this higher recognition.   (1950 [1890]: 316)

Once one starts down the path of seeking recognition, there seems to be a natural progression to an ideal sphere, one in which God recognizes one's actions. This is not to suggest that James dismisses the empirically spiritual. It is to ask how we are to understand the genesis of the moral self. If one remains non-metaphysical, then it appears that James's examination of these issues leads him in the direction of the social genesis of Adam Smith's man in the breast, the impartial spectator (1982 [1759]: 137).

For James, the development of this wider, ideal, impartial self is linked to broadening our horizons through sympathy, and it would be impossible to develop this "wider" self if we were incapable of basic sympathetic attachments to others, that is, if we lacked an ability to place ourselves in the positions of others. Without such sympathy, the impartial spectator could not evolve. Impartiality is equated here with a form of cosmopolitanism, a broadening of one's horizons, a capacity for seeing things from the vantage point of others. More specifically, sympathy in the sense of compassion for others assists in the growth of the self through felt relations. Du Bois utilizes both notions of sympathy in *Souls*. These notions are blended in the following passage from James's *Principles*, which will help shed light on some of Du Bois's assumptions in *Souls*. In reading James's words, consider how Du Bois may have viewed their applicability to the children and grandchildren of freed slaves and the white southerners of his generation.

All narrow people *intrench* their Me, they *retract* it. ... People who don't resemble them, or who treat them with indifference, people over whom they gain no influence, are people on whose existence, however meritorious it may intrinsically be, they look with chill negation, if not with positive hate. Who will not be mine I will exclude from existence altogether; that is, as far I can make it so, such people shall be as if they were not. Thus may a certain absoluteness and definiteness in the outline of my

Me console me for the smallness of its content. Sympathetic people, on the contrary, proceed by the entirely opposite way of expansion and inclusion. The outline of their self often gets uncertain enough, but for this the spread of its content more than atones. *Nil humani a me alienum.* Let them despise this little person of mine, and treat me like a dog, *I* shall not negate *them* so long as I have a soul in my body. They are realities as much as I am. What positive good is in them shall be mine too, etc., etc.   (1950 [1890]: 312–13)

Du Bois was in basic agreement with the sentiments that James espoused in the passage, which is evident in the passage quoted earlier, which began, "The nineteenth century was the first century of human sympathy,—the age when half wonderingly we began to descry in others that transfigured spark of divinity which we call Myself" (1989 [1903]: 178). However, Du Bois understood that this broadening of the self is seriously undermined, if not made impossible, by the Color Line. As long as the Veil is present, one cannot sympathize with the other. Thus the Color Line prevents the "expansion" of the self. But the issue for Du Bois is not only a matter of getting individuals to expand their horizons by sympathizing with individuals who are members of other races. It is a matter of understanding that individuals have identities that are tied to their membership in a race, and that these races have a life of their own. We must learn to recognize and treat other races, as well as individuals, "sympathetically".

II

Du Bois accepts the notion that there are great races. In a fashion similar to Herder, he wants to see the actualization of the potentialities of these different races. As Siegland Lemke points out (2000: 63–4), there is good reason to believe that Du Bois was directly familiar with and influenced by Herder, whose ideas found their way into nineteenth-century German letters.[7] It is

---

[7] Lemke states: "Obviously, it would be simplistic to ascertain a direct connection between Herder and Du Bois. But it is very likely that Du Bois came across Herder's writings in William James's philosophy course at Harvard and in Wilhelm Dilthey's lectures on the history of philosophy at the University of Berlin. Herder's insistence on the elevating effect of poetry, his definition of the *Volk*, and his sustained concept of *Seele* literally resonate throughout *The Souls of Black Folk*" (Lemke 2000: 63–4)—although it should be noted in passing that Herder actually opposed the notion of race. He argued that there is in fact only one human race, with an almost endless number of *Volk*. See Herder 1968 [1784–91]: 6–7.

worth comparing Herder's words with those of Du Bois. First, Herder from *Reflections on the Philosophy of the History of Mankind*, and then Du Bois from an address entitled "The Conservation of the Races", that he gave in 1897 to the American Negro Academy.

In every one of their inventions, whether of peace or war, and even in all the faults and barbarities that nations have committed, we discern the grand law of nature: let man be man; let him mould his condition according as to himself shall seem best. For this nations took possession of their land, and established themselves in it as they could. ... Thus we everywhere find mankind possessing and exercising the right of forming themselves to a kind of humanity, as soon as they have discerned it.   (Herder 1968 [1784–91]: 84)

The following are the first two of seven points that Du Bois recommends as a creed for the Academy (1996 [1897]: 46).[8]

1. We believe that the Negro people, as a race, have a contribution to make to civilization and humanity, which no other race can make.
2. We believe it the duty of the Americans of Negro descent, as a body, to maintain their race identity until this mission of the Negro people is accomplished, and the ideal of human brotherhood has become a practical possibility.

It appears that Du Bois relies not only on a Herderian notion of *Volk* and its right to self-determination, but also on a similar notion of Humanity (*Menschheit* or *Humanität*) in order to give African Americans their due as a people and to argue for their contribution to a common humanity. According to Frank E. Manuel, "For Herder Humanity is one, and a *Volk*—unless corrupted (this is the implicit caveat)—can express only fully human values and ideas. Progress is the gradual expression of all possible *Volk* configurations" (1968: pp. xx–xxi). While it is true that Herder views this process as unfolding over time, the central moral imperative of his vision is close to that of Du Bois

---

[8] In the same speech Du Bois makes the following claims about race. "If this be true [the division of human beings into races], then the history of the world is the history, not of individuals, but of groups, not of nations, but of races, and he who ignores or seeks to override the race idea in human history ignores and overrides the central thought of all history. What, then, is a race? It is a vast family of human beings, generally of common blood and language, always of common history, traditions and impulses, who are both voluntarily and involuntarily striving together for the accomplishment of certain more or less vividly conceived ideals of life" (1996 [1897]: 40).

While there is little doubt that Du Bois insisted on racial difference during the period when he wrote *Souls*, it is also the case that he was familiar with challenges to strict, essentializing definitions of race. This can be seen in his report on "The First Universal Races Congress" (1996 [1911]).

in the period in which he wrote *Souls*.[9] The dignity of each race is linked to a common humanity that finds expression through each race. But if we were to stop here, then Jamesian sympathy, combined with the rationality of the broad-minded impartial spectator and a Herderian notion of Humanity, would appear to be sufficient to develop the interracial communication and respect that Du Bois supports. If Anglos in the USA developed these sensibilities, it would allow African Americans the space to nurture their own culture.

Yet Du Bois himself complicates matters through his analysis of double-consciousness in the first chapter of *Souls*. The sort of sympathy or impartiality that we have been discussing thus far suggests that reciprocity can be achieved through a degree of good will and education. However, the experience of double-consciousness undermines these goals. With the introduction of the notion of double-consciousness, Du Bois takes his place in a tradition that extends back at least to Rousseau: namely, one that addresses the damage to the psyches, the "souls", of those who have been debased by slavery and servitude. For Du Bois, the threats to the self-actualization of black peoples and individuals are due not only to the explicit barriers of Jim Crow, but to the psychological repercussions of racism.

Zamir argues that Du Bois's notion of double-consciousness can be directly linked to Hegel's analysis of self-consciousness in the *Phenomenology of Spirit* (1977 [1807]: 104–38). Specifically, he argues that we should understand double-consciousness as a form of "unhappy consciousness" (1995: 144), the mode of consciousness with which Hegel closes his chapter on self-consciousness. There is good deal of evidence that Du Bois had studied the *Phenomenology*, and in all likelihood this study took place with George Santayana during Du Bois's second year at Harvard (Zamir 1995: 113, 248–9 n. 2). No doubt Zamir is correct regarding Hegel's influence. However, it is misleading to tie Du Bois's double-consciousness to Hegel's "unhappy consciousness". The latter entails a split between the changeable and the unchangeable; it is a religious consciousness that is lost to itself. Du Bois is drawing in a more general way on the alienation and doubleness found throughout the chapter, especially in the master and slave dialectic, as well as on Hegel's notion of recognition.[10]

---

[9] It is worth highlighting the reference to corruption in Manuel's account of Herder. Peoples can be tarnished and damaged by outside forces. This is a problem that Du Bois worries about in terms of the repercussions of slavery, which he believes may have left some African Americans with unacceptable sexual mores and a general lack of discipline.

[10] Hegel's master and slave dialectic is sufficiently familiar to require little by way of introduction. However, given the previous discussion of James and Du Bois's relationship to Scottish philosophy, it

In brief, the Hegelian background to Du Bois's discussion can be located in the development of self-consciousness for Hegel. The process of becoming self-conscious entails a split within the individual; there is a distance between the consciousness that is aware and that of which it is aware. This consciousness experiences itself as alienated from itself and the world. In the master and slave dialectic, we discover that the "splitting" of self-consciousness results in the master's "essence" being found outside the master in the slave, and vice versa. The goal is to overcome this alienation of self in the other. This will occur only in a society in which mutual recognition is present, and Hegel provides a foretaste of this mutuality in the *Phenomenology* when he declares:

What still lies ahead for consciousness is the experience of what Spirit is—this absolute substance which is the unity of the different independent self-consciousnesses which, in their opposition, enjoy perfect freedom and independence: 'I' that is 'We' and 'We' that is 'I'.   (1977 [1807]: 110)

Du Bois drew on Hegel's dialectical account of the alienation of the individual's consciousness from itself. This does not mean that he forsook the Jamesian view of the self as potentially an ideal, impartial self. Rather, he used Hegel and James to augment each other. Hegel demonstrated how a consciousness could be divided and experienced as a "twoness", and Du Bois drew on his insights in one of the most famous passages of *Souls*.

After the Egyptian and Indian, the Greek and Roman, the Teuton and Mongolian, the Negro is a sort of seventh son, born within a veil, and gifted with second-sight in this American world,—a world which yields him no true self-consciousness, but only lets him see himself through the revelation of the other world. It is a peculiar sensation, this double-consciousness, this sense of always looking at one's self through the eyes of others, of measuring one's soul by the tape of a world that looks on in amused contempt and pity. One ever feels his twoness,—an American, a Negro; two souls,

---

is worth noting that Hegel was familiar with Adam Smith as well as with the Scottish theorists of sentiment. Smith's influence can readily be seen, for example, in the introduction to Hegel's *Lectures on the Philosophy of History*. The notion that the self can judge itself only through the looking glass provided by the other would have been well known to any reader of Smith. Of course, the influences on Hegel are legion. But let us speculate. Let us consider the possibility that when Hegel was thinking about the relationship of master and slave, and developing his model of mutual recognition, he drew on the social interactionism of Smith. No doubt Hegel radicalized the interaction, for instead of assuming that the self learns about what is right and wrong from its interactions with others, the self is viewed as coming into being through its interactions with others. And it does this in such a way that the spirit of different times informs its constitution. We are only selves insofar as we are recognized as selves, and this is precisely why neither master nor slave can be said to have a fully developed sense of self. Each self is contaminated by its relationship with an other who is either idealized or seen as less than human. Only the power of the negative, of living contradictions that must be overcome, leads to the eventual sublation of the asymmetry between master and slave.

two thoughts, two unreconciled strivings; two warring ideals in one dark body, whose dogged strength alone keeps it from being torn asunder.   (1989 [1903]: 5)[11]

The problem is clear. If one has to expend too much of one's resources trying to see oneself through the eyes of the other, one loses oneself, or one becomes split, a divided self. So the Jamesian model that claims that impartiality is generated through individuals taking multiple perspectives must come to terms with the reality that seeing oneself through the eyes of others can in fact be a damaging experience. Under certain conditions the self can as easily become alienated from itself as it can be led to expand its horizons through taking the perspectives of others.

Those who have a double-consciousness are in a unique position to achieve the impartiality of the spectator, because of a heightened awareness of otherness and multiplicity. This in fact can be a resource for marginalized peoples. Multiple standpoints can lead to a breadth of vision and insight not possessed by dominant groups. Yet this advantage can be undermined through the alienation inherent in dominate/subordinate relationships. The participants in these relationships are not disembodied spirits. Those who are subordinate become frustrated and angry with those who compel them to see the world as they do. Du Bois confronts us with how asymmetry in power relations, which in his analysis is tied to racism, can undermine the best intentions of actors regarding sympathetic or impartial responses to others. To state the obvious, one cannot expect individuals to respond sympathetically under the yoke of oppression. In fact, the oppressed are confronted with a hostile, invasive "critic", who often appears under the guise of an impartial spectator. This is crucial. Those in the dominant position often have the luxury of *appearing* to be impartial or benevolent. But if there is no mutuality, no basic respect for the humanity of the other, the result is not impartiality but paternalism. The undermining of the "impartiality" of those who are subordinate through the interior "critic" cannot be separated from the way

---

[11] In Du Bois's article, "The Strivings of the Negro People", on which the first chapter of *Souls* is based, he refers to "self-consciousness" in this passage (1897: 194), and not to "true self-consciousness" as he does in *Souls*. From a Hegelian vantage point this is a significant clarification. Forms of alienated self-consciousness are "self-consciousnesses" for Hegel, but they are not yet truly and fully self-conscious. This achievement requires historical development. Du Bois's addition of "true" can be interpreted as an attempt to avoid leaving his readers with a false impression about those who experience double-consciousness: namely, that they lack any form of self-consciousness. What they lack is *true* self-consciousness. Du Bois tells us that "The history of the American Negro is the history of this strife—his longing to attain self-conscious manhood, to merge his double self into a better and truer self. In this merging he wishes neither of the older selves to be lost" (1989 [1903]: 5).

the veil prevents those who dominate, those who see themselves as more human than the other, from truly sympathizing with others. Asymmetrical relations undermine "natural" sympathetic responses for all those involved. For those who dominate, pity can become conflated and confused with sympathy. And pity infantalizes. It is no accident, then, that Du Bois lashes out against pity and the denial of "manhood" to the black race.

Du Bois has drawn on his experiences, his own standpoint as an African American, to challenge the possibility of mutuality and reciprocity, even as he promotes the latter. To place this in the context of contemporary debates about the relevance of recognition to our moral and political lives, on the one hand Du Bois comes through as an advocate of mutual recognition, of symmetrical relationships of respect. On the other hand he is a keen observer of the concrete conditions that make the realization of mutuality impractical or at a minimum exceedingly difficult. The general framework of the problem, of course, would not be news to Hegel, given his analysis of the master and slave relationship. However, what Du Bois has accomplished is to generate an account of the repercussions of having a "consciousness" that is split between cultural or group identities in a society that is inherently racist, one in which the veil remains opaque. Under these circumstances the Color Line promotes the presence of an invasive "critic", not a benign, impartial one. Du Bois has made explicit the psychological impact of this interaction. This challenges Hegel's optimism that history is moving in the direction of a society of mutual recognition and Herder's great hope that all *Volk* will have their day. In fact, Du Bois's challenge plays on one of Herder's fears: namely, the corruption of a *Volk* by "foreign" influences. Du Bois is telling us that there has been a corruption of the African-American *Volk* through the continuous internal gaze of the other. Unless this gaze is overcome, self-actualization for African Americans as a people will remain unrealized. And, *mutatis mutandis*, the same is true for Anglos.

Yet *The Souls of Black Folk* is a testament to the hope that a way can be found around this impasse. Du Bois speaks of double-consciousness in the first chapter. But he doesn't end the book on this note. Perhaps, given the right conditions, Whites and Blacks can view each other with sympathy, as complements in a larger American nation, so that double-consciousness will be overcome. The worlds of Blacks and Whites can be enlarged to include the experiences of each other. Herder's notion of Humanity will prevail. This is very much in keeping with James's program, and to a large extent that of other American pragmatists such as John Dewey and G. H. Mead, regarding the enlargement of the self. As a matter of fact, in the first chapter of *Souls*, Du Bois presents a notion of complementarity that draws on the latter tradition, as well as a notion of development through the inclusion of differences that bears the mark of Hegel and of the humanism of Herder.[12]

Work, culture, liberty,—all these we need . . . all striving toward that vaster ideal that swims before the Negro people, the ideal of human brotherhood, gained through the unifying ideal of Race; the ideal of fostering and developing the traits and talents of the Negro, not in opposition to or contempt for other races, but rather in large conformity to the greater ideals of the American Republic, in order that some day on American soil two-world-races may give each to each those characteristics both so sadly lack. We the darker ones come even now not altogether empty-handed: there are to-day no truer exponents of the pure human spirit of the Declaration of Independence than the American Negroes . . . all in all, we black men seem the sole oasis of simple faith and reverence in a dusty desert of dollars and smartness.   (1989 [1903]: 11–12)

The last line is perhaps a harbinger of Du Bois's future orientation, in which he came to question his early views; and in so doing he moved from psychology or cultural sociology to political economy. This is too large a topic for this chapter, but I would be remiss in not mentioning, however briefly, Du Bois's later work, for he came to understand racism primarily in terms of economic exploitation. In his autobiography, *Dusk of Dawn*, written many years after *The Souls of Black Folk*, Du Bois states:

[E]ven in the minds of the most dogmatic supporters of race theories and believers in the inferiority of colored folk to white, there was a conscious or unconscious determination to increase their incomes by taking full advantage of this belief. And then gradually this thought was metamorphosed into a realization that the income-bearing value of race prejudice was the cause not the result of theories of racial inferiority.   (2002 [1940]: 129)

I introduce these comments neither to take a stand on Du Bois's later Marxist turn, nor to defend the position that racism can be explained primarily in economic terms, but to provide an idea of how Du Bois came to question his earlier position. His comments speak to the limitations of notions of culture and race that Du Bois utilized in his earlier work. In order to understand oppression, we must focus more directly on an economic analysis of capital.

---

[12] Both Herder and Hegel would have a problem with how Du Bois conceptualizes historical "progress" in this passage, but for different reasons. For Herder, Du Bois would be insufficiently attuned to cultural differences, blending what should not be blended. For Hegel, Du Bois's treatment would be insufficiently dialectical. It would be mere edifying discourse.

REFERENCES

Du Bois, W. E. B. (1996 [1897]). "The Conservation of the Races". *American Negro Academy, Occasional Papers #2*. In Sundquist (1996), 38–47.

—— (1897). "The Strivings of the Negro People". *Atlantic Monthly*, 80: 194–8.

—— (1996 [1899]). *The Philadelphia Negro: A Social Study*. Philadelphia: University of Pennsylvania Press.

—— (1996 [1904]). "On the Souls of Black Folk". *The Independent*, 17 Nov. In Sundquist (1996), 304–5.

—— (1989 [1903]). *The Souls of Black Folk*. "Introduction" by Donald B. Gibson. New York: Penguin Books.

—— (1996 [1911]). "The First Universal Races Congress". *The Independent*, 70, 24 Aug., In Sundquist (1996), 55–9.

—— (2002 [1940]). *Dusk of Dawn, An Essay Toward an Autobiography of a Race Concept*. New Brunswick, NJ, and London: Transaction Publishers.

Hegel, G. W. F. (1977 [1807]). *Phenomenology of Sprit*, trans. A. V. Miller. Oxford: Oxford University Press.

Herder, Johann Gottfried von (1968 [1784–91]). *Reflections on the Philosophy of the History of Mankind*, trans. T. O. Churchill, ed. Frank E. Manuel. Chicago: University of Chicago Press.

James, William (1950 [1890]). *The Principles of Psychology*, i. New York: Dover Publications.

Lemke, Sieglinde (2000). "Berlin and Boundaries: *Sollen* versus *Geschehen*". *boundary 2*, 27/3: 45–77.

Manuel, Frank E. (1968). "Editor's Introduction". In Herder (1968 [1784–91]), pp. ix–xxv.

Mead, George Herbert (1934). *Mind, Self and Society: From the Standpoint of a Social Behaviorist*. Chicago: University of Chicago Press.

Reed, Adolph L., Jr. (1977). *W. E. B. Du Bois and American Political Thought: Fabianism and the Color Line*. Oxford: Oxford University Press.

Smith, Adam (1982 [1759]). *The Theory of Moral Sentiments*, ed. D. D. Raphael and A. L. Macfie. Indianapolis: Liberty Press.

Sundquist, Eric J. (ed.) (1996). *W. E. B. Du Bois: A Reader*. Oxford: Oxford University Press.

Zamir, Shamoon (1995). *Dark Voices, W. E. B. Du Bois and American Thought, 1888–1903*. Chicago: University of Chicago Press.

CHAPTER 10

....

THE PRAGMATIST
FAMILY ROMANCE

....

ROBERT WESTBROOK

THE RELATIONSHIP between American pragmatists—Charles S. Peirce, William James, John Dewey, Richard Rorty, Hilary Putnam, and others—and their critics has often been marked by sharp conflict. Those philosophers wedded to the conceptions of meaning and truth that pragmatists would displace have, not surprisingly, been ill-disposed to go quietly. Yet conflict *among* pragmatists has been no less sharp, leaving some to wonder whether it really makes sense to speak of "pragmatism" as such.

It does, but only with some care. Pragmatism is best conceived less as a well-defined, tightly knit school of thought than as a loose, contentious family of thinkers who have always squabbled, and have sometimes been moved to disown one another. Indeed, the history of pragmatism can perhaps best be narrated as what Freud called the "family romance" of the neurotic child, in which imagined doubts about paternity and sibling rivalry are front and center. Here, as Freud said, the tale becomes one of each child (or philosopher) hero asserting his or her own legitimacy "while his brothers and sisters are got out of the way by being bastardized" at best (1909: 77).

No sooner did James announce the birth of pragmatism in 1898, than questions of legitimacy and confraternity were raised. James (1978 [1898]: 123–4) credited his boyhood friend Peirce with initially forging the pragmatic method in the series of articles on the logic of science that the latter published in the *Popular Science Monthly* in 1877–8. Peirce quickly denied paternity of pragmatism as James characterized it, and announced that he would hence-forth refer to his own doctrine, properly understood, as "pragmaticism", a term "ugly enough to be safe from kidnappers" such as James. Dewey, though deeply indebted to James in some respects, nonetheless took care to distinguish his own "instrumentalism" from what he took to be James's unconvincing efforts to mobilize pragmatism on behalf of religious belief. At the same time, the ever-difficult Peirce responded to Dewey's praise of his essay on "What Pragmatism Is" (1998 [1905]) with a puzzled letter complaining that Dewey's work in logic "forbids all such researches as those which I have been absorbed in for the last eighteen years" (*CP* 8. 243–4). Undeterred by all this, the ever-generous James extended a brotherly welcome to Europeans such as F. C. S. Schiller and Giovanni Pappini, who were drawn to some of the very elements of his thinking that most troubled Peirce and Dewey.

Subsequent generations of pragmatists have been no less quarrelsome and fractious, and contemporary "neo-pragmatism" is even more variegated than its predecessors. Arthur Lovejoy's early estimate of "thirteen pragmatisms" now seems improbably low. For example, Richard Rorty and Hilary Putnam, the two most distinguished contemporary "neo-pragmatists", eyed one another warily. Putnam rebuffed Rorty's gestures of fraternal affection and has remained "appalled" at some of Rorty's views (1998: 10). Today we are confronted with an often bewildering array of efforts by philosophers, political theorists, legal scholars, and literary critics to reappropriate, recast, and reconstruct pragmatism in a sometimes surprising fashion. These projects not only contrast with one another but differ significantly from those of the founding pragmatists (Kloppenberg 1996).

What, then, is a plausible family tie among pragmatists? How might we, at least, constitute pragmatism as a lineage of contentious siblings, stepchildren, and bastards if not a gathering of more tightly knit kin. Obviously, we have to cast the family tie at a fairly high level of abstraction—not so high as to blur the distinction between pragmatists and those clearly outside the tribe, but not so low as to produce a gathering of kinsfolk any less internally contentious than the pragmatists have proven to be. A harmonious pragmatist family would be one without many of those who have a fair claim to the family name. That is, one could not construe this family as a happy one without simply taking sides in the legitimacy debates that have wracked it—insisting, for example, that Peirce or James or Putnam or Rorty should be disowned, and not merely bastardized (see, e.g., Haack 1997).

The fiercest debates between pragmatists and non-pragmatists and among pragmatists have centered on the pragmatist conception of truth. It is here that the principal family tie abides, and here as well that intra-family squabbles have usually begun.

As Putnam said, all pragmatists seek to avoid "both the illusions of metaphysics and the illusions of skepticism" (1992: 180). Consequently, they have been most often attacked by metaphysicians on the one hand and skeptics on the other, neither of whom regard themselves as the victims of illusions. And the most common charges that pragmatists have leveled at one another are those of regressing into dubious metaphysical claims or of falling into an abyss of skepticism.

By the "illusions of metaphysics", Putnam is referring to what is often termed "foundationalism", the belief that knowledge, if it is to be secure, must rest on certain, fixed, and incorrigible foundations. Those foundations must lie in the way the world is apart from the human effort to know about it. Foundationalists—be they realists or idealists—insist that belief is true if and only if it accurately represents or "corresponds" to that world. On this view, as Matthew Festenstein says, "the way the world is, including the way human beings are, constitutes an object which is accessible from a 'God's-eye view,' independently of actual human emotions, choices, self-understandings" (1997: 4). Only if we attain such a view against which to measure current belief, foundationalists argue, will our knowledge have the absolute, universal, and incorrigible grounds that, they contend, truth requires. If, as James said, "the trail of the human serpent is over everything" (1975 [1907]: 37), then, for the foundationalist, truth will forever elude us.

Pragmatists uniformly deny that human beings can secure such a God's-eye view of the world and reject the sort of "correspondence theory of truth" that requires it. For them, the attempt to find foundations for human knowledge outside human practices is, as Dewey (1929) said, a futile, self-defeating "quest for certainty". And "God's-eye view" is a particularly apt phrase for this quest, since some pragmatists—most notably, Dewey and Rorty—have suggested that the correspondence theory of truth is an unfortunate holdover from a theological age in which true knowledge was said to be knowledge of the world as God made it. To know the truth was to understand reality just as God intended; it was a pious act.

Foundationalism, pragmatists argue, has persisted despite its failure to deliver on its promise of objective truths corresponding to a mind-independent world because we fear that the only alternative to it is wholesale skepticism. We are in thrall to what pragmatist Richard Bernstein has termed "the Cartesian anxiety", the phobia we have inherited from Descartes that disaster awaits us if we are unable to discover an Archimedean point on which to rest our knowledge. We fear "*either* there is some support for our being, a fixed foundation for our knowledge, *or* we cannot escape the forces of darkness that envelop us with madness, with intellectual and moral chaos" (1983: 18).

All pragmatists reject this Cartesian either/or. Just because we cannot attain a God's-eye view of the world, they say, does not mean that we must fall into despairing skepticism. Doubt as well as belief, they argue, requires justification. "Let us not pretend to doubt in philosophy what we do not doubt in our hearts," Peirce wrote (1992 [1868]: 29). Universal doubt is a philosopher's game of pretend doubt, and while we may well doubt any particular belief on any particular occasion, we cannot doubt all beliefs all at once, since particular beliefs require a background of undoubted convictions if they are to be tested.

Thus, at the core of pragmatism is an attack on what Dewey termed the "intellectual lockjaw" (1977 [1908a]: 138 n.) of the insoluble epistemological conundrums of a "representationalist" conception of knowledge that holds that the aim of knowledge is to somehow (there's the rub, Dewey noted) represent or mirror the world as it really is, a conception that Dewey derided as a "Kodak fixation" (1977 [1908a]: 129). In its place, pragmatists substitute a conception of knowledge that owes much to the intellectual revolution fostered by Darwin and evolutionary theory, which had a profound effect on the classical pragmatists, and remains a touchstone for many neo-pragmatists. In this naturalized and historicized conception of the quest for knowledge, intelligence is an attribute of human beings that emerged and developed over the course of the evolution of the species in the service of its survival, adaptation, and flourishing. A belief is warranted not if it mirrors the world, but if it serves to resolve what Dewey termed the doubt-filled "problematic situations" in human experience. As Alan Ryan has said, "Pragmatism claims that human thinking and acting, from the least sophisticated to the most sophisticated, are driven by the need to respond to problems: all thought and action are provoked by a tension between ourselves as needy organisms on the one side and, on the other, the environment that must satisfy these needs. We think and act to reduce that tension" (2001: 16).

As pragmatists see it, the alternative to foundationalism is not skepticism, but fallibilism—the conviction that belief, though never certain, is not therefore necessarily dubious. Fallibilism says that we may rest content with less than certain yet confident belief. It allows us to affirm our settled convictions, as long as we do so provisionally. We may not claim absolute certainty for any belief; but neither need we doubt any belief without good reasons for doing so (Flanagan 1998). "Fallibilism does not require us to doubt *everything*," Putnam observes; "it only requires us to be prepared to doubt *anything*—if good reason to do so arises" (1995: 21). As therapist Peirce advised, "Your problems would be greatly simplified if, instead of saying that you want to know the 'Truth,' you were simply to say that you want to attain a state of belief unassailable by doubt" (1998 [1905]: 336).

As Peirce's advice indicates, pragmatists do not capitalize "Truth". Theirs, as Cheryl Misak has nicely put it, is a deflationary, lower-case, "low profile" conception of truth, one that nests it wholly within the confines of human inquiry (2000: 14). Inquiry is the means to resolve doubt and to sort out true from false beliefs. "A minimal characterization of good inquiry" is that it "takes experience seriously" (2000: 78). And because, to be adequately tested, beliefs must be subject to the widest possible range of experience, inquiry to be effective must, as Peirce said, be communal. "What fits with *my* experience is not of paramount importance as far as truth is concerned," Misak says. "What is important is what fits with all the experience that would be available, what the community of inquirers would converge upon" (2000: 95). Inquiry is our means of subjecting belief to the challenge of reasons, argument, and evidence. A belief that fully meets this challenge is true. This is what pragmatists (usually) mean when they say that the truth of a belief is to be measured by its practical consequences; this is what pragmatists (usually) mean when they say that truth is made, not found; this is what pragmatists (usually) mean when they say that a true belief is one that works.

Truth for pragmatists, then, is the upshot of exhaustive inquiry. As Misak observes:

Pragmatism thus abandons the kind of metaphysics which is currently in so much disrepute—it abandons concepts which pretend to transcend experience. Truth and objectivity are matters of what is best for the community of inquirers to believe, "best" here amounting to that which best fits with the evidence and argument. On the pragmatist view of truth, when we aim at empirical adequacy, predictive power, understanding the way things work, understanding ourselves, and the like, we aim at the truth. For a true belief is the belief which best satisfies those and other particular aims in inquiry.   (Misak 2000: 1)

For the pragmatist, then, "a true belief is one that would withstand doubt, were we to inquire as we fruitfully could on the matter. A true belief is such that, no matter how much further we were to investigate and debate, that belief would not be overturned by recalcitrant experience and argument" (2000: 49). But since no inquiry can be exhaustive, we can never know for sure that any of our beliefs are true, however indubitable they may seem at present or in present company. Truth is thus a "regulative ideal" (Emmet 1994), an ideal that is unrealizable, yet serves a valuable function—in this case, that of keeping the road of inquiry open. Truth, Misak concludes, is "what inquirers must *hope* for if they are to make sense of their practices of inquiry" (2000: 69). Truth is the aim of inquiry, but the best that can be secured at any moment in its course is well-justified belief, which is not necessarily true. It is *rational* nonetheless to adopt well-justified beliefs, even if these beliefs later prove to be false. Beliefs about matters that are in doubt are always forged against a background of beliefs about matters that, for the moment at least, are not—these fallible yet undoubted beliefs provide the warrants for new belief. Hence, beliefs can be deeply embedded in history and established cultural practices and nonetheless be well justified (if not necessarily true).

In abandoning representational conceptions of truth, pragmatists have not so much solved the problems plaguing foundationalists and skeptics as set them aside. Pragmatism, as Louis Menand has said, is "an effort to unhitch human beings from what pragmatists regard as a useless structure of bad abstractions about thought". As such, it "has a kind of ground-clearing sweep to it that gives many readers the sense that a pressing but vaguely understood obligation has suddenly been lifted from their shoulders, that some final examination for which they could never possibly have felt prepared has just been canceled" (1997: pp. xi–xii).

But foundationalists and skeptics have been loathe to permit pragmatists to escape the examinations they have set for each other, and consequently, pragmatists have periodically been embroiled in epistemological debates marked by uncomprehending efforts to enlist pragmatists in one camp or another of those they are trying to flee. Most often (usually by realist metaphysicians), they have been charged with an "idealism" that refuses to acknowledge the existence of a mind-independent world, and hence locks human beings up in an imaginary, solipsistic—even narcissistic—inner world of their own collective imagining.

A good example of this sort of incomprehension is a debate that Dewey had early in the twentieth century with the realist James Pratt, a dogged critic of pragmatism, over true knowledge of past events. Pratt contended (as would many critics subsequently) that pragmatists confused truth and verification. By showing that a belief "worked", inquiry might confirm its truth; but this working was not, as pragmatists contended, in itself the truth of the belief. Truth was antecedent to its verification: ideas were not true because they worked; they worked because they were true. In explaining the truth of belief about past events, the pragmatist conception of truth implied the fantastic assertion that such events could not be said to have occurred unless and until the belief that they had had been verified. Using one of Dewey's own examples, Pratt remarked: "Professor Dewey cites an idea that a certain noise comes from a street-car; this idea being investigated and verified *becomes* true. Had it not been verified it never would have been true—even if as a fact the noise *had* really come from the car" (1908: 125). By this same logic, critics such as Pratt observed, the fact that Columbus landed in America in 1492 would rest, improbably, on the future working of a belief about his voyage.

Dewey acknowledged in his response to Pratt that there was a sense in which the truth of a belief could be said to antecede its testing. Prior to its verification (as its verification revealed), a true belief has "the property of *ability to work*" (1978 [1909]: 8). This sort of functional capacity *was* a property of beliefs organically connected to verification; hence Dewey did not see how any difficulties were posed for pragmatism by insisting on *this* sort of antecedent truth. He suspected that pragmatism's critics meant to say something more than that an idea worked because it was workable. Pratt and other such "metaphysical" critics, he argued, confused the occurrence of an event with ideas or judgments about such occurrences. "Truth" was not a substantial property of the former, but a functional property of the latter. "Some conviction, some belief, some judgment with reference to [events] is necessary to introduce the category of truth and falsity," and it was important not to "confuse the content of a judgment with the *reference* of that content" (1978 [1909]: 6–7). The occurrence of noises from streetcars and of transatlantic voyages by fifteenth-century mariners did not wait upon successful verification of the judgments that "the noise came from the street-car" or "Columbus landed in America in 1492" (that *would be* fantastic), though the truth of our judgments about those occurrences did. Events did not "truly" happen, though true judgments about their happening could be made as long as these events left effects against which our judgments could be tested.

So much for the ties that bind the pragmatists and divide them from non-pragmatists. What about the internecine quarreling? Why, despite these common convictions about truth, are pragmatists forever disagreeing with one another on the subject? What has remained to argue about at family gatherings?

Plenty, it would seem. First of all, as I say, pragmatists have attacked one another for backsliding into foundationalism or plunging heedlessly into skepticism. And, at times, they have done so for good reason. On the one hand, Peirce, whom Rorty periodically ventured to kick out of the family, could sometimes scratch his metaphysical itch and say things such as "all science must be a delusion and a snare, if we cannot in some measure understand God's mind" (1958 [1903]: 129). On the other hand, Rorty, whose thinking Peirce would no doubt have found as horrendous as do many contemporary Peirceans, could cozy up uncomfortably close to some fashionable forms of "postmodern" skepticism. When Rorty said such things as "James and Dewey . . . are waiting at the end of the road which, for example, Foucault and Deleuze are currently traveling" (1982: p. xviii), many pragmatists were inclined to say something like: "Well, if so, they are there to tell them to apply the brakes before they drive off a cliff." One might say that pragmatists can be divided into those who navigate the pragmatist boat through the straits of epistemological debate by tacking closer to the Scylla of foundationalism and those who cut a channel closer to the Charybdis of skepticism.

Second, pragmatism has suffered from some notorious, widely broadcast formulations by two of its most provocative, well-known, and adventuresome bastards, James and Rorty. In *Pragmatism* (1907), James boldly argued that "the true is the name of whatever proves itself to be good in the way of belief, for definite, assignable reasons" (1975 [1907]: 42). Many critics understandably took him to mean that whatever beliefs we take to be good for us may, by virtue of that fact, be said to be true—an interpretation to which James lent credence with further claims such as "if theological ideas prove to have a value for concrete life, they will be true, for pragmatism, in the sense of being good for so much" (1975 [1907]: 40). These arguments were the product of the marriage of pragmatism with James's notion of the "will to believe", his contention that we have a right to beliefs for which the evidence is inconclusive if such beliefs are for us alive, forced, and momentous (1979 [1896]). James's concern here was to leave a logical space in which religious faith could flourish.

This argument drew a chorus of complaint from pragmatists as well as non-pragmatists, at the time and since. Although not necessarily hostile to religious faith, pragmatism cannot authorize its truth claims, Dewey said in a gentle, brotherly rebuke to James. The happy consequences for a believer of a belief in God "can not prove, or render more probable, the existence of such a being, for, by the argument, these desirable consequences depend upon accepting such an existence" (1977 [1908b]: 106). True ideas, Dewey said, were good in the sense that they solved the problems of inquiry, but this did not mean, as James sometimes implied, that *any* good that flowed from acceptance of a belief was evidence of its truth. James quickly backtracked from these claims, though the incautious *Pragmatism* has drawn far more readers than its more circumspect sequel, *The Meaning of Truth* (1909).

Among neo-pragmatists, pride of place in eliciting the sort of dismay that James's arguments did early in the century, is Rorty's assertion in *Philosophy and the Mirror of Nature* that truth is "what our peers will, *ceteris paribus*, let us get away with saying" (1979: 176). This remark is the sort of thing that Putnam—who thinks of pragmatism as "realism with a human face"—finds most appalling about Rorty's thinking, evidence of a skepticism that collapses truth into mere prevailing, consensual taste, ignoring the fact that many a consensual belief has proved false and/or morally repugnant (1990: 19–26).

Rorty, like James, worked hard to answer critics such as Putnam, while at the same time warning them of what he saw as metaphysical temptations lurking in their criticism (1998). He made clear that he had no doubt about the existence of a mind-independent world and its capacity to occasion beliefs about it, if not "in itself" justify beliefs that purport to "represent" it. "We can never be more arbitrary than the world lets us be," he said. "So even if there is no Way the World Is, even if there is no such thing as 'the intrinsic nature of reality,' there are still causal pressures. These pressures will be described in different ways at different times and for different purposes, but they are pressures none the less" (1999: 33). Rorty also acknowledged that "true" is an absolute, context-independent term, and that it makes no sense to say "true for me but not for you". It has, he admitted, a useful "cautionary" role to play in inquiry, since it warns us that however well justified we think a belief may be, it may turn out to be unjustified at some future date to some future community.

While such qualifications, perhaps, preserved Rorty's standing as at least a black sheep in the pragmatist family, he still seemed to many pragmatists to underestimate, as no pragmatist should, the usefulness of a functional concept of truth. Huw Price, for example, argues forcefully that someone as committed as Rorty to the displacement of representation by "conversation" should realize how much the norm of truth adds to inquiry over and above that of justified belief. Truth, he says, is for a pragmatist a norm that supplies assertoric dialogue with "its essential esprit de corps". Without a shared commitment to truth, we would have no investment in settling our differences in inquiry: "Truth is the grit that makes our individual opinions engage with one another. Truth puts the cogs in cognition, at least in its public manifestations" (Price 2003: 169). Rorty died apparently unconvinced (Rorty and Engel 2007).

Finally, pragmatists have often disagreed sharply about what the wider implications of their common understanding of meaning and truth might be for ethics, politics, and other realms of human experience. For example, a strenuous debate has emerged of late about whether or not pragmatism provides what Putnam termed "an epistemological justification for democracy" (1992: 180; cf. Westbrook 2005: 175–200). That is, some pragmatists such as Putnam, Misak (2000), and Robert Talisse (2005, 2007) have argued forcefully that, by virtue of its commitment to free and inclusive experimental inquiry, pragmatism has a tropism for democratic politics. "Democracy is a requirement for experimental inquiry," Putnam says. "To reject democracy is to reject the idea of being experimental" (1994: 64). Other pragmatists such as Rorty and Richard Posner (2003) have vigorously disagreed. Rorty went so far as to contend that pragmatism is "neutral between democrats and fascists" (1991: 75). This too was apparently a view he took with him to the grave (2006).

Its history thus suggests that it is likely that the pragmatist family will remain a contentious one. But it is a family that is likely as well, in spite of and to some extent because of its fractious nature, to sustain its position as one of the more significant intellectual clans on the terrain of modern life.

References

Bernstein, R. (1983). *Beyond Objectivism and Relativism: Science, Hermeneutics, and Praxis*. Philadelphia: University of Pennsylvania Press.

Dewey, J. (1977 [1908a]). "Does Reality Possess a Practical Character?". In *The Middle Works of John Dewey*, ed. Jo Ann Boydston, Carbondale, IL: Southern Illinois University Press, 4: 125–42.

_____ (1977 [1908*b*]). "What Pragmatism Means by Practical". In *The Middle Works of John Dewey*, ed. Jo Ann Boydston, Carbondale, IL: Southern Illinois University Press, 4: 98–115.

_____ (1978 [1909]). "A Short Catechism Concerning Truth". In *The Middle Works of John Dewey*, ed. Jo Ann Boydston, Carbondale, IL: Southern Illinois University Press, 6: 3–11.

_____ (1984 [1929]). *The Quest for Certainty*. In *The Later Works of John Dewey*, ed. Jo Ann Boydston, Carbondale, IL: Southern Illinois University Press, 4: 1–250.

Emmet, D. (1994). *The Role of the Unrealisable: A Study in Regulative Ideals*. New York: St Martin's Press.

Festenstein, M. (1997). *Pragmatism and Political Theory: From Dewey to Rorty*. Chicago: University of Chicago Press.

Flanagan, O. (1998). "Moral Confidence: Three Cheers for Naturalized Ethics". In R. Fox and R. Westbrook (eds.), *In Face of the Facts: Moral Inquiry in American Scholarship*, Cambridge: Cambridge University Press, 83–111.

Freud, S. (1909). "Family Romances". In *Sigmund Freud: Collected Papers*, ed. J. Strachey, New York: Basic Books, 5: 74–8.

Haack, S. (1997). "Vulgar Rortyism". *New Criterion*, 16 (Nov.): 67–70.

James, W. (1975 [1907]). *Pragmatism*. In *The Works of William James*, ed. F. H. Burkhardt, F. Bowers, and I. K. Skrupskelis, Cambridge, MA: Harvard University Press.

_____ (1978 [1898]). "The Pragmatic Method". In *Essays in Philosophy*, in *The Works of William James*, Cambridge, MA: Harvard University Press.

_____ (1979 [1896]). "The Will to Believe". In *The Will to Believe and other Essays in Popular Philosophy*, in *The Works of William James*, ed. F. H. Burkhardt, F. Bowers, and I. K. Skrupskelis, Cambridge, MA: Harvard University Press.

Kloppenberg, J. (1996). "Pragmatism: An Old Name for Some New Ways of Thinking?". *Journal of American History*, 83: 100–38.

Menand, L. (1997). "Introduction". In Menand (ed.), *Pragmatism: A Reader*, New York: Vintage Books, pp. xi–xxxiv.

Misak, C. (2000). *Truth, Politics, Morality*. London: Routledge.

Peirce, C. S. (1931–58). *Collected Papers of Charles Sanders Peirce*, i–vi, ed. C. Hartshorne and P. Weiss; vii and viii, ed. A. Burks, Cambridge, MA: Harvard University Press. Cited as *CP* plus volume and paragraph number.

_____ (1958 [1903]). "Draft of Review of J. J. Baldwin, *Dictionary of Philosophy and Psychology*". In *Collected Papers of Charles Sanders Peirce*, ed. A. Burks, Cambridge, MA: Harvard University Press, 8. 168.

_____ (1992 [1868]). "Some Consequences of Four Incapacities". In Peirce Edition Project (eds.), *The Essential Peirce*, Bloomington, IN: Indiana University Press, i: 28–55.

_____ (1998 [1905]). "What Pragmatism Is". In Peirce Edition Project (eds.), *The Essential Peirce*, Bloomington, IN: Indiana University Press, ii: 331–45.

Posner, R. (2003). *Law, Pragmatism, and Democracy*. Cambridge, MA: Harvard University Press.

Pratt, J. (1908). "Truth and Ideas". *Journal of Philosophy*, 5: 122–31.

Price, H. (2003). "Truth as Convenient Fiction". *Journal of Philosophy*, 100: 167–90.

Putnam, H. (1990). *Realism with a Human Face*. Cambridge, MA: Harvard University Press.

——— (1992). *Renewing Philosophy*. Cambridge, MA: Harvard University Press.

——— (1994). "Between the New Left and Judaism". In G. Borradori (ed.), *The American Philosopher: Conversations with Quine, Davidson, Putnam, Nozick, Rorty, Cavell, MacIntyre, and Kuhn*, Chicago: University of Chicago Press, 55–69.

——— (1995). *Pragmatism: An Open Question*. Oxford: Blackwell.

——— (1998). "A Politics of Hope". *Times Literary Supplement*, 22 May.

Rorty, R. (1979). *Philosophy and the Mirror of Nature*. Princeton: Princeton University Press.

——— (1982). *Consequences of Pragmatism*. Minneapolis: University of Minnesota Press.

——— (1991). "The Professor and the Prophet". *Transition*, 52: 70–8.

——— (1998). *Philosophical Papers*, iii: *Truth and Progress*. Cambridge: Cambridge University Press.

——— (1999). *Philosophy and Social Hope*. London: Penguin.

——— (2006). "Dewey and Posner on Pragmatism and Moral Progress". Unpublished Dewey Lecture in Law and Philosophy, University of Chicago Law School, 10 April.

——— and Engel, P. (2007). *What's the Use of Truth?* New York: Columbia University Press.

Ryan, A. (2001). "The Group". *New York Review of Books*, 31 May.

Talisse, R. (2005). *Democracy after Liberalism: Pragmatism and Deliberative Politics*. New York: Routledge.

——— (2007). *A Pragmatist Philosophy of Democracy*. New York: Routledge.

Westbrook, R. (2005). *Democratic Hope: Pragmatism and the Politics of Truth*. Ithaca, NY: Cornell University Press.

CHAPTER 11

THE RECEPTION OF EARLY AMERICAN PRAGMATISM

CHERYL MISAK

1. INTRODUCTION

PRAGMATISM is America's homegrown philosophy. The thought at its core is that we must look to the consequences of a concept in order fully to understand it. The view that is most associated with pragmatism is its inquiry-centered, anti-foundationalist account of truth, on which truth is not a relationship between our beliefs and the believer-independent world, but rather is the best we human inquirers can do. Although the early pragmatists made very significant contributions to other branches of philosophy and to other fields of investigation (Peirce in logic, James in psychology, Dewey in education), I will confine myself in this essay to what most philosophers think

This paper was improved by comments from the Philosophy Department at Vanderbilt University, especially from Rob Talisse. Doug Anderson and Russell Goodman also provided very helpful feedback.

of when they think of pragmatism. As Bertrand Russell put it, 'the cardinal point in the pragmatist philosophy' is 'its theory of truth' (1992 [1909]: 261).

Pragmatism originated in Cambridge, Massachusetts, in the early 1870s in the Metaphysical Club—an informal reading group in which Oliver Wendell Holmes, William James, Chauncy Wright, Charles Sanders Peirce, and others thrashed out their views. James's *Pragmatism: A New Name for Some Old Ways of Thinking* appeared in 1907, 'cometlike on our intellectual horizon' (Carus 2001*a* [1911]: 44). The view shone brightly right through to John Dewey's death in 1959. But then it seemed quickly to burn out. In the 1970s, when Richard Rorty brought about a renaissance of a certain kind of pragmatism, there were very few pragmatists or students of American philosophy in major American universities.

The trajectory of pragmatism is an interesting one, although not as interesting as Louis Menand makes it out to be in his best-selling and Pulitzer Prize-winning book *The Metaphysical Club*. He asserts that the early pragmatists 'taught a kind of skepticism that helped people cope with life in a heterogeneous, industrialized, mass market society'—a skepticism which helped 'free thought from thralldom to official ideologies, of the church or the state or even the academy' (2001: p. xii). Pragmatism, he says, 'belongs to a disestablishmentarian impulse in American culture' (2001: 89). Menand's classical pragmatists look a lot like the contemporary pragmatist Richard Rorty, arguing that there is no certainty, no truth, and no objectivity to be had, only solidarity with others, agreement within a community, or what our peers will let us get away with saying.

Menand's claim is that the American Civil War was, amongst other things, a failure of ideas. It 'swept away almost the whole intellectual culture of the North', and 'it took nearly half a century for the United States to find a culture to replace it, to find a set of ideas, and a way of thinking, that would help people cope with the conditions of modern life' (2001: p. x) That set of ideas, he asserts, was found in pragmatism. After the trauma of the Civil War, in which the lesson was 'that certitude leads to violence', people were not in the mood for absolutist philosophies (Menand 2001: 61). Pragmatism thus flourished until fallibilism and tolerance were made suspicious by the intellectual climate of the Cold War of the 1950s and 1960s (Menand 2001: 438).[1] James and Dewey came to be seen as 'naïve, and even a little dangerous'

---

[1] Menand does say that there were more mundane reasons as well for the change in status of the reputations of James and Dewey—their disciples were less impressive, and other ways of doing

(Menand 2001: 439). With the end of the Cold War, uncertainty was allowable again—hence Rorty's revival of pragmatism during the 1980s and 1990s. 'For in the post-Cold War world, where there are many competing belief systems, not just two, skepticism about the finality of any particular set of beliefs has begun to seem to some people an important value again' (Menand 2001: 441).

This is a rather breath-taking thesis. In this essay, I will show that it is not the best understanding of the early reception of pragmatism. The accurate story is less grandiose, but it is actually more interesting, in terms of the evolution of modern analytic philosophy.

2. CHARLES PEIRCE (1839–1914) AND WILLIAM JAMES (1842–1910)

Here is one way in which Peirce articulates the principle at the very core of pragmatism:

[W]e must not begin by talking of pure ideas,—vagabond thoughts that tramp the public roads without any human habitation,—but must begin with men and their conversation.   (*CP* 8. 112; 1900[2])

In order to get a complete grasp of a concept, we must connect it to that with which we have 'dealings' (*CP* 5. 416; 1905). Peirce and James each famously apply this principle to the concept of truth—in order to get a grip on the notion of truth, philosophers have to link the concept to our practices of believing, inquiring, and asserting.

The story of the reception of classical pragmatism is mostly a story of the reception of James's application of the pragmatic maxim to the concept of truth. For Peirce was very much in the background—under-employed, under-published, and under-read. He was by all accounts a difficult man.[3] That, and a now opaque scandal over his infidelity, divorce, and quick remarriage, combined to lock him out of academia. He spent a brief time on the faculty at

philosophy seemed 'more obviously suited to academic modes in inquiry' (2001: 438). But the main reason remains one about the 'intellectual climate of the Cold War' (2001: 439).

[2] References to Peirce's work are in standard form as follows: *CP*: volume number, followed by paragraph number; *W*: volume number, followed by page number; *MS*: manuscript number, as identified by Robin (1967).

[3] On this score, Menand 2001 is excellent. See also Brent 1993.

Johns Hopkins, but the Harvard position he craved was never to be offered. As a result, he had a day job as a scientist for the Coast Survey and worked on his philosophical contributions after hours.

James, on the other hand, was widely published, widely translated (nine books into French in the decade around the turn of the century, for instance), and widely known. It was James, for instance, who was the contact with the Italian pragmatists, and James who had an impact in France (see Shook 2006).

But it was also James who attracted what was to become rather fatal attention from England. First, he delivered a series of lectures at Oxford in 1908 on 'The Pluralistic Universe: The Present Situation in Philosophy', a wide-ranging discourse which brought in Hegel, Fechner, Bergson, descriptive psychology, and religious experience. It did not go over well. Second, his *Pragmatism* sparked the critical attention of Bertrand Russell and G. E. Moore, who, we shall see, leveled devastating criticisms of it. Finally, the Oxford-educated F. C. S. Schiller spent 1893–7 teaching at Cornell, where he became exposed to and enamored of James's pragmatism. Schiller's 'humanism' had as its slogan 'Man is the measure of all things', a slightly stronger governing sentiment than James's own 'the trail of the human serpent is over everything'. Schiller returned to teach at Oxford, where he engaged in highly contentious debates with Bradley and attracted Russell's scorn. (Russell, for instance, was put into 'a state of fury' over Schiller's 'impertinence' in writing a book on logic when 'he neither knows nor respects the subject' (1992 [1909]: 292).) Schiller's reputation dragged down James's, as the two seemed happy to be identified with each other.

The fact that James was so famous in many quarters (and infamous in others) put Peirce even deeper in the shadows. Paul Carus is one of the few philosophers who actually read and engaged Peirce in the early 1900s.[4] But even he airbrushes Peirce out of pragmatism in his influential and critical book titled *Truth on Trial*. Carus was attuned to the differences between Peirce and James:

Our readers may have noticed that since "pragmatism" has become the watchword of a new and popular movement with which Mr. Peirce, the inventor of the term, does not appear to be in full accord, he has introduced the word "pragmaticism" as if to point out the difference between his own philosophy and that of Professor James.   (Carus 2001a [1911]: 36)[5]

---

[4] He was locked in an intense but respectful debate with Peirce about chance and laws in *The Monist*.

[5] Peirce thought that 'pragmaticism' was a name 'ugly enough to be safe from kidnappers' (*CP* 5. 414; 1905). The trouble was that it was so ugly that it failed to catch on with anyone.

Carus calls Peirce 'the real founder of pragmatism' (2001*a* [1911]: 114), but he somehow finds it acceptable to hardly mention him in the rest of the book. Pragmatism might have been a comet on our intellectual horizon, but '[t]he nucleus of the comet is Professor James, brilliant but erratic; and he is attended by a tail of many admirers and imitators, all aglow with the stir of their master's enthusiasm and the world stands open-eyed at the unprecedented phenomenon' (2001*a* [1911]: 44).[6]

Similarly, James Pratt (1909) offers us a refutation of pragmatism by taking James to be the star, with John Dewey and Schiller the supporting cast, and Peirce as a mere walk-on part. Like many others at the turn of that century, Pratt doesn't even spell 'Peirce' correctly.[7] And William Caldwell, in *Pragmatism and Idealism*, tells us that 'Pragmatism ... rests in the main upon the work of three men, Professors James and Dewey of America, and Dr. Schiller of Oxford' (2001*a* [1913]: 3). He allows that Peirce is 'canonized as the patron saint of the movement by James' (2001*a* [1913]: 3), but doesn't rate him as worth much more of a reference in the rest of the book.[8]

This phenomenon continues to the present. Rorty, the inheritor of the James/Dewey pragmatist torch (see Misak, forthcoming), asserts that Peirce's 'contribution to pragmatism was merely to have given it a name, and to have stimulated James' (Rorty 1982: 61).

While Peirce is the archetype of what James called a 'technical' philosopher, James makes it clear at the beginning of *Pragmatism* that he is not interested in being one: 'the philosophy which is so important to each of us is not a technical matter; it is our more or less dumb sense of what life honestly and deeply means' (1949 [1907]: 5). He goes on: 'I have heard friends and colleagues try to popularize philosophy in this very hall, but they soon grew dry, and then technical, and the results were only partially encouraging.'

James was very successful in getting philosophy to the educated masses. His view was discussed extensively in the popular literature of the day. As Harvey Cormier says, of a humorous attack on James's view of truth, 'the most remarkable thing about this ... is that it exists at all. It's as if the *Daily Show* were to take on Quine or Habermas' (Cormier 2001: p. xi). Of course, this popularizing ambition tended not to impress professional philosophers. In his

---

[6] The essay from which this quote is taken was first published in 1908.

[7] In the Open Court Papers housed at Southern Illinois University, Peirce's name is actually misspelled several times on proofs of his own essays. I thank Doug Anderson for pointing this out to me.

[8] The defenders of pragmatism also ignored Peirce. See, e.g., Murray (2001 [1912]).

rather bad-tempered (indeed, generally bad) *Anti-Pragmatism*, Albert Schinz rants: 'Popular science, popular art, popular theology—only one thing was lacking—popular philosophy. And now they give that to us. What a triumph for a weak cause!' (Schinz 2001*a* [1909]: p. xvi).

That James thought that Peirce was prone to objectionable dry and technical philosophy is brought out beautifully in a rather bad-tempered exchange between the two in 1898, the same year in which James officially unveiled pragmatism in a lecture in California. James had charitably set up some paying lectures in Cambridge for his impoverished friend and, upon learning that Peirce intended to speak about logic, asked him to 'be a good boy and think a more popular plan out'.[9] Peirce, no doubt struggling with the shame of having to rely on James's kindness and bitter about being shut out of academia, is in turn scathing in his lectures about the Harvard philosophers and their lack of training in logic. Even after his dear friend James had died, Peirce couldn't resist saying that he had an 'almost unexampled incapacity for mathematical thought' (*CP* 6. 182; 1911).

We shall see below that two very different versions of the pragmatic account of truth and objectivity arise from applying the pragmatic maxim to the concept of truth—from linking the concept of truth to our practices. One version is Peirce's. He focuses on the practices of inquiry and tries to capture our cognitive aspirations to objectivity. The other is James's, the view which in substance took root in Dewey and then in Rorty, and which is only now being gradually overtaken by a more Peircean brand of pragmatism.[10]

3. Peirce: Truth as Indefeasibility

Peirce, along with every other pragmatist—classical and contemporary—argues against 'transcendental' accounts of truth, such as the correspondence theory, on which a true belief is one that corresponds to, or gets right, the believer-independent world. These views of truth are examples of those

---

[9] See Trammell 1972 for an account of the dispute.
[10] See, e.g., the essays collected in Misak 2007. Douglas Anderson notes in this volume that Peirce at times asserted that James and Schiller 'had a clear grasp of the leading ideas of pragmatism' and that 'they are doing splendid work beneficial to a wider public'. But note the underlying not entirely positive tone: 'they sincerely want to learn, and are learning in truth and actuality certain difficulties under which they labor' (MS 387a: 00309).

'vagabond thoughts'. They make truth 'the subject of metaphysics exclusively'. For the very idea of the believer-independent world, and the items within it to which beliefs or sentences might correspond, seem graspable only if we could somehow step outside our corpus of belief. We would do better to illuminate truth by considering its linkages with inquiry, assertion, and belief. For those are the human dealings relevant to truth. All pragmatist views of truth, that is, are naturalist views—we should not add anything metaphysical to science, or to any other first-order inquiry.[11] We have to extract the concept of truth, as it were, from our practices of inquiry, reason giving, and deliberation.

Peirce argues that a belief is true if it would be 'indefeasible'; or would not be improved upon; or would never lead to disappointment; or would forever meet the challenges of reasons, argument, and evidence. A true belief is the belief we would come to, were we to inquire as far as we could on a matter. Peirce initially put this idea in the following unhelpful way: a true belief is one which would be agreed upon at the hypothetical or 'fated' end of inquiry (see W3. 273; 1878). But his considered and much better formulation is this: a true belief is one which would withstand doubt, were we to inquire as far as we fruitfully could into the matter. A true belief is such that, no matter how much further we were to investigate and debate, it would not be overturned by recalcitrant experience and argument (CP 5. 569, 1901; 6. 485, 1908). On the whole, he tries to stay away from unhelpful ideas such as the final end of inquiry, perfect evidence, and the like.

Anticipating recent moves in philosophical debates about truth, he was also very careful to stay away from a reductive definition of truth: he did not want to *define* truth as that which satisfies our aims in inquiry. A dispute about definition, he says, is usually a 'profitless discussion' (CP 8. 100; 1910). His pragmatist project is to try to get us to see the difference between two respectable tasks. The first is to provide an analytic or 'nominal' definition of a concept like truth, which at best might be of use to someone who has never encountered the notion before. The second is to provide a pragmatic elucidation of the concept of truth on an account of the role the concept plays in practical endeavors. This is clearly the project that the pragmatist thinks is important.

---

[11] Peirce wasn't against metaphysics *tout court*. He engaged in a fair bit of metaphysical inquiry himself, and he thought that our practices are accompanied by metaphysical outlooks, whether we know it or not. But he was against metaphysical speculation or metaphysical theories that are unconnected to any experience that could speak for or against them. See Misak 1995.

Along with the pragmatist view of truth comes a fallibilist epistemology. Peirce famously argued (in, e.g., the 1887 'The Fixation of Belief') that inquiry begins with the irritation of doubt and ends with a stable doubt-resistant belief. If we were to have a belief which would always be immune to doubt—which would forever fit with experience and argument—then that belief is true. Since we can never know when a belief is like that, our beliefs are fallible. Any one of them might be shown to be false.

Fallibilism, however, does not entail that we ought to follow Descartes and try to bring into doubt all beliefs about which error is conceivable. Such doubts would be, Peirce argued, 'paper' or 'tin'—not the genuine article. He says:

there is but one state of mind from which you can 'set out', namely, the very state of mind in which you actually find yourself at the time you do 'set out'—a state in which you are laden with an immense mass of cognition already formed, of which you cannot divest yourself if you would . . . Do you call it doubting to write down on a piece of paper that you doubt? If so, doubt has nothing to do with any serious business.   (CP 5. 416; 1905)

Our body of background beliefs is susceptible to doubt on a piecemeal basis if that doubt is prompted by surprising or recalcitrant experience. We must *regard* our background beliefs as true, until some surprising experience throws one or some group of them into doubt. The inquirer

is under a compulsion to believe just what he does believe . . . as time goes on, the man's belief usually changes in a manner which he cannot resist . . . this force which changes a man's belief in spite of any effort of his may be, in all cases, called a *gain of experience*.   (MS 1342, p. 2; undated)

So, on the Peircean epistemology, an inquirer has a fallible background of 'commonsense' belief which is not in fact in doubt. Only against such a background can a belief be put into doubt and a new, better belief be adopted. All our beliefs are fallible, but they do not come into doubt all at once. Those which inquiry has not thrown into doubt are stable, and we should retain them until a reason to doubt arises.

Peirce links the scientific method to this epistemology. It is the method which pays close attention to the fact that beliefs fall to the surprise of recalcitrant experience. Inquiry 'is not standing upon the bedrock of fact. It is walking upon a bog, and can only say, this ground seems to hold for the present. Here I will stay till it begins to give way' (CP 5. 589; 1898).

The first step in the scientific method is what Peirce famously called an abductive inference: a hypothesis or a conjecture is identified that explains some surprising experience. Consequences are then deduced from this hypothesis and are tested by induction. If the hypothesis passes the test of experience, then it is accepted—it is stable and believed until upset by experience.

On Peirce's view, we aim at beliefs which would be forever stable—we aim at getting the best beliefs we can. We have in our various inquiries and deliberations a multiplicity of local aims—empirical adequacy, coherence with other beliefs, simplicity, explanatory power, getting a reliable guide to action, fruitfulness for other research, greater understanding of others, increased maturity, and the like. When we say that we aim at the truth, what we mean is that, were a belief really to satisfy all of our local aims in inquiry, then that belief would be true. There is nothing over and above the fulfillment of those aims, nothing metaphysical, to which we aspire. Truth is not some transcendental, mystical thing which we aim at for its own sake.

4. JAMES: TRUTH AND THE USEFUL

The pragmatist view of truth finds a different kind of expression in the hands of James. I choose my words carefully. It may well be that James was putting forward more or less the same view of truth as was Peirce—indeed, we shall see that at times he comes very close to articulating a view similar to Peirce's. But two facts about the context in which James placed himself result in a different expression of it. First, as we have seen, James was very concerned to make his view accessible, so he often describes the pragmatist account of truth in crisp, well-written, snappy sentences, designed to make a splash. This doesn't allow for much nuance.

Second, James, with Schiller, took himself to be arguing against the absolute idealism of F. H. Bradley at Oxford and Josiah Royce at Harvard. This is the view that there is one overarching or all-absorbing mind or unitary consciousness which includes everything else that exists. Peirce was less concerned with contrasting his position with idealism, and so the pragmatist view of truth, in his hands, has a different look to it.

James thinks that pragmatism will make short work of many long-standing and seemingly intractable philosophical problems: 'If no practical difference whatsoever can be traced, then the alternatives mean practically the same thing, and all dispute is idle' (1949 [1907]: 45). Thus we have the pragmatic maxim as voiced by James.

He sets out his view on truth and objectivity as: 'Any idea upon which we can ride . . . any idea that will carry us prosperously from any one part of our experience to any other part, linking things satisfactorily, working securely, simplifying, saving labor, is . . . true *instrumentally*' (1949 [1907]: 58). 'Satisfactorily', for James, 'means more satisfactorily to ourselves, and individuals will emphasize their points of satisfaction differently. To a certain degree, therefore, everything here is plastic' (1949 [1907]: 61). Sometimes he puts his position as follows: 'True ideas are those that we can assimilate, validate, corroborate and verify'; 'truth *happens* to an idea' (1949 [1907]: 200). He rather infamously suggested that if a belief in God made a positive or a good impact on someone's life, then it could reasonably be taken as true by that person.

We shall see that it is this kind of statement of pragmatism that inspired so much vitriol. But a few words of caution are required at the outset. First, a careful reading of James shows, first, that when James speaks of truth not being static, but rather, plastic, what he is quite clearly talking about is not truth, but what we take as knowledge. In *Pragmatism* he says:

[T]he great assumption of the intellectualists is that truth means essentially an inert static relation. When you've got your true idea of anything, there's an end of the matter. You're in possession; you *know*; you have fulfilled your thinking destiny.   (1949 [1907]: 200)

Second, like Peirce, James was concerned to characterize truth as something that was of human value, without making a true belief what this or that human found valuable at this or that time. He sometimes tries to correct a misunderstanding of his position by arguing that, contrary to his critics, he holds that the true is 'the expedient', but the expedient 'in the long run and on the whole, of course' (1914 [1909]: p. vii). That is, James too wants to argue that true beliefs are beliefs which survive because they deserve to survive (see Kappy Suckiel 1982: 105–15).

'The Moral Philosopher and the Moral Life' is perhaps James's clearest and most subtle presentation of the pragmatist view of truth. He speaks here of truth in ethics, but gestures at the general pragmatist account of truth: 'there can be no final truth in ethics any more than in physics, until the last man has had his experience and his say' (1979 [1897]: 184). He argues that society may be seen as a long-running experiment aimed at identifying the best kind of conduct. Its conventions thus deserve respect. Our background beliefs, while remaining fallible, capture the experience of generations (1979

[1897]: 206). James thinks that 'ethical science is just like physical science, and instead of being deducible all at once from abstract principles, must simply bide its time, and be ready to revise its conclusions from day to day' (1979 [1867]: 208).

Here we see a more careful James. He and Peirce think that, as with any kind of inquirer, the ethical deliberator might be hesitant to revise her beliefs, and this hesitation can be justified. But it is not always justified, says Peirce:

Like any other field, more than any other [morality] needs improvement, advance...But morality, doctrinaire conservatist that it is, destroys its own vitality by resisting change, and positively insisting, This is eternally right: That is eternally wrong.   (*CP* 2. 198; 1902)

For both Peirce and James, moral judgments are connected to experience in the way that all of our genuine judgments are: 'just as reasoning springs from experience, so the development of sentiment arises from the soul's Inward and Outward Experiences' (*CP* 1. 648; 1898). As with every other kind of experience, '[t]hat it is abstractly and absolutely infallible we do not pretend; but that it is practically infallible for the individual—which is the only clear sense the word "infallibility" will bear—in that he ought to obey it and not his individual reason, *that* we do maintain' (*CP* 1. 633, 1898). We take our body of background belief to be practically infallible, until the course of experience weighs in against it.

In *Pragmatism*, James offers us a clutch of metaphors for the growth of knowledge. One likens the change in belief to house renovations: 'You may alter your house *ad libitum*, but the ground plan of the first architect persists—you can make great changes, but you can not change a Gothic church into a Doric temple' (1949 [1907]: 170). Here is another: 'You may rinse and rinse the bottle, but you can't get the taste of the medicine or whisky that first filled it wholly out' (1949 [1907]: 170). All of his metaphors have the pragmatist theme that 'we patch and tinker more than we renew' (1949 [1907]: 169).

5. JOHN DEWEY AND INSTRUMENTALISM

John Dewey (1859–1952) was younger than Peirce and James and outlived them by four decades. He was a graduate student at Johns Hopkins during

Peirce's brief tenure there and had plenty of exposure to Peirce's ideas.[12] After James's death in 1910, he was the standard-bearer for pragmatism. Like James, he was an extremely high-profile public intellectual in America, thoroughly enmeshed in the important debates of his time. So pragmatism's fortunes seemed entirely secure.

Already in 1903 Dewey had published *Studies in Logical Theory*,[13] which was being referred to by James as the foundation for pragmatism in America (James 1949 [1907]: p. xiv). In it, he starts to formulate his epistemology, fully worked out in his *Logic: The Theory of Inquiry* of 1938. For Dewey, epistemology is the 'theory of inquiry' or 'experimental logic'. He adopts, pretty much wholesale, Peirce's doubt–belief model of inquiry.[14] Inquirers begin with a problematic situation, arrive at hypotheses which might explain or solve that problematic situation, and then test these hypotheses in action. If the candidate hypotheses are successfully employed in action, enabling us to meet our goals, they are true, or as Dewey later put it, we can assert them with warrant. Dewey's special twist on the Peircean account of inquiry is that he takes as his focus the idea of an organism trying to maintain stability or harmony in its environment.

With James, Dewey thinks that we make truth. Truth is not a 'ready-made' property of propositions:

The pragmatist says that since every proposition is a hypothesis referring to an inquiry still to be undertaken (a proposal in short) its truth is a matter of its career, of its history: that it becomes or is made true (or false).   (1998 [1911]: 114)

Again with James, he takes pragmatism to be a species of empiricism. But, unlike British empiricism, Dewey argues that pragmatism

does not insist upon antecedent phenomena but upon consequent phenomena; not upon the precedents but upon the possibilities of action. And this change in point of view is almost revolutionary in its consequences.   (1998 [1925]: 8)

So for Dewey, as for James, truth and knowledge are not static phenomena—it is not the case that our beliefs either mirror reality (and hence are true) or fail to do so (and hence are false). Peirce thought that truth was

---

[12] Menand 2001 is excellent on this score.

[13] This was a joint effort with his Chicago philosophy colleagues, but Dewey's four introductory chapters are the core of it.

[14] There are significant differences between Dewey and Peirce, differences that I shall gloss over here. For one thing, Dewey tended towards metaphysically heavy interpretations of doubt, belief, and inquiry.

static in the sense that a belief either would or would not survive the rigors of inquiry. But all three of the classical pragmatists speak with one voice when they suggest that we are always immersed in a context of inquiry, where the decision to be made is a decision about what to believe from here, not what to believe were we able to start from scratch—from certain infallible foundations.

Dewey, even more than James, extended his views of truth and objectivity to ethics and politics. Indeed, this is where he most distinguishes himself from his predecessors. He argued that 'the problems of men' could be brought under the sweep of science or inquiry. Thus Dewey characterized his view as being experimentalist through and through.

Dewey thought a lot about democracy, and it is fitting that his reputation in political theory is still hearty. Democracy fits hand in hand with the kind of experimentalism that Dewey put forward. For democracy, he argued, is the use of the experimental method to solve practical problems (Dewey 1981 [1939]). We propose solutions to problems, try to predict the consequences of the solutions' implementation, and ask whether our reactions to those consequences would be positive or negative. We then test the solution that has withstood the challenge of the first round of testing (in the imagination). That is, we see what the results actually are. Throughout this process, the emphasis is on testing, fallibility, and revision.

6. The Response to James

The reaction to James's *Pragmatism* set the tone for how pragmatism was viewed for decades to come. Whether fair or not, James's critics latched on to the most simple and clear statements of his view. Indeed, there is a striking uniformity about the view that pragmatism's critics take themselves to be reacting to. They all argue against the ideas that we make truth and that a true belief is one that is useful or works.

William Caldwell (2001*a* [1913]), for instance, identifies two essential elements of pragmatism. First is the idea that truth and reality are 'made', plastic, or modifiable; second is the rejection of the distinction between appearance and reality. Paul Carus agrees. Pragmatism replaces 'the belief in the stability of truth, in its persistence and eternality' with 'a more elastic kind of truth which can change with the fashions and makes it possible that we need no longer trouble about inconsistencies; for what is true to one need no longer be true to others, and the truth of to-day may be the real now, and yet it may become the error of the to-morrow' (2001a [1911]: 110). Hence pragmatism has put truth on trial, with James as the hapless prosecutor.

When anyone bothers to think about Peirce, he is excused from this charge. Carus says that James's mistake was that he 'calls truth what in Mr. Peirce's language is merely "the fixation of belief"'. (2001a 1911: 58). Peirce's argument, we have seen, is that were we to settle or fix belief permanently so that it would never disappoint us, then that would be the truth. Carus takes James to hold that if we have a belief that currently doesn't disappoint us, that is the truth.

It was the criticisms leveled by Russell and Moore that really sunk pragmatism's reputation. It is not that their objections were different or better than those of the American critics of pragmatism. It was, one assumes, that they were coming from Russell and Moore, perhaps the most important philosophers in the English-speaking world.[15]

Russell noted that he too was an empiricist, and so was sympathetic with much of James's view—especially the idea that pragmatism is a method that turns its back on a priori reasoning and turns towards concrete facts and consequences (1992 [1966]: 196). Nonetheless, he thought that James's account of truth was seriously defective. Sometimes he attacked a pragmatist straw man in a pretty irresponsible way. For one thing, Russell will sometimes quip, 'The skepticism embodied in pragmatism is that which says "Since all beliefs are absurd, we may as well believe what is most convenient"' (1992 [1909]: 280). James never went near that thought.

For another, Russell took James to be asserting a criterion of truth—a way of determining whether a particular belief is true—and then accused James of not seeing the difference between the criterion for truth and the meaning of truth (1992 [1966]: 202). Sometimes he exhibits nuance when he tries to tell us what James's criterion is: 'a belief is to be judged true in so far as the practical consequences of its adoption are good' (1992 [1966]: 199).

---

[15]   There was a striking anomaly in the reaction of Oxbridge to James. Whereas Russell and Moore scorned pragmatism, the most enduring of the Oxbridge philosophers, Wittgenstein, had a more complex relationship with James's work. As Russell Goodman has shown, while many of James's views came in for criticism by Wittgenstein, and while Wittgenstein disclaimed pragmatism, he read James's work intently for forty years, making frequent glowing remarks about it (Goodman 2002: 10, 12). Indeed, in *On Certainty*, one of the last things Wittgenstein wrote, we find: 'So I am trying to say something that sounds like pragmatism. Here I am being thwarted by a kind of Weltanschauung' (1969: 54).

Notice that here we have not a criterion of a belief's being true, but rather a criterion of a belief's being judged to be true. It is not implausible to think that we ought to look to a belief's practical consequences in order to judge it true or false, and it seems that this is what James, in his more careful moods, means. But a few pages later, Russell reverts to the most easily criticized version of James, where he has James asserting that 'A truth is anything which it pays to believe' (1992 [1966]: 201). James, in his less careful moods, does indeed make this move, but it isn't clear that Russell is right to take his less careful statements as representing his view.

But some of Russell's objections were more measured. For instance, he turned the pragmatist account of truth on itself, as it were, and noted that if it itself is to be useful, there must be a way of telling when the consequences of a belief are useful or good (1992 [1966]: 201):

We must suppose that this means that the consequences of entertaining the belief are better than those of rejecting it. In order to know this, we must know what are the consequences of entertaining it, and what are the consequences of rejecting it; we must know also what consequences are good, what bad, what consequences are better, and what worse.

This, of course, is a very tall order, which Russell immediately illustrates with two examples. First, the consequences of believing the doctrine of the Catholic faith might make one happy 'at the expense of a certain amount of stupidity and priestly domination' (1992 [1966]: 201). It is unclear how we are to weigh these benefits and burdens against each other. Second, the effects of Rousseau's doctrines were far-reaching—Europe is a different place from what it would have been without them. But how do we disentangle what the effects have been? And even if we could do that, whether we take them to be good or bad depends on our political views. The question of whether the consequences of believing are on the whole good or bad is an extraordinarily difficult one.

In a related objection, Russell points that one can take 'works' or 'pays' in two very different ways. In science, a hypothesis works if we can deduce a number of verifiable hypotheses from it. But for James, a hypothesis works if

the effects of believing it are good, including among the effects . . . the emotions entailed by it or its perceived consequences, and the actions to which we are prompted by it or its perceived consequences. This is a totally different conception of 'working', and one for which the authority of scientific procedure cannot be invoked.   (1992 [1966]: 210)

G. E. Moore reviewed James's *Pragmatism* in the 1907 *Proceedings of the Aristotelian Society*. The review is harsh and rather labored, with Moore identifying James's main assertions as things that he is 'anxious' to say, then picking them apart at length, and in the end finding them to be, despite James's protests to the contrary, 'silly' (1992 [1907]: 161, 174). He strikes a theme and a tone present in many of the commentaries on James:

> He may protest, quite angrily, when a view is put before him in other words than his own, that he never either meant or implied any such thing, and yet it may be possible to judge, from what he says, that this very view, wrapped up in other words, was not only held by him but was precisely what made his thoughts seem to him to be interesting and important.   (1992 [1907]: 174)

Here is a catalogue of Moore's pressing objections to James's view.

First, he points to a problem that dogs all pragmatist views of truth. If truth is tightly connected to what we can verify, how do we think of statements for which the evidence has been destroyed, or statements that are so trivial that no one has bothered to collect any evidence for them, or statements the evidence for which lies buried deep in the past? (1992 [1907]: 165, 179).[16]

Second, with Russell, Moore interrogates the linkage between the true and the useful.[17] If usefulness is a property that may come and go (in James's own words), then 'a belief, which occurs at several different times, may be true at some of the times at which it occurs, and yet untrue at others' (1992 [1907]: 183). The truth of a belief, that is, seems to vary from time to time and from culture to culture. Truth is not a stable property of beliefs, and that is an anathema, in Moore's view.

Third, Moore takes on James's claim that we make the truth: 'I think that he certainly means to suggest that we not only make our true beliefs, but also that we *make* them true' (1992 [1907]: 191). But Moore thinks it's crazy to suggest that my belief that *p* makes it true that *p*. My (correct) belief that it rained today did not make it rain today.

One can see that under a barrage of well-formed criticism such as this, pragmatism's reputation across the Atlantic was bound to suffer. But it came under similar stress in America.

James Pratt is the critic who, in my view, takes the most care with James's view. He sees two ambitious claims at the heart of pragmatism. The first is

---

[16] Peirce worried about this set of issues. See Misak (2004 [1991]).

[17] Here are two other ways in which he tries to disconnect the true and the useful: first, sometimes keeping truth front and center can be detrimental (as when you focus on your weaknesses); and second, believing trivial truths is not useful.

about truth: 'in morality and metaphysics and religion, as well as in science, we are justified in testing the truth of a belief by its usefulness' (2001*a* [1909]: 13). A true claim is a 'verified human claim' (2001*a* [1909]: 83). The second is about meaning: 'the meaning of any philosophical proposition can always be brought down to some particular consequence in our future practical experience' (2001*a* [1909]: 25). He takes both the pragmatist view about truth and the pragmatist view about meaning to be the views of James and Schiller. (Dewey gets a mention, but not Peirce.)

Pratt asked whether the pragmatist account of truth was itself true. It is certainly useful to pragmatists, he says, but not to others (2001*a* [1909]: 127). The fact that pragmatists will want to respond by saying that the truth of pragmatism consists in something more robust shows that they too think that there is some more transcendental account of truth in play—the pragmatist is 'making use of the very conception of truth which he is trying to refute' (2001*a* [1909]: 129).

Pratt also tackles James's view that religious hypotheses are true if they are good for us to believe. Here he echoes Moore's distinction between the two senses of what works or what is good. Pragmatism, Pratt says,

seeks to prove the truth of religion by its good and satisfactory consequences. Here, however, a distinction must be made; namely between the 'good', harmonious, and logically confirmatory consequences of religious concepts as such, and the good and pleasant consequences which come from believing these concepts. It is one thing to say a belief is true because the logical consequences that flow from it fit in harmoniously with our otherwise grounded knowledge; and quite another to call it true because it is pleasant to believe. (2001*a* [1909]: 186–7)

The difference between the views of Peirce and James can be nicely summarized by Pratt's distinction. Peirce holds that 'a belief is true because the logical consequences that flow from it would fit in harmoniously with our otherwise grounded knowledge', and James at times seems to hold that a belief is true 'because it is pleasant to believe'. There are two caveats, however. The first is that Peirce insisted on a subjunctive formulation: a belief is true if the logical consequences *would* fit harmoniously with our otherwise grounded knowledge, were we to pursue our investigations as far as they could fruitfully go.

The second caveat is that James, as his protests suggest, and as we have seen, sometimes put forward a more careful and subtle account of truth, one that was much closer to Peirce's. He was concerned to characterize truth as something that was of human value, without making a true belief what this or that human finds valuable at this or that time. The true, he says, is 'the expedient', but the expedient 'in the long run and on the whole, of course' (1914 [1909]: p. vii).

An equally pressing set of objections, again echoing Moore, was brought against James's claim about meaning—that the meaning of a sentence consists in its consequences for future experience.[18] Pratt notes that it is not clear whether 'our experience' means my own experience, the experience of all human beings of all times, or the experience of any possible rational or sentient being. On any of these options, sentences buried in the past (e.g., 'an ichthyosaurus, who perished ages before the birth of the first man, suffered pain') seem to be meaningless, as they don't have any future experiential consequences (Pratt 2001a [1909]: 25 ff.).[19] This issue continues to be one that any pragmatist—Peircean, Jamesian, Rortyian—struggles with.

James railed against these often harshly put objections, claiming that they had a 'fantastic' and 'slanderous' character and were based on willful misinterpretation (1914 [1909]: pp. xv, 180). He responds, for instance, to Russell by asserting that it would be an 'obvious absurdity', one that he was never tempted by, to hold that someone who believes a proposition p must first determine that its consequences are good, and then his belief must be a belief that the consequences of p are good (1914 [1909]: 272).

His protests, however, had very little impact. We have already seen Moore's treatment of James's disclaimers. Carus is similarly left cold by them: 'He seems to be in the habit of sometimes saying what he does not mean and then blames the world for misunderstanding him' (2001a [1911]: 23). He argues that if James is misunderstood, the misunderstanding can be laid at the feet of 'his own carelessness' (2001a [1911]: 127). He is glad to hear that James doesn't hold the view attributed to him by Russell, 'but I cannot help thinking that his explanations of the meaning of pragmatism go pretty far to justify Professor Russell in thinking so' (2001a [1911]: 128).

The tone of the reaction to James is vitriolic. Perhaps James had become so famous that no one thought twice about being brutal with him. William Caldwell, in his not unsympathetic *Pragmatism and Idealism*, notes that even in America, pragmatism encountered in its first decade of life 'at least something

---

[18] Peirce's view was that pragmatic meaning was but one aspect of meaning, not the whole of it. See Misak 2004 [1991]: ch. 1.

[19] Pratt concludes that pragmatism must be interpreted broadly, as taking into account any experience—actual or possible and past, present, or future. Then he says that it is indistinguishable from idealism (Pratt 2001a [1909]: 37 f.).

of the contempt and the incredulity and the hostility that it met with elsewhere, and also much of the American shrewd indifference to a much-advertised new article' (2001a [1913]: 49). Of its second decade Caldwell says that it is receiving in America 'the sharpest kind of official rationalist condemnation of Pragmatism as an imperfectly proved and a merely "subjective" and a highly unsystematic philosophy' (2001a [1913]: 51).

Carus, who warmly dedicates his *Truth on Trial* to the memory of James, and who says that James 'was a fascinating personality, original and interesting in his very vagaries, genial and ingenious, versatile and learned', is a good example of what Caldwell is talking about. For Carus continues: 'Exactness of method seems to have hampered his mind and naturally appeared to him as pedantry. He loved to indulge in the *chiaroscuro* of vague possibilities, and so he showed a hankering for the mysteries of psychic phenomena, whether due to telepathy or spirit communication' (2001a [1911]: 42–3). 'With all my admiration for Professor James I ... must openly confess that his loose way of philosophizing does not exercise a wholesome influence on the young generation' (2001a [1911]: 42).

Some of James's pragmatically inclined students turned out to be at the forefront and center of philosophy in the United States—the most striking example is C. I. Lewis, who studied with James and Royce at Harvard in the early 1900s. But, for the most part, James contributed to pragmatism's reputation at the beginning of the twentieth century for having, in Pratt's words, 'a looseness of thought' (2001a [1909]: 245). It is a reputation that it is still trying to shake.

7. THE RESPONSE TO DEWEY

Dewey was for a long time the most influential public intellectual in America. His influence within America was overwhelming and his critics were, on the whole, kinder to him than James's critics were to James.[20] Russell, for instance, distinguishes Dewey's pragmatism from James's and is much more favorably disposed to Dewey's. Unlike the Jamesian will to believe, he takes Dewey's view of truth to be marked by an appealing 'very genuine scientific temper' (Russell 1977 [1919]: 245). Nonetheless, Dewey seems to have presided over

---

[20] See the essays collected in Morgenbesser 1977.

the great slide of American pragmatism into near oblivion. As Bruce Kuklick (2001: 191) notes, none of Dewey's students went on to outstanding careers in which they promoted pragmatism.

Some of the complaints against James are made against Dewey. Woodbridge (1977 [1930]: 56), for instance, puts to Dewey the charge that knowing p can't be the cause of p's being true. But many of Dewey's critics focused on parts of Dewey's corpus that were less clearly aligned with the pragmatist account of truth and objectivity. The pragmatist account of truth and objectivity, in the minds of professional philosophers, seems to remain identified with James.

The received view of Dewey's fate is that the logical empiricists, who arrived from Germany and Austria after Dewey's retirement from Columbia in 1929 but while he was still very active, simply eclipsed him. As Richard Rorty puts it:

Along about 1945, American philosophers were, for better or worse, *bored* with Dewey, and thus with pragmatism. They were sick of being told that pragmatism was the philosophy of American democracy, that Dewey was the great American intellectual figure of their century, and the like. They wanted something new, something they could get their philosophical teeth into. What showed up, thanks to Hitler and various other historical contingencies, was logical empiricism, an early version of what we now call "analytic philosophy".   (Rorty 1995: 70)

But the story is not, as Rorty would have it, a straightforward replacement of pragmatism with what was seen as a new, better, and more exciting view. As Scott Soames writes in this volume, the pragmatist reverence for logic (at least Peirce's reverence), respect for science, suspicion of metaphysics, and emphasis on practical consequences made for fertile soil in which logical empiricism could grow.

Indeed, the affinities between pragmatism and logical empiricism were noticed during the rise of logical empiricism. In 1933, before the scattering of the Vienna Circle, Otto Neurath started *The International Encyclopedia of Unified Science*, and this, teamed with a set of influential conferences on the unity of science, was for a long time the official forum for logical empiricism—it is 'organized contemporary expression', as Neurath *et al.* put it (1938: 2). Once the logical empiricists hit the shores of America, Dewey was immediately seen as a kindred spirit. He was on the *Encyclopedia*'s Advisory Committee, he was one of the introducers (alongside Otto Neurath, Niels Bohr, Bertrand Russell, Rudoph Carnap, and Charles Morris) of the very first volume of the new series, published by University of Chicago Press, and he was the sole author of a volume in 1939. That volume was entitled *Theory of Valuation*. There is an obvious and natural link between, on the one hand, Dewey's attempt to unify all inquiry via the experimental method and, on the other hand, logical empiricism's attempt to unify all inquiry through the method of science and logic. One critical difference of course is that the empiricists thought that their unifying project left little room for a theory of value, and Dewey thought that his unifying project left plenty of room.

But it wasn't just Dewey who was brought into the logical empiricist fold. C. I. Lewis (1977 [1930]), for one, saw the similarity between pragmatism and verificationism. And strikingly, Peirce was the subject of a talk at the Fifth International Conference for the Unity of Science held at Harvard in 1940. (This was the first of the conferences held in the USA.) Ernest Nagel, the Columbia philosopher of science, who was not himself a logical empiricist but who had strong connections with the players and the positions, gave a quite masterful paper entitled 'Charles S. Peirce: Pioneer of Modern Empiricism'. Nagel pointed out the affinities between logical empiricism and pragmatism: the antipathy to metaphysical speculation, the emphasis on cooperative scientific research, and the fact that the pragmatic maxim 'was offered to philosophers in order to bring to an end disputes which no observation of facts could settle because they involved terms with no definite meaning' (1940: 73).

The relationship between classical American pragmatism and logical empiricism most definitely requires more work, work which happily is now being conducted (see Ch. 17 below). But this much is clear already: there is not a clean break between pragmatism and logical empiricism. Although there are significant differences between pragmatism and logical empiricism (pragmatism was friendly to ethics, to context, and to the history of philosophy, for instance), pragmatism's fate did not hinge on its being displaced by a radically different kind of view.

8. CONCLUSION

Two things are striking in the response to pragmatism in the early 1900s. First, Menand's suggestion is not borne out. The difficulties encountered by pragmatism had everything to do with the logical and philosophical problems that their critics homed in upon. They had very little, if anything, to do with a felt need, arising in response to the Civil War, for anti-authoritarian world views. Pratt says, with a bit of a sneer, that pragmatists will call his objections '"logic-chopping"—a simple and useful device when one has been reduced to unavoidable self-contradiction' (2001a [1909]: 128). Such objections, I suggest, were so strenuously put that pragmatism has never been able fully to shake off the reputation it attracted in the early 1900s.

Second, the difficulties articulated for James's view, so clearly seen at the outset, continue to press in on the inheritor of that view today. The kinds of criticisms that were put to James are put again and again to Rorty[21]—and just as harshly. (Susan Haack (1995), for instance, calls Rorty's view 'vulgar pragmatism'.) The charge is that, despite his claims to the contrary, Rorty is really is a relativist, holding that one belief is no better than another, and that one must 'treat the epistemic standards of any and every epistemic community as on a par' (Haack 1995: 136).

Indeed, some of the problems presented to James continue to press in on all contemporary pragmatists—Jamesian or not. The issue of buried secrets—the truth of sentences the evidence for which is buried in the past—remains, for instance, something that pragmatists must address. This is not to say that pragmatism—either the Jamesian or the Peircean branch—has been unresponsive to the force of criticism. It is to say, rather, that the deep problems that adhere to it have staying power. Pragmatists continue to grapple with them. It is important to note in this regard that relativists, correspondence theorists, etc. also grapple with their own set of problems. Heath Bawden was pressing one such set on the correspondence theory in 1910: 'But it is obvious, upon reflection, that the facts as they are in themselves are a mere abstraction. They have become facts only in the process of knowledge, and cannot therefore be used as an external test of the validity of that process' (2001b [1910]: 197 f.). This kind of thought continues to plague the correspondence theorist today.

Indeed, reviews of Pratt's What is Pragmatism (A. W. Moore 1909; Woolley 1909) object to his quick and easy applauding of the correspondence theory of truth. The reviewers quite rightly point out that he assumes that the correspondence theory is unproblematic and fails to feel the force of the pragmatists' objections to it. This leaves Pratt in precisely the position we currently find ourselves in. Both the correspondence theory and the pragmatist

---

[21] See Misak (forthcoming) for a sustained argument. Rorty says that his narratives about pragmatism 'tend to center around James's version (or, at least, certain selected versions out of the many that James casually tossed off) of the pragmatic theory of truth' (Rorty 1995: 71).

theory face pressing objections, and the question as to which one will survive its challenges requires great subtlety. Pragmatism is in a better position now than it was at the start of the twentieth century, as Peirce's views have been excavated and are starting, finally, to have some impact.

One way, far from the only way, to make this point is to see how Quine is linked to the classical pragmatists.[22] He was taught by C. I. Lewis (who was taught by William James), and the impact of Lewis on Quine's thinking was significant. Quine arrived at Harvard in 1930 as a graduate student in philosophy, but his BA was in mathematics. Two of his courses during that first intense graduate introduction to philosophy were taught by Lewis. (One was on Kant, and one was on the Theory of Knowledge.) It was here that he acquired his respect for the pragmatist pillars of anti-foundationalism and naturalism.[23] He then spent two years in Europe, where he attended some of the Vienna Circle's meetings and attended Carnap's lectures in Prague.

In the abstract of his famous 'Two Dogmas of Empiricism', Quine asserts that one upshot of the paper is 'a shift towards pragmatism' (1980 [1951]: 20). This is most apparent when one looks at Quine's naturalism, holism, and fallibilism. He argues that our entire belief system must be seen as an interconnected web. Mathematics and logic are at the center, gradually shading into the theoretical sentences of science, and then to specific observation sentences at the periphery. When faced with recalcitrant evidence, we must choose where to make adjustments in our web of belief—no sentence is immune from revision. Indeed, it was Quine who made famous Neurath's metaphor: we are like sailors adrift at sea, never able to return to dry dock to reconstruct our boat out of the finest materials. We work with what we have, replacing our boat of knowledge plank by plank, as required by the surprise of experience. The resonances with the metaphors offered by the early pragmatists are striking. James has us renovating a house, Peirce has us proceeding along a bog, only able to say that this ground holds for the present.

Quine's naturalism is still hearty today, in America and elsewhere. The emphasis on science and first-order inquiry is continued in the work of

[22] See Klein (forthcoming) for a discussion. Other pragmatist lineages that do not immediately succumb to the objections lobbed at James might include those now represented by Hilary Putnam, Isaac Levi, or Robert Brandom.

[23] He indicates this in 1990: 292. Quine's relationship to pragmatism, however, is complicated, perhaps because of pragmatism's Jamesian reputation. See Quine 1981.

new pragmatists who argue that the fact that standards of objectivity are historically situated (they come into being and evolve over time) does not detract from their objectivity.[24] The trail of the human serpent is over everything—standards of truth and objectivity are *our* standards—but this does not toss us into the sea of postmodern arbitrariness, where truth varies from person to person and from culture to culture. Nor does it require us to abandon our concepts of truth and objectivity. As Peirce and Dewey stressed, we are always immersed in a context of inquiry, where the decision to be made is a decision about what to believe from here, not what to believe were we able to start from scratch—from certain infallible foundations. But of course, we do not go forward arbitrarily. The central and deep pragmatist question is how we should go from present practice to a future practice, where our very standards themselves may be thrown into question (see Fine 2007).[25] That is a question that is quite rightly still getting a tremendous amount of attention in contemporary epistemology. It is resulting in a second renaissance for pragmatism—for a kind of new pragmatism which is really the oldest kind of pragmatism.

References

Bawden, Heath (2001 [1910]). *The Principles of Pragmatism*. Repr. in Shook (2001*b*), i.

Brent, Joseph (1993). *Charles Sanders Peirce: A Life*. Bloomington, IN: Indiana University Press.

Caldwell, William (1913). *Pragmatism and Idealism*. London: Adam and Charles Black. Repr. in Shook (2001*a*), iv. 59–85.

Carus, Paul (2001 [1911]). *Truth on Trial: An Exposition of the Nature of Truth*. Chicago: Open Court. Repr. in Shook (2001*a*), iii.

Cormier, Harvey (2001). Introduction. In Shook (2001*a*), iii.

Dewey, John (1998 [1911]). 'The Problem of Truth'. In Hickman and Alexander (1998), ii. 101–30.

_____ (1981 [1939]). 'Creative Democracy: The Task Before Us'. In *The Later Works of John Dewey 1925–1953*, xiv: *Essays*, ed. J. A. Boydson, Carbondale, IL: Southern Illinois University Press, 224–30.

---

[24] See the essays collected in Misak 2007, especially Hacking (2007: 39) for nice discussions along these lines.

[25] We are in the position, Fine says, of Kuhn's revolutionary scientist 'who must choose how to project the values of established practice into new terrain and, at the very same time, must oversee how things go and adjust accordingly' (2007: 56).

_____ (1998 [1925]). 'The Development of American Pragmatism'. In Hickman and Alexander (1998), 3–13.

_____ (1939). *International Encyclopedia of Unified Science*, ii, no. 4: *Theory of Valuation*. Chicago: University of Chicago Press.

Fine, Arthur (2007). 'Relativism, Pragmatism, and the Practice of Science'. In Misak (2007), 50–67.

Goodman, Russell (2002). *Wittgenstein and William James*. Cambridge: Cambridge University Press.

Haack, Susan (1995). 'Vulgar Pragmatism: An Unedifying Prospect'. In H. J. Saakamp (ed.), *Rorty and Pragmatism: The Philosopher Responds to his Critics*, Nashville: Vanderbilt University Press, 126–47.

Hacking, Ian (2007). 'On Not Being a Pragmatist: Eight Reasons and a Cause'. In Misak (2007), 32–49.

Hickman, L. and Alexander, T. (eds.) (1998). *The Essential Dewey: Pragmatism, Education, Democracy*, i and ii. Bloomington, IN: Indiana University Press.

James, William (1979 [1897]). 'The Moral Philosopher and the Moral Life'. In *The Will to Believe and Other Essays in Popular Philosophy*, Cambridge, MA: Harvard University Press, 141–62.

_____ (1949 [1907]). *Pragmatism: A New Name for Some Old Ways of Thinking*. New York: Longmans, Green and Co.

_____ (1914 [1909]). *The Meaning of Truth: A Sequel to Pragmatism*. New York: Longmans, Green and Co.

Kappy Suckiel, Ellen (1982). *The Pragmatic Philosophy of William James*. Notre Dame, IN: Notre Dame University Press.

Klein, Alexander (forthcoming). *The Rise of Empiricism: William James, Thomas Hill Green, and the Struggle over Psychology*.

Kuklick, Bruce (2001). *A History of Philosophy in America: 1720–2000*. Oxford: Clarendon Press.

Lewis, C. I. (1977 [1930]). 'Pragmatism and Current Thought'. In Morgenbesser (1977), 32–40.

Menand, Louis (2001). *The Metaphysical Club: A Story of Ideas in America*. New York: Farrar, Straus and Giroux.

Misak, Cheryl (2004 [1991]). *Truth and the End of Inquiry: A Peircean Account of Truth*, 2nd edn. Oxford: Oxford University Press.

_____ (1995). *Verificationism: Its History and Prospects*. London: Routledge.

_____ (ed.) (2007). *New Pragmatists*: Oxford: Oxford University Press.

_____ (forthcoming). 'Richard Rorty's Place in the Pragmatist Pantheon'. In Randal Auxier (ed.), *The Philosophy of Richard Rorty*, The Library of Living Philosophers, Carbondale, IL: University of Southern Illinois Press.

Moore, Addison W. (2001 [1909]). 'What is Pragmatism? *American Journal of Theology*, 13/3: 477–8. Repr. in Shook (2001*b*), i.

Moore, G. E. (1992 [1907]). 'Professor James's "Pragmatism"'. *Proceedings of the Aristotelian Society*, 8: 33–77. Repr. in Olin (1992), 161–95.

Morgenbesser, S. (ed.) (1977). *Dewey and his Critics*. Lancaster: Lancaster Press.

Murray, David (2001 [1912]). *Pragmatism*. Shook (2001*b*), iii.

Nagel, Ernest (1940). 'Charles S. Peirce: Pioneer of Modern Empiricism'. *Philosophy of Science*, 7/1: 69–80.

Neurath, Otto, Bohr, Niels, Dewey, John, Russell, Bertrand, Carnap, Rudolph, Morris, Charles (1938). *Encyclopedia and Unified Science, International Encyclopedia of Unified Science*, i/1. Chicago: University of Chicago Press.

Olin, Doris (1992). *William James: Pragmatism in Focus*. London: Routledge.

Peirce, Charles Sanders (1931–58). *Collected Papers of Charles Sanders Peirce*, i–vi, ed. C. Hartshorne and P. Weiss; vii and viii, ed. A. Burks. Cambridge, MA: Belknap Press. Cited as *CP* plus volume and paragraph number.

—— (1900–). *The Writings of Charles S. Peirce: A Chronological Edition*, ed. E. Moore. Bloomington: Indiana University Press.

—— Charles S. Peirce Papers, Houghton Library, Harvard University.

Pratt, James B. (2001 [1909]). *What is Pragmatism?* Repr. in Shook (2001*a*), i.

Quine, Willard van Orman (1951). 'Two Dogmas of Empiricism'. *Philosophical Review*, 60/1: 20–43. Repr. in *From a Logical Point of View*, 2nd edn, Cambridge, MA: Harvard University Press, 1980, 20–46.

—— (1981). 'The Pragmatist's Place in Empiricism'. In R. Mulvaney and P. Zeltner (eds.), *Pragmatism: Its Sources and Prospects*, University of South Carolina Press, 21–40.

—— (1990). 'Comments on Parsons'. In R. Gibson and R. Barrett (eds.), *Perspectives on Quine*, Oxford: Blackwell, 291–3.

Robin, Richard (1967). *Annotated Catalogue of the Papers of Charles S. Peirce*. Worcester, MA: University of Massachusetts Press.

Rorty, Richard (1982). *Consequences of Pragmatism*. Minneapolis: University of Minnesota Press.

—— (1995). 'Response to Richard Bernstein'. In H. J. Saatkamp (ed.), *Rorty and Pragmatism: The Philosopher Responds to his Critics*, Nashville: Vanderbilt University Press, 68–71.

Russell, Bertrand (1992 [1909]). 'Pragmatism'. In *Logical and Philosophical Papers, 1909–13*, and repr. in 1994.

—— (1992 [1966]). 'William James's Conception of Truth'. In *Philosophical Essays*, London: Allen and Unwin. Repr. in Olin (1992), 196–211.

—— (1994). *The Collected Papers of Bertrand Russell*. London: Routledge.

Schinz, Albert (2001 [1909]). *Anti-Pragmatism: An Examination into the Respective Rights of Intellectual Aristocracy and Social Democracy*. Boston: Small, Maynard and Company. Repr. in Shook (2001*a*), ii.

Shook, John (ed.) (2001*a*). *Early Critics of Pragmatism*, i–v. Bristol: Thoemmes Press.

—— (ed.) (2001*b*). *Early Defenders of Pragmatism*, i–v. Bristol: Thoemmes Press.

—— (2006). 'F. C. S. Schiller and European Pragmatism'. In J. Shook and J. Margolis (eds.), *A Companion to Pragmatism*, Oxford: Blackwell, 44–53.

Trammell, R. (1972). 'Religion, Instinct, and Reason in the Thought of C. S. Peirce'. *Transactions of the Charles. S. Peirce Society*, 8/11: 3–25.

Wittgenstein, Ludwig (1969). *On Certainty*. Oxford: Blackwell.

Woodbridge, Frederick (1977 [1930]). 'Experience and Dialectic'. In Morgenbesser (1977), 52–9.

Woolley, Helen Thompson (1909). Review of Pratt: *What is Pragmatism?*. *Journal of Philosophy*, 6/11: 300–2.

WHITEHEAD'S METAPHYSICAL SYSTEM

JOHN W. LANGO

WHITEHEAD IN AMERICA

BORN IN ENGLAND, and having held positions in mathematics at Cambridge University and the University of London, Alfred North Whitehead (1861–1947) became an American philosopher at the age of 63, by crossing the Atlantic to hold a position in philosophy at Harvard.[1] A main theme of this chapter on the American Whitehead is that his philosophical writings at Harvard are not merely of antiquarian interest but instead have considerable relevance for a variety of current philosophical topics. The focus is on the metaphysical system in his magnum opus, *Process and Reality: An Essay in Cosmology* (1929).[2]

---

[1] For a biography of Whitehead, see Lowe 1985, 1990.

[2] *Process and Reality* has been interpreted very differently. For instance, my defense of the contemporary relevance of the later Whitehead in this chapter is very different from the argument for Whitehead's contemporary relevance in Griffin 2007. For divergent interpretations of Whitehead, see the new *Handbook of Whiteheadian Process Thought* (Weber and Desmond 2008). Additionally, see the potpourri of articles about Whitehead in the journal devoted to process thought, *Process*

In the preface to that book, he acknowledged his great indebtedness both to "the two founders of Western thought, Plato and Aristotle" and to the "phase of philosophic thought which began with Descartes and ended with Hume" (Whitehead 1978 [1929]: p. xi). Note, for example, his famous remark that "[t]he safest general characterization of the European philosophical tradition is that it consists of a series of footnotes to Plato" (Whitehead 1978 [1929]: 39). Additionally, he acknowledged indebtedness to some American philosophers, for instance: "I am also indebted to [...] William James, and John Dewey" (Whitehead 1978 [1929]: p. xii).[3]

Ancient Greek philosophy is, or appears to be from our distant vantage point, self-contained, but American philosophy is not. In particular, such American philosophers as James and Dewey were influenced by European philosophers. In the case of Whitehead, the American Whitehead was strongly influenced by the European Whitehead. There is significant continuity between his earlier European writings—e.g., *Principia Mathematica* (1910–13, co-authored with Bertrand Russell), *An Enquiry Concerning the Principles of Natural Knowledge* (1919), and *The Concept of Nature* (1920)—and his later American writings—e.g., *Science and the Modern World* (1925), *Process and Reality* (1929), and *Adventures of Ideas* (1933). (For a bibliography of Whitehead's writings, see Schilpp 1951 [1941].)

WHITEHEAD'S PARTLY ANALYTIC METAPHYSICS

This last claim is often challenged. Against this continuity thesis there is a discontinuity thesis: namely, that the earlier Whitehead was analytic, whereas

Studies, the website of which is <http://web2.uwindsor.ca/courses/cmllc/whitney/blw.process.html>. For a relatively neutral introduction to Whitehead's metaphysics, see Kraus 1998. To find writings about Whitehead, consult the bibliographies available online through the Center for Process Studies at <http://www.ctr4process.org>.

 [3] The word omitted is "Bergson". Whitehead also acknowledged indebtedness to other American philosophers (e.g., Santayana). Concerning his indebtedness to such classic philosophers as Plato and Descartes, he warned readers that his metaphysical system in *Process and Reality* was "apt to emphasize just those elements in the writings of these masters which subsequent systematizers have put aside" (Whitehead 1978 [1929]: p. xi). In general, his interpretations of the philosophers who influenced him are difficult to summarize briefly. Consequently, I am not able to summarize in this chapter how he was influenced by such American philosophers as James and Dewey. For an illustration of how his metaphysical system was apt to emphasize unfamiliar elements in the writings of a great philosopher who influenced him, see my discussion of his indebtedness to Plato in Lango 2008.

the later Whitehead was not analytic but instead was speculative. Very roughly, his later speculative philosophy involves "the play of a free imagination" to obtain a "synoptic vision" of reality (Whitehead 1978 [1929]: 5).

In *Principia Mathematica*, Whitehead and Russell elaborated a mathematical theory (or logic) of relations, a theory basic to "the logical-analytic method in philosophy" that Russell championed in *Our Knowledge of the External World* (1914). In the preface to the latter book, Russell declared how his method was beholden to Whitehead: "I owe to him the definition of points, the suggestion for the treatment of instants and 'things,' and the whole conception of the world of physics as a *construction* rather than an *inference*" (Russell 1993 [1914]: 7). Such a method of logical construction was utilized by Whitehead in *Principles of Natural Knowledge*. Termed "the method of extensive abstraction", he utilized it to define points, straight lines, moments, time systems, and so forth by means of formal properties of "the fundamental relation of extension" (Whitehead 1982 [1925]: 101). The earlier Whitehead was analytic, in that he utilized an analytic method of logical construction.

Admittedly, the later Whitehead was speculative. In the second edition (1925) of *Principles of Natural Knowledge*, he made this remark about the first edition (1919): "But the true doctrine, that 'process' is the fundamental idea, was not in my mind with sufficient emphasis. Extension is derivative from process, and is required by it" (Whitehead 1982 [1925]: 202). The idea of process is fundamental to his metaphysical system in *Process and Reality* (1929). Moreover, he utilized in the latter book a "method" of "speculative philosophy" (Whitehead 1978 [1929]: 3), a method that is starkly different from the method of extensive abstraction. In explaining the new method, he made this remark: "Philosophy has been misled by the example of mathematics" (Whitehead 1978 [1929]: 8). In terms of these two remarks, the discontinuity thesis can be supported as follows. The earlier Whitehead was misled by the mathematical theory of relations in *Principia Mathematica*. Having discovered that the idea of process is fundamental, the later Whitehead developed a speculative metaphysical system in *Process and Reality*. Whitehead's later speculative philosophy superseded his earlier analytic philosophy.

In opposition to the discontinuity thesis, let me sketch a defense of the continuity thesis. Instead of entirely superseding his earlier analytic philosophy, his later speculative philosophy incorporated (but also revised) some of his earlier analytic philosophy. Among the five parts of *Process and Reality*, the fourth part is entitled "The Theory of Extension" (Whitehead 1978

[1929]: 283–333). A revised method of extensive abstraction is utilized there to define points, straight lines, and other geometrical elements (Whitehead 1978 [1929]: 287, 299, 306). Furthermore, some temporal concepts are defined by means of the theory of relations (Whitehead 1978 [1929]: 319–21).[4] Indeed, the later Whitehead was speculative, but he was also analytic.

To avoid overstatement, this defense of the continuity thesis needs to be qualified. "Speculative Philosophy is", Whitehead held, "the endeavor to frame a coherent, logical, necessary [metaphysical] system of general ideas" that is "applicable" and "adequate" (Whitehead 1978 [1929]: 3). In the first part of *Process and Reality*, entitled "The Speculative Scheme", he tentatively framed a metaphysical system concisely as a "categoreal scheme"—that is, a system (or "scheme") of "categories" (Whitehead 1978 [1929]: 20–8). What he meant by the term "logical" includes "the definition of constructs in logical terms" (Whitehead 1978 [1929]: 3). What he meant by the term "coherent" is, briefly, that the general ideas in a metaphysical system must "presuppose each other" (Whitehead 1978 [1929]: 3). What he meant by the term "adequate" is, roughly, that a metaphysical system must be capable of interpreting "every element of our experience" (Whitehead 1978 [1929]: 3). Rather than being limited to sense experience, the term "experience" should be understood very inclusively. (For brevity, the terms "necessary" and "applicable" are ignored.)

Utilizing the method of speculative philosophy, Whitehead endeavored in *Process and Reality* "to construct a [metaphysical] system of [general] ideas which brings the aesthetic, moral, and religious interests into relation with those concepts of the world which have their origin in natural science" (Whitehead 1978 [1929]: p. xii). Ideally, such a system must be adequate; it must be capable of interpreting both our scientific experience and our aesthetic, moral, and religious experience. Whereas *Principles of Natural Knowledge* was confined to concepts originating in natural science, *Process and Reality* encompassed both concepts originating in natural science and concepts originating in the stated interests of human beings.

Accordingly, the continuity thesis is that his later speculative metaphysical system incorporated (and revised)—but was not limited to—some of his earlier analytic philosophy of the natural world. For it also incorporated philosophical concepts obtained from the human world. In this qualified sense, his later metaphysics might be called *partly analytic*. But there are problems of coherence. How do analytic concepts originating in natural

---

[4] I discuss such temporal concepts in Lango 2000.

science and concepts originating in the stated human interests presuppose each other? (Cf. the traditional mind–matter problem.) More broadly, how can his speculative metaphysical system have an analytic facet? It might be thought that the analytic facet has to be distinctly subordinate. Enigmatically, however, in admitting that his metaphysical system in *Process and Reality* contained only "tentative formulations" of the general ideas, he made this remark: "We do not yet know how to recast the [metaphysical] scheme into a logical truth" (Whitehead 1978 [1929]: 8).[5] A metaphysical system should be coherent and adequate, but it should also be (in his wide sense of the term) logical. The earlier Whitehead was analytic, and the later Whitehead was both analytic and speculative.[6]

WAS WHITEHEAD A PROCESS PHILOSOPHER?

It has become customary to classify the American Whitehead as a "process philosopher", and his metaphysical system as a "process metaphysics".[7] These classifications are suggested by his remark (cited above) about "the true doctrine, that 'process' is the fundamental idea" (Whitehead 1982 [1925]: 202). A complementary remark in *Process and Reality* is that "[t]he elucidation of meaning involved in the phrase 'all things flow' is one chief task of metaphysics" (Whitehead 1978 [1929]: 208).

Nevertheless, there are other remarks about other fundamental ideas that suggest other classifications. The general idea of process is fundamental to Whitehead's speculative metaphysical system, but so are other general ideas. In the first section, it was implied that he should not be classified one-dimensionally as an American philosopher; in the preceding section, it was argued that he should not be classified one-dimensionally as a non-analytic philosopher; and, in the present section, it is maintained that he should not be classified one-dimensionally as a process philosopher.

Notably, a general idea of subjectivity is also fundamental, as the following remark indicates. Whitehead's metaphysical system "fully accepts Descartes'

---

[5] Disputably, in *Modes of Thought* (1938), he abandoned such a quest, but I cannot engage in this dispute here.

[6] Whitehead's metaphysics and analytic philosophy are compared in Lucas 1989.

[7] For a comprehensive introduction to process philosophy, see Rescher 1996. The chapters in Rescher 1996 are examined individually in Weber 2004.

discovery that subjective experiencing is the primary metaphysical situation which is presented to metaphysics for analysis" (Whitehead 1978 [1929]: 160). In addition to an analytic facet, which stemmed primarily from concepts of mathematics and natural science, there is a subjectively experiential facet, which stemmed primarily from a phenomenology of human experience. Whitehead was a process philosopher, but he was also a philosopher of subjective experience.

Additionally, a general idea of time is fundamental.[8] Among his earlier European writings was *The Principle of Relativity, with Applications to Physical Science* (1922), a book devoted to "an exposition of an alternative rendering of the [i.e., Einstein's] theory of relativity" (Whitehead 2004 [1922]: p. v). The American Whitehead was especially influenced by the European Whitehead's work on the scientific theory of relativity. In his speculative metaphysical system, he remarked, "the influence of the 'relativity theory' of modern physics is important" (Whitehead 1978 [1929]: 65). In particular, that a relativistic idea of time is fundamental is evidenced by this remark: "I shall always adopt the relativity view [of time]" (Whitehead 1978 [1929]: 66). He was also a philosopher of relativistic time.[9]

Process and Reality is replete with neologisms, among which perhaps the most well known is the term "actual occasion" (or the almost synonymous term "actual entity"). Central to Whitehead's metaphysical system are some ontological categories, "The Categories of Existence", the first of which is "Actual Entities (also termed Actual Occasions)" (Whitehead 1978 [1929]: 22). In conformity with the "spatiotemporal thinking" inspired by the theory of relativity (Quine 1960: 172), he included in his metaphysical system an ontology of events. Actual occasions are, roughly, the most elementary events (cf. the point events of relativity theory). Another fundamental idea is that of elementary (or atomic) events, an idea evidenced by his remark that his metaphysics is "an atomic theory of actuality" (Whitehead 1978 [1929]: 27). "An actual occasion is", he also remarked, "the limiting type of an event" (Whitehead 1978 [1929]: 73). In a brief biography of Whitehead, C. D. Broad appraised *Process and Reality* as "one of the most difficult philosophical books that exist; it can vie in this respect with the works of Plotinus and of Hegel" (Broad 1948: 144). And, let me add, one of the most difficult concepts in

---

[8] I compare Whitehead's philosophy of time and analytic philosophies of time in Lango 2007.
[9] In the Whitehead chapter in another collection about American philosophy, I focus on the general ideas of subjectivity and relativistic time (Lango 2004).

Process and Reality is the concept of actual occasions. For instance, reflecting the subjectively experiential facet, actual occasions are epitomized as "drops of experience" (Whitehead 1978 [1929]: 18). They are both event atoms and experience atoms. Abstrusely, Whitehead was also a metaphysical atomist (cf. Leibniz's monadology and Russell's logical atomism).

Furthermore, Whitehead was a relation philosopher. In his metaphysical system, he remarked, " 'relatedness' is dominant over 'quality' " (Whitehead 1978 [1929]: p. xiii). A general idea of relatedness is also fundamental. Specifically, among the categories of existence, the second is "Prehensions *or* Concrete Facts of Relatedness" (Whitehead 1978 [1929]: 22). An actual occasion is concretely related to other entities by means of its prehensions of them. The fundamental idea of relatedness and the fundamental idea of subjectivity are interlinked, for an actual occasion is the "subject" of its prehensions (Whitehead 1978 [1929]: 23). And these fundamental ideas are interlinked with the fundamental idea of time. Corresponding to the relativistic concepts of absolute past, absolute future, and absolute elsewhere (Hawking 1988: 25–8), an actual occasion has its "causal past", its "causal future", and its "contemporaries" (1978 [1929]: 123, 319). An actual occasion is concretely related to the actual occasions in its causal past by means of its prehensions of them. Such prehensions are termed "simple physical feelings" (Whitehead 1978 [1929]: 236). "All complex causal action can be reduced", he remarked, "to a complex of such primary components" (Whitehead 1978 [1929]: 236). Coherent with the atomism of events, there is an atomism of causal relations. Another difficult concept in *Process and Reality* is this concept of concrete relatedness through prehensions.

There are other fundamental ideas, some of which can be adumbrated as follows. For instance, a general idea of final causation is fundamental: "One task of a sound metaphysics is to exhibit final and efficient causes in their proper relation to each other" (Whitehead 1978 [1929]: 84). Whitehead's speculative metaphysics is a teleological metaphysics. Relatedly, his metaphysics is a theistic metaphysics: "God is the primordial creature" (Whitehead 1978 [1929]: 31). A particular idea of God is fundamental.[10] Additionally, his metaphysics includes a realist idea of universals. Having invented the neologism "eternal objects", in place of the traditional term "universals", he remarked that, in his categories of existence, "actual entities and eternal

---

[10] Whitehead's idea of God has greatly influenced a movement in theology called "process theology". See, e.g., Hartshorne 1972.

objects stand out with a certain extreme finality" (Whitehead 1978 [1929]: 22). For brevity, although there are additional general ideas in his metaphysical system, the question of whether any of them is comparably fundamental has to be set aside.

In summary, Whitehead was not simply a process philosopher. In addition to the fundamental idea of process in his metaphysical system, there are fundamental ideas of subjective experience, relativistic time, event atomism, concrete relatedness, final causation, God, universals, and so forth. No single fundamental idea is primary.[11] Instead, his "system of general ideas" (Whitehead 1978 [1929]: 3) is a system of fundamental ideas. In accordance with the requirement of coherence, these fundamental ideas must "presuppose each other" (Whitehead 1978 [1929]: 3). His speculative metaphysics is preeminently a systematic metaphysics. Most significantly, he was a systematic philosopher.

WHITEHEAD'S SYSTEMATIC METAPHYSICS

Why should a philosopher today read a book as difficult and abstruse as *Process and Reality*? The later Whitehead's philosophical writings—especially *Science and the Modern World* (1925)—were widely read and highly regarded by his contemporaries. At the end of his philosophical career, his philosophy was the subject of the third volume of the series "The Library of Living Philosophers". In the preface, the editor Paul A. Schilpp stated that *The Philosophy of Alfred North Whitehead* was "a volume the importance of which will be immediately apparent to every philosopher and student of philosophy" (Schilpp 1951 [1941]: p. xiii).[12]

Today the importance of Whitehead is not immediately apparent. As a historical event, the eclipse of Whitehead had a variety of causes, but a main cause was, I suspect, the influence of mid twentieth-century skepticism

---

[11] It might be objected that Whitehead's "category of the ultimate" is the most fundamental category. Indeed, he remarked that this category "expresses the general principle presupposed in the three more special [sets of] categories" (Whitehead 1978 [1929]: 21). However, in accordance with his conception of coherence, my reply to the objection is that the other categories express ideas presupposed in the category of the ultimate.

[12] For a writing illustrating the influence of Whitehead, see Fitch 1961. Frederic B. Fitch was well known as a logician, but he was also a sort of Whiteheadian. I compare Fitch and Whitehead in Lango 2002.

about metaphysics.[13] In recent decades, there has been a revival of interest in metaphysics, focused on particular topics—for example, the mind–body problem, the problem of universals, and the problem of persistence through time. Moreover, in focusing on one particular topic, there is a tendency to abstract from other particular topics. By contrast, interest in systematic metaphysics has not revived appreciably.

However, it would not be correct to assert that there is no interest today in systematic metaphysics. For example, in some earlier writings, David Armstrong discussed particular metaphysical topics—notably, the mind–body problem and the problem of universals. More recently, he has produced a sort of metaphysical system in his book *A World of States of Affairs*. In his introduction to this book, he declares that "[t]he chief novelty from my own point of view will lie in bringing the topics together in a systematic framework" (Armstrong 1997: 3). Echoing his words, my own point of view in this chapter is that a chief novelty that philosophers today should find in Whitehead's *Process and Reality* is the bringing together of particular topics in a systematic framework.

Indeed, in *Process and Reality*, Whitehead was concerned with particular topics: for instance, the topics "of time, of space, of perception, and of causality" (Whitehead 1978 [1929]: p. xii). However, instead of "a detached consideration of various traditional philosophical problems", he endeavored to frame a metaphysical system "in terms of which all particular topics find their interconnections" (Whitehead 1978 [1929]: p. xii). A main point is that, if an interest in systematic metaphysics were to revive sufficiently, the importance today of the later Whitehead would become considerably more apparent.

Granted, many philosophers today might not profit by reading selectively in *Process and Reality* with the exclusive aim of studying Whitehead's view about a particular topic, in abstraction from his views about other particular topics. Selective reading is hampered, especially because there is not in *Process and Reality* a "successive treatment of particular topics" (Whitehead 1978 [1929]: p. xii). Instead, passages relevant to any particular topic are widely dispersed: for instance, "the doctrines of time, of space, of perception, and of causality are recurred to again and again" (Whitehead 1978 [1929]: p. xii). Nevertheless, many philosophers today might profit, I submit, by investigating how a particular topic is interconnected with other particular topics in

---

[13] Concerning the eclipse of Whitehead, see Lucas 1989.

Whitehead's metaphysical system. Even though difficult and abstruse, *Process and Reality* illustrates instructively how a particular topic can be illuminated by a metaphysical system.[14]

REFERENCES

Armstrong, D. M. (1997). *A World of States of Affairs*. Cambridge: Cambridge University Press.

Broad, C. D. (1948). 'Alfred North Whitehead (1861–1947)'. *Mind*, 57: 139–45.

Fitch, Frederic B. (1961). 'Sketch of a Philosophy'. In Ivor LeClerc (ed.), *The Relevance of Whitehead*, London: George Allen & Unwin, 93–106.

Griffin, David Ray (2007). *Whitehead's Radically Different Postmodern Philosophy: An Argument for Its Contemporary Relevance*. Albany, NY: State University of New York Press.

Hartshorne, Charles (1972). *Whitehead's Philosophy: Selected Essays, 1935–1970*. Lincoln, NE: University of Nebraska Press.

Hawking, Stephen (1988). *A Brief History of Time: From the Big Bang to Black Holes*. London: Bantam Press.

Henning, Brian G. (2005). *The Ethics of Creativity: Beauty, Morality and Nature in a Processive Cosmos*. Pittsburgh: University of Pittsburgh Press.

Kraus, Elizabeth M. (1998). *The Metaphysics of Experience: A Companion to Whitehead's Process and Reality*, 2nd edn. New York: Fordham University Press.

Lango, John W. (2000). 'Time and Strict Partial Order'. *American Philosophical Quarterly*, 37: 373–87.

——— (2002). 'Fitch's Method and Whitehead's Metaphysics'. *Transactions of the Charles S. Peirce Society*, 38: 581–603.

——— (2004). 'Alfred North Whitehead, 1861–1947'. In A. T. Marsoobian and J. Ryder (eds.), *The Blackwell Guide to American Philosophy*, Oxford: Blackwell, 210–25.

——— (2007). 'Whitehead's Philosophy of Time through the Prism of Analytic Concepts'. In G. Durand and M. Weber (eds.), *Alfred North Whitehead's Principles of Natural Knowledge*, Frankfurt: Ontos Verlag, 137–56.

——— (2008). 'Plato (427–347 BCE)'. In Weber and Desmond (2008).

Lowe, Victor (1985, 1990). *Alfred North Whitehead: The Man and His Work*, 2 vols. Baltimore: Johns Hopkins University Press.

Lucas, George R. Jr. (1989). *The Rehabilitation of Whitehead: An Analytic and Historical Assessment of Process Philosophy*. Albany, NY: State University of New York Press.

Palmer, Clare (1998). *Environmental Ethics and Process Thinking*. Oxford: Oxford University Press.

Quine, Willard van Orman (1960). *Word and Object*. Cambridge, MA: MIT Press.

---

[14] Recently, some writings in environmental ethics have utilized ideas from Whitehead's metaphysical system. See, e.g., Henning 2005 and Palmer 1998.

Rescher, Nicholas (1996). *Process Metaphysics: An Introduction to Process Philosophy*. Albany, NY: State University of New York Press.

Russell, Bertrand (1993 [1914]). *Our Knowledge of the External World: As a Field for Scientific Method in Philosophy*. New York: Routledge.

Schilpp, Paul Arthur (ed.) (1951 [1941]). *The Philosophy of Alfred North Whitehead*, 2nd edn. New York: Tudor Publishing Co.

Weber, Michel (ed.) (2004). *After Whitehead: Rescher on Process Metaphysics*. Frankfurt: Ontos Verlag.

____ and Desmond, William Jr. (eds.) (2008). *Handbook of Whiteheadian Process Thought*, 2 vols. Frankfurt: Ontos Verlag.

Whitehead, Alfred North (1919). *An Enquiry Concerning the Principles of Natural Knowledge*. Cambridge: Cambridge University Press.

____ (1982 [1925]). *An Enquiry Concerning the Principles of Natural Knowledge*, 2nd edn. Mineola, NY: Dover Publications.

____ (1971 [1920]). *The Concept of Nature*. Cambridge: Cambridge University Press.

____ (2004 [1922]). *The Principle of Relativity, with Applications to Physical Science*. Mineola, NY: Dover Publications.

____ (1997 [1925]). *Science and the Modern World*. New York: Free Press.

____ (1978 [1929]). *Process and Reality: An Essay in Cosmology*, corrected edn. ed. D. Griffin and D. Sherburne. New York: Free Press.

____ (1967 [1933]). *Adventures of Ideas*. New York: Free Press.

____ (1968 [1938]). *Modes of Thought*. New York: Free Press.

____ and Russell, Bertrand (1925–27 [1910–13]). *Principia Mathematica*. Cambridge: Cambridge University Press.

CHAPTER 13

THORSTEIN VEBLEN AND AMERICAN SOCIAL CRITICISM

JOSEPH HEATH

THORSTEIN VEBLEN is perhaps best thought of as America's answer to Karl Marx. This is sometimes obscured by the rather unfortunate title of his most important work, *The Theory of the Leisure Class* (1899), which is misleading, insofar as it suggests that the book is just a theory of the "leisure class". What the book provides is in fact a perfectly general theory of class, not to mention property, economic development, and social evolution. It is, in other words, a system of theory that rivals Marx's historical materialism with respect to scope, generality, and explanatory power. Furthermore, it is a system of theory whose central predictions, with respect to the development of capitalism and the possibilities for emancipatory social change, have proved to be essentially correct. When stacked up against Marx's prognostications, this success clearly provides the basis for what might best be described as an *invidious comparison*.

For example, it is Veblen who, at the close of the nineteenth century, observed that

The exigencies of the modern industrial system frequently place individuals and households in juxtaposition between whom there is little contact in any other sense than that of juxtaposition. One's neighbors, mechanically speaking, often are socially not one's neighbors, or even acquaintances; and still their transient good opinion has a high degree of utility. ... It is evident, therefore, that the present trend of the development is in the direction of heightening the utility of conspicuous consumption as compared with leisure.   (1994 [1899]: 86)

One could search long and hard to find a single paragraph in Marx's work that is as prescient, or that reveals a more profound grasp of the underlying dynamics of the capitalist system.

Apart from the merits of his general analysis of social class, Veblen also pioneered a style of critical theory, in many ways distinctively American, but in any case quite different from the European traditions that went on to dominate twentieth-century intellectual history. Karl Marx and Sigmund Freud became, via the Frankfurt School, the most influential figures in the European stream of critical theory. Veblen, by contrast, initiated a more theoretically parsimonious style of social criticism, which remained a powerful force throughout the same period yet was seldom identified as part of a cohesive movement or school of thought. On can see the influence clearly, though, in subsequent works of American social criticism ranging from Jane Jacobs's *The Life and Death of Great American Cities* (1961) to Thomas Frank's *The Conquest of Cool* (1997).

Although Veblen was not himself a pragmatist, he took two of the central ideas that helped shape the pragmatist ethos in the USA in the late nineteenth century—the importance of instrumental action and the evolutionary adaption of social institutions—and showed how they could be developed into a critical theory of society. Veblen's precise relationship with pragmatism has been the subject of considerable debate (Ayres 1961: 27 ff.; McFarland 1985; Tilman 1996: 109–41). He studied philosophy at Carlton College (BA, 1880), Johns Hopkins, and Yale (Ph.D., 1884). After seven years of unemployment, he went to study economics at Cornell, where he simply showed up one day, "wearing a coonskin cap and corduroy trousers" (Dorfman 1966: 80) and talked his way in. Before graduating, he received a faculty appointment at the University of Chicago, and went on to teach at Stanford University, the University of Missouri, and finally the New School for Social Research. Although he studied briefly with Charles Sanders Peirce at Johns Hopkins, and interacted with John Dewey and George Herbert Mead as colleagues, he always maintained an arm's-length relationship to pragmatism. (Indeed, the emphasis that he placed over the years on "idle curiosity" was intended precisely to distance himself from the pragmatist insistence that all knowledge be practical.) His dominant intellectual influences could perhaps best be described as a blend of Herbert Spencer and Edward Bellamy. Nevertheless, his work was sufficiently imbued with the pragmatist ethos that Europeans, including various members of the Frankfurt School, had difficulty seeing the difference (Adorno 1941; Tilman 1992: 191). This made his work relatively easy to dismiss, on the grounds that the "scientism" of the pragmatist perspective (such as the preference for Darwinian over "dialectical" methods) deprived it of the potential for radical insight. Yet, in retrospect, it seems clear that many of these critics were simply appalled at how many of their own "leisure class" habits Veblen's critique unmasked. (His classification of "high culture" as merely another form of conspicuous consumption was a particular sticking point with Theodor Adorno, who described Veblen's attitude in this regard as "splenetic", "misanthopic", and "melancholy" (1941: 393, 407).)

In this paper, my goal is to identify and explain some of the characteristic features of the style of social criticism that Veblen pioneered. In order to do so, I must first set aside several of the misconceptions that have arisen about his work. The first concerns its generality, as I have already suggested. Veblen must be understood not merely as a critic of an obsolete "aristocratic" pattern of upper-class consumption, but rather as the progenitor of a general theory of the relationship between class, status, private property, and social inequality. The second major misunderstanding of Veblen's work arises from the assumption that he is engaged in *moralizing* social criticism. On the contrary, Veblen shared with both Marx and Freud the desire to refrain from making simple value judgments. Yet, at the same time, he sought to avoid the pitfall that both Marx and Freud fell into: namely, relying upon elaborate theoretical constructions in lieu of moral claims (a strategy that violates one of the most fundamental rules of argument, viz. that one cannot derive plausible conclusions—e.g., workers are badly treated, people are sexually repressed—from anything that is intrinsically less plausible—e.g., Hegelian dialectics, the struggle of Eros and Thanatos). Veblen, by contrast, attempts to ground his critical theory in a set of minimal or platitudinous normative claims. In particular, he presents the first clear-cut instance of a theorist using the diagnosis of an unsuspected collective action problem as a strategy of social and cultural criticism.

I

Status is the central concept in Veblen's analytical framework. Status is, in his view, more fundamental than class, private property, or any other economic concept. Indeed, a proper understanding of status is essential to understanding any of the routine assumptions made by economists, such as the "irksomeness" of labor and the desirability of leisure (Veblen 1898). Veblen conceives of status among humans as a stratification system, no different in principle from the hierarchies that structure social relations throughout the animal kingdom (from the "pecking order" among chickens to the dominance relations among our closest primate relatives). It is grounded in judgments that establish an *invidious comparison*, which Veblen defines as a "comparison of persons with a view to rating and grading them in respect of relative worth or value" (1994 [1899]: 34).

Human action, in Veblen's view, is governed by two fundamental instincts, or "proclivities". The first is the "instinct of workmanship", which he regards as a fairly direct outgrowth of the instrumentality, or "teleological" character, of human action. Because our actions are always aimed at some objective, we acquire "a sense of the merit of serviceability or efficiency and of the demerit of futility, waste, or incapacity" (1994 [1899]: 15). In other words, thanks to the generic structure of instrumental rationality, which is concerned with finding the most appropriate means to the realization of our ends, we come to value that which is useful and effective, and to disparage that which is useless or wasteful. The second fundamental instinct is the "predatory proclivity", which expresses itself in the form of fighting, "practices of exploit", and dominance in social relations (Tool 1998: 309).

The exercise of each of these proclivities serves as a basis for invidious comparison among persons, and thus the emergence of status hierarchy. Workmanship can be judged with respect to degrees of skill, and predation with respect to degrees of "prowess". Thus, even in a hunter-gatherer society with no explicit class differentiation, everyone knows who the most skilled hunter is, and honors him accordingly. However, there is an asymmetry between the workmanly and the predatory proclivities. The latter can be turned against fellow human beings, which then serves as the basis for a new invidious comparison: that between dominator and dominated. It is through this mechanism that the status hierarchy acquires the characteristics of a dominance hierarchy. This transition to a "predatory culture" marks a change "from a struggle of the group against a non-human environment to a struggle against a human environment" (1994 [1899]: 220).

The first consequence to emerge from this inward turn is the gendered division of labor. Since economic returns are sufficiently close to the subsistence minimum in the early stages of human social evolution, it is impossible for an entire class to sustain itself through predation alone (except externally, through "raiding" and warfare). Thus men and women both work, yet male effort is reserved for domains of activity that involve some element of "exploit" (and thus "cannot without derogation be compared with the uneventful diligence of the women" (1994 [1899]: 5)). The concept of "property", extending beyond mere personal possession, emerges also during this stage, modeled on the relationship of domination toward women. Ownership begins with the domination of women (what we would now call "mate-guarding behavior"), and is subsequently extended to encompass physical objects. It is therefore, first and foremost, a system of rank. "Ownership began and grew into a human institution on grounds unrelated to the subsistence minimum. The dominant incentive was from the outset the invidious distinction attaching to wealth" (1994 [1899]: 26).

When the size of the economic surplus becomes sufficiently great to permit stable relations of exploitation, the stage is set for the emergence of an explicit class society. The predatory character of the upper class is reflected in the fact that it is not only exempt from any "industrial" employment, but positively barred from it. This produces a sort of transvaluation of values, in which the useless becomes celebrated, precisely because it serves as a sign that one is a member of the dominant class—hence the social significance of leisure. Of course, the instinct of workmanship is never entirely extinguished. Once the predatory class is sufficiently entrenched, fewer opportunities present themselves for displays of prowess. Thus this class invents for itself new, labor-intensive activities, which may involve great effort and skill, but which are demarcated from the activities of the laboring classes by virtue of being explicitly futile in their aim. Sport is the most obvious example, but, more controversially, Veblen also includes under this rubric religious observances, etiquette, esoteric learning (such as classical languages), aesthetic appreciation, "domestic music", and a variety of other activities (1994 [1899]: 45). Hence the perverse spectacle of the best (if not necessarily the brightest) applying themselves with boundless energy and selfless commitment, developing advanced competencies in activities that have absolutely no redeeming social value. The term "leisure class" is, in this respect, somewhat misleading, since members of this class often find their lives to be just as hectic and demanding as those of the laboring classes. This is why Veblen describes leisure not as mere "indolence", but as a "performance" (1994 [1899]: 58). (For example, he observes that "good breeding requires time, application and expense" (1994 [1899]: 49).)

There is considerable fodder here for social criticism, and Veblen might easily have used this analysis as the basis for a moralizing critique of the class structure of the society in which he lived. Yet he chose to keep his powder dry. In order to see this, however, it is essential to distinguish the *satirical* from the *critical* elements of Veblen's work. When he suggests that members of the "hereditary leisure class" are rivaled only by "lower-class delinquents" in their retention of barbarian traits and a "bellicose frame of mind" (1994 [1899]: 247), it is difficult to interpret this as anything other than criticism. Or consider his "explanation" for the relatively high social status accorded to lawyers (despite the fact that they are usually propertyless):

The profession of law does not imply large ownership; but since no taint of usefulness, for other than the competitive purpose, attaches to the lawyer's trade, it grades high in the conventional scheme. The lawyer is exclusively occupied with the details of predatory fraud, either in achieving or in checkmating chicane, and success in the profession is therefore accepted as marking a large endowment of that barbarian astuteness which has always commanded men's respect and fear.   (1994 [1899]: 231)

Given that the book is replete with such passages, many readers have been inclined to dismiss Veblen's assurances that he is not engaged in any sort of condemnation (Dorfman 1966: 192). (Similarly, when Marx writes that "capital is dead labor which, vampire-like, only lives by sucking living labor" (1990 [1867]: 342), it speaks against his claim that "exploitation" is a purely technical concept, and that he is not engaged in a moralizing critique of capitalism.) Indeed, it is easy to read such high-minded assurances as just another satirical aspect of the work, mimicking the way that conventional economists adopted the mantle of "positive" social science, while peddling works that consisted of little more than thinly veiled right-wing ideology. (After all, those who are scandalized by any deviation from the ideal of "value-neutral" social-scientific inquiry tend to react, not to the presence of value judgments *per se*, but rather to the occurrence of value judgments with which they disagree.)

In Veblen's case, however, the claim is slightly more credible than it is with Marx. This is for two reasons. First, there is the fact that whatever intuitive abhorrence we may feel for the excesses of the predatory class is, according to

Veblen's own analysis, merely an expression of the "instinct of workmanship" acting in our own person. This immediately relativizes the judgment and deprives it of some force. Who is to say that one instinct is better than the other? As Veblen is at pains to point out, the sort of temperament induced by the instinct of workmanship is considered just as contemptible by those with a greater endowment of the predatory proclivities, and they have chosen their activities with the specific intention of distancing themselves from it. For example, members of the predatory class don't work, not because they are lazy, but because of a moral revulsion that they experience at the very thought of gainful employment, or any other activity afflicted by a "taint of usefulness". Thus Veblen's own analytical framework has a tendency to undercut whatever normative grounds there may be for straightforward moral criticism of the leisure class. The problem of "the standpoint of the critic", which preoccupied critical theorists throughout the twentieth century, arises here with considerable force.

The second reason to take seriously Veblen's protestations of neutrality is that his work does contain a second strain of explicitly critical reflections, which he is more forthright in acknowledging. In particular, Veblen develops a critique of two features of the leisure class—namely, its "wastefulness" and its "conservativism"—based upon normative foundations that are *not* merely the expression of some instinctual reactions. On these particular points, he tries to develop what we might refer to, anachronistically, as a "freestanding" normative basis for critique. These arguments are distinguished by the fact that they are far more formal in structure and employ a conceptual apparatus that goes on to be developed and refined in later work. This suggests that Veblen intended these two lines of critique to be taken much more seriously than the sarcastic asides and *bon mots* that set the overall tone of the work.

II

Reading through *The Theory of the Leisure Class*, it is clear that Veblen disapproved of many things. He disapproved of duels (a "barbarian recrudescence"), sports ("serviceable evidence of an unproductive expenditure of time"), manners ("the voucher of a life of leisure"), dogs ("the filthiest of the domestic animals"), corsets ("crucifixion of the flesh"), churches ("the priestly vicarious leisure class"), captains of industry ("quasi-predatory careers of fraud"), cap and gown in academia ("atavistic conformity"), and so on. Yet, beyond mere disapproval, there are also some things that he *criticized*. The primary difference is that, in cases where he criticized, he also provided an explicit articulation of the normative basis for his claims.

Consider the case of waste—or, to be more specific, the particular sort of waste generated by conspicuous consumption. Veblen's criticism here is relatively simple. Some goods are valued and consumed for their intrinsic properties. Thus the "advance of industrial efficiency" leads to improvements in the quality and comfort of life. Yet property is accumulated, not just to satisfy our basic physical needs, but also for its honorific qualities. It serves as a basis for invidious comparison, with respect not just to quantity, but also to quality. This sort of accumulation is collectively self-defeating, for the simple reason that not everyone can be above average. The result is that, regardless of how much the standard of living rises, "the normal, average individual will live in chronic dissatisfaction with his present lot" (1994 [1899]: 31).

One way of articulating the problem is to say that status (along with all its derivative concepts, such as self-respect, esteem, honor, and merit) is essentially an ordinal ranking system, and thus the quest for status is a zero-sum game.

In the nature of the case, the desire for wealth can scarcely be satiated in any individual instance, and evidently a satiation of the average or general desire for wealth is out of the question. However widely, or equally, or "fairly," it may be distributed, no general increase of the community's wealth can make any approach to satiating this need, the ground of which is the desire of every one to excel every one else in the accumulation of goods. If, as is sometimes assumed, the incentive to accumulation were the want of subsistence or of physical comfort, then the aggregate economic wants of a community might conceivably be satisfied at some point in the advance of industrial efficiency; but since the struggle is substantially a race for reputability on the basis of an invidious comparison, no approach to a definitive attainment is possible.   (1994 [1899]: 32)

Because status is zero-sum, the production and consumption of status goods is negative-sum, since effort and resources are channeled toward applications where they do not generate "an enhancement of life and well-being on the whole" (1994 [1899]: 97). It is because these economic activities have a real cost, yet fail to produce any benefit, that they can be referred to as "wasteful". Veblen is clear, however, that this description is not intended to impugn the motives of individuals who engage in consumption governed by "the canon of conspicuous waste". From the "standpoint of the individual consumer" it is not wasteful. "Whatever form of expenditure the consumer chooses, or whatever end he seeks in making his choice, has utility to him by virtue of his preference" (1994 [1899]: 98). Thus the use of the term "waste" "implies no deprecation of the motives or of the ends sought by the consumer" (1994 [1899]: 98). The problem is that, because of the collective action problem induced by conspicuous consumption, this gain in utility is ephemeral. It is undone the moment a "fresh increase in wealth" gives rise to "a new standard of sufficiency" and "a new pecuniary classification of one's self" (1994 [1899]: 31). Thus the outcome of competitive consumption is unsatisfactory, not according to some "external" standard imposed by the critic, but according to the preferences of the consumers themselves. It is for this reason that waste of this sort fails to satisfy what Veblen calls "the economic conscience" (1994 [1899]: 98).

There is of course an influential line of thinking, descended from antiquity, that emphasizes the insatiability of human desire. This was based upon a commonly observed psychological tendency whereby the satisfaction of one desire gives rise to several more. The significance of Veblen's analysis lay in his redirection of our attention away from the psychological toward the social, and away from the mental state toward the object of desire. From this perspective, it is natural to expect that the rate of growth of "the pecuniary standard of decency" would be a function of the rate of growth of the economy. This was not at all obvious at the time. Joseph Schumpeter, for instance, as late as 1942, predicted that further economic growth would make "provision for the unemployed . . . not only a tolerable but a light burden" (1942: 69). He was of course aware that what we conceive of as poverty has a tendency to ratchet up over time. He simply assumed that the two rates of growth would be independent—such that the increase in "total output" could outstrip the growth of expectations. People would literally become swamped with goods. Under such conditions, it would be difficult to imagine the persistence of "chronic dissatisfaction" of the sort that Veblen predicted.

Veblen, on the other hand, argued that "the need of conspicuous waste . . . stands ready to absorb any increase in the community's industrial efficiency or output of goods, after the most elementary physical wants have been provided for" (1994 [1899]: 110). This sounds like hyperbole. However, the widely reported finding that economic growth produces no measurable increase in average happiness after the "plateau" of US$10,000 GDP per capita has been reached (while there remains a weak but consistent correlation between *relative* wealth and individual happiness) appears to bear out Veblen's assessment

(Stutzer and Frey 2001). In part, the failure to appreciate the plausibility of Veblen's claim stems from a tendency to adopt an unnecessarily narrow interpretation of the sort of preference structures that lead to competitive consumption. This has something to do with Veblen's order of exposition, since his discussion of "chronic dissatisfaction" makes reference only to the competitive accumulation of wealth. Thus it is sometimes thought that "conspicuous waste" arises only when individuals use consumption as a way of displaying their wealth. Harvey Leibenstein (1950), for instance, introduced the term "Veblen effect" to describe cases in which the preference for a good increases as the price increases. (This is similar, but not identical, to a Giffen good (Marshall 1895: 208), in which the quantity demanded increases as a function of price. The Veblen effect involves a shift in the demand curve, while the Giffen good is merely one with an upwardly sloping demand curve.) Yet Veblen was quite clear that the sort of preferences that motivate competitive consumption depend only in an indirect way upon the costliness of these items. It is the "canons of taste" and "decency" that determine preference. Price is relevant only insofar as it influences these standards. With respect to clothing, for instance, he claims that "This spiritual need of dress is not wholly, nor even chiefly, a naïve propensity for display of expenditure. The law of conspicuous waste guides consumption in apparel, as in other things, chiefly at the second remove, by shaping the canons of taste and decency" (1994 [1899]: 168).

Veblen considers the status hierarchy, as a system of invidious comparison, to be more fundamental than other major categories of contrastive judgment, such as aesthetic taste or the moral sense. For example, "the superior gratification derived from the use and contemplation of costly and supposedly beautiful products is, commonly, in great measure a gratification of our sense of costliness masquerading under the name of beauty" (1994 [1899]: 128). This is because "our higher appreciation of the superior article is an appreciation of its superior honorific character", not its brute aesthetic qualities, and its honorific character arises from the way in which its consumptions "fits" into the background status hierarchy. Veblen provides a variety of examples of this, such as the appreciation shown for flowers:

In this way it has happened, for instance, that some beautiful flowers pass conventionally for offensive weeds; others that can be cultivated with relative ease are accepted and admired by the lower middle class, who can afford no more expensive luxuries of this kind; but these varieties are rejected as vulgar by those people who are better able to pay for expensive flowers and who are educated to a higher schedule of pecuniary beauty in the florists' products; while still other flowers, of no greater intrinsic beauty than these, are cultivated at great cost and call out much admiration from flower-lovers whose tastes have been matured under the critical guidance of a polite environment.   (1994 [1899]: 132)

Cheap flowers are despised not because they are cheap, but because they are ugly. The point is that they are perceived to be ugly because they are classified as ugly, and they are classified as ugly because they are cheap. (One can see this clearly in the case of goldenrod, which grows wild in North America, where it is therefore treated as a weed, but is imported to Europe, where it is prized by gardeners.) This phenomenon also underlies what Pierre Bourdieu describes as "the miracle of the unequal class distribution of the capacity for inspired encounters with works of art and high culture in general" (1984: 29). The important point is that there may be nothing competitive, envious, or even ostentatious about the individual consumer's preferences. Consumers, in Veblen's view, need not be preoccupied with status. The mere fact that they are attracted to the "beauty" or "style" of an object can be enough to generate competitive consumption, because "the canon of taste under which the designer works is a canon formed under the surveillance of the law of conspicuous waste, and . . . this law acts selectively to eliminate any canon of taste that does not conform to its demands" (1994 [1899]: 164).

Far too many of Veblen's readers come away from the book convinced that they are exempt from the habits of conspicuous waste, because their everyday consumption habits are not informed by any desire to put on a display of wealth (or to demonstrate "pecuniary strength"). This represents a singular failure to appreciate the force of Veblen's argument. Consider, for instance, the contemporary countercultural style that David Brooks (2000) refers to as "one-downmanship". The imperative is something like this:

Cultivated people are repelled by the idea of keeping up with the Joneses. Nothing is more disreputable than competing with your neighbors by trying to more effectively mimic the style of the social class just above you. Instead, as members of the educated class, you reject status symbols in order to raise your status with your equally cultivated peers. Everything about you must be slightly more casual than your neighbor. Your furnishings must be slightly more peasanty. Your lives should have a greater patina of simplicity. So your dinnerware will not have the sort of regal designs they use at Buckingham Palace. It will be basic white, like what they sell at Pottery Barn. Your shoes won't be snazzy pumps; they'll be simple but expensive penny loafers from Prada. Ostentation is a disgrace, but anything unadorned is a sign of refreshing honesty.   (2000: 93–4)

This pattern of "anti-consumerist" consumption is just as powerfully motivated by the concern for invidious distinction, and therefore has the same collectively self-defeating character as any other form of competitive consumption (Heath 2001). Yet, perversely, Brooks takes these observations as evidence that "the Thorstein Veblen era is over" (Brooks 2000: 84; see also Schor 1998: 8). There has of course been an inversion of the value schema since Veblen's time—partly as a consequence of Veblen's own work—so that the canons of taste now place an exaggerated emphasis upon usefulness, rather than uselessness (hence the popularity of restaurant-grade stainless steel stoves in homes, or the vogue for using trucks as passenger vehicles). Yet the fact that these items are potentially useful does not mean that they are actually put to good use. Thus the level of "conspicuous waste" involved in their production and consumption has not been affected at all by the transition from "bourgeois" to "bohemian" values. It is precisely because it is independent of any particular system of values that the logical structure of Veblen's analysis and the force of his critique remain valid (indeed, it provides the key to understanding the underlying dynamic of these changing patterns of consumption).

III

The second major charge that Veblen lays upon the doorstep of "the wealthier class" is that it is "conservative", or, more specifically, that it "comes to exert a retarding influence upon social development far in excess of that which the simple numerical strength of the class would assign it" (1994 [1899]: 200). The analytical basis for this claim and the normative foundations for the implied criticism are supplied by Veblen's theory of social evolution. Of course, the modern reader cannot help but approach any exercise in late nineteenth-century social Darwinism with considerable trepidation. Nevertheless (and despite his rather anxiety-provoking speculations about the origins of the dolichoblond 'race' and Aryan culture), much of what Veblen says on the subject is perfectly reasonable, and can easily be reconstructed within a modern evolutionary framework.

Veblen was an early proponent of what is now referred to as a "dual inheritance" or a "gene-culture co-evolutionary" theory (Richerson and Boyd 2004; Hodgson 1998: 188–9). Social action is subject to the influence of two distinct inheritance systems: the biological, which provides the individual with a set of *instincts*, and the cultural, which contributes a set of *habits* (Weed 1981). The most significant sets of habits form *institutions*, which are "not only themselves the result of a selective and adaptive process", but also "efficient factors of selection" insofar as they "make for a further selection of individuals endowed with the fittest temperament" (1994 [1899]: 188). The inheritance system, in the case of institutions, is based upon the human propensity toward emulation, which Veblen regarded as absolutely fundamental. Simply put, people imitate one another, and, as a result, habits or patterns of action developed by individuals get passed down from generation to generation. Thus there is an inertial tendency in the cultural sphere (1994 [1899]: 191).

More recent evolutionary theory has shown that these sorts of co-evolutionary models do not necessarily diverge from sociobiological models in any interesting way. It all depends upon how individuals choose the person that they intend to imitate. Most obviously, if children simply imitate their parents, then no pattern of behavior can emerge at the cultural level that could not also be sustained as a biological trait (since the cultural pattern will enjoy greater reproductive success only if it increases an individual's chances of becoming a parent, which is to say, if it enhances biological fitness). Perhaps more surprisingly, if individuals choose a role model through some random (or unbiased) sampling from the population, then culture will still evolve in lockstep with biology. It is only if there is some bias in the sampling procedure that the dynamics of the two inheritance systems can diverge in interesting ways.

Contemporary discussion has largely focused upon the suggestion, made by Robert Boyd and Peter Richerson, that cultural reproduction is subject to a "conformist" or a "frequency-dependent" bias, such that individuals choose to adopt the pattern of behavior exhibited by the majority of the population (Boyd and Richerson 2005: 31). This creates, among other things, "tipping point" effects that are far more dramatic in the cultural sphere than in the biological. Veblen's suggestion, on the other hand, is that imitation is biased by the status system. Individuals have a propensity to imitate those who are directly above them in the status hierarchy (hence the phenomenon of "pecuniary emulation"). Because of this, behavioral patterns and "spiritual attitudes" are propagated downward through the status hierarchy, giving the dominant class a wholly disproportionate influence upon the more general characteristics of the culture.

In modern civilized communities the lines of demarcation between social classes have grown vague and transient, and wherever this happens the norm of reputability imposed by the upper class extends its coercive influence with but slight hindrance down through the social structure to the lowest strata. The result is that the members of each stratum accept as their ideal of decency the scheme of life in vogue in the next higher stratum, and bend their energies to live up to that ideal.   (1994 [1899]: 84)

Thus what Marxists have been inclined to describe as the "hegemony" of the ruling class is not so much a consequence of straightforward domination as a product of this imitative "micromotive" generating a rather dramatic form of "macrobehavior" (Schelling 1978). Indeed, one of the reasons why Veblen's work received such a guarded, if not hostile, reception among socialists is that he claimed that *every* stratum of society was complicit in reproducing the class structure.

No class of society, not even the most abjectly poor, forgoes all customary conspicuous consumption. The last items of this category of consumption are not given up except under stress of the direst necessity. Very much of squalor and discomfort will be endured before the last trinket or the last pretense of pecuniary decency is put away. There is no class and no country that has yielded so abjectly before the pressure of physical want as to deny themselves all gratification of this higher or spiritual need.   (1994 [1899]: 85)

There is an even more disquieting suggestion made here: namely, that status, like any other good, is subject to diminishing marginal returns, and it is therefore the *lower* classes who are more likely to make serious compromises in their standard of living in order to engage in competitive consumption. Our natural inclination is to think of conspicuous consumption as a vice that is most common among members of the upper class. We forget that because these individuals already have so much status, they are unlikely to make great sacrifices in order to achieve some small increment (R. Frank 1985: 144). Hence the explosive suggestion that competitive consumption may in fact be a greater social problem among the poor than among the rich.

More importantly, Veblen argues that the upper classes cannot be held responsible for the *structure* of the class system, since that structure is upheld and reproduced through a system of emulation that occurs at all levels of society. What they can be held responsible for is the specific *content* that gets propagated through this system of emulation—the habits and ideas that are promoted. It is here that its most pernicious influence is felt. The problem arises as a consequence of what Veblen describes as the "industrial exemption" of the upper classes.

Veblen views culture—and in particular, the prevailing set of economic institutions—as an adaptive system. This means that it changes over time in response to environmental pressures. Veblen regards "the industrial process"—by which he means something very similar to what Marx called "social labor"—as the primary point at which these environmental pressures are felt, and thus the domain in which adaption occurs most readily. The problem is that those who are most directly involved in the industrial process, and who are therefore most likely to abandon old habits when those habits become maladaptive, are at the bottom of the status hierarchy. As a result, the most useful exercises of what Boyd and Richerson call "guided variation" (2004: 116) occur in the class of society that is the *least* likely to exercise any influence upon others. Furthermore, the higher one goes up the status hierarchy, the more out of touch people become with the material constraints imposed by the environment. The class system serves as a sort of internal buffer within the culture that insulates individuals from environmental pressures. This explains what Veblen calls "the conservation of archaic traits" among members of the upper classes. The problem is that these individuals are the *most* likely to be imitated. As a result, there will be a constant *lag* in the adaptation of the culture to its environment. Useful innovations will be ignored, while entrenched patterns of behavior will persist long after they have become maladaptive, simply because the most conservative class is also the most culturally influential.

In Veblen's view, Marx was quite wrong to regard the "reactionary" nature of the upper classes as a consequence of the threat posed to its material interests. It is, on the contrary, almost entirely "spiritual":

The opposition of the [upper] class to changes in the cultural scheme is instinctive, and does not rest primarily on an interested calculation of material advantages; it is an instinctive revulsion at any departure from the accepted way of doing and of looking at things—a revulsion common to all men and only to be overcome by stress of circumstances. All change in habits of life and of thought is irksome. The difference in this respect between the wealthy and the common run of mankind lies not so much in the motive which prompts to conservatism as in the degree of exposure to the economic forces that urge a change.   (1994 [1899]: 199)

Thus Veblen's critique of upper-class conservatism is not a moralizing critique. While he makes it clear that he disapproves of their "barbarian" habits, he uses this only as a basis for satire. His formal criticism is considerably more restrained. The problem with the institution of the leisure class is that it "acts to lower the industrial efficiency of the community and retard the adaptation of human nature to the exigencies of modern industrial life" (1994 [1899]: 244). One might almost say that the leisure class "fetters" the development of the forces of production. Whether or not one thinks that this is a good thing will, of course, depend substantially upon the position that one occupies in the status hierarchy, and one's degree of exposure to leisure-class values.

IV

One of the peculiar things about the rules governing status is that they must often remain tacit in order to be effective. This is why people react with such hostility to the *arriviste*. Newer members of a social class tend to be acting out, quite consciously, a script that older members of the class have long ago internalized—like an apprentice driver who needs to remind himself to shoulder-check every time he changes lanes. The *arriviste* or the *nouveau riche* is often accused of vulgarity. Yet often the problem is not that they are doing anything *wrong*, it's that they are doing it all too *consciously*. This leaves more entrenched members of the class feeling exposed, because it reveals the artifice underlying what they prefer to regard as a purely natural form of behavior. (What Bourdieu calls "the ideology of natural taste" has correlates within all of these hierarchies: from "the ideology of good breeding" to "the ideology of natural cool".)

As a result, the conventions associated with any given status hierarchy often cannot survive explicit articulation, simply because this exposes the artificiality of the practice. Thus the most immediate impact of Veblen's *The Theory of the Leisure Class* arose from the way in which he, somewhat relentlessly, exposed these subterranean features of the status system to the harsh light of day. Veblen played an important role in undermining *the particular pattern of behavior* that was dominant among the upper classes at the time. But of course, this sort of critique does nothing to undermine the *structure* of the status system. It just forces people to find some new way of demarcating themselves from their social inferiors. It creates the need for a system of distinctions that can serve this function without being too obviously *intended* to serve this function.

Thus the pattern of conspicuous waste has changed, from conspicuous leisure to conspicuous consumption, as Veblen predicted, and now to what we might call "conspicuous authenticity". Brooks provides a nice example of this, in showing how the formal sitting room at the front of the home, reserved for entertaining guests, became unsustainable as soon as its artificiality became too obvious. As a result, it became customary in middle-class homes to invite guests into the kitchen upon arrival. This quickly led to an explosion of spending on kitchens, which are now easily the most expensive rooms in North American homes (featuring granite countertops, restaurant-grade appliances, furniture-style cabinetry, and kitchen cupboards with glass doors—like old-fashioned china cabinets). The underlying principle is that "spending on conspicuous display is evil, but it's egalitarian to spend money on parts of the house that would previously have been used by servants" (Brooks 2000: 89). While the "canons" of conspicuous waste have changed, the "law" has not.

The fact that the content of our practices has changed over the past century proves to be an advantage when it comes to interpreting Veblen's work. For it allows us to distinguish with greater ease the logical structure of his critique from the volley of more specific cultural criticisms that he launched—precisely because the latter have become dated, while the former has not. I have tried to show that Veblen presents two "official" criticisms of the status system: first, that it generates collectively self-defeating patterns of consumption; and second, that it makes our social institutions maladaptive with respect to the environment. To the extent that these claims are justified, they are as valid today at they were at the time Veblen made them.

From a methodological standpoint, what is important about these two criticisms is that they both reflect an attempt on Veblen's part to steer clear of straightforwardly moralizing critique. His strategy was to start with normative claims that are, from a pragmatist perspective, platitudinous. The critical aspect of the theory then involves showing how these norm-ative intuitions can be deployed in unobvious ways, via a more general social theory: we all condemn waste, we simply fail to realize how much of our economic activity is wasteful; we all support progress, yet we fail to appreciate the extent to which our social habits impede the adaptiveness of our institutions. Thus fairly radical social criticism emerges as a con-sequence of this analysis. In this respect, Veblen's greatest work, *The Theory of the Leisure Class*, can be thought of as an attempt to leverage common sense—or at least, what the pragmatists thought of as common sense—into critical theory.

REFERENCES

Adorno, Theodor W. (1941). "Veblen's Attack on Culture". *Studies in Philosophy and Social Science*, 9: 389–413.

Ayres, Clarence (1961). *Towards a Reasonable Society*. Austin, TX: University of Texas Press.

Bourdieu, Pierre (1984). *Distinction*, trans. Richard Nice. Cambridge, MA: Harvard University Press.

Boyd, Robert, and Richerson, Peter J. (2004). *The Origin and Evolution of Cultures*. Oxford: Oxford University Press.

Brooks, David (2000). *Bobos in Paradise*. New York: Simon & Schuster.

Dorfman, Joseph (1966). *Thorstein Veblen and His America*. New York: Augustus Kelly.

Frank, Robert (1985). *Choosing the Right Pond*. New York: Oxford University Press.

Frank, Thomas (1997). *The Conquest of Cool*. Chicago: University of Chicago Press.

Heath, Joseph (2001). "The Structure of Hip Consumerism". *Philosophy and Social Criticism*, 27: 1–17.

Hodgson, Geoffrey M. (1998). "Veblen's *Theory of the Leisure Class* and the Genesis of Evolutionary Economics". In Warren J. Samuels (ed.), *The Founding of Institutional Economics*, London: Routledge, 170–200.

Jacobs, Jane (1992 [1961]). *The Death and Life of Great American Cities*. New York: Random House.

Leibenstein, Harvey (1950). "Bandwagon, Snob, and Veblen Effects in the Theory of Consumers' Demand". *Quarterly Journal of Economics*, 64: 183–207.

Marshall, Alfred (1895). *Principles of Economics*, 3rd edn. London: Macmillan & Co.

Marx, Karl (1990 [1867]). *Capital*, i, trans. Ben Fowkes. London: Penguin.

McFarland, Floyd B. (1985). "Thorstein Veblen versus the Institutionalists". *Review of Radial Political Economics*, 17/4: 95–105.

Richerson, Peter J., and Boyd, Robert (2005). *Not be Genes Alone*. Chicago: University of Chicago Press.

Schelling, Thomas C. (1978). *Micromotives and Macrobehavior*. New York: W. W. Norton.

Schor, Juliet (1998). *The Overspent American*. New York: Basic Books.

Schumpeter, Joseph (1942). *Capitalism, Socialism and Democracy*. New York: HarperCollins.

Stutzer, Alois, and Frey, Bruno (2001). *Happiness and Economics*. Princeton: Princeton University Press.

Tilman, Rick (1992). *Thorstein Veblen and his Critics, 1891–1963*. Princeton: Princeton University Press.

——— (1996). *The Intellectual Legacy of Thorstein Veblen*. Westport, CT: Greenwood.

Tool, Marc R. (1998). "A Neoinstitutional Theory of Social Change in Veblen's *The Theory of the Leisure Class*". In Warren J. Samuels, *The Founding of Institutional Economics*, London: Routledge, 302–19.

Veblen, Thorstein (1898). "The Instinct of Workmanship and the Irksomeness of Labor". *American Journal of Sociology*, 4: 187–201.

_____ (1994 [1899]). *The Theory of the Leisure Class*. London: Penguin.

Weed, Frank J. (1981). "Interpreting 'Institutions' in Veblen's Evolutionary Theory". *American Journal of Economics and Sociology*, 40: 67–78.

CHAPTER 14

PRAGMATISM AND THE COLD WAR

ROBERT TALISSE

In the years following World War II, relations between the United States and its Western European allies, on the one hand, and the Soviet Union and its allies, on the other, grew increasingly tense. The term *Cold War* was introduced by Truman advisor Bernard Baruch to refer to the period in international relations, running roughly from the mid-1940s to the early 1990s, during which the world's two superpowers—the United States and the Soviet Union—were locked in military, social, ideological, and economic struggles which constantly threatened, but ultimately fell just short of, all-out conventional, or *hot*, war. The period was marked by a general breakdown of diplomatic relations between the two nations, resulting in a nuclear arms race, massive military spending, and a series of proxy wars within smaller states between factions representing the interests of (and often funded by) the superpowers.

In the United States, the Cold War precipitated a period of social anxiety popularly described as the *McCarthy Era*. Running from the late 1940s to the late 1950s, the McCarthy Era was driven by increasing suspicion that key social and political institutions of the United States were being infiltrated by Communists and anti-Americanists of other stripes on behalf of a Soviet-controlled international Communist organization devoted ultimately to the dissolution of American democracy. The concern over Communist infiltration developed into outright paranoia following Senator Joseph McCarthy's 1950 speech in West Virginia in which he claimed to have a compiled a substantial list of known Communists working in the State Department of the United States. This led to the formation of the Tydings Committee (whose official charge was to investigate the alleged Communist infiltration of the State Department) and eventually to the McCarthy-led Senate Permanent Subcommittee on Investigations and the House Committee on Un-American Activities, which conducted the now infamous public hearings on Communist influence on American society that brought intellectuals, artists, librarians, military officers, and Hollywood actors, among others, under suspicion of disloyalty.

How did these tumultuous times impact America's indigenous school of philosophy? According to a narrative that dominates contemporary work on pragmatism, the Cold War era saw in professional philosophy an "eclipse" of pragmatism by more technical forms of philosophizing described variously as "logical positivism", "scientism", or, most generally, "analytic philosophy". Some have suggested that the concurrence of this eclipse with the Cold War is not coincidental. John McCumber (2001), for example, has argued that the Cold War in general, and McCarthyism in particular, produced strong institutional incentives for academics in the United States to retreat from the public sphere and adopt more insular concerns and methodologies. According to McCumber, analytic philosophy, which he describes as being focused on technical issues concerning language and logic, provided an apolitical safe haven for philosophers in America, while pragmatism, a philosophical school that insists that philosophers must attend to what Dewey called the "problems of men" (*MW* 10: 46)[1] and be publicly engaged, was a natural casualty of the Cold War.[2]

We need not take up the issue of whether McCumber is correct to hold that the Cold War played a direct causal role in the eclipse of pragmatism. What is central to our present purpose is the eclipse narrative itself, the view that pragmatism was marginalized and dormant in the years roughly corresponding to the Cold War, and was resuscitated in the 1980s.

---

[1] References to Dewey follow the standard formula: abbreviation, volume number, then page number.
[2] Menand suggests a similar account, stating that the "intellectual climate of the Cold War" (2001: 439) was hostile to pragmatic ways of thinking.

The eclipse narrative is a resurrection story of a familiar stripe. The original pragmatists arrive on the scene around the turn of the century and attempt to overturn the past by exposing the untenable assumptions underlying traditional philosophy. They offer a radical and new kind of philosophy, one which upsets traditional assumptions and dethrones the status quo. Pragmatism prevails for a brief while, but then the force of tradition reemerges and forces pragmatism underground. Darkness descends. But eventually pragmatism reemerges, due in large measure to the publication of Richard Rorty's ground-breaking 1979 work *Philosophy and the Mirror of Nature*, which restored the philosophical reputation of John Dewey and opened the field to new work in pragmatism.[3]

Like many resurrection stories, the eclipse narrative is also a persecution story. It contends that pragmatism was not refuted but "eclipsed". This element of the story runs as follows: Advances in formal logic associated with Russell and Frege gave rise to faddish intellectual trends that placed the analysis of language at the core of philosophy, thereby making it seem more scientific and rigorous; consequently, the pragmatists, who emphasized experience rather than language, were simply dismissed as confused, imprecise, irrelevant, or worse. The story continues, that now we see that the "linguistic turn" characteristic of analytic philosophy was simply an error and that pragmatism has been all along "waiting at the end of the dialectical road" which analytic philosophy had taken fifty years to traverse (Rorty 1982: p. xviii).

Hence the renaissance of pragmatism is often seen as a kind of *vindication* of pragmatism, a *victory* over analytic philosophy. In this way, the eclipse narrative identifies analytic philosophy as a philosophical *villain* and places pragmatism in opposition to it. Even today, it is widely held that the degree to which analytic philosophy represents the mainstream of philosophy in America is the extent to which pragmatism is being marginalized. Consequently, the eclipse narrative tends to foster an attitude of resentment towards professional philosophy which manifests itself in the tendency to demonize analytic philosophy as "narrow", "irrelevant", and "nihilistic", a tendency

---

[3] It is nearly impossible to find a current work on pragmatism that does not present some version of this story. See, e.g., West 1989: 3; Bernstein 1987; Festenstein 1997: 2; Dickstein 1998: 1; Hickman 1998: p. xii; Caspary 2000: 1; Wilshire 2002; Capps 2003: 1; Fesmire 2003: 2; Hildebrand 2003: 1; McDermott 2004; and Westbrook 2005: p. xii. Good (2003) argues that the eclipse narrative is flawed because pragmatism was never a dominant philosophical movement in America; see also Eldridge 2004.

which Richard Bernstein has rightly criticized as unpragmatic and parochial (1995: 62).[4]

Though it is the dominant self-understanding among contemporary scholars of pragmatism, the eclipse narrative is highly questionable. For one thing, those who promote the narrative rarely clarify what they mean by "analytic philosophy", and when a description is offered, it often rings hollow. Bruce Wilshire, for example, identifies analytic philosophy with "scientism", the view that "only science can know" (2002: 4; cf. McCumber 2001: 49 ff.), but it is clear that only the most extreme of the logical positivists, if anyone, ever held such a stark position. More importantly, if we examine the work of the most influential figures in mainstream philosophy from the past sixty years—Ludwig Wittgenstein, Nelson Goodman, C. I. Lewis, Ernest Nagel, W. V. O. Quine, Donald Davidson, Wilfrid Sellars, Hilary Putnam, John Rawls, John Searle, Daniel Dennett, Crispin Wright, Michael Dummett, David Wiggins, Jürgen Habermas, and Robert Brandom—we find that they either explicitly acknowledge a distinctively pragmatist inheritance or take themselves to be responding critically to identifiably pragmatist arguments. Judged by the centrality of distinctively pragmatist theses concerning meaning, truth, knowledge, and action to ongoing debates in philosophy, pragmatism is easily among the most successful philosophical trends of the past two centuries. It seems, then, that the eclipse narrative is demonstrably false; pragmatism was alive and well throughout the Cold War, and it continues to be a major force on the philosophical scene.

Purveyors of the eclipse narrative will respond that the argument above employs the wrong criterion; they will reject the idea that the centrality of pragmatist claims to perpetual debates *within* professional philosophy is an appropriate metric of philosophical success. They will contend that even though Quine, Sellars, Putnam, and the rest clearly borrow from the pragmatisms of Peirce, James, and Dewey, they nonetheless represent an abandonment of pragmatism because they reject the central pragmatist commitment to doing philosophy in a way that is *publicly engaged*. The response continues that it is the *nature of the concerns* to which Quine and the others are attending which constitutes a rejection of pragmatism. Again, the view is that true pragmatism must be addressed to the "problems of men"; pragmatists must be public philosophers.

---

[4] See Talisse 2007: ch. 7 for further discussion.

But this defense of the eclipse narrative is problematic. What does it mean to be doing philosophy in a publicly engaged way? If by "public philosopher" we mean something robust such as *public intellectual on the scale of Dewey*, then we confront the fact that Peirce and arguably James were not public philosophers in this sense. Moreover, if highly visible public political engagement is a necessary condition for being a pragmatist, there are almost no pragmatists today, for, since the death of Richard Rorty, Cornel West is the only self-described pragmatist who can plausibly claim to be a public intellectual on such a scale. Yet if we adopt a more modest sense of "public philosopher", it is difficult to see why figures heavily influenced by pragmatism, such as Habermas, Putnam, and Dennett, should not qualify.

One might respond that Habermas and the others have taken up the role of public philosopher only recently, and that during the Cold War era there were no public philosophers, and thus no true pragmatists. But this response fails. During the years in which pragmatism was supposedly in "eclipse", the pragmatist philosopher Sidney Hook was a powerful force in professional philosophy and also among America's most influential public intellectuals.

It is curious that contemporary pragmatists who promote the eclipse narrative often fail to notice Hook. Indeed, he has been almost completely written out of the history of pragmatism.[5] This oversight is unfortunate: due consideration of his work instantly casts doubt on the eclipse narrative. Consider that throughout the 1950s and 1960s, much of Hook's academic work was aimed towards defending pragmatic naturalism against objections raised by Marxists, existentialists, Thomists, and others, that pragmatism is narrowly instrumentalist, anti-humanist, ruthlessly capitalist, and, in a word, the intellectual expression of the vulgarities of American culture. In a 1956 essay which reads like a manifesto of pragmatism, "Naturalism and First Principles", Hook contends that there are standards of rationality that are "not limited to our culture and to our time", but arise out of

---

[5] Hook's absence from the recent literature on pragmatism is easily documented. Despite the explosion of new work in pragmatism over the past fifteen years, there has been almost no attention paid to Hook. For example, there is no substantial discussion of Hook in Murphy 1990; Campbell 1992; Festenstein 1997; Hart and Anderson 1997; Mounce 1997; Rosenthal, Hausman, and Anderson 1999; Gunn 2001; Menand 2001; Kuklick 2001; MacGilvray 2004; and Stout 2004; John Diggins offers some helpful comments on "Hook's disappearance from the history of pragmatism" (1998: 224). For many years, the sole exception to this trend was West 1989; but now see Westbrook 2005: ch. 5, and the essays collected in Cotter 2004. See also Haack and Lane (2006), who include Hook in their anthology of pragmatist writings.

processes of "practical living" (2002 [1956]: 47). Citing scientific method as the "refinement" of these "canons of rationality", Hook argues that naturalism is the commitment to applying scientific method to all human problems (2002 [1956]: 47). Accordingly, pragmatism is not the attempt somehow to reduce everything to science, as critics allege, but rather the attempt to further develop and systematize the habits of inquiry already embedded in our "successful working practice in solving problems concerning the nature of things" (2002 [1956]: 66).

This kind of encapsulation of pragmatism often raises the charge that it is naïvely optimistic. Hook fixed on this kind of criticism in his presidential address to the American Philosophical Association in 1959—and note that this is at the supposed high point of analytic philosophy's hegemony. In "Pragmatism and the Tragic Sense of Life", Hook argues that the moral question "What should I do?" arises "in a situation in which good conflicts with good", or good conflicts with right (2002 [1960]: 78 f.), or right conflicts with right (2002 [1960]: 81). Accordingly, Hook rebuffs the charge of optimism by the concept of conflict—not between good and evil, but among goods and rights—at the center of pragmatist ethics. In fact, one of the distinctive characteristics of Hook's pragmatism is the emphasis he places on conflict.[6]

Most important for present purposes, however, is the fact that, throughout this period of supposed eclipse, and indeed until his death in 1989, Hook engaged in public and sometimes highly visible debates on philosophical and political topics with the likes of Albert Einstein, Bertrand Russell, Noam Chomsky, William F. Buckley, Mortimer Adler, and Herbert Marcuse. That is, *pace* the eclipse narrative, perhaps the most visible and influential public intellectual of the Cold War era was a self-avowed pragmatist philosopher.

It is tempting to conclude that the exclusion of Hook is deliberate, that Hook is ignored precisely because he cannot be fitted into the eclipse narrative. The temptation is heightened by the fact that, among the few who acknowledge Hook at all, some have gone so far as to cite Hook's "failings as a pragmatist philosopher" (Good 2003: 79) as a *cause* of the eclipse of pragmatism. Along these lines, John Capps contends that Hook hastened pragmatism's demise by adopting during the Cold War era argumentative strategies that are

---

[6] See also Hook 2002 [1975] and 2002 [1940]. The sensitivity to the importance of conflict may be the result of his early work on Marx's philosophy.

"touchstones of analytic philosophy" and therefore "at odds" with Hook's "philosophical identity as a pragmatist" (Capps 2003: 73). The eclipse narrative is preserved by denying that Hook was a pragmatist.

This maneuver is implausible, but it is worth dwelling on Hook's encounter with the Cold War. According to Capps, the fateful episode which brought about pragmatism's eclipse was Hook's public defense in the early 1950s of the view that members of the Communist Party (CP) were unfit to teach in public schools in the United States. Capps claims that Hook's argument represents the moment at which pragmatism "lost the sensitivity to context which, in happier times, had been one of its defining characteristics" (2003: 62). Capps alleges that once Hook abandoned this "sensitivity to context", pragmatism was lost.

Let us examine Hook's infamous position. In several essays and the book, *Heresy, Yes—Conspiracy, No* (1953), Hook argued that the CP was not merely a political party, but a conspiratorial organization under the direct control of a dictator who expressly sought to dismantle Western democracy (1953: 21–34). According to Hook, the CP explicitly cited educational indoctrination as among the means by which it sought to undermine the United States (1953: 181 f.), and it *required* of its members full endorsement of its objectives and methods (1953: 183). Hence membership in the CP signaled an individual's allegiance to the objectives of the CP (1953: 28 ff.). Hook concluded that CP members were *prima facie* unfit to hold "sensitive" positions, including that of teacher in a public college, advocating the removal of CP members from the relevant positions.

It is important to notice the nuances of Hook's view. Three preliminary clarifications are worth emphasizing. First, Hook's argument was not intended to apply to Communists *per se*, but only to members of the CP.[7] Hook had no problem with *Communist* teachers (1987: 503). Second, Hook did not object to CP members in all areas of society, but only to those who held "sensitive" or "strategic" posts; Hollywood actors were of no concern to Hook (1953: 72). Third, Hook did not argue that CP membership should be *outlawed* or that CP members should be imprisoned for their membership (1953: 26). More importantly, it must be added that Hook argued that CP members should be *suspended* from their positions until a proper inquiry into their activities could be conducted (1987: 504). Hook did not advocate

---

[7] Hook himself was for a long time a self-declared Communist, but never a member of the CP (Phelps 1997: 31–2).

the *automatic* dismissal from a post of a suspected CP member; there was always to be an inquiry into the nature and extent of the person's involvement.[8]

In a nutshell, then, Hook held the following. The CP is a conspiratorial organization under the direct control of a dictatorship that expressly aims to undermine American democracy. Membership in the CP is granted only after one has pledged allegiance to the CP and its stated aims and methods. Among the methods endorsed by the CP for undermining American democracy is the indoctrination of students in the views officially endorsed by the CP. Accordingly, CP members are *prima facie* committed to instilling the CP positions in students regardless of the evidence or arguments that can be marshaled in their support. Thus CP members are doctrinally bound to reject inquiry as such; they are therefore unable to meet their primary responsibility as professors (Hook 1953: 206–7).

Hook's position is certainly open to challenge, but, *pace* Capps, there is nothing unpragmatic, anti-contextualist, or distinctively "analytic" about the argument. Casting the position in more familiar contexts, Hook's argument is equivalent to the view that airport baggage-checkers who belong to al-Qaeda but have not as yet been shown to have committed terrorist acts should be, at the very least, suspended. When taken in the context of the Cold War and the threat which the CP was then reasonably believed to pose, Hook's position seems a fully pragmatist response.

It is worth emphasizing further that Hook's position presents no conflict with his *democratic* commitments. Let us assume for the sake of argument that Hook was *justified* in believing that the CP was a powerful conspiratorial organization devoted to the undermining of democracy in part by means of educational indoctrination that required of its members full and continuing obedience to its dictates. On this assumption, it is hard to see how Hook's argument represents a democratic failing. Again, Hook's position makes as much sense as a policy of suspending airport baggage inspectors whom we have good reason to believe are members of al-Qaeda, and of dismissing those who prove to be members. Is the latter policy anti-democratic?

Someone might object that the policy of suspending CP teachers—and per-haps even that of dismissing al-Qaeda baggage inspectors—is anti-democratic

---

[8] Cf. "Even though I believed that membership in the [CP] rendered an individual unfit ... to be a member of the teaching staff, I did *not* believe that their mere fact of membership should result in automatic dismissal (Hook 1987: 504).

because it violates the core democratic value of freedom of speech. Hook's proposal, a critic might say, punishes criticism and dissent; yet democracy must keep itself open to such activities. Thus, the critic concludes, Hook's position constitutes a betrayal of democracy.

But this kind of criticism fails to countenance a crucial distinction that Hook insisted upon between *internal* and *external* opposition to democracy. Opposition to a policy or action of a democratic community is internal if it complies with the "rules of the game" of democracy and of democratic discourse (Hook 2002 [1959]: 264). By contrast, opposition is external to the democratic framework if it violates these rules. Hook writes:

Opposition of the first kind, no matter how mistaken, must be tolerated, if for no other reason than that we cannot be sure that it is not we who are mistaken. Opposition of the second kind, no matter what protective coloration it wears . . . must be swiftly dealt with if democracy is to survive.   (2002 [1938]: 296)

A distinction of this kind is essential to any viable conception of democracy. That is, any democratic view must draw a distinction between tolerable and intolerable modes of dissent, between *civil* disobedience and *uncivil* disobedience, between opposition and revolt, or, in Hook's nomenclature, between heresy and conspiracy. Hook's position is that modes of political action that attempt to accomplish political aims by means of methods that overtly reject or circumvent standing democratic procedures are *ipso facto* undeserving of tolerance. The bulk of Hook's writings just about the CP is devoted to showing that the CP is engaged in *external* opposition to the democratic status quo, and therefore is conspiratorial, and hence intolerable.

One may judge with the hindsight of fifty years that Hook overestimated the threat that the CP posed. But the pragmatic question concerns what *Hook* was justified in believing, not what we should *now* believe—again, with all the clarity of hindsight—about the severity of the threat. Hence our concern is not whether Hook was correct about the threat the CP posed; rather, it is whether Hook was correct to think that a commitment to democracy requires the kind of measures he advocated when faced with the kind of threat he believed was prevalent. As I have indicated, I find it difficult to disagree with Hook on this score. I conclude, then, that Hook's position concerning CP teachers is fully consistent with his pragmatic commitments.

But, as the view that Hook was not really a pragmatist collapses, so too does the entire eclipse narrative. Once Hook is brought into the picture, we see that not only did pragmatist arguments and theses continue to shape the character of mainstream philosophy, but also that pragmatism was very well represented in the public arena. Again, once we have a clear view of the matter, we find that pragmatism is among the most successful philosophical movements ever. But where does this leave our discussion of pragmatism and the Cold War?

Rorty has claimed that in the years following World War II "all that happened was that the philosophy professors got bored with James and Dewey and latched on to something that looked new and promising" (2004: 284). Although Rorty is correct to reject the eclipse narrative, this rather blasé alternative cannot be the entire story. For one thing, Rorty's account leaves one to wonder why James and Dewey began to look boring, and why other options seemed promising. I think Rorty's account should be supplemented along the following lines.

To begin, it is worth reminding ourselves of two related facts. First, the alleged eclipse of pragmatism coincides not only with the Cold War, but also with Dewey's gradual withdrawal from the intellectual scene and eventual death in 1952. Second, the pragmatism that was allegedly eclipsed was primarily Deweyan pragmatism.[9] Accordingly, in order to fill in the story of pragmatism and the Cold War, we need to look at Dewey's version of pragmatism.

Dewey explicitly conceived of his pragmatism in revolutionary terms. He thought that the truth of Darwinism required a comprehensive reconstruction of philosophy in which traditional problems of philosophy, and the categories which they presumed, would be discarded; Dewey declared that "we do not solve" the traditional problems of philosophy, we "get over them" (MW 4: 14). Consequently, Dewey's philosophy begins from a sweeping attack on all the standard philosophical schools and positions: rationalism, idealism, absolutism, essentialism, sense data empiricism, epistemic foundationalism, metaphysical realism, correspondence theories of truth, mind–body dualism, logical atomism, utilitarianism and deontology in ethics, social contractarianism, and so on. Perhaps the novelty of Dewey's critique took proponents

---

[9] Peirce was always highly regarded among professional philosophers; however, the full import of his thought could not be estimated, due to the unavailability of a systematic edition of his writings. For this reason, Peirce's pragmatism was never the dominant version. As for James, his pragmatism was never regarded as canonical, and his own articulations of pragmatist themes were largely rejected by subsequent pragmatists, including Dewey. On Dewey's reaction to James's pragmatism, see especially his 1908 essay "What Pragmatism Means by 'Practical'" (MW 4: 98–115).

of these positions by surprise; for Dewey did not simply introduce new considerations into the standing debates, he criticized the presuppositions underlying the debates themselves. Typically, Dewey argued that all parties to any given long-standing debate in philosophy had presupposed some dualism—man and nature, permanence and change, reason and emotion, ideal and real, mind and body, individual and community, subject and object (*LW* 4: 195)—that had been rendered obsolete by Darwinism. Hence, according to Dewey, philosophy's past is composed of a series of mere "puzzles" (*LW* 1: 17) to be discarded as "chaff" (*LW* 1: 4).

Unlike Rorty, who saw pragmatism as a rejection of philosophy altogether, Dewey's project was not merely critical. Dewey spent his career building a comprehensive philosophical framework based in a distinctive brand of pragmatism that he called *empirical naturalism* or *experimentalism*. By the early 1940s, Dewey had constructed a grand and integrated—almost Hegelian—system of metaphysics, logic, psychology, epistemology, ethics, aesthetics, politics, and theology. Indeed, many of Dewey's contemporary followers see the "organic unity" (Fesmire 2003: 70) of Dewey's philosophy as a principal virtue.

What we see in the mid-twentieth century, however, is a series of new articulations of the old positions that Dewey claimed to have dissolved. Frequently, these new articulations were designed to respond to precisely the kind of objections that Dewey had proposed. Consider just a few examples. In the 1950s and 1960s, John Rawls proposed a new methodology for moral theory and a new defense of contractarianism which rejected intuitionism, egoism, utilitarianism, and the metaphysical extravagances of Kantianism. In the late 1950s and following, Roderick Chisholm devised foundationalist epistemology that was also fallibilist. In the 1960s, philosophers of language such as Jerrold Katz and Jerry Fodor drew on Chomsky's work in linguistics to devise a new kind of rationalism and nativism rooted in empirical data; around the same time, John Searle resuscitated mind–body dualism in a form consistent with naturalism. By the 1970s, powerful new versions of nearly all of the traditional philosophical positions, and, importantly, compelling new studies of key historical figures—including Dewey's principal foes, Descartes and Kant—had emerged.

The availability of ostensibly viable new instantiations of traditional positions challenged Dewey's strategy of dismissing entire philosophical schools as premised on a single simple error. New Kantians relied upon the method of reflective equilibrium, not transcendental metaphysics; new foundationalists did not need to embark on a "quest for certainty"; new rationalists could appeal to scientific data in support of their semantics; philosophers of mind could adopt a *property* dualism of mind and body, thereby eschewing the Cartesian metaphysics of dual substances. Whether any of these new positions is philosophically successful is of course debatable. To repeat, my point is that the development of these views rendered unsustainable Dewey's claim that Darwinism supplied a perspective from which centuries of philosophy could be swept away with a single intellectual gesture; it no longer seemed plausible to assert, with Dewey, that his philosophical approach was "the way, and the only way . . . by which one can freely accept the standpoint and conclusions of modern science" (*LW* 1: 4). Accordingly, those who favored the kind of pragmatism and naturalism associated with Dewey were driven to abandon Dewey's style of criticism. They had to engage the new developments piecemeal, argument by argument.

This in turn led to a general distrust of the kind of comprehensive philosophical system building in which Dewey engaged. It no longer seemed useful to erect what John Stuhr calls, in characterizing Dewey's philosophy, "a comprehensive account of experience, inquiry, logic, education, morality, religion, and art" (1998: 85). Most of those active in professional philosophy had come to see that no set of philosophical premises full-bodied enough to support a system was non-controversial enough to justify the effort of grand system building. The most philosophers could pursue was a defensible account of some more or less specific phenomenon, with the hope that such an account could be shown to hang together with similar accounts of related phenomena. But note that this humbling of philosophical ambition is driven by the utterly *pragmatic* insight that, when no single approach can plausibly claim to be the only responsible way of proceeding, philosophy itself must advance dialectically and in piecemeal fashion, by way of meeting the arguments, challenges, and counterexamples raised by those who do not share one's fundamental philosophical orientation.

Hence it seems more accurate to say that in the 1950s and 1960s Deweyan pragmatism, his "comprehensive account", was in *crisis*, not eclipse. What was clear at that time was that if the tradition of pragmatic naturalism was to survive, it needed to be reworked, revised in light of new challenges. Here, the post-Deweyan pragmatists *par excellence* are Hook and Quine. Hook offers no grand system, but rather highly focused attempts to articulate and defend a generally naturalist and experimentalist approach to very specific problems in philosophy and politics. Similarly, Quine's corpus presents an ongoing development of a few key pragmatist and naturalist insights about science, language, and ontology, and an attempt to fit them together. Importantly, both Hook and Quine proceed by way of critical engagement with non-naturalist critics and interlocutors. It is unsurprising that after Dewey's death Quine quickly rose to become so influential among professional philosophers in America; for he understood, with Hook, that the case for pragmatic naturalism was to be made on a case-by-case basis, not by way of a "comprehensive account" of everything under the sun. For similar reasons, it is no surprise that the Dewey that emerges heroic in Rorty's work is a "therapeutic" Dewey (Rorty 1977: 73), a Dewey shorn of system.

Hence, what is seen by those committed to the eclipse narrative as a turn towards insularity, irrelevance, and technicality-for-its-own-sake is actually a pragmatically responsible reaction to the sheer plurality of philosophically forceful competitors, a plurality that Dewey had explicitly denied. The Cold War era saw no eclipse or abandonment of pragmatism; rather, the Cold War coincided with the period in which pragmatism was forced to confront powerful challenges from opponents who had the opportunity to revise and rework their positions in light of pragmatist criticisms. Once again, we see that, far from being marginalized or excluded, pragmatism remained highly influential throughout the second half of the twentieth century.

References

Bernstein, Richard (1987). "One Step Forward, Two Steps Backward". *Political Theory*, 15/4: 538–63.

——— (1995). "American Philosophy as a Conflict of Narratives". In Herman Saatkamp (ed.), *Rorty and Pragmatism*, Nashville: Vanderbilt University Press, 54–67.

Campbell, James (1992). *The Community Reconstructed: The Meaning of Pragmatist Social Thought*. Urbana, IL: University of Illinois Press.

Capps, John (2003). "Pragmatism and the McCarthy Era". *Transactions of the Charles S. Peirce Society*, 39/1: 61–76.

Caspary, William (2000). *Dewey on Democracy*. Ithaca, NY: Cornell University Press.

Cotter, Matthew (ed.) (2004). *Sidney Hook Reconsidered*. Amherst, NY: Prometheus Books.

Dewey, John (1969–91). *The Collected Works of John Dewey: The Early Works [EW], The Middle Works [MW], The Later Works [LW]*, ed. Jo Ann Boydston, 37 vols. Carbondale, IL: Southern Illinois University Press.

Dickstein, Morris (1998). "Introduction: Pragmatism Then and Now". In Dickstein (ed.), *The Revival of Pragmatism*, Durham, NC: Duke University Press, 1–18.

Diggins, John P. (1998). *The Promise of Pragmatism*. Chicago: University of Chicago Press.

Eldridge, Michael (2004). "Dewey's Bulldog and the Eclipse of Pragmatism". In Cotter (2004), 129–46.

Fesmire, Steven (2003). *John Dewey and Moral Imagination*. Indianapolis: Indiana University Press.

Festenstein, Matthew (1997). *Pragmatism and Political Theory*. Chicago: University of Chicago Press.

Good, James A. (2003). "The 'Eclipse' of Pragmatism: A Reply to John Capps". *Transactions of the Charles S. Peirce Society*, 39/1: 77–86.

Gunn, Giles (2001). *Beyond Solidarity*. Chicago: University of Chicago Press.

Haack, Susan, and Lane, Robert (eds.) (2006). *Pragmatism: Old and New*. Amherst, NY: Prometheus Books.

Hart, Richard, and Anderson, Douglas (eds.) (1997). *Philosophy in Experience*. New York: Fordham University Press.

Hickman, Larry (1998). "Introduction". In Hickman (ed.), *Reading Dewey*, Indiananpolis: University of Indiana Press, pp. ix–xx.

Hildebrand, David (2003). *Beyond Realism and Anti-realism*. Nashville: Vanderbilt University Press.

Hook, Sidney (2002 [1938]). "The Democratic Way of Life". In Talisse and Tempio (2002), 275–88.

_____ (2002 [1940]). "Conflicts in Ways of Belief". In Talisse and Tempio (2002), 267–74.

_____ (1953). *Heresy, Yes—Conspiracy, No*. New York: John Day.

_____ (2002 [1956]). "Naturalism and First Principles". In Talisse and Tempio (2002), 46–67.

_____ (2002 [1959]). "The Philosophical Heritage of the Atlantic Democracies". In Talisse and Tempio (2002), 250–66.

_____ (2002 [1960]). "Pragmatism and the Tragic Sense of Life". In Talisse and Tempio (2002), 68–90.

_____ (2002 [1975]). "The Place of Reason in an Age of Conflict". In Talisse and Tempio (2002), 91–108.

_____ (1987). *Out of Step: An Unquiet Life in the Twentieth Century*. New York: Harper and Row.

Kuklick, Bruce (2001). *A History of Philosophy in America*. New York: Oxford University Press.

MacGilvray, Eric (2004). *Reconstructing Public Reason*. Cambridge, MA: Harvard University Press.

McCumber, John (2001). *Time in the Ditch*. Evanston, IL: Northwestern University Press.

McDermott, John J. (2004). "Epilogue: The Renascence of Classical American Philosophy". In Armen Marsoobian and John Ryder (eds.), *The Blackwell Companion to American Philosophy*, Oxford: Blackwell, 397–405.

Menand, Louis (2001). *The Metaphysical Club*. New York: Farrar, Straus, and Giroux.

Mounce, H. O. (1997). *The Two Pragmatisms*. New York: Routledge.

Murphy, John P. (1990). *Pragmatism: From Peirce to Davidson*. Boulder, CO: Westview Press.

Phelps, Christopher (1997). *Young Sidney Hook*. Ithaca, NY: Cornell University Press.

Rorty, Richard (1977). "Dewey's Metaphysics". Repr. in Rorty (1982), 72–89.

——— (1979). *Philosophy and the Mirror of Nature*. Princeton: Princeton University Press.

——— (1982). *Consequences of Pragmatism*. Minneapolis: University of Minnesota Press.

——— (2004). "Afterword". In Cotter (2004), 281–6.

Rosenthal, Sandra, Hausman, Carl, and Anderson, Douglas (eds.) (1999). *Classical American Philosophy: Its Contemporary Vitality*. Urbana, IL: University of Illinois Press.

Stout, Jeffrey (2004). *Democracy and Tradition*. Princeton: Princeton University Press.

Stuhr, John (1998). "Dewey's Social and Political Philosophy". In Larry Hickman (ed.), *Reading Dewey*, Indianapolis: Indiana University Press, 82–98.

Talisse, Robert B. (2007). *A Pragmatist Philosophy of Democracy*. New York: Routledge.

——— and Tempio, R. (eds.) (2002). *Sidney Hook on Pragmatism, Democracy, and Freedom*. Amherst, NY: Prometheus Books.

West, Cornel (1989). *The American Evasion of Philosophy*. Madison: University of Wisconsin Press.

Westbrook, Robert (2005). *Democratic Hope*. Ithaca, NY: Cornell University Press.

Wilshire, Bruce (2002). *Fashionable Nihilism: A Critique of Analytic Philosophy*. Albany, NY: SUNY Press.

CHAPTER 15

PRAGMATISM AND THE GIVEN: C. I. LEWIS, QUINE, AND PEIRCE

CHRISTOPHER HOOKWAY

1. INTRODUCTION: PRAGMATISM AND EXPERIENCE

IT IS EASY to lose sight of the importance of C. I. Lewis's contributions to twentieth-century philosophy. They provide a bridge between the writings of the classical pragmatists such as Peirce, James, Royce, and others, on the one hand, and philosophers like Quine, who influenced the emergence of 'neo-pragmatism' in the final decades of that century, on the

I am grateful to Cheryl Misak and Jennifer Saul whose comments on an earlier version of this paper have led to substantial improvements.

other. As Murray Murphey's recent magisterial study makes clear, Lewis's contributions to logic and epistemology provided a rigorous development of the pragmatist epistemology that had been developed by Peirce and James. Indeed, he had access to Peirce's manuscripts when he returned to Harvard in 1920 (Murphey 2005: 111), and his early exposure to the work of Royce led to an understanding of the relations between logic and metaphysics that has been of lasting importance. And, over many years, his teaching at Harvard exposed succeeding philosophical generations to pragmatist ideas, even if their response was often to reject or qualify them. Books such as *Mind and the World Order* (1929) and *An Analysis of Knowledge and Valuation* (1946) articulated a pragmatist epistemology that has had a substantial influence even if it is now too little studied.

The subtitle of Murphey's book, *The Last Great Pragmatist*, carries a double message. First, there is an invaluable reminder that we must approach Lewis as a member of the pragmatist tradition rather than, as is often the case among analytical philosophers, as a foundationalist epistemologist whose links to pragmatism were incidental. Second, there is the suggestion that, after Lewis, pragmatism had no 'great' exponents. This implies that if Lewis's version of pragmatism proves problematic, there is no significant later development of the tradition that takes pragmatism further. That the living tradition of pragmatism comes to an end with Lewis's work is supported by the fact that, faced by extensive criticism of his epistemological and metaphysical views in the 1950s, Lewis appears to have lost heart and did not return to the defence of 'conceptualistic pragmatism'. His later writings were almost exclusively concerned with ethics and value theory. However, there is also considerable evidence that the pragmatist tradition did not die, and that it has prospered into the twenty-first century.

There is one respect in which much of the most influential work in pragmatism after the 1950s does mark a break with the tradition of 'classical pragmatism' which, Murphey suggests, came to an end with the work of Lewis. There is a very striking difference between the philosophical positions of the classical pragmatists and those of at least some recent philosophers who have been described as 'neo-pragmatists' or who are seen as fellow travellers of pragmatism. This concerns the role of experience in philosophy. Peirce, James, and Dewey all insist that perceptual experience has a rich phenomenological character. When James describes himself as a 'radical' empiricist, he is both drawing our attention to the fact that experience has much more content than earlier empiricists had allowed and endorsing a metaphysical view that treats experiences as the fundamental components of reality. Peirce, especially in his later writings, defends a form of empiricism that allows that we directly perceive external things, that we can experience the causal impact of one thing upon another, and that our experience presents the world as containing generality, for example as governed by laws. Moreover, these features of the content of perceptual experience have an important role in explaining how we participate in inquiry, evaluating beliefs and theories and solving theoretical problems. So the classical pragmatists were typically empiricists, and one thing that made them distinctive was the rich content they found in experience. For philosophers such as Rorty, Sellars, Quine, and Davidson—all thinkers who are described as contributing to the revival of pragmatism in the last decades of the twentieth century—experience appears to have a much more limited role. All these neo-pragmatists accept that the only kind of thing that can serve as a reason for belief is another belief. Perception may have a role in the causation of beliefs, but it has no role in justifying them. Nowhere in their writings do we find the careful sensitivity to the phenomenology of experience that characterizes the work of classical pragmatists. Most of these thinkers seem to think that their position results from their rejection of the 'myth of the given'. Once we abandon that mistaken idea, it seems, the phenomenology of perceptual experience has little to contribute to epistemology and the theory of inquiry. An important intermediate figure here is C. I. Lewis. Unlike these other philosophers, he was unembarrassed about embracing the given, and thinkers like Sellars were explicit that books like *Mind and the World Order* were primary sources for the idea of *givenness* that they were rejecting. Moreover, when Lewis was developing his epistemological ideas, he claimed to be drawing on ideas that he had found in the published writings and manuscripts of James and, especially, Peirce. This raises a question about whether the conceptions of experience employed by the classical pragmatists were similarly committed to the *given*. Have these recent thinkers shown us how to retain the insights of pragmatism while abandoning what was taken to be a flawed conception of the given? Or have they thrown away the baby with the bathwater, losing track of deep insights that are contained in the earlier pragmatist views about experience? Indeed, how far was Lewis's epistemology a backward step, reintroducing Kantian dichotomies?

2. THE GIVEN IN TWENTIETH-CENTURY EPISTEMOLOGY

For most contemporary philosophers, the concept of the *given* is intimately connected with two philosophical positions: empiricism and epistemological foundationalism. Those who reject the given identify Lewis as a paradigm empiricist foundationalist. Such a reading of Lewis's work is almost certainly mistaken, but we should begin by identifying what this 'standard reading' of the given involves.

Foundationalism is an account of the structure of justification. Many of our justified beliefs obtain their justification from the fact that they are inferred from, or dependent upon, other justified beliefs. Concerned to avoid a regress of justification, foundationalists hold that this is not the case for all of our beliefs. There are basic or foundational beliefs whose justification is non-inferential, and these provide the ultimate first premises for the inferences upon which our other beliefs depend. There is then a question about just how these basic beliefs are justified. There are many ways of answering this question, but the one that is relevant to the reading of Lewis has two components, described by Eric Dayton as follows:

Certainty: These [basic] beliefs are certain, self-evident, cannot be mistaken.

Sensuousness: [Basic] beliefs are about (or are) sensuous episodes of epistemic awareness (typically awareness of sensuous kinds, objects or events). [Dayton prefers 'self-justified' to 'basic']   (Dayton 1995: 257)

Somehow our basic beliefs respond to sensory experience that is independent of our thoughts and concepts: we are the passive recipients of such experiences; they are *given* to us and are thus often referred to as 'the given'.

There are many reasons for rejecting this sort of foundationalist epistemology (see, e.g., Haack 1993), but at this point I want to mention just one issue, suggested by Wilfrid Sellars's famous exposure of the 'myth of the given' (1963: 41 f.). Somehow the elements of my experience justify or constitute my basic knowledge. Any perceptual judgement that I form will involve interpretation of the given—I judge that I see something as red and triangular, or I see something as a blue book on the desk. The given was characterized as something which does not depend upon or reflect our concepts; hence, we might suppose, it lacks the sort of structure possessed by the judgements which it is supposed to justify. If the given is to *justify* our basic beliefs, then it must occupy a normative role: somehow it must make the interpretation we offer a correct or appropriate one. Indeed, given *Certainty* above, it must justify an interpretation that will be infallible. Unless the given itself has a conceptual or propositional content, it is impossible to see how it can fill this normative role. The given might *cause* us to form particular interpretations, but it cannot *justify* them. The dilemma is: either our experience has a kind of conceptual structure, so it is not the given; or it lacks conceptual structure, in which case it cannot justify our beliefs.

There is plenty of evidence that many people read Lewis as a defender of a foundationalist approach to epistemology according to which the given provides justification for the foundationalist beliefs. Eric Dayton, whose paper 'C. I. Lewis and the Given' criticizes such readings, lists a number of examples of those who endorse them. As an example, he quotes Roderick Firth, who identifies as Lewis's best-known doctrine the view that 'our knowledge of the external world can be justified, in the last analysis, only by the indubitable apprehensions of the immediate data of sense' (Firth 1968: 329; Dayton 1995: 254.) This presents Lewis as a foundationalist, and we find something similar in Laurence BonJour's characterization of the two theses 'at the core of Lewis's epistemology':

First, that the justification for empirical knowledge depends essentially on a foundation of "given" experience; and, second, that empirical knowledge itself consists in what Lewis calls the "interpretation" of the given, where this involves hypothetical predications of future given experience on the basis of what is currently given together with hypothesized apparent actions of various sorts.   (BonJour 2004: 195)

As we shall see in the next section, this reading does not fit Lewis's 1929 book, *Mind and the World Order*. The epistemology defended in that book is coherentist, not foundationalist, and the role of the given is not to provide justifiers for our basic beliefs. In his 1989 paper 'Two Concepts of the Given in C. I. Lewis: Realism and Foundationalism', Christopher Gowans emphasized this point about Lewis's earlier views while suggesting that, by the time he wrote *An Analysis of Knowledge and Valuation* in 1946, Lewis's views had evolved and, without noticing what had happened, he had adopted a position that fitted Firth's reading of Lewis as a foundationalist. More recently, in the paper mentioned above, Eric Dayton has endorsed Gowans's reading of *Mind and the World Order*, but disputed the claim that Lewis was ever a foundationalist, even in *An Analysis of Knowledge and Valuation*. He sees very little change or evolution in Lewis's thought on this topic. In order not to get involved in scholarly issues about the development of Lewis's views, I shall be mostly concerned with the views of the earlier book.

3. C. I. Lewis and the Given

Early in chapter 2 of *Mind and the World Order*, C. I. Lewis announced:

There are, in our cognitive experience, two elements; the immediate data, such as those of sense, which are presented or given to the mind, and a form, construction, or interpretation, which represents the activity of thought. Recognition of this fact is one of the oldest and most universal of philosophic insights.   (Lewis 1929: 38)

He immediately acknowledged that, obvious and fundamental as this distinction is, exactly how it should be described and understood is extremely uncertain. Interestingly, this passage says nothing about the structure of *justification*; the claim it makes concerns the nature of cognitive *experience*—for example, the experience of seeing that something is the case. This passage already prepares us for the suggestion. Indeed, we can note that saying that this claim that cognition contains two elements says nothing about the structure of justification. Its importance for his philosophy is suggested by the very Kantian observation: 'If there be no datum given to the mind, then knowledge must be contentless and arbitrary' because 'there would be nothing to be true to', while 'if there be no interpretation or construction which the mind itself imposes, then thought is rendered superfluous, the possibility of error becomes inexplicable, and the distinction of true and false is in danger of becoming meaningless' (1929: 39). Thus we are presented with a philosophical distinction between the 'immediate data' or 'given', on the one hand, and the interpretation of that data, on the other. And we are presented with a reason for taking it seriously: unless the distinction between given and interpretation holds, we cannot make sense of some fundamental features of cognition.

Lewis wrote about the given on a number of occasions, including his Ph.D. thesis in 1910, *Mind and the World Order* in 1929, and *An Analysis of Knowledge and Valuation* in 1946. His views about the nature of the given and its role in cognition evolved, but the general shape of his views remained largely constant, and, for present purposes, we do not need to understand the details of the later modifications they received. Indeed, Lewis's most important claims about the given did not depend upon the details of one or other of his published accounts. We can identify a view of the given which did not change substantially; we can also ask why it was so important to him that there be immediate data; and we can examine what evidence there is for thinking that there is, indeed, a given.

Lewis's first characterization of his dichotomy in *Mind and World Order*, at the beginning of chapter 2, identifies two fundamental features in the given:

There is, in all experience, that element which we are aware that we do not create by thinking and cannot, in general, displace or alter. As a first approximation, we may designate it as "the sensuous".   (1929: 48–9)

The 'criteria of givenness' that he offers at the end of the chapter have a similar flavour:

These are, first, its specific sensuous or feeling-character, and second, that the mode of thought can neither create nor alter it—that it remains unaffected by any change of mental attitude. It is the second of these criteria which is definitive; the first alone is not sufficient.   (1929: 66)

When he criticizes idealists who, he suggests, try to get by without acknowledging the given, it is evident that they thereby commit themselves to denying that 'the fact of my seeing this moment a sheet of white paper instead of a green tree is a datum which is beyond the power of my thought to alter' (1929: 45). He complains that idealists duck the question 'Does the activity of thinking create what would ordinarily be called the data of sense?'

So the most important features of the given include:

1. The given is not created by our thinking.
2. The given cannot be destroyed or altered by our thinking.
3. The given has a 'sensuous' or qualitative character.

So what reason is there to accept that there is a given? Lewis's distinction can seem more obvious than it, perhaps, is, if we are deceived by an ambiguity in the concept of *experience* that Lewis draws to our attention. There is a clear distinction between my seeing something and my arriving at an opinion as a result of conscious deliberation. And it is plausible that I have more active control over my deliberations than I do over what I see, although I can control the latter by, for example, closing my eyes or looking in a different direction.

The ambiguity is between 'the thick experience of the world of things' and the 'thin given of immediacy' (1929: 54). What we *see*, and 'what we most certainly know', are 'objects and full-blooded facts about them which could be stated in propositions': 'we do not see patches of colour, but trees and houses'. And philosophical reflection on knowledge takes off from facts of these kinds. But if this is the subject matter of our 'pre-analytic data', it is still possible, on the basis of reflection about this data, to make contact with the thing given by abstraction from our everyday experience. The given, then, is not what we see, but it is a crucial element of our seeing it. Philosophical reflection is required to establish that my seeing the computer on my desk involves my having a presentation of various phenomenal shapes, hues, and so on. This means, of course, that we do not have immediate reflective knowledge of which elements of cognition are immediate or given. The claim that the given is *immediate* means, presumably, that the given element in cognition is not itself the result of inferences or other cognitive activities. That something is given is not mediated through other cognitive operations, although the *knowledge* that something is given may indeed be so mediated.

Before exploring this further, we need to examine the second element of our empirical cognitions, interpretation. Lewis does this through an example which involves describing some element of his present experience as a fountain pen, making use of a term with which he is already familiar. What this entails is: (a) '[abstracting] this item from the total field of [his] present consciousness'; (b) 'and [relating] it to what is not just now present'; (c) 'in ways which [he] has learned'; (d) 'and which reflect modes of action which [he has] acquired'. (1929: 49).

When I see something as a fountain pen, I interpret it as something that can be used for distinctive purposes, that will behave in distinctive ways if it is acted on in certain ways, and that is expected to behave in distinctive ways in the future. This interpretation goes beyond what is presented in the given, the content of which does not reach forward into the future or present itself as relevant to our purposes. The given is not, *qua* given, interpreted, but it is *interpretable*, and, presumably it is features of the given which make it appropriate to interpret it as, say, of a white table rather than a green tree.

This suggests some more features of the given:

4. What is given, independently of the active intervention of attention and thought, is a total field of consciousness, which is 'undifferentiated', and is perhaps something rather like William James's 'stream of consciousness' (cf. Murphey 2005: p. x).[1]

---

[1] The influence of James may also be present in Lewis's observation that we describe 'items' of experience by exploring their relations to other actual or possible experiences in ways that reflect our

5. The given must have some sort of 'implicit' structure which makes it possible to refer to, or abstract, different 'items' that it contains, and which somehow ensures that some interpretations are more appropriate than others (cf. Murphey 2005 and Lewis 1910).

If we accept that the given forms part of every 'cognitive experience', and that it has a role in prompting interpretation through the use of concepts, thereby contributing to the generation of 'thick experience', then we have to face a question about just how it can do this. How does the given guide or make possible interpretation? How is it that the given gives rise to the rich, 'thick' perceptual experience of things like fountain pens? If the given provides content for cognition, then the given must have some character that makes some conceptual interpretations appropriate and others inappropriate. This emerges as early as his Ph.D. thesis, where Lewis holds that 'the bases for discriminations are implicit in the given and are made explicit by attention' (Murphey 2005: 37). In interpreting the given, in attending to items in the given, we respond to its character, but we change neither its qualitative character nor its sensuous feel. Somehow the given is apt for interpreting in some ways but not others, but it contains nothing general or conceptual. It is a common objection to the given that we can make no sense of how a non-conceptual 'thin given' can legitimate some interpretations and not others.

In *Mind and the World Order*, Lewis gestures towards a metaphysical explanation of how this occurs (1929: 60 ff.). Having pointed out that the content of a 'presentation' is not something repeatable or universal, he observes that the content 'is either a specific quale (such as the immediacy of redness or loudness) or something analyzable into a complex of such' (1929: 60). These qualia, while not to be confused with the general properties of being red or being loud, are 'recognizable from one to another experience'. Unlike these properties, they do not have names; nor do they have a temporal spread. It follows from this that we cannot *describe* our experience without interpreting it, but the fact that the given is a complex of qualia is somehow able to explain the possibility of our interpreting it and bringing it under general concepts. It is a major source of puzzlement here that the components that explain what we can do with the given are repeatable without being general, and given, fundamental sources of our knowledge without being describable. And this

interests in action: successful interpretation, we might say, puts us into a satisfactory relation to our experience, leading us 'prosperously' from one part of experience to another.

makes it all the more important that we can find good reason to think that such things exist.

We can now raise an issue about how to interpret Lewis's claim that the given cannot be created, destroyed, or adapted through thought. Lewis writes of 'active thought' here, which may suggest that he is concerned solely with the possibility of our exercising control over presentations through active conscious deliberation. It would be compatible with that, that the given could still bear the traces of habitual or automatic cognition, perhaps being influenced unconsciously by background knowledge. There is an interesting passage in which Lewis observes that our interpretation of the fountain pen exploits knowledge and habits of behaviour that we have learned, and that someone from a different culture or with very different interests and experience would not classify it in the same way (1929: 49). They would describe what we know to be a pen in very different terms. In spite of this, Lewis tells us, 'what I refer to as "the given" in this experience is, in broad terms, qualitatively no different than it would be if I were an infant or an ignorant savage' (1929: 50), which suggests that what is given does not bear traces of the unconscious effects of our interests and knowledge. The given could only bear such traces if our cognitive position could influence what qualia were available to function as parts of the given. I am not aware of anywhere that Lewis considers that possibility.

We must now return to the important issue: what reasons are there to think that there is a 'given', an element in experience and cognition, which is not created by, or controlled by, active thought, yet which provides, as it were, the *material* for interpretation? We can consider three ways of arguing for this view. The first is to claim that the presence of the given is somehow self-evident, perhaps obvious to introspection. A second possibility is that the presence of a given element in cognition can be established through psychological inquiry. The third possibility is that it is established through a distinctively philosophical investigation. As was suggested by the quotations at the beginning of this section, we can make no sense of our thoughts having a content, or of there being a distinction between true and false beliefs, if there is not a given.

A passage in Lewis's Ph.D. thesis may support the first kind of argument:

We actually find in consciousness, at any one time, a sensuous, qualitative content, an undifferentiated complex of that which is simply presented, and which no purpose of ours can create.   (Lewis 1910: 78; Murphey 2005: 36)

I doubt whether this is true. We can certainly distinguish what we see, for example, from the reflective thoughts we form about what we see. But it is compatible with this that the content of our perceptions is shaped by our concepts and interests. It is not evident to introspection that the sensory experience of Lewis when he looks at his pen is the same as that of someone who has no experience of fountain pens and their uses. Moreover, since Lewis then admitted that the awareness of the given 'does not exist by itself in the mind of any rational being' (Lewis 1910: 78–81; Murphey 2005: 36–7), but is always accompanied by 'the mode of attention' which is 'superimposed upon it', it is an open question whether we have the capacity to inspect and make sense of there being such a thing as the given element.

It is useful here to recall the argument of Peirce's 1867 paper 'Questions Concerning Certain Faculties Claimed for Man' (*EP* 1. 11–27). This is concerned with whether there are any 'intuitions', these being 'cognitions' which are determined solely by the external object, bearing no influence from inference or from our background knowledge. He draws on familiar psychological phenomena to show that many states that we might initially identify as intuitions are, in fact, the results of unconscious inference. If there are intuitions, then our belief in them must be grounded in an explanatory inference; and Peirce's conclusion is that there is no reason to think that there are any such states. It is likely that Lewis's given would count as an intuition on Peirce's definition.

Lewis argues at length against the second kind of answer. Psychological investigations will not reveal how the *given* is interpreted and how it gives rise to thick perceptual experience: psychology and philosophy have different sorts of goals. Lewis tells us that, from the psychological point of view, a state of apprehending the given, or a Kantian manifold, 'is probably a fiction' (1929: 55). The given, we are told, is 'in experience', not some separable psychological state which has a causal role in determining the nature of experience. Lewis insists that the investigation that leads us to identify the given (for example) is 'antecedent to the special sciences'. But how this works is not made very clear in Lewis's text: he mostly relies on the fact that the given is 'what remains unaltered, no matter what our interests, no matter how we think or conceive' (1929: 52). It is natural to conclude that he is in the grip of a philosophical picture according to which, if we are to have knowledge at all, this is how things *must be*.

In closing this section, we should ask just what explanatory work the given is supposed to do in subsequent chapters. But first, consider Lewis's two 'criteria' of givenness. The first points to the fact that the given normally has a sensuous or feeling-quality; this is related to its being composed of qualia. The second emphasizes that the given is not under our control: active thought and deliberation cannot affect the given. Why does Lewis mention both of them? And why should they go together? He holds that just the second of these is 'essential', in which case we might wonder why he bothers to mention the first. What role does each have in the sort of explanatory work that the given is supposed to do?

According to Lewis, 'If there be no datum given to the mind, then knowledge must be contentless and arbitrary', because 'there would be nothing to be true to' (1929: 39). How does the given ensure that there is something for knowledge 'to be true to?' Consider three different ways in which this connection might be understood. First, the fact that the given is identified as something which is independent of the knower's active thinking may provide the explanation of how we can obtain knowledge of a mind-independent reality. It may help him to defend a kind of empirical realism, one that echoes Berkeley's attempts to make sense of our concept of reality. The given resists our attempts to change it and constrains our opinions. Second, obtaining knowledge of the empirical world requires us to apply concepts to things that are given to us in experience, and, indeed, it requires us to have a shared understanding of those concepts and to expect others to agree with our applications of them. Third, the given has a further epistemological role, that of providing foundations for our reasoning about what is the case. Why, in each case, should he need to appeal to something with the special features of the 'thin given'?

The thin given captures a strong sense of mind independence, especially when we allow that there are no idiosyncratic variations in the presentations that different people, and people who belong to different cultures, receive. The elements of the given, qualia, are, again, likely to be universal and available to all. As we shall see later, even if the strategy of explaining *reality* in terms of resistance to the will is correct, it is not clear why this insight *has* to be explained in terms of the thin given.

If the given is to serve any of these roles, then it must be something that we are aware of. We must be able to attend to its features and obtain information about it that can provide certain foundations for the rest of our empirical knowledge. This *seems* to be in tension with other features of the given. The given is not an object of knowledge; nor can it be described. This is because description and knowledge involve interpretation, and thus involve treating the object of knowledge as something that is spread out in time rather than given in an instant. We see fountain pens and trees by interpreting the given, but we are not aware of the given by interpreting something else: immediate presentations are signs that need to be understood or interpreted, but they do not themselves involve the interpretation of some other sign. In spite of this, we can *report* on what is given, saying things that indicate the presence of qualia in terms of their ability to elicit particular interpretations. We cannot know that we are attending to a quale that *is* red, but we can announce that it *looks red*; this captures the idea that the particular given tends to elicit a particular kind of interpretation. In such cases, Lewis thinks, the only risk of error lies in the possibility that we may misuse words.

4. THE ROLE OF THE GIVEN

An alternative to the claim that Lewis was trying to defend a form of epistemological foundationalism suggests that he was concerned with some metaphysical questions about the nature of knowledge: should we be realists, idealists, phenomenalists, or what? The answer Lewis offers to this question is Kantian in shape, and it is reflected in one theme mentioned by BonJour. Our cognitive achievements provide interpretations of the given, of our experience. The role of the given is to provide objects for our knowledge, not to provide foundations for the justification of such knowledge. All our beliefs—and thus any that enter into justification—are fallible interpretations of the given. And they are all fallible: we cannot rule out the possibility that our interpretations will turn out to clash with other interpretations. The epistemology is coherentist: our beliefs are justified because they do not clash with other beliefs. But the given acquaints us with the objects of our knowledge. And it can do the latter without occupying a justificatory role.

Lewis's distinction between the given and our systems of concepts is reminiscent of the Kantian distinction between intuitions and concepts. This too is not a distinction between different kinds of justification that beliefs can receive. We might express it, rather, as a distinction between the objects that our knowledge is about and what we know about these things. Intuitions are passive, providing objects to which we apply concepts. The fundamental issue concerns just how we can apply concepts to the sensory intuitions we receive. On this reading, Lewis differs from other 'great pragmatists' by being willing to embrace the sort of Kantian dichotomies that other pragmatists treat with great suspicion. How well does such a reading fit Lewis?

Lewis embraces a pragmatic conception of the a priori. A priori knowledge reflects the conceptual resources we have. The classifications we employ in interpreting the given are not *dictated* by a mind-independent reality. Rather, they reflect our interests and needs, and on any occasion we apply systems of concepts that best suit our purposes. This involves a denial of realism about classifications: they are not mind-independent; we might even think of them as our constructions. Knowledge always involves interpretation; and interpretation is creative. This is the pragmatist component of Lewis's philosophy.

But Lewis wants to combine his pragmatism with realism. The things to which we apply our concepts are mind-independent. The given is a model of something that is not determined by the mind of the knower. So we apply our concepts to something that is not shaped by our minds, unlike Kantian intuitions, which are determined by the forms of inner and outer sense. We interpret real things in ways that suit our purposes. Perception embodies interpretation of the given, so the contents of ordinary perception are not fully mind-independent. Thick experience is thus not fully real and mind-independent. But the *thin* given captures something which is fully mind-independent, unaffected by our beliefs, expectations, and interpretations. This provides a way of vindicating realism.

If this is what is going on, it explains some of the more puzzling features of Lewis's discussion of the given. First, it explains why Lewis was so anxious to insist that the given did not vary across cultures. When considering our experience of a fountain pen, he noted that 'what I refer to as "the given" in this experience is, in broad terms, qualitatively no different than it would be if I were an infant or an ignorant savage' (1929: 50), which suggests that what is given does not bear traces of the unconscious effects of our interests and knowledge. If it is essential to the given that it is an element in cognition which is wholly mind-independent, then we cannot explain differences in the given, as it strikes different people, by appeal to their mental attitudes or their knowledge. So this claim about the constancy of the given across very different people is required if the doctrine is to enable him to embrace realism.

Secondly, it explains why Lewis denied that we can use psychology to identify features of the given. The given is not something that is picked out in terms of its place in the psychological processes of cognition. It is, rather, an aspect or feature of the complex processes of thick experience and cognition, something that is abstracted with a metaphysical or philosophical purpose in mind. It is a feature of the whole thick experience, but, presumably, there is no reason why this should correspond to a psychological component of this process. It is better to think of the investigation as logical or phenomenological.

Thirdly, it might explain Lewis's claims about the metaphysical structure of the given, about its being composed of qualia. If Lewis is to combine realism with pragmatism in the way that I have described, it is important that the interpretation of the given is not simply free-floating. Even if reality cannot dictate how it should be interpreted, it must possess features that constrain how we will interpret it. It is compatible with this that there is room for manoeuvre when interpretation occurs, but interpretation must not be free-floating. But it is important that in the context of this more Kantian project, it is not required that these features of the given *justify* the interpretation. Interpretations are evaluated according to how well they cohere with other interpretations, not in terms of how well they fit 'the given'. Our beliefs are mostly not about the given; they are about tables, chairs, fountain pens, and the like. But it is only because our experience contains a component that is given that we can possess and test these opinions.

Lewis's claims make most sense when we see the *given* as something with a role in metaphysics rather than as something with a place in foundationalist epistemology. Is it any more defensible when taken in that way? In the final section, I shall argue that, in its metaphysical guise, it is unstable, likely to be pulled in two different directions. Understanding why this is the case helps us to understand some of the differences between classical pragmatism and contemporary neo-pragmatism.

5. THREE PRAGMATISTS AND THE GIVEN

In order to identify what I find unsatisfactory in Lewis's notion of the given, we need to recall the difference between 'the thick experience of the world of things' and the 'thin given of immediacy' (1929: 54). What we *see*, and 'what we most certainly know', are 'objects and full-blooded facts about them which could be stated in propositions'. When we describe the phenomenology of our visual experience, for example, it involves interpretation. For example, my experience of the fountain pen rolling over the edge of the desk involves an element of anticipation, guided by my knowledge of pens and similar objects, which means that, were the pen to remain suspended in the air after leaving the desk, I would experience a real sense of perceptual dislocation. What we see reflects what we know. As Lewis insists, 'we do not see patches of colour, but trees and houses'. I take it to follow from this that it would be wrong to say that we see the patches of colour and draw conclusions about trees and houses from premises about the patches of colour. So, in paying attention to the thin given, we allow that what we can see extends far beyond what is given to us.

As we understand Lewis, the fact that the given forms part of our cognitive experience enables us to understand how the objects of our knowledge are mind-independent, even if our interpretations of those things reflect our purposes, our cognitive habits, and our background beliefs and attitudes. Just how does the idea of *givenness* capture the idea of mind independence? Lewis's discussions emphasize a number of features which contribute to the explanation of this:

a. We have no control over the given element in experience.
b. It bears no traces of our cognitive activity.
c. It has a distinctive *sensuous* character.
d. It is *the same for everyone*: this sensuous character is shared with anyone else who observed the same scene from the same position, however different from ours may be their interests, habits, and conceptual apparatus.

The fact that it is the same for everyone provides evidence that it is independent of our cognitive activity. In this section, I shall compare Lewis's way of making room for the mind independence of the objects of our knowledge to those of two philosophers. These are C. S. Peirce, a classical pragmatist acknowledged by Lewis to be an influence upon his work, and W. V. O Quine, a student of Lewis's who has had a considerable influence upon neo-pragmatist thought. Neither would accept all of (a)–(d); but they differ in which ones they reject.

When we think about the impact of reality upon us, the evidence of our cognitive contact with real things outside ourselves, we can characterize this impact in a number of ways. Lewis's was to identify some aspect or feature of our experience that is somehow indicative of this impact: namely, the thin given. An alternative possibility is suggested by Quine's writings (1960: chs. 1 and 2; 1990: *passim*): even if our experiences and interpretations are idiosyncratic, it is possible that different agents, whatever their skills and background, will suffer the same irritations or stimulations of their retinas or other sensory surfaces. This offers a clear basis for distinguishing the impact of external things upon us from the various interpretations (conscious and unconscious) that are built up from them. The thin given and the surface irritations serve similar roles in marking the fact that we are the passive recipients of information about our surroundings. Moreover, we can't control these retinal stimulations, and they do not seem to be affected by our concepts or beliefs. What is missing from Lewis's account is the idea that the given has a distinctive sensuous character.

Once this step has been taken, we may be tempted to take another: one that is associated with neo-pragmatists like Richard Rorty and defended in some detail by Donald Davidson. So long as our senses are affected by the same external objects and states of affairs, it does not seem to matter whether the retinal stimulations we receive are exactly the same. We can all obtain knowledge of a fountain pen by interpreting the information that is received from it, even if the constitution of our eyes, for example, is very different. Possession of a prosthetic eye that lacked anything corresponding to the retina, for example, would not impair our cognitive contact with the pen. We must be in contact with external things, but it matters not a jot whether we all receive the same sensuous inputs or have exactly the same kind of sensory organ (Davidson 2005: 64–5). Quine came to accept this in his last writings (Quine 1996).

It is a natural view that we encounter reality through experience; we are able to attend to the things that we see, and we exploit this in learning more about our surroundings. Although this is a view that is rejected by neo-pragmatists influenced by Quine, classical pragmatists such as Peirce, James, and Dewey would not have disputed it. But when we study Peirce's account of perception or James's radical empiricism, we see that the pragmatists seem to begin from the riches of 'thick experience' and show no inclination to accept Lewis's thin conception of the given. Since most would have been sympathetic to Lewis's realism, they need ways of understanding the mind independence of the objects of perceptual knowledge without appealing to a thin given which is the same for all people. In considering Peirce's views, we are looking for an account which (1) takes seriously the phenomenology of perception, (2) allows that we have direct perceptual knowledge of mind-independent things, and (3) does not include the thin Lewisian given.

In one of his earliest published papers, 'Questions Concerning Certain Faculties Claimed for Man', Peirce discussed whether we ever possess 'intuitions', which he explained as 'cognitions' which were are determined solely by their external object and are not determined at all by our other cognitions. Although Lewis would insist that the given is an *aspect* of a cognition rather than a cognition in itself, Peirce's reasons for denying that there are cognitions may also be applied to show that there is no thin given. He appeals to some familiar psychological phenomena to suggest that we are very poor at judging whether cognitions are mind-independent. For example, information about the blind spot on the retina shows that the continuous qualitative character of our perceptual experience depends upon cognitive processes that fill the gap (*EP* 1. 15). It is never evident to introspection, for example, that an experience or a cognition does not involve the effects of cognitive elaboration. If there are intuitions (or if there is a given component in experience), we can know this only as the result of an explanatory inference; we need to show that perceptual knowledge would be impossible if there were no given, for example. It is Peirce's view that no such explanatory argument is required or available.

However, Peirce does insist that our ability to have knowledge of external things depends upon our being able to attend to things when we perceive them, and refer to them using indexical expressions. (See Hookway 2000: ch. 4.) Peirce agrees with Lewis that it is a mark of the perceptual that we cannot control the nature of our experience: 'the perceiver is aware of being compelled to perceive what he perceives' (*CP* 4. 541). Moreover, this is connected to a 'double consciousness' that he finds in perception: we experience the percept and its elements as *other* than ourselves. The things that we perceive manifest what Peirce calls *Secondness*: the phenomenological character of perception involves a sense of external objects as things other than ourselves; phenomenology reveals that we stand in a dyadic relation to them. It is part of the richness of experience that we take ourselves, fallibly, to experience external things directly. We may put this by saying that we experience things as mind-independent although, on any particular occasion, we may be wrong to do so. On occasion, Peirce expresses his view by saying that the external object is itself a constituent of the percept, of the immediate objects of perception (*CP* 7. 619).[2] The phenomenological feature of perception that supports realism about its objects is thus not the fact that experience contains an element that would be the same for all, but rather the fact that we experience things as *other*, as external. In one sense we might

---

[2] These passages are taken from an unpublished manuscript from 1903 entitled 'Telepathy and Perception'. This is in the *Collected Papers* at 7. 619.

describe such experiences as 'given to us'; their phenomenology presents them as the effects on us of other things.

But this is compatible with denying that there is a sensuous 'given' of the kind that Lewis describes. We are aware that we experience processes developing through time in patterned ways. Although we cannot control our perceptions at the time when they occur, and although we are 'compelled' to make our perceptual judgements without having any *reason* to do so (*CP* 4. 541, 7. 622), there are familiar examples showing that how things look is influenced by background knowledge and the concepts we employ. Perceptual experience always involves an element of anticipation, which usually coheres with future experience but sometimes clashes with it. Peirce offers a plausible example:

Sometimes when I have been seated in a railway-car that was stationary and another train has been slowly passing by, I have been vexed at the unreasonableness of its appearing to me that our train was moving and the other train was at rest. I have reasoned with the perception. I have asked "Is there jarring such as there is when one is in a moving car?" No. "Is there any noise of the wheels?" No. . . . "Then why do I have the idea that the train is at rest and that we are moving?" There is no answer except that such is the percipuum, and I cannot help it. (*CP* 7. 643)

Usually we cannot control these processes, but there are intermediate cases where we can: Peirce refers to examples like the Schroeder stair, but the duck–rabbit would also serve as an example of a case where how things look is under control (see Hookway 1985: ch. 5). So we interact with real things, and we can refer to them demonstratively by exploiting the ways in which we interpret them as other. We are aware that we cannot control how they look. We are aware that how things actually are may not be the same as the ways we believe them to be. So we are aware both of the risks of error that we run and of the ways in which we can attempt to identify and correct our errors. The phenomenology of experience has a realist character, and we can recognize this without having to distinguish thick experience from the sort of thin given that Lewis defends. Once again, it is hard to see why we need to follow Lewis in accepting the thin given as a way of vindicating realism.

6. Conclusion

It is interesting to ask why Lewis found it so obvious (and necessary) that there be a given. Part of the answer is that he was too much of a Kantian and too little of a pragmatist. Although Peirce saw his pragmaticism as the view that Kant would have accepted had he avoided some fundamental errors (*EP* 2. 353–4), he still rejected the Kantian dichotomy between intuitions and other kinds of cognitions from very early in his career. Other pragmatists, such as Dewey, rejected other Kantian dichotomies. Lewis's philosophy loosened up Kant by defending a pragmatist account of the a priori; but the dichotomies between given and concept, and between analytic and synthetic propositions, were still there. His defence of the given can be seen as an effect of this. In comparing Lewis with Quine and Peirce, I compare his positions with those of philosophers who, in very different ways, freed themselves from the Kantian dichotomies.

References

BonJour, Laurence (2004). 'C. I. Lewis on the Given and its Interpretation'. In *Midwest Studies in Philosophy*, vol. 28, 195–209.

Davidson, Donald (2005). *Truth and Predication*. Cambridge, MA: Belknap Press.

Dayton, Eric (1995). 'C. I. Lewis and the Given'. *Transactions of the Charles S. Peirce Society*, 31: 254–87.

Firth, Roderick (1968). 'Lewis on the Given'. In Schilpp (1968), 329–50.

Gowans, Christopher W. (1989). 'Two Concepts of the Given in C. I. Lewis: Realism and Foundationalism'. *Journal of the History of Philosophy*, 27: 573–90.

Haack, Susan (1993). *Evidence and Inquiry*. Oxford: Blackwell.

Hookway, Christopher (1985). *Peirce*. London: Routledge & Kegan Paul.

—— (2000). *Truth, Rationality, and Pragmatism: Themes from Peirce*. Oxford: Clarendon Press.

Lewis, C. I. (1910). 'The Place of Intuition in Knowledge' (Harvard University, Ph.D. thesis).

—— (1929). *Mind and the World Order: Outline of a Theory of Knowledge*. New York: Charles Scribner's Sons.

—— (1946). *An Analysis of Knowledge and Evaluation*. La Salle, IL: Open Court.

Murphey, Murray G. (2005). *C. I. Lewis: The Last Great Pragmatist*. Albany, NY: SUNY Press.

Peirce, Charles Sanders (1931–58). *Collected Papers of Charles Sanders Peirce*. Cambridge, MA: Harvard University Press. References take the form *CP* 7. 416 (numbered para. 416 of vol. 7).

—— (1992, 1998). *The Essential Peirce*, ed. Peirce Edition Project, 2 vol. Indianapolis: Indiana University Press. References take the form *EP* followed by volume and page nos.

Quine, W. V. O. (1960). *Word and Object*. Cambridge, MA: MIT Press.

—— (1990). *Pursuit of Truth*. Cambridge, MA: Harvard University Press.

____ (1996). 'Progress on Two Fronts'. *Journal of Philosophy*, 93: 159–63.

Schilpp, Paul Arthur (ed.) (1968). *The Philosophy of C. I. Lewis.* La Salle, IL: Open Court.

Sellars, Wilfrid (1963). *Science, Perception and Reality.* London: Routledge & Kegan Paul.

CHAPTER 16

....

W. V. QUINE

....

ARIF AHMED

Quine's philosophy is the continuation of British empiricism by other means. At any rate, his epistemology is; and that is what motivates his most important and notorious theses, concerning ontological relativity, indeterminacy of translation, and analyticity.

Before describing that, it is worth briefly comparing Quine's general outlook with that of those who shared it most: the pragmatists and the logical positivists. I am not attempting to trace any influence, however. Certainly the American pragmatists—Peirce, James, and Dewey—had little direct influence on him (1990b: 292[1]).

One relevant pragmatist doctrine is *semantic behaviourism*: linguistic meaning is not *mental*, but *behavioural*. As Dewey said: 'Meaning . . . is not a psychic existence; it is primarily a property of behaviour' (quoted in 1968a: 27). People who would use a word identically must mean it identically, however their mental associations vary. Quine agrees with this (see further 3.1 below) but draws distinctive as well as momentous conclusions from it (see further 3.2–3).[2]

One relevant pragmatist attitude is disengagement from sceptical doubt. Here Quine endorses Peirce, for whom 'we should recognize that we are

I am most grateful to Prof. Misak for very helpful comments. I have also found much enlightenment in Prof. Gibson's and Prof. Hylton's writings on Quine.

[1] All references are to Quine except where indicated, and use reprint pagination.
[2] On Quine and Dewey see further Murphy 1990: 83.

born into a going conceptual scheme . . . and we should work critically within it, doubting when conflicts arise' (1981*d*: 35; cf. 1951: 46). But Quine's reasons are different. Peirce thought that Cartesian doubt is psychologically impossible, and so impotent to motivate genuine inquiry (Misak 2004: 50–5). For Quine it is unanswerable: there is no doctrine at once firmer than empirical science and capable of justifying it. This despair seems in turn to have arisen from Carnap's failure (Carnap 1967) to reduce external-world statements to logical constructions from sensory experience. But the lesson Quine draws is naturalism: we should not cease or doubt scientific inquiry but pursue it in full awareness that no firmer discipline can justify it. (See further 1.2.2.)

There are also overlaps between Quine's doctrine and method and those of the logical positivists: Neurath, Schlick, Hahn, Frank, and, above all, Carnap. Two of their cardinal doctrines—both associated with classical pragmatism too—are especially relevant.

The first is verificationism: the meaning of a sentence is its means of empirical confirmation. We shall see that Quine does not accept the doctrine in precisely this form, but prefers one that is compatible with his holism. (See further 2.5.3, 3.3.3.)

The second and perhaps fundamental doctrine is empiricism. I describe Quine's distinctive version in 1.3 below; but a formulation acceptable to all parties would be this: the world reveals itself only through sensory experience. As well as *motivating* much of Quine's most important work, it is also a premiss in his arguments for both semantic behaviourism (see 3.1) and verificationism (see 3.3.3).

Methodologically, what unites Quine and the logical positivists is a preoccupation with language. For the positivists this stemmed from their *Tractatus*-inspired conception of philosophy as analysis aimed at eliminating meaningless 'metaphysical' statements. Quine shared the interest but not the motivation: language was of interest because his naturalistic epistemology mandated investigation of it (1990*c*: 3; see also 2.1.2 below). Moreover, it was a field in which a thoroughgoing empiricism was yet to be realized.

For what is most important about Quine is that he saw the consequences of empiricism with more clarity than anyone since Hume. To be sure, *Quine's* empiricism is not quite like anyone else's; but it *is* recognizable as such. Here I describe that empiricism, the epistemological project that it motivates, and the deep consequences for our understanding of language.

Section 1 sketches Quine's overall epistemological project and the empiricism that drives it. Section 2 describes his pursuit of that project, and section 3 explains its consequences for language. For the sake of smoothness, my discussion of his critics is largely confined to footnotes.

1 EMPIRICISM

1.1 Empiricism and its Aims

A helpful initial statement of empiricism is the scholastic one: *Nihil in mente quod non prius in sensu*. It is helpful not because it has one precise meaning, but because it has many: which one you accept determines your brand of empiricism. There are three issues. What is it to be 'in the mind'? How are the things 'in the mind' supposed to be related to what is in the senses? And what is it to be 'in the *senses*'? We consider these issues in turn.

For present purposes I take what is 'in the mind' to be your *theory* of the external world: that is (initially at least), what you *believe* about it (rather than, e.g., a concept or a sensation).

There are three relations that an empiricist might uphold between what is in the mind and what is in the senses; each generates a distinctive empiricist project.

(i) *Justification.* Beliefs about the external world are justified by just as much of it as is available to the senses. If anything justifies my belief that a table is in front of me, then it is what I *see* of the table. But how many such beliefs and, more generally, how much science *does* sensory experience justify? The empiricist tries to justify as much as he can.

(ii) *Reduction.* Knowable or not, what is *graspable* in the content of my beliefs cannot reach me except through my senses. If they are not nonsense, these beliefs must therefore be analysable in sensory terms. The empiricist tries to effect the analysis.

(iii) *Explanation.* Regardless of whether they can be justified or reduced, my beliefs can only have *arisen* from sensory input. The empiricist therefore tries to explain how the sensory input *produces* the beliefs.

All three projects are central to the empiricist tradition. With regard to (i), both Berkeley and Russell (Russell 1922) sought in experience the tribunal that would vindicate everyday beliefs against scepticism. With regard to (ii), they both thought that reduction was the way to do it: if external-world statements are just constructs out of sensory ones, then they might inherit their certainty from the latter (see Berkeley 1975: 90 (*Principles*, §3); Quine 1966: 83–4). Independently of (i), some regard (ii) as mandatory for certifying our theory as *meaningful* (Schlick 1936: 148; Quine 1969a: 76). With regard to (iii), Berkeley tried to explain how belief in three dimensions arose from visual perception of only two (Berkeley 1975: 7 (*New Theory of Vision*, §2)). Berkeley and Hume both sought to explain in terms of what *is* perceived the everyday and problematic conviction that it always could and some-times does exist *unperceived* (Berkeley 1975: 90–1 (*Principles*, §§4–5); Hume 1949: I. iv. 2).

The third issue was: what for empiricists is 'in the *senses*'? Traditionally, it was at least this: what is available without presupposition to *conscious awareness*. For Berkeley and Hume, it was 'ideas' and 'impressions'; for Russell, 'sense data'; for Carnap, 'elementary experiences'. Demanding awareness is hardly surprising in light of project (i): you can be justified only by what can impinge upon consciousness (1969a: 84).

1.2 Quine's Rejection of the Traditional Aims of Empiricism

Quine departs from traditional empiricism at two points. He thinks we should abandon the justificatory and reductive projects (i) and (ii), and also that the traditional understanding of sensory input is impotent to answer (iii), the explanatory demand.

1.2.1 Rejecting the Traditional Project of Justification

With regard to (i) there are two points. First, Humean scepticism about induction is unanswerable. We cannot justify on the basis of present experience (or anything else) our beliefs about its future course: appeals either to experience or to its uniformity are respectively impotent and question-begging. 'The Humean predicament is the human predicament' (1969a: 72).[3] But *inductive* scepticism is not yet scepticism about the *external world*. Even if experience allows no rational inference to its future course, there may still be one to its present objects.

But second, sensory justification of external-world beliefs demands the pursuit of (ii): that is, reductive analysis of those beliefs into ones enjoying the

---

[3] See further Fogelin 2004.

certainty of immediate experience. This reduction *would* offer those beliefs independent validation (1966: 84). If the statement that a table is before me is equivalent to one about my present sense data, then I can determine its truth-value with certainty. So let us turn to project (ii): sensory or phenomenalistic reduction.

1.2.2 Rejecting the Traditional Project of Reduction

The most important attempt at reduction is the *Aufbau* of Carnap: according to Quine, its failure indicates why any such programme is doomed in principle. The key point is the derivation of objective assignments of colours to space-time points from some course of experience (Carnap 1967: §126; see esp. 126. 10). For Carnap a course of experience E warrants the statement 'Colour C is at point X' if the latter belongs to that overall assignment (of colours to distances from the eye) that implies maximal overall stability in the external world amongst all assignments compatible with E. But then no such assignment could be final. Some further experience might warrant revision of that assignment because now a different assignment might be the most stable one compatible with this extended range of experience. An analogy: the statement 'There is a table at point X' cannot be *finally* settled by any course of experience E, because any such experience (e.g., as of an oblong sense datum) might be succeeded by one that forced revision (e.g., as of sensory evidence that one had been drinking). Now the open-ended character of the proposed method is not a ground for rejecting *it*; but it *is* grounds for denying its reductive status.

Roughly summarized, the plan was that qualities should be assigned to point-instants in such a way as to achieve the laziest world compatible with our experience... I think this is a good schematization... of what science really does; but it provides no indication, not even the sketchiest, of how a statement of the form 'Quality q is at $x; y; z; t$' could ever be translated into Carnap's initial language of sense data and logic.   (1951: 40; see also 1966: 84–5, 1969a: 76–7)

In short, the fact that statements about the external world are always open to revision in light of *further* experience implies their inevitable immunity to phenomenalistic reduction. This indefiniteness or open texture of object statements (Waismann 1945: 121) is not Quine's famous doctrine of *holism*, which is rather what *explains* the indefiniteness (1969a: 79; see 2.5.2 for more on holism). But whatever you call it, indefiniteness means abandoning (i) as well as (ii).

The scepticism thus engendered puts scientific inquiry under a cloud. Our beliefs about the external world, whether commonsensical or scientific, cannot all be justified in terms of something more certain. But *abandoning* science is the wrong reaction. Scepticism, unanswerable though it be, is a counsel not of inactivity but only of modesty. It says that there is no justification for science before some neutral bar of experience. But we do not *need* the justification to continue the activity. This combination of modesty and optimism constitutes *naturalism*:

[N]atural science [is] an inquiry into reality, fallible and corrigible but not answerable to any supra-scientific tribunal, and not in need of any justification beyond observation and the hypothetico-deductive method.   (1981*b*: 72)

What we must therefore abandon are the reductive and the justificatory projects. But the resultant scepticism loses much of its sting. Like Hume, Quine thinks that we can retain our scientific beliefs and methods notwithstanding the absence of independent certification.

1.2.3 Amending the Traditional Project of Explanation

Despite these concessions, the empiricist can still envisage an *explanatory* connection running from sensory inputs to beliefs: that is, project (iii). But Quine rejects this too *if* 'sensory inputs' denotes objects of immediate awareness: that is, sense data. He has three arguments.

(a) He denies that one's beliefs about the external world are responses to a pure *stream* of sense data over time. On this picture a sequence of sense data prompts the positing of physical objects 'behind' it. I have temporally separated sense impressions, as of a table; but their resemblance and the surrounding sensory patterns prompt me to posit a single table existing between glimpses. That is roughly the story offered by Hume (Hume 1949: I. iv. 2, 6), and also by any *explanatory* analogue of Carnap's reductive proposal (1.2.2). It is wrong because we are *not* normally aware of temporally extended sensory sequences as data. And that is because our memories are not faded sensory relics of the sense data they commemorate. But that is what they would have to be if we were ever to be aware of a temporally extended and purely sensory sequence.

Ordinarily we do not remember the trapezoidal sensory surface of a desk, as a colour patch extending across the lower half of the visual field; what we remember is *that* there was a desk meeting such-and-such approximate specifications of form and size in three-dimensional space.   (1953*b*: 224)

The present picture therefore gets things backwards. Awareness of sensory sequences cannot explain our positing of objects 'behind' them. If anything, one has *already* posited objects behind the *momentary* data; and the memory that there *were* such objects, surviving in linguistic form, is what explains belief in the sensory sequence itself.

It is not an instructive oversimplification, but a basic falsification, to represent cognition as a discernment of regularities in an unadulterated stream of experience. Better to conceive of the stream itself as polluted, at each succeeding point of its course, by every prior cognition.   (1953*b*: 224)

This shows that awareness of a sensory sequence cannot explain beliefs about what it represents. The only alternative is a *synchronic* explanatory strategy running from *momentary* sense data to simultaneous or immediately succeeding beliefs about their external causes.

   (b) The second argument attacks this synchronic proposal. Quine argues that momentary visual or tactile sense data cannot explain belief in, for example, depth or external objects, because the awareness of the objects normally precedes the awareness of the sense data.

What are given in sensation are smells, noises, feels, flashes, patches of col-our, and the like: such were the conditions of the problem for Berkeley and Hume. ... Experiment suggests, and introspection as well, that what are sensed are not primarily those sensory elements, but significantly structured wholes. ... Confronted with a solid, [a subject] directly senses a body in depth. He goes through none of Berkeley's inferential construction of the depth dimension, for he is unaware of the two-dimensional data of that construction.   (1974: 1–2; see also 1960*b*: 1; 1970*a*: 1)

We cannot explain the belief in depth, solidity, etc. in terms of sense data, for awareness of the sense data is not there soon enough to do the explaining. 'Sense data' are not really data at all.

   (c) The third argument is that sense data are in any case unnecessary to account for our belief in physical objects, as there is an alternative route that eschews them (1960*b*: 235). That alternative is Quine's own explanatory story, discussed at length in the sequel.

   So Quine rejects traditional versions of all three empiricist projects: justification, reduction, and explanation. Is there then nothing for empiricism to do, and nothing worthy of its name? There is. On Quine's view, empiricists can attempt the explanatory project (iii); but only if we revise our understanding of sensory input.

1.3 Quine's Empiricism

Two things are striking about our actual sense organs. One is that their doings are present to awareness; but we rejected this as a basis for extrapolation. The other is not their effect but their topology. If you include touch, then our sense organs or nerve-endings form a closed surface around the body. Impressed by this, we extrapolate 'what is given to the senses' as follows: it is restricted to what goes on at the *surface* of our bodies. The senses are literal—that is, spatial—interfaces between our bodies and the rest of the world; and what is given to them is just what goes on *at* those surfaces.[4]

That is Quine's interpretation: sensory input is just nerve-triggerings or 'surface irritations' (1957: 229).[5] In particular, 'what is given to the senses' has *nothing* to do with awareness: the epistemologist 'can appeal to physical receptors of sensory stimulation and say that what is distinctive about sense data is mere proximity to those receptors, without regard to awareness. Better still, he can drop the talk of sense data and talk rather of sensory stimulation' (1974: 3).

Now Quine's empiricism is that, on this interpretation of 'in the senses', there is always an *explanatory* connection between what is in the mind and what is in the senses:

All I am or ever hope to be is due to irritations of my surface, together with such latent tendencies to respond as may have been present in my original germ plasm. And all the lore of the ages is due to irritation of the surfaces of a succession of persons, together, again, with the internal initial conditions of the several individuals.   (1957: 228–9)

So understood, empiricism says that all my beliefs about the external world are due to what goes on on my surface. It is true if and only if there is no relevant action at a distance—that is, if the external world cannot act on me except via our common interface. This *does* appear true, as our senses confirm. Empiricism is empirically confirmed. It is also empirically disconfirmable: clairvoyance and telepathy would be counterexamples, if they existed (1992a: 20–1).[6]

---

[4] One might wonder what privileges *this* closed surface over, e.g., the surface of the brain. Quine says that the choice is pragmatic artifice (1993: 113 f.). Nothing significant in what follows turns on this choice.

[5] Two historical points: (i) this conception of experience appears to have post-dated 'Two Dogmas' (1951); (ii) in *Word and Object* the terminology changed—'triggering of sensory receptors' replaced 'surface irritations'—but the underlying conception did not. For (i) see 1981c: 39–40; for (ii) see 1981c: 40.

[6] Van Fraassen claims against Quine that empiricism (i) cannot be empirically confirmed and (ii) cannot be empirically disconfirmed. (i) He says that we cannot rely on experience to show

Now that we have recast our conception of what is in the senses, we can resurrect the explanatory project (iii). The problem is to explain our beliefs about the external world—that is, our scientific theory—in terms of sensory input—that is, our superficial nerve firings. The answer is hardly obvious. What is given to our senses (what goes on at our surfaces) is no more than 'various impacts of airwaves on the eardrums and some gaseous reactions in the nasal passages and a few kindred odds and ends' (1974: 2); what do *not* go on there are those external events of which we take the superficial ones to inform us.

Although its statement was novel, the empiricism itself, and the explanatory project that it drives, were implicitly there all along. For instance, Berkeley was right to worry that depth is unavailable to the senses; only not because depth is unavailable to *awareness* but rather because depth cannot affect a bi-dimensional ocular surface (1974: 2; 1960b: 2). Quine's empiricism, unlike Berkeley's own, suffices to generate the problem about depth that so exercised the latter. More to the point, Quine's version appears also to be necessary for the problem. Berkeley's best argument that we do not see depth (Berkeley 1975: 7 (*New Theory of Vision*, §2)) relies on the bi-dimensionality of the ocular surface. But this is relevant *only* if there is no relevant action at a distance. Otherwise, the distance of a point from my retina could by itself affect visual centres in my brain without making any difference to the intervening retinal pattern.

How, then, does our theory about the world arise from its glancing impacts upon us? Answering this question is the aim of what Quine calls 'naturalized epistemology'. Let us see how he pursues it, and what conclusions he reaches.

---

that experience is a good source of information: once that assumption has been questioned, then so too have our empirical methods of assessing it (van Fraassen 1995: 79–81). His argument for (ii) appears to be as follows. He considers a supposed counterexample to empiricism: a person is placed in a sensory deprivation tank and, because of daydreams that he has there, he makes novel and reliable claims about (say) pterodactyls. This appears to falsify empiricism, but van Fraassen says not: the subject *has* derived his beliefs from experiences, i.e. daydreams. 'As a result, we are unable to find examples of a person gaining information in any other way—for whatever looks like that is classified as an indirect, derivative way of gaining information through experience alone' (van Fraassen 1995: 77).

These criticisms do not apply to Quine's empiricism. *Ad* (i) Quine's empiricism is not that experience is *a* good source of information, but the converse: 'whatever evidence there *is* for science *is* sensory evidence' (1969a: 75). There is no more difficulty in empirically confirming that than in using one reliable organ of sight to confirm that there are no others. And *ad* (ii): although they are objects of awareness, daydreams are not sensory input in Quine's topological sense; so the result that van Fraassen describes *would* count for Quine as empirical disconfirmation of empiricism.

2 Epistemology

2.1 Methodology

Before describing the elements of Quine's theory it is worth making three points about his method.

2.1.1 Scientific Method of Explanation

First, there is no obstacle to using our scientific theory in naturalized epistemology. That *would* have been circular if we had wanted to *justify* the theory, but we gave up on that (1.2.1); it is not circular if we are aiming only at an explanation of our belief in them. 'Unlike Descartes, we own and use our beliefs of the moment, even in the midst of philosophizing, until by what is vaguely called scientific method we change them here and there for the better' (1960b: 24–5).[7]

It is worth noting that Quine's actual method is more speculative than one would expect. His account of the connection between observation and theory relies only lightly and intermittently on actual experimental results. Partly this is because the speculative stage must come first in naturalized epistemology, 'in order to isolate just the factual questions that bear on our purposes' (1975b: 78). But in addition, an imaginative reconstruction is enough for certain purposes, in particular for vindicating empiricism. If we can show how one's theory of the external world *could* have arisen from sensory stimulations,

---

[7] In a judicious and penetrating recent study BonJour argues that naturalized epistemology is impotent to answer scepticism (BonJour 1998: 89–97). But it was never meant to. Quine is clear that scepticism about, e.g., external bodies could never be met by an epistemology that assumed them (see, e.g., 1969a: 75–6). Nor is it a criticism of Quinean epistemology that it doesn't even *try* to answer scepticism. Accepting that scepticism is unanswerable need not involve the abandonment of science, but only an appreciation that nothing that could justify science is firmer than it. In short, Quine's naturalism is what Kripke calls a 'sceptical' rather than a 'straight' response to scepticism (Kripke 1982: 66 ff.).

BonJour may have been misled by certain remarks of Quine's to the effect that scepticism about science assumes science itself: we must assume, e.g., material bodies in order to make sense of illusion, and hence to argue that belief in them is unjustified (e.g., 1974: 2–3; 1975b: 67). On the basis of Quine's claims that (i) scepticism is thus parasitic upon science and (ii) naturalized epistemology *also* assumes science, BonJour attributes to Quine, and then has great fun with, the thesis (iii) that 'naturalized epistemology is in principle adequate to deal with scepticism' (BonJour 1998: 86–7). But all that follows from (i) and (ii) is that we must assume the truth of our scientific beliefs in order *both* to explain them *and* to show them unjustified. This *is* Quine's position (1975b: 67 f.), and it is quite coherent. More to the point, it contains no hint that the explanatory project either is or is meant to be any sort of counter to the sceptical one.

then we will have shown that empiricism has the explanatory resources to account for our scientific beliefs.

2.1.2 The Explanandum

Quine seems to be trying to explain *beliefs*. But beliefs of any complexity are not observable—and a theory explaining them could not be tested—except in so far as expressed in language (1981*f*: 2). Quine's explanation is therefore directed not at beliefs but at their linguistic counterparts: dispositions to produce or assent to *sentences* (1974: 34–5). That is why epistemological inquiry motivates much of Quine's interest in language (1990*c*: 3).

This shift from beliefs to sentences may appear to be a skirting of the main issue in favour of an empirically tractable one. But Quine argues that belief attributions are so unobjective as to be disqualified from a properly austere science. This is as follows.

There are three ways of construing 'A believes that *p*': as relating a person A to the *objects* mentioned by *p*, to a *proposition*, or to a *sentence*.

What rules out the first proposal is *intensionality* (1995*a*: 90 f.). According to that proposal, 'Tom believes that Tully denounced Catiline' reports a relation between Tom and Tully. If it reports truly, then the same relation *must* hold between Tom and Cicero, who *is* Tully. But 'Tom believes that Cicero denounced Catiline' may be false: for Tom might think that Cicero and Tully are distinct (1960*b*: 145). So the first proposal is wrong.

So perhaps belief ascriptions relate the believer to what his words *mean*: that is, a proposition. 'Tom believes that Tully denounced Catiline' and 'Tom believes that Cicero denounced Catiline' therefore relate Tom to distinct entities: respectively, the proposition that Tully denounced Catiline and the proposition that Cicero did. So the possibility that the two ascriptions differ in truth-value no longer presents a threat. Quine rejects the proposal, because he is dubious that there are propositions—that is, meanings common to sentences of different languages. Propositions are suspicious for reasons to do with translational indeterminacy, though we shall see (3.3 below) that these are not really conclusive.

In any case Quine takes the third line: belief ascriptions relate persons to the *sentence* following 'that'. Of course the embedded sentence will always be in English if the belief ascription is. But it can truly be so related even to non-Anglophones: 'Tacitus believes that Tully denounced Catiline' is just as true as the ascription relating Tom to the same sentence 'Tully denounced Catiline'.

For the relation asserted in a belief ascription is roughly this: the *speaker* would assent to the embedded sentence if *he* were in the ascribee's position (1995*a*: 92–3). Belief ascriptions are therefore inescapably empathetic.

But a consequence of this line is indeterminacy. For when trying to exercise empathy, there is in general no correct answer as to how many of my own beliefs I should hold constant. Thus, 'we can usually expect to rate [belief reports] only as better or worse, more or less faithful, and we cannot even hope for a strict standard of more and less; what is involved is evaluation, relative to special purposes, of an essentially dramatic act' (1960*b*: 219). Therefore we should bypass, in scientific studies, the beliefs themselves and settle for what *is* objectively ascribable: linguistic dispositions. The question of explaining our *beliefs* therefore gives way to that of explaining their linguistic expression. In parallel, and in particular, the question of explaining belief *in* external objects gives way to the question of explaining our linguistic *reference* to them (1981*f*: 2). Thus questions of reference loom large for Quine (see 2.5.3).

2.1.3 Learning of Language

Quine thinks that an explanation of our theoretical talk is an explanation of its *acquisition* (1974: 38). This seems implausible: surely learning what a sentence means is one thing, and assenting to it is another. Yes; but what are *not* different things according to Quine are learning what a sentence means and learning *when* to assent to it. When you learn a sentence, you learn how experience bears on it, either directly or via other sentences. To learn a sentence is at least to learn what experiences bear on it.[8] Therefore an account of how you learn a sentence will *ipso facto* be an account of how experience prompts assent to it.

But this is doubtful: when I learn or invent a new method for detecting neutrinos, have I learnt or invented a new *meaning* for 'There are neutrinos'? However, this doubt is relevant less to Quine's actual method than to his description of it. His theory explains how we learn what *verifies* our sentences. If the theory is correct, then the epistemological question has been answered; it hardly matters whether we add that this theory about sentences is about no more than their meaning. For instance, Quine's discussion of the interanimation of theoretical sentences (see 2.5.1) tells us how assent to a

---

[8] This is not verificationism but its converse. See further 3.3.3 below.

sentence S can prompt assent to another sentence T. This is obviously relevant to explaining why we believe T, *however* much or little it has to do with T's meaning.

To summarize these three points: Quine aims to account *scientifically* for our *acquisition* of scientific *discourse*.

2.2 Simple Observation Sentences

We learn our first words through simple conditioning: this may be explained as follows.

An *episode* is a particular total sensory stimulation: an event consisting of some distribution of neural firings across one's surface (1974: 16). Episodes are *receptually similar* to the extent that they share neural firings (1974: 17). A subject can learn to respond to receptual similarity. He can be conditioned by judicious rewards and punishments to respond in one way (e.g., barking) to all episodes that are receptually sufficiently similar to a particular one (e.g., one caused by a ringing bell). Then *perceptual similarity* is partially explained thus: an episode *a* is perceptually more similar to *b* than to *c* if the subject, having learnt to respond in one way to *b* and in another way to *c*, then responds in the first way to *a* (1974: 17–18). A rough illustration: a subject who says 'A' when shown a yellow flower and 'B' when shown a red ball, then says 'A' when shown a yellow ball. He finds the 'yellow ball' episode more perceptually similar to the 'yellow flower' episode than to the 'red ball' episode. Perceptual similarity is an *holistic* or *overall* similarity relation between episodes considered *globally*: there is no question of 'parts' of the stimulation having perceptual similarity (1974: 16; cf. 1995a: 18). This consciously echoes Carnap's relation of recollected similarity between *global momentary experiences* (Carnap 1967: §78).

The subject has an animal drive to increase perceptual similarity between a given episode and a past one. Its strength varies positively with the pleasure involved in the past episode and with the perceptual similarity *already* obtaining between the episodes. And it has an animal drive to *decrease* perceptual similarity between a given episode and a past one whose strength varies positively with the *dis*pleasure involved in the past episode and the perceptual similarity already obtaining (1974: 28).

So a child says 'Red' in the conspicuous presence of a red flower. The parent seeing both child and flower will reward the former. This strengthens the child's drive to increase perceptual similarity between future episodes and this one. Most of all, it strengthens the drive to increase the perceptual similarity of episodes that are *already* somewhat perceptually similar to this one. Especially reinforced, therefore, will be the drive to increase the perceptual similarity of those future episodes produced when a red flower is conspicuous. Hence the child increases the similarity by making sure that he hears his own voice saying 'Red' on such occasions also (1974: 29). Of course no single reward or punishment can single out just one drive for reinforcement; but a *pattern* of rewards and punishments can reinforce one drive above all—for example, to say 'Red' just when confronted by red things. By similar means he will then learn not to *say* 'Red' in all such circumstances but to *assent* to it then (1974: 45 ff.). That is how primitive language arises from animal drives.

The procedure works only if two conditions are satisfied. First, there must be a good chance that if one of them finds the episodes produced on two occasions to be perceptually similar, so does the other—so that, for example, things that look the same colour to either will look the same colour to both. For the parent is aiming to reinforce the child's drive to respond in the same way on occasions that produce episodes in the parent that the *parent* finds perceptually highly similar to the present one. And this intention will be frustrated unless the child finds the corresponding episodes produced in *himself* to be perceptually highly similar. Otherwise he will appear to his teacher as Wittgenstein's recalcitrant student does to his (Wittgenstein 1967: §185), for example, applying 'green' to grue things. The requisite agreement cannot be taught, because all teaching relies on it. Quine calls it *pre-established harmony* (1996: 160).

Pre-established harmony is unsurprising in an evolutionary context: for the perceptual similarities that underlie language learning also underlie our inductive practices (1969c: 121). Yesterday's emerald, which was grue and green, is for us more perceptually similar to today's green grass than to today's grue sky. So, given the obvious survival value of inducing in the right direction, it is perhaps unsurprising that our perceptual similarity spaces are in harmony. They all respond alike to nature's baton.

The second, more obvious and fundamental, necessary condition on conditioning is that the child's cues must typically be *intersubjectively* available. The parent can assess and fairly reward the child's response 'Red' to a red flower only if the parent sees *what* the child is seeing and *that* the child is seeing it. That is why a child's first sentences will depend for assent or dissent upon conditions that affect both his *and* other people's sensoria (1960b: 7).

The requirement is of interest because Quine once suggested that it helps explain belief in an *external* world:

Sensitivity to redness will avail the child nothing, in learning 'red' from the mother, except insofar as the mother is in a position to appreciate that the child is confronted with something red. Hence, perhaps, our first glimmerings of an external world. The most primitive sense of externality may well be a sense of the mother's reinforcement of likenesses and contrasts in the first phases of word learning.   (1957: 232)

But this shows only that redness must *be* intersubjectively available, and not at all that the child must believe it. I will argue shortly that the *next* phase of language learning is what ushers in our 'first glimmerings of an external world'.

Expressions that may be learnt thus are *observation sentences*. For present purposes we define these as follows. The stimulus meaning of a sentence S (*any* sentence) is an ordered pair (M1, M2) where M1—S's positive stimulus meaning—is (roughly) the set of episodes that would prompt assent to a query of S; and M2—its negative stimulus meaning—is (roughly) the set of episodes that would prompt *dissent* (for more precision, see 1960*b*: 32). Then an observation sentence for an individual is one whose stimulus meaning is invariant: that is, his assent or dissent to it supervenes upon his current episode. 'Red', if learnt in the way imagined, is an observation sentence.[9] One's willingness to assent or dissent depends only on current neural stimulation.[10]

---

[9] We speak of a *sentence*, not a *word*, because it is all by itself a 'move in the language game': one says something by saying *it* in a way that one fails to achieve by saying, e.g., 'if'. According to Hylton, Quine has at this stage rejected Russell's view that the sole meaning of a word like 'Red' is a *reference* with which we are *acquainted* (Hylton 2004: 118). But if we consider languages containing only one-word observation sentences, and if we transpose Russell's 'acquaintance' into a Quinean key (so that it involves neural commerce rather than awareness), then I do not know what harm there is in calling the stimulus meaning of an observation sentence both its reference and an object of acquaintance. The harm arises only when empirical data force us to supply a theoretical notion of reference *contradistinguished* from stimulus meaning. I cannot see how a language as restrictive as what is here imagined could exhibit such data. Modulo 'acquaintance', it therefore seems that the difference between Quine and Russell is at *this* stage only nominal (cf. 1970*a*: 8).

[10] It is perhaps worth sketching the vicissitudes of 'observation sentences'. A stricter rendition is: a sentence S is observational, (a) if assent to S varies from one occasion to another (it is an occasion sentence); (b) *to the extent that* assent and dissent to it upon a given episode depend only on the neural firings involved in that episode. Observationality is both idiosyncratic and a matter of degree. That is roughly Quine's 1981 definition (1981*a*: 25): call it EC-observationality. In 1960 he had explained it in *communitarian* terms: a sentence is observational, (a) if it is an occasion sentence, and (b) to the extent that its stimulus meaning coincides for *different* speakers (1960*b*: 43). Call this WO-observationality. Dissatisfaction with intersubjective comparison of stimulus meanings (1968*b*: 157; 1974: 23–4) led to a third definition: an occasion sentence is observational to the extent that many witnesses would agree

2.3 Compound Observation Sentences

2.3.1 Their Acquisition

The account so far applies to one-word observation sentences: 'Red', 'Mama', 'Water', 'Square', 'Windy'. The next complication is the observational compound: a sentence containing two observation sentences: for example, 'Red water', 'Yellow paper'. These examples are compound *predications*: they apply when the water *is* red or the paper *is* yellow. But the term 'observational compound' also covers sentences containing prepositional connectives ('Mama in garden', 'Dog chase cat'). They are all observation sentences: each *could* be learnt on the pattern of the simple ones.

But in fact they are not. Quine speculates on them as follows:

Perhaps the child learns such a connective by first learning a compound observation sentence outright as a whole by direct ostension. Then, having learned also each of the component sentences independently, he catches on to the trick and proceeds to apply the connective by analogy to other pairs.   (1995a: 23–4)

I might, for example, learn 'Fido in garden' as follows. I associate certain stimulatory patterns with the sentences 'Fido' and 'Garden', also 'Mama' and 'Kitchen'. Then I learn 'Mama in kitchen', 'Fido in kitchen', and 'Mama in garden' as similarly inarticulate observation sentences (so initially 'Mama' occurs in the third as 'itch' does in 'Kitchen'). But then episodes involving *linguistic* features become perceptually similar for me: that is, those accompanied by utterance of these long observation sentences. The basis of the newfound similarity is that the 'occasions for the "in" compound resemble one another by virtue of all having this complex trait: terms are uttered whose associated portions of the scene are embedded the one in the other'

on it on a given *occasion* (i.e., a given common cause of their possibly unalike episodes) (1974: 39). Call this RR-observationality.

These notions are distinct. Bergstrom pointed out that a sentence can be highly EC-observational without being highly RR-observational: e.g., 'It's cold' in a community where people possess different sensitivities to cold (Bergstrom 1990: 39). Davidson's scenario involving systematically rearranged sensoria shows in effect that a sentence may be both highly EC- and RR-observational without being highly WO-observational (Davidson 1990: 74).

It is true that RR-observationality is what matters for intersubjective *justification* (1974: 39–40): more highly RR-observational sentences are more likely to be fixed points in theoretical disputes. But what matters for *explanatory* epistemology is EC-observationality. Sentences that are learnt first can be grasped independently of others. These sentences will be keyed directly to episodes of the *subject*: hence they are highly EC-observational, but need not be highly RR-observational or WO-observational. Given the aim of following Quine's main epistemological thread, 'observational' here means EC-observational.

(1974: 62). On this basis, I learn to assent to 'Fido in garden' when the portion of the visible scene associated with 'Fido' is embedded in that associated with 'Garden'; similarly for compounds involving other prepositions ('Sea below sky') or none ('Black dog', 'Smiling Mama'). This illustrates 'analogical substitution' (1960*b*: 11).

2.3.2 Their Significance

The observational compound has this epistemological significance: *its* mastery is what first evinces a glimmering of an external world. This appears as follows.

From observation of someone's use of *simple* observation sentences alone there is no reason to treat them as applying to external objects. On observing that 'Red' gets assent just when something red is visibly present, we *could* interpret 'red' as a predicate true of all and only red things. But we could *also* interpret this and all his other observed terms as predicates that are intermittently true, not of external objects, but of *him*: they describe his sensory state. 'Red!' is as if to say 'I am in a sensory state of red-detection'. Nothing that we observe will rule this out, for he is typically in a sensory state of red-detection when and only when something red is visible. We could therefore do all justice to his verbal behaviour by saying that it reports his own state, just as a thermometer reports its own temperature. Nothing in *this* part of it therefore rules out a Berkeleian or monadistic interpretation of human language: statements supposedly about external objects in fact merely describe one's own sensory state.

But now consider the speaker's mastery of novel compound predications. *Without* explicit instruction, he learns to assent in the normal way to *compound* observation sentences ('Red water', 'White rabbit') upon learning their components. For instance, he assents to 'Red water?' when and only when some visible water is red. This is of course what normally happens (1970*a*: 9). But how can we explain it?

Here the notion of the application of a predicate becomes useful. Suppose we say that the component terms of a compound ('red', 'water') apply to particular objects: then our explanation is that once he has grasped their respective applications, the speaker then accords with the rule that a binary *compound* predicate applies to whatever *both* components apply to. This simple rule allows us smoothly to generate the application conditions of compound predications from those of their components: a speaker will assent to a query 'FG?' whenever 'F' and 'G' both apply to the same thing.

But if that is the point of assigning applications to the component terms, then we must *now* reject the conjecture that the latter are predicates that intermittently apply only to *him*. On that conjecture he assents, for example, to 'Red' whenever 'red' denotes *him*: that is, whenever *he* is red-detecting. So if 'red' denotes him whenever he is red-detecting, and 'water' denotes him whenever he is water-detecting, the simple explanatory rule of the last paragraph implies assent to 'Red water?' whenever he is both red-detecting *and* water-detecting. And that is wrong. If he is like the rest of us, the speaker will not assent in *all* such cases, but only when *red water* is visible: for example, when red ink spills into a swimming pool. On other occasions he will be red-detecting *and* water-detecting, but will *deny* the compound (e.g., if a red buoy is afloat).

So if the assignment of applications to its components is to explain the use of novel compounds, the former *must* be to objects other than the speaker. And this retrospectively rules out the idea that his simple observation statements predicate a sensory state of himself. We must treat them as reports about other objects. In short, interpreting a speaker's simple observation sentences as reports of his own sensory states rules out the simplest explanation of his use of novel compounds. It is mastery of novel *compounds* and not simple observation sentences that evinces our first glimmering of an external world.[11]

2.4 Observation Categoricals

We now consider observation categoricals.[12] Like observational compounds, these combine two (or more) observation sentences. But their truth-value is constant across occasions—they are what Quine calls *standing* as opposed to *occasion* sentences (1992*a*: 3, 10). Two kinds of categorical—free and focal—are distinguished (1992*a*: 11; 1995*a*: 27).

---

[11] I note three points about this argument. (i) If it works, then it also rules out interpreting our terms as predicates of a single substance of *any* sort: our language no more embodies a Spinozan metaphysic than a Berkeleian or Leibnizian one. (ii) I appealed to compound *predication*, but could equally well have used any observational compound: e.g., ones involving the term 'in'. (iii) The argument is modelled on one of Evans's (Evans 1975: 33–7); but it is different, because directed at a quite different sort of indeterminacy. The argument shares this premiss with Evans's: a semantic theory helps explain linguistic behaviour; hence a theory that yields a simpler explanation is preferable. Quine would reject this premiss on the grounds that the *real* explanation can be only in terms of an underlying physiological mechanism (1975*a*: 95). See further Hookway 1988: 159 ff.

[12] These are not observation *conditionals*: see 1992*a*: 10 n. 2; 1981*a*: 26.

2.4.1 Free Categoricals

These are 'the first step beyond ordinary observation sentences, namely a generalized expression of expectation. . . . They are our first faltering scientific laws' (1995a: 25). The free categorical combines two observation sentences into a sentence that is true if and only if the second is true whenever the first is: 'When it rains it is cold' from 'Rain!' and 'Cold!'; 'When the sun rises the birds sing' from 'Sunrise!' and 'Birdsong!'

Quine says little about the learning of free categoricals, but he is clear on their importance. Communicating observation sentences shares the benefit of momentary sensory stimulations; but communicating free categoricals shares the benefit of *inductions* (1995a: 25).

Although not observation sentences, free categoricals can be tested against observation. At least, observation can *refute* them: any episode belonging to the positive stimulus meaning of 'Sunrise!' and the negative one of 'Birdsong!' refutes 'Whenever the sun rises the birds sing'. Free categoricals are thus the simplest theories and the closest to experience. So we are some way towards our explanatory goal:

We have a sketch of a causal chain from the impacts of rays and particles on our receptors to a rudimentary theory of the external world. For the observation categoricals are indeed a theory of the world, complete with empirical checkpoints subject to the experimental method.   (1995a: 26)

Exactly how categoricals relate to sentences deeper within the theory is the subject of 2.5.1–2 below.

2.4.2 Focal Categoricals

Consider the free categorical joining 'Raven!' and 'Black raven!'. It says that whenever a raven is in view, a black one is, but *not* that every raven is black. It is compatible with white ravens that always accompany black ones (1995a: 27). The statement that all ravens are black, 'Whenever there is a raven *it* is black', is a *focal* categorical. Crucially it involves pronominal cross-reference: 'it' refers back to what 'raven' denoted. Its empirical content is as follows: episodes falling in the positive stimulus meaning of 'Raven!' and the negative one of 'Black raven!' disconfirm 'All ravens are black'.

Quine speculates that this sort of expression first arose through 'pronouns of laziness'; that is, such abbreviatory devices as 'it' in 'I banged my head and it hurts'. Here 'it' simply stands in for the *words* 'my head'; and it may be that

'Whenever there is a raven it is black' originally abbreviated 'Whenever there is a raven a raven is black' (1995a: 27–8).

2.4.3 The Significance of Categoricals

Two points about observation categoricals are relevant to epistemology. The first is their location on the interface between observational input and theoretical output. The observation categorical is the consequence of a theory that gets directly tested by experience. If we confirm it by observing an instance (i.e., a case where the antecedent and the consequent are both true), then we have to some slight extent confirmed what implies it. If we refute it by observing that the antecedent is true and the consequent is false, then we have refuted what implies it (1992a: 12). That is how the mass of theory, which is *not* about experience, can be related to experience.

The second point is that the testing of observation categoricals depends only on the stimulus meanings of their component *sentences*. This means that the interface between theory and experience is *holophrastic*: they are connected via whole sentences, and not their component terms. A difference over the denotations of a theory's terms therefore makes no difference to the bearing of experience upon it as long as the sensory meaning of its peripheral sentences remains undisturbed. I discuss the deeper significance of this point at 3.2.2 below.

2.5 The Web of Belief

We now consider what might be called the interior of the theory. Most sentences—the law of gravity, or the dates of the Thirty Years' War, or 'London is the capital of Great Britain'—are *not* learnt by direct or analogous associations with stimuli; neither are they compounded from such sentences as may be. Three doctrines concerning these *theoretical* sentences are of special interest: their interanimation, their holistic manner of confirmation, and their relation to reference.

2.5.1 Sentential Interanimation

The first important point about theoretical sentences is that we learn them by grasping their direct connections not with non-verbal experience but with *other sentences*.

We can illustrate this situation through its advantages. A purely phenomenalistic language, whose sentences are all observational or observation
categoricals, has a severely limited capacity to store information. Experiences
typically survive not as lingering images, but rather as stored sentences (recall
1.2.3(a)). Hence I could not draw present conclusions from past experiences
unless some sentences were associated not only with sensory stimulations, but
with other sentences. For example, on Monday I see Mr Jones put on a red
hat, and on Tuesday I see him put on a blue one; the experiences survive only
as sentences. On Wednesday I can say 'Somebody who put on a red hat put
on a blue one' only because that sentence is associated with other *sentences*,
in this case 'Mr Jones put on a red hat' and 'Mr Jones put on a blue hat'.
'Association of sentences is wanted not just with non-verbal stimulation, but
with other sentences, if we are to exploit finished conceptualizations and not
just repeat them' (1960b: 10). A phenomenalistic language could not properly
exploit memory itself.

How are these associations learnt? Clearly we make too many to have managed it through explicit conditioning. For instance, we all accept the existential
inference just stated, but nobody gave any thought to its sentences until just
now. Quine's answer: *analogical synthesis.* We learn novel interconnections by
analogy between them and ones already grasped. Thus someone who learns
by direct conditioning to infer (i) 'Something is wearing a hat' from 'Mr Jones
is wearing a hat' and from 'Mr Smith is wearing a hat' and (ii) 'Something is
hungry' from 'Mr Smith is hungry', will by analogy pick up on the trick of
inferring a sentence of the form 'Something is F' from any sentence of the
form 'a is F'. (It is crucial for recognizing this form that sentences be made
up of interchangeable units, i.e. words. See 1981f: 3; Hylton 2004: 137.) The
general means for learning the vast majority of sentences in the theoretical
interior is therefore an implicit or transferred conditioning connecting them
with one another and ultimately with experience (see further 1969e; Chomsky
1969: 57).

Here, then, is a sketch of the route by which one ultimately comes to accept
theoretical sentences in response to sensory inputs. Selective rewarding of
response to sensory input conditions us to associate sentences to stimulations
(2.2). We make further such associations through analogical substitution
(2.3). We associate sentences with other *sentences* through (largely implicit)
conditioning; they ultimately relate to experience via associated observation
categoricals (2.4). But there is one crucial further point regarding this last
relation.

2.5.2 Holism

(a) *Its Content.* A theoretical statement typically does not by itself imply any observation categoricals that might therefore be used to test it in isolation. Only many theoretical sentences together will do that. So the connection just sketched is not between each sentence of theory and experience; it is between a 'critical mass' of theory and experience. This doctrine, that experience tests our sentences only *in blocks,* is *holism* (1981c: 70–1; see also 1969a: 79–80, 1998e: 619; for a more extreme version see 1951: 37 ff.).

Holism thus described is hard to deny. It is clear that even empirically applicable sentences like Ohm's law (voltage = current × resistance) or Newton's laws of motion do not *alone* yield observational consequences, but only together with others—for example, sentences describing the values of certain theoretical parameters in some experiment.

(b) *Its Consequences.* We shall see that holism motivates both translational indeterminacy (3.3.3) and the epistemological irrelevance of analyticity (3.4).

It also implies a certain freedom in our responses to observation. If theoretical sentences lack proprietary observational consequences, then any of various amendments of an observationally falsified theory will square it with observation (1951: 42–3).[13] Quine once asked (1960b: 5): how much of our theory of the world does it force upon us? Well, if holism is true, it is almost none. Man's conceptual sovereignty reaches throughout science saving only the edges—that is, observation categoricals and sentences. Just about *any* other statement, including highly theoretical ones of mathematics and logic, can at our discretion suffer revision in the face of experience. Certainly experience itself teaches nothing to the contrary. 'Man proposes; the world disposes, but only by holophrastic yes-or-no verdicts on the observation sentences that embody man's predictions' (1995c: 351). We therefore conform in revision only to *pragmatic* ideals: simplicity, economy, and an unwillingness to make sweeping changes where a minor one will do (1951: 46).[14]

---

[13] This is not underdetermination of theory by data (on which see 3.3.2 below), for it does not imply that the alternative revisions are empirically equivalent, but only that both are compatible with actual observation. For further discussion see 1975c.

[14] It is frequently said that a holistic system in which every sentence and rule of inference was empirically revisable would be inoperable even by pragmatic criteria. For in order to decide what by *pragmatic* lights to revise, one must keep *some* statement or rule immune to revision: one describing a connection between an observation statement and the theory it refutes, or the logic in which the pragmatic consequences of theoretical choices are calculated and evaluated (Wright 1986: 192–4; BonJour 1998: 92; Shapiro 2000: 338–9, Glock 2003: 93; possibly also Strawson 1983: 89). If it were

(c) *Its Explanation.* Given its momentous consequences it would be worth knowing *why* holism is true.

Perhaps it is because of the tenuous and analogical means by which we acquire most of language. One might, for example, acquire certain associations between sentences about molecules and others through an imperfect analogy with the dynamics of visible particles (1960*b*: 15). Holism is the outcome:

[A] person's progress in learning his or her language is not a continuous derivation, which, followed backward, would enable us to reduce scientific theory to sheer observation. It is a progress rather by short leaps of analogy. No wonder any of the statements of a theory can be adhered to, come what may, by revising the truth value of other statements in the theory. Empirical evidence simply cannot be allocated to the individual sentences of a theory in a unique way.   (Gibson 1982: 82)

But this won't explain why sentences learnt that way have *no* proprietary empirical content, but only why it is vague. If anything is learnt by a leap of analogy (a big one), it is the application of emotional adjectives ('cheerful', 'sad', etc.) to musical themes. It does not follow that, for example, 'This tune is cheerful' has no observational consequences of its own, but only that they are probably not clear-cut.[15]

My suggested explanation may be introduced by posing the same problem in a slightly different way. We want to know why theoretical sentences lack

optional to deny that this observation occasioned revision *at all*, then the idea of its being recalcitrant in the first place, hence the very connection between experience and theory, would be lost. And if it were optional to reject the rules for comparing theoretical options, we should be unable even to *apply* our pragmatic criteria.

But first: distinguish the claim that on each occasion of revision *every* sentence/rule is vulnerable and the claim that every sentence/rule is vulnerable on *some* occasion. The criticism affects only the first claim, but even the strong holism of 'Two Dogmas' commits Quine only to the second. Quine has repudiated the first, saying that on any occasion of inquiry some beliefs *are* immune to revision—1998*a*: 94 (see further my 2000).

Second: there may be a distinction between *sentences* and their *interconnections*. It may be that Quine would not have denied that certain interconnections are unrevisable, even though no sentence is; it could be the interconnections that express the logic required for evaluating revisions.

In 'Two Dogmas' he says: 'Reevaluation of some statements entails reevaluation of others, because of their logical interconnections—the logical laws themselves being in turn simply certain further statements of the system' (1951: 42). This seems to mean that every interconnection is equivalent to some statement (Shapiro 2000: 337), which appears contrary to my second point. But it is not: it could be that, when revised, certain sentences simply cease to express the unrevisable interconnections they once did. In that case it is consistent with 'Two Dogmas' that certain interconnections are unrevisable, even though no sentence is.

[15] Nozick speculates that holism arises because 'the facts that evolution selects for attentiveness to ... lie athwart those with specific experiential content' (Nozick 1998: 341). Quine rejects that (1998*c*: 364–5), but his remark that holism sets in with the hypothetico-deductive method does not say how the two are connected, and neither does Gibson's expansion of that account (Gibson 1988: 147–8).

specific empirical consequences. Now consider the smallest items of our language that *are* open to direct empirical disconfirmation (i.e., whole chunks of theory if holism is true). Then we can put the question like this: why are *those* items articulated into units (sentences) that are empirically tested only via the theories they belong to?

Well, this articulation has an advantage: division of confirmational labour. Consider a language whose standing sentences α, β, γ, and δ and observation sentences O_1–O_5 have the following optimal translations:

α = Anything struck by a spear is frightened.

β = Frightened lions attack.

γ = Anything attacked by a tiger is frightened.

δ = Frightened rabbits flee.

O_1 = Lion struck by spear!

O_2 = Rabbit struck by spear!

O_3 = Lion attacked by tiger!

O_4 = Attacking lion!

O_5 = Fleeing rabbit!

The language is holistic: none of α, β, γ, or δ has proprietary observational consequences. But the block (α & δ) implies an observation categorical that we may write $O_2 \supset O_5$; similarly (β & γ) implies $O_3 \supset O_4$. We can test these blocks without risk by throwing spears at rabbits and setting tigers on lions. (Throwing spears at lions is far more dangerous.) If observation confirms them, it also indirectly confirms the component sentences, and in particular α and β. We therefore have indirect confirmation for a *third* block (α & β), which implies $O_1 \supset O_4$. This is useful, because we can thereby predict what happens if you throw a spear at a lion without having to risk trying it out. In short, the articulation of blocks (α & δ) and (β & γ) into recombinable components makes it possible to confirm a new theory without checking its specific consequences.

In a non-holistic counterpart language the directly testable theoretical blocks are indivisible: one cannot discern any confirmable element common to (α & δ) and (α & β). These blocks are then better written simply as 'X' and 'Y'. Speakers of *that* language could test Y only *directly*, since it draws no support from studies confirming X. Speakers of the non-holistic language could test Y only by throwing spears at lions.

This illustrates the practical advantage of a language whose confirmable components (theoretical sentences) are individually too small to imply observation categoricals. One might conjecture that similar advantages (perhaps involving the reduction of time and expenditure as much as risk) apply to larger and more complex languages. The calculus that is a chapter of an empirically confirmed physics needs no separate confirmation as a chapter of economics. And such practical advantages as these may ultimately belong to an evolutionary account of holism.

2.5.3 Reference and Ontological Commitment

Let us return to the question: in virtue of what do our terms *refer* to particular external *objects*? To answer this question is to say what it is to be committed to those objects (2.1.2). For Quine the question has not yet been answered; for he would reject the argument at 2.3.2 (see further n. 11).

Much of language lacks reference altogether. 'Hello' and 'Thank you' are no more *about* their causes than about anything else (1957: 230). And the same may initially be said about observation sentences: for example, 'Mama' or 'Water' (1958: 7). How then does one reach the point of referring to Mama or water?

We have so far observed linguistic distinctions only at the theoretical periphery: between simple and compound observation sentences and between these and observation categoricals. We treated of the theoretical interior as a mass because holism sees no distinctions amongst the ways in which different theoretical sentences relate to sensory input. But in order to trace the emergence of *reference*, we must consider stages in the learning of theory itself.

The first is the learning of standing sentences conjoining observation sentences: for example, 'Snow is white'. (Unlike observational compounds, these are not themselves observation sentences.) Quine conjectures that we learn these through transferred conditioning: whenever one sees snow, one sees white; assent to 'white' is then transferred from the presence of snow to the presence of 'snow'. When the parent queries 'Snow is white?', the word 'snow' makes the child assent to 'white'. So on hearing the whole query, he assents (1974: 65). What prompts the response is not just the compresence of white and snow but their visible intersection; the resulting emphasis on a bounded region of the scene prefigures the typical compactness of the ultimate objects of reference (1981*f*: 7). But there is no need to say that 'snow' or 'white' refers: they are just responses to visibly snowy or white tracts of reality.

The next stage is predication on *individuative* terms. Such terms (e.g., 'dog' but not 'red') do not apply to every visible part of what they apply to: Fido is a dog, but Fido's head is not (1981*f*: 4–5). The individuativeness of 'dog' is not apparent from the observation sentence 'Dog!'. But a child who grasps 'Fido is a dog' is manifesting grasp of an integral object (1974: 66). For he exhibits such patterns of behaviour as this: assent to 'Fido is a dog' but not to 'Schmido is a dog', where 'Schmido' and 'Fido' have the same stimulus meanings. This will give us reason to say that 'Fido' refers to *Fido* but 'Schmido' refers *not* to Fido but (say) to his undetached head. There is then some point in saying that 'dog' refers to—or, as Quine says, 'denotes'—dogs. It indicates that 'dog' divides the doggy part of reality into discrete chunks spatially coterminous with dogs. The child assents to 'Fido is a dog' just in case pointing to *any* part of *some* such chunk, but no other, will prompt assent to both 'Fido?' and 'dog?' (Hence he will not assent to 'Schmido is a dog'.)

But for Quine the relation of 'dog' to dogs is not yet *full* denotation, for it does not denote *persistent* individuals (1995*c*: 350). Although any denotation of 'dog' is *spatially* coterminous with a dog, its *temporal* individuation remains obscure. Assent to 'Fido?' on temporally separated occasions shows nothing to the contrary; only that he responds alike to what *resembles* Fido (1981*f*: 7; 1995*c*: 351). Mastery of 'Fido' or 'Fido is a dog' therefore gives no reason to think that 'dog' denotes chunks of reality that each have the *temporal* extension of a dog; hence no reason to say that 'dog' denotes *dogs*.

The same point applies to focal categoricals (2.4.2): 'Whenever there is a raven it is black'. It is true that its mastery motivates the assignment of *some* reference. 'The pronoun "it" is a vital new link in the component observation sentences "Lo, a raven" and "Black" or "Lo, black". It posits common carriers of the two traits, ravenhood and black' (1995*a*: 25). But there is no reference to persisting external bodies: accounting for, for example, 'All ravens are black' or 'All dogs have tails', demands denotation not of ravens or dogs but only their temporal slices.

What *does* impose that demand is cross-*temporal* pronominal reference: for example, 'If *a* dog eats a spoiled fish and sickens, then *it* will thereafter avoid fish'. Of a child who has grasped such sentences we *can* say that his 'dog' denotes dogs: he can discern the temporal boundaries of dogs as well as their spatial ones. Otherwise he could not tell whether some dog that is now eating fish *is the same as* one that ate a spoilt one; and hence he could not tell when to reject the sentence. Mastering generalizations of this sort is what signals full reference to persisting individuals. The child has absorbed our 'elaborate schematism of space, time, and conjectural hidden careers or trajectories on the part of causally interacting bodies' (1992*b*: 7). That is what *reference* to physical bodies amounts to; hence that is what it takes to *commit* to them.

So much for what commitment to bodies *is*. How is it achieved? We have already answered that: mastery of sentences involving cross-temporal pronominal reference, like that of other theoretical sentences, is a matter of properly associating such sentences with others, and ultimately with observations. The network of associations itself arises through conditioning, both explicit and analogical (see 2.5.1 above).

This completes in outline the explanatory project of 1.3. We traced a path from the superficial influence upon us of physical objects to a theory treating of those very objects. I turn now to the startling conclusions about language that Quine reaches from certain points on that path.

3 LANGUAGE

Quine's most famous doctrines are (i) ontological relativity; (ii) translational indeterminacy; (iii) rejection of analyticity. Both (i) and (ii) appear to be *epistemological* theses in the traditional sense: we cannot tell (i) what some-body's terms denote or (ii) the correct translation of his sentences. That is how I initially present them. But Quine also defends *metaphysical* versions: (i) there is no *fact* about denotation; (ii) there is no *fact* about the right translation. To get from the epistemological to the metaphysical claim, he appeals in each case to Dewey's premiss: semantic behaviourism. So we start with that.

3.1 Semantic Behaviourism

Semantic behaviourism:

[T]here are no meanings, nor likenesses nor distinctions of meaning, beyond what are implicit in people's dispositions to overt behaviour.   (1968*a*: 29)

Why should we believe this?

Quine rests it upon 'our observation of linguistic acquisition and the implausibility of supplementary channels such as telepathy' (2000: 421). Passages such as this come closest to a more explicit argument:

Meanings are, first and foremost, meanings of language. Language is a social art which we all acquire on the evidence solely of other people's overt behaviour under publicly recognizable circumstances. Meanings, therefore, ... end up as grist for the behaviourist's mill.   (1968*a*: 26; see also 1987: 5, 1992*a*: 38)

The argument appears to be:

(1) Meaning is linguistic. (premiss)
(2) Language can be acquired only through observation of overt behaviour in observable circumstances. (premiss)
(3) Semantic behaviourism is true. (from (1), (2))

We may grant premiss (1) (if you doubt it, then read 'linguistic meaning' for 'meaning' in the rest of this paper). Premiss (2) appears to follow from Quine's empiricism (see 1.3). Since I can learn only from what affects my sensory surfaces, I can learn language from others only through the aspects of *their* usage that impinges on my sensory surfaces. But *another's* surface, and hence his behaviour, screens off what is going on inside him or his mind from *my* surface. I can therefore learn from another only what I can learn from his observable behaviour in observable circumstances.

So the argument is sound if valid; but it is not valid.[16] For shared aspects of linguistic meaning may exist that are *not* acquired but which are (a) innate and (b) never manifest in linguistic behaviour. Suppose that every speaker associated with 'red' some private idea that he encountered on learning the word; and suppose that everyone was innately disposed to believe when taught 'red' in the normal manner that everyone else associated with 'red' the same idea as himself. This association might be forever undetectable in behaviour; but it cannot without begging any questions about the meaning of 'meaning' be excluded from the meaning of 'red'.

For instance, one could not exclude the private image from the meaning of 'red' on the grounds that linguistic meaning is essentially *correctable* by others (as Quine requires at 1992*a*: 38). For why accept the latter unless it is already agreed that linguistic meaning is exhausted by behaviour? Nor could one say that Quine's empiricism itself rules out the idea of a private idea (1969*b*: 58):

---

[16]   The following argument against Quine parallels one of Craig's against both Schlick and Dummett. See Craig 1982: 552–5; Schlick 1936: 148; Dummett 1973: 216 f. For the similarity between Quine and Dummett on this point see Misak 1995: 144.

the empiricist thesis that what is *acquired from others* of language mastery is acquired through the senses leaves it open that some elements of language mastery are not acquired from others.

Still, many philosophers nowadays deny any private ingredient of meaning: this is perhaps due less to Quine than to Wittgenstein (on whom see Kripke 1982: 41–51). Semantic behaviourism may then be inescapable. Let us now consider Quine's use of it.

3.2 Ontological Relativity

The thesis of ontological relativity—that is, 'inscrutability of reference' (1998*d*: 459)—divides into three claims of increasing strength. First, certain redistributions of the denotations of one's terms—of one's ontology—leave unaltered the *truth-value* of sentences in one's theory. Second, they leave intact the *evidence* for that theory. Third, there is no *fact* about what one's terms denote. I consider these in turn.

3.2.1 Ontology and Truth-Value

The first point is established by considering a function taking each of the old denotations to one of the new ones—what Quine calls a *proxy function* (1964: 217).[17] Things are simplest when the function is one to one, and its range and domain coincide (i.e., it *permutes* its domain). Suppose, for instance, that every physical object O has a *cosmic complement* O*: a physical object consisting of the entirety of space and time other than the spatiotemporal region taken up by O (so every object both has and is a cosmic complement). Let *f* take every object to its cosmic complement. It suffices to show that

---

[17] His other and more famous argument in this connection involves 'gavagai'. A native of an alien tribe utters or assents to 'Gavagai!' when a rabbit runs past. Does 'gavagai' then denote rabbits, their temporal stages, or their undetached parts? We could perhaps establish the first possibility by asking him whether this 'gavagai' and that 'gavagai' were one and the same (pointing at different parts of the rabbit at different times). But being able to ask *that* presupposes the equally indeterminate answer to the question whether the native sign that we translate as identity—call it 'blub'—is not better translated in 'gavagai' contexts as follows: 'blub gavagai' denotes pairs of rabbit stages belonging to the same rabbit (1960*b*: 51–3, 71–2).

Evans has objected that reference is discernible in the native tongue prior to isolating an apparatus of identity: it appears in the use of compound predication involving individuatives (1975: 34 f.). This, together with the application of internal negation, tense, etc., rules out Quine's alternative translations (Evans 1975: 40–7). For a gesture at Quine's response see n. 11 and the reference therein; in any case the argument in the main text is immune to Evans's point.

reinterpreting each expression as denoting the image under f of what it used to denote leaves intact the truth-values of the reinterpreted sentences.

Consider then any one-place predicate or general term, represented as 'P', and any singular term 'a'. Under the permutation, 'a is a P' comes to mean that the proxy of a is a proxy-of-a-P. But these two sentences are clearly alike in truth-value. The same reasoning applies to many-place predicates, hence to atomic sentences generally, and so, up the tree of logic, to sentences generally.   (1994: 495)

Thus 'Fido is a dog' is true when reinterpreted if and only if the reinterpreted predicate 'dog' denotes Fido's *cosmic complement*. But the reinterpreted 'dog' denotes *cosmic complements* of dogs. Hence 'Fido is a dog' is true when reinterpreted if and only if Fido's cosmic complement is the cosmic complement of a dog, hence if and only if Fido is a dog, hence if and only if 'Fido is a dog' is true on the *old* interpretation.

This argument from proxy functions is decisive but relatively anodyne: it is unsurprising that a theory can be interpreted in many ways. But we are in reach of something more disturbing.

3.2.2 Ontology and Epistemology

Quine argues that proxy-functional reinterpretation leaves intact not only sentences' truth-values but also their *evidence*.

Recall that the evidence for a sentence in a theory—that is, what sensory inputs bear upon its acceptance or rejection—depends on two kinds of association.

One is the association of observation sentences with episodes belonging to their stimulus meanings (2.2–3). That settles what counts as evidence for or against the observation categoricals (2.4). The other type of association is intersentential (2.5.1): we assent to 'Today is Tuesday' not because of fresh stimulation but simply because of present willingness to assent to 'Yesterday was Monday'. Through these two kinds of association a block of sentences can be tested via the observation categoricals that they imply.

But proxy-functional reinterpretation leaves both types of association unaffected. With regard to the first sort Quine says: '[T]he association of observation sentences with ranges of neural input is holophrastic. It is independent of reifications, independent of whatever objects the observation sentences or their parts may be taken to refer to as terms' (1992*b*: 8). Nothing in one's use of observation sentences or categoricals forces us to assign one denotation scheme to its terms in preference to a permutation thereof.

Nothing in one's use of 'Rabbit!' shows that 'rabbit' denotes rabbits and not their proxies. 'But I say "Rabbit!" when I see a *rabbit*, not a proxy of one!' True, but you say 'Rabbit!' when you *proxy-see* the *proxy* of a rabbit, where to 'proxy-see' something is to see what it is a proxy of. The position of rabbits *vis-à-vis* their proxies is symmetrical: nothing in your use of 'Rabbit!' shows that 'rabbit' denotes the things whose sight causes you to say 'Rabbit!' rather than the things whose *proxy-sight* causes you to say it. The same goes for observation categoricals. The reason, as Quine indicates, is that confirmation is holophrastic: it is only as *sentences* that these expressions are associated with sensory input (2.4.3). Any reinterpretation of their terms that leaves sentential meaning (stimulus meaning) intact is therefore indifferent with regard to that association.

With regard to the intersentential associations whereby theory implies observation categoricals, Quine says that the 'implication hinges only on *logical* structure and is independent of what the objects, the values of the variables, may be' (1992*b*; my emphasis). Hence intersentential association is indifferent to proxy-functional reinterpretation.

This does not establish the point. Certainly *if* an inference from some sentence to another depends only on their *logical* structure, it is indifferent to uniform reinterpretation of non-logical terms. The inference from 'No proxy of a rabbit is a rabbit' to 'No rabbit is a proxy of a rabbit' is indifferent to whether 'rabbit' denotes rabbits or their proxies (or anything else). All that matters is the logical form: 'No Fs are Gs, therefore no Gs are Fs.'

But Quine himself points out that not all intersentential associations are logical (1960*b*: 11). I might be conditioned to pass from 'John is taller than James' and 'James is taller than Simon' to 'John is taller than Simon'. But the inference depends on more than *logical* structure: it turns on the transitivity of the relation *taller than*. And I may well be ignorant about transitivity whilst still accepting the inference, which cannot therefore be an enthymematic one that *does* turn on logical structure.

It is clear how Quine could respond. Even *non*-logical associations are indifferent to proxy-functional reinterpretation. The point is not that the implications are always *logical* (they are not), but that they connect *sentences*. And any association between *whole sentences* that accords with one denotational scheme will *also* accord with any permutation of it. Thus the inference in the last paragraph turns on the transitivity of *taller than*. But when reinterpreted, 'taller than' denotes just the ordered pairs (x, y) such that *x is the proxy of something taller than that which y is the proxy of*. And this too is transitive.

More generally, note that any reinterpretation that *guarantees* truth-*values* of all sentences (see 3.2.1 above) can never affect the plausibility of inferences amongst them. The intersentential associations would therefore have been exactly the same if my terms had been denoting proxies of what they actually denote.

So both kinds of association are indifferent to proxy-functional reinterpretation. So if theory and sensory input are related solely via the sentential links described at 2.2–2.5.1, the evidential relation is indifferent to what one's terms denote. If the evidence supports an interpretation of a theory, then it equally supports a permuted reinterpretation. All that matters to epistemology is whatever structure is preserved by any such permutation. Hence Quine's conclusion: 'save the structure and you save all' (1992*b*: 8).[18]

3.2.3 Ontology and the Facts

Quine affirms not only the epistemological irrelevance but also the *non-factuality* of ontology: there is simply no fact about whether 'dog' denotes dogs or their proxies (1968*a*: 48).

The argument assumes that if one overall assignment of denotations to my terms fits my dispositions to verbal behaviour, then so does a proxy-functional permutation thereof (see, e.g., 1968*a*: 38). The conclusion does not follow from this premiss alone, but it *does* if we grant semantic behaviourism (see 3.1).

(1) If an assignment of denotations to my terms fits my dispositions to verbal behaviour, then so does a permutation of that assignment. (premiss)

---

[18] This shows that evidence for a theory does not discriminate one assignment of denotations from proxy-functional *permutations* thereof. But the same reasoning shows that the evidence does not discriminate one assignment of denotations from *any* one-to-one reassignment of denotations, including the assignment of wholly alien entities, as long as there is one new entity for every old one. Quine's talk of 'structure' therefore seems empty: the evidence for any ontology is equally evidence for another of the same cardinality. There would seem to follow the apparently disastrous conclusion that Newman drew on similar grounds from Russell's structuralism (Russell 1927): 'The doctrine that *only* structure is known involves the doctrine that *nothing* can be known that is not logically deducible from the mere fact of existence, except ("theoretically") the number of constituting objects' (Newman 1928: 144).

Quine can accept that the evidence is indifferent between ontologies of the same cardinality, and even the scepticism that follows. He will deny that we should in response *withhold* from the ontology that we hitherto accepted: to accept that ontology is underdetermined by evidence is not to repudiate the ontology in terms of which that recognition took place (1981*f*: 21). This stance is of course simply a consequence of naturalism (see 1.2.2 above).

(2) There are no meanings, nor likenesses nor differences in meanings, beyond what is implicit in my dispositions to verbal behaviour. (premiss)

(3) There is no difference between one assignment of denotations to my terms (on which, e.g., my term 'dog' denotes dogs) and a permutation of it (on which, e.g., my term 'dog' denotes cosmic complements of dogs). (from (1) and (2))

Premiss (1) gains support from two points. First, we know that what sensory stimulations bear on acceptance or rejection of a theory is indifferent to permutation of its terms' denotations. Second, Quine accepts that the only verbal behaviour relevant to assigning a denotational scheme 'comes in the form of facts about what events or situations in the world cause, or would cause, speakers to assent to, or dissent from, each sentence in the speaker's repertoire' (Davidson 1979: 230; cf. Quine 1958: 4–5). It follows from the second point that assignments of denotation need be sensitive only to what counts as evidence for the theory. But then it follows from the first point that premiss (1) is true.

With regard to premiss (2), semantic behaviourism: the implausibility of (3) might tempt one to interpret the argument from (1) and (2) thereto as a *reductio* of (2). But first, we have (3.1) an argument for (2) which, though not irrefragable, puts a price on (2)'s rejection that many are unwilling to pay. And second, the argument to (3) can coherently be treated as a *reductio* of (2) only by one who thinks that something *other* than verbal behavioural dispositions suffice to fix denotations—for example, something in one's mind. But well-known arguments, not due to Quine, make it plausible that nothing *other* than those dispositions can fill this office (Kripke 1982: 57; McGee 2005: 398–400).

So Quine appears to have strong grounds for (3): there is no fact about what one's terms denote.

But then what was going on in 2.5.3? There I described what it takes for 'dog' to denote *dogs* and indicated how this came about. Was I not stating or trying to account for the *facts*?

I was. The facts are behavioural: the complex linguistic dispositions to which mastery of, for example, 'Dogs that eat spoiled fish will thereafter avoid them' amounts. The proxy argument shows that assigning 'Fido' to Fido and 'dog' to dogs does no more—and no less—justice to these facts than reassigning 'Fido' to Fido's proxy and 'dog' to dogs' proxies. It does not show that *what* these assignments are doing justice to—the speech dispositions themselves—are not facts: they are, and *they* are what we sought to explain.

Very well: but I didn't only gesture at an account of how these dispositions arose—I *also* tried to say at what point in their development reference is *achieved*—at what point 'dogs' denotes dogs. Certainly there is a fact about whether or not one has a given speech disposition—proxy functions were never going to threaten *that*. But the following remains under threat: whether 'dog' in the mouth of a speaker with given speech dispositions is denoting dogs or their proxies. To repeat: if no facts settle *that*, then what were we arguing for in 2.5.3?

We can reply as follows. When speaking of our *own* language, let us reserve 'reference', 'denotation', etc. for a disquotational relation: 'London' refers to London and 'dog' denotes dogs (1992*a*: 52; 1998*d*: 460). The question, at what stage in the development of linguistic dispositions do we reach denotation, now becomes perfectly meaningful. It is this. Consider the speech dispositions of an English speaker: at what point in their development do we do full (though not unique) justice to these facts by assigning his words their *reference* or *denotation*: that is, by assigning 'London' to London and 'dog' to dogs? That perfectly meaningful question is what we spent 2.5.3 trying to answer (see further 1974: 83–4).

Of course this disquotational understanding of 'reference' is available only for one's *own* language. So ontological relativity is compatible with genuinely factual investigations into reference only at the cost of a certain parochiality (1960*b*: p. ix).

3.3 Translational Indeterminacy

Quine's conjecture of translational indeterminacy:

Manuals for translating one language into another can be set up in divergent ways, all compatible with the totality of speech dispositions, yet incompatible with one another.   (1960*b*: 27)

Before describing the arguments for this claim, it is worth saying something about its content and significance.

3.3.1 Its Meaning and Consequence

A translation manual specifies a correlation of sentences in some unknown 'source' language with those in a known 'target' language. Assuming an infinitude of source sentences, such a manual must proceed (if it is itself finite) not only by explicit correlations of source sentences with target ones, but also by explaining the source vocabulary and grammar in the target language (1958: 3); the resulting correlations of source words with target words are *analytical hypotheses* (1960*b*: 68).

The first argument (3.3.2) focuses on manuals for *radical* translation. Translation is radical if no continuity between source and target language may be assumed beyond their speakers' common humanity (1960*b*: 28). The Anglophone radical translator cannot take such hints from interlinguistic homophony as are available to translators of a language culturally related to English. The idea (to anticipate) is that facts available to the radical translator—native speech dispositions—are all the facts about meaning that there are. So to cast doubt on interlinguistic sameness of meaning for *any* two languages (Quine's aim), it suffices to show that *radical* translation manuals may do all justice to the facts in any of many incompatible ways.

But what is it for translation manuals to be *incompatible*? In *Word and Object* Quine said that incompatible manuals take a single source sentence to target sentences that stand in no 'sort of equivalence, however loose' (1960*b*: 27). He has since explicated it thus: translation of a single source text produced by applying the two manuals to alternate sentences thereof yields an incoherent *target* language output (1992*a*: 48).

Why does translational indeterminacy matter? Given semantic behaviourism, it implies that there is no *fact* about which translation manual is correct: divergent manuals do equal justice to speech dispositions, and hence by semantic behaviourism to *all* relevant facts.[19] Translational indeterminacy

---

[19] Suppose without loss of generality that the domain of both the theory of translation and physics itself consists of space-time points. The characteristic predicates of translation theory would be, e.g., *x belongs to some person stage whose utterance 'Gavagai!' is translatable as 'Rabbit!'*. Call a theory of translation *weakly reducible to physics* if its predicates F_i are each co-extensional with some (possibly infinite) disjunction $\beta(F_i)$ of physical predicates; call a theory of translation *strongly reducible to physics* if its predicates F_i are each co-extensional with some single physical predicate $\alpha(F_i)$. Weak reducibility is the position of a functionalist about translation theory; strong reducibility is the position of an identity theorist about translation theory.

Then according to Friedman (1975: 367–8), Quine's argument for semantic behaviourism does not show that *only* behaviour is relevant to translation: translation theory might even be strongly reducible to physics by virtue of its predicates each being co-extensional with some physical *non-behavioural* predicate. It needs only that this physical predicate is *itself* co-extensional with some behavioural one.

Now that is true, but it makes no difference to Quine's argument. We will see that the totality of facts about behavioural dispositions will not settle which of two conflicting translation manuals is correct. In order to warrant the further conclusion that *no* facts settle it, the ancillary premiss that no facts *other* than behavioural ones could settle it will suffice. Friedman is right to think that

therefore casts doubt on propositions (1990*a*; 1992*a*: 102). We normally think that sentences of different languages can express the same proposition: that is, their common meaning. But equally correct and conflicting translation manuals defeat this idea. If we can equally well translate 'Das Neutrinoe hät keine Masse' as either 'Neutrinos have mass' or 'Neutrinos do *not* have mass', then no fact settles which English sentence expresses the same proposition as the German sentence; and they cannot *both* do so. Here we see a reason for rejecting propositions as objects of belief, and therefore in part for rejecting beliefs as the *explananda* of naturalized epistemology (see 2.1.2).

We consider two arguments for translational indeterminacy: 'from above' and from holism.[20]

3.3.2 The Argument from Above

Physics may be empirically underdetermined: incompatible physical theories might be compatible with just the same observational data. But to the extent that choice between such theories is underdetermined by the data, so too the choice of which theory to attribute to a radically foreign physicist is underdetermined by his linguistic dispositions. A translation manual that attributes one theory to him will therefore be incompatible with one that attributes the other; yet both are adequate to his dispositions. Such is Quine's argument (1970*b*).

Quine has not established *this*. But what the argument of 3.1 *has* established—modulo the quite different objection presented there—is this: any predicates (physical or not) whose extension is relevant to settling translational indeterminacy must *themselves* co-vary with the behavioural ones or combinations thereof, for there can be no difference in meaning without difference in behavioural disposition. And *this* ancillary premiss is all that Quine needs at present. For if it is true, and if we know that the extensions of the predicates of translation theory are underdetermined by those of one's behavioural predicates, it follows that they are underdetermined by *any* facts.

In short, in order to get from the premiss that translation is behaviourally underdetermined to the conclusion that it is non-factual, Quine seems to need the additional and undefended premiss that *only* behavioural phenomena settle facts about translation. In fact he does not: he needs only the defended premiss that only those phenomena *that themselves co-vary with behavioural ones* settle facts about translation.

[20] A third argument appears in *Word and Object*: the so-called argument 'from below'. This is the 'gavagai' argument of n. 17 above. Quine later made clear (1970*b*) that this was not his preferred argument: it is easy enough to see why. In the 'gavagai' example, terms of the source language are so translated by the two manuals that disagreement over how to translate 'gavagai' gets *compensated* by disagreements over other terms, so that translations of any given native *sentence* are equivalent (or even identical: 1992*a*: 51). So translating a source text by alternating the two manuals is unlikely to yield an incoherent text in the target language.

'Underdetermination' of physical theory here means only *epistemic* underdetermination: *not* that no fact settles which physical theory is true. When it comes to physics, Quine himself is straightforwardly realistic: there *is* a true theory even if it is in principle empirically indistinguishable from certain false ones (1969*e*: 303).

Of course when it comes to questions of meaning and translation, he takes a different view: namely, semantic behaviourism. But here he argues (i) from the epistemic underdetermination of physics to the *epistemic* underdetermination of radical translation by speech dispositions; given semantic behaviourism, we *then* (ii) infer *factual* indeterminacy of translation. We have already considered semantic behaviourism; it remains to examine step (i).

Suppose, then, that two observationally equivalent physical theories are incompatible. Quine describes the stages by which a radical translator determines which to impute to a radically foreign physicist:

As always in radical translation, the starting point is the equating of observation sentences of the two languages by an inductive equating of stimulus meanings. In order afterward to construe the foreigner's theoretical sentences we have to project analytical hypotheses, whose ultimate justification is substantially just that the implied observation sentences match up. But now the same old empirical slack, the old indeterminacy between physical theories, returns in second intension. Insofar as the truth of a physical theory is underdetermined by observables, the translation of the foreigner's physical theory is underdetermined by translation of his observation sentences. If our physical theory can vary though all possible observations be fixed, then our translation of his physical theory can vary though our translations of all possible observation reports on his part be fixed.   (1970*b*: 179–80)

Observation sentences are the starting points of translation for the same reason that they initiate one's first language: their association with publicly available stimulatory occasions is independent of any hidden collateral information (see 2.2 above). Translating the native's term 'Red!' requires no more than a record of the visible circumstances accompanying his assent and dissent to 'Red?'. That changes when we translate the (empirically under-determined) theoretical interior. There are two empirically equivalent theories attributable to the foreign physicist. Given that they imply the same observation sentences (or rather categoricals), how could he show us which one he meant? Observation can reveal to us only his dispositions to respond to stimuli produced by observable circumstances; it is unclear how this could have a differential bearing on the two theories, given their observational equivalence.

Here is an artificial example.[21] We saw (3.2.2) that one assignment of denotations to our words is empirically indistinguishable from a proxy-functional reassignment. Now the same is true, for the same reason, of an assignment to the *foreigner's* words: there is no empirical difference between a scheme assigning his 'gavagai' to rabbits and a permuted one that assigns it to their proxies. In this example the two schemes play the role of empirically equivalent but incompatible physical theories.

Imagining some syntactical means of identifying direct quotation and the category of referring expressions in the language, suppose further that we observe the foreigner's term 'bongo' to parallel our 'denotes'. Thus he assents to, for example, ' "gavagai" bongo gavagai' and in general to any instance of ' "X" bongo X' where 'X' is a referring expression.

Now we have a choice: we can translate 'bongo' either as 'denotes' or as 'denotes the proxy of'. Each translation manual correlates the foreign theory of denotation with one of two empirically equivalent domestic theories. And it is quite unclear what foreign speech disposition could show just one manual to be wrong. And yet the two manuals are incompatible: used in alternation on a native text, they produce nonsense. Consider the text: ' "Hesperus" bongo Hesperus et Hesperus eadem Phosphorus. Hinc "Hesperus" bongo Phosphorus.' That text, perfectly coherent according to either manual alone, now gets translated into the incoherent: ' "Hesperus" denotes Hesperus and Hesperus is Phosphorus. Hence "Hesperus" denotes the proxy of Phosphorus.'

It would be hasty to conclude that *no* foreign speech dispositions could support one such translation manual at the expense of its rival in the case Quine actually considers. There *may* be possible patterns of behaviour that we have ignored and which could do just that.[22] But Quine was not out to

---

[21] I should emphasize that Quine would *not* have used this example in this context, because it involves empirically equivalent theories that are not only not *physical* theories; they are ones that by his own lights do not even differ over the *facts* (see 3.2.3 above). Still, it gives a feel for the structure of the problem.

[22] One such, it is claimed, is the inferential structure of the rival theories (see, e.g., Hylton 2007: 219). Surely the radical translator can tell (by putting sentences to him, etc.) what the foreigner is prepared to infer from what. And it may be that one of our two empirically underdetermined (target language) theories contains sentences whose inferential connections better match the foreigner's than the other. And this would be a reason for preferring the better-matched theory. On the other hand, if the target language theories are structurally isomorphic, then in what sense are they different?

This is not compelling. In our example concerning proxy functions, the two manuals are compatible with just the same inferences on the foreigner's part. Yet they clearly conflict by the criterion of 3.3.1; i.e., they produce nonsense if used on a single text in alternation. (See further Kirk 1986: 188–90.)

prove that such determinants *never* exist, only that there is no reason to think they *must*. At any rate, that is all he seems to need. For in that case radical translation *can* smoothly and unimprovably assign source to target sentences *without* presupposing an interlinguistic proposition common to every pair of correlated sentences. And if translation of a native sentence *can* be as good as it gets without capturing any proposition underlying the latter, why think that things are *ever* otherwise? Inconclusive as the argument is, it apparently suits Quine's aim of *challenging* the 'uncritical notion of meanings and, therewith, of introspective semantics' (1987: 9).[23]

3.3.3 *The Argument from Holism*

The argument from above sought to establish the *epistemological* thesis that two translation manuals might conflict but fit foreign speech dispositions to perfection; given semantic behaviourism, there follows the *metaphysical* thesis that the facts leave unsettled which manual is right. The holism argument proceeds directly to the latter thesis. But it still relies, in another way, on semantic behaviourism.

The argument is from *holism* and *verificationism*. Holism says that *sentences of a theory have empirical implications only as a body*. And Quine's verificationism says that *the meaning of a linguistic item consists in its net empirical implications*: that is, what difference its truth makes to possible experience (1969a: 78). He argues as follows.

These considerations raise a philosophical question even about ordinary unphilosophical translation, such as from English into Arunta or Chinese. If the English sentences of a theory have their meaning only as a body, then we can justify their translation into Arunta only together as a body. There will be no justification for pairing off the component English sentences with component Arunta sentences, except as these correlations make the translation of the theory as a whole come out right. Any translations of the English sentences into Arunta sentences will be as correct as any other, so long as the net empirical implications of the theory are preserved in translation. But it is to be expected that many different ways of translating

---

[23] This is, I think, the correct response to Wright, who argues plausibly that someone who (consistently with the premises of 1970b) holds 'that only very high-level physical theory is subject to underdetermination will be under no pressure to concede indeterminacy of translation except for vocabulary which occurs exclusively in such theory' (Wright 1997: 417). That may be true; the most that Quine has shown, therefore, is that indeterminacy is to be expected at a very high level of physical theory. But this is all he needs: if translation of high-level theory can proceed in cheerful disregard of propositions, then what feature of the practice of lower-level translations should make us think that propositions set the standard *there*?

the component sentences, essentially differing individually, would deliver the same empirical implications for the theory as a whole; deviations in the translation of one sentence could be compensated for in the translation of another component sentence. Insofar, there could be no ground for saying which of two glaringly unlike translations of individual sentences is right.   (1969a: 80)

We may summarize it thus:

(1) Each sentence of a given English theory has empirical implications only together with the others. (holistic premiss)

(2) A sentence's meaning consists in its empirical implications. (verificationist premiss)

(3) Many conflicting translations of its sentences preserve equally the empirical implications of a theory containing them. (premiss)

(4) Any translation of the English theory into Arunta preserves its sentences' meanings if it preserves their empirical implications. (from (2))

(5) Any translation of the theory preserves its sentences' meanings equally well if it preserves the empirical implications of the theory. (from (1), (4))

(6) Many conflicting translations of the component sentences will preserve *their* meanings equally well. (from (3), (5))

This does not prove (6) but appears to make it at least as likely as (3), assuming (1) and (2). Hence in so far as (3) is 'to be expected', so is (6), which is the metaphysical thesis: the facts leave it unsettled which translation is correct.[24]

The language of 2.5.2(c) illustrates the point. I said that we could translate its theoretical sentences α, β, γ, and δ respectively as: 'Anything struck by a spear is frightened', 'Frightened lions attack', 'Anything attacked by a tiger is frightened', and 'Frightened rabbits flee'. But precisely because of the (modest) holism there in sway, an equally adequate translation manual is just like this one except that 'angry' replaces 'frightened' throughout. The observation

---

[24] Kirk has objected that from (1) and (2) it follows that sentences of the source language do *not* have empirical meaning. But this is inconsistent, he says, with the conclusion that rival translation manuals preserve sentence meanings equally well (Kirk 1986: 83). But there is no inconsistency if we understand the empirical meaning assigned by a translation manual to a sentence of the source language to be relative to the sentences it assigns to the *other* source sentences. So the empirical meaning assigned by a translation manual M to any sentence S in the target language theory is the empirical implications of S under M *given all the other target language sentences assigned by M to the source theory*. Then each manual M will assign the same non-null empirical meaning to each such sentence S: i.e., the empirical meaning of the whole theory. There remains no reason to expect that all the manuals assigning the source theory's actual empirical meaning to each such sentence will be compatible with one another by the standard of the alternation test.

categoricals implied by each theoretical block big enough to imply any will be the same under each manual; whatever facts there are about the sentences' meaning are therefore got equally right by both.

Is the argument sound? We have already discussed the holistic premiss. What about the verificationist one? Quine argues thus:

Should the unwelcomeness of the conclusion persuade us to abandon the verification theory of meaning? Certainly not. The sort of meaning that is basic to translation, and to the learning of one's own language, is necessarily empirical meaning and nothing more. A child learns his first words and sentences by hearing and using them in the presence of appropriate stimuli. These must be external stimuli, for they must act both on the child and on the speaker from whom he is learning. Language is socially inculcated and controlled; the inculcation and control turn strictly on the keying of sentences to shared stimulation. Internal factors may vary *ad libitum* as long as the keying of language to external stimuli is undisturbed.   (1969a: 81)

It is difficult to interpret this argument as one for *verificationism*, though plainly it is meant to be. Here is my reconstruction.

> (7) There is no more to linguistic meaning than what can be inculcated and controlled by another. (premiss)
>
> (8) Linguistic meaning can be inculcated and controlled by another only to the extent that it consists in observable responses to stimuli observable by the other. (premiss)
>
> (9) Stimuli that are observable by the other must be external to the learner. (premiss)
>
> (10) Stimuli that are external to the learner only impinge on him via sensory channels. (premiss)
>
> (11) There is no more to linguistic meaning than dispositions to observable responses to stimuli observable by another. (from (7), (8))
>
> (12) There is no more to linguistic meaning than dispositions to observable responses to external stimuli. (from (9), (11))
>
> (13) There is no more to linguistic meaning than dispositions to observable responses to sensory input. (from (10), (12))

Premiss (7) follows from semantic behaviourism. Premiss (8) is falsified inasmuch as we can inculcate and control a child's use of 'Ouch!' without observing its distal *stimulus* (which may be in his bowels) so long as we observe the stimulus's side effects (1960b: 5–6). This does not matter if we focus on sentences about the external world: verificationism about *these* is verification enough. Premiss (9) is a fact of experience. Premiss (10) follows from Quine's empiricism. The conclusion (13) implies that one means no more by a sentence than is settled by one's disposition to use it in response to sensory input. Since this is settled by its empirical implications, it follows that premiss (2) is true.

Modulo the doubts about semantic behaviourism expressed in 3.1, the verificationist premiss thus appears plausible. It is therefore plausible that translational indeterminacy is to be expected at least as much as (3) is to be expected. Whilst the argument hardly proves indeterminacy, it does give reason to expect it; this may be enough for Quine's purposes as outlined at the end of 3.3.2.

3.4 Analyticity

I want to conclude with Quine's most famous paper (1951). It is directed at the doctrine of analyticity: the claim that some sentences are true, or better, *held* true, because of what they mean. These include 'All bachelors are unmarried', 'Tuesday is the day before Wednesday', and perhaps '$2 + 2 = 4$'.

Such sentences have been something of an embarrassment for empiricism. It is quite unclear what *sensory* experience confirms them; and to postulate non-sensory experience—'some doctrine of ultimate and inexplicable insight into the obvious traits of reality' (1960a: 113)—is to abandon empiricism altogether. So it is easy to see how the doctrine, that we grasp their truth simply by grasping their meanings, might have seemed liberating. Following Kant, we call such truths *analytic*; those grounded in non-linguistic fact are *synthetic* (1951: 20).

There has been much dispute over what Quine's 1951 objection to analyticity was. On one view, he thought 'analytic' unintelligible because its standard definition was circular (Grice and Strawson 1956: 147–8); on another, that it makes sense but that *every* sentence is synthetic (Harman 1967: 125); on a third, that it makes sense, but no sentences are *either* analytic *or* synthetic (Dummett 1974: 351–2).

Certainly Quine did try to make something of the circularity involved in defining 'analytic' (1951: 27–30). But by 1953 he was not inclined to take this line seriously (1953a: 138). The enduring, or at any rate real, difficulty with 'analytic' was neither its intelligibility nor its extension, but its redundancy. The problem it was meant to solve—what makes us hold certain sentences true—can be solved without it.

I now perceive that the philosophically important question about analyticity and the linguistic doctrine of logical truth is *not* how to explicate them: it is the question rather of their relevance to epistemology.   (1998b: 207)

What 'Two Dogmas' teaches is how holism supports this conclusion.

We should note that the holism stated in 'Two Dogmas' is stronger than the moderate version at 2.5.2. The stronger position is not that *many* sentences lack proprietary empirical consequences, but that they *all* do:

Any statement can be held true come what may, if we make drastic enough adjustments elsewhere in the system. Even a statement very close to the periphery [i.e., a highly observational one] can be held true in the face of recalcitrant experience by pleading hallucination or by amending statements of the kind called logical laws.   (1951: 43)

But this difference makes no difference to the argument that I want now to highlight (1998*e*: 619).

Epistemology attempts to connect our experience of the world with our theory of it. Denying moderate holism raises a difficulty for that project. If holism is false, then each sentence has its own fixed sensory content. This is the *second* dogma of empiricism, the first being the doctrine of analyticity (1951: 40 f.). Now what about truths of mathematics, or 'Every bachelor is unmarried'? *If* experience confirms or disconfirms sentences in isolation, then what experience confirms or disconfirms *them*? And if the answer is 'none', then why do we hold them true?

What saves the second dogmatist from embarrassment is the point that not experience alone but it *and* language together are what make for confirmation (in the following replace 'truth' with 'confirmation'[25]): 'For there can be no doubt that sheer verbal usage is in general a major determinant of truth. Even so factual a sentence as "Brutus killed Caesar" owes its truth not only to the killing but equally to our using the words as we do' (1960*a*: 108). The second dogmatist can now explain mathematics and logic as a sort of limiting case: their confirmation is owed *purely* to the linguistic component that plays *some* role in confirming *every* sentence. Such limiting cases are the analytic truths. And this is the first dogma.

Holism, being incompatible with the second dogma, eliminates the *motivation* for calling some statements analytic in this epistemologically relevant sense. The holist says that *most* sentences lack proprietary sensory content: the fact that mathematical and logical truths lack it therefore raises no special problem for *them*. What confirms them and all these other statements, is the

---

[25] As we should. The quoted passage is about what makes 'logical *certainty*' possible. So the (second dogmatist's) answer should be that sentences that are logically certain are automatically *confirmed* 'by virtue of their meaning', not that they are automatically *true*. For a similar complaint about other passages, see McDermott 2001: 978–9.

confirmation as a whole of the theories in which they partake (1951: 42). And the tenacity of mathematics and logic is not explained by their being a by-product of linguistic use. What explains it is our 'conservative preference for revisions that disturb the system least' (1998*b*: 208).

That it was its epistemological relevance, and not its intelligibility or extension, that concerned Quine is partly confirmed by the fact that he himself has defined analyticity: a sentence is analytic if everyone learns its truth by learning its words (1974: 79). This notion of analyticity is intelligible and non-empty ('Bachelors are unmarried men' is plausibly analytic). But 'we have here no such radical cleavage as was called for by Carnap and other epistemologists' (1974: 80). On the contrary, the notion is epistemologically sterile. The fact that the past use of a sentence happened to introduce one of its words is irrelevant to its *present* confirmation:

When in relativity theory momentum is found to be not quite proportional to velocity, despite its original definition as mass times velocity, there is no flurry over redefinition or contradiction in terms, and I don't think there should be. The definition served its purpose in introducing a word for subsequent use, and the word was thereafter ours to use in the evolving theory, with no lingering commitments.   (1991: 272)

In short, there is nothing wrong with calling a sentence 'analytic'. Only it does nothing to explain why we believe it.[26]

That concludes my discussion of Quine's linguistic theses. They are ultimately derived from his empiricism and the epistemology it inspired. Semantic behaviourism itself (3.1) allegedly follows from Quine's empiricism (1.3). Ontological relativity (3.2.2–3) follows from the holophrastic nature of confirmation (2.4.3) together with semantic behaviourism. Translational

---

[26] McDermott considers whether Quine was arguing from holism to the epistemological irrelevance of analyticity, and comments: 'But the question is, now, is it an argument from *holism*? Apparently not. A *non*-holistic system would have rules linking each of its sentences, directly or indirectly, with certain experiences, so that occurrence of those experiences would require abandonment of the sentence. These rules would be rationally revisable in pursuit of a system which was simpler, clearer, and empirically adequate. If, in the interests of easy communication, it proved useful to classify some of these rules as "rules of meaning", that would still be irrelevant to the merits of revising a rule in pursuit of the aims designated by Quine as *epistemologically* relevant—just as in the holistic case' (McDermott 2001: 1004).

But on a non-holistic model, each sentence will have its *own* confirming and disconfirming experiences. There will therefore be no *choice*, in face of any experience, over which statements to drop and which ones to retain. Hence simplicity, clarity, etc. cannot on this model account for theoretical adjustments in the face of experience. The apparent immunity of mathematics and logic—if they exist in this language—will therefore remain unexplained unless we resort to confirmation in virtue purely of linguistic rules or use: i.e., analyticity.

indeterminacy (3.3.3) is a consequence of verificationism and holism (2.5.2); verificationism itself an alleged consequence of empiricism. And as we have just seen, Quine's treatment of analyticity (3.4) is a consequence of his holism.

Thus reference, meaning, and analyticity join material substance, spiritual substance, inductive knowledge, and necessary connection on the casualty list of empiricism. Quine's naturalistic reformulation of that doctrine was a major and enduring contribution. But his greatest contribution was the direction of its—probably inherent—destructive tendencies at the semantic and logical preoccupations of his own era.

REFERENCES

Ahmed, A. (2000). 'Hale on some Arguments for the Necessity of Necessity'. *Mind*, 109: 81–91.

Barrett, R., and Gibson, R. (eds.) (1990). *Perspectives on Quine*. Oxford: Blackwell.

Bergstrom, L. (1990). 'Quine on Underdetermination'. In Barrett and Gibson (1990), 38–52.

Berkeley, G. (1975). *Philosophical Works*, ed. M. R. Ayers. London: Everyman.

Boghossian, P., and Peacocke, C. (eds.) (2000). *New Essays on the A Priori*. Oxford: Clarendon Press.

BonJour, L. (1998). *In Defense of Pure Reason*. Cambridge: Cambridge University Press.

Butterfield, J. (ed.) (1986). *Language, Mind and Logic*. Cambridge: Cambridge University Press.

Carnap, R. (1967). *The Logical Structure of the World*, trans. Rolf A. George. London: Routledge & Kegan Paul.

Chomsky, N. (1969). 'Quine's Empirical Assumptions'. In Davidson and Hintikka (1969), 53–68.

Craig, E. (1982). 'Meaning, Use and Privacy'. *Mind*, 91: 541–64.

Davidson, D. (1979). 'The Inscrutability of Reference'. *Southwestern Journal of Philosophy*, 10: 7–19; repr. in Davidson (1984), 227–41.

——— (1984). *Inquiries into Truth and Interpretation*. Oxford: Oxford University Press.

——— (1990). 'Meaning, Truth and Evidence'. In Barrett and Gibson (1990), 68–79.

——— and Hintikka, J. (eds.) (1969). *Words and Objections*. Dordrecht: D. Reidel.

Dummett, M. A. E. (1973). 'The Philosophical Basis of Intuitionistic Logic'. In H. E. Rose and J. C. Shepherdson (eds.), *Logic Colloquium 1973*, Amsterdam: North Holland, 5–40; repr. in Dummett (1978), 215–47.

——— (1974). 'The Significance of Quine's Indeterminacy Thesis'. *Synthese*, 27: 351–97.

_____ (1978). *Truth and Other Enigmas*. London: Duckworth.

Evans, G. (1975). 'Identity and Predication'. *Journal of Philosophy*, 72: 343–63; repr. in Evans (1985), 25–48.

_____ (1985). *Collected Papers*. Oxford: Clarendon Press.

Feigl, H., and Sellars, W. (eds.) (1949). *Readings in Philosophical Analysis*. New York: Appleton-Century-Croft.

Fogelin, R. (2004). 'Aspects of Quine's Naturalized Epistemology'. In Gibson (2004), 19–46.

Foster, L., and Swanson, J. W. (ed.) (1970). *Experience and Theory*. London: Duckworth.

Friedman, M. (1975). 'Physicalism and the Indeterminacy of Translation'. *Noûs*, 9: 353–74.

Gibson, R. (1982). *The Philosophy of W. V. Quine: An Expository Essay*. Tampa, FL: University of South Florida Press.

_____ (1988). *Enlightened Empiricism: An Examination of Quine's Theory of Knowledge*. Tampa, FL: University Presses of Florida.

_____ (ed.) (2004). *The Cambridge Companion to Quine*. Cambridge: Cambridge University Press.

Glock, H. (2003). *Quine and Davidson on Language, Thought and Reality*. Cambridge: Cambridge University Press.

Grice, P., and Strawson, P. F. (1956). 'In Defense of a Dogma'. *Philosophical Review*, 65: 141–58.

Guttenplan, S. (ed.) (1975). *Mind and Language*. Oxford: Clarendon Press.

Hahn, E., and Schilpp, P. (eds.) (1998). *The Philosophy of W. V. Quine*. Chicago and La Salle, IL.: Open Court.

Hale, R. V., and Wright, C. (eds.) (1997). *Blackwell Companion to the Philosophy of Language*. Oxford: Blackwell.

Harman, G. (1967). 'Quine on Meaning and Existence, I'. *Review of Metaphysics*, 21/1: 124–51.

Hook, S. (ed.) (1969). *Language and Philosophy*. New York: New York University Press.

Hookway, C. (1988). *Quine: Language, Experience and Reality*. Cambridge: Polity.

Hume, D. (1949). *Treatise of Human Nature*, ed. with an analytical index by L. A. Selby-Bigge. Oxford: Clarendon Press.

Hylton, P. (2004). 'Quine on Reference and Ontology'. In Gibson (2004), 115–50.

_____ (2007). *Quine*. London: Routledge.

Kirk, R. (1986). *Translation Determined*. Oxford: Clarendon Press.

Kotatko, P., and Orenstein, A. (eds.) (2000). *Knowledge, Language and Logic: Questions for Quine*. Dordrecht: Kluwer.

Kripke, S. A. (1982). *Wittgenstein on Rules and Private Language*. Oxford: Blackwell.

Leonardi, P., and Santambrogio, M. (eds.) (1995). *On Quine*. Cambridge: Cambridge University Press.

Lewis, D. K. (1973). *Counterfactuals*. Oxford: Blackwell.

McDermott, M. (2001). 'Quine's Holism and Functionalist Holism'. *Mind*, 110: 977–1025.

McGee, V. (2005). 'Inscrutability and its Discontents'. *Noûs*, 39/3: 397–425.

Misak, C. J. (1995). *Verificationism: Its History and Prospects*. London: Routledge.

———(2004). *Truth and the End of Inquiry: A Peircean Account of Truth*, expanded paperback edn. Oxford: Clarendon Press.

Mulvaney, R. J., and Zeltner, P. M. (eds.) (1981). *Pragmatism: Its Sources and Prospects*. Columbia, SC: University of South Carolina Press.

Murphy, J. P. (1990). *Pragmatism: From Peirce to Davidson*. Oxford: Westview Press.

Newman, M. H. A. (1928). 'Mr Russell's "Causal Theory of Perception"'. *Mind*, 37: 137–48.

Nozick, R. (1998). 'Experience, Theory and Language'. In Hahn and Schilpp (1998), 339–63.

Quine, W. V. (1951). 'Two Dogmas of Empiricism'. *Philosophical Review*, 60: 20–43; repr. in Quine (1980): 20–46.

———(1953a). 'Mr Strawson on Logical Theory'. *Mind*, 62: 433–51; repr. in Quine (1976), 137–57.

———(1953b). 'On Mental Entities'. *Proceedings of the American Academy of Arts and Sciences*, 80: 198–203; repr. in Quine (1976), 221–7.

———(1957). 'The Scope and Language of Science'. *British Journal for the Philosophy of Science*, 8: 1–17; repr. in Quine (1976), 228–45.

———(1958). 'Speaking of Objects'. *Proceedings and Addresses of the American Philosophical Association*, 31: 5–22; repr. in Quine (1969d), 1–25.

———(1960a). 'Carnap and Logical Truth'. *Synthese*, 12: 350–74; repr. in Quine (1976), 107–32.

———(1960b). *Word and Object*. Cambridge, MA.: MIT Press.

———(1964). 'Ontological Reduction and the World of Numbers'. *Journal of Philosophy*, 61: 209–16; repr. in Quine (1976), 212–20.

———(1966). 'Russell's Ontological Development'. *Journal of Philosophy*, 63: 657–67; repr. in Quine (1981e), 73–85.

———(1968a). 'Ontological Relativity'. *Journal of Philosophy*, 65: 185–212; repr. in Quine (1969d), 26–68.

———(1968b). 'Propositional Objects'. *Critica*, 2/5: 3–22; repr. in Quine (1969d), 139–60.

———(1969a) 'Epistemology Naturalized'. In Quine (1969d), 69–90.

———(1969b). 'Linguistics and Philosophy'. In Hook (1969), 95–8; repr. in Quine (1976), 56–8.

———(1969c). 'Natural Kinds'. In Quine (1969d), 114–38.

———(1969d). *Ontological Relativity and Other Essays*. New York: Columbia University Press.

———(1969e). 'Reply to Chomsky'. In Davidson and Hintikka (1969), 302–11.

———(1970a). 'Grades of Theoreticity'. In Foster and Swanson (1970), 1–17.

———(1970b). 'On the Reasons for the Indeterminacy of Translation'. *Journal of Philosophy*, 67: 179–83.

____ (1974). *The Roots of Reference*. Chicago and La Salle, IL: Open Court.

____ (1975a). 'Mind and Verbal Dispositions'. In Guttenplan (1975), 83–95.

____ (1975b). 'The Nature of Natural Knowledge'. In Guttenplan (1975), 67–81.

____ (1975c). 'On Empirically Equivalent Systems of the World'. *Erkenntnis*, 9: 313–28.

____ (1976). *The Ways of Paradox and Other Essays*. Cambridge, MA: Harvard University Press.

____ (1980). *From a Logical Point of View*, 2nd edn. Cambridge, MA: Harvard University Press.

____ (1981a). 'Empirical Content'. In Quine (1981e), 24–30.

____ (1981b). 'Five Milestones of Empiricism'. In Quine (1981e), 67–72.

____ (1981c). 'On the Very Idea of a Third Dogma'. In Quine (1981e), 38–42.

____ (1981d). 'The Pragmatists' Place in Empiricism'. in Mulvaney and Zeltner (1981), 21–39.

____ (1981e). *Theories and Things*. Cambridge, MA: Harvard University Press.

____ (1981f). 'Things and Their Place in Theories'. In Quine (1981e), 1–23.

____ (1987). 'Indeterminacy of Translation Again'. *Journal of Philosophy*, 84: 5–10.

____ (1990a). 'Comment on Hintikka.' In Barrett and Gibson (1990), 176.

____ (1990b). 'Comment on Parsons'. In Barrett and Gibson (1990), 291–3.

____ (1990c). 'Three Indeterminacies'. In Barrett and Gibson (1990), 1–16.

____ (1991). 'Two Dogmas in Retrospect'. *Canadian Journal of Philosophy*, 21/3: 265–74.

____ (1992a). *Pursuit of Truth*, 2nd edn. Cambridge, MA: Harvard University Press.

____ (1992b). 'Structure and Nature'. *Journal of Philosophy*, 89: 5–9.

____ (1993). 'In Praise of Observation Sentences'. *Journal of Philosophy*, 90: 107–16.

____ (1994). 'Responses'. *Inquiry*, 37: 495–505.

____ (1995a) *From Stimulus to Science*. Cambridge, MA: Harvard University Press.

____ (1995b). 'Naturalism, Or, Living Within One's Means'. *Dialectica*, 49: 251–61.

____ (1995c). 'Reactions'. In Leonardi and Santambrogio (1995), 347–61.

____ (1996). 'Progress on Two Fronts'. *Journal of Philosophy*, 93: 159–63.

____ (1998a). 'Reply to Bohnert'. In Hahn and Schilpp (1998), 93–5.

____ (1998b). 'Reply to Hellman'. In Hahn and Schilpp (1998), 206–8.

____ (1998c). 'Reply to Nozick'. In Hahn and Schilpp (1998), 364–7.

____ (1998d). 'Reply to Roth'. In Hahn and Schilpp (1998), 459–61.

____ (1998e). 'Reply to Vuillemin'. In Hahn and Schilpp (1998), 619–22.

____ (2000). 'Quine's Responses'. In Kotatko and Orenstein (2000), 407–30.

Romanos, G. D. (1983). *Quine and Analytic Philosophy: The Language of Language*. Cambridge, MA: MIT Press.

Russell, B. (1922). *Our Knowledge of the External World*. London: Allen & Unwin.

____ (1927). *The Analysis of Matter*. London: Allen & Unwin.

Schlick, M. (1936). 'Meaning and Verification'. *Philosophical Review*, 45: 339–69; repr. in Feigl and Sellars (1949), 146–70.

Shapiro, S. (2000). 'The Status of Logic'. In Boghossian and Peacocke (2000), 333–67.

Strawson, P. F. (1969). 'Singular Terms and Predication'. In Davidson and Hintikka (1969), 97–117.

——— (1983). *Skepticism and Naturalism: Some Varieties*. New York: Columbia University Press.

——— (1998). 'Reference and its Roots'. In Hahn and Schilpp (1998), 519–32.

Van Fraassen, B. (1995). 'Against Naturalized Epistemology'. In Leonardi and Santambrogio (1995), 68–88.

Waismann, F. (1945). 'Verifiability'. *Proceedings of the Aristotelian Society,* suppl. vol. 19: 119–50.

Wittgenstein, L. (1967). *Philosophical Investigations*, trans. G. E. M. Anscombe, 3rd edn. Oxford: Blackwell.

Wright, C. (1986). 'Inventing Logical Necessity'. In Butterfield (1986), 187–209.

——— (1997). 'The Indeterminacy of Translation'. In Hale and Wright (1997), 397–426.

CHAPTER 17

··

PHILOSOPHY OF SCIENCE IN AMERICA

··

ALAN RICHARDSON

As we enter the heart of the twentieth-first century, philosophy of science is a well-entrenched subdiscipline within philosophy, not just in the United States but throughout the world. The US-based Philosophy of Science Association holds a conference biennially that attracts hundreds of scholars from around the world; every four years the Division of Philosophy of Science of the International Union for History and Philosophy of Science holds an even larger conference on Logic, Methodology, and Philosophy of Science. There are several general philosophy of science journals dotted throughout the world, and many more specialist journals dealing with the philosophy of particular sciences. Several leading American universities, including Indiana and Pittsburgh, employ philosophers of science not only in their philosophy departments but in departments or programs of history and philosophy of science.

It was not always thus. One hundred years ago there were few professional journals in philosophy at all, and none that specialized in philosophy of science. What is now *The Journal of Philosophy* was, until about 1920, called

The Journal of Philosophy, Psychology and Scientific Method, but it did not announce itself as a journal in philosophy of science but as a journal in "scientific philosophy". In 1895, the first recognizable professional position in philosophy of science was created, but it was created at a fair distance from both the USA and academic philosophy: it was the chair in "Philosophy, in particular the history and theory of the inductive sciences", a position in the Science Faculty at the University of Vienna taken up by the physicist, psycho-physiologist, and philosopher, Ernst Mach (Stadler 2001). Mach was one of several scientists at the beginning of the twentieth century whose reflections on the nature of the scientific enterprise formed the bulk of what we would recognize today as philosophy of science; he was joined in this endeavor by Pierre Duhem, Henri Poincaré, Frederigo Enrigues, Max Planck, Wilhelm Ostwald, Ludwig Boltzmann, and others. At the time, the USA was something of a scientific backwater compared with France, Germany, and Britain; thus, it is not surprising that the most reflective scientists were found in Europe. Of course, reflection on the nature of scientific knowledge has been, arguably, a part of the philosophical enterprise since the Greeks. However, in American philosophy before the turn of the twentieth century it would have been unusual for a philosopher interested in the nature of scientific knowledge to refer to his (far less often, her) concern as "philosophy of science", and even more rare for him to call himself a "philosopher of science".[1]

This is not inexplicable, since the formation of a subdiscipline of philosophy properly called "philosophy of science" requires preconditions which were fulfilled only in the late nineteenth and early twentieth centuries. Until the 1830s or so, philosophy was not itself carefully distinguished from science, and so science was not considered an object of study distinct from either philosophy itself or from any attempt to acquire systematic knowledge of the world. Before the schism, "philosophy of science" would be a redundancy, a peculiar new name either for "first philosophy" (the inquiry into the possibility of knowledge in general) or for a general theory of knowledge. Once it was generally accepted that the sciences were specialist subjects distinct from philosophy, it became possible for a philosopher interested in knowledge to become interested in the particularities and peculiarities of

---

[1] Unusual but not unheard of: Edgar Singer taught a course at the University of Pennsylvania from 1896 onward called "Philosophy of Science" (Hatfield 2002). As early as 1865, C. S. Peirce lectured on "the logic of science" at Harvard (Peirce 1982– , [1865]: i. 162–336).

knowledge-making in the special sciences. It also became possible, given that the specialist sciences were, so it seemed, progressing by leaps and bounds while philosophy was not, for a philosopher to become worried about the scientific status of philosophy. When the *Journal of Philosophy, Psychology, and Scientific Method* announced in 1904 that it was a journal in "scientific philosophy", it was announcing that it was concerned not merely to promote philosophical reflection on the nature of science, but also to establish and promote the proper scientific status of philosophy. Of course, those concerned to promote scientific philosophy would need an account of science upon which to test and establish the scientific status of philosophy. Once inquiry into the nature of scientific knowledge was given the imprimatur of leading scientists, and especially after the revolutionary changes in the physical sciences in the early twentieth century, it became possible for scientifically trained philosophers to take providing an account of scientific knowledge as their primary task. These philosophers became the first generation of philosophers to think of themselves as primarily philosophers of science.

In light of these general remarks, the structure of this essay is as follows. First, there will be a brief description of some work in natural philosophy and philosophy of nature in the USA in the era before and around the split between science and philosophy. Second, there will be a description of some salient features of the American philosophical reflection on science from 1877, when C. S. Peirce offered the first American philosophy of knowledge trained primarily on the question of scientific method, until roughly 1930, when the logical positivists began their move to American shores. Third, the rise of logical positivism and the era of professionalization of philosophy of science will be discussed. Fourth, the main lines of the decline of logical positivism will be outlined. Finally, some major themes in the philosophy of science in the post-positivist era in the United States will be presented.

Natural Philosophy and Philosophy of Nature in Early America

Until well into the nineteenth century, systematic study of nature, particularly when that study sought to discuss causes and explanations, was called either "science" or "natural philosophy"; its practitioners were called natural philosophers. Sir Isaac Newton's (1686) *Principia Mathematica Philosophiae Naturalis*—Mathematical Principles of Natural Philosophy—was only the most famous work of natural philosophy written during the time when America was a colony. The discovery and exploration of a new world rich in natural resources and which had many plant and animal species unknown in Britain and Europe excited early modern natural philosophers. Thus, the systematic investigation of nature in the American colonies was an ongoing activity. Natural history and natural philosophy were activities passionately engaged in by many of the founding fathers of the United States, including George Washington and Thomas Jefferson. America also produced some natural philosophers of note, including the materialist Cadwallader Colden (1688–1776) and, notably, the polymath and diplomat Benjamin Franklin. Colden and Franklin were among the founders, in 1742, of the American Philosophical Society, a group of natural philosophers who self-consciously took on the task, "the promotion of useful knowledge", for the colonies that the Royal Society had discharged in Britain since its founding in 1662.[2]

Most academic philosophy in the colonies was concerned, however, largely with moral and theological philosophy. Philosophy in the colleges often took the form of apologetics for particular sects of Protestant religion (for example, Unitarianism at Harvard and Presbyterianism at Princeton). Moral philosophy and natural philosophy in the eighteenth century, however, intersected in mental philosophy, or "the science of man". One prominent American contributor to the eighteenth-century natural philosophy of morals was Benjamin Rush (1745–1813), a signatory of the Declaration of Independence and a chemist and physician in Philadelphia. His 1786 address to the American Philosophical Society, "The Influence of Physical Causes on the Moral Faculty" (Rush 1946), was a broadly naturalistic treatment of material causes of the action of the will.

The contours of American philosophy at the beginning of the nineteenth century were largely in accord with those of Scottish Enlightenment philosophy. The only aspect of the natural philosophical views put forward

---

[2] Colden's ambitious project in natural philosophy is given voice in, e.g., Colden (1751). On Colden, see Hayes (2003); on Franklin's natural historical and natural philosophical work see I. B. Cohen (1990).

that is notably American was the oft expressed view that the physical conditions in the American colonies (and new American state) provided the conditions of material and, thus, mental and moral improvement of humanity. The broad outlines of evolving Scottish philosophy continued to dominate American academic natural and mental philosophy through much of the nineteenth century, especially in the field of mental and moral philosophy. This is evidenced in the influence of Thomas Reid and Dugald Stewart on generations of American treatises in mental philosophy such as Thomas Upham's (1831) *Elements of Mental Philosophy*, Noah Porter's (1868) *The Human Intellect*, and, especially, James McCosh's (1886) *Psychology*. Meanwhile, American exceptionalism as a moral and intellectual matter continued to animate the philosophical thoughts of amateur philosophers and polymaths in the first half of the nineteenth century. In addition to Ralph Waldo Emerson's well-known "The American Scholar" delivered to the Phi Beta Kappa Society in Cambridge, Massachusetts, in 1837 (Emerson 1983 [1837]), we can see this in remarks of, for example, Charles Jared Ingersoll's (1946 [1823]) "The Influence of America on the Mind", delivered to the American Philosophical Society in 1823.[3]

In the Romantic period, European natural philosophy had a more metaphysical rival, philosophy of nature, or *Naturphilosophie*. Perhaps most associated with the German philosopher Schelling, philosophy of nature is hard to characterize, but it sought to offer a metaphysics, moral philosophy, and aesthetics based on a comprehensive understanding of the nature of nature. Characteristic of the various versions of philosophy of nature is an energetic or dynamic point of view inspired by the awesome forces of nature. The vastness and splendor of the American West often inspired philosophies of nature, and thus it is not surprising that philosophy of nature, often filtered through the work of T. S. Coleridge, also had American variants. It is certainly to be found in the place of nature in the transcendentalism of Emerson and Henry David Thoreau. Perhaps the most peculiar(ly) American version of it is in the electrical energism of Edgar Allan Poe's astonishing 1848 oration before the New York Academy of Science, "Eureka" (Poe 2004 [1848]).[4]

---

[3] On Scottish mental philosophy in America, see Schneider (1946) and Kuklick (2001).
[4] Kuklick (2001) provides some guidance *re* Emerson, Thoreau, and *Naturphilosophie*.

Pragmatism, Naturalism, and the Philosophy of Science in America, 1870–1930

While science and nature (the most comprehensive object studied by science) were topics of philosophy in the USA from the beginning, it was not until the last third of the nineteenth century that something recognizably continuous with contemporary philosophy of science began to emerge. In the last third of the nineteenth century it was uncontroversial that established natural sciences such as physics and chemistry were enterprises distinct from philosophy; this was both an accomplished achievement in the divisions of the disciplines and a consequence of philosophical positivism. Biological science, meanwhile, had, with the theories of Charles Darwin, issued a challenge both to established theology and to any philosophy that argued that human morality or mental life were beyond the pale of natural scientific explanation. Similar and not unrelated challenges to dominant mental philosophy were issued also from the "new psychology" which emphasized experimental and physiological approaches to explaining human mental life. By the beginning of the twentieth century, moreover, advances in the exact sciences had become increasingly visible topics of discussion by both scientists and lay promoters of scientific thought. Science had both co-opted much of the territory of philosophy and offered itself as the progressive force in reliable knowledge of the world. It was time for philosophers to take science as an object of philosophical discussion.

Moreover, these discussions came at a time when American universities were expanding their research mission, modeling themselves on the great German research universities of the age. First at Johns Hopkins and then at other universities such as Harvard, Michigan, and Chicago, philosophical training was continued up to the doctoral level. Philosophers were meant to be researchers as much as teachers. This drive toward professionalization and research was seen also in the founding of academic research journals in philosophy, starting with *Mind* in England in 1876. On American shores, the principal publications were *The Philosophical Review*, published by the Sage School of Philosophy at Cornell University starting in 1891, *The International Journal of Ethics*, and the aforementioned *Journal of Philosophy, Psychology, and Scientific Method*, published by the Columbia University Philosophy

Department from 1904. American philosophers also organized themselves into a national professional organization, the American Philosophical Association, in 1901.[5]

Among the earliest as well as the most influential and clearest arguments that philosophy would do well to attend to the processes of scientific thinking was a series of essays written by Charles Sanders Peirce (1839–1914) in 1877–8 in the *Popular Science Monthly*. In these essays, Peirce, who would soon be appointed to the philosophy department at Johns Hopkins (and almost as soon be dismissed), announced what have since often been taken to be the two most fundamental ideas of pragmatism. First, he offered an account of truth as that upon which beliefs would settle at the ideal limit of inquiry—and affirmed the scientific method to be the best method for achieving this permanent fixation of belief. Second, he offered an account of the meaning of ideas as confined to the sensible effects of things:

I only desire to point out how impossible it is that we should have an idea in our minds which relates to anything but conceived sensible effects of things. Our idea of anything *is* our idea of its sensible effects.... Consider what effects, which might conceivably have practical bearings, we conceive the object of our conception to have. Then, our conception of these effects is the whole of our conception of the object.   (Peirce 1958 [1877/8]: 5.401)

Peirce argued that these doctrines follow from a proper conception of scientific method. And then it follows from these doctrines that many disputes in theology and philosophy are not really disputes at all.

Peirce was as much a working scientist as he was a philosopher, and he did not rest content with providing very high-level methodological advice. He also engaged in fundamental research in formal logic and in probabilistic and statistical inference. Indeed, his work helped to create one of the first specialist research communities in American philosophy working in the fields of algebraic logic and the foundations of statistical and probabilistic inference. He explicitly claimed that Darwin's achievement lay in large part in invoking the statistical method in biology:

The Darwinian controversy is, in large part, a question of logic. Mr. Darwin proposed to apply the statistical method to biology.... Darwin, while unable to say what the operation of variation and natural selection in every individual case will be, demonstrates that in the long run they will adapt animals to their circumstances.

---

[5] The early history of the American Philosophical Association is recounted in Wilson (1990) and Campbell (2006).

Whether or not existing animal forms are due to such action, or what position the theory ought to take, forms the subject of a discussion in which questions of fact and questions of logic are curiously interlaced.   (Peirce 1958 [1877/8]: 5.364)

Peirce here expresses two salient things for the history of philosophy of science at this time. First, he serves notice that the central topic of logic or scientific method for him and his successors will be the logic of statistical reasoning, a logic that stands in complicated relations to concepts like individual causation. Second, he notes how, in central and difficult cases of scientific theorizing, questions of fact and questions of method are both at stake.

As wielded by Peirce in these early papers, the pragmatist doctrines and concern with the proper logic and method of science were meant to diagnose and rectify certain peculiarly philosophical confusions. Thus, Peirce illustrated the account of what a concept means with a discussion of force, in order to disabuse the reader of any sense that there is some mysterious essence of force that physics cannot illuminate. Of course, this is a philosophical perspective offered by prominent physicists at the time, and Peirce himself targets Kirchhoff in his discussion. The proper understanding of meaning will rid of us such unanswerable philosophical worries:

The idea which the work 'force' excites in our minds has no other function than to affect our actions, and these actions can have no reference to force other than through its effects. Consequently, if we know what the effects of force are, we are acquainted with every fact which is implied by saying that force exists, and there is nothing more to know.   (Peirce 1958 [1877/8]: 5.404)

Even decades later, Peirce was to claim that pragmatism was a form of "prope-positivism" that "will serve to show that almost every proposition of ontological metaphysics is either meaningless gibberish . . . or else is downright absurd; so that all such rubbish being swept away, what will remain of philosophy will be a series of problems capable of investigation by the observational methods of the true sciences" (Peirce 1958 [1905]: 5.423).

This sort of eliminativism with regard to "ontological metaphysics" was welded, a bit uneasily, to an account of scientific theorizing that stressed the creativity of science. In Peirce's hands that became an insistence on a form of reasoning that he called "abduction", a sort of inference to the best explanation. Peirce was quite clear on both the difficulty and the promise of viewing this creative aspect of science as an *inference*, since it was neither deduction nor induction. It was not induction precisely because it was creative—typically scientific theorizing goes conceptually beyond what is available in the mere report of perception or even of experimental procedures and results. By 1903, Peirce argued that pragmatism importantly *was* an abductive account of scientific theorizing, that the fate of pragmatism as a philosophical project depended on there being an adequate account of abduction (Peirce 1958 [1903]: 5.180–212). His own account of proper scientific theorizing brought metaphysics—a form of scholastic realism about universals—back into the philosophy.

The nature and fate of the philosophical project of pragmatism aside, Peirce's achievements for American philosophy of science are mainly technical. Having argued forcefully that science proceeded neither wholly inductively nor wholly deductively but through inferences by abduction, he made the logic of abduction a going concern among technically minded American philosophers and scientists. He had a similar effect in the fields of statistical reasoning and mathematical logic. His philosophical projects shaded off into technical projects in statistics, algebra, and logic.

Peirce was not the only significant figure working in philosophy of science in America in the late nineteenth century. Frequently these figures were on the margins of American academic philosophy, if affiliated with it at all. One such figure was the German-born American polymath and politician John Bernhard Stallo (1823–1900). Stallo had been a teacher of German and mathematics at St Francis Xavier College and at St John's College (now Fordham University) in the 1840s, but had settled into life as a lawyer and politician in Cincinnati thereafter. In contrast to his youthful Hegelian philosophy of nature, Stallo's 1882 book *The Concepts and Theories of Physics* (Stallo 1960), expressed a sort of idiosyncratic positivism that stressed the provisionality of physical concepts and theories. This work, mainly in its later editions, became influential well beyond American shores; it was read and cited by Bertrand Russell, Ernst Mach, Rudolf Carnap, and others. The work was later reissued under the editorship of the American Nobel Prize-winning physicist Percy Bridgman.

Another figure who was influential, due to his own philosophical work but mainly due to his indefatigable publishing efforts, was another German-American, Paul Carus. Carus was original editor and publisher of *The Monist*, a journal of philosophy that began publishing in 1890. This journal was an important venue for work in philosophy of science in America until the mid-1930s, when it ceased publication (until it was revived again in 1962). As the name suggests, the journal was connected to American monism, which grew out of European monist movements connected to the thought of Ernst Haeckel, Ernst Mach, and others. Carus's own work was extremely wide-ranging—he wrote on topics from Buddhism to philosophical monism to Christian doctrine to topics in the philosophy of science to Nietzschean philosophy. In the early decades of the twentieth century he wrote books on vitalism and mechanism and on the theory of relativity (Carus 1913a, 1913b). The Open Court Publishing Company, founded by Carus in 1887, was one of the leading American publishers of European science and philosophy of science; it was the main publisher in English of the work of Ernst Mach.[6]

Meanwhile, within academic philosophy, philosophy of science was not much of a going concern in the 1890s and 1900s. There were a few figures who took up philosophy of science in the classroom: Edgar A. Singer at the University of Pennsylvania taught courses under that rubric in the 1890s; Josiah Royce (1855–1916) taught courses on themes in philosophy of science at Harvard already from the 1880s (Hatfield 2002). Reflection on scientific method in general or the methods of the special sciences in particular continued, of course, but they were often directed toward the philosophical lessons to be learned from the (putative) truth of certain scientific doctrines. As early as the 1860s, Chauncey Wright (1830–75), a mentor of Peirce (and James) at Harvard, offered a non-teleological, anti-Spencerian Darwinian naturalism to American philosophy (Wright 1865).[7] Naturalism continued to be a going concern in fin-de-siècle American philosophy in the work of philosophers such as F. J. E. Woodbridge (1867–1940) at Columbia and George Santayana (1863–1952) at Harvard. Among the special scientific issues that attracted much attention at the time were issues around vitalism and mechanism in biology, as well as many issues in psychology. Indeed, the empirical sciences of the mind seemed to many to have particular relevance to philosophy, and Peirce's pragmatist successors William James (1842–1910) and John Dewey (1859–1952) were just two of many American philosophers writing about both content and method of psychology in the 1880s and 1890s.

The concerns among American philosophers regarding the scientific status of the specific cases of psychology and vitalist biology are instructive for considering the place of philosophy of science in American philosophy at the time. These areas of study were of specific interest to philosophers because

---

[6] For more on Carus, see Henderson (1993).   [7] On Wright, see Menand (2001).

they were sciences whose content would tell us, so it was thought, important things about humanity, sciences whose results would speak to long-standing philosophical issues about the nature of life and the workings of the mind. The methodological interest in these sciences specifically, thus, was derivative from the perceived philosophical interest of the sciences themselves. These sciences were, however, both controversial as science and problematic in their relations to philosophy. Thus, interest in, for example, psychology as a science that might tell us something important in epistemology often resulted in the need to get clear about methodological, conceptual, and metaphysical issues in the sciences themselves: what sort of psychology is properly scientific, what is the relation of brain processes to mental processes, etc.? Thus, there are issues in the philosophy of science suffused throughout works such as James's 1890 *The Principles of Psychology*, even though the work itself would scarcely be accurately or adequately characterized as a treatise in the philosophy of science.

The nature of science took on a new significance in the pragmatism of Dewey in the first decades of the twentieth century. Unlike Peirce, Dewey did not often concern himself with the technical details of scientific methodology or inference. Dewey's project was largely to promote scientific thought as the method of critical intelligence and to promote the value of such scientific thought within the province of philosophy. Dewey was particularly concerned that the method of scientific intelligence be enforced in the realms of social and moral philosophy. Indeed, completing the scientific revolution by bringing the moral and social realms into properly scientific investigation was, he suggested on more than one occasion, the peculiar task of twentieth-century philosophy. This was a pressing problem for Dewey, given that the modern world had altered the structure of society and robbed the modern person of much of what had provided a sense of human value. Social, political, and moral philosophy had to become areas of experimental activity if the modern citizen was not to become unmoored, unable to locate relatively permanent values that could direct his or her life (Dewey 1982 [1920]; 1984 [1927]).

Although not technical like Peirce's project, in some ways Dewey's project did follow along Peircean lines. It was as important to Dewey's project as it was to Peirce's that the world revealed by science was a world of probability and chance, a world in which a priori demonstrative reason or the quest for certainty was misplaced. Accordingly, Dewey also stressed, as Peirce had done before him, the creativity and intelligence as well as the provisionality of scientific procedure. Toward the end of his life, Dewey decided that these aspects of his philosophy were important enough that he eschewed calling it "pragmatism", preferring instead to use the term "experimentalism". Dewey's vision was more naturalist and less idealist than was Peirce's, however. Dewey stressed the biological, psychological, and social conditions in which the empirical human agent engaged in scientific inquiry (Dewey 1986 [1938]). Indeed, Dewey's Darwinian naturalism stressed the ontological plasticity of the world—the Darwinian world possessed no fixed, permanent forms. It was a world in which humanity could remake itself morally and politically (Dewey 1982 [1920]).

Dewey's project captured the interest of a wider American audience than any philosophical project before or since. It spoke to American progressive liberalism in an era when the USA was understood to be the vanguard of modernity. Despite, and in part because of, the wider popularity of the Deweyan project, it attracted critics across academic philosophy. Among the complaints were two that are relevant to our concerns here. The first was that Dewey was importantly wrong about the nature of science, especially scientific methods. The second was that he was wrong to try to import scientific methods into philosophy. Both of these objections required a countervailing philosophy of science to the one Dewey offered— and the second required a countervailing philosophy of philosophy in addition.

Among those who contested either Dewey's philosophy of science or his imposition of that philosophy of science onto an account of philosophy itself were leading American philosophers of the time such as Morris Raphael Cohen (1880–1947) and George Santayana. For Santayana, patron saint of American naturalism and, by the second decade of the twentieth century, advocate of so-called critical realism, Dewey's account of philosophy depended on a "half-hearted" naturalism (Santayana 1925). The world seen aright for Santayana is not a world centered on human striving—a properly naturalized metaphysics is a vision of a world in which human striving is a small and insignificant part. Santayana's dispute with Dewey mainly centered on the question of what a properly scientific or naturalized metaphysics says about the world. Cohen's complaints were more clearly centered on Dewey's account of science, but led him to similar conclusions. At stake for Cohen was the disinterestedness of Dewey's philosophical vision. Cohen saw Dewey as promoting a scientific philosophy, but doing so for political and social reasons; this, for Cohen, was a violation of the spirit of disinterested inquiry in both science and philosophy.

Echoing the Weberian ideal of value-free science, Cohen wrote in 1940, in an article explicitly critical of Dewey, that

Ardor for social reform is admirable in anyone, but detachment and a critical attitude are the special duties of those who as scientists or philosophers have to maintain the canons of intellectual integrity. Too often has devotion to temporal causes turned philosophical light into partisan heat.   (M. R. Cohen 1949 [1940]: 175)

Independently of his criticism of Dewey, Cohen's work in philosophy of science was both wide-ranging and, in the American context, unusual. Cohen did not emphasize the connections between philosophy and biology or psychology, and his concerns in philosophy of science were directed toward logic, mathematics, and physics as much as toward the social and life sciences. He was an early American voice in the philosophical interpretation of Einstein's theory of relativity. Indeed, although his interests ranged across the broadest sweep of philosophical topics, and although he might be best remembered as a philosopher of law, Cohen preferred to call himself a 'logician'. His two books, *Reason and Nature: The Meaning of Scientific Method* (1931) and, with Ernest Nagel (1901–85), *An Introduction to Logic and Scientific Method* (1934), can fairly be said to represent the state of the art in American philosophy of science in the early 1930s.[8]

ENTER LOGICAL POSITIVISM: AMERICAN PHILOSOPHY OF SCIENCE IN THE 1930S AND 1940S

Two processes occurred in the early 1930s that altered the face of philosophy of science in the USA. First, starting in 1930 and moving with increasing momentum throughout the 1930s, the thought and the scholars associated with logical positivism moved from Europe to the USA. Second, and only partially connected with the first, a new professionalism was achieved in American philosophy of science. The principal fruit of this endeavor was the founding in 1934 of a new professional journal, *Philosophy of Science*, under the editorship of the biochemist William Malisoff, in which a community of self-described philosophers of science could interact among themselves and

---

[8] For more on M. R. Cohen, see Hollinger (1975).

with scientists. It was around the mid-1930s that American philosophy of science began to look very much like a precursor of contemporary philosophy of science in America, an explicit subdiscipline of philosophy with its own problems, methods, research community, journals, and professional organizations. Moreover, with logical empiricism arose a sensibility about the proper topics and methods of philosophy of science that, however much it may be disputed or superseded in contemporary philosophy of science, is clearly important for establishing the main lines of research in philosophy of science even up to today.

'Logical positivism' is a name we can use to refer to the philosophical projects of the Vienna Circle organized around Moritz Schlick (1882–1936) in Vienna in the mid-1920s and with associated groups, especially the Berlin philosophers around Hans Reichenbach (1891–1953).[9] The name was also coined for an American audience in a paper written by the young Vienna Circle member Herbert Feigl (1902–88), together with American recruit to the project Arthur Blumberg, that was published in *The Journal of Philosophy* in 1931 (Blumberg and Feigl 1931). Feigl was also the first Vienna Circle member—and the first logical positivist—to emigrate from Europe to the USA in advance of the rise of fascism in the German-speaking countries of Europe. Feigl arrived at the University of Iowa in 1931. By the late 1930s, logical positivism had gone from a fringe movement among scientifically oriented philosophers in middle Europe to a prominent feature of the American philosophical landscape. Émigrés to the United States included, in addition to Feigl, Gustav Bergmann (1906–87), Rudolf Carnap (1891–1970), Carl Hempel (1905–97), Hans Reichenbach, Karl Menger (1902–85), Philip Frank (1884–1966), Kurt Gödel (1906–78), and Alfred Tarski (1901–83). In the USA in the 1930s, they found a welcoming group of young American philosophers interested in logic and philosophy of science, including Charles Morris (1901–79), Ernest Nagel, and W. V. Quine (1908–2000).[10]

The logical positivism that traveled to America in the 1930s was a philosophically robust program of research. It argued that the new formal logic that had been developed by Gottlob Frege and Bertrand Russell was the proper tool for establishing a sophisticated philosophical understanding of empirical science combined with a rejection of super-empirical knowledge claims. Thus,

---

[9]   It is a contentious name. Within the project itself, it was largely superseded by Hans Reichenbach's favored term, "logical empiricism". I use "logical positivism" here because it is more common in the secondary and tertiary literature.

[10]   By far the most historically complete documentation of the Vienna Circle is Stadler (2001).

it offered an empiricist understanding of the proper scope and limits of knowledge and an epistemology trained on the successes of the empirical sciences. Moreover, that epistemology was used to reject any claims to know anything that went in principle beyond what could be known in science—giving the logical positivists a position from which to reject any non-empirical metaphysics and any ethics referring to an allegedly super-sensible realm of values. This rejection of the metaphysical is logical positivism's chief connection to historical positivism of a Machian or even Comtean vintage. All of this was presented in a technical language of formal logic which provided the logical positivists with both an epistemologically unproblematic standpoint from which to do philosophy and a means for generating detailed, technical research projects in, for example, the logic of confirmation or probabilistic inference.[11]

The philosophical vision of the logical positivists reflected the training that most of them received, which, as was common in the German-speaking world at the time, was both deeply and broadly scientific. Many of the leading logical positivists had much more training in the sciences than in philosophy; Schlick earned a Ph.D. in Physics under Max Planck in 1905. Within the sciences, with a few exceptions (such as Otto Neurath (1882–1946)), the logical positivists were much more knowledgeable about and interested in developments in mathematics and physics than those in psychology and biology, the sciences of primary interest to most of their American philosophical contemporaries. Indeed, the general features of logical positivist philosophy were largely worked out by Moritz Schlick, Hans Reichenbach, and Rudolf Carnap in a series of methodological ruminations on Albert Einstein's theory of relativity. Einstein had revealed, according to the logical positivists, that the development of exact empirical science depended upon conventional choices of the meanings of empirical terms that allowed the coordination of empirical matters of fact with pure mathematical structures. This, in turn, permitted the enunciation of laws of physics in the language of mathematics and rendered those laws empirically testable. One Einsteinian example of this was the conventional definition that Einstein used for "simultaneity of events at a distance from one another"—Einstein revealed both that some conventional choice was necessary to give this concept empirical import and the way in which the

---

[11] Much recent scholarship has been dedicated to providing a more sophisticated understanding of logical positivism than it has typically enjoyed. See especially Friedman (1999), Coffa (1991), and Richardson (1998).

choice he himself offered led to the mathematical development of the special theory of relativity.[12]

These lessons from physics were broadened into a general logical and epistemological project by the time of the mature logical positivism of the 1930s. The place of conventions in making knowledge claims possible was developed into a general framework in which the language of science was divided into the conventionally chosen meaning postulates that constituted the empirical meanings of the terms in the language and the specific empirical claims made in that language. The first were understood to be analytic truths, whose truth was due to the meanings of the non-logical vocabulary in them, while the second were understood to be synthetic claims. These terms from semantics had epistemological import—only certain meaning postulates allowed the formation of synthetic sentences that could be tested. The point of the project was to make precise the meanings of scientific claims and to show how those precise meanings gave science its robust connection to experience, while enabling a critique of metaphysics as involving empirically meaningless terms.

At its most forceful, the logical positivist project of the early 1930s echoed aspects of the view put forward by Peirce two generations earlier, claiming that the meaning of a proposition was its method of verification.[13] The verificationist period of logical positivism was brief, however, having been thoroughly critiqued within debates inside the Vienna Circle—and providing a criterion of empirical meaningfulness adequate to both explaining the successes of science and criticizing metaphysics became a project for the logical positivists. They similarly worked out in debate both in private and in print their views about the relations of the foundations of knowledge to experience in the famous "protocol sentence debate".[14]

In the 1930s and 1940s, certain essays and books by the logical positivists helped establish their philosophical project as the central one in philosophy of science, logic, and philosophy of language. Within philosophy of science,

---

[12] See Schlick (1979 [1922]) and Reichenbach (1958 [1928]). Sklar (1974) provides an excellent introduction to conventionalism regarding the metric geometry of space(-time); Friedman (1999) provides the philosophically richest account of conventionalism within the early work of the logical positivists.

[13] There was an aspect of verificiationism, as we have seen above, in Peirce's views on meaning. This was not the extent of Peirce's own account of meaning. For details and complications, see Misak (1995: 99 f.).

[14] On the protocol sentence debate, see Uebel (1992); on the liberalization of the criterion of empirical meaningfulness, see Hempel (1950, 1951) and Mormann (2007).

one can point to the publication in 1936 in *Philosophy of Science* of Carnap's important programmatic paper for the question of the empirical significance of scientific concepts, "Testability and Meaning", as well as the publication shortly thereafter of a translation (and augmentation) of his *Logical Syntax of Language* (Carnap 1936–7; 1937 [1934]). The 1930s also saw the publication of Hans Reichenbach's *Experience and Prediction* (Reichenbach 2006 [1938]). In the 1940s, the bona fides of logical positivism were further strengthened by the publication of other technically masterful but philosophically rich works such as Carl Hempel and Paul Oppenheim's "Studies in the Logic of Explanation" (1948), as well as Hempel's "Studies in the Logic of Confirmation" (Hempel 1945). These works served to illustrate the fecundity of the technical philosophy of science promoted by the logical positivists; no one interested in philosophical aspects of science in the USA could ignore them.

While the specifics of the logical positivist project were not in line with the specifics of the American pragmatism of the 1920s and 1930s, there was a kinship of scientific modernism that allowed strategic alliances to be formed. Much as did Dewey, the logical positivists subscribed to the idea that an increasingly scientized world was an increasingly rational and progressive world. This social progressive aspect of logical positivism was especially important to Otto Neurath's unity of science project. While Neurath did not himself emigrate to the United States, his *International Encyclopedia of Unified Science* was co-edited by Carnap and Morris, both of whom in the late 1930s were at the University of Chicago, and published by the University of Chicago Press. Neurath, on a visit to New York in the mid-1930s, successfully recruited Dewey to the project, for which Dewey ultimately wrote two pieces.[15]

While Dewey reluctantly permitted himself—despite many doctrinal differences between his position and those of the logical positivists—to participate in what was the main joint publishing project for the logical positivists in the USA, ambitious young American philosophers gave logical positivism a more enthusiastic reception. Indeed, but for the efforts of some of these young scholars, it would have been substantially more difficult for the logical positivists to achieve academic positions at major American universities. We have already mentioned Arthur Blumberg, whose joint work with Feigl was the first substantial introduction to logical positivism published in the

---

[15] On Neurath's life and politics see Cartwright *et al.* (1996) and Reisch (2005). On the *Encyclopedia*, see Reisch (1995, 2003). On Dewey's participation in the *Encyclopedia*, see Reisch (2005: ch. 4).

USA for American readers. Four young American philosophers in the 1930s deserve special attention in considering the reception of logical positivism in America: Charles Morris, W. V. Quine, Nelson Goodman (1906–98), and Ernest Nagel.

Charles Morris had done his Ph.D. in philosophy at Chicago in the 1920s under the last great Chicago pragmatist, George Herbert Mead. (The Chicago pragmatists were so named by William James in a review of Dewey *et al.*'s *Studies in Logical Theory*. They included Dewey, Mead, James Angell, and Adrian Moore. Dewey decamped to Columbia shortly in 1904, leaving Mead as the most central philosophical figure among the pragmatists in Chicago.[16]) After a few years at Rice University, Morris was able to secure employment at the University of Chicago in the mid-1930s. At the time, Chicago was moving increasingly in a more traditionally humanistic direction than one would have associated with the Chicago pragmatism of the early years of the twentieth century. Under the leadership of its president, Robert M. Hutchins, and the departmental leadership of Richard McKeon and Mortimore Adler, Chicago was becoming much more of a historically oriented—indeed, neo-Thomist—department. Despite this, Morris was able through his own professional activities and through a series of publications on the relations between logical positivism and American pragmatism, to secure an appointment for Rudolf Carnap at Chicago in 1936. In various essays written in the 1930s, Morris argued that American pragmatism and logical positivism were intimately related forms of "scientific empiricism" that agreed that philosophy should train its attention on the production of knowledge in the sciences and also organize itself as a scientific discipline (Morris 1937). Morris especially connected the semiotic wing of pragmatism that descended from Peirce through Mead with the logico-linguistic orientation of logical positivism. This allowed him to accept Carnap's claim that the principal topic of the philosophy of science was an investigation of the language of science while also arguing that pragmatism offered to logical positivism a neglected branch of such investigation: pragmatics, an investigation of the relations of scientific language to the users of that language. Morris first made the tripartite division between semantics, syntax, and pragmatics that Carnap came to accept and that subsequently became a canonical division not only in philosophy of language but also in linguistics. In addition to his own intellectual labors in the 1930s and 1940s, Morris did much editorial and

---

[16] See Menand (2001: 358 ff.) for more on Chicago pragmatism.

organizational work that aided logical positivism in gaining a foothold in America.[17]

W. V. Quine was the greatest American recruit to logical positivism in the 1930s. As a very young Ph.D. graduate of Harvard University in the early 1930s, Quine went on a tour of central Europe, then the leading area for research in logic. He spent some time in Vienna with the Vienna Circle, but the Circle's leading logical light, Rudolf Carnap, had already moved to Prague in 1931 to become Chair of the Philosophy of the Natural Sciences at the German university there. Thus, Quine went in 1933 to Prague, where Carnap was writing the original German version of *The Logical Syntax of Language*. Quine became a committed Carnapian, lecturing on Carnap's philosophy upon his return to Harvard in 1934 and succeeding in garnering for Carnap an honorary doctorate at the 1936 tricentennial of Harvard College.[18] Quine had been a student at Harvard of the American pragmatist epistemologist and logician C. I. Lewis and the British algebraist, logician, and metaphysician A. N. Whitehead. Quine saw Carnap's work as epistemologically in substantial agreement with Lewis's. Like Lewis, Carnap argued that a linguistic framework was not justified by experience but overlaid upon the experientially given, imposing upon the given enough structure that articulate, empirically meaningful thought becomes possible. Carnap and Lewis agreed that more than one logical system was possible, and that the choice of such a system was not a matter of empirical confirmation or disconfirmation but an entirely pragmatic matter, a matter of convenience.[19]

Quine's own logical work in the 1930s and 1940s helped establish the reputation of logical positivism as a productive movement in philosophy. Quine was one of Carnap's closest philosophical confidantes and came to see Carnap as his greatest mentor. Nonetheless, already in 1936, Quine had expressed in print some concerns with whether the notion of convention could account for the peculiar nature of logical truth (Quine 1936). As we shall see in the next section, by the early 1950s, Quine had become the most trenchant and influential critic of Carnap's account of logical truth and, with it, Carnap's very understanding of the nature of philosophy. Together with a similar trajectory away from a logic-based understanding of logical positivist philosophy of science in the work of Carl Hempel, Quine's work by the 1950s

[17] On Morris, see Reisch (1995, 2003, 2005).

[18] Quine's lectures on Carnap are in Creath 1990: 47–103.

[19] For more detail on Quine's life, see Quine (1985, 1986). The secondary literature on Quine is vast; Gibson (2004) serves as a good point of entry.

became emblematic of an internal critique of the presuppositions of logical positivist philosophy of science and helped usher in a new era in American philosophy of science.

Quine's slightly younger Harvard colleague Nelson Goodman may have been the first significant American philosopher to take up some of the work of the logical positivists in his dissertation research. Goodman's dissertation, in part, examined and criticized the construction of the physical world from the elements of sensation as it was presented in Carnap's *Logischer Aufbau der Welt* (Carnap 1967 [1928]).[20] His work brought to light some of the technical difficulties inherent in the attempt to use the tools of formal logic to account for knowledge of the external world. In addition to this work, Goodman also collaborated with Quine in the late 1930s in an attempt to construct a nominalist understanding of mathematics that would allow an empiricist to embrace how classical mathematics is used in science (Quine and Goodman 1940). Goodman and Quine's ontological concerns were at the heart of discussions among them, Carnap, Tarski, Russell, and Feigl during the academic year 1940–1 when they all spent at least part of the year at Harvard (Frost-Arnold 2007).

Ernest Nagel was in the 1930s one of the few young American philosophers who, through the mediation of Cohen, was attempting to further something like the historical and technical aspects of Peirce's philosophy of science. Nagel had done significant work in the foundations of probability theory in the 1930s and, thus, was one of the few American philosophers with the technical competence to comment upon the work on the foundations of the theory of probability and the place of probability in the sciences by Hans Reichenbach. Morris and Carnap ultimately recruited Nagel to write the monograph on probability theory in the *International Encyclopedia of Unified Science* (Nagel 1939). Nagel's philosophical trajectory seems to have been something of the opposite of Quine's. Whereas he was in the 1930s someone of technical competence, he also had very broad historical interests and, in line with his sympathy for pragmatism, a generally naturalist philosophical project. His magnum opus of 1961, however, *The Structure of Science* (Nagel 1961) has been understood as something of a monument to the formalist philosophy of science that logical positivism had made canonical; the book

---

[20] The dissertation is Goodman (1990 [1941]); it became the core of his influential book, Goodman 1951. Goodman (1963) gives his account of the philosophical significance of Carnap's *Aufbau*.

helped make some topics, such as intertheoretical reduction, into central topics of such a technical philosophy of science.

While logical positivism was in the 1930s busy establishing itself in the New World, there were some American philosophers who were busy establishing the discipline of philosophy of science as a going concern in their home country. The most interesting and successful group of such American philosophers were centered at the University of Pennsylvania around the elder statesman for American philosophy of science at the time, Edgar Singer. Singer had been trained as an engineer and, as we have noted, had been teaching courses in philosophy of science at Penn for forty years by the time the mid-1930s rolled around. He viewed himself as a pragmatist, but of a hard-edged quantitative scientific bent (Butts 2000). His students in the 1930s, such as C. Westman and Russell Ackoff, were interested in topics such as the logic of experimental inference (Churchman 1948; Churchman and Ackoff 1950). He had strong professional relations with scientists. It was this group around Singer who established the journal *Philosophy of Science* and the Philosophy of Science Association, which was at the time a subscription society for the journal. The journal was first under the editorship of Singer's student and colleague William Malisoff and then edited by a series of students of Singer—Churchman, Richard Rudner, Robert Butts. While the logical positivists certainly published prominently in the journal, they did not dominate the editorial board or the pages of the journal. The first editorial and advisory boards for the journal contained roughly fifty philosophers of science, scientists, and other scholars. It included biologists such as H. J. Muller, R. A. Fisher, J. B. S. Haldane, T. H. Morgan, and Sewell Wright; physicists such as Henry Margenau, Percy Bridgman, and E. Wigner; psychologists such as Wolfgang Köhler and R. C. Tolman; as well as historians of science and mathematics such as E. T. Bell and George Sarton. Two logical positivists (Carnap and Feigl) were on the editorial board; Reichenbach and Moritz Schlick were on the advisory board. Other American philosophers on the boards included Blumberg, Cohen, A. O. Lovejoy, W. P. Montague, Singer, and Paul Weiss.

The contents of the early volumes also indicate the eclectic nature of the journal, which featured important essays by the logical positivists (including essays by Carnap and Feigl to lead off volume 1, number 1) but also many essays from many different philosophical and scientific points of view. Malisoff remarks on this breadth in his introduction to the first issue, appending these comments to a series of quotations about philosophy of science that expressed very different points of view:

In our group we have representatives of practically all the shades of opinion suggested by the quotations—radicals, progressives, a few tried veterans of established philosophic fashion, but no reactionaries—a coalition dominated by the unorthodox. In style we allow the greatest latitude.... In content we require accuracy, thoroughness, and rigor—in the fashion of a research journal.   (Malisoff 1934: 3)

He then provides the following tentative and personal listing of of subject headings for a program of research in philosophy of science (1934: 3–4):

1. Studies in the analysis of meaning, definition, symbolism.
2. Studies in presuppositions—axioms, postulates, maxims.
3. Studies in method.
4. Studies in the nature and formulation of theoretical principles.
5. Studies in the structure of the sciences, their hierarchies.
6. Studies in the function and significance of science within various contexts.

This list of topics is not at all inconsistent with the vision of logical empiricism, but in both principle and practice was more wide-ranging. Many of the essays in the early issues were principally advances in scientific concept formation or elucidation of explanatory problems offered by scientists for their science; this begins in the first issue with an essay on "Indeterminism and Natural Selection" by Fisher (1934). Many of the essays, especially those by scientists such as Margenau, would have been considered too metaphysical by the logical positivists.

Arguably, the most important contributions to philosophy among Americans at this time were by scientists. Indeed, the single most significant contribution to philosophy of science in the 1920s and 1930s among the Americans was the operationalism promoted by Bridgman (1927), which also found favor among other American scientists, especially behaviorist psychologists like B. F. Skinner and S. S. Stevens. Operationalism is close kin to verificationist lessons about scientific concepts in both logical positivism and American pragmatism, but was mainly a contribution to proper empirical control of theorizing by scientists for scientists. The rich interaction between working scientists and philosophers of science at this time period is well represented in the pages of the journal.[21]

---

[21] On Bridgman, see Holton (1993); on Stevens and operationalism, see Hardcastle (1995).

A TALE OF TWO DOGMAS: AMERICAN PHILOSOPHY OF SCIENCE IN THE 1950S AND 1960S

The 1950s were the best of times and the worst of times in the life of logical positivism. In many ways, the project was still attaining its canonical status as the central project in American philosophy of science in that decade. Many of the greatest works in the logical positivist *œuvre* were published or translated in the 1950s; these include Carnap's *Logical Foundations of Probability Theory* and his "Empiricism, Semantics, and Ontology" (Carnap 1950a, 1950b), Reichenbach's *The Direction of Time* and *The Philosophy of Space and Time* (Reichenbach 1956; 1958 [1928]), and Hempel's *Fundamentals of Concept Formation in Empirical Science* (Hempel 1952). Moreover, especially through the efforts of Herbert Feigl, logical positivism was the central focus of teaching anthologies and book series. Logical positivism was at the core of Feigl's anthology, jointly edited with Wilfrid Sellars, *Readings in Philosophical Analysis* (Feigl and Sellars 1949), and his anthology, jointly edited with May Brodbeck, *Readings in the Philosophy of Science* (Feigl and Brodbeck 1953). These anthologies became central in graduate training in analytic philosophy and philosophy of science in the USA in the 1950s and 1960s. Feigl's Minnesota Center for Philosophy of Science began publishing volumes of the series Minnesota Studies in the Philosophy of Science in 1956, again with the logical positivists very well represented. In addition to these newer projects, Carnap and Morris continued to edit the *International Encyclopedia of Unified Science* in the 1950s, even though it was vastly scaled back from original plans. Moreover, it was not just the émigré scholars associated with logical positivism that put logical positivism at the center of teaching in analytic philosophy—logical positivism, especially the work of Carnap and Reichenbach, is second only to the work of Bertrand Russell as focus of Arthur Pap's textbook *Elements of Analytic Philosophy* (Pap 1949), for example. The decade ended with the publication of A. J. Ayer's influential anthology *Logical Positivism* (Ayer 1959).

Moreover, it was at this time that logical positivism was clearly beginning to shape the advanced training of a younger generation of scholars. Reichenbach's doctoral students in this period included important philosophers of science such as Hilary Putnam and Wesley Salmon. Carnap's students included

Richard Jeffrey, Howard Stein, and Abner Shimony. Frank's group at Boston recruited philosophers of science such as Robert S. Cohen and Marx Wartofsky (and historians of science such as Gerald Holton). A young generation of technical philosophers of physics such as Adolf Grünbaum, Shimony, and Stein were students of logical positivists and inspired by other logical positivists. These students became leaders in philosophy of science; several of them are still active leaders in the field today.

Notwithstanding all this positive activity, the 1950s was also a time in which the account of the philosophy offered by the logical positivists was subjected to searching criticism. In Britain, a decidedly less formal and less scientifically inclined version of analytic philosophy was advanced by the late Wittgenstein and his students at Cambridge as well as by the ordinary language philosophers at Oxford. In the USA, some of the figures most associated with logical positivism began to offer highly influential internal criticisms with wide-ranging consequences. The most important critical pieces were written by W. V. Quine and Carl Hempel in the early 1950s. Quine's "Two Dogmas of Empiricism" (Quine 1951) argued that the division between analytic and synthetic sentences crucial to logical positivist understanding of the methods of science and their whole conception of philosophy as "the logic of science" could not be maintained. For Quine the lessons were that empiricism had to become naturalistic (studying how in fact people like us learned things like science), and that the strict distinction between science and metaphysics offered by the logical positivists could not be maintained. No essay was more central in altering analytic philosophy's sense of its projects and alternatives than was this one by Quine. In a similar fashion, Carl Hempel wrote articles in the early 1950s in which he maintained that the logical positivist criterion of empirical significance could not be drawn using the logical tools of logical positivists or with the consequences for securing science without metaphysics that the logical positivists desired (Hempel 1950, 1951). Hempel's arguments and the lessons he drew from them were in substantial agreement with Quine's and indicated that some of the central features of logical positivist philosophy of science could no longer gain universal support even among those sympathetic to it.

Throughout the 1950s and into the 1960s, alternative projects in American philosophy of science were also being developed. Whereas according to logical positivism metaphysical issues such as the reality of theoretical posits in science were considered pseudo-problems, several philosophers of science in the 1950s and 1960s began arguing for a form of scientific realism. Often the argument took the form of meta-abduction about science, that only scientific realism could explain the progress of science. In the American context, forms of scientific realism were prominently offered by, for example, Wilfrid Sellars (1967) and Hilary Putnam (1965).

Even more important for the development of non-positivist philosophy of science in the 1950s and early 1960s were theorists who argued that, for various reasons, philosophy of science had to be more informed by history of science than it had been for the logical positivists. One American example of this sort of argument was offered by N. R. Hanson, who wanted to bring back the question of the processes of scientific discovery as a proper topic of philosophical concern (Hanson 1958). In so doing, Hanson drew on history of science but also on a number of scientific and philosophical projects that were off limits to the logical positivists, including late Wittgensteinian philosophical analysis and Gestalt psychology. The most searching example of this sort of argument, however, was offered within the confines of the *International Encyclopedia of Unified Science* itself, when, in 1962, Thomas Kuhn's *The Structure of Scientific Revolutions* (Kuhn 1996 [1962]) appeared under the *Encyclopedia*'s auspices.[22] Kuhn himself and his early reviewers understood that the "image of science by which we are possessed" (Kuhn 1996 [1962]: 1), against which he argued, was given its most prominent philosophical voice in the work of the logical positivists. In this work, which became the most famous and influential work in philosophy of science in the second half of the twentieth century, Kuhn argued that the principal task of philosophy of science was to explain the historical development of science, a development that was at odds, so Kuhn argued, with a simple progressivist or accumulationist account. Kuhn's problem of the rational development of science across revolutionary changes and his vision of a thoroughly historically informed philosophy of science fundamentally altered the field's sense of its central problems and methods.

One further significant problem for logical positivist philosophy of science was raised in the 1960s, when a group of formally minded philosophers began to argue against the specific conception of scientific theories as axiom systems that was canonical in logical positivism (Suppe 1974). These philosophers argued that this was the incorrect formal understanding of theories, which

---

[22] On the publication history of Kuhn's book, see Reisch (1991). On Kuhn's relations to logical positivism more generally, see Earman (1993), Friedman (1993, 2003), Irzik and Grünberg (1995), and Richardson (2007).

ought to be understood rather as sets of models that are sometimes, but not always, described by propositional structures. The most essential formal tool for philosophy of science is not, according to this model-theoretic or semantic view of theories, syntax or proof theory, but semantics or model theory. Taken altogether, one can say that by the late 1960s logical positivist philosophy of science had been importantly argued against regarding its technical methods, its sense of the central philosophical questions about science, and its philosophical ambitions. If not refuted, logical positivism had by 1970 become widely perceived as decisively superseded.

Even when philosophers of science took up explicit themes from logical positivist work, their results led them to reject the views of the logical positivists. For example, Wesley Salmon's work on scientific explanation, especially within the context of statistical and probabilistic theories, was instrumental in leading to a rejection of the logic-based accounts of explanation offered by Hempel in favor of more metaphysically robust causal alternatives (Salmon 1971, 1978). Similarly, technical work on the logic of decision and confirmation theory by figures such as Jeffrey (1965) and Henry Kyburg (1961) pointed beyond the logic of confirmation offered in the work of Carnap. Perhaps most famously, Nelson Goodman's work on the problem of induction led to a widespread conviction that logical relations alone could not account for either the notion of a scientific law or the relation of confirmation of laws by empirical evidence (Goodman 1965 [1955]).

This important development took place against an evolving professional background. Programs and centers in philosophy of science or history and philosophy of science were being established at leading institutions such as Pittsburgh, Indiana, Boston, and Minnesota. The journal *Philosophy of Science* was increasingly pitched to a professional research community in philosophy of science; as Don Howard (2003) has detailed, the number of important works in sociology and history of science and in values and science as well as essays and editorial work by scientists in the journal decreased markedly through the 1950s. The Philosophy of Science Association increased its activity throughout this period, holding meetings with the American Association for the Advancement of Science (Section L) in the 1950s, eventually holding its first stand-alone biennial meeting in 1968. The Boston Colloquium for the Philosophy of Science began around 1960, followed by the publication series Boston Studies in the Philosophy of Science, from 1962. Thus, philosophy of science became an increasingly professionalized, but also isolated, research community in philosophy just as that community's sense of a unified philosophical project was decreasing. Moreover, the first generation of logical positivist philosophers was aging and dying—Reichenbach died in 1953; Frank retired in the mid-1950s and died in 1966; Carnap retired in the 1960s and died in 1970. Of the original émigré community, only Hempel and Feigl were actively engaged in philosophy of science into the 1970s.

POST-POSITIVIST PHILOSOPHY OF SCIENCE IN AMERICA AFTER 1970

Thomas Kuhn's *Structure of Scientific Revolutions* is one of the most influential and widely cited works in the humanities in the twentieth century. While professional philosophers of science were often not convinced by Kuhn's arguments, the work ultimately succeeded in altering the landscape of philosophy of science. Kuhn's historical concerns transformed the main epistemological topic in philosophy of science from confirmation or disconfirmation of scientific theories to the dynamics of theory change in science. His vision of normal science punctuated by seemingly irrational periods of revolutionary change made issues of conceptual change and the possibility of historically invariant canons of rationality key issues for philosophy of science. His views—along with those of his colleague at Berkeley in the 1950s, Paul Feyerabend—on incommensurability raised the possibility that no global story of rational progress in science was possible.[23] Moreover, Kuhn's ways of specifying incommensurability, which became increasingly less practice-oriented and more language-oriented, brought philosophy of science into greater contact with new views in philosophy of language developed in the 1970s by philosophers such as Saul Kripke (1972) and Hilary Putnam (1975).

Kuhn's work also brought in its wake a number of projects in sociology and cultural studies of science (as well as in non-standard philosophy of science, especially in the later work of Feyerabend) that philosophers of science usually understood as attempts to debunk the authority of science, attempts to claim that science was not objective, not reliable, and not privileged compared with

---

[23] Feyerabend's early views on incommensurability were expressed in Feyerabend (1965).

other "ways of knowing".[24] Advocates of such projects sometimes delighted in tweaking the noses of philosophers of science, who, in turn, delighted in decrying the irrationalism of such projects and defending the virtue of science.[25] Kuhn's work had already been, in the radical era of the 1960s, often associated with very different work that was critical of science and technology, such as the critical theory of Herbert Marcuse (1964). For his impact on liberalizing of critical perspectives and the tools of philosophical analysis of science, as well as in his specific claims about temporally bounded paradigms giving structure to scientific work, Kuhn was important also for early feminist philosophers of science such as Sandra Harding's standpoint theory (Harding 1986).

Moreover, given their vociferous response to Kuhn and their attempts to offer a different account of the historical development of science, Karl Popper, Imre Lakatos, and their philosophical followers in Britain became more important figures in the philosophical landscape in the late 1960s and throughout the 1970s.[26] Attempts in the 1970s at a more historically informed philosophy of science were issued on American shores, also; the most prominent American contributors to such attempts were Dudley Shapere (1965, 1980) and Larry Laudan (1977). This period became one of (only in part fruitful) interchange between philosophers and historians of science, with philosophers of science (cf. Lakatos and Zahar 1976; Zahar 1973) at times presenting historical cases as tests of various philosophies of science in the field.

With prominent exceptions, especially the work of Clark Glymour (1980) as well as various Bayesian accounts of scientific theory confirmation, by the late 1970s and into the 1980s, the response of more technically minded philosophers of science in the USA to the large-scale changes being wrought by attacks on logical positivism was to go local. High-level technical work proceeded apace in fields such as philosophy of quantum theory and

[24] The sociological project that philosophers, and ultimately also Kuhn himself, found most objectionable was the "strong programme"—see Barnes and Bloor (1982); for its relations to Kuhn, see Barnes (1982). Feyerabend's "anarchist" views in theory of scientific knowledge were expressed in Feyerabend (1975).

[25] Barnes (1974) is an example of delight in dismissing the concerns of philosophy in the name of relativism and skepticism.

[26] Popper had, of course, been well known since the 1930s, but his magnum opus in philosophy of science, *The Logic of Scientific Discovery* of 1934, was not translated until 1959. The early intervention of the Popperians in objecting to Kuhn was a 1965 conference on Kuhn's work later published as Lakatos and Musgrave (1970). Lakatos (1970) offered a different historical philosophy of science from Kuhn's.

philosophy of space-time physics; in the 1970s, fields like philosophy of biology and philosophy of psychology came to be well established. Relatively moribund fields like philosophy of history and philosophy of social science seemed to draw new life in the 1970s from explicit rejections of Carl Hempel's account of historical explanation or Ernest Nagel's rejection of functionalism in social science.

General philosophy of science did not disappear, of course. Bas van Fraassen's *The Scientific Image* (1980) attempted to provide a new empiricism in philosophy of science wedded to a semantic conception of theories and a pragmatic account of explanation. Other work in the 1980s introduced important concern with experimental practice (Hacking 1983), with idealization in science (Cartwright 1983), with the varieties of scientific representation (Giere 1988), and with the variety of evidential standards and practices in the sciences (Keller 1983). The consequence of such work was again specialization, as philosophers began to look in more detail at specific episodes in scientific theory construction or experimental or other evidentiary practice. If there were larger projects in the 1980s and into the 1990s that philosophers of science signed on to, they were highly programmatic. Giere (1985) and Philip Kitcher (1991) were prominent in following Quine and calling for *naturalized* philosophy of science—although no standard account of what naturalizing amounts to has been accepted. Kitcher (1990, 1993), Giere (1988), David Hull (1988), and Helen Longino (1990) were prominent in calling for a more social philosophy of science in which the social aspect of science is seen not as calling into question the rationality of science but as explaining it. Again, philosophers sympathetic to this view have not come to substantial agreement on what a socialized philosophy of science is committed to, or on how such a philosophy of science relates to sociology of science. A prominent movement inspired by the work of Hacking, Cartwright, Giere, and Longino has focused on the disunity of science; philosophers here attempt to come to terms with the varieties of scientific practice and modes of scientific representation and the consequences of the multiplicity of such practices for general claims about, for example, scientific realism or "the nature" of scientific explanation (Galison and Stump 1996; Kellert *et al.* 2006).

In consequence, philosophy of science has wide scope and a variety of different foci today. Almost all of the projects continue to have some reference back to the days of logical positivism, if only to distinguish themselves from it. In addition to esoteric projects in the philosophy of the special sciences, there are prominent general projects in naturalized philosophy of science, social philosophy of science, the semantic conception of theories, the disunity of science, feminist theories of science—these projects often colliding or overlapping in interesting ways. Moreover, there is now a robust project in history of philosophy of science, one that has had an important impact on accounts of the proper topics of philosophy of science offered by leading figures in the field today such as Michael Friedman (2001) and Bas van Fraassen (2002). It is an era of eclecticism and detail work in philosophy of science, an era in which each philosopher of science can find interesting issues to work on, but in which a coherent overall sense of the importance of thinking philosophically about science is largely absent.

References

Ayer, Alfred Jules (1959). *Logical Positivism*. New York: The Free Press.

Barnes, Barry (1974). *Scientific Knowledge and Sociological Theory*. London: Routledge & Kegan Paul.

—— (1982). *T. S. Kuhn and Social Science*. London: Macmillan.

—— and Bloor, David (1982). "Relativism, Rationalism, and the Sociology of Knowledge". In M. Hollis and S. Lukes (eds.), *Rationality and Relativism*, Oxford: Blackwell, 21–47.

Blumberg, Albert E., and Feigl, Herbert (1931). "Logical Positivism: A New Movement in European Philosophy". *The Journal of Philosophy*, 28: 281–96.

Bridgman, Percy W. (1927). *The Logic of Modern Physics*. New York: Macmillan.

Butts, Robert E. (2000). "The Reception of German Scientific Philosophy in North America: 1930–1965". In *Witches, Scientists, Philosophers: Essays and Lectures*, Dordrecht: Kluwer, 193–204.

Campbell, James (2006). *A Thoughtful Profession: The Early Years of the American Philosophical Association*. Chicago: Open Court.

Carnap, Rudolf (1967 [1928]). *The Logical Structure of the World*, trans. R. George. Berkeley and Los Angeles: University of California Press.

—— (1936–7). "Testability and Meaning". *Philosophy of Science*, 3: 419–71; 4: 1–40.

—— (1937 [1934]). *The Logical Syntax of Language*, trans. A. Smeaton. London: Kegan Paul.

—— (1950a). "Empiricism, Semantics, and Ontology". *Revue Internationale de Philosophie*, 11: 20–40.

—— (1950b). *Logical Foundations of Probability*, 2nd edn. 1962. Chicago: University of Chicago Press.

Cartwright, Nancy (1983). *How the Laws of Physics Lie*. Oxford: Oxford University Press.

_____ Cat, Jordi, Fleck, Lola, and Uebel, Thomas E. (1996). *Otto Neurath: Philosophy between Science and Politics*. Cambridge: Cambridge University Press.

Carus, Paul (1913*a*). *The Mechanistic Principle and the Non-Mechanical*. Chicago: Open Court.

_____ (1913*b*). *The Principle of Relativity in the Light of the Philosophy of Science*. Chicago: Open Court.

Churchman, C. West (1948). *Theory of Experimental Inference*. New York: Macmillan.

_____ and Ackoff, Russell (1950). *Methods of Inquiry: An Introduction to Philosophy and Scientific Method*. St Louis, MO: Educational Publishers.

Coffa, J. Alberto (1991). *The Semantic Tradition from Kant to Carnap: To the Vienna Station*, ed. L. Wessels. Cambridge: Cambridge University Press.

Cohen, I. B. (1990). *Benjamin Franklin's Science*. Cambridge, MA: Harvard University Press.

Cohen, Morris Raphael (1931). *Reason and Nature: The Meaning of Scientific Method*. Glencoe, IL: The Free Press.

_____ (1949 [1940]). "Some Difficulties in John Dewey's Anthropocentric Naturalism". In *Studies in Philosophy and Science*, New York: Henry Holt and Company, 139–75.

_____ and Nagel, Ernest (1934). *An Introduction to Logic and Scientific Method*. London: Routledge & Kegan Paul.

Colden, Cadwallader (1751). *The Principles of Action in Matter, the Gravitation of Bodies, and the Motion of the Planets, Explained from Those Principles*. London: R. Dodsley.

Creath, Richard (ed.) (1990). *Dear Carnap, Dear Van: The Quine–Carnap Correspondence and Related Work*. Berkeley and Los Angeles: University of California Press.

Dewey, John (1982 [1920]). *Reconstruction in Philosophy*. In *John Dewey: The Middle Works, 1899–1924*, xii. Carbondale and Edwardsville: Southern Illinois University Press.

_____ (1984 [1927]). *The Public and Its Problems*. In *John Dewey: The Later Works, 1925–1953*, ii. Carbondale and Edwardsville: Southern Illinois University Press.

_____ (1986 [1938]). *Logic: The Theory of Inquiry*. In *John Dewey: The Later Works, 1925–1953*, xii. Carbondale and Edwardsville: Southern Illinois University Press.

Earman, John (1993). "Carnap, Kuhn, and the Philosophy of Scientific Methodology". In P. Horwich (ed.), *World Changes: Thomas Kuhn and the Nature of Science*, Cambridge, MA: MIT Press, 9–36.

Emerson, Ralph Waldo (1983 [1837]). "The American Scholar". In *Essays and Lectures*, New York: Library of America, i. 51–71.

Feigl, Herbert, and Brodbeck, May (1953). *Readings in the Philosophy of Science*. New York: Appleton-Century-Croft.

Feigl, Herbert, and Sellars, Wilfrid (1949). *Readings in Philosophical Analysis*. New York: Appleton-Century-Croft.

Feyerabend, Paul K. (1965). "On the 'Meaning' of Scientific Terms". *Journal of Philosophy*, 62: 266–74.

—— (1975). *Against Method*. London: New Left Books.

Fisher, R. A. (1934). "Indeterminism and Natural Selection". *Philosophy of Science*, 1: 99–117.

Friedman, Michael (1993). "Remarks on the History of Science and the History of Philosophy". In P. Horwich (ed.), *World Changes: Thomas Kuhn and the Nature of Science*, Cambridge, MA: MIT Press, 37–54.

—— (1999). *Reconsidering Logical Positivism*. Cambridge: Cambridge University Press.

—— (2001). *Dynamics of Reason: The 1999 Kant Lectures at Stanford University*. Stanford: CSLI.

—— (2003). "Kuhn and Logical Empiricism". In T. Nickles (ed.), *Thomas Kuhn*, Cambridge: Cambridge University Press, 19–44.

Frost-Arnold, Greg (2007). "Carnap, Tarski, and Quine's Year Together: Discussions of Logic, Science, and Mathematics" (unpublished Ph.D. dissertation, University of Pittsburgh).

Galison, Peter, and Stump, David (1996). *The Disunity of Science: Boundaries, Contexts, and Power*. Stanford, CA: Stanford University Press.

Gibson, Roger F. (ed.) (2004). *The Cambridge Companion to Quine*. Cambridge: Cambridge University Press.

Giere, Ronald N. (1985). "Philosophy of Science Naturalized". *Philosophy of Science*, 52: 331–56.

—— (1988). *Explaining Science: A Cognitive Approach*. Chicago: University of Chicago Press.

Glymour, Clark (1980). *Theory and Evidence*. Princeton: Princeton University Press.

Goodman, Nelson (1990 [1941]). *A Study of Qualities*. New York: Garland.

—— (1951). *The Structure of Appearance*. Cambridge, MA: Harvard University Press.

—— (1965 [1955]). *Fact, Fiction, and Forecast*, 2nd edn. London: Athlone Press; Indianapolis: Bobbs-Merrill Co.

—— (1963). "The Significance of *Der logische Aufbau der Welt*". In P. A. Schilpp (ed.), *The Philosophy of Rudolf Carnap*, Chicago: Open Court, 545–58.

Hacking, Ian (1983). *Representing and Intervening*. Cambridge: Cambridge University Press.

Hanson, Norwood Russell (1958). *Patterns of Discovery*. Cambridge: Cambridge University Press.

Hardcastle, Gary L. (1995). "S. S. Stevens and the Origins of Operationalism". *Philosophy of Science*, 62: 404–24.

Harding, Sandra (1986). *The Science Question in Feminism*. Ithaca, NY: Cornell University Press.

Hatfield, Gary (2002). "Psychology, Philosophy, and Cognitive Science: Reflections on the History and Philosophy of Experimental Psychology". *Mind and Language*, 17: 207–32.

Hayes, Kevin J. (2003). "Cadwallader Colden". In P. B. Dematteis and L. B. McHenry (eds.), *American Philosophers before 1945*, The Dictionary of Literary Biography, 270, Farmington Hills, MI: The Gale Group, 49–55.

Hempel, Carl G. (1945). "Studies in the Logic of Confirmation". *Mind*, 54: 1–26, 97–121.

_____ (1950). "Problems and Changes in the Empiricist Criterion of Meaning". *Revue Internationale de Philosophie*, 11: 41–63.

_____ (1951). "The Concept of Cognitive Significance: A Reconsideration". *Proceedings of the American Academy of Arts and Sciences*, 80: 61–77.

_____ (1952). *Fundamentals of Concept Formation in Empirical Science. International Encyclopedia of Unified Science*, ii, no. 7. Chicago: University of Chicago Press.

_____ and Oppenheim, Paul (1948). "Studies in the Logic of Explanation". *Philosophy of Science*, 15: 135–75.

Henderson, Harold (1993). *Catalyst for Controversy: Paul Carus of Open Court*. Carbondale and Edwardsville: Southern Illinois University Press.

Hollinger, David A. (1975). *Morris R. Cohen and the Scientific Ideal*. Cambridge, MA: MIT Press.

Holton, Gerald J. (1993). "A Personal View of Percy W. Bridgman, Physicist and Philosopher". *Methodology and Science*, 26: 1–5.

Howard, Don (2003). "Two Left Turns Make a Right: On the Curious Political Career of North American Philosophy of Science at Midcentury". In G. L. Hardcastle and A. W. Richardson (eds.), *Logical Empiricism in North America*, Minneapolis: University of Minnesota Press, 25–93.

Hull, David (1988). *Science as a Process: An Evolutionary Account of the Social and Conceptual Development of Science*. Chicago: University of Chicago Press.

Ingersoll, Charles J. (1946 [1823]). "The Influence of America on the Mind". In J. L. Blau (ed.), *American Philosophical Addresses, 1700–1900*, New York: Columbia University Press, 20–59.

Irzik, Gürol, and Grünberg, T. (1995). "Carnap and Kuhn: Arch Enemies or Close Allies?" *British Journal for the Philosophy of Science*, 46: 285–307.

James, William (1983 [1891]). *The Principles of Psychology*. Cambridge, MA: Harvard University Press.

Jeffrey, Richard C. (1965). *The Logic of Decision*, 2nd edn. 1983. Chicago: University of Chicago Press.

Keller, Evelyn Fox (1983). *A Feeling for the Organism: The Life and Work of Barbara McClintock*. New York: W. H. Freeman.

Kellert, Stephen H., Longino, Helen E., and Waters, C. Kenneth (eds.) (2006). *Scientific Pluralism*. Minneapolis: University of Minnesota Press.

Kitcher, Philip (1990). "The Division of Cognitive Labor". *The Journal of Philosophy*, 87: 5–22.

Kitcher, Philip (1991). "The Naturalists Return". *The Philosophical Review*, 101: 53–114.

—— (1993). *The Advancement of Science*. Oxford: Oxford University Press.

Kripke, Saul (1972). *Naming and Necessity*. Cambridge, MA: Harvard University Press.

Kuhn, Thomas S. (1996 [1962]). "The Structure of Scientific Revolutions". *International Encyclopedia of Unified Science*, ii, no. 2, 3rd edn. Chicago: University of Chicago Press.

Kuklick, Bruce (2001). *A History of American Philosophy, 1720–2000*. Oxford: Oxford University Press.

Kyburg, Henry (1961). *Probability and the Logic of Rational Belief*. Middletown, CT: Wesleyan University Press.

Lakatos, Imre (1970). "Falsification and the Methodology of Scientific Research Programmes". In Lakatos and Musgrave (1970), 91–196.

—— and Musgrave, Alan (eds.) (1970). *Criticism and the Growth of Knowledge*. Cambridge: Cambridge University Press.

—— and Zahar, Elie (1976). "Why did Copernicus's Programme Supersede Ptolemy's?" In R. Westman, *The Copernican Achievement*, Los Angeles: University of California Press, 354–83.

Laudan, Larry (1977). *Progress and Its Problems*. Los Angeles: University of California Press.

Longino, Helen E. (1990). *Science as Social Knowledge: Values and Objectivity in Scientific Inquiry*. Princeton: Princeton University Press.

Malisoff, William M. (1934). "What is Philosophy of Science". *Philosophy of Science*, 1: 1–4.

Marcuse, Herbert (1964). *One-Dimensional Man: Studies in the Ideology of Advanced Industrial Society*. Boston: Beacon Press.

McCosh, James (1886). *Psychology*. London: Macmillan.

Menand, Louis (2001). *The Metaphysical Club: A Story of Ideas in America*. New York: Farrar, Straus, and Giroux.

Misak, Cheryl (1995). *Verificationism: Its History and Prospects*. London: Routledge.

Mormann, Thomas (2007). "The Structure of Scientific Theories in Logical Empiricism". In A. Richardson and T. Uebel (eds.), *The Cambridge Companion to Logical Empiricism*, Cambridge: Cambridge University Press, 136–62.

Morris, Charles (1937). *Logical Positivism, Pragmatism, and Scientific Empiricism*. Paris: Hermann.

Nagel, Ernest (1939). "Principles of the Theory of Probability". *International Encyclopedia of Unified Science*, i, no. 6. Chicago: University of Chicago Press.

—— (1961). *The Structure of Science*. New York: Harcourt, Brace, and World.

Newton, Isaac (1999 [1686]). *Principia Mathematica Philosophiae Naturalis*, trans. I. B. Cohen and A. M. Whitman. Berkeley and Los Angeles: University of California Press.

Pap, Arthur (1949). *Elements of Analytic Philosophy*. New York: Macmillan.

Peirce, Charles S. (1931–58). *Collected Papers of Charles S. Peirce*, i–vi, ed. C. Hartshorne and P. Weiss; vii–viii, ed. A. Burks. Cambridge, MA: Belknap Press.

_____ (1982–). *The Writings of Charles S. Peirce: A Chronological Edition*, ed. E. Moore. Bloomington, IN: Indiana University Press.

Poe, Edgar Allan (2004 [1848]). *Eureka*, ed. S. Levine and S. F. Levine. Urbana, IL: University of Illinois Press.

Popper, Karl (1959 [1934]). *The Logic of Scientific Discovery*. New York: Basic Books.

Porter, Noah (1868). *The Human Intellect; with an Introduction upon Psychology and the Soul*. New York: Charles Scribner.

Putnam, Hilary (1965). "How Not to Talk about Meaning." In R. S. Cohen and M. Wartofsky (eds.), *In Honor of Philipp Frank*, New York: Humanities Press, 205–22.

_____ (1975). "The Meaning of 'Meaning'". In K. Gunderson (ed.), *Language, Mind, and Knowledge*, Minneapolis: University of Minnesota Press, 131–93.

Quine, Willard van Orman (1936). "Truth by Convention". In O. H. Lee (ed.), *Philosophical Essays for A. N. Whitehead*, New York: Longmans, 90–124.

_____ (1951). "Two Dogmas of Empiricism". *Philosophical Review*, 60: 20–43.

_____ (1985). *The Time of My Life*. Cambridge, MA: MIT Press.

_____ (1986). "Autobiography of W. V. Quine". In L. E. Hahn and P. A. Schilpp (eds.), *The Philosophy of W. V. Quine*, Chicago: Open Court, 3–46.

_____ and Goodman, Nelson (1940). "Elimination of Extra-logical Postulates". *Journal of Symbolic Logic*, 5: 104–9.

Reichenbach, Hans (1958 [1928]). *The Philosophy of Space and Time*, trans. M. Reichenbach and J. Freund. New York: Dover.

_____ (2006 [1938]). *Experience and Prediction*. South Bend, IN: Notre Dame University Press.

_____ (1956). *The Direction of Time*. Berkeley and Los Angeles: University of California Press.

Reisch, George A. (1991). "Did Kuhn Kill Logical Empiricism?". *Philosophy of Science*, 58: 264–77.

_____ (1995). "A History of the *International Encyclopedia of Unified Science*" (unpublished Ph.D. dissertation, University of Chicago).

_____ (2003). "Disunity in the International Encyclopedia". In G. L. Hardcastle and A. W. Richardson, *Logical Empiricism in North America*, Minneapolis: University of Minnesota Press, 197–215.

_____ (2005). *How the Cold War Transformed Philosophy of Science: To the Icy Slopes of Logic*. Cambridge: Cambridge University Press.

Richardson, Alan (1998). *Carnap's Construction of the World: The* Aufbau *and the Emergence of Logical Empiricism*. Cambridge: Cambridge University Press.

_____ (2007). " 'That Sort of Everyday Image of Logical Positivism': Thomas Kuhn and the Decline of Logical Empiricist Philosophy of Science". In A. Richardson and T. Uebel (eds.), *The Cambridge Companion to Logical Empiricism*, Cambridge: Cambridge University Press, 346–69.

Rush, Benjamin (1946 [1786]). "The Influence of Physical Causes on the Moral Faculty". In J. L. Blau (ed.), *American Philosophical Addresses, 1700–1900*, New York: Columbia University Press, 315–43.

Salmon, Wesley C. (1971). *Statistical Explanation and Statistical Relevance*. Pittsburgh: University of Pittsburgh Press.

—— (1978). "Why ask, 'Why?'?". *Proceedings and Addresses of the American Philosophical Association*, 51: 683–705.

Santayana, George (1925). "Dewey's Naturalistic Metaphysics". *The Journal of Philosophy*, 22: 673–88.

Schlick, Moritz (1979 [1922]). *Space and Time in Contemporary Physics*, trans. H. Brose and P. Heath. In *Moritz Schlick: Philosophical Papers*, ed. H. L. Mulder and B. van de Velde-Schlick, Dordrecht: Reidel, i. 207–69.

Schneider, Herbert W. (1946). *A History of American Philosophy*. New York: Columbia University Press.

Sellars, Wilfrid (1967). *Science and Metaphysics: Variations on Kantian Themes*. London: Routledge & Kegan Paul.

Shapere, Dudley (1965). "Meaning and Scientific Change". In R. Colodny (ed.), *Mind and Cosmos*, Pittsburgh: University of Pittsburgh Press, 41–85.

—— (1980). "The Character of Scientific Change". In T. Nickles (ed.), *Scientific Discovery, Logic and Rationality*, Dordrecht: Reidel, 61–116.

Sklar, Lawrence (1974). *Space, Time, and Spacetime*. Berkeley and Los Angeles: University of California Press.

Stadler, Friedrich (2001). *The Vienna Circle: Studies in the Origins, Development, and Influences of Logical Empiricism*, trans. Camilla Nielson *et al.* Vienna: Springer.

Stallo, J. B. (1960 [1882]). *Concepts and Theories of Modern Physics*. Cambridge, MA: Harvard University Press.

Suppe, Fredrick (ed.) (1974). *The Structure of Scientific Theories*. Urbana, IL: University of Illinois Press.

Uebel, Thomas E. (1992). *Overcoming Logical Positivism from Within: The Emergence of Neurath's Naturalism in the Vienna Circle's Protocol Sentence Debate*. Amsterdam: Rodopi.

Upham, Thomas (1831). *Elements of Mental Philosophy*. Boston: Willis and Lilly.

Van Fraassen, Bas C. (1980). *The Scientific Image*. Oxford: Oxford University Press.

—— (2002). *The Empirical Stance*. New Haven: Yale University Press.

Wilson, Daniel C. (1990). *Science, Community, and the Transformation of American Philosophy, 1860–1930*. Chicago: University of Chicago Press.

Wright, Chauncey (1865). "The Philosophy of Herbert Spencer". *North American Review*, 100: 423–76.

Zahar, Elie (1973). "Why did Einstein's Research Programme Supersede Lorentz's?". *British Journal for the Philosophy of Science*, 24: 95–123.

CHAPTER 18

THE INFLUENCE OF WITTGENSTEIN ON AMERICAN PHILOSOPHY

HANS-JOHANN GLOCK

DURING his lifetime, Ludwig Wittgenstein (1889–1951) published only one significant philosophical work, the *Tractatus*. Nevertheless, some fifty years after his death, many regard him as the greatest philosopher of the twentieth century. A fairly comprehensive bibliography up to 1995 has in excess of 9,000 entries (Philipp 1996), and the stream of publications has not abated since then. At the same time, however, there is a pervasive feeling that his influence is in decline. What is more, this impression is not confined to Wittgenstein's detractors but is shared by many of his admirers.

Some of Wittgenstein's metaphilosophical and philosophical ideas have never found favor within the mainstream of Anglophone philosophy, notably the distinction between saying and showing in the *Tractatus*, the comparison

I gratefully acknowledge help from Jack Canfield, Max de Gaynesford, John Hyman, Javier Kalhat, Cheryl Misak, and David Stern.

of philosophy to a kind of therapy in the *Philosophical Investigations*, and his anthropocentric conception of mathematics in *Remarks on the Foundations of Mathematics*. Nevertheless, at the height of his influence—between the 1940s and the 1970s—many of his views were common currency, and even those who did not subscribe to them treated them with respect. This held not just for his philosophy of mind—notably his attack on Cartesianism—and his philosophy of language—especially his linking of linguistic meaning to use—but also for *some* of his metaphilosophical contentions: for instance, that there is a qualitative difference between the conceptual investigations pursued by philosophy and the factual investigations pursued by science.

Wittgenstein's attack on Cartesianism continues to carry favor. But the contemporary mainstream of analytic philosophy rejects most of his other ideas. In both substance and spirit it seems alien, if not downright hostile, to Wittgenstein's legacy. That mainstream, moreover, has increasingly been dominated by North American philosophy: more specifically, philosophy done in the USA. Neither Quinean naturalism nor Kripkean essentialism is hospitable to Wittgensteinian philosophy. It might seem, therefore, that the story of Wittgenstein's influence on American philosophy is a short one, or at any rate more of a history than an account of its current impact. This appearance is not entirely unfounded. It seems that concentrating on Wittgenstein is considered to be a bad career move for aspiring graduate students in the USA (see Putnam, forthcoming: 2). But the relation between Wittgenstein and Wittgenstein studies, on the one hand, and American philosophy and intellectual life, on the other, is much more complex, intense, and intriguing than might appear at first.

The present is very much included in this verdict. Wittgenstein is the only philosopher to have made it on to the *Time Magazine* list of the '100 most important people of the [twentieth] century', where he is portrayed by Dennett <http://www.time.com/time100/scientist>. And though it may come as a shock, in a recent poll among professional philosophers in *North America*, the *Investigations* was ranked as the most important philosophical work of the twentieth century, and the *Tractatus* came in fourth (Lackey 1999: 331–2). A poll undertaken in Europe might not yield similar results; and a poll of philosophers from Australia and New Zealand would almost certainly be less favorable to Wittgenstein. Furthermore, Wittgenstein scholars and Wittgensteinians continue to find employment in major philosophy programs.[1] Finally, many of the leading mainstream American philosophers of the second half of the twentieth century have engaged with Wittgenstein in a spirit that is at least partly positive or constructive. What is more, this roll-call includes not just followers like Cavell and McDowell, and 'mainstream' sympathizers like Dennett, Sellars, and Searle, but also thinkers whose ideas are generally contrasted with Wittgenstein's, such as Kripke, Davidson, Putnam, and Kaplan.

In what follows I shall sketch the complex connections between Wittgenstein and North America from their beginnings to the present. Section 1 deals with the impact of the *Tractatus* on logical positivism and American post-positivism, and section 2 concerns his personal connections with American philosophers. Section 3 surveys the impact of his later work on post-war philosophical debates in America, and section 4, American contributions to Wittgenstein studies and exegesis. I end with brief reflections on the relationship between Wittgenstein and two prominent American philosophical trends, pragmatism and naturalism.

One can distinguish between *American* philosophy and philosophy *in America* (Marsoobian and Ryder 2004: p. xv). There are three reasons for this. The first is the decisive role played by European refugees from Nazism in establishing analytic philosophy of a positivist and post-positivist bent as the dominant force within American academic philosophy (see section 1 below). The second is the influx of philosophical talent (mainly, though not exclusively, from Britain) to the United States encouraged by the expansion of the tertiary education sector from the 1960s onwards. The final one is rarely noted. Logical positivism was not the only European import. Phenomenology, existentialism, critical theory, and postmodernism were introduced to America from the 1930s onwards.

Though least significant, even this last phenomenon is relevant to Wittgenstein's role in American philosophy. Furthermore, like philosophy in general, Wittgensteinian philosophy and Wittgenstein studies have become an international field, with people moving back and forth freely. (Judging by citation indexes, being a native speaker of German appears to be a distinct disadvantage, but otherwise it's a level playing field.). The aforementioned brain drain included such figures as Paul Grice, Stuart Hampshire, J. O. Urmson, and Philippa Foot. Grice was officially hostile to Wittgenstein. But even he was

[1] There is also a North American Wittgenstein Society founded by Merrill Ring, <http://www.humboldt.edu/~jwp2/naws>.

decisively shaped by conceptual analysis and hence indirectly by Wittgenstein. And among (temporary or permanent) imports of a later vintage are philosophers who are *bona fide* Wittgensteinians and/or Wittgenstein scholars: notably Hintikka, Ishiguro, McDowell, Pears, Sluga, Stern, and Winch. As a result, I shall not confine my discussion to native citizens of North America, but will include contributions made by philosophers while working in America.

1. THE *Tractatus*, LOGICAL POSITIVISM, AND AMERICAN POST-POSITIVISM

The *Tractatus* revolves around the relation between *thought* and *language*, on the one hand, and *reality*, on the other. But its interest differs fundamentally from the epistemological concerns that dominated modern philosophy. Instead, the focus is on logical or semantic questions that are in some respects prior to those of epistemology and metaphysics. The issue is not: How can we represent reality accurately, i.e. arrive at beliefs that are true and justified? It is, rather: How can we represent reality *at all*, whether truly or falsely? What gives content to our beliefs and sentences? What enables them to be about something?

For Wittgenstein, the essence of *representation* or *intentionality* is intimately linked to the nature of *logic*, since logic comprises the most general preconditions for the possibility of representation. We represent reality through thought. But the *Tractatus* breaks with the traditional view that language is merely a medium for transmitting pre-linguistic thoughts. Thought is intrinsically linked to the linguistic expression of thought. The *Tractatus* features a striking account of the essence of symbolic representation—the picture theory of the proposition—which at the same time furnishes a metaphysical account of the basic constituents of reality—logical atomism—a novel understanding of logic, and a revolutionary conception of philosophy itself. All meaningful propositions can be analyzed into logically independent 'elementary propositions'. The ultimate constituents of such propositions are unanalyzable 'names' (the simplest components of language). These names have as their meaning, i.e. stand for, indestructible 'objects' (the simplest components of reality). An elementary proposition depicts a possible combination of objects—a possible 'state of affairs'—by arranging names in a certain manner. If that possible state of affairs actually obtains, that proposition is true.

Empirical propositions have sense by virtue of depicting possible states of affairs. By contrast, logical propositions are vacuous 'tautologies', since they combine empirical propositions in such a way that all factual information cancels out. 'It is raining' says something about the weather—true or false—and so does 'It is not raining'. But 'Either it is raining or it is not raining' does not. The necessity of tautologies simply reflects the fact that they do not make any claims the truth-value of which depends on how things actually are. The pronouncements of metaphysics, finally, are not just senseless but 'nonsensical'; for, contrary to the criterion of sense implicit in the picture theory, they do not depict a state of affairs which may or may not obtain. What such metaphysical 'pseudo-propositions' try to *say* is *shown* by empirical propositions properly analyzed. In fact, the pronouncements of the *Tractatus* itself are in the end condemned as nonsensical. They lead one to appreciate the essence of symbolic representation. Once this is achieved, however, one must throw away the ladder which one has climbed up. Philosophy cannot be a 'doctrine', since there are no meaningful philosophical propositions. It is an 'activity', a 'critique of language' by means of logical analysis. Positively, it elucidates the meaningful propositions of science; negatively, it reveals that metaphysical statements are nonsensical (4.0031, 4.112, 6.53 f.).

The reception of Wittgenstein's early ideas started even before the book was published, through Russell. An American audience might conceivably have heard of Wittgenstein as early as 1914. In the preface to *Our Knowledge of the External World*, which Russell delivered as Lowell Lectures in Boston, Russell mentions that 'in pure logic' he has had 'the benefit of vitally important discoveries, not yet published, by my friend Mr. Ludwig Wittgenstein' (1914: 9). The German–English edition of the *Tractatus* appeared in 1922. But easily the most important American reception of Wittgenstein's early work was indirect. In 1924 the *Tractatus* had come to the attention of the Vienna Circle, a group of scientifically minded philosophers led by Moritz Schlick. It was recognized by some of them as a turning point in the history of philosophy. But their grasp of it was partial (see Hacker 1996: ch. 3): for instance, when they assimilated the account of mathematical equations to that of logical tautologies. The idea that metaphysical pronouncements are nonsensical pseudo-propositions appealed to their anti-metaphysical zeal, and they dismissed the suggestion that there are ineffable metaphysical and ethical truths. They harnessed the restriction of philosophy to the analysis

of language, in particular of the propositions of science, to their scientistic
conviction that science is the only source of genuine knowledge. Wittgenstein
himself found this view offensive, even though his restriction of meaningful
discourse to the empirical 'propositions of natural science' (1961[1922]: 6.53)
sold the ticket on which the logical positivists were traveling. As committed
empiricists, they welcomed the idea that all necessary propositions are tau-
tologous or 'analytic', and hence do not express knowledge of reality. Unlike
earlier versions of empiricism (Mill, Mach), this *logical* empiricism promises
to do justice to the necessity of logic and mathematics while avoiding both
Platonism and the Kantian idea of synthetic a priori truths.

Although Wittgenstein did not take part in the weekly meetings of the
Circle, he met a select few—Schlick, Waismann, and, initially, Carnap and
Feigl. Together with the *Tractatus*, these discussions (recorded in Wittgenstein
1979) were formative influences on the development of logical positivism in
the interwar years. In the course of these discussions, Wittgenstein developed
the now notorious principle of verification, according to which the meaning
of a proposition is the method of its verification. Like Schlick and Carnap,
he combined verificationism with phenomenalism, thereby strengthening
further the impression that the *Tractatus* had been an empiricist overture to
logical positivism, an interpretation recently revived by Merrill and Jaakko
Hintikka (1986).

Logical positivism became what is by common consent—though not
necessarily common acclaim—the most influential philosophical school of
the last hundred years, mainly through its large-scale exodus to America (Feigl
1981: 57–94; Hacker 1996: sect. 7.1; Friedman 1998). Its emphasis on formal
logic and admiration for natural science decisively shaped the mainstream of
American analytic philosophy, which in this respect is post-positivist.

By far the most eminent positivist import was Rudolf Carnap. He distinguished between a 'left' and a 'right wing' of the Vienna Circle, and not
just along political lines. The former comprised Neurath, Hahn, and himself;
the latter Schlick and Waismann, 'who remained in personal contact with
Wittgenstein and were inclined to maintain his views and formulations' (1963:
57–8). Furthermore, he was taken aback by Wittgenstein's authoritarian style
of debate, which tolerated 'no critical comment' and treated insights as a kind
of divine inspiration.

I sometimes had the impression that the deliberately rational and unemotional
attitude of the scientist and likewise any idea which had the flavour of 'enlightenment'
were repugnant to Wittgenstein.   (1963: 25–9).

At the same time Carnap continued to regard Wittgenstein as 'the philosopher who, apart from Russell and Frege, had the greatest influence on my thinking' (1963: 24). Perhaps Carnap realized that on one crucial issue he himself was a 'right-winger': namely, the status of philosophy *vis-à-vis* science. All logical positivists believed that philosophy should emulate the rigor and the cooperative spirit of the formal and empirical sciences. But whereas Neurath adopted a naturalistic stance according to which philosophy itself dissolves into a unified physicalist science, thereby anticipating Quine, Carnap held fast to a qualitative distinction between the empirical investigation of reality and the philosophical analysis of the propositions and methods of science. The *Tractatus* had portrayed philosophy as a second-order discipline. Unlike science, philosophy does not itself represent reality, but sets 'limits to the disputable sphere of science'. Without propounding any propositions of its own, it clarifies meaningful propositions, and demonstrates that metaphysical propositions violate the rules of logical syntax (4.112 ff., 6.53). In exact parallel for Carnap, philosophy is not a doctrine consisting of propositions but a method, namely of logical analysis. Negatively, it reveals metaphysical nonsense. Positively, it turns into the 'logic of science': namely, the linguistic analysis or explication of scientific propositions, concepts, and methods (1937: 279). This demarcation of philosophy and science underlies Carnap's distinction between analytic and synthetic propositions in *The Logical Syntax of Language* and his distinction between internal and external questions in 'Empiricism, Semantics and Ontology' (1956). He reaffirmed it towards the end of his life. Scientific philosophy is not philosophy that meddles in the scientific investigation of reality. Instead, it is philosophy that reflects on this investigation in the same rationalistic and collaborative spirit as the one which guides the first-order explorations of the scientists themselves (1964: 133–4). Accordingly, Quine's famous attack on Carnap also pits him against Wittgenstein (see section 5).

On other issues, Carnap increasingly diverged from the *Tractatus* after his move to the USA in 1935. He had originally been impressed by Wittgenstein's strictures against any attempt to talk about the relation between language and reality, and he had therefore restricted the analysis of language to logical *syntax*, the intra-linguistic rules for the combination of signs. Tarski's resolution of the semantic paradoxes persuaded Carnap to drop the restriction to syntax. His subsequent attempts to explicate semantic notions—notably through the idea of possible worlds (1956)—laid the foundations for intensional semantics, perhaps the most 'American' of all semantic theories. Still, that impetus was indebted not just to C. I. Lewis's modal logic and to Frege's sense/meaning distinction, but also to the *Tractatus*. The basic idea of all truth-conditional semantics, intensional semantics included, is that the meaning of a sentence consists in, or is determined by, the conditions under which it is true. That idea was first expressed clearly in the *Tractatus* (4.022, 4.024, 4.061–4, 5.101–21). Furthermore, Wittgenstein's technical apparatus (logical space, truth possibilities, range) influenced not just Carnap's theory of probability but also his notion of an 'L-state' (1956: 9–10) or possible world, and thereby intensional semantics, which identifies the meaning of a sentence with the set of possible worlds in which it is true.

At the same time, there is also an important difference which is generally overlooked. Like Frege, Russell, and Quine, Carnap was a *bona fide* 'ideal language' philosopher. He regarded his logical calculi as artificial ideal *languages* that replace natural languages for the purposes of science and scientific philosophy. By contrast, the early Wittgenstein regarded formal logic as an ideal *notation* which brings out the *underlying logical structure* which sentences in the vernacular possessed all along. In this respect he is a clear forerunner of another project of abiding importance to American philosophy: namely, that of a *theory of meaning for natural languages*. This project is pursued not just by intensional semanticists like Montague, but also by Davidson. Just as the *Tractatus* maintains that the depth structure of ordinary language is given by Russellian logic, so Davidson maintains that it is given by Tarski's formal theory of truth. Like the early Wittgenstein, and in explicit opposition to Quine, Davidson aims to bring out the 'metaphysics implicit in natural language'. He is interested not in 'improving on natural language, but in understanding it'. Alluding to a simile of the later Wittgenstein, he describes 'the language of science not as a substitute for our present language, but as a suburb of it' (2001[1984]: 203; 1985: 172, 176). Formal logic is philosophically important because it reveals the underlying structure of natural languages (see Glock 1996: 223–5; 2003b: 17).[2]

2. WITTGENSTEIN IN AMERICA

After Wittgenstein's return to Cambridge in 1929, he subjected his own earlier work to a withering critique. He came to realize that there are logical

---

[2] In analyzing vernacular constructions, Davidson deliberately sticks to the predicate calculus because he forswears intensional notions like those employed in modal logic. This inveterate

relations between propositions which cannot result from the truth-functional combination of simpler propositions, and hence that the logically independent elementary propositions he had postulated were a myth. Similarly, the atomistic idea of indecomposable objects and unanalyzable names is a chimera. This collapse of logical atomism also undermines the picture theory. The explanation of how propositions represent reality cannot be that they are arrangements of logical atoms which share a logical form with an arrangement of metaphysical atoms. Moreover, meaningful propositions do not presuppose a one-to-one correlation between words and things. The underlying referential conception of meaning is doubly wrong. Not all words refer to objects. Indeed, even in the case of referring expressions, their meaning is *not* the object they stand for. The meaning of a word is not an entity of any kind, but its use according to linguistic rules (1953: §43).

Wittgenstein held on to the idea that ordinary language is alright, but *not* because analysis reveals it to be *au fond* 'a calculus according to definite rules'. Language is not the self-sufficient abstract system which is presented in the *Tractatus*. Rather, it is a human practice which in turn is embedded in a social 'form of life'. Wittgenstein also continued to believe that philosophical problems are rooted in misunderstandings of language. But he rejected logical depth analysis as a means of achieving clarity. Many philosophically contested concepts cannot be defined analytically by reference to necessary and sufficient conditions. They are united by 'family-resemblances', overlapping similarities, rather than by a common characteristic mark. To fight the 'bewitchment of our understanding through the means of our language' we require neither the construction of artificial languages nor the uncovering of logical forms beneath the surface of ordinary language. Instead, we need a description of our public linguistic practices, which constitute a motley of 'language-games' (1953: §§23, 81, 108).

The initial influence of Wittgenstein's later ideas was through his teaching, and through the circulation of lecture notes and dictations. As a result, it was largely confined to his colleagues and pupils at Cambridge. But among the latter were American visitors such as Alice Ambrose. She was working in the philosophy of mathematics, and planned to present what she took to be Wittgenstein's views in an article for *Mind* (1935). But Wittgenstein

extensionalism is immediately owed to Quine. But it continues the *Tractatus*'s 'thesis of extensionality', according to which simple propositions occur in a complex one only in such a way that the truth-value of the latter depends solely on those of the former (5, 5.54).

was paranoid about distortions of his unpublished ideas (see 1953: preface; Malcolm 1984: 49–50). He tried to sabotage the publication by interceding with both Ambrose and Moore, then editor of the journal. When these attempts failed, he broke off all contacts with her (Monk 1990: 346). Ambrose later taught at Smith College, together with her husband Morris Lazerowitz. Both of them had an abiding interest in the topic of logical necessity, and their publications clarified and developed Wittgenstein's iconoclastic claims about the necessary propositions of logic, mathematics, and metaphysics, (e.g. Lazerowitz and Ambrose 1985).

By far the most important North American pupil of Wittgenstein, however, was Norman Malcolm. He had studied at the University of Nebraska with Bouwsma, an ardent admirer of Moore and acquaintance of Wittgenstein's, and later at Harvard. Before setting off for Cambridge in 1938, he went to say goodbye to the logician Henry Sheffer. 'He said to me, in a mocking tone, that when I met Wittgenstein I should make a low bow and exclaim: "There is but one Tautology, and Wittgenstein is its prophet"' (1984: 86). This remark attests not just to an ironical skepticism towards the *Tractatus*, but also to a keen appreciation of one aspect of its account of logical propositions—that they all say the same: namely, nothing.

On arrival at Cambridge, Malcolm soon became one of Wittgenstein's most devoted disciples and a trusted friend. After returning to the USA, Malcolm eventually acquired a position at Cornell. He managed to turn Cornell into one of America's leading departments and into its premier center for Wittgenstein studies. This development was aided by Wittgenstein's only visit to the USA, between July and October 1949, when he stayed with the Malcolms. Given the rationing and extreme austerity of post-war Britain, most visitors would have cherished the creature comforts afforded by the land of plenty. Predictably, Wittgenstein proved entirely immune to such temptations. According to Malcolm, 'he would more or less eat bread and cheese at all meals, largely ignoring the various dishes that my wife prepared. Wittgenstein declared that it did not much matter to him *what* he ate, so long as it was always the *same*' (1984: 69).

While at Cornell, Wittgenstein met for discussions several American philosophers. Among them were Max Black and Malcolm's former teacher, Bouwsma. Black's influential work in the philosophy of language was partly shaped by both the early and the later Wittgenstein. He tried to show how philosophical problems concerning analysis, metaphor, and vagueness could be solved by linguistic methods that combine the formal analysis envisaged by the *Tractatus* with a conceptual analysis influenced by the *Philosophical Investigations* (see Black 1949). Bouwsma, for his part, published an account of the conversations he had with Wittgenstein at Cornell in 1949 and Oxford in 1950–1 (Bouwsma 1986). In it he denies that Wittgenstein pursued philosophical arguments of any kind. Instead, Bouwsma stresses the therapeutic side, assimilating Wittgenstein's method to psychoanalysis. In this he is in line with other American interpreters, such as his former pupil Lazerowitz, and with the new Wittgensteinians (see section 4). According to Malcolm, however, Wittgenstein repeatedly repudiated the suggestion that, on his conception, philosophy was a form of psychoanalysis: 'The two are different techniques', he insisted (1984: 48).

The sojourn at Cornell also had one important consequence, which was noted only recently. Wittgenstein's final manuscripts, written in 1950–1, feature seminal discussions of epistemological themes that were posthumously published under the title *On Certainty*. Important parts of *On Certainty* engage with Moore's refutation of idealism and skepticism, and with the truistic propositions that Moore regarded as certain. For this reason, it has generally been assumed that these remarks were based on reading Moore's 'Defense of Common Sense' and 'Proof of an External World', and on personal discussions between Moore and Wittgenstein at Cambridge. As Kober (1996) has shown, however, it is more probable that they were the reflection of discussions between Malcolm and Wittgenstein at Cornell. These discussions were based on an article that Malcolm had recently completed (1949; see 1984: 70–5), in which he tried to reconstruct Moore's refutation of skepticism from a Wittgensteinian perspective. So the intellectual traffic between Wittgenstein and his American followers was not all one-way.

3. Wittgensteinianism in America

Wittgenstein's influence through hearsay was decisively superseded by the posthumous publication of the *Investigations* in 1953. Just as the *Tractatus* had shaped logical positivism, so Wittgenstein's later work was a guiding force behind so-called ordinary language philosophy (Hacker 1996: sect. 6.3). This movement flourished between the 1930s and the 1960s, and is more aptly called 'conceptual analysis'. Like Wittgenstein and the logical positivists, the conceptual analysts took a linguistic turn by regarding philosophical problems as conceptual and concepts as embodied in language. Again like Wittgenstein, but unlike the logical positivists, they thought that traditional philosophical problems are to be solved or dissolved not by constructing artificial languages, but by describing the ordinary use of philosophically contested terms. Finally, like Wittgenstein but unlike the logical positivists, most of them were suspicious of large-scale quasi-scientific theory construction in philosophy.

Conceptual analysis is closely associated with Oxford, and commonly contrasted with American analytic philosophy. To be sure, under the leadership of Carnap, Hempel, Reichenbach, and Quine, many American philosophers concentrated on the logical construction of artificial languages. But for one thing, Wittgenstein's influence on post-war American philosophy was not confined to the later work. For instance, next to Whitehead and Cassirer, the early Wittgenstein was also a major influence on Susanne K. Langer. Her influential *Philosophy in a New Key* applies a theory of symbolism inspired by the *Tractatus* to problems in aesthetics. More importantly, to this day there are plenty of American philosophers who devote at least part of their efforts to the task of analyzing concepts rather than constructing formal languages. And most of these have been inspired by or are sympathetic to Wittgenstein (an exception is Ebersole 1979).

Between the late 1950s and the late 1960s, respect for Wittgenstein's achievements was at its peak. The emphasis was on two areas. One was his later philosophy of language, especially the slogan that meaning is use and the idea of family resemblance, which were regarded as central to the proper conduct of philosophical analysis. The other was Wittgenstein's philosophy of mind, especially the private language argument and the idea of a criterion, which were recognized as powerful challenges to Cartesian dualism, phenomenalism, and skepticism about other minds.

American philosophers were major contributors to these debates, variously interpreting, developing, attacking, or defending Wittgenstein's views, or what they took to be his views. Malcolm was the leading American advocate of Wittgenstein. His writings, mainly on epistemology and the philosophy of mind, were renowned for their clarity and intellectual honesty even among his opponents. He sought to clarify Wittgenstein's philosophical psychology and to defend it against the charge of logical behaviorism (1972). He used Wittgensteinian methods to combat both imagist and neurophysiological causal theories of memory (1977). In a scintillating debate with Armstrong he also employed Wittgensteinian ideas against the identity theory of mind (Armstrong and Malcolm 1984). Malcolm's attempts to extract from Moore and *On Certainty* a response to skepticism have already been mentioned. His book *Dreaming* (1959) pursued a somewhat different line to reveal that Cartesian doubt is senseless, inspired by remarks in *Philosophical Investigations* (Part II: 184, 222). It argues that one cannot think or judge during sleep, and hence, a fortiori, one cannot judge falsely during a dream that one is awake.

The book provoked a vehement backlash. Critics such as Putnam (1975: chs. 15–16), Fodor and Chihara (1965) accused it of relying on indefensible assumptions like logical behaviorism and verificationism. What is more, the actual or alleged flaws in his reasoning were regarded as reflecting fundamental flaws in Wittgensteinian philosophy.[3] Wittgenstein's anti-Cartesian philosophy of mind was widely accused of resting on mistaken semantic assumptions. Malcolm in turn attacked the functionalist and representationalist alternatives of his critics. He objected especially to the Chomskian idea that genuinely cognitive and symbolic activities could be inaccessible in principle to consciousness, in the way in which neurophysiological processes are. His own animadversions against popular assumptions in cognitive science fell largely on deaf ears. But they are not so very unlike Searle's high-profile attacks on strong artificial intelligence and on 'deep unconscious' rule-following. Searle's approach to these issues is indebted to the conceptual analysis of his teachers Austin and Grice, who disliked Wittgenstein. Searle himself, however, has at times employed and developed Wittgensteinian ideas, in particular on rule-following and proper names (1987). Like Wittgenstein, he holds that even the most evolved mental life presupposes a background of non-representational and non-theoretical capacities and dispositions.

One crucial bone of contention between Malcolm and his critics was the relation between the meaning of mental terms and behavioral criteria. Like Rogers Albritton (1959), a highly resourceful yet less prolific Wittgensteinian, Malcolm maintained that behavioral criteria provide non-inductive evidence for the truth of third-person psychological statements, and thereby furnish the wherewithal for a refutation of skepticism about other minds. When Susan displays pain behavior under certain circumstances, there remains no room for intelligible doubt.

By contrast, the Harvard philosopher Stanley Cavell resisted the attempt to dissolve skepticism conclusively by appeal to fixed rules of language.[4] For

---

[3] For a qualified defense of Malcolm's own approach, see Schroeder 1997.
[4] Cavell pioneered an 'unruly' reading, which downplays or qualifies Wittgenstein's talk of language as constituted by 'grammatical rules'. See also sects. 4 and 5.

him Wittgenstein's criteria do not underpin the certainty of third-person psychological statements, but determine the applicability of mental concepts. Put differently, their role is semantic, rather than epistemic. Cavell first came to fame through an article 'The Availability of Wittgenstein's Later Philosophy' (1962). In it he points out the complex obstacles facing a reader of *Philosophical Investigations*, and defends the book against the charge of revolving around dogmatic appeals to ordinary language or common sense. In both style and content his approach to Wittgenstein differs sharply from that of Malcolm and Albritton, and displays the influence of so-called continental philosophy. According to Cavell, the *Investigations* manifests existential tensions typical of the modern subject. Wittgenstein is torn between the deep human need to transcend the limitations of the ordinary and the realization that such attempts are ultimately futile (1969, 1979, 2001).

Cavell's admiration for Wittgenstein and Austin was shared by Burton Dreben, whose other icon was his colleague Quine. Because of the two, Harvard became a center of Wittgensteinian thought in North America, Quine's pre-eminence notwithstanding. Even Putnam came to recognize affinities with Wittgenstein as part of his more general move towards a kind of neo-pragmatism. From its inception, Putnam's work—notably his functionalist approach to the mind—emphasized the role or function of the notions or phenomena he investigated, as opposed to their constitution or essence. Like Wittgenstein, he tried to elucidate so-called analytic propositions not by asking what they are about, but by inquiring into their role within human thought and discourse. Later he extended this approach to meaning and intentionality, insisting that the question of how words and concepts are used is more illuminating than the question of what they are or what they refer to (1975: chs. 2, 4, 9; see Gaynesford 2006: 51–5). Cavell and Dreben were two driving spirits behind the so-called New Wittgenstein, and Putnam's latest reflections on Wittgenstein gravitate towards the same direction.

This can also be said of McDowell, who came to Pittsburgh from Oxford. Apart from participating in the debate about rule-following, McDowell's initial contribution to Wittgensteinian thinking was yet another gloss on criteria (1998: ch. 17). The standard approach acknowledges that criterial evidence falls short of entailment, and is therefore defeasible. This threatens to reopen the flood gates to skepticism about other minds. To close them, McDowell suggested that criteria are neither defeasible nor evidential. If we see Susan screaming and writhing, we do not infer—consciously or unconsciously—that she is in pain from behavioral evidence; we simply *see* her writhing in agony. Like straightforward perception of material objects, this observation does not adduce evidence; it specifies a perceptual capacity which directly shows us how things are. McDowell's *Mind and World* (1994) employs the idea that normal perception is non-inferential in an avowed exercise in Wittgensteinian therapy. It serves as a remedy for the excesses of the empiricist myth of the given, on the one hand, and rationalist approaches verging on idealism, on the other.

This Kantian theme already had strong roots in Pittsburgh, where Sellars had coined the dismissal phrase 'myth of the given' for sense-data empiricism. Sellars may have encountered the *Tractatus* as a Rhodes scholar at Oxford. Or he may have become acquainted with Wittgenstein through his one-time colleague Feigl, at Minnesota. In any event, he can be regarded as the founding father of a semantic approach inspired by Wittgenstein that is highly influential at present (see Sellars 1963: chs. 7 and 11). Conceptual or inferential role semantics starts out from Wittgenstein's slogan that meaning is use. But that slogan suffers from the fact that the notion of meaning is highly unspecific. Conceptual role semantics therefore refines it by identifying a more narrowly specified kind of use: namely, its use in inferences. By contrast to some versions of conceptual role semantics, the one initiated by Sellars and further developed by Brandom also goes back to Wittgenstein in another respect: namely, its emphasis on the normative dimension of language. An expression has a meaning only insofar as it is subject to conditions of its correct application. Linguistic behavior is guided by rules of a specifically semantic (Wittgenstein would have said 'grammatical') kind. These are only implicit in our practices and need to be made explicit, as in the title of Brandom's blockbuster (1994).

Rules and rule-following are also the topic of Kripke's stimulating discussion of Wittgenstein's so-called rule-following considerations. Kripke does not purport to provide an accurate account of the primary texts, but to propound 'Wittgenstein's argument as it struck Kripke' (1982: 5). As regards its content, Kripke's interpretation is characterized by two features. First, like Fogelin (1976) before him, he portrays Wittgenstein as constructing a skeptical paradox in the style of Hume, one which questions the possibility of distinguishing between following and violating a rule, and thereby casts doubt on the very phenomenon of meaning. Secondly, he adopts a *communitarian* reading according to which rule-following and language are inherently social. Kripke's book was the starting point for a debate about 'Kripkenstein' on rule-following, a debate which is now conducted largely in blissful disregard of Wittgenstein's own writings (see Miller and Wright 2002). Kripke's quasi-interpretation provoked hostile reactions from several scholars (Baker and Hacker 1984; Winch 1987). But while the skeptical interpretation of Wittgenstein is wrong, and the community interpretation contentious at best, as regards the *normativity of meaning* Kripke has highlighted and ably defended a genuinely Wittgensteinian idea (see section 5). In any event, Kripke's book placed rule-following at the center of attention, and led to Malcolm's and McDowell's communitarian yet non-skeptical readings.

It also helped to rekindle interest in Wittgenstein's philosophy of mathematics. Unlike Wittgenstein's philosophy of mind and language, the former immediately received a hostile reception on publication of *Remarks on the Foundations of Mathematics*, from American commentators (Chihara 1961) among others. Weighing in on the opposite side, Barry Stroud wrote a prominent response to Dummett's influential attack. He defended Wittgenstein in particular against the accusation of espousing a 'full-blooded conventionalism' according to which anything goes in novel mathematical proofs, interpreting him instead as a naturalist who detects the roots of logical compulsion in human nature (for an alternative, Kantian reading of Wittgenstein's invocation of forms of life, see Garver 1994). More recently, North American philosophers have defended Wittgenstein by drawing on both the historical context and the *Nachlass* sources (Shanker 1987; Marion 1998). Others have elaborated Wittgenstein's underlying denial that linguistic rules must pay heed to reality (Schwyzer 2001; Forster 2004). Wittgenstein's claims about logic and mathematics are often baffling, and have been accused of containing definite technical errors. On closer scrutiny, however, the alleged errors turn out to be *philosophical challenges* to cherished assumptions about the nature of mathematics. But while these challenges are ingenious and radical, they have yet to receive a compelling justification.

4. WITTGENSTEIN STUDIES IN AMERICA

American philosophers have not just debated the merits of Wittgensteinian ideas; they have also contributed substantially to Wittgenstein scholarship and philology. To Ambrose, Diamond, and Klagge we owe valuable editions of parts of his output. To Black (1964) we owe the only commentary on the *Tractatus*, and to Hallett (1977) the first commentary on the *Investigations*. American scholars have also taken a lead in important exegetical debates.[5]

The first readers of *Philosophical Investigations* were struck by the sharp contrast with the *Tractatus*. This even gave rise to the postulation of two literary personae—early Wittgenstein, author of the *Tractatus*, and later Wittgenstein, author of the *Investigations* (Pitcher 1964). Against this dichotomy, scholars like Fann (1969) pointed to a whole catalogue of ideas that run through Wittgenstein's entire work, notably his conviction that philosophy is *toto caelo* different from science, and that it has to do with problems of language rather than matters of fact. Their hand was strengthened by the increasing availability of writings following Wittgenstein's return to Cambridge in 1929. However, instead of unifying Wittgenstein's *œuvre*, these discoveries lend succour to the idea of a distinct 'transition' or 'middle period' (see Pitcher 1968: pp. v–vi; Arrington 1983; Stern 2005). Even more recently, the idea of a 'Wittgenstein' postdating the *Investigations* has been launched (Moyal-Sharrock 2004), partly because American interpreters like Stroll (1994) have hailed *On Certainty* as Wittgenstein's third work of genius, and one which adopts a distinct outlook.

The alternative tack has been to deny any fundamental change. Thus Hintikka has maintained that Wittgenstein continued to hold on to the ineffability of semantics and the privacy of experience, merely switching from a phenomenological to a physicalist language grounded in our everyday language-games (1996). An even greater continuity is assumed by the New Wittgensteinians, who deny that the *Tractatus* was ever committed to any metaphysical claims from which the later Wittgenstein could have distanced himself. In my judgment, it is best to steer a middle course between the Scylla of multiplying Wittgensteins *sine necessitate* and the Charybdis of 'Mono-Wittgensteinianism' (Conant 2007). Wittgenstein's explicit pronouncements, most notably in the preface of *Philosophical Investigations*, support the impression one gets from reading his manuscripts and typescripts in sequence, that there was a single major, though gradual, change in philosophical outlook (as opposed to manner of representation or focus of attention): namely, from the logico-metaphysical vision of the *Tractatus* to its dialectic demolition in the *Investigations*.

---

[5] For a more comprehensive survey of exegetical controversies, see Glock 2007.

The most contested topic in recent American Wittgenstein scholarship is his attitude towards reason. Was he a proponent of the claims of reason, of rational argument, justification, and clarification? Or was he an enemy of such Enlightenment ideals? Was he even a philosopher at all, or was he a sage, prophet, or guru, seeking therapy or salvation rather than wisdom?

Opinion on these matters divides roughly into two camps: *rationalist* and *irrationalist* interpretations. While the former detect arguments in Wittgenstein's *œuvre*, the latter view it as a therapeutic or aesthetic exercise. This division does not coincide with Chihara's division (1982; also Stern 2005: 176–7) between 'left-' and 'right-wing interpretations'. Some rationalists do not qualify as right-wingers, since they acknowledge that Wittgenstein tried to avoid doctrines and theses while insisting that he engaged in rational argument, albeit of a critical and elenctic/dialectical rather than constructive and demonstrative kind. Finally, the distinction does not run between analytic and continental interpretations (cp. Biletzki 2003: ch. 10). Explaining these misleading categories in a coherent manner is a substantial task (undertaken in Glock 2008). More importantly, the label 'continental' would be particularly misleading in our context. For many irrationalist interpretations have prominent American roots, such as:

- Therapeutic interpretations. On account of the comparisons with psychoanalysis, it is held that Wittgenstein's later work features not conceptual clarifications but only therapeutic attempts to make us abandon philosophical problems for the sake of intellectual tranquility (Bouwsma 1986).
- Nonsense interpretations, to which I return below.
- Pyrrhonian interpretations, according to which Wittgenstein does not just aim to overcome metaphysical philosophizing by a better, 'critical' variety, but refuses to take a stance on any philosophical issue whatever (Fogelin 1976: ch. 15; Stern 2004).
- Genre interpretations. The *Philosophical Investigations* must not be read as a philosophical treatise that contains if not theories or theses then at least some definite philosophical questions and arguments, but as an album or part of a 'hypertext' consisting of the whole *Nachlass* that is meant to inspire and resonate in wholly diverse directions (Stern 1994, 1996).

- Postmodern interpretations: a position inaugurated by Rorty (1979), according to which Wittgenstein, along with Heidegger and the pragmatists, paves the way for an 'edifying philosophy' in which the traditional concern with truth and objectivity is abandoned in favor of the hermeneutic attempt to keep a conversation going. According to Rorty, Wittgenstein supports Dewey's and Quine's attack on the idea that philosophy is a subject distinct from the empirical sciences (1982: pp. xviii, 28).

Irrationalist interpretations are not necessarily irrational. Postmodern irrationalism is indeed postmodern: that is to say, it is entertainingly ludicrous. Given Wittgenstein's adamant and abiding separation of philosophical from factual problems and investigations, the suggestion that he was keen to dissolve philosophy into science is a travesty.

The irrationalist interpretation which has made the most splash in recent years is the nonsense interpretation. It was inspired by Cavell and Dreben, and is currently epitomized by Cora Diamond (1991, 2000) and James Conant (2001, 2002).[6] Starting out from these avowedly American origins (McCarthy and Stidd 2001), it has, under the title the 'New Wittgenstein' (Crary and Read 2000), led to a debate which is overheated, over-hyped and . . . over here in Europe.

What sets the New Wittgensteinians apart from other irrationalist approaches are two points.[7] The first is a reading of the *Tractatus*. In the final sections, Wittgenstein condemns the propositions of the *Tractatus* itself as nonsensical (6.54–7). According to a standard interpretation, his reason was that these propositions try to express truths about the essence of language which, by Wittgenstein's own lights, cannot be expressed in meaningful propositions, but which show themselves in logical propositions and in empirical propositions properly analyzed. According to the New Wittgensteinians, by contrast, the *Tractatus* is meant to consist not of illuminating nonsense that

---

[6] One can distinguish different branches of New Wittgensteinianism. There is a Cavellian branch, which assimilates Wittgenstein to continental thinkers, especially Kierkegaard, and a Drebenian branch—which includes Goldfarb (1997) and Ricketts (1996)—which reads Wittgenstein as reacting to difficulties inherent in Frege's conception of logic.

[7] Claims to the contrary notwithstanding, it is neither the stress on the therapeutic character of the *Investigations* nor the non-metaphysical picture of the *Tractatus* that distinguishes the New Wittgensteinians, but exclusively the issue of nonsense. By contrast to metaphysical readings of the *Tractatus* (e.g. Malcolm 1986), 'linguistic' interpreters like Ishiguro (2001) treat the so-called essence of reality as a mere projection of the structure of language. But they differ from the New Wittgensteinians in that they portray the book as committed to the idea that the essence of linguistic representation cannot be said but can be shown.

tries to hint at logico-metaphysical truths, but of 'plain nonsense' (Diamond 1991: 181; Conant 1992: 198), nonsense in the same drastic sense as gibberish like 'piggly tiggle wiggle'. The purpose of the exercise is therapeutic. By producing such sheer nonsense, Wittgenstein tries to unmask the idea of metaphysical truths (effable or ineffable) as absurd, and to wean us off the temptation to engage in philosophy. The second claim is that Wittgenstein's conception of nonsense, both early and late, was 'austere' rather than 'substantial' (Crary 2000: 12–13; Diamond 1991: 111–12; Conant 2002: 380–3). There is just one kind of nonsense: namely, plain nonsense. For it is illusory to suppose that a special kind of nonsense—notably metaphysical nonsense like 'The true is the whole'—could result from combining meaningful words in a way that transgresses the rules of logical syntax or grammar.

The 'plain nonsense' interpretation finds some support from the text, and it promises to rescue the *Tractatus* from the charge of being self-defeating. Alas, it has fatal drawbacks, which have been pointed out by American scholars, among others (Proops 2001; Williams 2004; see also Hacker 2001: ch. 4).[8] It is at odds with the external evidence, writings and conversations in which Wittgenstein states that the *Tractatus* is committed to the idea of ineffable insights. Secondly, unlike the illuminating nonsense detected by orthodox interpretations, sheer gibberish cannot be in any way superior to the philosophical nonsense resulting from 'misunderstanding the logic of our language' (4.003). Consequently, if the pronouncements of the *Tractatus* were meant to be mere nonsense, Wittgenstein would have to be neutral between, for example, Frege's and Russell's idea that propositions are names of objects and the idea that they differ from names in saying something, or between their claim that the propositions of logic describe abstract objects and the claim that they are tautologies. In fact, however, Wittgenstein continued to defend the latter ideas even after abandoning the *Tractatus*. Finally, the nonsense interpretation employs hermeneutical double standards. On the one hand, it must reject as deliberate nonsense remarks which insist that

---

[8] Hacker (2003: 1) further complains that unlike the 'Old American Wittgensteinians' the 'New American Wittgensteinians' tend to be preoccupied with a relatively narrow range of issues evolving around nonsense. He has a point with respect to theoretical philosophy, the branch with which Wittgenstein's writings are almost exclusively concerned. On the other hand, the New Wittgensteinians have been in the forefront of applying Wittgenstein's ideas to ethics (e.g. Crary 2007). But a 'practical' interest in Wittgenstein is evident among Old American Wittgensteinians as well. Thus Arrington (1989) has done pioneering work on how moral relativism can be improved through Wittgenstein's idea of the autonomy of grammar.

philosophical propositions are attempts to say something that can only be shown. On the other hand, it must accept as genuine those remarks that provide the rationale for declaring philosophical pronouncements to be illegitimate. Yet these two types of remarks are inextricably interwoven in the text. Furthermore, *any* concession that some parts of the book furnish the standards by which the *Tractatus* in particular, and metaphysics in general, qualify as nonsense reintroduces a distinction between illuminating and non-illuminating nonsense, a distinction which the New Wittgensteinians condemn as 'irresolute' (Goldfarb 1997: 64) or even a case of 'chickening out' (Diamond 1991: 181, 194). The only consistent *interpretation* is one which acknowledges *the text itself* to be *inconsistent*, because it consciously advances sentences which, by its own standards, cannot make sense. Hence, if we are resolutely committed to consistency ourselves, this is the interpretation we are bound to accept.

Whereas most orthodox interpreters do not condone the position they detect in the *Tractatus*, the New Wittgensteinians not only ascribe the afore-mentioned views to Wittgenstein, they also *subscribe* to them. They endorse the austere conception of nonsense.[9] They also think that the statements of the *Tractatus* are indeed gibberish, yet nonetheless capable of establishing the futile nature of all philosophy. How precisely this combination is to be effected remains unclear. For gibberish cannot state a reason for anything, least of all for dismissing a venerable intellectual enterprise like philosophy. Indeed, *if* Wittgenstein *had* intended to produce hokum and succeeded, this fact would provide a reason for abandoning *not* philosophy but the philosophical study of his writings.[10]

The rational line for both rationalist and irrationalist *interpreters* is to acknowledge that Wittgenstein's work combines rationalist and irrationalist elements. The rational line for *philosophers* is to explore the arguments, insights, and instructive errors it has to offer. This exhortation presupposes, of course, that philosophy is an enterprise based on reasoning. But since one cannot reason against this presupposition without self-refutation, it is one to which we should commit.

---

[9] On the basis of semantic doctrines which I have argued to be untenable and at odds with Wittgenstein's own later insights (Glock 2004).

[10] One might then pass on the baton to *psychopathological* investigations of Wittgenstein's *frame of mind* (Sass 2001; Hintikka and Hintikka 2002). From amnesia to Asperger's, from dyslexia to schizophrenia, there is hardly a mental disorder that he has not been diagnosed with. Lack of acquaintance with the patient is no obstacle, it would appear, which just goes to show that while armchair philosophy is regarded as dubious, armchair psychology is a thriving discipline.

5. WITTGENSTEIN AND AMERICAN PHILOSOPHY

But what is the relation between Wittgenstein's contributions to rational philosophizing and those of distinctively American modes of philosophizing?

Wittgenstein has often been associated with pragmatism. Yet the American pragmatists were not a major positive influence on his thought. Wittgenstein was impressed by James's *Variety of Religious Experience* (Monk 1990: 112); yet it left no mark, even on his occasional ruminations about religion. Admittedly, James's *Principles of Psychology* is one of the few works he discusses frequently, but mainly to attack its introspectionist methodology and its empiricist account of the will.

American pragmatists and neo-pragmatists are famous for their 'debunking of dualisms' (Rorty 1986: 333, 339), including distinctions dear to Wittgenstein, like that between empirical and a priori propositions, and between philosophy and science. After all, one of Wittgenstein's mottoes was *Lear*'s 'I'll teach you differences'. Like the pragmatists, Wittgenstein repudiated distinctions without a difference, notably those invoked in skeptical scenarios. His complaint was not, however, that it makes no *practical* difference, for instance, whether the world has existed for billions of years or whether it was created five minutes ago, complete with records of the past. Instead, he objects that the purported difference lacks genuine semantic content. Insofar as pragmatism sidesteps skeptical doubts as impractical, he regarded it as a *Weltanschauung* to be avoided (1975: §422). For better or worse, his anti-skeptical strategy is more verificationist than utilitarian. And his conception of truth is deflationary, and precludes any definition by reference to consensus or utility (Glock 1996: 365–8, 382–5; 2006).

At the same time there are grand-strategic similarities: the resistance to metaphysical myths, the aspiration to overcome philosophical problems by reference to human practice, the stress on the social dimension of that practice, and a holistic conception of language.

Quine credits Dewey with having anticipated Wittgenstein's slogan 'meaning is use'.[11] It is undeniable that while Wittgenstein was still trying to rescue the picture theory, Dewey and Mead had already rejected the idea of language

---

[11] Quine 1969: 27. On the relationship between Wittgenstein and Quine, see Arrington and Glock 1996.

as a medium for picturing reality, and replaced it by the view that language is predominantly an instrument or tool serving social purposes. Similarly, the pragmatists rejected Cartesianism long before Wittgenstein. But the route is rather different. Pragmatists like James and Dewey often operated through more or less dogmatic assertion and utility considerations.

In comparison, Wittgenstein's dialectical procedure of teasing out conceptual confusions and tensions inherent in philosophical problems and theories is subtle to a fault. Nor is the destination always the same. Like the pragmatists, Wittgenstein sought the solution to the puzzle of meaning in linguistic practice. But his account is less behaviorist than that of Dewey and Mead. He did not subscribe to a causal theory of meaning by identifying the meaning of a word with either the causes or the effects of its utterance. Similarly, his comparison of words to tools notwithstanding, his conception of meaning was not genuinely instrumentalist. He was not concerned with the practical effects of the use of a word, but with the role or function that it has within a system of rules.

This normativist perspective on language sets him apart from strong naturalistic tendencies within American philosophy in the wake of Quine. Even Davidson, who professes sympathy for Wittgenstein's slogan that meaning is use and for the repudiation of the idea of a private language, rejects the idea that language is an activity guided by shared conventions (Glock 2003*b*: chs. 3 and 5).

At the same time, there is an equally impressive normativist strand both in American pragmatism and in contemporary American philosophy. Peirce's semiotic distinction between index, icon, and symbol is congenial to Wittgenstein's claim that signs acquire a genuine linguistic meaning through the roles they play in a conventional practice.[12] Norms are also pivotal for current attempts to avoid *both* epistemological naturalism, the view that there is no knowledge outside natural science, *and* ontological supernaturalism, the view that there are supernatural entities such as God, Platonic Forms, or Cartesian souls (in addition to Sellars, Brandom, McDowell, and Putnam, see Williams 1999). The basic idea is that human beings are special not because they are connected to a reality beyond the physical world of space, time, and matter, but because they can only be adequately understood from a

---

[12] Both approaches can be combined to combat Fodor's idea that there is a 'language of thought' involving signs the tokens of which are neural firings that are not and cannot be employed by speakers or hearers and which are not subject to convention and interpretation by cognitive subjects (Glock 2003*a*).

normative perspective alien to the natural sciences. For this reason, there is knowledge outside natural science—knowledge of language and meaning, for example—even though it does not deal with supernatural entities.

This 'third way' goes back to Wittgenstein's comparison of language to a game like chess. On the one hand, a chess-piece is a piece of wood whose constitution can be described by physics. On the other hand, one cannot explain what a chess-piece or what the game of chess is in purely physical terms. Yet the difference between a chess-piece and a simple piece of wood is not that the former is associated with an abstract entity or with a process in a separate mental realm. Rather, it is that the chess-piece has a role in a rule-guided practice (1953: §108).

That practice in turn presupposes agents with special and distinctively human capacities. Yet, while these capacities cannot be adequately characterized in physical terms, they do not transcend the natural world. They are perfectly intelligible features of animals of a unique kind; and their causal prerequisites and evolutionary emergence can be explained by science. In spelling out this inspiration, American proponents of the third way will face severe challenges from both Quinean naturalists and Kripkean metaphysicians.[13] But that will help to keep them on their toes.

References

Albritton, R. (1959). 'On Wittgenstein's Use of the Term "Criterion"'. *Journal of Philosophy*, 61: 845–57.

Ambrose, A. (1935). 'Finitism in Mathematics'. *Mind*, 44: 186–203.

Armstrong, D. M. and Malcolm, N. (1984). *Consciousness and Causality*. Oxford: Blackwell.

Arrington, R. L. (1983). 'Representation in Wittgenstein's *Tractatus* and Middle Writings'. *Synthese*, 56: 181–98.

——(1989). *Rationalism, Realism and Relativism*. Ithaca, NY: Cornell University Press.

——and Glock, H. J. (eds.) (1996). *Wittgenstein and Quine*. New York: Routledge.

Baker, G. P., and Hacker, P. M. S. (1984). *Scepticism, Rules and Language*. Oxford: Blackwell.

Biletzki, A. (2003). *(Over)Interpreting Wittgenstein*. Dordrecht: Kluwer.

Black, M. (1949). *Language and Philosophy*. Ithaca, NY: Cornell University Press.

---

[13] The relation of Wittgensteinian ideas to the new theory of reference spearheaded by Kripke need not be antagonistic through and through, as Wettstein (2004) shows.

_____ (1964). *A Companion to Wittgenstein's 'Tractatus'*. Ithaca, NY: Cornell University Press.

Bouwsma, O. K. (1986). *Wittgenstein Conversations*. Indianapolis: Hackett.

Brandom, R. (1994). *Making it Explicit*. Cambridge, MA: Harvard University Press.

Carnap, R. (1937). *The Logical Syntax of Language*. London: Routledge & Kegan Paul.

_____ (1956). *Meaning and Necessity*. Chicago: University of Chicago Press.

_____ (1963). 'Intellectual Autobiography'. In P. Schilpp (ed.), *The Philosophy of Rudolf Carnap*, Library of Living Philosophers, 11, La Salle, IL: Open Court, 1–84.

_____ (1964). 'Interview mit Rudolf Carnap (1964)'. In W. Hochkeppel (ed.), *Mein Weg in die Philosophie*, Stuttgart: Reclam, 138–47.

Cavell, S. (1962). 'The Availability of Wittgenstein's Philosophy'. *Philosophical Review*, 71: 67–93. Repr. in Pitcher (1968), 151–85.

_____ (1969). *Must We Mean What We Say?* New York: Scribner.

_____ (1979). *The Claim of Reason*. Oxford: Oxford University Press.

_____ (2001). 'The *Investigations*' Everyday Aesthetics of Itself'. In McCarthy and Stidd (2001), 250–66.

Chihara, C. S. (1963). 'Mathematical Discovery and Concept-Formation'. *Philosophical Review*, 72: 17–34. Repr. in Pitcher (1968), 448–68.

_____ (1982). 'The Wright-Wing Defence of Wittgenstein's Philosophy of Logic'. *Philosophical Review*, 90: 99–108.

Conant, J. (1992). 'Kierkegaard, Wittgenstein and Nonsense'. In T. Cohen, P. Guyer, and H. Putnam (eds.), *Pursuits of Reason*, Lubbock, TX: Texas Tech University Press, 195–224.

_____ (2001). 'Two Conceptions of *Die Überwindung der Metaphysik*'. In McCarthy and Stidd (2001), 13–61.

_____ (2002). 'The Method of the *Tractatus*'. In E. Reck (ed.), *From Frege to Wittgenstein*, Oxford: Oxford University Press, 374–462.

_____ (2007). 'Mild Mono-Wittgensteinianism', in Crary (2007), 31–142.

Crary, A. (2000). 'Introduction'. In Crary and Read (2000), 1–18.

_____ (ed.) (2007). *Wittgenstein and the Moral Life*. Cambridge, MA: MIT Press.

_____ and Read, R. (eds.) (2000). *The New Wittgenstein*. London: Routledge.

Davidson, D. (2001 [1984]). *Inquiries into Truth and Interpretation*. Oxford: Oxford University Press.

_____ (1985). 'Reply to Quine on Events'. In E. Lepore and B. McLaughlin (eds.), *Actions and Events: Perspectives on the Philosophy of Donald Davidson*, Oxford: Blackwell, 172–6.

Diamond, C. (1991). *The Realistic Spirit*. Cambridge, MA: MIT Press.

_____ (2000). 'Ethics, Imagination and the Method of Wittgenstein's *Tractatus*'. In Crary and Read (2000), 149–73.

Ebersole, Frank B. (1979). *Language and Perception*. Washington: University Press of America.

Fann, K. T. (1969). *Wittgenstein's Conception of Philosophy*. Oxford: Blackwell.

Feigl, H. (1981). *Inquiries and Provocations,* ed. R. S. Cohen. Dordrecht: Reidel.

Fodor, J., and Chihara, C. (1965). 'Operationalism and Ordinary Language: A Critique of Wittgenstein'. *American Philosophical Quarterly*, 2: 281–95.

Fogelin, R. F. (1976). *Wittgenstein*. London: Routledge; 2nd edn. 1987.

Forster, M. N. (2004). *Wittgenstein on the Arbitrariness of Grammar*. Princeton: Princeton University Press.

Friedman, M. (1998). 'Logical Positivism'. In E. Craig (ed.), *The Routledge Encyclopedia of Philosophy*, London: Routledge, 789–95.

Garver, N. (1994). *This Complicated Form of Life*. La Salle, IL: Open Court.

Gaynesford, M. de (2006). *Hilary Putnam*. Chesham: Acumen.

Glock, H. J. (1996). *A Wittgenstein Dictionary*. Oxford: Blackwell.

—— (ed.) (2001). *Wittgenstein: A Critical Reader*. Oxford: Blackwell.

—— (2003a). 'Neural Representationalism'. *Facta Philosophica*, 5: 147–71.

—— (2003b). *Quine and Davidson*. Cambridge: Cambridge University Press.

—— (2004). 'All Kinds of Nonsense'. In E. Ammereller and E. Fischer (eds.), *Wittgenstein at Work*, London: Routledge, 221–45.

—— (2006). 'Truth in the *Tractatus*'. *Synthese*, 148: 345–68.

—— (2007). 'Perspectives on Wittgenstein: An Intermittently Opinionated Survey'. In G. Kahane, E. Kanderian, and O. Kuusela (eds.), *Wittgenstein and his Interpreters*, Oxford: Blackwell, 37–65.

—— (2008). *What is Analytic Philosophy?* Cambridge: Cambridge University Press.

Goldfarb, W. (1997). 'Metaphysics and Nonsense'. *Journal of Philosophical Research*, 22: 57–73.

Hacker, P. M. S. (1996). *Wittgenstein's Place in Twentieth-Century Analytical Philosophy*. Oxford: Blackwell.

—— (2001). *Wittgenstein: Connections and Controversies*. Oxford: Oxford University Press.

—— (2003). 'Wittgenstein, Carnap and the New American Wittgensteinians'. *Philosophical Quarterly*, 53: 1–23.

Hallett, G. (1977). *A Companion to Wittgenstein's "Philosophical Investigations"*. Ithaca, NY: Cornell University Press.

Hintikka, J. (1996). *Ludwig Wittgenstein: Half-Truths and One-and-a-Half-Truths*. Boston: Kluwer.

—— and Hintikka, A. M. (2002). 'Wittgenstein: The Bewitched Writer'. In R. Haller and K. Puhl (eds.), *Wittgenstein and the Future of Philosophy*, Vienna: öbv & hpt, 131–50.

Hintikka, M. B., and Hintikka, J. (1986). *Investigating Wittgenstein*. Oxford: Blackwell.

Ishiguro, H. (2001). 'The So-called Picture Theory: Language and the World in *Tractatus Logico-Philosophicus*'. In Glock (2001), 26–46.

Kober, M. (1996). 'Certainties of a World-Picture: The Epistemological Investigations of *On Certainty*'. In Sluga and Stern (1996), 411–41.

Kripke, S. (1982). *Wittgenstein on Rules and Private Language*. Cambridge, MA: Harvard University Press.

Lackey, D. (1999). 'What are the Modern Classics? The Baruch Poll of Great Philosophy in the Twentieth Century'. *Philosophical Forum*, 4: 329–46.

Langer, Susanne K. (1948). *Philosophy in a New Key*. Cambridge, MA: Harvard University Press.

Lazerowitz, M., and Ambrose, A. (1985). *Necessity and Language*. London: Croom Helm.

Malcolm, N. (1949). 'Defending Common Sense'. *Philosophical Review*, 48: 201–20.

_____ (1959). *Dreaming*. London: Routledge & Kegan Paul.

_____ (1972). *Problems of Mind*. London: Allen & Unwin.

_____ (1977). *Memory and Mind*. Ithaca, NY: Cornell University Press.

_____ (1984). *Wittgenstein—A Memoir*. Oxford: Oxford University Press.

_____ (1986). *Nothing is Hidden*. Oxford: Blackwell.

Marion, M. (1998). *Wittgenstein, Finitism, and the Foundations of Mathematics*. Oxford: Clarendon Press.

Marsoobian, A., and Ryder, John (2004). *The Blackwell Guide to American Philosophy*. Oxford: Blackwell.

McCarthy, T., and Stidd, S. C. (eds.) (2001). *Wittgenstein in America*. New York: Oxford University Press.

McDowell, J. (1994). *Mind and World*. Cambridge, MA: Harvard University Press.

_____ (1998). *Mind, Value and Reality*. Cambridge, MA: Harvard University Press.

Miller, A., and Wright, C. (eds.) (2002). *Rule-Following and Meaning*. Chesham: Acumen.

Monk, R. (1990). *Wittgenstein: The Duty of Genius*. London: Cape.

Moyal-Sharrock, D. (ed.) (2004). *The Third Wittgenstein: The Post-Investigations Works*. Aldershot: Ashgate.

Philipp, P. (1996). *Bibliographie zur Wittgenstein-Literatur*. Bergen: Wittgenstein Archives.

Pitcher, G. (1964). *The Philosophy of Wittgenstein*. Englewood Cliffs, NJ: Prentice-Hall.

_____ (ed.) (1968). *The Philosophical Investigations*. London: Macmillan.

Proops, I. (2001). 'The New Wittgenstein: A Critique'. *European Journal of Philosophy*, 9: 375–404.

Putnam, H. (1975). *Mind, Language and Reality*. Cambridge: Cambridge University Press.

_____ (forthcoming). 'Is Analytic Philosophy a Good Thing? Why I am Ambivalent'.

Quine, W. V. (1969). *Ontological Relativity and Other Essays*. New York: Columbia University Press.

Ricketts, T. (1996). 'Pictures, Logic and the Limits of Sense in Wittgenstein's *Tractatus*'. In Sluga and Stern (1996), 59–99.

Rorty, R. (1979). *Philosophy and the Mirror of Nature*. Princeton: Princeton University Press.

_____ (1982). *Consequences of Pragmatism*. Minneapolis: University of Minnesota Press.

_____ (1986). 'Pragmatism, Davidson and Truth'. In E. LePore (ed.), *Truth and Interpretation*, Oxford: Blackwell, 333–55.

Russell, B. (1914). *Our Knowledge of the External World*. Chicago: Open Court.

Sass, L. (2001). 'Deep Disquietudes'. In J. Klagge (ed.), *Wittgenstein: Philosophy and Biography*, New York: Cambridge University Press, 98–155.

Schroeder, S. (1997). 'The Concept of Dreaming: On Three Theses by Malcolm'. *Philosophical Investigations*, 20: 15–38.

Searle, J. (1987). 'Wittgenstein'. In B. Magee (ed.), *The Great Philosophers*, Oxford: Oxford University Press, 320–47.

Schwyzer, H. (2001). 'Autonomy'. In Glock (2001), 289–304.

Sellars, W. (1963). *Science, Perception and Reality*. London: Routledge & Kegan Paul.

Shanker, S. (1987). *Wittgenstein and the Turning Point in the Philosophy of Mathematics*. London: Croom Helm.

Sluga, H., and Stern, D. (eds.) (1996). *The Cambridge Companion to Wittgenstein*. Cambridge: Cambridge University Press.

Stern, D. (1994). 'The Wittgenstein Papers as Text and Hypertext'. In K. Johannessen (ed.), *Wittgenstein and Norway*, Oslo: Solum, 251–74.

—— (1996). 'The Availability of Wittgenstein's Philosophy'. In Sluga and Stern (1996), 442–76.

—— (2004). *Wittgenstein's Philosophical Investigations: An Introduction*. Cambridge: Cambridge University Press.

—— (2005). 'How Many Wittgensteins?'. In A. Pichler, and S. Säätelä (eds.), *Wittgenstein: The Philosopher and his Works*, Bergen: Wittgenstein Archives, 164–88.

Stroll, A. (1994). *Moore and Wittgenstein on Certainty*. New York: Oxford University Press.

Wettstein, H. (2004). *The Magic Prism*. New York: Oxford University Press.

Williams, M. (1999). *Wittgenstein, Mind and Meaning*. New York: Routledge.

—— (2004). 'Nonsense and Cosmic Exile'. In M. Kölbl and B. Weiss (eds.), *Wittgenstein's Lasting Significance*, New York: Routledge, 6–31.

Winch, P. (1987). *Trying to Make Sense*. Oxford: Blackwell.

Wittgenstein, L. (1961 [1922]). *Tractatus Logico-Philosophicus*. London: Routledge & Kegan Paul.

—— (1953). *Philosophical Investigations*. Oxford: Blackwell; 3rd edn. 1967.

—— (1975). *On Certainty*. Oxford: Blackwell.

—— (1979). *Wittgenstein and the Vienna Circle*. Oxford: Blackwell.

PLACING IN A SPACE OF NORMS: NEO-SELLARSIAN PHILOSOPHY IN THE TWENTY-FIRST CENTURY

MARK LANCE

WILFRID SELLARS was surely one of and, in my view, the most important philosopher of the twentieth century. Though his influence is neither as obvious to the general philosophical community, nor as wide in academia at large as that of, for example, Quine and Rawls, it is arguably deeper and of more enduring significance. Sellars made fundamental, systematic, and deeply original contributions to philosophy of language, epistemology, metaphysics, philosophy of mind, and pragmatism, and lesser but still important contributions to meta-ethics and philosophical logic.

There are many ways one might approach a survey of the influence of Sellars's work on contemporary philosophy. The most obvious would be to offer a survey of his own ideas; but given the broad and systematic nature of his work, this would be most difficult in a short essay, and in any event good discussions of Sellars's work have been published recently. The most systematic of these is William DeVries's recent book (2005). While I certainly do not agree with DeVries's reading of Sellars in all particulars, he has done a wonderful job of capturing the major themes in Sellars's work for a twenty-first-century audience.

Another possibility would be to survey the many research programs that have grown out of Sellars's work. The problem here is the sheer scope of the project. Sellars's ideas have been deeply influential in the work of such diverse philosophers as Paul Churchland, Hector-Neri Castañeda, Bas van Fraassen, John McDowell, Jay Rosenberg, Laurence BonJour, Robert Brandom, and Daniel Dennett. Each of these philosophers has highlighted different elements of Sellars's work, and while such a focus has often led them in significantly "un-Sellarsian" directions, this is neither to criticize the importance of the work, nor to underplay the Sellarsian influence. The ability to inspire new and diverse research programs is surely one important measure of the importance of a philosopher.

In what follows, I propose a more modest project. I sketch a single trajectory—or at least, a cluster of closely related trajectories—that take off from the Sellarsian corpus. Perhaps it is better to say that this trajectory incorporates the Sellarsian corpus as a significant moment in its historical development, since the ideas I explain here trace their influence also to such philosophers as Wittgenstein, the classical American pragmatists, Heidegger, Hegel, and Kant. Indeed, one of the important thematic innovations of the Sellarsian legacy is the tracing of an intelligible historical thread that moves through and discerns common themes from these figures and others. (Less obvious figures who are nonetheless arguably intelligible in terms of this tradition include Merleau-Ponty and Foucault.)

The last period of Sellars's life roughly coincided with the emergence of a remarkable intellectual community at the University of Pittsburgh, a community whose discussions centered on key Sellarsian ideas. In the period from 1980 to 1995 (Sellars died in 1989), each of the following was at Pitt as either a professor or a graduate student: Wilfrid himself, Bob Brandom, Joe Camp, John McDowell, John Haugeland, Jim Conant, Nuel Belnap, Michael Kremer, Ken Gemes, Bill Blattner, Danielle Macbeth, Marc Lange,

John MacFarlane, Johanna Seibt, Rebecca Kukla, and myself. Of course there were many other extraordinary philosophers around at the time—Gauthier, two Baiers, two Salmons, Glymour, Earman, Grünbaum, Rescher, Gupta, and Nehamas, to name just a few—and the tradition I lay out in what follows had other important contributors not present in this period at Pitt—Rorty, Rouse, Pinkard, Taylor, etc.—but the above group formed a central basis for a conversation that I believe is now coming into its own as a major tradition in American philosophy, as one of the viable ways of doing, understanding, and thinking about philosophy, a tradition often simply referred to as "Pittsburgh philosophy".

1. NORMATIVE FUNCTIONALISM

Sellars is rightly credited with being one of the originators of functionalism in the philosophy of mind, but the typical understanding of functionalism is quite distinct from Sellars's own conception of mental kinds. To understand the first key distinction, let's begin with two jokes:

Joke 1

Q: What do you call a boomerang that doesn't come back to you?

A: A stick.

Joke 2

Q: What does an orthopedic surgeon call an athlete's knee that won't bend?

A: College tuition for the kids.

The distinction is straightforward. A "descriptive functionalist type" is one in which an entity is a member of the type just in case it actually plays a certain functional role in the architecture of an appropriate larger whole. In this sense of "function", something only functions as a boomerang if it plays the role characteristic of boomerangs. A non-functioning boomerang is not a boomerang at all.

Despite its prominence in the philosophical literature on functionalist approaches to philosophy of mind, both pro and con, descriptive functionalism is not the only, or the most common, way that we invoke function in the individuation of types in either ordinary language or science. When my computer breaks, I do not think of it as no longer a computer. (That it is now an expensive paper-weight is usually meant *merely* as a joke.) We do not think of a non-functioning heart—say, in a recent heart-attack victim—as not a heart. Rather, we see these as "defective" instances of the kind, but instances nonetheless. The fact that they are not fulfilling the relevant function is reason not for reclassification, but for repair. This use of functional kind-terms, on the surface, seems to commit one to "normative functionalism", according to which a kind is defined by the function that instances *ought to* perform, or *properly* perform. To individuate entities in terms of normative function is to treat a function as a sort of ideal against which the item in question is measured, and to draw various implications about the way the entity should function, and the way in which others should relate to it in light of that *telos*.

Of course, classical descriptive functionalism does not simply ignore the fact that functional classification goes on in cases in which the entity in question does not continue to function in the relevant manner. One might look to "typical" function as definitive of the nature of the object. (Though here one is at a loss to understand the sense in which an ill-manufactured part—one that will never function in the proper way—is of the relevant functional kind.) Or one might look to the intentions of the creator of the object as definitive of the kind. That is, for the object to be of the functional kind is for it to have been created with the intention of its fitting that kind. (But here, barring explanatory resort to theism, one is at a loss to explain the functional status of objects that have no creator.)[1]

In the end, what marks the fundamental difference between the two sorts of functionalism is how seriously, and ineliminably, one makes use of normative notions. The descriptive functionalist either eschews or reduces any reference to normative status, or normative function, while the normative functionalist takes such an idea as essential and irreducible, defining function in terms of it.

For our purposes, an important example of normative functionalism occurs in games and sports. Sellars himself makes frequent use of the example of chess.[2] To understand something as a pawn is to understand it in terms of the role it properly plays in a game governed by rules. A pawn need not always be functioning as a pawn. One can, after all, make illegal moves. That they are

---

[1] I do not, of course, take myself to have refuted descriptive functionalism in this short comment. There are many moves that are made. The goal here is to remind the reader of the considerations that lead philosophers to normative functionalism. Indeed, my goal throughout this paper is expository rather than argumentative. I want to give a general outline of how things are seen by proponents of a current in contemporary American philosophy, certainly not to argue against other approaches.

[2] For example, in understanding the meaning of a sentence in Sellars 1950 and 1954.

illegal—that they are improper, moves one should not make—simply entails that the object is still at that moment functioning as a pawn, because there is no sense in which it is wrong to move a piece of plastic from one side of a board to another all at once. To be a pawn, that is, is to be the sort of thing that is subject to the rules of chess governing pawns, not necessarily something that is actually following those rules.

Such normative functional kinds are importantly holistic. That is, there is an important ontological dimension in which the game of chess is prior to the pawn. This is not to say that there could be games of chess without pawns, but rather to say that what it is to be a pawn is essentially tied to its role *in the game.* It is not merely a contingent epistemic fact that one cannot understand a pawn except by understanding what the game is and the role the pawn plays in that game. Rather, that a pawn is understood by its role in the game is of the essence of the kind.[3] Thus, there is a constitutive tie between the overall point of the game and the normative role played by the pawn.

Similar points can be made regarding sports. Here, not only are objects understood in terms of their role in the game—balls, goals, fields of play, etc. are what they are in terms of their proper function in soccer—but we see normative functionalist conceptions of agents as well. How do we understand the kind "batter" (in baseball)? One could discuss the typical physiology or perhaps the chemical makeup of batters, but this would utterly miss the point. Closer to the mark would be to discuss how they typically function within the social practice of baseball—they try to hit pitches, run to first base when they do, etc. But here we are met with the usual objections to descriptive functionalism. Some batters routinely fail. (In games against young children, they fail even in following the rules far more often than they succeed.) Others are unmotivated. But these must count as defects. An unmotivated batter is a bad batter, not merely a guy who stands around near home plate.

On the normative functionalist construal, to take someone to be a batter is to take them to be subject to certain rules (three strikes and you are out), committed to certain constitutive goals (getting on base), appropriately responsive to the judgments of certain other agents in the game (umpires), related in appropriate ways to other players (pitchers, catchers, etc.), and

---

[3] The idea of an ontological category defined in epistemic terms is familiar from Descartes's definition of the mental in terms of privileged introspective access. Despite other radical differences between the Cartesian and Sellarsian traditions, this kind of privileging of the epistemic is an important and little noted similarity.

ultimately to the entire game. To take something to be a batter, one might well put the point, is to *place them* within the game of baseball.

That is, while one can understand the object that is a batter as an object, as a biological organism, etc., one can also take up a different *stance* towards them: the baseball stance.[4] To do so is to understand their actions as *plays*, their role as *position*, the events in the world as happenings in a game to which they are normatively accountable. And there is nothing more to being a batter than such a stance being appropriate. To be a batter is to be someone to whom one appropriately applies the relevant rules, interpretations, descriptions, and evaluations. It is to be someone for whom a ball thrown by the guy on the mound is a pitch by a pitcher, for whom standing still in response to that flying ball is "taking" the pitch, itself a substantive action with a concrete normative significance depending on the specific trajectory the pitch takes.[5]

2. MEANING

It is in just this sense that we should understand the Sellarsian idea that to treat something as a person is to place it within the space of reasons.

When God created Adam, he whispered in his ear, 'In all contexts of action you will recognize rules, if only the rule to grope for rules to recognize. When you cease to recognize rules, you will walk on four feet.'   (Sellars 1950: 313)

Though I claim that it permeates the entire Sellarsian tradition, we see the normative functionalist approach most obviously in Sellarsian accounts of linguistic meaning. According to Sellars, saying what a sentence means is not offering a descriptive account of the sentence, but rather characterizing it in terms of its role, where this is understood in normative terms. Without going into detail, Sellars distinguishes three types of moves that occur in "language-games": language entrances, language–language moves, and language exits. The first are, paradigmatically, observations—moving from an

---

[4] The notion of a stance—of a broad practice of taking things in certain ways, subject to a distinctive system of normative appropriateness—is probably most familiar from Strawson's distinction between the objective and the participant stance; but Dennett has applied the idea in ways that are closer in topic—though not necessarily in final view—to the uses by Sellars. I discuss this approach, and apply it to the idea of human freedom, in Lance and White 2007.

[5] For a detailed discussion of the way in which the individuation of actions is dependent upon such practical placing, and to be understood in terms of such normative significance, see Maher 2007.

act of observation to a linguistic claim. A classic example would be seeing a rabbit and saying "That's a rabbit". Language–language moves are, roughly, inferences, but inferences understood quite broadly to include not only moving from "That's a rabbit" to "That's a rabbit or that's a squirrel" but also to "That's a mammal" and even to "The garden is in danger". These latter substantive moves, in distinction to logical inferences, are called "material inferences". Language exit moves are moves that take us from performances in language to other sorts of actions—say, stating an intention and doing it, or giving an order and its being followed.

Thus, to talk about meaning, for Sellars, is to talk about how words function within a normative system that governs a practice in which we make such moves and are governed by proprieties relating to them. So, according to Sellars, to say that "Schnee ist Weiss" (in German) means that snow is white is to say that "Schnee ist Weiss" (in German) is a •snow is white•. Here "dot quotes" are Sellars's technical device that functions as an operator that takes a sentence of a language to the normative functional role played by that sentence. Thus, what we are doing in making such a meaning claim is explaining the proper role of a German sentence. But we are doing it not by spelling out that role in theoretical terms—say, by giving a partial account of the inferential proprieties applying to it—but by relating it to another sentence playing (roughly) the same role, where it is pragmatically assumed that the person we are speaking to already understands this latter sentence (generally implicitly) in its normative role. That is to say, I perform a speech act which takes your prior tacit understanding of how to use "Snow is white" and turns this into an understanding of the role of "Schnee ist weiss" in German: "That German sentence works like this English one you know how to use." Similarly, we might point to a piece of equipment designed for alien physiology by holding up a hammer and saying "It is one of these".

The project of turning this idea about the nature of meaning into an explicit theory of such normative roles has been taken up in greatest detail by Robert Brandom. In a series of articles culminating in his massively influential *Making It Explicit* (1994), Brandom develops this idea in the direction of "inferentialism", which is the view that semantic content is a function of inferential role, where, as in Sellars, inferential role is a matter of various normative proprieties attaching to material inferential moves.

In Brandom's work, the Kantian principle of the priority of the propositional takes on a decidedly pragmatic tone. In line with the fundamental normative functionalist project, the primary elements of language are the sorts of performances that can be governed by practical norms. For Brandom, the central move in the language-game is that of asserting. To assert is to commit oneself to a justificatory burden—to responding to appropriate linguistic challenges, to providing evidence, etc.—and to offer to others an inference license—to endorse, that is, claims that can appropriately be inferred from the assertion in question and to take up a stance of challenge or incompatibility to a range of contrary assertions. (Compare: to be a batter is to take on as a constitutive responsibility the goal of hitting a pitch. Asserting, for Brandom, is stepping up to the plate on behalf of a claim.)

Starting with the idea of such a normatively constrained linguistic perform-ance, and manipulating in various ways the normative statuses of commitment and entitlement, as well as the pragmatic stances of undertaking (commit-ment) and attributing (either commitment or entitlement), Brandom develops detailed explanations of a range of linguistically and philosophically important phenomena. First among these is the definition of several sorts of inference in normative terms.[6] Using this, he defines various sorts of inferential role. In terms of so-called substitution inferences, sub-sentential content comes into view. The basic idea here is to understand the role of a part of a sentence in terms of the contribution it makes to the inferential role of sentences in which it occurs. The overall result is a program in formal semantics which, though far less developed, deserves to be seen as a serious competitor to truth-conditional and possible-worlds semantics.

The role of logical vocabulary is important to this program. Since it is the inferential role of sentences that make them what they are, in the relevant sense, we should expect that the ability to state these proprieties explicitly would be particularly important. In order to give any sort of theory of the meaning of sentences, one will have to make use of various conditional locutions. If we are, that is, to render theoretically the sorts of roles that are captured in the Sellarsian dot-quote schemas, we will say things like "If that is a rabbit, then it is a mammal". Such logical vocabulary, according to Brandom, is paradigmatic of vocabulary that "makes explicit" a normative propriety previously implicit in a normatively constrained game.

The familiar rules of a logical system—inferential proprieties governing sentences with logical vocabulary—emerge as proposals for how to institute

---

[6] For more on this aspect of the program, see both *Making It Explicit* and the recent Locke Lectures, as well as my "Two Concepts of Entailment" (1995).

a content on a bit of language—'and', 'or', 'if...then...', 'it is not the case that', etc.—that would allow it to play this expliciting role. This conception of logic has spawned a small literature in philosophical logic of its own.[7]

3. Objections to Brandomian Semantics

We consider here three objections to the inferentialist development of Sellarsian normative inferentialism about language. The first comes from outside the program, while the other two are internal.

A number of writers, notably Fodor, have attempted to dismiss inferentialism as implying a pernicious form of holism. The argument goes roughly like this: If meaning is a function of material inferential role, then any two claims which stand in different inferential relations to any claim whatsoever must mean something different. Thus, a relation to any claim whatsoever is, in principle, relevant to the meaning of a given claim P. Thus, since no two people will ever relate claims in precisely the same way across the entire language, no claim can ever mean the same in my mouth as it does in yours. Fodor and others have claimed that this objection requires that Brandom somehow divide the inferences involving P into those relevant to meaning and those not, which is to introduce the analytic/synthetic distinction discredited by Quine.

I mention this objection not because it is a serious worry for the program, but simply because it is heard frequently and to make clear the difference between descriptive and normative functionalism. In fact, the objection is based entirely on reading the Brandomian project as descriptive. Once we realize that what is at issue is not the inferences people are disposed to make (or some such), but the inferences that are proper within the relevant practice, the issue disappears. There is no need to invoke any analytic/synthetic partitioning of the space of acceptable inferences for these purposes at all. My use of "spin angular momentum" and that of the physicist mean the same thing, not because *we are disposed* to make the same inferences from assertions, for example, of "Some quarks have 1/3 integral spin angular momentum" but

---

[7] Peregrin 2000, 2001, 2007; Lance and Kremer 1994, 1995; Lance 2001; Restall 1993, 2004.

because the same things *properly* follow from my assertion of this declarative as follow from the physicist's assertion.[8]

The second worry about the Brandomian program is much more serious, and one that arises from within the Sellarsian project. John McDowell has repeatedly and forcefully challenged the idea that inference can be a sufficient ground for empirical meaning, since it leaves out entirely the role of the world in receptivity. Our claims are, after all, meant to be about an empirical world, and as such, their correctness must in the end be owed to that world. But if all one has to work with is relations between sentences, it seems that correctness must be an entirely intra-linguistic affair. Our conceptual scheme is left, in McDowell's memorable phrase, spinning in the void.

This objection is aimed as much at Sellars as at Brandom, for while both—in different ways—acknowledge the causal role of the non-linguistic world in bringing about our assertions, influencing their ongoing revision, and similarly the causal role of our discursive activity, via action, on the non-linguistic world, it is a core commitment of all parties to this debate that mere causal connections cannot constitute genuine linguistic or epistemic normativity. This, as we will see below, is the essence of the myth of the given. So McDowell's challenge is to show how genuine receptive encounters with an empirical world can be part of the normative functional story. We return to this challenge below.

The final objection concerns the nature of the normativity that plays such a crucial role in Brandom's work. Brandom claims that normativity, in a sense sufficient to ground meaning and epistemic entitlement, is implicit in linguistic practice. Importantly, it is implicit in practice in a way that is independent of the logical, semantic, and epistemic vocabulary that serves to make such normativity explicit. In *Making It Explicit*, he is clear that a practice lacking explicitating vocabulary could exist and would be genuinely meaningful. But as we will see—and as Danielle Macbeth, among others, has argued—this raises very serious problems for how one is to understand normativity. Brandom is clear that semantic normativity is not reducible to behavior, whether first-order linguistic behavior or this together

---

[8] And it is worth noting that the viability—and equally important the *point*—of an analytic/synthetic distinction looks altogether different when the issue arises within the context of normative functionalism. For an account of the pragmatic significance of drawing such a distinction in ordinary argumentative practice, see Lance and O'Leary-Hawthorne 1997: ch. 2. Of course the resurrection of this distinction attempted there provides no aid and comfort to foundationalism.

with patterns of reinforcement of such behavior.[9] But one wonders what else there is. If normativity is not instituted as some pattern of linguistic behavior, and is not given by the non-linguistic world, then how are we to understand it?

Closely related, we can ask what exactly this relation of "making explicit" is meant to be. It simply cannot be that a claim makes a normative propriety explicit if it accurately captures what is done in the underlying practice, for this would just be regularism—the idea that normativity is understood as a regularity of use—which Brandom rightly condemns. It appears that the relation must be somehow normative itself, but there is a great challenge in retaining both pragmatism and full-blooded normativity here.

Note, that Sellars himself does not see things in this way. "[A]nything which can properly be called conceptual thinking can occur only within a framework of conceptual thinking in terms of which it can be criticized, supported, refuted, in short, evaluated" (1963b: 6). "Rule obeying behavior contains, in some sense, both a game and a metagame, the latter being the game in which belong the rules obeyed in playing the former game as a piece of rule obeying behavior" (1954: §16).

The second of these comments means that it is not enough for claims themselves to be criticizable; the norms that govern them must be so as well. So for Sellars, conceptually significant moves can exist only in a context in which the norms governing them can be challenged, evaluated, etc. That is, there can be no language without the ability to make explicit the inferential proprieties that lend content to that language. Why Sellars would claim that, and how it contributes to our ability to make sense of normativity itself, requires that we explain a final twist on normative functionalism and the Sellarsian critique of the given.

---

[9] I, for one, do not find any clear and consistent position on this issue in Sellars's own work. Once in the mid-1980s, when we were graduate students at Pitt, Ken Gemes and I went to talk to Sellars about this issue. Ken laid out for him what we called the distinction between "right-" and "left-" Sellarsianism. Right-Sellarsianism took it that norms—especially those constitutive of meaning—are reducible to a pattern of behavior, reinforcement and criticism of behavior, reinforcement and criticism of reinforcing and critical behavior, etc. Left-Sellarsianism takes the normative to be irreducible—"norms all the way down". Simply put, we never got a straight answer as to which view he endorsed; Sellars always insisted that this distinction was too crude and that we needed to read more. Sadly, his prescription—no doubt good in itself—was not sufficient to cure the puzzlement in my own case, though, as we will see, Sellars's denial of the Brandomian claim that explicitating vocabulary is optional suggests a way to move towards a plausible left-Sellarsianism that may not involve a fundamental ontological commitment to norms.

4. HISTORICIST NORMATIVE FUNCTIONALISM

A number of Sellars's most famous and novel accounts are put in historical terms. We are told a story—often called a "myth"—about the origin and development of an idea as a way of explicating what the idea is. Sellars is always careful to emphasize that he is not purporting to do armchair history, that what is being made explicit by the quasi-historical narrative is a certain logical structure, or a dimension of logical dependence. What exactly can this mean? Here is one idea that is clear enough and at least part of what is going on in key Sellarsian accounts.

Sometimes we find a social practice that can only be understood as dependent upon another practice. That is to say first that we have an asymmetrical dependence—practice A could exist without practice B, but not vice versa—but also to say that the functional identity of B involves its relation to the structure within which A functions. Consider the genre of realistic fiction. One could not understand the idea of a fictional portrayal, say in a movie, of a sort of situation if one did not understand the kinds of performances involved in the fiction in their more fundamental context. Or again, consider the linguistic category of irony. An ironic utterance is one that functions so as to indicate the opposite of the conventional meaning of the same sentence used declaratively. ("This Iraq invasion has sure turned out well.")

But crucially, irony is not merely a species of ambiguity, with a string of words meaning one thing in one tone of voice and the negation of this in another. Rather, it is essential to the ironic use that it "wear its reversal on its sleeve". The practice of irony is essentially derivative. It can be understood only as a normative system that rides as an optional add-on to the normative practice of conventional declarival speech.

The most natural way to explain a structure like this is in historical stages. One would first give an account of the functional structure of declarival speech, and then explain how such a system could be made more complex by adding another layer of practice to it, one in which sentences are used for particular effect in an ironic manner.

Such an account is clearly at work in Sellars's argument in his 1997 that looks-talk (talk of how things appear to one) is derivative on is-talk. For Sellars, looks-talk is both epistemically and conceptually dependent—in one important dimension of dependence—on is-talk. That is, only someone who understands the proper function of claims about how things are can so much as meaningfully utter claims about how things appear to her. Further, any knowledge of how things appear is dependent upon lots of knowledge about how things are. Telling this story in historical normative functionalist terms—building the structure of the practice of looks-judgments as a logically derivate add-on to a practice of is-judgments—is supposed to make clear how this dimension of dependence is compatible with the fact that appearances can be genuinely non-inferential and stand as evidence for claims about the world.

5. HEGELIAN HISTORICAL NORMATIVE FUNCTIONALISM

One of the key ideas that emerges in Hegel's account of the historical development of consciousness is that later stages in the development of a conceptual scheme change the status of earlier ones.[10] One might think, for example, that legal normativity is essentially derivative on moral normativity. Without a practice, that is, of taking each other to be persons subject to moral norms, there could not be such a thing as an institutionalized practice of law. Of course one group of hominids could knock another group around when they did not act in accordance with some rule or other, but that would not be normativity, certainly not law. (What matters for present purposes is only that such a view is understandable, not that it is ultimately correct.)

Indeed, one might take legal norms to be a particular sort of institutionalization of a portion of (what a society takes to be) the moral law within a structure of governance. But to think of legal norms in this way is quite compatible with thinking that the character of moral practice is quite different when it exists in the context of a system that includes the practice of law. The function of "moral norm" may be intelligible within a practice not including the law, but at the same time it could be seen to be fundamentally different in the more complex structure. Further, so this line of thought goes, even actions performed at earlier points in history—acts performed before the

---

[10] I call this sort of functionalism "Hegelian" as a way of crediting the philosopher whom I take to have first developed such an idea, not because anything in this section is meant as a reading of Hegel. When I speak of 'historical stages' in this section, I mean this, of course, in the sense of sect. 4.

institutionalization of law—have a different function because of the fact that they were performed within a practice that would, in the future, involve the more complex structure.[11]

However this might be for the relation between law and morality, I think this structure is what Sellars is getting at in the above quotes. A practice without normative explicitating vocabulary can involve rules in fairly robust ways. Sellars (1950) distinguishes three notions of an act's dependence upon rules. The thinnest is simply acting "in accord with" rules. The most robust is following, or obeying, a rule, something one does only when one is aware of the rule, capable of citing it as the justification of the action, etc. Between these is what Sellars speaks of as action "because of" a rule.

[W]e have tacitly accepted a dichotomy between (a) *merely conforming to rules*; doing A in C, A′ in C′ etc., where these doings "just happen" to contribute to the realization of a complex pattern; (b) *obeying rules*; doing A in C, A′ in C′, etc. with the intention of fulfilling the demands of an envisaged system of rules. But surely this is a false dichotomy! . . . Let me use a familiar analogy to make my point. In interpreting the phenomena of evolution, it is quite proper to say that the sequence of species living in the various environments on the earth's surface took the form it did because this sequence maintained and improved a biological *rapport* between species and environment. It is quite clear, however, that saying this does not commit us to the idea that some mind or other envisaged this biological *rapport* and intended its realization. . . . What would it mean to say of a bee returning from a clover field that its turnings and wigglings occur *because* they are part of a complex dance? . . . It is open to us to give an evolutionary account of the phenomena of the dance, and hence to interpret the statement that *this* wiggle occurred because of the complex dance to which it belongs.   (1954: 225)

In another essay, he says:

. . . a rule is an embodied generalization which to speak loosely but suggestively, tends to make itself true. Better, it tends to inhibit the occurrence of such events as would falsify it . . .   (1950: 299)

But if one can be in such a non-accidental relation to rules in virtue of practices that lack explicitating vocabulary, there is another important and richer sense of normativity that is lacking for creatures such as bees. However rich this normative structure becomes, however embedded and institutionalized the function of the rules in bringing about the evolution of behavior in accord with them, one is still *merely bound by* rules in such a

---

[11] Certain readers may recognize this as an instantiation of what is known as "semantic temporal externalism".

practice. It is in this sense that a dog can learn bits of human language, learn where it ought to eat and defecate, understand that it shouldn't jump on people, etc. Namely, it can come to competently act in accord with such rules in virtue of the bindingness of those rules. But for all this, the dog's relation to norms is fundamentally different from that of a person.

A person, in a slogan, is not merely the subject of norms, but the author of them as well. That is, when told that I oughtn't to do something, I can react by obeying or not, just like the dog. But I have as well another crucial move open to me in the normative practice of action evaluation: I can insist that the person telling me what I ought to do *is wrong*. I can argue that the putative norm is mistaken, demand a reason, provide counter reasons, etc. I submit that it is plausible that normativity which functions within a practice in which it can be "criticized, supported, refuted, in short, evaluated" is normativity in a fundamentally different sense from normativity which functions in a practice without these possibilities, despite the fact that norms governing such criticizing, supporting, etc. are clearly derivative on a more basic practice of normative evaluation. Indeed, one sense in which norms are not merely imperatives—in which oughts are grounded in the space of reasons rather than on personal authority—is that they are subject to such critical evaluation.[12]

Of course, saying that normativity is fundamentally different when operating in a context in which explicit normative claims can be made, challenged, evaluated, and defended is not yet to say what those claims are. If we must understand them in terms of what Derrida calls "the metaphysics of presence"—namely, in terms of the object that they purport to describe—it is unclear that the historicist project is getting anywhere.[13] We have to understand the speech act of "stating a normative propriety" as *doing* something other than merely describing.

This is what we identified above as the second objection to the Brandomian program. Recall that Brandom wants, on the one hand, to preserve the core pragmatist idea that all normativity is fundamentally instituted through skillful practice, that knowledge of rules is a derivative phenomenon, one that makes underlying normativity explicit. But, on the other hand, Brandom doesn't want to fall into any sort of descriptivist relativism that would identify

---

[12] For a detailed discussion of this distinction see Kukla and Lance 2008*b*: esp. ch. 5.

[13] Indeed, at least some of what Derrida is up to can be seen quite naturally as cohering with the Sellarsian program.

normative propriety with what is actually done. But if normative claims are essentially tied in their normative function to underlying normatively constrained practices, but are not descriptive of them, it simply seems inescapable that normative claims must have a fundamentally different pragmatic function from ordinary declarative judgments. They cannot be seen as simply semantically distinct—which would be to abandon pragmatism by taking normativity to be a kind of thing that floats free of practice (the metaphysics of presence). So they must be pragmatically distinct, their utterance functioning differently at the level of pragmatics from the declarative. But how, one wonders, can such an idea be developed without moving down well-discredited roads mapped out by classical prescriptivism in moral philosophy?

Answering this question, and developing a pragmatics of normative utterances is one of the main goals taken up in Kukla and Lance (2008b). Whether or not that account is successful, it seems clear that the viability of some such account is a precondition on the viability of the whole project. That a Sellarsian explanation of normativity must move through the pragmatic distinction between the kind of move involved in making a deontic claim and the more ordinary act of declaring explains, I think, why it is crucial to the Sellarsian program to say that only a structure in which there exists vocabulary with which to make explicit normative proprieties can be one in which norms exist in the full-blooded sense at all.[14]

But it is equally important to the Sellarsian program that even performances which took place at a point in the historical development of the agent—early childhood, say—before they were competent with the use of explicitating vocabulary can count as fully normative in virtue of the fact that they will in the future play a role in a practice that includes normativity in its full sense.[15] A similar structure is found in the relation between the mental and the linguistic on the Sellarsian approach. Sellars says that to take brain events to be instances of mental kinds is to understand them on an analogy with the

[14] Brandom once put a point similar to this one to me in the form of the slogan that a child is not a person until she has mastered conditionals.

[15] This is the point of Sellars's unpacking in his 1997 of the apparent circularity of the dependence of our knowledge of generalizations on our knowledge of particular facts, and the dependence of these on knowledge of generalizations. For a sophisticated discussion of the logic of such mutual dependence see Kukla 2000.

roles played by utterances in natural language. This idea of something that is essentially analogical is another instance of the sort of historicist normative dependence we have been discussing.

The general point of the myth of Jones, in Sellars 1997, is that our entitlement to say that things appear thus and so depends on our having knowledge of various generalizations that themselves could have epistemic status only within a practice of making and justifying claims about the world. Further, the identification of mental states in propositional terms is an identification that is essentially parasitic on the normative functional roles played by external speech acts. Roughly, to treat an internal event as a belief that P, for example, is to take it to be the sort of event that properly leads to an assertion that P, where this latter is understood in terms of its external role in the game of giving and asking for reasons.

Of course, everyone agrees that beliefs give rise to assertions. If we are justified in believing P, it is epistemically appropriate to say that P. But the question is one of conceptual priority. For the Sellarsian, there is no independent route to content that does not move through public linguistic practice, which is the only place in which normative systems can function. The function of mental states in such a system is to serve as background to, license, make inappropriate, etc. external linguistic performances. And for each category of speech act there is a corresponding internal performance that amounts to being in an occurrent state that warrantedly gives rise to the corresponding public speech act. What it is to think, in a slogan, is to be in a state of potential speaking.

Again, however, the account is Hegelian, for a normativity that operated exclusively on publicly available performances would be a singularly thin one. In our fully developed space of reasons, the vast majority of relevant propositional attitudes are not spoken. Whether I'm justified in believing P depends crucially on an enormous amount of knowledge that I have, but haven't *said*. So crucial is the tie between the mental and the linguistic that we can say that the sense of epistemic normativity that attaches to public utterances is simply different when this occurs within a practice that also individuates mental states in propositional terms, however derivative that individuation is on the practice of public speech.

6. KNOWLEDGE AND THE MYTH
OF THE GIVEN

To see mental states, including perceptual states, in these normative functionalist terms requires rejecting any framework that supposes there to be an atomistic, purely descriptive account of perceptual states that captures their relevance to epistemology. Indeed, the suggestion that the mere occurrence of some event—described in a way that does not already situate it functionally within a space of pre-existing knowledge within which it can be "criticized, supported, refuted, in short, evaluated"—can constitute justification is what Sellars means by the myth of the given. In his classic essay "Empiricism and the Philosophy of Mind" (in Sellars 1997), he lays out a number of objections to "the framework of givenness" and discusses in detail many specific forms of the myth. But for our purposes the fundamental idea is that one cannot begin with a purely descriptive, non-normative *individuation of mental states* and build out of these anything resembling genuine knowledge. Knowledge is irreducibly normative.

This is not, of course, to deny that one can attribute contents to animals, say, as part of a theory of behavior. There is certainly a sense in which a dog, or even a cat, has the idea of a walk, or of dinner, or of an opening in a wall. As John McDowell (2005) puts the point:

For instance: any animal—rational or not—with suitable sensory equipment, engaged in getting from one place to another, can be expected, other things being equal, to respond to the affordance constituted by a sufficiently large opening, in a wall that otherwise blocks its path, by going through the opening. But the truth about a human being's exercise of competence in making her way around, in a performance that can be described like that, need not be *exhausted* by the match with what can be said about, say, a cat's correspondingly describable response to a corresponding affordance. The human being's response is, if you like, indistinguishable from the cat's response *qua* response to an affordance describable in those terms. But it does not follow that the human being's response cannot be unlike the cat's response in being the human being's rationality at work.

Again, the idea is that to take the human to be seeing a door is to take them to be engaging in a skillful interaction with the world that gives rise to a state that essentially functions to justify various beliefs, assertions, and actions. As such, it is also essentially the sort of state that normatively situates the perceiver as open to challenges of various sorts—demands for evidence, suggestions of error, etc. (Compare: by taking a pitch which is the third strike, a batter becomes subject to the norm that if the catcher drops the pitch, he should run to first base.) Even if the cat's actions do not merely conform to a regularity, but do so because of the regularity in the Sellarsian sense, the fact that the cat is not occupying states that function within a normative space of rationality implies that they are contentful in a fundamentally different, a fundamentally impoverished, way by comparison to descriptively similar states in a person.

A neuroscientific description of what goes on in human visual processing, or any other aspect of intelligent human behavior—the sort of description that might apply equally well to non-rational, non-discursive creatures—stands in contrast to a genuinely conceptual account itself rooted in the epistemic project in roughly the way that an anatomical account of the muscular process of moving one's arms when swinging a baseball bat relates to an account of the sport of baseball. Here, too, there are no doubt quite interesting things to be discovered, things having to do with how animals like us implement practices that have various normative significances, whether that implementation is in the brain or elsewhere. And if we were to train gorillas, for example, to behave in accord with the norms of baseball, we might well expect that there would be quite similar muscular, as well as neuropsychological, structures operating in our successful subjects as operate within members of the Mets. But none of this suggests that by interrogating these physiological structures in the right way we would ever gain an understanding of what it is to be a batter or to swing at a pitch. Such performances are fundamentally understood in normative inferentialist terms, and to think otherwise is to embrace the framework of givenness. Swings *qua* the kinds of things that can generate runs, just as thoughts *qua* the kinds of things that generate assertions, are justified or unjustified, make truth claims, etc., are not categories which show up in scientific explanation, but in the meta-practice of evaluating our first-order performances.

7. THE PRIMACY OF SKILLS
TO EPISTEMOLOGY

One of the most important ways in which post-Sellarsian philosophy has gone beyond what one can find in Sellars's own work is the development of the notions of skillful embodied coping by such philosophers as Dreyfus,

Haugeland, and (primarily in his discussions of moral knowledge) McDowell. Though we cannot begin to get into the details of the account here, these philosophers draw on the work of Heidegger and Merleau-Ponty (and more distantly, Aristotle) in developing an account of knowing-how as engaged coping. Such skills exhibit a number of characteristics: they are deeply contextual—one knows how to play soccer on grass fields, not ice, in environments with a normal complement of gravity, oxygen, etc., in which the field is relatively level, the opponents recognizably human in their own skills, etc. At the same time, they are flexible within this contextual range. A skill is no rote repetition of a behavior according to an input–output rule. One adapts competently to changes in the environment. Similarly, skills are kinds of understanding that can be put together, assembled, disassembled, etc. Thus, one puts together dribbling, running, kicking, and passing in a typical sequence of play in soccer. Finally, as Haugeland (1998b) emphasizes in perhaps the most developed discussion of this view of skills, they involve a deep interdependence, a functional interconnection, of agent and environment.

Despite some unfortunate suggestions by Dreyfus to the effect that skillful coping is simply distinct from, perhaps even in competition with, rationality or propositional knowing-that as a mode of human engagement with the world, the bulk of work within the Sellarsian tradition has sought to utilize this idea of skillful coping to *account for* propositional knowledge. The leading pragmatist idea here is that knowledge is a practical skillful accomplishment. Speaking is, at bottom, a skillful negotiation of the sport of language,[16] one in which sentences show up as equipment that must be dealt with in competent ways—this is what is involved in making moves within the space of reasons—and knowledge is just the relevant sort of success in such an involved practice. Inference, then, is not generally to be understood as something mechanistic—on a model with the sort of purely formal inference that goes on in introductory logic proofs—but as an engaged, contextual, flexible, and structurally complex system of movements through the space of language. Such, in any event, is the leading idea pursued by Brandom, Haugeland, and philosophers of science such as Joe Rouse,[17] in thinking about the activity of theoretical justification.

---

[16] The idea of a *sport* of language is developed in my 1998, where I explain the importance of the distinction between sports and games to an understanding of language in Sellarsian terms.

[17] See especially Rouse 2002.

8. RECEPTIVITY

So how does the world impinge normatively on this social practice of justifying our claims? According to Brandom, the context within which propositions function normatively is an inferential one. But inferences occur only between statements, or thoughts, and other statements or thoughts. So in what sense can we see this whole practice as empirical, as vindicated ultimately by the deliverances of the world in receptivity? For Brandom, the answer is causal. The space of reasons is impinged upon causally at the periphery.

But as McDowell argues forcefully, this is to embrace the myth of the given. What we want is a genuinely normative constraint by the world, not mere beating about of our conceptual behavior. (One way to look at the central point is that the world can cause irrational changes of belief just as well as rational ones. So if all we have to work with is causal impingement upon an inferential structure, we aren't going to have any sort of explanation of the normative significance of genuine receptivity, even if we could cook up a descriptive property that tracks genuinely correct observation.) We want, that is, for the world to matter to our justifications in the way that the lines on the field matter to whether a ball is in play or out. For McDowell, this involves a "re-animation" of the world according to which the world is genuinely propositional in itself. McDowell references Aristotle's discussion of second nature in trying to make such a notion plausible and consistent with a scientific understanding of nature as having no such things in it, but it is fair to say that few philosophers claim to fully understand how this story goes.

Despite McDowell's frequent suggestions that this is not the case, it would seem that what is needed is some account of the sort that Haugeland tries to give in his 1998c. We want a pragmatic account of the particular skillful act of perceiving—itself an engaged act in the world—that makes clear how our practice institutes some such interactive performances as contentful and normatively significant, and also how the linguistic structure of human practice is structured so as to take up these significant performances as normatively relevant to practices of inferential justification. I'm not convinced by the particulars of Haugeland's version—especially his division of competence into two categories of social creation and receptive responsibility, and his treatment of truth as a normative status—but attempt to do better in Kukla and Lance 2008*b*.[18]

9. Truth

One issue upon which there is substantial disagreement among Sellarsians is truth. Sellars himself maintained that truth insofar as it involved relations to the world was irrelevant to semantics. Content was a matter solely of the normative appropriatenesses governing linguistic moves. But it was a crucial part of the (admittedly rather idiosyncratic) Sellarsian account of how beings compatible with the scientific image could come to be competent knowers, perceivers, and language-users that there be a substantial language–world picturing relation.

Both Haugeland and McDowell, in different ways, have taken truth to be a substantive part of the normative structure of linguistic practice, essentially seeing truth as a kind of external norm governing assertion. Rorty, on the far end of things, rejects the very idea of a relation between language and the world, and embraces a sort of irrealist elimination of truth in favor of such pragmatic virtues as "democratic availability".

Brandom and I are in the "deflationary" camp. We follow the seminal account of Grover, Camp, and Belnap in claiming that truth-talk plays a fundamentally non-descriptive role, essentially arguing that "it is true that" is a way to construct a sort of sentential variable. Such variables—anaphoric pro-sentences—are quite useful in the expression of many claims about the world, claims that could not be made without truth-talk. There is no way to say things like "Everything the oracle says is true" without something in the language that functions as a sentential-level variable (and quantificational cases are not the only example). Further, there is a detailed explanation in the work of Brandom for why it is useful to have an operator on sentences that forms such anaphoric sentential variables. Thus, on this version of deflationism, truth-talk is not at all empty, or eliminable from the language. But for all that, it does not function to describe anything or to predicate a substantive property of objects.

---

[18] The account there—see especially chs. 2 and 3—is, however, only a beginning, focusing on the linguistic end of the receptive transaction, on how something such as observing must be taken up pragmatically in language. Nonetheless, this account identifies whole dimensions of the phenomenon that go missing on traditional accounts.

What all Sellarsian philosophers agree on is that truth is not a descriptive notion, say of correspondence with reality. Sellars himself believed that there is a crucial sense in which language does picture reality, but for Sellars this picturing was neither something that constituted truth nor something that played a role in semantics. Rather, it was necessary for the descriptive story of how it was that an organism could manage to function as a competent player within the normative space of semantics. Though no one doubts that such a causal story will involve positing all sorts of relations between the agent and the world, the question is whether there is one single relation that language, in all its diversity, bears to the world. As Brandom once put his skepticism on this point in conversation, "asking for the relation between language and the world is like asking for the relation between me and China. The problem isn't that there isn't one, but that there are rather too many."

10. CONCLUSIONS

Even with the strict limits I have imposed on our topic—essentially drawing out a single roughly coherent trajectory of work departing from the Sellarsian corpus—there is a great deal more that could be discussed. I have said next to nothing about the crucial Sellarsian theme of the relation between the manifest and the scientific images. This was absolutely central to Sellars's own philosophy, and though it figures less centrally in the work of the "Pittsburgh School" philosophers, the question of how the conception of the world that emerges in the natural sciences relates to that of ordinary human interaction is an important one. Here, too, some form of the historicist normative functionalist conception is common currency. One wants to understand the inferential structure and the involved practical social space of science as a riff on a more basic mode of dealing with the world. To my mind, the two most interesting philosophers working specifically on the practice of science within a recognizably Sellarsian framework are Marc Lange and Joe Rouse.

Nor have I said much at all about Sellars's work on phenomenal states. Here there has been much less effort to pick up on Sellarsian themes within this tradition. Sellars's own emphasis on color perception, "sensa", and the like seems to have dropped off the map for most of the philosophers discussed here (though not entirely in the case of Haugeland). But the problems that led

Sellars to devote so much attention to these phenomena have not gone away, and the issue is well due for a resurgence.

All in all, however, I hope it is clear that neo-Sellarsian philosophy—a project centering on the methodological move of placing in a space of norms—is a rich and rapidly developing project in contemporary American philosophy. (And largely due to Brandom's influence, a growing emphasis on the European continent as well.) It begins from a very different place than, for example, traditional scientific realist projects, and departs also quite centrally from classical pragmatism. It is a tradition, as I said, that draws inspiration as much from Hegel, Heidegger, Wittgenstein, and Merleau-Ponty, as it does from Kant, Sellars, and the pragmatists, while at the same time being deeply influenced by and respectful of contemporary natural science and mathematics.

This will seem odd to philosophers trained in either the "analytic" or the "continental" tradition. Both have been taught to think of the distinction in terms of a dispute over the centrality of science and mathematics to the intellectual project. For typical analytic philosophy, at least since the positivists and Quine, the philosopher is epistemically duty-bound to respect the deliverances of science, having no standing from which to offer anything epistemically more secure or more basic. Thus, insofar as there is substantive philosophical work to be done, it must amount to some sort of vindication—of which reduction is the paradigm—in the terms of science.

Typical continental philosophers reject this approach as science worship, and insist on the autonomy of philosophy as a critical discipline. But in so doing, they accept the same underlying premise: namely, that if one takes science to be epistemically autonomous—challengeable only by more science—then one must assume that it is hegemonic, that essentially all intellectually respectable work must take place in its terms. Rebecca Kukla and I—following on ideas of Belnap's—attribute this to the "declarival fallacy". This is the assumption that at the level of linguistic practice, declaratives are both autonomous and foundational for all of language. But one need not accept this. One can develop a functionalist understanding of all sorts of discourse, one that takes normativity fully seriously, and at the same time takes scientific accomplishments seriously. One can be as committed to rigor and consistency with the scientific image as Sellars, yet think that the practice of science is not all we do, or even something that can be understood in isolation from other aspects of human practice.

As with any philosophical approach, this one remains a work in progress.

References

Austin, J. L. (1962). *How To Do Things with Words.* Cambridge, MA: Harvard University Press.

Belnap, N. (1990). "Declaratives Are Not Enough". *Philosophical Studies,* 59: 1–30.

Brandom, R. (1994). *Making It Explicit: Reasoning, Representing, and Discursive Commitment.* Cambridge, MA: Harvard University Press.

de Vries, William (2005). *Wilfrid Sellars.* Montreal and Kingston: McGill–Queen's University Press.

Dreyfus, H. L. (1991). *Being-in-the-World: A Commentary on Heidegger's Being and Time, Division I.* Cambridge, MA: MIT Press.

——— (1992). *What Computers Still Can't Do: A Critique of Artificial Reason.* Cambridge, MA: MIT Press.

Gibbard, A. (2003). *Thinking How to Live.* Cambridge, MA: Harvard University Press.

Haugeland, John (1998a). *Having Thought,* Cambridge, MA: Harvard University Press.

——— (1998b). "Mind Embodied and Embedded". In Haugeland (1998a), 207–40.

——— (1998c). "Truth and Rule-Following". In Haugeland (1998a), 305–62.

Heidegger, M. (1996). *Being and Time: A Translation of Sein und Zeit.* Albany, NY: State University of New York Press.

Kukla, Rebecca (2000). "Myth, Memory and Misrecognition in Sellars' 'Empiricism and the Philosophy of Mind' ". *Philosophical Studies,* 101: 161–211.

——— and Lance, M. (2008a). "Perception, Language, and the First Person". Forthcoming in Bernard Weiss and Jeremy Wanderer (eds.), *Reading Brandom: Making It Explicit,* London: Routledge.

——— ——— (2008b). *'Yo!' and 'Lo!': The Pragmatic Topography of the Space of Reasons.* Cambridge, MA: Harvard University Press.

Lance, Mark (1995). "Two Concepts of Entailment". *Journal of Philosophical Research,* 20: 113–37.

——— (1996). "Quantification, Substitution and Conceptual Content". *Nous,* 30/4: 481–507.

——— (1997). "The Significance of Anaphoric Theories of Truth and Reference". In Enrique Villanueva (ed.), *Truth,* Philosophical Issues, 8, Atascadero, CA: Ridgeview Publishing Company, 181–99; repr. in Bradley Armour-Garb and J. C. Beall (eds.), *Truth,* La Salle, IL: Open Court Press, 2001, 282–98.

——— (1998). "Some Reflections on the Sport of Language". In Jim Tomberlin (ed.), *Language, Mind, and Ontology,* Philosophical Perspectives, 12, Oxford: Blackwell, 219–40.

——— (2001). "The Logical Structure of Linguistic Commitment III: Brandomian Scorekeeping and Incompatibility". *Journal of Philosophical Logic,* 30/5: 439–64.

——— and Kremer, Philip (1994). "The Logical Structure of Linguistic Commitment I: Four Systems of Non-Relevant Commitment Entailment". *Journal of Philosophical Logic,* 23: 369–400.

Lance, Mark, and Kremer, Philip (1995). "The Logical Structure of Linguistic Commitment II: Systems of Relevant Commitment Entailment". *Journal of Philosophical Logic*, 25/4: 425–49.

———and May, Todd (1994). "Two Dogmas of Post-empiricism, Anti-theoretical Strains in Rorty and Derrida". *Philosophical Forum*, 25/4: 273–309.

———and O'Leary-Hawthorne, John (1997). *The Grammar of Meaning*. Cambridge: Cambridge University Press.

———and White, Heath (2007). "Stereoscopic Vision: Reasons, Causes, and Two Spaces of Material Inference". *Philosophers' Imprint*, 7/4: 1–21.

Lange, Marc (2004). *Natural Laws in Scientific Practice*. New York: Oxford University Press.

Macbeth, Danielle (1994). "The Coin of the Intentional Realm". *Journal for the Theory of Social Behavior*, 24: 143–66.

———(2005). "Inferentialism and Holistic Role Abstraction in the Telling of Tales". *European Journal of Philosophy*, 13: 409–20.

———(forthcoming). "Pragmatism and Objective Truth". In Cheryl Misak (ed.), *New Pragmatism*, Oxford: Oxford University Press.

Maher, Chauncey (2007). "Individuating Actions" (dissertation, Georgetown University).

May, Todd (1993). *Between Genealogy and Epistemology: Psychology, Politics, and Knowledge in the Thought of Michel Foucault*. Philadelphia: Penn State University Press.

McDowell, J. (1994). *Mind and World*. Cambridge, MA: Harvard University Press.

———(1998). "Having the World in View: Sellars, Kant, and Intentionality". *Journal of Philosophy*, 95: 269–305.

———(2005). "Reply to Dreyfus: What Myth?" APA symposium presentation.

Peregrin, J. (2000). "The 'Natural' and the 'Formal' ". *Journal of Philosophical Logic*, 29: 75–101.

———(2001). *Meaning and Structure*. Aldershot: Ashgate.

———(2007). "Semantics as Based on Inference". In J. van Bentham, G. Heinzmann, M. Rebuschi, and H. Visser (eds.), *The Age of Alternative Logics*, Dordrecht: Kluwer, 25–36.

Restall, Greg (1993). "Simplified Semantics for Relevant Logics (and Some of their Rivals)". *Journal of Philosophical Logic*, 22: 481–511.

———(2004). "Logical Pluralism and the Preservation of Warrant". In S. Rahman *et al.* (eds.), *Logic, Epistemology, and the Philosophy of Science*, Dordrecht: Kluwer, 162–73.

Rosenberg, Jay (1974). *Linguistic Representation*. Dordrecht: D. Reidel.

Rorty, R. (1982). *Consequences of Pragmatism: Essays, 1972–1980*. Minneapolis: University of Minnesota Press.

Rouse, J. (2002). *How Scientific Practices Matter: Reclaiming Philosophical Naturalism*. Chicago: University of Chicago Press.

Seibt, J. (1990). *Properties and Processes (A Synoptic Study of Wilfrid Sellars's Nominalism)*. Atascadero, CA: Ridgeview Publishing Company.

Sellars, W. (1950). "Language, Rules and Behavior". In S. Hook (ed.), *John Dewey: Philosopher of Science and Freedom*, New York: Diall Press, 289–315.

_____ (1953). "Inference and Meaning". *Mind*, 62: 313–38.

_____ (1954). "Some Reflections on Language Games". *Philosophy of Science*, 21: 204–28.

_____ (1963a). "Abstract Entities". *Review of Metaphysics*, 16: 627–71.

_____ (1963b). *Science, Perception and Reality*. London: Routledge & Kegan Paul.

_____ (1969). "Language as Thought and as Communication". *Philosophy and Phenomenological Research*, 29: 506–27.

_____ (1974). "Meaning as Functional Classification". *Synthese*, 27: 417–37.

_____ (1980). *Pure Pragmatics and Possible Worlds: The Early Essays of Wilfrid Sellars*, ed. Jeffrey Sicha. Atascadero, CA: Ridgeview Publishing Company.

_____ (1992). *Science and Metaphysics*. Atascadero, CA: Ridgeview Publishing Company.

_____ (1997). *Empiricism and the Philosophy of Mind*. Cambridge, MA: Harvard University Press.

Todes, S. (2001). *Body and World*. Cambridge, MA: MIT Press.

....

RORTY, DAVIDSON, AND THE FUTURE OF METAPHYSICS IN AMERICA

....

BJØRN RAMBERG

1. THE FIGHT against metaphysics has been a hallmark of much philosophy during the last century and a half. The fight has been futile, and it is by now well established that metaphysics, like capitalism, co-opts all opposition. Nietzsche railed against metaphysics, while Heidegger, in the end, simply wanted to leave it alone; but neither the railing nor the leaving has turned out to yield viable research programs. The logical positivists did try to do serious philosophy against metaphysics, but managed thereby to establish only that metaphysics is pretty much inevitable. Contemporary mainstream Anglophone philosophy is happy to acknowledge this; whether one is a realist or an anti-realist in ethics, a reductionist or an anti-reductionist regarding the mental, a naturalist or an anti-naturalist in epistemology, and no matter what one's view of truth, one proceeds content with the thought that metaphysics and philosophy are one. True, there remain pockets of right-wing Quineans who hold that any question of fact in the end is—or must be converted

into—a properly scientific question. The common attitude, however, is sensible, relaxed, enlightened; what, in the end, was all that anti-metaphysical fuss about? What *were* those self-castigating Europeans so afraid of?

In the present chapter, I will consider one recent, last stab at metaphysics. Not, of course, with any notion of pulling off what Nietzsche, Heidegger, Neurath, Ayer, and Hempel conspicuously failed to do. Indeed, the future of metaphysics in America is assuredly bright—given the pressure to produce distinctively philosophical publications in distinctively philosophical journals. What I shall try to do, rather, is to restate the point of the struggle against metaphysics in terms of certain recent developments in American philosophy. My aim is to suggest why someone might still take the struggle against metaphysics *seriously*, and not simply dismiss that struggle as an odd historical phase—the temporary alienation of philosophy from itself—or as a pathological form of intellectual Puritanism, of *scientism*. This struggle, as I conceive of it here, is the effort to think of philosophy and metaphysics as *distinct activities*, and, moreover, to show that a commitment to the former may give reason for being wary of the latter.

These reflections take the form of commentary on Richard Rorty's efforts to rearticulate pragmatism. In the course of forty years of philosophical writing, Rorty, at different times, manifested both a recognizably Heideggerian and a recognizably Nietzschean attitude to metaphysics. These are not my focus here. Rather, I consider the points of Rorty's work where he comes closest to passing as a mainstream Anglophone philosopher. This aspect of Rorty's thought may be discerned most readily in his appropriation of the work of Donald Davidson. It is in grappling with arguments from Davidson—in his metabolizing them—that Rorty's *struggle with* (as opposed to a railing at and a leaving of) metaphysics is most palpable. In the context of this struggle, Rorty conceives of pragmatism as an attitude to philosophy that *opposes* metaphysics. Pragmatism, in this context, is the idea of philosophy without metaphysics.

Immediately below, in section 2, I distinguish two strands of polemic against metaphysics in *Philosophy and the Mirror of Nature* (Rorty 1979). I then marshal specific points for the sake of which Rorty relies on Davidson, in *Philosophy and the Mirror of Nature* and in later essays. Considering these points in terms of Rorty's meta-philosophical agenda, however, it would seem that a more ambivalent attitude to Davidson would be warranted than Rorty has ever displayed. It would anyway appear, as I then claim in section 3, that there are patent difficulties befalling one who attempts to draw in Davidson as an ally in a struggle against metaphysics; it seems hard, as I explain, to deny him the status, if not of *positive* metaphysician, then at least of *default* metaphysician. However, as I suggest in section 4, Rorty's thinking about metaphysics, and about pragmatism as a source of resistance to metaphysical thinking, develops in interesting ways after *Philosophy and the Mirror of Nature*. These may be brought out precisely in relation to the very difficulties that Davidson presents for the pragmatist reader. A radicalization occurs, which obviates the tension remaining in *Philosophy and the Mirror of Nature* with regard to metaphysics, as Rorty increasingly allows political, ethical, and even esthetical terms to bear the full weight of the claims he advances. The result is a recasting of the stakes in Rorty's struggle against metaphysics, construed now in terms of the idea of the *autonomy* of philosophy, and also of the relation between Rorty and Davidson. The very contestability of Davidson's position *vis-à-vis* metaphysics, I conclude in section 5, serves to emphasize the consistency and depth with which Rorty's anti-essentialist attitude to philosophy may finally be carried through.

2. It is useful to think of Rorty's attack on metaphysics in *Philosophy and the Mirror of Nature* along two different lines—one highly generalized and abstract, the other directed at specific metaphysical constructions. The former turns on a key meta-philosophical opposition of the book: namely, that between systematic and edifying philosophy (Rorty 1979: 365 ff.). Edifying philosophers—Dewey, Heidegger, and Wittgenstein are the heavily idealized mantle-bearers of therapeutic philosophy in *Philosophy and the Mirror of Nature*—do not build philosophical systems. They are fifth columnists, renegades, who deploy a current vocabulary of philosophy in a manner that turns it against its own presuppositions and undermines the coherence of the very problems around which the vocabulary has evolved. This is *therapy*, insofar as it allows us to see that specific problems that have us in their thrall are intrinsically connected to specific vocabularies, and that these vocabularies are, in Rorty's term, *optional*. There is an obvious and explicit link to Wittgenstein and the idea that philosophical problems are what we get when we are somehow taken in by language, and also a faint echo of the logical positivists' notion that trouble arises when we think we grasp meanings that aren't really there to be grasped. There is an important difference between the idea that language may fool us into seeing problems that are not really there, as the logical positivists wanted to suggest, and the Rortyan idea, more in line with Wittgenstein, that our mistaking philosophical problems consists in our

taking them as mandatory, inescapable challenges to our ingenuity. At least to Rorty, they are not illusions to be seen through, but dead ends, to be backed out of. The backing out is achieved, if at all, precisely by a reworking and transformation of the vocabulary that got us into the fix in the first place. And while the positivists clung to the idea of a permanent cure, Rorty offers no such hope. New or transformed vocabularies will bring their own dead ends. Successful therapy creates conditions for further systematic construction.

At this level of abstraction, metaphysics appears as the will to do constructive philosophy. In Rortyan terms, this is the will to create a maximally encompassing perspective, expressible in one coherent vocabulary, with the capability of *resolving* questions about what sorts of beings there are and how—and to what extent—we can know them. The basic presupposition of this project, which Rorty characterizes as *epistemology*, is "that all contributions to a given discourse are commensurable" (Rorty 1979: 316). Commensurability, in turn, is tied to rationality: "By 'commensurable' I mean able to be brought under a set of rules which will tell us how rational agreement can be reached on what would settle the issue on every point where statements seem to conflict' (Rorty 1979: 316).

Metaphysics, then, becomes the search for *commensuration*. Though Rorty in *Philosophy and the Mirror of Nature* urges us in no uncertain terms to forgo this ideal of meta-level agreement, and so to drop the idea of a common ground of knowledge, his attitude to metaphysics nevertheless seems not fully resolved. One the one hand, there is a sense in which systematic, constructive philosophy and edifying, therapeutic philosophy are portrayed as partners in perpetual crime, with one creating and re-creating opportunity for the other. On the other hand, Rorty explicitly proposes a mode of philosophical discourse—*hermeneutics*, as he calls it—which is intended to replace the commensurability-seeking discourse of Western metaphysics, a successor discipline to epistemology, where the point is, along Nietzschean lines, to invent and sustain varied perspectives, to be juxtaposed but not pressed into a unified whole. Rorty is never able to convey, however, how such hermeneutic conversation would actually proceed. Drawing on Thomas Kuhn's famous distinction between normal and revolutionary science, forging the derivative notion of abnormal—that is, non-commensurating—discourse, Rorty simply makes it harder, not easier, to conceive of an alternative to a perpetual dialectic of systematic and edifying philosophy, insofar as Kuhn's opposition is a dialectical one, where revolutionary science emerges from the tensions in successfully normalized science. Nor will the explicit appeal to Hans-Georg

Gadamer get us very far in the direction of a clear view of a successor discipline to epistemology-based, commensuration-seeking philosophy. For Gadamer's contribution, if it is to be summed up, is the elaboration of the insight that in reaching a common understanding with others, we must allow ourselves to be transformed. Hermeneutics certainly recognizes the situatedness of any contribution to a discourse and makes a point of the incommensurability that may ensue across both time and space. This perspective is maintained consistently also with regard to the position of the understanding subject, whose *prejudices* accordingly are just as much at stake as is the nature of the object of understanding. No priority is given, in Gadamerian terms, to subjective consciousness. However, though it is achieved, if at all, in a dynamically evolving and subject-transforming language, Gadamerian dialogue surely seeks a commensuration of standpoints. This is inherent in the famous ideal of a *fusion of horizons*.

The upshot of this is that the generalized contrast between metaphysics and non-metaphysical conversation that Rorty seeks to provide in the third part of *Philosophy and the Mirror of Nature* remains largely unsubstantiated. We are left with no clear sense of how a discursive genre could be philosophical yet not be geared, somehow, to the achievement of commensuration. Anticipating the main point of section 4, we might say that Rorty, at this stage of his thinking, tries unsuccessfully to capture a difference between metaphysics and philosophy in *philosophical* terms, and that this is exactly why the effort fails.

The other line of attack in *Philosophy and the Mirror of Nature*, however, addresses not metaphysics in vague generality, but specific edifices of Western philosophy, chief among them representationalism, the subject–object dichotomy, and the scheme–content distinction. These three are really just different labels for, or manifestations of, the same basic metaphoric, the mind as mirror of nature. With regard to this image, Rorty's strategy is twofold; he tells a story of its genesis, but also enters into close combat, deploying philosophical arguments from within analytic philosophy to make explicit and to undermine the assumptions that, on his diagnosis, the mirror imagery has saddled us with. It is at this point in the campaign that Davidson is brought to bear.

The thumbnail version of the relevant claims developed in *Philosophy and the Mirror of Nature* is that once you take in the full force of Sellars's attack on the myth of the given, and juxtapose it with Quine's extinguishing of a principled distinction between the analytic and the synthetic, matters of meaning and matters of fact, then what you end up with is the philosophy of

Davidson. The pinnacle of the expression of this happy synthesis is Davidson's rejection of the scheme–content distinction (cf. Davidson 1974). This paper, as Rorty reads it, deploys and deepens (in a Sellarsian direction) the Quinean third-person perspective on meaning and mind with devastating consequences for the representationalist ideas that have sustained epistemology since Kant. In Davidson's view, we simply cannot make sense of the idea that we produce representations of a given world by structuring through operations of subjectivity the input provided by an objective source. So questions concerning the adequacy of our conceptual schemes or the accuracy of our representational capacities must simply be abandoned as resting on an incoherent view of how thinking agents relate epistemically to the world they operate in.

Rorty hails the resulting "pure philosophy of language" (Rorty 1979: 259–62), where truth is construed in purely semantic terms and no notion of reference with epistemic or ontological implications can get any traction at all. This is philosophy of language shorn of the metaphysical significance afforded it by Michael Dummett and other enthusiasts of the linguistic turn. It will not enter into alliances with either ontology or epistemology. As Rorty puts it, "The actual results of the hard work on adverbial modification and the like which would result from concerted efforts to carry out Davidson's suggestions would do little to help or hinder any solution of any of the text-book problems of philosophy" (Rorty 1979: 261).

Nevertheless, by telling us something about what it takes for a creature to be a user of language, Davidson's account of "how language works" contains the core of a philosophical anthropology of wide scope and great cohesion. As Davidson's account unfolds, developing from engagements with specific and delimited problems in philosophy of language, of mind and of action, to the at times sweeping vistas of later papers, a systematic philosophy of great ambition emerges. Rorty, however, remains enthusiastic. During the 1980s, he writes a series of papers in which he comes increasingly to rely on Davidson to clarify and articulate his own philosophical views. As he puts it in "Non-Reductive Physicalism", "I see Davidson as the culmination of the holist and pragmatist strains in contemporary analytic philosophy: These motifs, in turn, are the culmination of a long struggle (which extends far outside the boundaries of 'analytic' philosophy) against Platonic and religious conceptions of the world" (Rorty 1987a: 117).

How can it be that Rorty's oppositional meta-philosophical stance, his notion of therapeutic philosophy, can be served by—can enthusiastically embrace—one of the most systematic and comprehensive philosophical edifices raised during the second half of the twentieth century? One explanation might be that for all Rorty's sweeping meta-philosophical rhetoric and brazen historicizing, he is at heart a pretty conventional philosopher, content to embrace any doctrine, metaphysical or not, that is supported by arguments he finds persuasive. So it is not systematic and constructive philosophy *per se* that bothers him in *Philosophy and the Mirror of Nature*, it is *erroneous* systematic and constructive philosophy. Davidson, by contrast, is alright, because, tuned in to both Quinian and Sellarsian thought, he is both sufficiently naturalistic and sufficiently anti-scientist to appeal to Rorty's philosophical sensibilities. Another possible explanation, however, is that Rorty has moved beyond the polarization of philosophy into constructive and therapeutic endeavors, and that the contrast between systematic and edifying philosophy critical to the anti-metaphysical line of *Philosophy and the Mirror of Nature* no longer defines Rorty's pragmatic stance. The struggle against metaphysics may no longer be the struggle against systematic philosophy as such. But if that is so, what is now the point of pragmatist resistance toward metaphysics? What is at stake, meta-philosophically speaking? Before addressing this question more directly, in section 4, it will be useful to consider some features of the Davidsonian philosophical edifice that Rorty exploits, and to juxtapose Rorty's use of Davidson with the kind of reception that Davidson has received among notable analytic philosophers. We will see that while Davidson provides Rorty with critical elements in his articulation of a pragmatic view of truth and language, his relation to metaphysics is ambiguous, at best.

3. When Rorty turns to Davidson for anti-metaphysical argument beyond the case he makes in *Philosophy and the Mirror of Nature*, he extends and develops the anti-representationalist line described in the previous section. A good place to start is with Rorty's articulation of a pragmatic form of naturalism, in "Non-reductive Physicalism" (1987a). In this paper he succinctly treats three Davidsonian theses that remain of lasting significance for his views: reasons can be causes; things in the world do not make sentences (nor, a fortiori, beliefs) true; metaphors do not have meanings (Rorty 1987a: 113 ff.). Let us consider these in turn. Davidson's famous argument for monism (Davidson 1970) turns on the claim that a mental state—a combination of beliefs and desires—providing a reason for an action properly explains that action only if it is also the cause of it (Davidson 1963). In Rorty's reading, this "amounts to the claim that a given event can be described equally well in physiological and psychological, non-intentional and intentional, terms"

(Rorty 1987a: 114). The pragmatist lesson, for Rorty, is that there is no essence in the thing that makes it be either a mental thing or a physical thing. What makes one form of description (not, of course, a particular claim) apt rather than another is human purpose, interest, and need. Nevertheless, this "is to grant the materialist everything he should want". It is, Rorty claims, "to gratify all his legitimate needs, to permit him to pay all the compliments to the physical sciences which they deserve. But it will not permit him to gratify all his metaphysical, reductionist needs. It will not permit him to claim that he has finally grasped the 'essence' of the world of human beings" (1987a: 116–17).

The pay-off of Davidson's doctrine is clear; linking the mental–physical distinction to kinds of vocabularies and choice between vocabularies to human purpose, there is no longer any motivation to pursue distinctively metaphysical questions of the sort that later became known as "placement problems".

Similar gains are extracted from the Davidsonian perspective on truth. With regard to the thought that there are no truth-makers, that there is nothing that makes a sentence true, Rorty remarks:

This doctrine may seem clearly paradoxical. . . . It also seems paradoxical not to make a distinction between "the way the world really is" and "convenient, but metaphorical, ways of talking about the world." Yet Davidson is willing to accept both paradoxes in order to escape from the traditional Western philosophical picture, the picture dominated by what he calls, "the dualism of scheme and content." (Rorty 1987a: 116)

Indeed, Davidson's work on the concept of truth is pivotal for Rorty's articulation of pragmatism. Ten years later, he writes,

The greatest of my many intellectual debts to Donald Davidson is my realization that nobody should even try to specify the nature of truth. . . . Davidson has helped us realize that *the very absoluteness of truth is a good reason for thinking "true" indefinable and for thinking that no theory of the nature of truth is possible.*   (Rorty 1998b: 3)

However, while Rorty, inspired by Davidson, quickly abandons the pragmatist theory of truth, he still has things to say about the notion. In "Pragmatism, Davidson and Truth" (1986b), he elaborates, somewhat in the spirit of early work by Robert Brandom (1976), the uses to which the notion of truth is put: (a) an endorsing use, (b) a cautionary use, (c) a disquotational use (Rorty 1986b: 128).

On this picture, we can explain why we use "true" when we do, and to what ends. We can show the connection between understanding a language and understanding how sentences acquire their particular truth conditions as a result of their parts and the way they are combined. What we cannot do is appeal to the concept of truth to illuminate our epistemic practices. Davidson, in Rorty's view, has given us an account of truth that meets our explanatory needs, insofar as we can articulate the purposes for which a competent speaker deploys the concept of truth, "while eschewing the idea that the expediency of a belief can be explained by its truth" (Rorty 1986*b*: 128).

Like the first two, the final thesis that Rorty extracts from Davidson is deployed to undermine the framework of assumptions that gives rise to representationalist epistemology. To Davidson's account of metaphor as an essentially non-semantic phenomenon, Rorty adds the idea that metaphors are nevertheless basic to our linguistic practice; metaphor is what keeps language alive and adaptable, because, while

they have no place in the language-game which has been played prior to their production ... they may, and indeed do, have a crucial role in the language-games which are played afterwards. For, by being literalized, becoming "dead" metaphors, they enlarge logical space. So metaphor is an essential instrument in the process of reweaving our beliefs and desires; without it, there would be no such thing as a scientific revolution or a cultural breakthrough, but merely the process of altering the truth-values of statements formulated in a forever unchanging vocabulary.   (Rorty 1987*a*: 124)

Whatever one thinks of this view of how language changes or how metaphor works, it is clear that the idea serves Rorty's purposes well. If literal truths in general depend on semantic material hardened into literal service through a process that is not itself tractable in semantic terms, but rather is hostage to contingencies, force of circumstance, and changing proclivities in a speech community, and so not subject to anything like explicit rational deliberation, then it is hard to see how literal truths could come to stand in a correspondence relation with the way things are in themselves. An established vocabulary might well allow sentences that are both true and literal; but, given their non-rational genesis, it is difficult to see how a set of dead metaphors could secure any form of ontological privilege for a particular vocabulary with respect to competing forms of description.

Even if one grants Rorty his three Davidsonian theses, however, it remains questionable in what sense these constitute an attack on metaphysics as such. What Davidson does away with, if one follows Rorty's reading, is a certain framework of epistemology, a certain broad, and broadly Cartesian, understanding of the problems we encounter in accounting for ourselves as putative knowing subjects. We lose our motivation to think of truth as a substantive goal or achievement (cf. Rorty 1995), and also the opportunity to frame general skeptical worries (cf. Rorty 1998a). These are certainly grand claims, and, if true, of great significance for the agenda of philosophy. But they do not impugn metaphysics as such. Indeed, as many of Davidson's interlocutors have assumed, it is natural to take Davidson precisely as offering metaphysical views. It may seem, then, that Rorty—or I—have dramatically overstated the anti-metaphysical ambition of the pragmatist line of thought that Rorty has pursued with Davidson's help.

To press this point home, we need only glance at two or three of the many debates and commentaries that Davidson has drawn over the years. Jaegwon Kim has for many years engaged Davidson's account of the mental–physical relation and his view of events (cf. Kim 1993 and 1997). In a recent discussion of Davidson's philosophy of mind and of psychology, Kim presses questions of a distinctively metaphysical flavor. Concluding a section on the alleged supervenience relation between mind and body, Kim says:

Thus, the question is open as to how anomalous monism can, by itself or with suitable strengthening, cope with the problem of mental causation, and there is some doubt whether this can be done. This is not surprising, because Davidson's strict law requirement on causation, combined with his view that strict laws can be found only in basic physics, appears to give the physical domain a special role in shaping the causal structure of the world. In fact, it can be interpreted, or perhaps misinterpreted, as implying that physical causation is the only causation that exists.   (Kim 2003: 132)

Now, the problem of mental causation—that is, whether mental states actually or only apparently cause our actions—is one that Davidson does appear to take seriously. It confronts us with the conceptual problem of devising an understanding of the mental, the physical, causation, laws, supervenience, etc., that makes it possible for us to legitimately take mental states as causes, in the appropriate way, of our actions. Davidson, it would seem, has for a long time been engaged in just this project.

Kim also presses Davidson on the ontology of mental states: "If beliefs are essentially normative and are posited because of our normative requirement, are there beliefs in the same sense in which there are physical objects and events, like trees and explosions?" (Kim 2003: 134). Kim's challenges are formulated in unabashedly metaphysical terms, yet they are not questions that Davidson dismisses. Indeed, to answer just these sorts of questions is what Davidson appears to be doing. In the same volume, Paul Pietroski concludes a detailed and sympathetic account of Davidson's views on events thus:

ordinary claims have implications about events; and claims about events are in turn crucially related to how we think about causation, space-time, ourselves, and how we are related to the physical world that we often talk about and occasionally comprehend. Davidson thus shows how apparently narrow and technical questions about the semantics of natural language sentences can bear on the more traditional questions of philosophy.   (Pietroski 2003: 160)

Pietroski provides a generous and favorable account, yet one that would appear to align nicely with Kim's and to be fundamentally at odds with the direction in which Rorty wants to travel with Davidson. If there is any single point that Rorty has emphasized over thirty years of reading Davidson, it is that his account of language helps us leave behind the traditional problems of philosophy.

This, however, is clearly a minority view. As Kirk Ludwig puts it in the introduction to the volume of commentaries from which I have just quoted: "[Davidson's papers] form a mosaic that presents a systematic account of the nature of human thought, action, and speech, and their relation to the natural world, that is one of the most subtle and impressive systems to emerge in analytic philosophy in the last fifty years" (Ludwig 2003: 1). Together with Ernest Lepore, Ludwig lays out and examines that system over 400 pages, with the third and final part being devoted to "Metaphysics and Epistemology" (Lepore and Ludwig 2005: part III). Among the metaphysical doctrines they scrutinize are "The Impossibility of Alternative Conceptual Schemes", "The Impossibility of Massive Error", and "Inscrutability of Reference", concluding generally that the arguments supporting these famous claims are at best incomplete. Scott Soames, devoting a chapter of his two-volume chronological account of analytical philosophy to Davidson's argument against the possibility of, as Soames also puts it, alternative conceptual schemes, finds that he has "little alternative but to conclude that Davidson's case against alternative conceptual schemes is a failure" (Soames 2003: 330).

It is possible that Rorty is right, and that these commentators, whether concluding critically or favorably, are reading Davidson in a direction that runs against the underlying current of his thought. This, however, is a very tough case to make out. Davidson, using language which is Kantian in tone, develops accounts of the conditions of objectivity, of thought, and of communication, drawing strong, anti-Cartesian conclusions (cf. *inter alia*, Davidson 1983, 1986, 1991).

The natural conclusion is that Davidson's contribution is, at best, to advance philosophy beyond the Cartesian presuppositions of traditional dualistic epistemology, or, more modestly, given the many critical assessments of his arguments, to deepen our understanding of those presuppositions and what they entail. That would appear to leave metaphysics pretty much as it was: an inquiry into the non-empirical presuppositions of knowing and doing, an inquiry where we will presumably continue to make progress, by continuing to correct our mistakes and misconceptions.

Perhaps, though, this conclusion is a little hasty. For irrespective of the question of genre, it does seem right that Davidson, if his views have merit, forecloses certain options. His case against conceptual schemes is not against *alternative* conceptual schemes, but against the idea that there is any clear point to thinking of what we do when we master language as mastering a conceptual scheme *at all*. It is, as Rorty continually emphasizes, the scheme–content dichotomy that Davidson attacks. And if the related considerations against massive error are plausible, then at least we have a significantly different conception of our metaphysical tasks at hand. For by closing the space required to doubt the representational adequacy of our concepts, Davidson also undermines what has arguably been an important metaphysical impetus, that of securing epistemic *legitimation*—and usually a selective legitimation. And here we are close to one of Rorty's deepest concerns; what he calls *secularization* is precisely the development of a human self-understanding that eschews the need for legitimation of human thought and sentiment by appeal to structures—modes of being—that transcend transitory, finite, situated human existence.

Let us call *positive metaphysics* the philosophical ambition that survives only as long as secularization fails; the project of legitimating, and thus hierarchizing, epistemic practices. Positive metaphysicians take seriously the idea that we could be fundamentally wrong about what kinds of things there are in the world, what kinds of beings we ourselves are, and how one is related to the other. Positive metaphysicians believe that it may be possible to alleviate this by discovering, through conceptual efforts, what it really is to be a subject, and object, a knower, an agent. They think that in order to tell whether, for instance, we really can be said to *be* agents, we need to determine what causality *really is*, and what conditions must be satisfied for any creature to be a minded creature. This is tough armchair work. Let us grant, now, that Rorty's use of Davidson at the very least poses a serious challenge to this conception of what philosophical reflection is aimed at. Still, Rorty's pragmatic stance toward metaphysics remains, for all I have said so far, not essentially different from that of earlier combatants. Call this stance *default metaphysics*. The defining feature of default metaphysics is that it addresses the question of the viability of positive metaphysics as an essentially and internally philosophical question. Varieties of naturalism that conceive of this doctrine as a philosophical response to philosophical questions would provide examples. But what is the harm in default metaphysics? If we are naturalists, isn't that enough to shut down the pernicious kind of metaphysics, the positive kind? If we can agree to be naturalists, to account for ourselves in philosophical terms in such a way that positive metaphysics is no longer a live option, then even if our account of ourselves is metaphysical, it would be a naturalized metaphysics. Why should a pragmatist balk at that?

4. The guiding idea, as we pursue that question, is this: the conception most fundamentally shaping Rorty's struggle is that metaphysics is what you get when you accept the idea that philosophy has a distinct set of problems. The positive and the default metaphysician disagree about what those questions are, or at least how they may be posed, but neither doubts that she is addressing problems of philosophy. A metaphysician, then, is apparently someone who believes in the reality of philosophical problems. A pragmatist, by contrast, is someone who doesn't. Two challenges, however, immediately threaten this way of putting the matter. Doesn't everyone believe in the reality of philosophical problems, *some* philosophical problems? One may disagree about their origin, their durability, and so on; but it is not as if philosophers have nothing to engage their minds except illusions of problems. Typically, when a philosopher declares a problem or a domain of philosophical inquiry to be illusory, that conclusion is arrived at by way of other problems or domains that are taken very seriously indeed. And, secondly and relatedly, what might Rortyan pragmatists take themselves to be addressing, if not philosophical problems?

The immediate lesson is that we ought to resist the temptation to capture the contrast we are after between metaphysics and pragmatism in terms of what is real and what is not. To deny that philosophy has its own distinctive set of problems—to deny that there is a set of questions which are essentially philosophical—is not to deny that philosophical questions are real questions. It is to deny that they must be philosophical, to suggest that we might treat them as questions of a different order. At a minimum, then, we must unpack the core issue—how to conceive of what we are doing when we engage in philosophy—without invoking a distinction between real problems and illusory problems. If a challenge about the nature of philosophical questions is to be issued, it cannot be, at least not when coming from those flying the standard of pragmatism, to the effect that a metaphysical mistake has been committed.

A statement of the anti-essentialist attitude toward philosophy that I would like to elucidate is offered in one Rorty's last essays, "Wittgenstein and the Linguistic Turn" (2007c). Contrasting "therapists"—James Conant, Cora Diamond, and others—with pragmatic Wittgenstenians (such as Rorty), he says:

> The therapists treat "philosophy" as the name of a disease that can be cured by recognizing that one has been uttering nonsense. The pragmatists, however, are not interested in getting rid of philosophical problems as such. They are dubious about the claim that philosophical problems constitute a natural kind. They are focused on certain particular problems—those that came into prominence in the seventeenth century. (Rorty 2007c: 165)

The point here, I take it, is that there is, for Rorty, no such thing as *philosophy* that *requires* of us a certain kind of response. That there is such a thing, and such a requirement, is what unites the therapists and both varieties of metaphysicians—what, indeed, makes them all metaphysicians, even though they have very different notions of the kind of response that is required. To follow Rorty here, we need not deny that there are philosophical questions. We need only deny that they must be taken and answered in a certain way—that is, as questions which are properly prior to, and independent of, concern with the contingencies of human affairs.

Metaphysicians are metaphysicians precisely because they do assert exactly this—or live by it. Rorty denies it. Certainly, many others have, too. Quine famously denies it, in asserting his naturalism; philosophy is continuous with and part of the same general project as science. Indeed, today the idea of continuity between philosophy and science, a continuity that tells us something important about philosophy and that philosophy does not share with other areas of culture, is widespread. For Rorty, however, the denial is not based on a scientistic understanding of philosophy, an understanding of philosophy as part of *inquiry* in this narrower sense. Philosophical questions have their genesis in contingent history, in plastic practice, and can be taken as referring back to that practice. Rorty's case against metaphysics, then, is that it just is a commitment to this autonomy thesis. Metaphysics may of course bear on human affairs, constraining or illuminating them; but this simply means that the normative practical commitments by which we form our lives and guide our conduct are depicted as derivative, dependent for their reasonableness on insight into something that transcends them. In short, metaphysics is a strategy for insulating the work of philosophy from the larger issues of cultural politics which are the locus of human action, choice, and suffering. The real point of the critique of metaphysics is that we risk diminishing our own powers—both our power to see new opportunities for engaging with the world and our power to act on suffering in ameliorating fashion. Fighting against metaphysics is to contribute to our ability and willingness to take responsibility for how we talk; this, to put it in Hegelian terms, is the pragmatist's way of spiritualizing the nature that we also are. It is this responsibility that gives us room to maneuver, reflectively to either embrace or alter some of the varied, complex ways that we language-using creatures have developed for handling ourselves in the world. The more we treat ourselves as subservient responders, mere representers of structures or contents that are determinately there irrespective of our interested interaction with them, the more we abdicate our potential for personal, social, and political creativity, for freedom.

What, then, of Rorty's appropriation of Davidson, who at least appears to proceed as a metaphysician in this regard? Let us turn once more to Rorty's interaction with Davidson's work. In "The Contingency of Language", the first chapter of *Contingency, Irony, and Solidarity* (1989), Rorty draws heavily on Davidson, but is less concerned with the destruction of metaphysics than he is in *Philosophy and the Mirror of Nature* and more concerned with drawing an alternative picture to the representationalist view that he rejects. For this purpose, he finds inspiration in Davison's "A Nice Derangement of Epitaphs" (1986), in which Davidson, according to Rorty, "dispenses with the picture of language as a third thing intervening between self and reality, and of different languages as barriers between persons or cultures" (Rorty 1989: 14). Rorty now aims to provide "an account of intellectual and moral progress which squares with Davidson's account of language". This account, elaborated in a number of essays from the late 1980s on, has provided us with some of the ideas for which Rorty is best known: the idea of objectivity as solidarity (cf., *inter alia*, Rorty 1991), the rejection of truth as a goal of inquiry (cf. Rorty 1995), the notion that irony is the appropriate attitude of a civilized person to her own deepest commitments (cf. Rorty 1989), the claim that liberal tolerance is fostered by ethnocentrism (or anti-anti-ethnocentrism—cf. Rorty 1986*a*). In Rorty's non-metaphysical account of human virtue—that is, the sort of behavior that tends to improve the conditions of life for people in general—appeal is made to standards of assessment that are immanent to experience and that have emerged historically through a non-teleological process. That, in turn, amounts, in Rorty's own words, to providing an "intellectual history viewed as the history of metaphor".

One way to look at this work is to see it as an application of Davidsonian doctrine to wider cultural and political concerns. However, it is possible to see Rorty as doing something different, something more radical. While exploiting to the fullest possible extent Davidson's account of communication, of objective thought as requiring a plurality of speakers, of knowledge of oneself, of others, and of the world as being a single structure where all points of the triangle mutually support one another, Rorty engages in a parallel project, which reverses the direction of support. Rorty's account of epistemic virtues in terms of solidarity (Rorty 1985, 1987*b*), of human interest, is not intended to provide a picture of objectivity or knowledge that is an alternative to Davidson's philosophical account. Rather, we should take Rorty's account of epistemic virtue as a matter of human solidarity as a demonstration of the possibility of taking philosophical questions as questions of cultural politics. What Rorty aims to do here is to derive motivation and support for his use of naturalizing Davidsonian theses to undermine representationalist thinking from the commitments of an ethical and political nature—and in the case of his treatment of self-creation, also of an esthetic nature—that he expresses in those papers that explicitly address questions of cultural politics and human progress. In this way the philosophical ideas that Rorty imports from Davidson become, increasingly, embedded in the project of directly confronting ourselves and our practices in ethical and political terms. This, I take it, is just what Rorty means when he asserts the priority of democracy over philosophy and describes philosophy itself as a species of cultural politics. From the point of view of this radical pragmatism, the question of the autonomy of philosophy is not a matter to be settled by theoretical reflection, determined by philosophical understanding. It is a question of ethical choice of direction. As he puts the point in the preface to his final collection of essays, "The more philosophy interacts with other human activities—not just natural science, but art, literature, religion and politics as well—the more relevant to cultural politics it becomes, and thus the more useful. The more it strives for autonomy, the less attention it deserves" (Rorty 2007*b*: p. x).

Metaphysics in philosophy is the wish to entrench the autonomy that Rorty fears will make philosophy increasingly useless in human terms. It is the construction of authority beyond human practice, unmalleable and immune to change. Metaphysics, from this point of view, appears as a variant of authoritarian alienation. Pragmatism, in Rorty's hands, finds its deepest expression as anti-authoritarianism (cf., for instance, Rorty 2000: 62). It opposes metaphysics as one opposes authoritarianism—through discreditation, by handling philosophical questions in terms that recover them from this alienation and treats them in—and as a part of—a context of ethical, political, and esthetical choice.

5. The emphasis on the *humanizing* aspect of Davidson's account of thought and of objectivity becomes increasingly central to Rorty's reading and deployment of Davidson. His enthusiasm for the constructive and systematic work of Brandom serves to highlight this point. Resting normativity on human conduct, Brandom leaves no room for a source of authority or responsibility beyond efforts and travails of historically situated human beings. The pragmatist's point, then, is not that metaphysics is illusory or that metaphysical questions are meaningless. The claim, rather, is that metaphysics and philosophy are *possibly* distinct activities. No one disputes the fact that one *may* take philosophical questions metaphysically—that is, as questions that are raised and answered as if they spring from prior constraints on the contingencies of our existence and our practices. The *positive metaphysician* does this explicitly. The positive metaphysician seeks to map the non-empirical necessities by which all beings, all forms of life, are constrained. The *default metaphysician* takes questions metaphysically simply by neglecting to thematize or reflect the historicity and practice-rootedness of the concepts—the vocabulary—under investigation, rendering the knowledge produced as of something non-human, something *autonomous*. The *pragmatist* urges us, by contrast, explicitly to take philosophical questions as if they arise out of those very contingencies, resting on them and expressing them—that is, as questions to ourselves about ourselves. This is the content of the pragmatist's efforts to persuade us to "stop talking about ontology" and "to turn everything over to sociology", to borrow the admonitions of the later Rorty—or, as he also puts it, to let philosophy be cultural politics.

Davidson's systematic philosophy—a daring, constructive account of what it takes to be an acting, communicating, thinking being—provides such a pragmatist with two central elements of this campaign. The first consists of that network of philosophical arguments to the effect that our capacities to act and communicate in the world do not presuppose either subjective or objective essences, the stuff of which positive metaphysics is built. The second element is an opportunity, a challenge to *demonstrate* that metaphysics is not compulsory even for problem-oriented, constructive philosophy. This demonstration, the fundamental goal of Rorty's developing engagement with Davidson, consists in integrating Davidson's arguments into an account which precisely thematizes the historicity and practice-rootedness of the complex view that is developed, without creating tensions between that pragmatist story and the content of the view of human agency and thought that is being appropriated. Success in this endeavor would also illustrate the further—important—pragmatist point that whether or not Davidson's work is positive metaphysics, default metaphysics, or pragmatist, will depend on its effective history. For the pragmatist—though not for the metaphysician—this is only to be expected. For rejecting the autonomy thesis along pragmatist lines cuts both ways; if metaphysics does not carve out any specific non-contingent preserve of inquiry—that is, if it has no essence—then no amount of philosophizing could ever get us securely past it. Metaphysics continues, as any genre will, as long as it can be adapted to the purposes of prevailing needs and interests. And as it does so, pragmatists, for their part, will persist in construing those needs and interests as thoroughly human, thoroughly practical, and thoroughly non-metaphysical.

REFERENCES

Brandom, Robert (1976). "Truth and Assertibility". *Journal of Philosophy*, 73: 137–49.
____ (2000). *Rorty and his Critics*. Oxford: Blackwell.
Davidson, Donald (1963). "Actions, Reasons, and Causes". In Davidson (1980), 3–20.
____ (1970). "Mental Events". In Davidson (1980), 207–24.
____ (1974). "On the Very Idea of a Conceptual Scheme". In Davidson (1982), 183–98.
____ (1980). *Essays on Actions and Events*. Oxford: Oxford University Press.
____ (1982). *Inquiries into Truth and Interpretation*. Oxford: Oxford University Press.
____ (1983). "A Coherence Theory of Truth and Knowledge". In Davidson (2001), 137–53.
____ (1986). "A Nice Derangement of Epitaphs". In Davidson (2005), 89–107.
____ (1991). "Three Varieties of Knowledge". In Davidson (2001), 205–20.
____ (2001). *Subjective, Intersubjective, Objective*. Oxford: Oxford University Press.
____ (2005). *Truth, Language and History*. Oxford: Oxford University Press.
Kim, Jaegwon (1993). *Supervenience and Mind: Selected Philosophical Essays*. Cambridge: Cambridge University Press.

Kim, Jaegwon (1997). *Mind in a Physical World*. Cambridge, MA: MIT Press.

——— (2003). "Philosophy of Mind and Psychology". In Ludwig (2003), 113–36.

Lepore, Ernest, and Ludwig, Kirk (2005). *Donald Davidson: Meaning, Truth, Language and Reality*. Oxford: Oxford University Press.

Ludwig, Kirk (ed.) (2003). *Donald Davidson*. Cambridge: Cambridge University Press.

Pietroski, Paul (2003). "Semantics and the Metaphysics of Events". In Ludwig (2003), 137–62.

Rorty, Richard (1979). *Philosophy and the Mirror of Nature*. Princeton: Princeton University Press.

——— (1985). "Solidarity or Objectivity". In Rorty (1991), 21–34.

——— (1986a). "On Ethnocentrism: A Reply to Clifford Geertz". In Rorty (1991), 203–10.

——— (1986b). "Pragmatism, Davidson, and Truth". In Rorty (1991), 126–50.

——— (1987a). "Non-Reductive Physicalism". In Rorty (1991), 113–25.

——— (1987b). "Science as Solidarity". In Rorty (1991), 35–45.

——— (1989). *Contingency, Irony, and Solidarity*. Cambridge: Cambridge University Press.

——— (1991). *Philosophical Papers*, i: *Objectivity, Relativism, and Truth*. Cambridge: Cambridge University Press.

——— (1995). "Is Truth a Goal of Inquiry? Donald Davidson versus Crispin Wright". In Rorty (1998b), 19–42.

——— (1998a). "Antiskeptical Weapons: Michael Williams versus Donald Davidson". In Rorty (1998b), 153–63.

——— (1998b). *Philosophical Papers*, iii: *Truth and Progress*. Cambridge: Cambridge University Press.

——— (2000). "Response to Jürgen Habermas". In Brandom (2000), 56–64.

——— (2007a). "Naturalism and Quietism". In Rorty (2007b), 147–59.

——— (2007b). *Philosophical Papers*, iv: *Philosophy as Cultural Politics*. Cambridge: Cambridge University Press.

——— (2007c). "Wittgenstein and the Linguistic Turn". In Rorty (2007b), 160–75.

Soames, Scott (2003). *Philosophical Analysis in the Twentieth Century*, ii: *The Age of Meaning*. Princeton: Princeton University Press.

CHAPTER 21

....

ANALYTIC PHILOSOPHY IN AMERICA

....

SCOTT SOAMES

THE LEADING pre-analytic philosopher in America, and one of its giants of all time, was Charles Sanders Peirce (1839–1914). Receiving a scientific education (including a Harvard B.Sc. in chemistry in 1863), he lectured on logic and philosophy of science at Harvard (1864–5, 1869–71) and Johns Hopkins (1879–84), after which he moved to Milford, Pennsylvania, where he continued to write prodigiously. His greatest contributions were in logic, including a syntax for quantification theory (1870 and 1883) and a truth-functionally complete system based on what later came to be called "the Sheffer stroke". Though his contributions were, in many respects, parallel to those of Gottlob Frege, the two logicians worked independently, with the writing of Frege, through its influence on Bertrand Russell, becoming the more widely known. Still, Alfred North Whitehead was an admirer, whose knowledge of quantification theory was said to have come substantially from Peirce, while Hilary Putnam (1982: p. xiii) observes that much that is "quite familiar in modern logic actually became known to the logical world through the efforts of Peirce and his students". In 1985, W. V. Quine identified Peirce as sharing credit with Frege for the development of modern quantification theory, and cited his influence on Schröder and Peano (see Houser *et al.* 1997).

Outside logic, Peirce's philosophy of pragmatism—or, as he called it, "pragmaticism"—was widely admired. In epistemology, he was an anti-foundationalist, resisting the idea of a privileged starting point of maximally certain statements (e.g. of private sensation), and adopting, as a guiding hypothesis, the idea that the application of scientific method to intersubjectively verifiable claims would, through a process of self-correction, lead different investigators to converge on a common result, no matter what their starting points. While not definitively identifying truth with that which would be confirmed in the limit of ideal (scientific) inquiry, he did think that the practical consequences of true beliefs provided grounds for expecting them to be confirmed by continuing investigation. Correspondingly, he took the meaning of a theoretical claim to be its experiential "cash value"—the collection of possible empirical observations that would verify it. He had little patience with metaphysical speculation about "things in themselves" underlying observed phenomena, or grand metaphysical systems. In all these ways, Peirce exerted a strong influence on those who would follow. Peircean reverence for logic, respect for science, suspicion of a priori metaphysics, and emphasis on the practical consequences of theoretical differences found fertile soil, and took root in America, creating a hospitable environment for the later growth, and distinctive shape, of analytic philosophy there (see Misak 2004).

The other great American pragmatist was William James (1842–1910). Like Peirce, James had a scientific education in chemistry, anatomy, and medicine at Harvard, where he received an M.D. in 1869. He taught physiology in 1872, and in 1875 set up the first laboratory for experimental psychology in America. Between 1885 and 1907 he was professor of psychology and philosophy at Harvard, giving *The Varieties of Religious Experience* (1902) as the Gifford Lectures at Edinburgh, and publishing *Pragmatism* in 1907. Though influenced by Peirce, his outlook was less scientific, and his audience broader. Whereas, for Peirce, truth and meaning rest on the intellectual foundation of possible observation, for James they rest on what it is beneficial to believe. To the extent that religious beliefs help us live better lives, they pass the Jamesian pragmatic test for truth, just as scientific beliefs do.

Third in the trio of pre-analytic pragmatists was John Dewey (1859–1952), who received his Ph.D. in philosophy in 1884 from Johns Hopkins, where he encountered Peirce. Between 1884 and 1930, he taught at the universities of Michigan, Minnesota, Chicago, and (for the last twenty-four years) Columbia. Like Peirce, he was an anti-foundationalist and a believer in the self-correcting nature of empirical investigation in a community of inquirers. Like Quine, who was to follow, he held that there are no absolute first principles that are either known with certainty or beyond rational revision in light of new experience. Truth, for Dewey, was warranted assertibility. Though less influential than Peirce in the later development of analytic philosophy, his views on education and other social issues had a large and controversial impact.

Along with pragmatism, realism and naturalism characterized much American philosophy between Peirce and Quine. Peirce wrote in 1896, "Nothing can be more completely false than that we can experience only our own ideas. That is indeed without exaggeration the very epitome of *all* falsity" (*CP* 6.95). The independence of the perceived from the perceiver, and the known from the knower, was emphasized in *The New Realism* (1912) by philosophers such as E. B. Holt and R. B. Perry. As Passmore (1957) notes, their conception of perception was similar to that given in G. E. Moore's "The Refutation of Idealism" (1903), while their rejection of "internal relations" paralleled a similar rejection, central to the rebellion of Moore and Russell against absolute idealism. (The importance of the rejection for New Realists was in their observation that when a knows b, the relational properties of knowing b, and of being known by a, are not essential to a and b, respectively.) By 1920, another brand of realism, Critical Realism, was on the scene. Advocated by A. O. Lovejoy, G. Santayana, and R. W. Sellars, among others, it struggled to reconcile the objective physical world, revealed in perception, with an irreducible Kantian residue added by the perceiver to the content of experience. Although disputes between these varieties of realism have now lost much of their force, it is striking how congenial the broad themes of naturalism, respect for science and common sense, and suspicion of idealism and other a priori speculation were to the growth of analytic philosophy in America.

THE TRANSITION TO ANALYTIC PHILOSOPHY

The American transition to analytic philosophy was mediated by several pivotal figures, institutions, and events. One such figure was Morris Cohen (1880–1947). Born in Russia, educated at City College of New York, with a 1906 Harvard Ph.D., he taught at City from 1912 to 1938, and at the University of Chicago from 1938 to 1941. Known for his interest in logic and the philosophy of science, he was a committed naturalist who recognized no non-scientific methods capable of attaining knowledge in philosophy. One of his students was the Czechoslovakian-born Ernest Nagel (1901–85), who, after earning his B.A. at City, got his Ph.D. in 1931 (under Dewey) from Columbia, where (with the exception of a year at Rockefeller University in the 1960s) he spent his career teaching and writing about the philosophy of science and explaining the centrality of logic to philosophy. His little book *Gödel's Proof* (1958), co-authored with James R. Newman, introduced the incompleteness theorems to many students, while his main work, *The Structure of Science* (1961) summed up the results of decades of teaching and research on the nature of explanation and the logical structure of scientific knowledge.

Of all the transitional figures, the greatest was C. I. Lewis (1883–1964). Receiving his B.A. (1905) and Ph.D. (1910) from Harvard, he worked with, and was influenced by, William James, Josiah Royce, and Ralph Barton Perry. After teaching at Berkeley for nine years, he returned to take up a position at Harvard in 1920, from which he retired thirty-three years later, having taught many who would become leading analytic figures—including Quine, Roderick Chisholm, Roderick Firth, William Frankena, Nelson Goodman, and Norman Malcolm. He finished his career at Stanford University in 1960. An eclectic thinker and system-builder, Lewis combined an element of perceptual realism, filtered through Perry, a Kantian element, filtered through Josiah Royce, and a pragmatic element, filtered through Peirce (whose work he encountered when given the job of cataloging the latter's vast unpublished writings). Like Perry, he believed that perception and knowledge require an independent reality given in experience. Like Royce, he was convinced that experience is the result of structuring and interpreting the given in terms of "a priori" concepts added by the mind. Like Peirce, he held (i) that our concepts—even the "a priori" ones—are not fixed by the nature of the mind, but are revisable in light of experience; and (ii) that the meanings of concepts, thoughts, and experience lie in their pragmatic success in anticipating and predicting new experience and grounding successful action. These ideas were worked out in his two major works, *Mind and the World Order* (1929) and *An Analysis of Knowledge and Valuation* (1946), which were among the most widely read of their day—the former being the subject of a memorable seminar at Oxford led by J. L. Austin and Isaiah Berlin in the 1936–7 academic year.

Lewis's relation to the logical positivists was ambiguous. On the one hand, he shared their scientific naturalism, their emphasis on logical analysis, and their view of testable consequences as the basis of empirical significance. On the other, he vigorously opposed their non-cognitivism about value, their physicalism, and their embrace of "the linguistic turn". For him, the primary bearers of meaning and truth were mental: thoughts, concepts, and experiences. Of most importance for analytic philosophy was his pioneering work in modal logic, included in his widely read *Symbolic Logic* (1932), co-authored with C. H. Langford. His main contribution was in formulating a series of increasingly strong axiomatic systems (the S-systems) of the modal propositional calculus (with operators for necessity and possibility)—which provided the basis for (i) later axiomatic extensions to the predicate calculus by Ruth Marcus (1946) and Rudolf Carnap (1946); (ii) the fledgling semantic treatment by Carnap (1947); and (iii) the revealing model-theoretic inter-pretations of the S-systems in Saul Kripke (1959 and 1963). For Lewis, the philosophical moral drawn from the competing axiomatic systems was that logical first principles are not decidable a priori, but must be judged by their pragmatic success—a conclusion which, no matter what its ultimate merits, was premature in light of later work. Finally, the distinction in Lewis (1946) between the different "modes of meaning of a term"—(i) its extension, con-sisting of things to which it refers or applies; (ii) its "comprehension" (now called its "intension"), consisting of a mapping of possible world-states to extensions; and (iii) its "signification", consisting of a concept or property determining (ii)—was an important forerunner of later developments in analytic philosophy of language.

In understanding the transition to the analytic period in America, it is important to remember that analytic philosophy is neither a fixed body of substantive doctrine, a precise methodology, nor a radical break with most traditional philosophy of the past—save for varieties of romanticism, theism, and absolute idealism. Instead, it is a discrete historical tradition stemming from Frege, Moore, Russell, Wittgenstein, and the logical positivists, characterized by respect for science and common sense, belief in the relevance of logic and language for philosophy, emphasis on precision and clarity of argumentation, suspicion of a priori metaphysics, and elevation of the goals of truth and knowledge over inspiration, moral uplift, and spiritual comfort—plus a dose of professional specialization. All of these tendencies were already present in America—preeminently at Harvard, but also at Columbia, City College of New York, the University of Michigan, and elsewhere. They were reinforced by repeated visits to the USA to teach and lecture by Moore (1940–4) and Russell (1896, 1914, 1924, 1927, 1929, 1931, 1938, 1939, 1940–2), and the addition to the Harvard philosophy faculty in 1924 of the co-author of *Principia Mathematica*, Alfred North Whitehead. Each had a noticeable impact on the locals. For example, Quine—whose first great paper, "Truth by Convention" (1936), appeared in a collection in honor of Whitehead—describes his 1931 encounter with Russell as his "most dazzling exposure to greatness", while his later Harvard colleague, Morton White, says that his experience of Moore at Columbia in the early 1940s was "one of the most refreshing episodes in [his] philosophical education". By then, all that was needed for America to enter the stream of analytic philosophy was for the works of its philosophers to regularly, and in large numbers, enter the torrent flowing from its British and European sources.

THE BEGINNINGS OF ANALYTIC PHILOSOPHY

The emergence of analytic philosophy in America was marked by three events above all others: (i) the arrival from Europe of leading logicians, philosophers of science, logical positivists, and other analytic philosophers; (ii) the transformation of the Harvard department led by Quine in the 1950s and 1960s; and (iii) the vast post-war expansion in higher education in America, which came to encompass a substantial drain in philosophical talent from Britain to the United States—including (for varying lengths of time) such figures as Paul Grice, Stuart Hampshire, J. O. Urmson, and Philippa Foot.

The first, and most dramatic, of these events was the arrival of an enormously gifted and distinguished group of émigrés from Europe. Among them were Herbert Feigl (1902–88), arriving from Vienna in 1931, Rudolf Carnap (1891–1970), arriving in 1935 from Prague, Carl Hempel (1905–97), arriving from Germany in 1937, Hans Reichenbach (1891–1953), arriving from Germany by way of Turkey in 1938, Gustav Bergman (1906–87), coming from Vienna in 1938, Alfred Tarski (1901–83), arriving from Poland in 1939, and Kurt Gödel (1906–78), arriving from Vienna in 1940.

Feigl, who studied philosophy of science and probability under Moritz Schlick, and was a member of the Vienna Circle, first taught at the University of Iowa from 1931 to 1940, and then at the University of Minnesota from

1940 to 1973. He is best known for his partnership with Wilfrid Sellars in (i) co-editing the collection *Readings in Philosophical Analysis* (1949), which was for decades a staple in the classrooms of analytic philosophers, and (ii) co-founding the journal *Philosophical Studies* in 1950 as a forum for the new school of "analytic philosophy".

Carnap, the world's premier logical positivist, taught at the University of Chicago from 1936 to 1952, with a year's visit to Harvard in 1941–2. From 1952 to 1954 he was at the Institute for Advanced Study in Princeton, after which he held a chair in philosophy at UCLA from 1954 to 1962. Having studied logic with Frege, Carnap's own students included such notable American philosophers as Richard Jeffrey (subjective probability) and David Kaplan (the logic of demonstratives). Among Carnap's major works published during his years in America were "Testability and Meaning" (1936–7), *Introduction to Semantics* (1942), *Meaning and Necessity* (1947), *The Logical Foundations of Probability* (1950*b*), and "Empiricism, Semantics, and Ontology" (1950*a*).

Reichenbach, another leading positivist and preeminent philosopher of science, studied civil engineering, physics, mathematics, and philosophy, working under, or attending lectures of, David Hilbert, Max Planck, and Albert Einstein. In the 1920s, he published several books interpreting relativity theory, and in 1930, together with Carnap, he took over editorship of *Erkenntnis*, the leading journal of logical positivism. In 1935, while in Turkey, he published *The Theory of Probability*. After moving to the United States, he accepted a position at UCLA, where he remained until his death in 1953. Among his students was Hilary Putnam, who was to become a leading philosopher at Princeton, MIT, and Harvard. Reichenbach's major American works include *Experience and Prediction* (1938), *Philosophic Foundations of Quantum Mechanics* (1944), *Elements of Symbolic Logic* (1947), and *The Rise of Scientific Philosophy* (1951).

In his first year in the USA, Hempel, who had been a well-known contributor to logical positivism in Europe, held a position as a research associate at the University of Chicago, arranged by Carnap. From 1939 to 1948, he taught in New York, at City College and Queens, after which he went to Yale, where he stayed until 1955. In that year he joined the Princeton department, where he became—with the renowned classical philosopher Gregory Vlastos—the nucleus of what was to become one of the world's great centers of analytic philosophy. Hempel remained at Princeton until his retirement in 1973, after which he spent another decade teaching at the University of Pittsburgh. Upon retiring from there, he returned to Princeton (which had kept his house and office for him), where he spent the rest of his life. His major American works include "Studies in the Logic of Confirmation" (1945), "A Definition of Degree of Confirmation", with Paul Oppenheim, (1945), "Studies in the Logic of Explanation", with Oppenheim (1948), "The Empiricist Criterion of Meaning" (1950), *Aspects of Scientific Explanation* (1965), and *Philosophy of Natural Science* (1966).

Bergmann, who had been associated with the Vienna Circle, taught at the University of Iowa from 1939 to 1974. President of the Western Division of the American Philosophical Association in 1967–8, his students went on to teach in many philosophy departments throughout the country.

Alfred Tarski had already done his path-breaking work on truth and logical consequence when he set off from Poland in August 1939 (on what turned out to be the last boat before the Nazi–Soviet invasion) to lecture at the Congress for Unified Science at Harvard University. Finding that he had no country to return to, he remained in the United States. Though initially unable to secure a regular faculty position, he held a two-year post as research associate at Harvard, arranged by Quine, and taught two courses in logic at the City College of New York. After spending 1941–2 (with Gödel) at the Institute for Advanced Study in Princeton, he moved to the mathematics department at Berkeley, where he remained. Acknowledged as one of the greatest logicians of all time, he was also a dedicated and influential teacher. As leader of the Ph.D. program in Logic and the Methodology of Science at Berkeley, Tarski both exercised a strong influence on his younger colleagues, like Dana Scott, and supervised twenty-four dissertations, including those of Richard Montague and Solomon Feferman, who substantially influenced the course of analytic philosophy, as well as the programs of their respective institutions (Scott at Princeton, Montague at UCLA, and Feferman at Stanford). The trio of Tarski, Gödel (at the Institute for Advanced Study in Princeton from 1940), and Alonzo Church (Princeton 1929–67, and UCLA 1967–90, whose students included Anthony Anderson, Leon Henkin, Stephen Kleene, Hartley Rogers, J. B. Rosser, Dana Scott, and Alan Turing) not only transformed the mathematical study of symbolic logic, but also exerted a powerful force on the study of philosophical aspects of logic by analytic philosophers.

The second factor leading to the triumph of analytic philosophy in America was the transformation of the Harvard department, led by Quine (1908–2000)—the one man more responsible than any other for the decisive analytic turn in America. In 1932, he finished his Ph.D. dissertation at

Harvard on Russell's *Principia Mathematica*. During the next year, he held a fellowship that allowed him to travel to Europe, where he met, or attended seminars given by, Carnap, Tarski, Lesniewski, Lukasiewicz, Schlick, Hahn, Reichenbach, Gödel, and Ayer. (He had already met Feigl in 1930.) The relationship with Carnap was the deepest. Back at the Harvard Society of Fellows for three years, he gave lectures expounding Carnap and published his well-known paper "Truth by Convention" (1936), which grew out of them. There, Quine attacked the linguistic theory of the a priori, then popular among the positivists. In opposition to the view that all a priori knowledge, including knowledge of logic, is knowledge of linguistic convention, he pointed out that the potentially infinite scope of logical knowledge would require it to be derived from a manageable set of allegedly conventional axioms. But since knowledge of logic is presupposed by such derivations, it cannot be explained by them. The objection, which to this day remains powerful, illustrates a characteristic feature of Quine's thought. Starting with the problems posed by his positivist mentors, he isolates a central tenet about meaning in their proposed solution, and exposes an inherent problem. Quine's reaction was not, of course, to give a non-linguistic account of the a priori, but to purify empiricism by giving up the a priori altogether.

The same dynamic is illustrated in his discussion of ontological commitment in "On What There Is" (1948) and of analyticity in "Two Dogmas of Empiricism" (1951), where his skepticism about analyticity and his holism about empirical content are on display. With Carnap and other positivists, he agrees (i) that the empirical content of our claims is to be found in the observations that would confirm them, and (ii) that necessity is to be identified with analyticity, if it exists at all. Unlike them, Quine rejects any account of empirical content, or meaning, that portions it out to sentences one by one, and, in so doing, he ends up discarding analyticity, apriority, and necessity in the bargain. The end result is a version of empiricism of the same sort as that of the logical positivists, only more radical, in which meaning plays no privileged epistemic role. Thus it was that philosophy in America entered the mainstream of analytic philosophy, altering its course.

By 1951 Quine was a world-renowned figure. However, despite having been tenured at Harvard for ten years (interrupted by a stint of military service in World War II), he was still in the minority there—as illustrated by the department's rejection of his 1948 proposal to offer a position to Carnap. In those years, his chief allies were, first, Henry Aiken, who joined the department in 1946, and later, Morton White, whose appointment in

1948 was instigated by Aiken and Quine. With these appointments, and the retirement of C. I. Lewis in 1953, the department was ready for change. In the 1950s and 1960s, largely under the philosophical leadership of Quine and the chairmanship of White, Harvard added Roderick Firth, Burton Dreben, Israel Scheffler, Rogers Albritton, Stanley Cavell, John Rawls, Nelson Goodman, Hilary Putnam, and Robert Nozick (see White 1999). By the end of that time they had gathered as fine a collection of philosophers as could be found anywhere.

The 1950s and 1960s also saw a lively interaction grow up between the philosophers at Harvard and those at Oxford. Having met Isaiah Berlin in 1949, White spent a year in Oxford, coming away deeply impressed, not only by Berlin, but also by Gilbert Ryle, John Austin, H. L. A. Hart, and Paul Grice. Shortly thereafter, Austin, Hart, and Grice were lecturing at Harvard. First, Austin spent the spring of 1955 at Harvard giving *How to Do Things with Words* (later published in 1962) as the William James Lectures. Then, Hart spent the 1956–7 academic year teaching philosophy and law, to be followed by Grice, who lectured at Harvard in the late 1950s before giving "Logic and Conversation" as the William James Lectures of 1967 (eventually published in Grice 1989). This interaction between the Quine-led descendants of Carnap and the Ryle–Austin–Grice-led descendants of Wittgenstein encompassed the most important strands of the analytic philosophy of the day. Both sides were well represented at Harvard, and nowhere in the philosophical world was the intellectual ferment more lively. What was true of Harvard was also increasingly true of America as a whole—as visits by, and longer-term professorships for, leading British philosophers, including Elizabeth Anscombe, Philippa Foot, Stuart Hampshire, David Pears, and J. O. Urmson, brought important non-positivist perspectives to the rapidly advancing ranks of analytic philosophers in America. Although in the end the Quinean–Peircean logical and scientific strand of analytic philosophy proved to be the strongest, both at Harvard and across America, the tradition was enlarged, implicitly refuting Quine's infamous echo, "philosophy of science is philosophy enough", of Carnap's original call to arms (from *The Logical Syntax of Language* (1937: 292)), "Philosophy is to be replaced by the logic of science—that is to say, by the logical analysis of the concepts and sentences of the sciences."

By the early 1970s analytic philosophy was dominant in America. Fueled by the enormous post-war expansion in higher education, the number of faculty positions in philosophy—to be filled overwhelmingly by analytic philosophers—expanded rapidly. Membership in the American Philosophical Association rose from 747 in 1940, to 1,248 in 1950, 1,984 in 1960, 2,725 in 1970, and 5,125 in 1980. With these numbers came the growth of several powerful analytic departments. Chief of these was Princeton, which—with Paul Benacerraf, John Burgess, Michael Frede, Gilbert Harman, Richard Jeffrey, Saul Kripke, David Lewis, Thomas Nagel, Thomas Scanlon, and Margaret Wilson, among others—was, by the end of the 1970s, widely regarded as the top of the heap. Close behind, specializing in the philosophy of science, was Pittsburgh, which had come into its own as a great department when Wilfrid Sellars arrived there from Yale in 1963, bringing with him a group of that institution's best young philosophers. Throughout the period, Michigan retained its reputation for preeminence in ethics and meta-ethics, a position it had held since the arrival of the famous emotivist Charles Stevenson in 1946 (from Yale). Two other programs, at UCLA and Cornell, also deserve special notice. Having welcomed Reichenbach and Carnap, acquired Montague and Church, and hired its own brilliant Ph.D. David Kaplan, UCLA was almost without peer in the study of philosophical logic. Adding Tony Martin, Tyler Burge, Rogers Albritton, and Philippa Foot, it became a powerhouse in the arsenal of analytic philosophy. Meanwhile, Cornell had become the home of Wittgensteinianism in America—under the influence of Norman Malcolm, who studied with Wittgenstein at Oxford, and Max Black, who wrote an important work on the *Tractatus*. With the addition of Sydney Shoemaker, Keith Donnellan, and (later) Robert Stalnaker, it attained a position of continuing strength. Other leading departments between 1940 and 1980 included Berkeley, Stanford, MIT, and Brown.

The staggering growth in the quality and quantity of analytic philosophy in that period, and the extent of its dominance throughout the country, is illustrated by a dramatic contrast between two departments at very different institutions. The first is the philosophy department at Wayne State University, located in downtown Detroit, serving a predominantly lower middle-class and working-class student population. Such was the abundance of available talent, and the enthusiasm of young philosophers entering the profession, that between 1955 and 1970 the philosophy department at Wayne acquired a reputation for precision, passion, and fierce analytical argumentation that had few rivals anywhere. Among the prominent philosophers who spent substantial portions of their careers at Wayne State were Richard Cartwright, Hector-Neri Castañeda, Edmund Gettier, Keith Lehrer, Michael McKinsey, George Nakhnikian, Alvin Plantinga, and Robert Sleigh. In 1967, the leading journal, *Nous*, was started at Wayne State by Castañeda (a student of Sellars). By contrast, philosophy at Yale, one of America's great, elite universities, suffered. Setting itself in the 1940s and 1950s resolutely against the rising tide of analytic philosophy, and fancying itself as the defender of a less scientific, more humanistic and metaphysical tradition, the department denied tenure to Stevenson in 1946, refused to promote Hempel in 1955, lost Sellars in 1963, and declined to renew Stalnaker's contract in the early 1970s. By the late 1980s, with only three senior professors, it was stripped of its power over appointments, and placed in receivership. At the dawn of the new century, it was only beginning to recover. Such was the contrast between embracing (Wayne State) and dismissing (Yale) analytic philosophy in America.

With the background set, and institutional terrain surveyed, it is time to turn to leading philosophical themes and figures in American analytic philosophy.

THE QUINE/CARNAP DEBATE ABOUT MEANING, REFERENCE, AND ANALYTICITY

The logical empiricist Carnap divided meaningful sentences into two classes— the analytic and the synthetic—the content of the later explicated in terms of observations that would verify them. Quine in part agreed and in part disagreed. While happy to identify the meanings of comprehensive theories with the observations that would confirm them, he attacked Carnap's distinction between sentences as based on the false presupposition that a scientifically defensible conception of meaning could sensibly be applied to individual sentences, taken one by one. This meant rejecting the idea that sentences, or other expressions, could be synonymous, as well as the idea that they could be true in virtue of meaning. Carnap replied that the intensional notions of meaning and synonymy could not be rejected without also rejecting the extensional notions of truth and reference. Regarding that course as too radical, he developed an account of the integrated connections between extensional and intensional notions, as well as an explanation of how empirical evidence bears on assignments of semantic values to expressions.

An early follower of Tarski, Carnap correctly distinguished Tarski's notion of truth from epistemic notions like certainty and confirmation, with which truth had often been confused—"Truth and Confirmation" (1949). Rightly noting that these confusions had prevented truth from playing a central role in earlier positivist accounts of meaning, he made it the basis for his own subsequent semantic theories—"Intellectual Autobiography" (1963). (Unfortunately, like other early theorists, he wrongly took the notion of truth needed for this task to be Tarski's own formal notion. Fortunately, his semantic theories do not depend on this error.) In *Introduction to Semantics* (1942) Carnap laid out his truth-conditional conception of meaning, extending it to modal languages in *Meaning and Necessity* (1947), where necessary truth is identified with analyticity. Later, in "Meaning and Synonymy in Natural Languages" (1956), he tried to show how the meaning of a term, over and above its reference, can play an important role in empirical theorizing about language users. He argued that although there are empirical uncertainties in establishing the meaning and reference of a given term, there are sound empirical methods for bringing evidence to bear on both questions. As a result, he concluded, meaning and reference are in the same boat. Thus, he thought, Quine was wrong to dismiss intensional notions like meaning and synonymy, while apparently retaining extensional notions like reference (and truth). Contrary to Quine, Carnap maintained that the intensional and the extensional are scientifically on a par—both required and both respectable.

Quine's response was to agree that meaning and reference are on a par, but to up the ante by rejecting both. This, in the end, was the legacy of his doctrine of the indeterminacy of translation and the inscrutability of reference—presented in *Word and Object* (1960), "Reply to Chomsky" (1969*b*), "Ontological Relativity" (1969*a*), and "On the Reasons for the Indeterminacy of Translation" (1970). The problem, as he saw it, was that neither theories assigning sameness of meaning to sentences, nor those assigning reference to sub-sentential expressions, are determined by possible (behavioral) data bearing on their confirmation. Moreover, he claimed, the addition of all truths statable in the language of physical science would not resolve the indeterminacy. Since he held (roughly) that all genuine truths are determined by physical truths, he concluded that statements attributing sameness of meaning to sentences, or reference to sub-sentential expressions, do not qualify as objective truths.

Though spectacularly provocative, this view did not command lasting assent. The argument for it suffers from implicit ambiguities involving the determination relation—no resolution of which seems capable of simultaneously vindicating all Quinean premises (Soames 2003: ch. 10). In addition, the indeterminacy theses appear to be self-undermining. Taken together, they amount to radical eliminativism about the ordinary notions of meaning, reference, and truth—coupled with a proposal to replace them with scientifically respectable notions of stimulus meaning, disquotational Tarski-reference, and Tarski-truth. The difficulty is that without the notions he proposes to eliminate, the crucial theses on which his doctrines depend appear to be unstatable (Soames 2003: ch. 11). Thus, it is not clear that his position is sustainable.

THE STRUGGLE OVER MODALITY AND THE RISE OF PHILOSOPHICAL LOGIC

As noted, in 1946 Marcus and Carnap independently extended Lewis's axiomatic treatment of the modal propositional calculus to the predicate calculus (with quantification). In 1947, Carnap coupled this with a primitive possible-worlds semantics. However, this extension of logic to include quantification over modal operators provoked vigorous Quinean objections (Quine 1943, 1947, 1953), which, unfortunately, were not carefully distinguished from one another for decades. Quine's strongest, and most justifiable, point was—as Burgess (1998) explains—that there was a mismatch between the formal innovation of quantifying into modal constructions and the informal, philosophical explanations given by modal logicians of the content of the necessity operator they employed. When asked, 'What notion is it the logic of which is formally captured by systems containing this operator?', the answer commonly given was that by *necessity* they meant *logical truth* or *analyticity*. Quine, of course, had problems with analyticity. However, what exercised him about quantified modal logic was that since analyticity is supposed to be a property of sentences, quantifying into a construction governed by the necessity operator amounts to attributing *truth in virtue of meaning* not to a sentence but to a pair consisting of a formula containing a free occurrence of a variable and an object serving as value of the variable. The idea that such a pair could be true in virtue of meaning, Quine thought, made no sense. Whether or not sense could, in principle, be made of it, modal logicians at the time were not doing so. Thus, he understandably concluded, quantified modal logic rests on a mistake.

More generally, he concluded that it is unintelligible to (objectually) quantify into any construction for which substitution of co-referential singular terms sometimes fails to preserve truth. This was a definite error, though one not clearly recognized for many years—Kaplan (1986), Kazmi (1987), Richard (1987), and Soames (1995). Distracted by this error, defenders of modal logic—Smullyan (1947 and 1948), Fitch (1949), Marcus (1960 and 1961), and Føllesdal (1961)—focused on what they took to be the need for logical languages to contain name-like terms (pure tags) that resisted failure of substitutivity (under co-reference) everywhere. However, the definitive response to Quinean objections to quantified modal logic was not to invent a special class of terms, but to stop viewing necessity as analyticity, to start thinking of it as truth at all counterfactually possible world states, and to explain what it is for a statement that a given object has, or lacks, a specified property at such a state to be true. Theses moves, hinted at in the formal Kripke-semantics for modal logic, were made explicit in Kripke's 1970 lectures that became *Naming and Necessity* (1980), and reinforced by David Kaplan's 1971 manuscript which became "Demonstratives" (1989).

After the development of the Kripke-semantics, progress in philosophical logic exploded. Similar treatments of tense logic, building on Arthur Prior's *Time and Modality* (1957), and intuitionist logic soon followed. The most comprehensive program was spelled out in a series of papers by Richard Montague, published in the 1960s and early 1970s, and collected in his *Formal Philosophy* (1974). There, Montague articulated a highly generalized system of intensional logic that served as a framework for analyzing the syntax, semantics, and pragmatics of large fragments of natural language. This work not only influenced the philosophical logicians who were to follow, but also provided the basis for an approach to semantics in theoretical linguistics that has lasted into the new century. Formal, truth-conditional semantics of the languages of modern symbolic logic began with Tarski in the 1930s. Now, with the philosophical logic of Marcus, Carnap, Prior, Kripke, Montague, and others, the range of linguistic constructions amenable to these techniques was expanded to include those expressing time and tense, necessity and possibility, and many others. David Kaplan's "Demonstratives" extended this program to include another essential feature of natural language—context-sensitive sentences containing indexicals like 'I', 'we', 'you', 'she', 'that', 'now', 'today', and 'actually'. By the end of the century, it had become possible to imagine the day when natural languages would be treatable in something close to their entirety by descendants of the logical techniques initiated by Tarski.

One of the most important philosophical applications of the new logic was the development of the Stalnaker–Lewis treatment of counterfactual conditionals, given in Robert Stalnaker (1968, 1975, 1978) and David Lewis (1973*b*). The problem, which had long been of interest to analytic philosophers, had been illuminated but not solved by Nelson Goodman in "The Problem of Counterfactual Conditionals" (1947) and *Fact, Fiction, and Forecast* (1954). On the Stalnaker–Lewis approach, widely credited as a significant advance, 'If it had been the case that A, then it would have been the case that B' is true iff among the world states at which A is true, those in which B is also true are more similar to the actual world state than those in which B is false (with the relevant similarity relation depending on aspects of the context of utterance). In addition to providing solutions to logical and semantic problems, this analysis had the effect of legitimizing and clarifying the role of counterfactuals in illuminating a variety of philosophically important concepts. See, for example, D. Lewis (1973*a* and 1986*a*) on causation, Stalnaker (1984) on mental content, and D. Lewis (1997) on dispositions.

THE DAVIDSONIAN PROGRAM

Similar in aim to modal semantics, but different in execution, the program of Donald Davidson (1917–2003) attempted to provide a philosophically revealing truth-conditional theory of meaning for natural language, based on the work of Tarski. However, whereas philosophical logicians in the Carnap–Kripke–Montague–Kaplan tradition employed complex systems of intensional logic—in which the truth of sentences is relativized to possible world states, plus, in many cases, times and contexts—Davidson worked within the simple extensional framework that Tarski had used. His aim—as indicated in Davidson (1965, 1967*b*, 1970, 1973*a* and 1973*b*)—was to construct finitely axiomatizable theories of truth for natural languages L that allow one to derive—from axioms specifying the referential properties of its words and phrases—a true T-sentence, ⌜'S' is a true sentence of L if and only if p⌝, for each sentence S of L. Since such a theory would give the truth conditions of every sentence on the basis of its semantically significant structure, it would, Davidson thought, count as a theory of meaning for L. He envisioned such a theory being empirically tested by comparing the conditions in which speakers hold particular sentences to be true with the truth conditions it assigns to those sentences. On his view, the correct theory of meaning is, roughly, the theory T_M according to which the conditions in which speakers hold sentences to be true most closely matches the conditions in which T_M, plus our theory of the world, predicts the sentences to be true. Roughly put, Davidson takes the correct theory to be the one according to which speakers of L turn out to be truth-tellers—*modulo* instances of explicable error—more frequently than on any other interpretation of L.

This bold idea generated responses of two sorts. The first attempted to implement the program by giving analyses of natural-language constructions in Davidsonian terms. Leading examples dealt with (i) event nominals and adverbial modification (Davidson 1967*a*; Higginbotham 1983); (ii) propositional attitude ascriptions (Davidson 1968; Larson and Ludlow 1993); (iii) metaphor (Davidson 1978); and (iv) pronouns (Evans 1977; Higginbotham 1980). The second sort of response to Davidson's program questioned his grounds for taking a theory of truth to be a theory of meaning. Emphasizing that theories of truth do not assign any entities to sentences to serve as their meanings, and also do not issue in theorems about what individual sentences mean, Davidson initially rested his claim that they, nevertheless, qualify as theories of meaning on the contention that one who knew that which they stated would thereby grasp the intricate system of connections relating the truth conditions of every sentence in the language to those of every other. It was the systematicity of this knowledge that convinced him that knowledge of an appropriate truth theory T_M for L would be sufficient for understanding its sentences. However, this was a mistake—as was shown by Foster (1976), who demonstrated that one could know that which was stated by T_M, while systematically misunderstanding its sentences. Although Davidson's "Reply to Foster" (1976) modified the original justification for taking his theories of truth to be theories of meaning, the new justification was shown to fail in Soames 1992. Since then, other attempted justifications have been offered—e.g. Higginbotham (1991, 2006); Larson and Segal (1995)—but the issue is yet to be conclusively resolved.

Today, the Davidsonian program continues as one approach among many to the semantics of natural language. As a historical matter, its larger place in the analytic tradition in America came from the role it played in connecting different strands of the tradition. Its concern with the application of logical techniques to the task of understanding natural language connected it to the technically more sophisticated work of the philosophical logicians. Its emphasis on explaining semantic competence in terms of a complex mapping between the surface structure of sentences and their underlying logical forms connected it to the ideas of linguistically minded philosophers, intent on making common cause with Chomskian generative grammarians. Davidson's avoidance of the intensional—and his determination to explicate both the meanings of sentences and the contents of the beliefs they are used to express in terms of the extensional notions of truth and reference, plus the slender attitude of an agent's holding a sentence to be true—connected him to Quine's naturalism and "flight from intension". Finally, Davidson's systematic, but logically quite simple, approach to the theory of meaning connected his work to those philosophers—particularly, but not exclusively, in Britain—who continued to believe that meaning had a central role to play in philosophy, and who were frustrated by the failure of earlier, ordinary language philosophers to provide a fruitful way of studying it.

Kripke and the End of the Linguistic Turn

The most important development in the last thirty years of the twentieth century was the challenge posed to theses (i)–(iv) growing out of the work of Saul Kripke (1980), Hilary Putnam (1970, 1975b), and David Kaplan (1989).

(i) The meaning of a term is not its referent, but a descriptive sense that encodes conditions necessary and sufficient for determining reference.

(ii) Since the meaning of a word is the descriptive sense that a speaker associates with it, meaning is transparent. If two words mean the same, then anyone who understands both should be able to figure that out by checking the sense that he or she associates with them. Word meanings and mental contents are determined by factors internal to agents.

(iii) A priori and necessary truth amount to the same thing. Both are grounded in meaning.

(iv) Metaphysical claims about objects having or lacking properties essentially—independently of how they are described—make no sense. Even if a term t designates an object o and ⌈Necessarily t is F (if t exists)⌉ is true, there will always be another term t* designating o for which ⌈Necessarily t* is F (if t* exists)⌉ is false. Since it would be arbitrary to give either sentence priority in determining the essential properties of o, the idea that objects have, or lack, such properties must be relativized to how they are described.

Prior to the Kripke-inspired attack on these doctrines, analytic philosophers typically regarded all possibility to be linguistic possibility, and the necessary, the a priori, and the analytic to be one. Even Quine, who rejected modality, took *necessity, apriority,* and *analyticity* to be different names of the same discredited notion. Those who rejected such austerity typically lumped the three notions together, and continued to view the job of philosophy as the discovery of illuminating conceptual—i.e. analytic–a priori–necessary—truths, through the analysis of meaning.

All that changed with Kripke's introduction of rigid designation, direct reference, and non-descriptionality. His argument that names and natural kind terms are rigid designators, and so not equivalent to descriptions associated with them by speakers, was the entering wedge. He next used rigid designation to rebut Quine's famous objection to essentialism, enshrined in (iv). A rigid designator t of an object o is one that picks out o in all possible circumstances in which o exists. Thus, when t is rigid, the question of whether o has the property expressed by F essentially is equivalent to the question of whether the sentence ⌈Necessarily t is F (if t exists)⌉ is true. The truth values of other sentences, containing non-rigid designators, are irrelevant. Once this was seen, the objection to the intelligibility of essentialism collapsed (Soames 2003: ch. 14).

With both a non-descriptive semantics and a rehabilitated conception of essentialism in place, Kripke next showed how to generate instances of the necessary a posteriori. If n is a name or indexical that rigidly designates an existing object o, F expresses an essential property of o, and knowledge that o has this property requires empirical evidence, then the proposition expressed by ⌈If n exists, then n is F⌉ is both necessary and knowable only a posteriori (see Soames 2006). All of a sudden, the necessary and the a priori were no longer the same, and the idea that one, or both, might arise from something beyond the linguistic became credible.

With this essentialist route to the necessary a posteriori came a distinction between conceivability and genuine possibility—between ways things could conceivably be versus ways things could really be (or have been). The distinction is typically drawn in terms of possible worlds, or better, possible world states. For the Kripkean, possible states of the world are not concrete universes, but abstract objects (see Stalnaker 1976, 1984). Metaphysically possible world states are maximally complete ways the real concrete universe could have been—maximally complete properties which the universe could have instantiated. Epistemically possible world states are maximally complete ways which the universe can coherently be conceived to be—maximally complete properties that the universe can be conceived of as instantiating, and that one cannot know a priori that it doesn't, or couldn't, instantiate (see Salmon 1989 and Soames 2003, 2005, and 2007). These two sets of properties are different. Just as there are properties that ordinary objects could have had and other properties that they couldn't have had, so there are certain maximally complete properties that the universe could have had—metaphysically possible world states—and other maximally complete properties that the universe couldn't have had—metaphysically impossible world states. Just as some of the properties that objects couldn't have had are properties that one can conceive of them as having, and that one cannot know a priori that they don't, or couldn't, have, so some maximally complete properties that the universe couldn't have had are properties that one can conceive of it as having, and that one cannot know a priori that it doesn't, or couldn't, have. These states of the world are epistemically, but not metaphysically, possible. On this picture, the reason why empirical evidence is required for knowledge of necessary truths that are knowable only a posteriori is to rule out metaphysically impossible, but epistemically possible, world states in which they are false.

This was the heart of the philosophical revolution led by Kripke and his allies. By the time it was over, (i)–(iv) had been called into question, and rejected by many. Most important, the decoupling of necessity, apriority, and analyticity enlarged the scope of philosophical inquiry—including metaphysical inquiry about essence—beyond that which could be grounded in the analysis of meaning. The linguistic turn, it appeared, had met its match.

RAWLS AND THE RESUSCITATION OF NORMATIVE THEORY

A similar transformation occurred at about the same time in ethics, political philosophy, and the philosophy of law. The period from the mid-1930s to the early 1960s had been the heyday of emotivism and evaluative non-cognitivism. For many years, one of America's most well-known analytic writers in ethics was Charles Stevenson, whose "The Emotive Meaning of Ethical Terms" (1937) and *Ethics and Language* (1944), had become classics. In these works, he argued that the function of evaluative terms—like *good, bad, right,* and *wrong*—was not to describe the world, or courses of action, but to express one's emotional attitude toward them. Sentences containing such terms were not, he maintained, used to make statements that could be true or false, but to express feelings and guide action. As a result, normative theories about the right and the good could not be objects of knowledge, or even rationally justified belief, and so were excluded from the proper domain of philosophy. As Stevenson put it at the end of his famous article, since "*x is good* is essentially a vehicle for suggestion, it is scarcely a statement which philosophers, any more than other men, are called upon to make. To the extent that ethics predicates the ethical terms of anything, rather than explains their meaning, it ceases to be a reflective study." Accordingly, he thought, the only job for the moral philosopher was to explain how evaluative language works. Ethics had been swallowed by meta-ethics.

This view, which had grown more sophisticated in the 1950s, was, at the end of that decade, subjected to a powerful objection known as *the Frege–Geach point*, forcefully advanced not only by the British philosopher Peter Geach (1960), but also by the American, John Searle (1962). The objection is based on the observation that when evaluative sentences like *that is good* occur as clauses in larger, descriptive sentences, their meanings make systematic contributions to the truth conditions of statements made by utterances of the larger sentences. Since evaluative sentences have the same meanings when used on their own as when they occur as clauses of larger sentences, their meanings cannot be identified with any set of emotional responses accompanying their use, or any action—like commending or guiding choices—that may be performed by uttering them on their own. Thus, the idea that evaluative sentences have descriptive content, or something like it, was revived, facilitating a renaissance in normative theory that was already under way.

One sees this renaissance in the writings of theorists like Joel Feinberg, Richard Brandt, Kurt Baier, and Thomas Nagel from the late 1950s through the early 1970s. But above all, one sees it in the work of John Rawls (1921–2002)—particularly "Justice as Fairness" (1958), "The Sense of Justice" (1963), and his classic, *A Theory of Justice* (1971). It is hard to exaggerate the impact of this book on the moral and political philosophy of the time. Fully informed by the relevant social science, guided by a plausible and self-conscious methodology, and deeply learned about the conceptual and historical underpinnings of utilitarianism, deontology, contractarianism, egalitarianism, and libertarianism, *A Theory of Justice* brought to analytic philosophy the most compelling and systematic study of fundamental normative questions it had ever seen.

The central idea is that a just society is one whose basic structure would be freely and unanimously chosen by rational, self-interested agents in a fair bargaining procedure for determining the fundamental rules governing their social interaction. The procedure involves the selection of principles under constraints defined by what Rawls calls *the original position*—a hypothetical situation in which one possesses all relevant knowledge of general facts about human nature and society, while being deprived of any knowledge of one's own abilities, desires, or place in the social order that could lead one to favor principles benefiting oneself. Given these constraints, Rawls argues that two general principles emerge as the basis for a just society: one guaranteeing to each citizen the most extensive set of basic liberties compatible with similar liberties for all, and the other (the so-called *difference principle*) stipulating that social and economic inequalities (attached to positions open to everyone under conditions of equality of opportunity) are to be tolerated only to the extent that the least well-off individuals in the system are better off than the least well-off would be under any alternative system. The elaboration of these principles involves balancing liberty, equality, and utility, while making room for rights, and rejecting classical utilitarianism. Rawls's argument can also be read as justifying a liberal-left (but not too far left), redistributionist version of modern democratic capitalism—a fact that prompted criticisms from both the socialist left and the libertarian right.

The most well known of these was the libertarian classic *Anarchy, State, and Utopia* (1974), written by Rawls's Harvard colleague Robert Nozick (1938–2002). In part a negative critique of Rawls, and in part a positive alternative, its central idea is that liberty is the dominant political value. For Nozick, the distribution of goods is governed by principles of historical entitlement, which, in contrast to Rawls's end-result principles, are entirely procedural. According to the entitlement theory, any distribution of goods that arises by a series of just steps—including the voluntary exchange of assets by parties entitled to them ("capitalist acts between consenting adults")—is itself just. Since any pattern of distribution can be disrupted by such voluntary exchanges, this means that no such pattern—strict equality, the difference principle, total utility, maximum average utility, or any other—can be constitutive of a just society. This was Nozick's most provocative conclusion.

Rawls and Nozick brought political philosophy in particular—and ambitious moral theory in general—squarely into the mainstream of the analytic tradition, both of which continue to be important foci of attention, as illustrated by Thomas Scanlon's contractarian approach to obligation in *What We Owe to Each Other* (1998). A similar revival, led (in America) by Ronald Dworkin's *Taking Rights Seriously* (1977) and *Law's Empire* (1986), took place in the philosophy of law. Dworkin, with B.A.s from Harvard (1953) and Oxford (1955) and an LL.B from Harvard Law School (1957), succeeded the great legal positivist H. L. A. Hart in the Chair of Jurisprudence at Oxford in 1969, where he soon became known as the chief critic of Hart's positivism—a view according to which legal validity is a matter of fidelity to the institutional sources of positive law, and, except at the margins, independent of substantive moral considerations. As opposed to this, Dworkin argues for a theory of "constructive interpretation" in which neither the contents of laws nor their applications to particular cases are, in principle, entirely determined by the routine application of conventional, legal rules—independent of any moral assessment of the consequences of particular applications, and any judgment about how those consequences bear on the social purposes of the laws and the intentions of those who enacted them. For Dworkin, all adjudication requires the judge to weigh substantive moral concerns with existing legal history, so as to arrive at the most just and morally desirable principles for achieving the legitimate ends of the law, while accommodating, so far as is reasonably possible, the results of past decisions and existing legal practices. Although this process may seem to allow extraordinary judicial discretion in determining both the results reached in particular cases and the contents of the laws involved in those cases—to the delight or consternation of partisans of different stripes—Dworkin doesn't view it that way. Insisting that the mix of normative and factual considerations required by his theory determines unique results even in "hard cases", he denies that judges have the authority to create new law (or to arrive at results outside the law), and he charges them with what he admits to be the difficult and complicated task of discovering the unarticulated law that he believes already to be there. In all of this, he provides a sophisticated, though controversial, philosophical rationale for the prevailing liberal-left practice of jurisprudence of the past half-century—in much same the way as Rawls provided a rationale for liberal-left understandings of modern democratic welfare states with free-market economies. Though the debate over Dworkin's views, led by such figures as Joseph Raz, has been vigorous, it does not seem to have been politically freighted in quite the way that the Rawls/Nozick debate was. Be that as it may, there has been no shortage of spirited controversy in which Dworkin—at New York University

Law School since 1975, and Frank Henry Sommer Professor of Law, with an appointment in philosophy since 1994—has been involved.

A COLLECTION OF SPECIALTIES

By the end of the twentieth century, analytic philosophy in America, and elsewhere, had broadened to include active research programs on nearly all topics of traditional philosophical concern. In metaphysics, physicalism, the nature of time and space, and problems of material constitution were hotly debated, and at least one full-blown metaphysical system—that of David Lewis (1941–2001)—commanded center stage. In epistemology, the Gettier problem (Gettier 1963) generated a vast literature on what, beyond true, justified belief, constitutes knowledge. One central idea—espoused in such works as Goldman (1967) and Dretske (1981)—is that knowledge is true belief that is caused in the right way. Another innovation was contextualism—pioneered by Cohen (1986, 1988, 1998) and DeRose (1992, 1995, 2002), and adopted by D. Lewis (1996). According to this view, standards of justification incorporated in the predicate *know* are sensitive to variations in the context of utterance, with important consequences for a variety of epistemological problems, including those posed by skepticism.

In the philosophy of mind, lively and intense discussion centered around a cluster of related topics: functionalism about mental states (e.g. Putnam 1967a, 1967b; Fodor 1968; and D. Lewis 1980), the computational theory of mind (e.g. Fodor 1975, 1979, 1983; Searle 1980, 1984), scientifically acceptable notions of mental content (e.g. Burge 1979; Fodor 1987, 1990), intentionalism (the view that all there is to the content of any mental state is its representational content) (e.g. Harman 1990; Dretske 1995; Tye 1995; Byrne 2002), the controversy over phenomenal qualities (so-called *qualia*) (e.g. Nagel 1974; Shoemaker 1982, 1994; Thau 2002), and the nature of consciousness (e.g. Lycan 1996). Ethics saw vigorous debates over utilitarianism (e.g. Scheffler 1982; Kagan 1989), as well as the development of sophisticated meta-ethical theories (e.g. Harman 1977; Gibbard 1990, 2003). In the philosophy of science, nothing attracted as much attention as Thomas Kuhn's *The Structure of Scientific Revolutions* (1962). However, the true sequel to the general conception of science espoused by the logical empiricists was probably the marriage of semantic realism with pragmatic verificationism found in the constructive empiricism of Bas van Fraassen's *The Scientific Image* (1980). Since then, overall characterizations of the scientific enterprise have largely been replaced by more specialized, and highly focused, studies of particular problems of individual sciences.

This is only a small sample of the immense range and variety of topics under active investigation by analytic philosophers in America. With a few exceptions—most notably religion, and perhaps also aesthetics—it is doubtful that any philosophical topics have ever received as much scrutiny as they do now. Even in religion and aesthetics, the situation has improved with the work of such distinguished analytic philosophers as Alvin Plantinga, William Alston, and Peter van Inwagen in the philosophy of religion, and Kendall Walton, Arthur Danto, Stanley Cavell, and Paul Ziff in aesthetics. If there is a systemic problem with analytic philosophy today, it does not lie in a neglect of subject areas, or in a paucity of approaches for dealing with different problems, but in the difficulty, in an age of unprecedented abundance, of formulating unifying synthetic overviews of the sort that philosophers have traditionally been known for.

QUALITY, QUANTITY, AND IDENTITY

At the beginning of the twentieth century, American philosophy was, with the exception of a solitary genius (Peirce) working alone in Milford, Pennsylvania, essentially the philosophy of the Harvard department, then dominated by the pragmatist William James, the absolute idealist Josiah Royce, and the realist Ralph Barton Perry (Kuklick 1977, 2001). Analytic philosophy did not yet exist in America, but its precursor, pragmatism, was at its zenith. A half-century later, in the early 1950s, the last of the great pre-analytic pragmatists—C. I. Lewis—retired from Harvard, leaving the department in the capable hands of Quine—the first world-class analytic philosopher in America. Although Harvard was still the center of things, and would remain so for another two decades, arrivals from Europe, supplemented by a growing number of home-grown products, had established firm analytic footholds at UCLA, Berkeley, Chicago, Columbia, Michigan, Cornell, Brown, the University of Pennsylvania, and elsewhere. Twenty years later, in the mid-1970s, philosophy in America was analytic philosophy, and the baton of leadership had been passed to the Princeton department of Saul Kripke and David Lewis.

By then, the vast expansion in higher education had produced a surge in the number of professional philosophers and the rise of many competing centers of philosophical excellence—including the powerful department at Pittsburgh and the small, but increasingly influential, department at MIT. These trends continued through the turn of the century, when two new departments—New York University and Rutgers—rose to the top, while the number of philosophers continued to grow. By then, the number of strong departments with highly effective graduate programs had risen to about twenty, with a great deal of impressive philosophical talent spread far beyond that. Philosophers were now thoroughly professionalized, and their work—the primary audience for which was other professional philosophers—was much more specialized.

Although the appearance of philosophical genius is unpredictable, and can hardly be quantified, the overall quality of philosophy done throughout the country appears to be higher than ever before. What is truly staggering, however, is the increase in quantity. As noted earlier, the membership reported by the American Philosophical Association rose from 747 in 1940 to 5,125 in 1980. In 1990 it was 8,336, in 2000 it was 10,474, and in 2006 it reached more than 11,200. These are not simply teachers. A large number are active in research and publish regularly. Thus, it is not surprising that the number of outlets for publication in philosophy has also grown to accommodate them. For example, the *Directory of American Philosophers 2004–2005* reported 267 journals publishing philosophy in the United States and 168 philosophical societies.

Even these numbers are misleadingly low. To focus only on the United States is to falsely presuppose that there is today a distinctively American philosophical community, producing its own recognizable type of philosophy. There isn't. Philosophy in America today is, overwhelmingly, philosophy in the analytic tradition. However, there is no longer an American strain of the tradition that is substantially different from what is found in Britain, Australia, New Zealand, Canada, or even in the increasingly large and numerous enclaves in non-English-speaking countries to which analytic philosophy has spread. The size and influence of philosophy done in America is, to be sure, considerably greater than that done elsewhere. But this philosophy is by no means done only by Americans. More and more, there is a single, integrated community of analytic philosophers from different countries, within which individuals move back and forth. America is the center of the community, but it doesn't define it.

References

Austin, J. L. (1962). *How to Do Things with Words*. Cambridge, MA: Harvard University Press.

Burgess, John (1998). 'Quinus ab omni naevo vindicatus'. In Ali Kazmi (ed.), *Meaning and Reference*, Calgary: University of Calgary Press, 25–65.

Burge, Tyler (1979). 'Individualism and the Mental'. In Peter French, Theodore Uehling Jr., and Howard Wettstein (eds.), *Midwest Studies in Philosophy*, 4, Minneapolis: University of Minnesota Press, 73–121.

Byrne, Alex (2002). 'Intentionalism Defended'. *Philosophical Review*, 110: 199–240.

Carnap, Rudolf (1936–7). 'Testability and Meaning'. *Philosophy of Science*, 3: 419–71; 4: 1–40.

—— (1937). *The Logical Syntax of Language*. London: Kegan Paul. Translation of *Logische Syntax Der Sprache* (1934).

—— (1942). *Introduction to Semantics*. Cambridge, MA: Harvard University Press.

—— (1946). 'Modalities and Quantification'. *Journal of Symbolic Logic*, 11: 33–64.

—— (1947). *Meaning and Necessity*. Chicago: University of Chicago Press; 2nd expanded edn. 1956.

—— (1949). 'Truth and Confirmation'. In Feigl and Sellars (1949), 119–27.

—— (1950*a*). 'Empiricism, Semantics, and Ontology'. *Revue Internationale de Philosophie*, 4: 20–40. Repr. and revised in Carnap, *Meaning and Necessity*, 2nd edn.

—— (1950*b*). *The Logical Foundations of Probability*. Chicago: University of Chicago Press.

—— (1956). 'Meaning and Synonymy in Natural Languages'. *Philosophical Studies*, 7: 33–47. Repr. in Carnap, *Meaning and Necessity*, 2nd edn.

—— (1963). 'Intellectual Autobiography'. In P. A. Schilpp (ed.), *The Philosophy of Rudolf Carnap*, La Salle, IL: Open Court, 1–84.

Cohen, Stewart (1986). 'Knowledge and Context'. *Journal of Philosophy*, 83: 574–83.

—— (1988). 'How to be a Fallibilist'. *Philosophical Perspectives*, 2: 581–605.

—— (1998). 'Contextualist Solutions to Epistemological Problems: Scepticism, Gettier, and the Lottery'. *Australasian Journal of Philosophy*, 76: 289–306.

Davidson, Donald (1965). 'Theories of Meaning and Learnable Languages'. In Yehoshua Bar-Hillel (ed.), *Logic, Methodology and Philosophy of Science: Proceedings of the 1964 International Congress*, Amsterdam: North-Holland Publishing Company, 383–94. Repr. in Davidson (2001*b*), 3–15.

—— (1967*a*). 'The Logical Form of Action Sentences'. In N. Rescher (ed.), *The Logic of Decision and Action*, Pittsburgh: University of Pittsburgh Press, 81–95. Repr. in Davidson (2001*a*), 105–21.

Davidson, Donald (1967b). 'Truth and Meaning'. *Synthese*, 17: 304–23. Repr. in Davidson (2001b), 17–42.

——(1968). 'On Saying That'. *Synthese*, 19: 130–46. Repr. in Davidson (2001b), 93–108.

——(1970). 'Semantics for Natural Languages'. In B. Visentini (ed.), *Linguaggi nella Società e nella Tecnica*, Milan: Edizioni di Comunità, 177–88. Repr. in Davidson (2001b), 55–64.

——(1973a). 'In Defense of Convention T'. In Hughes Leblanc (ed.), *Truth, Syntax, and Modality*, Amsterdam: North-Holland Publishing Company, 76–85. Repr. in Davidson (2001b), 65–76.

——(1973b). 'Radical Interpretation'. *Dialectica*, 27: 313–28. Repr. in Davidson (2001b), 125–40.

——(1976). 'Reply to Foster'. In Gareth Evans and John McDowell (eds.), *Truth and Meaning: Essays in Semantics*, Oxford: Clarendon Press, 33–41. Repr. in Davidson (2001b), 171–80.

——(1978). 'What Metaphors Mean'. *Critical Inquiry*, 5: 31–47. Repr. in Davidson (2001b), 245–64.

——(2001a). *Essays on Actions and Events*. Oxford: Clarendon Press.

——(2001b). *Inquiries into Truth and Interpretation*. Oxford: Clarendon Press.

DeRose, Keith (1992). 'Contextualism and Knowledge Attributions'. *Philosophy and Phenomenological Research*, 52: 913–29.

——(1995). 'Solving the Sceptical Problem'. *Philosophical Review*, 104: 1–52.

——(2002). 'Assertion, Knowledge and Context'. *Philosophical Review*, 111: 167–203.

Dretske, Fred (1981). *Knowledge and the Flow of Information*. Cambridge, MA: MIT Press.

——(1995). *Naturalizing the Mind*. Cambridge, MA: MIT Press.

Dworkin, Ronald (1977). *Taking Rights Seriously*. Cambridge, MA: Harvard University Press.

——(1986). *Law's Empire*. Cambridge, MA: Harvard University Press.

Evans, Gareth (1977). 'Pronouns, Quantifiers and Relative Clauses'. *Canadian Journal of Philosophy*, 7: 467–536.

Feigl, Herbert, and Sellars, Wilfrid (eds.) (1949). *Readings in Philosophical Analysis*. New York: Appleton.

Fitch, Frederic B. (1949). 'The Problem of the Morning Star and the Evening Star'. *Philosophy of Science*, 16: 137–41.

Fodor, J. A. (1968). *Psychological Explanation*. New York: Random House.

——(1975). *The Language of Thought*. New York: Crowell.

——(1979). *Representations*. Cambridge, MA: MIT Press.

——(1983). *The Modularity of Mind*. Cambridge, MA: MIT Press.

——(1987). *Psychosemantics: The Problem of Meaning in the Philosophy of Mind*. Cambridge, MA: MIT Press.

——(1990). *A Theory of Content and Other Essays*. Cambridge, MA: MIT Press.

Føllesdal, Dagfinn (1961). 'Referential Opacity and Modal Logic.' (Harvard University dissertation).

Foster, J. A. (1976). 'Meaning and Truth theory'. In G. Evans and J. McDowell (eds.), *Truth and Meaning*, Oxford: Clarendon Press, 1–32.

Geach, Peter (1960). 'Ascriptivism'. *Philosophical Review*, 69: 221–5.

Gettier, Edmund (1963). 'Is Justified True Belief Knowledge?'. *Analysis*, 23: 121–3.

Gibbard, Alan (1990). *Wise Choices, Apt Feelings: A Theory of Normative Judgment.* Cambridge, MA: Harvard University Press.

—— (2003). *Thinking How to Live.* Cambridge, MA: Harvard University Press.

Goldman, Alvin (1967). 'A Causal Theory of Knowing'. *Journal of Philosophy*, 64: 335–72.

Goodman, Nelson (1947). 'The Problem of Counterfactual Conditionals'. *Journal of Philosophy*, 44: 113–28.

—— (1954). *Fact, Fiction, and Forecast.* Cambridge, MA: Harvard University Press.

Grice, Paul (1989). *Studies in the Way of Words.* Cambridge, MA: Harvard University Press.

Harman, Gilbert (1977). *The Nature of Morality.* New York: Oxford University Press.

—— (1990). 'The Intrinsic Quality of Experience'. *Philosophical Perspectives*, 4: 31–52.

Hempel, Carl (1945). 'Studies in the Logic of Confirmation'. *Mind*, 54: 1–16, 97–121.

—— (1950). 'The Empiricist Criterion of Meaning'. *Revue Internationale de Philosophie* 4: 41–63. Repr. in A. J. Ayer (ed.), *Logical Positivism*, New York: Free Press, 1959, 108–29.

—— (1965). *Aspects of Scientific Explanation.* New York: Free Press.

—— (1966). *Philosophy of Natural Science.* Englewood Cliffs, NJ: Prentice-Hall.

—— and Oppenheim, Paul (1945). 'A Definition of Degree of Confirmation'. *Philosophy of Science*, 12: 98–115.

—— —— (1948). 'Studies in the Logic of Explanation'. *Philosophy of Science*, 15: 135–75.

Higginbotham, James (1980). 'Pronouns and Bound Variables'. *Linguistic Inquiry*, 11: 679–708.

—— (1983). 'The Logic of Perceptual Reports: An Extensional Alternative to Situation Semantics'. *Journal of Philosophy*, 80: 100–27.

—— (1991). 'Truth and Understanding'. *Iyyun*, 40: 271–88.

—— (2006). 'Truth and Reference as the Basis of Meaning'. In Michael Devitt and R. Hanley (eds.), *Blackwell Guide to the Philosophy of Language*, Oxford: Blackwell, 58–76.

Holt, Edwin; Marvin, Walter Taylor; Montague, W. P.; Perry, Ralph Barton; Pitkin, Walter; and Spaulding, Edward (1912). *The New Realism.* New York: The Macmillan Company.

Houser, Nathan; Roberts, Don; and Van Evra, James (eds.) (1997). *Studies in the Logic of Charles Sanders Peirce.* Bloomington, IN: Indiana University Press.

James, William (1902). *The Varieties of Religious Experience.* New York: Longmans, Green and Company.

—— (1907). *Pragmatism: A New Name for Some Old Ways of Thinking.* New York: Longmans, Green and Company.

Kagan, Shelly (1989). *The Limits of Morality*. New York: Oxford University Press.

Kaplan, David (1986). 'Opacity'. In Lewis E. Hahn and Paul A. Schilpp (eds.), *The Philosophy of W. V. Quine*, La Salle, IL: Open Court, 229–89.

—— (1989). 'Demonstratives'. In Joseph Almog, John Perry, and Howard Wettstein (eds.), *Themes from Kaplan*, Oxford: Oxford University Press, 481–564.

Kazmi, Ali (1987). 'Quantification and Opacity'. *Linguistics and Philosophy*, 10: 77–100.

Kripke, Saul (1959). 'A Completeness Theorem in Modal Logic'. *Journal of Symbolic Logic*, 24: 1–13.

—— (1963). 'Semantical Analysis of Modal Logic I, Normal Modal Propositional Calculi'. *Zeitschrift für Matematische Logik und Grundlagen der Mathematik*, 9: 67–96.

—— (1980). *Naming and Necessity*. Cambridge, MA: Harvard University Press.

Kuhn, Thomas (1962). *The Structure of Scientific Revolutions*. Chicago: University of Chicago Press.

Kuklick, Bruce (1977). *The Rise of American Philosophy*. New Haven: Yale University Press.

—— (2001). *A History of Philosophy in America*. Oxford: Oxford University Press.

Larson, Richard, and Ludlow, Peter (1993). 'Interpreted Logical Forms'. *Synthese*, 95: 305–56. Repr. in Peter Ludlow (ed.), *Readings in the Philosophy of Language*, Cambridge, MA: MIT Press, 1997, 993–1040.

—— and Segal, Gabriel (1995). *Knowledge of Meaning*. Cambridge, MA: MIT Press.

Lewis, C. I. (1929). *Mind and the World Order*. New York: Charles Scribner's Sons.

—— (1946). *An Analysis of Knowledge and Valuation*. La Salle, IL: Open Court.

—— and Langford, C. H. (1932). *Symbolic Logic*. New York: Appleton-Century Company.

Lewis, David (1973a). 'Causation'. *Journal of Philosophy*, 70: 556–67. Repr. in Lewis (1986b), 159–7.

—— (1973b). *Counterfactuals*. Cambridge, MA: Harvard University Press.

—— (1980). 'Mad Pain and Martian Pain'. In Ned Block (ed.), *Readings in the Philosophy of Psychology*, i, Cambridge, MA: Harvard University Press, 216–22. Repr. in Lewis (1983), 122–33.

—— (1983), *Philosophical Papers*, i. New York: Oxford University Press.

—— (1986a). 'Causal Explanation'. In Lewis (1986b), 214–40.

—— (1986b), *Philosophical Papers*, ii. New York: Oxford University Press.

—— (1996). 'Elusive Knowledge'. *Australasian Journal of Philosophy*, 74: 549–67. Repr. in Lewis (1999), 418–46.

—— (1997). 'Finkish Dispositions'. *The Philosophical Quarterly*, 47: 143–58. Repr. in Lewis (1999), 133–51.

—— (1999). *Papers in Metaphysics and Epistemology*. Cambridge: Cambridge University Press.

Lycan, William (1996). *Consciousness and Experience*. Cambridge, MA: MIT Press.

Marcus, Ruth (1946). 'A Functional Calculus of First Order Based on Strict Implication'. *Journal of Symbolic Logic*, 11: 115–18.

_____ (1960). 'Extensionality'. *Mind*, 69: 55–62.

_____ (1961). 'Modalities and Intensional Languages'. *Synthese*, 13: 303–22.

Misak, Cheryl (ed.) (2004). *The Cambridge Companion to Peirce*. Cambridge: Cambridge University Press.

Montague, Richard (1974). *Formal Philosophy: Selected Papers of Richard Montague*. New Haven: Yale University Press.

Moore, G. E. (1903). 'The Refutation of Idealism'. *Mind*, 12: 433–53.

Nagel, Ernest (1961). *The Structure of Science*. London: Routledge & Kegan Paul.

_____ (1974). 'What is it Like to be a Bat?'. *Philosophical Review*, 83: 435–50.

_____ and Newman, J. R. (1958). *Gödel's Proof*. New York: New York University Press.

Nozick, Robert (1974). *Anarchy, State, and Utopia*. New York: Basic Books.

Passmore, John (1957). *A Hundred Years of Philosophy*. London: Gerald Duckworth & Co.

Peirce, Charles Sanders (1870). 'Description for a Notation of the Logic of Relatives'. *Memoirs of the American Academy of Arts and Sciences*, 9: 317–78.

_____ (1883). 'Note B. the Logic of Relatives'. In C. S. Peirce (ed.), *Studies in Logic by Members of the Johns Hopkins University*, Boston: Little, Brown, and Company, 187–203.

_____ (1931–58). *Collected Papers of Charles Sanders Peirce*, i–vi, ed. C. Hartshorne and P. Weiss (1931–5); vii and viii, ed. A. Burks (1958). Cambridge, MA: Belknap Press.

Prior, Arthur (1957). *Time and Modality*. Oxford: Clarendon Press.

Putnam, Hilary (1967a). 'The Mental Life of Some Machines'. In H. Castañeda (ed.), *Intentionality, Minds, and Perception*, Detroit: Wayne State University Press, 177–200. Repr. in Putnam (1975a), 408–28.

_____ (1967b). 'The Nature of Mental States'. In W. H. Capitan and D. D. Merrill (eds.), *Art, Mind, and Religion*, Pittsburgh: University of Pittsburgh Press, 37–48. Repr. in Putnam (1975a), 429–40.

_____ (1970). 'Is Semantics Possible?'. In H. Kiefer and M. Munitz (eds.), *Language, Belief and Metaphysics*, Albany, NY: State University of New York Press, 50–63. Repr. in Putnam (1975a), 139–52.

_____ (1975a). *Collected Papers*, ii. Cambridge: Cambridge University Press.

_____ (1975b). 'The Meaning of "Meaning"'. In K. Gunderson (ed.), *Language, Mind and Knowledge*, Minneapolis: University of Minnesota Press, 131–93. Repr. in Putnam (1975a), 215–71.

_____ (1982). 'Peirce as Logician'. *Historia Mathematica*, 9: 290–301.

Quine, W. V. (1936). 'Truth by Convention'. In O. H. Lee (ed.), *Philosophical Essays for A. N. Whitehead*, New York: Longmans, 90–124. Repr. in *The Ways of Paradox*, New York: Random House, 1966, 70–99.

_____ (1943). 'Notes on Existence and Necessity'. *Journal of Philosophy*, 40: 113–27.

_____ (1947). 'The Problem of Interpreting Modal Logic'. *Journal of Symbolic Logic*, 12: 43–8.

_____ (1948). 'On What There Is'. *Review of Metaphysics*, 2: 21–38. Repr. in Quine (1980), 1–19.

Quine, W. V. (1951). 'Two Dogmas of Empiricism'. *Philosophical Review*, 60: 20–43. Repr. and revised in Quine (1980), 20–46.

—— (1953). 'Reference and Modality'. In Quine, *From a Logical Point of View*, Cambridge, MA: Harvard University Press, 139–59.

—— (1960). *Word and Object*. Cambridge, MA: MIT Press.

—— (1969a). 'Ontological Relativity'. In Quine, *Ontological Relativity and Other Essays*, New York: Columbia University, Press.

—— (1969b). 'Reply to Chomsky'. In Donald Davidson and Jaakko Hintikka (eds.), *Words and Objections*, Dordrecht: Reidel, 302–11.

—— (1970). 'On the Reasons for the Indeterminacy of Translation'. *Journal of Philosophy*, 67: 178–83.

—— (1980). *From a Logical Point of View*, rev. 2nd edn. Cambridge, MA: Harvard University Press.

—— (1985). 'In the Logical Vestibule'. *Times Literary Supplement*, 12 July. Repr. as 'MacHale on Boole', in Quine, *Selected Logic Papers*, enlarged edn., Cambridge, MA: Harvard University Press, 1995, 251–7.

Rawls, John (1958). 'Justice as Fairness'. *Philosophical Review*, 67: 164–94.

—— (1963). 'The Sense of Justice'. *Philosophical Review*, 72: 281–305.

—— (1971). *A Theory of Justice*. Cambridge, MA: Harvard University Press.

Reichenbach, Hans (1935). *Wahrscheinlichkeitslehre: eine Untersuchung über die logischen und mathematischen Grundlagen der Wahrscheinlichkeitsrechnung*. Leiden: Sijthoff. English trans.: *The Theory of Probability: An Inquiry into the Logical and Mathematical Foundations of the Calculus of Probability*. Berkeley: University of California Press, 1948.

—— (1938). *Experience and Prediction: An Analysis of the Foundations and the Structure of Knowledge*. Chicago: University of Chicago Press.

—— (1944). *Philosophic Foundations of Quantum Mechanics*. Berkeley: University of California Press.

—— (1947). *Elements of Symbolic Logic*. New York: Macmillan Company.

—— (1951). *The Rise of Scientific Philosophy*. Berkeley: University of California Press.

Richard, Mark (1987). 'Quantification and Leibniz's Law'. *Linguistics and Philosophy*, 10: 77–100.

Russell, Bertrand, and Whitehead, Alfred North (1910–13). *Principia Mathematica*. Cambridge: Cambridge University Press.

Salmon, Nathan (1989). 'On the Logic of What Might Have Been'. *Philosophical Review*, 98: 3–34.

Scanlon, Thomas (1998). *What We Owe to Each Other*. Cambridge, MA: Harvard University Press.

Scheffler, Samuel (1982). *The Rejection of Consequentialism*. Oxford: Clarendon Press.

Searle, John (1962). 'Meaning and Speech Acts'. *Philosophical Review*, 71: 423–32.

—— (1980). 'Minds, Brains, and Programs'. *Behavioral and Brain Sciences*, 3: 417–24.

—— (1984). *Minds, Brains, and Science*. Cambridge, MA: Harvard University Press.

Shoemaker, Sydney (1982). 'The Inverted Spectrum'. *Journal of Philosophy*, 79: 357–81.

_____ (1994). 'Phenomenal Character'. *Nous*, 28: 21–38.

Smullyan, A. F. (1947). 'Review of Quine's "The Problem of Interpreting Modal Logic"'. *Journal of Symbolic Logic*, 12: 139–41.

_____ (1948). 'Modality and Description'. *Journal of Symbolic Logic*, 13: 31–7.

Soames, Scott (1992). 'Truth, Meaning, and Understanding'. *Philosophical Studies*, 65: 17–35.

_____ (1995). 'Revisionism About Reference'. *Synthese*, 104: 191–216.

_____ (2003). *Philosophical Analysis in the Twentieth Century*, ii. Princeton: Princeton University Press.

_____ (2005). *Reference and Description*. Princeton: Princeton University Press.

_____ (2006). 'The Philosophical Significance of the Kripkean Necessary Aposteriori'. In Ernest Sosa and Enrique Villanueva (eds.), *Philosophical Issues*, 16: 288–309.

_____ (2007). 'Actually'. *Aristotelian Society*, suppl. vol. 81/1: 251–77.

Stalnaker, Robert (1968). 'A Theory of Conditionals'. In *Studies in Logical Theory*, American Philosophical Quarterly Monograph Series, 2, Oxford: Blackwell, 98–112. Repr. in Frank Jackson (ed.), *Conditionals*, Oxford: Oxford University Press, 1991, 28–45.

_____ (1975). 'Indicative Conditionals'. *Philosophia*, 5: 269–86. Repr. in Frank Jackson (ed.), *Conditionals*, Oxford: Oxford University Press, 1991, 136–54.

_____ (1976). 'Possible Worlds'. *Nous*, 10: 65–75. Revised and repr. as Stalnaker (1984), ch. 3.

_____ (1978). 'Assertion'. In Peter Cole (ed.), *Syntax and Semantics 9: Pragmatics*. New York: Academic Press, 315–32. Repr. in Stalnaker, *Context and Content*, Oxford: Oxford University Press, 1999, 78–96.

_____ (1984). *Inquiry*. Cambridge, MA: MIT Press.

Stevenson, Charles (1937). 'The Emotive Meaning of Ethical Terms'. *Mind*, 46: 14–31.

_____ (1944). *Ethics and Language*. New Haven: Yale University Press.

Thau, Michael (2002). *Consciousness and Cognition*. Oxford: Oxford University Press.

Tye, Michael (1995). *Ten Problems of Consciousness*. Cambridge, MA: MIT Press.

Van Fraassen, Bas (1980). *The Scientific Image*. Oxford: Oxford University Press.

White, Morton (1999). *A Philosopher's Story*. University Park, PA: Pennsylvania State University Press.

CHAPTER 22

LOGIC AND THE FOUNDATIONS OF MATHEMATICS

DANIELLE MACBETH

CATALYZED by the failure of Frege's logicist program, logic and the foundations of mathematics first became a philosophical topic in Europe in the early years of the twentieth century. Frege had aimed to show that logic constitutes the foundation for mathematics in the sense of providing both the primitive concepts in terms of which mathematical concepts were to be defined and the primitive truths on the basis of which mathematical truths were to be proved.[1] Russell's paradox showed that the project could not be completed, at least as envisaged by Frege. It nevertheless seemed clear to many that mathematics must be founded on *something*, and over the first few decades of the twentieth century four proposals emerged: two species of logicism—namely, ramified type theory as developed in Russell and Whitehead's *Principia* and Zermelo–Frankel set theory—and Hilbert's finitist program (a species of formalism), and, finally, Brouwerian

---

[1] As is well known, Frege himself took this logicist thesis to apply only to arithmetic, not also to geometry; more recent conceptions of geometry suggest that the logicist thesis, if it is applicable to mathematics at all, is applicable to all of mathematics.

intuitionism.[2] Across the Atlantic, already by the time Russell had discovered his famous paradox, the great American pragmatist Charles Sanders Peirce was developing a radically new *non-foundationalist* picture of mathematics, one that, through the later influence of Quine, Putnam, and Benacerraf, would profoundly shape the course of the philosophy of mathematics in the United States.

Three trends in the philosophy of mathematics as it is currently practiced in the United States will concern us. The first is the acknowledged mainstream, comprising the New World's non-foundationalist correlates to the Old World's 'big three' (logicism, formalism, and intuitionism): namely, structuralism, nominalism, and post-Quinean naturalism.[3] One of our central tasks will be to show that the difficulties that have given rise to these three schools can ultimately be traced to issues generated by the rise of a fundamentally new mathematical practice in the nineteenth century, the practice of deriving new results by reasoning from concepts alone: it was manifest that this new practice of reasoning from concepts yielded new, important, and contentful mathematical knowledge, and yet, for reasons that will become clear, it seemed impossible to understand how it *could*.

The second trend began to take off in the 1970s and is self-styled as a 'maverick' tradition.[4] It is one that is for the most part more radically naturalistic than even post-Quinean naturalism; and it has provided useful correctives to some of the excesses of the mainstream.[5] It has also become increasingly mainstreamed. With almost everyone in disagreement with almost everyone else, and an apparently endless stream of publications to explain why,

[2] The reasons for thinking that mathematics is founded on something may have varied considerably. Both Russell and Hilbert are on record as self-consciously searching for an indubitable ground for our knowledge of mathematics. Brouwer presumably had a more Kantian conception of foundations in terms of constructions, and Zermelo may have been after nothing more than a consistent set of axioms from which to derive all of arithmetic. Good introductions to these various positions are given in George and Velleman (2002) and Giaquinto (2002). Jacquette (2002) includes a selection of papers on intuitionism, and Shapiro (2005) contains recent appraisals of all three schools. Important original works are collected in Benacerraf and Putnam (1983), as well as in Ewald (1996) and van Heijenoort (1967).

[3] This is not to say that there is not important work being done by Americans on the more traditional big three. Certainly there is: e.g. Feferman (1998). But such work tends to be more mathematical: it aims to show how far one can get by pursuing a particular train of thought rather than what, precisely, mathematics is. So, e.g., Burgess (2005) takes up the neo-logicism of Crispin Wright not to assess whether or not it is right but to assess how much mathematics it can support.

[4] The term was first used by Aspray and Kitcher in their 'opinionated' introduction to Aspray and Kitcher (1988).

[5] It has also had some excesses of its own, among them Lakoff and Núñez (2000).

the distinction between mainstream and maverick has become a distinction without a difference.

The final trend we will consider is the burgeoning tradition of Frege studies in the United States, or, more exactly, some strands in that burgeoning tradition. Recent reappraisals of Frege's work are uncovering fundamental Peircean pragmatist themes at the heart of Frege's thought; and these themes, together with some Kantian ideas from Peirce, will help us to begin to understand how a radically new sort of resolution of the difficulties that have arisen in the wake of contemporary mathematical practice might be achieved, one that would not merely add yet another voice to the cacophony, but instead diagnose the root cause of the debates that are currently taking place throughout the philosophy of mathematics, both in the United States and around the world. We begin with Peirce.

At the heart of Peirce's pragmatism is a conception of sentential meaning focused not on what is the case if the sentence is true—that is, on truth conditions—but instead on what follows if the sentence is true—that is, on a sentence's inferential consequences. The basic idea can be found already in Kant's *Critique* (1781/7), in the idea that 'if the grounds from which a certain cognition should be derived are too manifold or lie too deeply hidden, then one tries whether they may not be reached through their consequences . . . one uses this kind of inference, though to be sure with some degree of care, if it is merely a matter of proving something as an hypothesis' (A790/B818). The difference between Kant and Peirce is that, according to Peirce, but not Kant, this kind of inference is the only way to establish truth in the sciences. Because such a method of proving something—by testing its consequences rather than by deriving it from its proper grounds—obviously cannot yield certainty, but only 'experimental' grounds for judgment (because it is impossible to be confident that one has exhausted the consequences of any given claim), it follows directly from this pragmatist conception of meaning in terms of consequences that there is no certain or indubitable truth. Anything we think we know, however self-evident it may seem, can turn out to have been mistaken. Nothing is or can be (as Sellars would say) Given—that is, absolutely unquestionable. On the other hand, there will always be a great deal that is not (currently) in question in our practice, a great deal that we currently do not have any reason to doubt. That is where our inquiries must start, from where we are, while at the same time recognizing that in our scientific inquiries we do not stand 'upon the bedrock of fact' but are instead 'walking upon a bog, and can only say, this ground seems to hold for the present' (*RLT* 176–7).

Peirce's pragmatism begins with a consequentialist conception of meaning, and hence a fallibilist conception of knowing. Peirce furthermore holds that this lack of any certain foundation is as true in mathematics as it is in the empirical or natural sciences. Indeed, for Peirce, mathematics is the *paradigm* of such an experimental science. As Ketner and Putnam explain in their introduction to Peirce's Cambridge lectures of 1898:

Epistemologically at any rate, mathematics was [for Peirce] an observational, experimental, hypothesis-confirming, inductive science that worked only with pure hypotheses without regard for their application in 'real' life. Because it explored the consequences of pure hypotheses by experimenting upon representative diagrams, mathematics was the inspirational source of the pragmatic maxim, the jewel of the methodological part of semeiotic, and the distinctive feature of Peirce's thought. As he often stated, the pragmatic maxim is little more than a summarizing statement of the procedure of experimental design in a laboratory—deduce the observable consequences of the hypothesis. And for Peirce the simplest and most basic laboratory was the kind of experimenting upon diagrams one finds in mathematics.   (*RLT* 2)

But although Peirce rejected the foundationalist picture according to which mathematics is founded on certain and unshakable truths, he did not thereby embrace, as James and Dewey (and later, Rorty) did, a conception of truth according to which it depends ultimately on our practices and interests. Although the trail of the human serpent is over all (just as James said), we can, Peirce thinks, nonetheless get things objectively right, know things as they really are. Like Sellars, Peirce saw the lack of foundations not as a *barrier* to a robust notion of objective truth but instead as *enabling* of it—however exactly this was to work.

By the early decades of the twentieth century, James's version of pragmatism had become well known in the United States. Nevertheless, it is the logicism of the logical positivists—that is, of the scientifically trained European philosophers making up the Vienna Circle, many of whom were to flee to the United States to escape the Nazis—that sets the stage for the philosophy of mathematics as it would unfold over the course of the twentieth century in the United States. Hempel explains, with characteristic clarity, the positivist's view of mathematics:

Mathematics is a branch of logic. It can be derived from logic in the following sense:
    a. all the concepts of mathematics, i.e. of arithmetic, algebra, and analysis, can be defined in terms of four concepts of pure logic.
    b. All the theorems of mathematics can be deduced from those definitions by means of the principles of logic (including the axioms of infinity and choice).

In this sense it can be said that the propositions of the system of mathematics as here delimited are true by virtue of the definitions of the mathematical concepts involved, or that they make explicit certain characteristics with which we have endowed our mathematical concepts by definition. The propositions of mathematics have, therefore, the same unquestionable certainty which is typical of such propositions as 'All bachelors are unmarried,' but they also share the complete lack of empirical content which is associated with that certainty: The propositions of mathematics are devoid of all factual content; they convey no information whatever on any empirical subject matter.   (Hempel 1945: 389–90)

Notice the implicit suggestion. The propositions of mathematics are devoid of factual content—but not of content *über haupt*. They convey no information on any empirical matter—but are nevertheless informative regarding some other, presumably appropriately mathematical, subject matter. They enjoy 'unquestionable certainty', but are nonetheless contentful pieces of knowledge; they are ampliative, extensions of our knowledge, but also a priori and analytic. It was a fine view. But it could not long stand up to the pragmatism that greeted it on its arrival in the New World. To understand why it could not, we need to start our story quite a bit further back, with some ideas about mathematical practice that were current before Kant appeared and changed everything.

Throughout its long history, mathematical practice has involved the use of written marks according to rules. To count, for example, is at its most basic to inscribe marks—say, notches in a bone, one for each thing counted. Similarly, in a demonstration in Euclid, one begins by drawing a diagram according to certain specifications. To learn basic arithmetic or elementary algebra is to learn to manipulate signs according to rules. And so on. But although all of mathematics uses signs, inscribed marks according to rules, not all of mathematics uses *symbols*. Whereas a collection of four strokes can be taken to be not merely a symbol but instead an actual instance of a number (conceived as a collection of units), the corresponding arabic numeral '4' can seem instead to be *only* a symbol, a sign that stands in for or is representative of the number, and is enormously useful in calculations, but nonetheless is not an instance of the thing itself. Even more obviously, a drawn circle can be seen as an instance, however imperfect, of a geometrical circle, as an instance of that which is only represented by the equation $x^2 + y^2 = r^2$ of elementary algebra.

There is a significant difference between our two pairs of examples, however. Whereas the arabic numeration system can be (and for a long time was) treated merely as a convenient shorthand by means of which to solve arithmetical problems, the rules of elementary algebra permit transformations that are, from the ancient and medieval perspective, sheer nonsense. If numbers are collections of units, and if the signs of arabic numeration are merely representatives of numbers otherwise given, then it will seem manifest that many apparent problems in arithmetic can have no solution, and so are not really arithmetical problems at all: although $3 + x = 5$ is a perfectly good arithmetical problem, $5 + x = 3$ is not, because there is nothing that one might add to five (things) to yield three (things). From the perspective of the rules of elementary algebra, in particular, for this case, the rule that if $a + x = b$, then $x = b - a$, the two cases are exactly the same: the solution in the first case is $x = 5 - 3$, and in the second, $x = 3 - 5$. The language of algebra introduces in this way something essentially new; whereas basic arithmetic is, originally, bounded by our intuitions regarding what makes sense, the rules of algebra seem to enable us somehow to transcend those bounds, to find a new kind of meaning in the rule-governed manipulation of signs.[6] Because it does, the introduction of the language of algebra inevitably generates a tension between two quite different conceptions of rigor and proof.

Algebra uses a system of signs governed by algorithms to solve problems; Euclidean geometry instead uses diagrams that involve (so it seems) instances of geometrical figures to demonstrate the truth of theorems and the solutions of problems. Arabic numeration, like algebra, uses a system of signs governed by algorithms to solve problems; pebble arithmetic involves not signs for, but instead actual instances of, numbers, conceived as collections of units. Standard arithmetic and algebra, on the one hand, and pebble arithmetic and geometry, on the other, are thus two very different sorts of systems; and they give rise in turn to two quite different conceptions of rigor and of proof. A Euclidean demonstration would seem to be a course of pictorial thinking, one that reveals connections to an attentive audience. It does not *require* assent, but to one attentive to what is being claimed and to what is depicted in the diagram, the chain of pictorial thinking shows the truth of the conclusion. The rigor of the demonstration thus crucially depends on intuition and meaning. From the perspective of this case, the often merely mechanical manipulation of signs according to rules in algebra can seem anything but

---

[6] In Macbeth (2004) I explore in detail just what it is that is new with the introduction of the symbolic language of algebra, and also argue that Descartes, not Viète, ought to be seen as the first truly modern mathematician.

rigorous, leading as it apparently does to the 'obscurity and paradox' of, for instance, numbers that are less than nothing, or worse the roots of numbers that are less than nothing.[7] But in a different sense it can seem that *only* a calculation in arithmetic or algebra is properly rigorous, because only such a calculation *requires* assent by anyone who knows the rules governing the use of the signs involved. From this perspective, rigor crucially depends on ignoring intuition and meaning because they are, or at least can be, a source of error and prejudice. Kant's contemporary Lambert championed just this conception of rigor and proof, arguing that a proof should 'never appeal to the thing itself . . . but be conducted entirely symbolically', that it should treat its premises 'like so many algebraic equations that one has ready before him and from which one extracts x, y, z, etc. without looking back to the object itself'.[8]

A Euclidean demonstration enables one to see why a conclusion holds by literally showing the connections that are the ground of its truth, but apparently does so at the expense of rigor in our second sense. An argument that proceeds by means of the often merely mechanical manipulation of symbols according to strict algorithms, by contrast, definitively establishes a truth, but seems to do so at the expense of understanding. It does not show, with the intuitive clarity of a Euclidean demonstration, why the conclusion should be as it is, and sometimes yields results that run directly counter to intuition. How extraordinary, then, that Kant should claim in the first *Critique* that *all* of mathematics functions in the same way: namely, through constructions in pure intuition, constructions that enable one literally to see, and so to understand, the necessity of the conclusion drawn. How *could* this be, given that in geometry one focuses on the things themselves, whereas in arithmetic and algebra one focuses not on the things but instead on arbitrary (rule-governed) signs?

Before Kant, we have seen, there were two incompatible ways to think about mathematical practice. The first, and more intuitive, more classical way was bottom-up: beginning with concrete sensible objects such as drawn geometrical figures or 'actual' numbers—that is, collections of things—the mathematician learns to abstract from these concrete cases and to reason about mathematical entities that are only imperfectly depicted in a Euclidean

---

[7] The description is John Playfair's in 'On the Arithmetic of Impossible Equations' (1778); quoted in Nagel (1935: 173).

[8] 'Theorie der Parallellinien' (1786); quoted in Detlefson (2005: 250).

demonstration or by a collection of strokes on a page. From this perspective, the manipulation of symbols according to algorithms in arithmetic and algebra was to be understood instrumentally; such systems of signs are useful, but not meaningful in their own right. The second way was top-down, beginning with the symbolic language of algebra and, by extension, that of arithmetic. On this view the meanings of the signs used in calculations are exhausted by the rules governing their use; they have no meaning or content beyond that constituted by the rules governing their use, and because they do not, our inability to imagine the results of certain computations—for example, that of taking a larger from a smaller number—is irrelevant to meaning. Euclidean geometry, dependent as it is on drawn figures rather than on rule-governed signs, is to be replaced by 'analytic geometry'—that is to say, algebra—because only as algebra is geometry properly rigorous.

Kant overcomes this either/or. According to him, all of mathematics—whether a Euclidean demonstration, a calculation in arithmetic, or a computation in algebra—functions in the same way, through the construction of concepts in pure intuition. The truths of mathematics are known, in every case, by reason 'guided throughout by intuition'—that is, through the construction of concepts in pure intuition. Because the intuition is pure, grounded in the forms of sensibility, space, and time, it follows immediately that mathematics is applicable in the natural sciences; although not itself empirical knowledge, mathematical knowledge, on Kant's view, is nonetheless knowledge about empirical objects. But if that is right, then both earlier accounts must have been wrong. If Kant is right, Euclidean geometry cannot function by picturing, however imperfectly, geometrical objects, as the first, bottom-up account would have it (as if arithmetic were some kind of empirical science), and the symbolic languages of arithmetic and algebra similarly cannot be *merely* symbolic, their meaning exhausted by the rules governing the use of their signs, as the second, top-down account would have it (as if mathematics were merely logic). Instead, if Kant is right, both sorts of systems of signs function to *encode information* (contained in the relevant concepts) in a way that enables rigorous reasoning *in* the system of signs, reasoning that is revelatory of new and substantive mathematical truths. We will later see in more detail how this is to work.

Kant provided an illuminating and intellectually satisfying account of the practice of early modern mathematics, one that revealed it to be rigorous *both* in the sense of compelling one's assent *and* in the sense of bringing one to see just why the results hold. It was an extraordinary philosophical achievement. Unfortunately, even as Kant was working out his philosophy of mathematics, mathematicians were coming more and more to eschew the sorts of constructive problem-solving techniques that Kant focuses on, in favor of a more conceptual approach. A new mathematical practice was emerging, and it did so, over the course of the nineteenth century, in roughly three, not strictly chronological, stages. First, mathematicians began to introduce new mathematical objects that could not, by any stretch of the imagination, be constructed in an intuition—for example, the projective geometer's points at infinity where parallel lines meet. Second, the focus was shifting more generally from algebraic representations of objects to descriptions of them using concepts. In the case of limit operations, for example, instead of trying to compute—that is, to construct—the limit as Leibniz had done, Cauchy, Bolzano, and Weierstrass aimed instead to describe what must be true of it. Riemann similarly did not require, as Euler had, that a function be given algebraic expression; it was enough to describe its behavior. And finally, a new sort of algebra was emerging, one that concerned not any particular mathematical objects, functions, or relations, but instead the kinds of structures they can be seen to exhibit—that is, groups, rings, fields, and so on. In each case, the focus was on reasoning from concepts; the construction of concepts in intuition was not needed, and intuition itself was coming to be seen as a 'foreign' element to be expelled from mathematics.[9]

Developments in the practice of mathematics over the course of the nineteenth century suggested that merely by reasoning from concepts one could extend one's knowledge. But if so, then either Kant was wrong to have thought that analytic judgments are only explicative, that all ampliative judgments are instead synthetic, or he was wrong to have thought that by reason alone only analytic judgments are possible—that is, that synthetic judgments inevitably involve intuitions as contrasted with concepts, whether pure or empirical. For Kant himself, of course, the analytic/synthetic distinction exactly lines up both with the explicative/ampliative distinction and with the by-logic-alone/involving-intuition distinction: analytic judgments are known

---

[9] Very helpful and illuminating discussions of these transformations can be found in Stein (1988), Nagel (1939), Wilson (1992), Ferreiros and Gray (2006), Gray (1992), Avigad (2006), and Tappenden (2006). One caveat: Stein describes this transformation of mathematics in the nineteenth century as 'so profound that it is not too much to call it a second birth of the subject—its first birth having occurred among the ancient Greeks' (1988: 238). This is misleading insofar as it ignores Descartes's transformation of mathematics in the seventeenth century, the transformation without which modern science would have been impossible. See Macbeth (2004).

by reason alone and are merely explicative, and synthetic judgments are ampliative, because an intuition serves in such judgments to connect the predicate to the concept of the subject. What the new mathematical practice of reasoning from concepts showed was that this picture of the analytic/synthetic distinction had to be wrong. What it did not settle was how it was wrong. The logical positivists, focusing on the knowledge produced, drew our first conclusion; they took it that what had been shown was that some analytic judgments, known by logic and reasoning alone, are in fact ampliative, not merely explicative. Peirce, focusing instead on the activity of mathematical inquiry, drew the second conclusion; he thought that the lesson of modern mathematical practice was that even reasoning from concepts by logic alone can involve constructions and so be synthetic, hence ampliative. The two responses will be considered in turn.

According to the positivists, developments in mathematics in the nineteenth century showed that there can be judgments—that is, judged (or judgeable) contents—that are true in virtue of the meanings stipulated in one's axioms, and so analytic a priori, but which are far from trivial, which can be proved only from a whole collection of axioms in what is perhaps a quite complex series of steps.[10] Although concepts do often contain contents that can be made explicit in trivial analytic judgments (the concept *human*, for example, contains a content that is made explicit in the analytic judgment that all humans are rational), it was coming to seem that concepts can also acquire meaning through their relations one to another, relations that can be made explicit in an axiomatization. Theorems that can be derived from a set of such axioms, solely in virtue of the stipulated relations, thus follow 'by meaning alone', and so are analytic in Kant's sense despite being ampliative—that is, significant extensions of our knowledge. Coffa explains the point this way:

If Kant was right, concepts without intuitions are empty, and no geometric derivation is possible that does not appeal to intuition. But by the end of the nineteenth century, Bolzano, Helmholtz, Frege, Dedekind, and many others had helped determine that Kant was not right, that concepts without intuitions are not empty at all. The formalist

---

[10]   One will perhaps think of Frege's familiar remark in 1980 [1884]: §88: 'the conclusions . . . extend our knowledge, and ought therefore, on Kant's view, to be regarded as synthetic; and yet they can be proved by purely logical means, and are thus analytic. The truth is that they are contained in the definitions, but as plants are contained in their seeds, not as beams are contained in a house'. In fact, we will see, Frege's own views were much closer to Peirce's than they were to those of the later logical positivists.

project in geometry was therefore designed not to expel meaning from science but to realize Bolzano's old dream: the formulation of non-empirical scientific knowledge on a purely conceptual basis.   (Coffa 1991: 140)

For the positivists, mathematical knowledge can be ampliative despite being analytic, because meaning can be determined for a set of expressions, assumed to be otherwise meaningless, through an axiomatization involving those expressions.

Peirce's response to these same developments in nineteenth-century mathematics was very different. His thought was not that what those developments show is that constructions are not needed in mathematics, but instead that even logic, even reasoning from concepts alone, can involve constructions. He explains in 'The Logic of Mathematics in Relation to Education' (1898):

Kant is entirely right in saying that, in drawing those consequences, the mathematician uses what, in geometry, is called a 'construction', or in general a diagram, or visual array of characters or lines. Such a construction is formed according to a precept furnished by the hypothesis. Being formed, the construction is submitted to the scrutiny of observation, and new relations are discovered among its parts, not stated in the precept by which it was formed, and are found, by a little mental experimentation, to be such that they will always be present in such a construction. Thus the necessary reasoning of mathematics is performed by means of observation and experiment, and its necessary character is due simply to the circumstance that the subject of this observation and experiment is a diagram of our own creation, the condition of whose being we know all about.

But Kant, owing to the slight development which formal logic had received in his time, and especially owing to his total ignorance of the logic of relatives, which throws a brilliant light upon the whole of logic, fell into error in supposing that mathematical and philosophical necessary reasoning are distinguished by the circumstance that the former uses constructions. This is not true. All necessary reasoning whatsoever proceeds by constructions; and the difference between mathematical and philosophical necessary deductions is that the latter are so excessively simple that the construction attracts no attention and is overlooked.   (CP iii. 350)

On Peirce's view, the lesson of the developments in mathematical practice in the nineteenth century is not that mathematics, which (as developments in the nineteenth century had shown) can involve reasoning from concepts alone, is for that reason analytic, rather than synthetic as Kant thought, but instead that reasoning from concepts alone is, like the rest of mathematical practice, synthetic—that is, ampliative—albeit a priori and necessary, because even reasoning from concepts involves constructions. We will come back to this.

For now, we need to return to the positivist view, and to Quine's utterly devastating critique of it.[11]

We have seen that, according to the positivists, the truths of mathematics are analytic despite being ampliative; they are contentful, non-trivial truths that, like any analytic truths, are known by appeal to meanings alone. Quine's essential, and fundamentally pragmatist, objection to the view is that if the judgments of mathematics really are analytic, founded on meaning alone, hence incorrigible and unrevisable, then they are not and cannot be *true*; alternatively, if they are true (or false), then they are not founded on meaning alone, because in that case they can be revised as needed. Quite simply, if it really is impossible to get it wrong (save by merely making a mistake in one's formal reasoning, in one's manipulation of signs according to rules), then there is no content to the claim at all. And this is true furthermore even of simple analytic judgments such as that all humans are rational. If that judgment is true by virtue of meaning, because being human is by definition being (say) a rational animal, then the judgment that all humans are rational is not a piece of knowledge of any kind. It is nothing more than a substitution instance of the logical schema 'all (A&B) is A', and this substitution instance absolutely must not be confused with a truth, however trivial, about humans; for if it were really a *truth* about humans, then it would be possible that it be mistaken. Insofar as it is not possible that one is mistaken (except in the trivial sense of having misapplied some rule governing one's use of signs), it is also not possible that what one has is an item of knowledge. What is unquestionable in principle is not knowledge but merely blind prejudice, merely (as Peirce would say) what one is inclined to think.[12]

This point can be hard to see, and it can be hard to see at least in part because there is a perfectly good distinction to be drawn between claims that are *believed* on the basis of meanings and claims that are believed on the basis of fact. I might, for example, believe that humans are rational on the grounds that in the language that I speak part of what it means to be human is to be rational. Quine's point is that either sort of belief, either belief on the basis of meanings or belief on the basis of fact, can turn out to have been mistaken and require revision. Even Kant himself took the contents of at least our empirical concepts to be subject to empirical inquiry, and hence subject to

---

[11] Quine's criticisms of the logical positivists' conception of mathematics first appeared in print in Quine (1937), but the most famous and influential formulation is given in Quine (1951), repr. in *From a Logical Point of View* (1953).

[12] See Lecture Four, 'The First Rule of Logic', of *RLT*, and also 'The Fixation of Belief' in *EP* i.

revision. In particular, if *human* (say) is an empirical concept, then there are, on Kant's view, no analytic truths about humans, but only synthetic ones that are discovered as we come to know more and more about the sorts of beings we are. Only an a priori, or non-empirical, concept could possibly ground an analytic truth on Kant's account. Given that the positivist rejects the notion of an a priori concept, there is simply no place left for the positivist to stand between infallible but empty logical forms, on the one hand, and corrigible, empirical contents, on the other. The judgments of mathematics, if they have any content at all, are contentful in virtue of facing the tribunal of experience in just the way any other claim does. The only tribunal is experience, and the only science is empirical—that is, a posteriori—science.

The situation, then, seems to be this. Mathematics starts with some definitions, either explicit or implicit (that is, given by a collection of axioms), and derives theorems using familiar rules of logic. The process can be understood merely mechanically—that is, as a process of formal, syntactic derivation. Such a process furthermore might seem to explain how we know that the theorems are true, indeed necessarily so given the axioms. Unfortunately, as Benacerraf (1973) argues, it is in that case utterly mysterious why we should say that those derived theorems are *true*; for to understand truth, in mathematics as in the rest of the language, we need to provide an interpretation, a semantics for the language, and as Tarski has taught us, this means providing a domain of objects for our names to refer to and for our quantifiers to range over. And here there would seem to be only two options: either those objects are everyday empirical objects, or they are abstract objects. Now, mathematics does not seem to be about empirical objects, because that would be incompatible with the characteristic necessity of its results; its timeless necessity suggests instead that its objects are likewise timeless and unchanging—that is to say, Platonic. But, mathematics aside, Platonism is incompatible with everything we have come to understand about the world: although Plato in his time may have had good reason to posit such objects, we in ours do not. We cannot in good conscience be Platonists about mathematical objects. But if that is so, then the content of mathematics, if it has any content at all, is empirical—just as Quine argues.

Mathematics seems to involve more than mere empty formalisms, the mere manipulation of signs; it seems, that is, to have content, and indeed content that is not empirical. On the other hand, it appears to be impossible to fit timeless, abstract objects into any robust and intellectually respectable picture of empirical reality. So how are we to account for the fact that mathematics has content? Quine's solution to the difficulty is to start with naturalism, and so with the rejection of abstract objects (hence with a kind of formalism in mathematics), but then to suggest that as we proceed with our natural, empirical scientific investigations, we discover that we cannot do without the sorts of things mathematicians talk about—for instance, sets. So, much as we posit unobservables such as electrons to make sense of our experience of the world, we can similarly posit sets, thereby providing distinctively mathematical content without falling into Platonism.[13]

In 'Mathematics without Foundations', Putnam (1967) offers a different way out of the difficulty. He suggests that there are available in mathematics two very different perspectives: that of modal logic and that of set theory. From the modal logic perspective, the propositions of mathematics appear to be logically necessary, albeit empty, and from the set theory perspective, they appear contentful, because about sets, though now it is hard to see why they are necessary. It is a bit, Putnam suggests, like the physicist thinking now in terms of particles and now in terms of waves; you can have it one way for some purposes and the other for other purposes, but never both together. The problem for such a suggestion, as well as for the Quinean attempt to have it both ways rehearsed above, is, as Benacerraf (1973) makes clear, that one does not really have any understanding either of necessity or of content in mathematics without at the same time having an understanding of both. And that, as work both within and outside the mainstream had made amply clear, is just what we do not know how to achieve.

We have seen that Quine aims to treat the ontological commitments of mathematics as continuous with those of science. His starting point is a naturalism of natural, empirical science, which requires the rejection of mathematical Platonism; but he thinks that he can then reintroduce a kind of relaxed Platonism on the basis of the needs of natural science. But, as Parsons (1980) argues, this seems to get the practice of mathematics wrong, and so to sin against naturalism for the case of the science of mathematics. It is for just this reason that post-Quinean naturalists such as Maddy and Burgess eschew legislating for mathematics from the outside (as Quine does) to pursue instead a naturalized mathematics. Unfortunately, they seem as a result to have no means of counteracting the unbridled Platonism of the practicing mathematician.[14]

---

[13] This is Quine's so-called indispensability argument, which appeared first in Quine (1948). Putnam also rehearses this argument (with an explicit nod to Quine) in Putnam (1971).

[14] For an introduction to the views of post-Quinean naturalists such as Maddy and Burgess, as well as further references, see Maddy (2005).

Nominalism is, then, a natural alternative, one that is pursued, for instance, by Field—though, as the discussion in Burgess (2004) shows, it is a natural alternative only if one is a post-Quinean rather than a Quinean naturalist.[15] Unfortunately, nominalism is just another way of being a formalist. What we wanted was to be able to dismount the Platonism/formalism seesaw, not to settle, however temporarily, on one end of it.

The post-Quinean naturalist seems to settle on the Platonist horn of our dilemma, and the nominalist on the formalist horn. What then of structuralism, the last of the big three in the mainstream of the American logic and foundations tradition? Structuralism seems originally to have been motivated by Benacerraf's well-known argument (in Benacerraf 1965) to show that numbers cannot be identified with sets—despite the fact that structuralism provides an obvious, albeit internal, answer to the question of what at least some contemporary mathematics is about.[16] And structuralism can seem to be the one position in the philosophy of mathematics that can go between the horns of Platonism and formalism. After all, one might think, surely there are structures, and not in any objectionable Platonist sense. In fact, just the same debates arise again, only now they are between formalists and Platonists within structuralism; and they are unresolvable for precisely the same reasons as before.[17] In the nature of the case, neither the formalist (focused on syntax alone) nor the Platonist (positing abstract structures for mathematics to be about) can provide what is wanted, a compelling and intellectually respectable account of the capacity of the mathematician to achieve interesting, new, and true results by reasoning alone.

We have seen that the mainstream has its roots in Quine's rejection of the positivist idea that mathematical judgments are truths that can be known to be necessary, a priori, and infallible because they are known by meanings alone. The maverick tradition, similarly, takes its starting point from the fact

[15] Chihara (2005) provides a lively introduction to nominalism, as well as further references. Field (1980) is perhaps the most famous nominalist essay.

[16] Bourbaki, e.g., explicitly suggests that mathematics concerns various sorts of structures. (See Corry (1992) for discussion of Bourbaki's notion structure). And many mathematicians are quite happy to describe mathematics as a science of structures, or of patterns. Nevertheless, as Parsons (1990) points out, the characterization nonetheless cannot serve, as the structuralist claims it does, for the whole of mathematics.

[17] Resnick (1997), Shapiro (1997), and Hellman (1989), e.g., are all structuralists, though they differ markedly in what they take the ontological commitments of structuralism to be. See Hellman (2001, 2005).

that mathematics is not at all infallible in its judgments.[18] Unfortunately, this tradition sometimes understands the fallibility of our mathematical knowledge, not in terms of the deep reason that, as Peirce and Quine saw, the possibility of error is built into the very fabric of inquiry, but instead in terms of the trivial reason that we can make mistakes in our calculations, mistakes that though they may go undetected, even for years, are nonetheless invariably detectable. The following passage, which otherwise makes a very good point, falls into just this error. Azzouni is responding to mavericks who suggest that mathematical practice is, like any other practice, essentially social; Azzouni's point is that mathematical practice is quite unlike any other social practice insofar as its standards are, as he puts it, robust.

Mistakes *can* persevere; but mostly they're eliminated, even if *repeatedly* made. More important, mathematical practice is *so* robust that even if a mistake eludes detection for years, and even if many later results presuppose that mistake, this won't provide enough social inertia—once the error *is* unearthed—to prevent changing the practice back to what it was originally: In mathematics, even after lots of time, the subsequent mathematics built on the 'falsehood' is repudiated.   (Azzouni 2006: 128)

Azzouni assumes that errors in mathematics can, with sufficient care and attention, be avoided by the practicing mathematician, that mathematicians are fallible but not essentially so. But think again of Peirce's picture according to which an error can lie hidden because the consequences that would at last reveal it have not been drawn—indeed, perhaps cannot (yet) be drawn because the additional premises that would be required have not yet been so much as formulated. Is it at all credible to think, for example, that Aristotle could have corrected his conception of number, could have come to have realized that zero is a perfectly good number, merely by more careful reflection? No. What Aristotle needed was not further and more careful attention to his mathematics, but instead a different conception of number, one that would become possible only in the light of the development of the symbolic language of algebra nearly 2,000 years after Aristotle lived. More generally put, the problem, in the interesting cases, is not that someone has made some error in reasoning, an error that could have been recognized and corrected had only more care been taken; it is that one's conceptions of things can be flawed in ways that can require hundreds, even thousands, of years of ongoing intellectual inquiry to reveal.

---

[18] An important early manifesto is Lakatos (1978). See also Putnam (1975), Kitcher (1983), and essays in Grosholz and Breger (2000).

What the Azzouni passage is right about, of course, is that there is only one right answer in mathematics: that truth, at least in mathematics, is not at all relative—to anything. It is the same for all cultures, all times, and all people, even (although Azzouni himself would not go this far) all rational beings. (Suppose that mathematical truth is not the same for all rational beings, but only for us. To explain that fact would require positing some form of cognitive 'hardwiring' in us that could, for all we know, be different in other rational beings. But that is just the Myth of the Given again: if we were hardwired to do mathematics as we do, then at a certain point there would no longer be any possibility of revision, and hence no longer any notion of truth. The fact of the matter is that we can make mistakes, and that we can correct our mistakes: truth is the same for all rational beings, just as Frege said. Anything less would not be truth.) Azzouni is enough of a maverick to avoid the word 'objective', but that is just what he seems to be pointing to, the fact that there are objective standards in mathematics, standards that all mathematicians are answerable to. Mathematics is clearly not just another social practice. What one would like, then, is an account of mathematical practice that explains that objectivity while avoiding Platonism, that explains what Wilson (1992: 111) has called mathematics' 'hidden essentialism'.

A further development within the maverick tradition is the emphasis it has put on the actual practice of mathematics, both at a given time and as it has evolved over its long history, and hence on informal as contrasted with formal proof, and on explanation and understanding as contrasted with proof and the establishment of truths.[19] Work in the mainstream as well has begun to look more carefully at what mathematicians actually do, and also at the history of mathematics.[20] Indeed, analytic philosophy more generally, which (historically) has been notoriously a- and sometimes even anti-historical, is coming more and more to realize that understanding must be historically

[19] See, e.g., Rota (1997: chs. 9–11). Coming from a quite different perspective, Manders (1987) calls for an account not just of the reliability of mathematical practice but of the fact that it yields understanding. Also relevant are Tappenden (1995a and b).

[20] There are two quite different ways to do this, however. The first, more superficial way is merely to 'check in' with mathematicians both past and present to see whether what they are doing is consistent with what one is saying about what they do. The second, deeper way is to recognize that the practice of mathematics, and thereby its historical unfolding, is the key to understanding mathematics itself; that it is the practice, not the product, that needs to be the focus of philosophical inquiry. (It is worth recalling in this context our discussion above of the differences between Peirce's and the positivists' response to the idea of reasoning from concepts alone that is nonetheless ampliative.)

informed. We turn finally to some fruits of that realization, the third strand in the tradition—which is to say, recent work on Frege insofar as it bears on the issues of concern here.

Benacerraf once again provides a critical point of orientation. As he argues in 'Frege: The Last Logicist' (1981), the tradition has profoundly misunderstood Frege's logicism; it has failed to distinguish Frege's logicism from that of the later logical positivist tradition. Also significant is Burge's recent collection of papers (2005), especially his 'Frege on Knowing the Foundation', which emphasizes some of the deeply pragmatist themes in Frege's thought—in particular his fallibilism and his essentially historicist understanding of intellectual inquiry. What I want to focus on, however, is the novel reading of Frege's strange two-dimensional notation that is developed in Macbeth (2005), because it is on the basis of this reading that we will be able to see most clearly both the connections to Peirce and the outlines of a way out of the impasse generated by the idea that through reasoning from concepts alone mathematicians can advance our knowledge and understanding. Frege's two-dimensional logical language, it will be suggested, is just what is needed to understand Peirce's idea that reasoning is a matter of construction and so in its way synthetic a priori despite being by concepts alone. And that in its turn will help us to understand the nature of mathematical reasoning in a way that avoids both formalism and Platonism. First, however, we need to understand better the role of constructions in Kant's account of the practice of mathematics.

Mathematics seems essentially to involve written marks. As one recent author has put it, 'one doesn't speak mathematics but writes it. Equally important, one doesn't write it as one writes or notates speech; rather, one "writes" in some other, more originating and constitutive sense' (Rotman 2000: p. ix). Already in 1764, in his 'Inquiry Concerning the Distinctness of the Principles of Natural Theology and Morality', Kant offers the beginnings of a theory about how such marks function in the practice of mathematics. He suggests, first, that the signs and marks employed in mathematics 'show in their composition the constituent concepts of which the whole idea... consists'. The arabic numeral '278', for example, shows (on this reading) that the number designated consists of two hundreds, seven tens, and eight units. A drawn triangle similarly is manifestly a three-sided closed plane figure; like the numeral '278', it is a whole of simple parts. These complexes are then further combined, according to Kant, to show 'in their combinations the relations of the . . . thoughts to each other'.[21] In mathematics, one combines the wholes that are formed out of simples into larger wholes that exhibit relations among them. The systems of signs thus have three levels of articulation: first, the primitive signs; then the wholes formed out of those primitives, wholes that constitute the subject matter of the relevant part of mathematics (the numbers of arithmetic, say, or the figures of Euclidean geometry); and finally, the largest wholes—for example, a Euclidean diagram or a calculation in arabic numeration—that are wholes of the (intermediate) wholes of the primitive parts. In the *Critique*, by which time Kant had discovered the logical and metaphysical distinction between intuitions and concepts, Kant further indicates that it is precisely because it is possible to reconceptualize at the second level, to see a collection of marks now this way and now that—possible, that is, to synthesize the given manifold of marks under different concepts—that one can come in the course of one's reasoning to see that the predicate of the judgment in question belongs necessarily to the concept of the subject despite not being contained in it.

Consider a demonstration in Euclid. Such a demonstration consists of a diagram constructed out of the primitives of the system (points, lines, angles, and areas) together with a commentary that, among other things, instructs one how to conceive various aspects of the diagram—a given line, for instance, now as a radius of a circle and now as a side of a triangle. What Kant saw is that such reconceptualizations are critical to the cogency of the demonstrations. The very first proposition in Euclid's *Elements* illustrates the essential point. The problem is to construct an equilateral triangle on a given finite straight line. To demonstrate the solution, one first constructs a circle with one endpoint of the given line as center and the line itself as radius, and then another circle with the other endpoint as center and the line as radius. Then, from one of the two points of intersection of the two circles, one draws two lines, one to each of the endpoints of the original line. Now one reasons on the basis of the drawn diagram: two of the three lines are radii of one circle and so must be equal in length, and one of those radii along with the third line are radii of the other circle, so must be equal in length. But if the two lines in each of the two pairs are equal in length, and there is one line that is in both pairs, then all three lines must be equal in

---

[21] All quotations are from Kant (1764: 251). In this passage Kant is in fact describing what the words of natural language that are used in philosophy cannot do. It is clear that he means indirectly to say what the signs and marks in mathematics can do.

length. Those very same lines, however, can also be conceived as the sides of a triangle. Because they can, we know that the triangle so constructed is equilateral. QED.

As this little example illustrates, a demonstration in Euclidean geometry works because the diagram has three levels of articulation that enable one to reconfigure at the second level, to see the primitive signs now as parts of this figure and now as parts of that. The diagram does not merely picture objects; it encodes information such as that two line lengths are equal (because they are radii of one and the same circle). And because it encodes information in a system of signs that involves not only complexes of primitives but (inscribed) relations among those complexes, it is possible to 'gestalt' the parts of a Euclidean diagram in a variety of ways, and thereby to identify new complexes in the diagram and new relations. What one takes out of the diagram, then, was already in it only, as Frege would say, as a plant is in the seed, not as beams are in a house. The demonstration is ampliative, an extension of knowledge, for just this reason.

One can similarly demonstrate a simple fact of arithmetic through the successive reconceptualizing of the units of a number. One begins, for instance, with a collection of seven strokes and a collection of five strokes. Again, there are three levels of articulation: the primitives (the individual strokes), the two collections of those primitives, and the whole array. Because the two collections are given in the array, it is possible to reconceive a unit of one collection as instead a unit of the other and in this way to 'add the units . . . previously taken together in order to constitute the number 5 one after another to the number 7, and thus see the number 12 arise' (B16).

Calculations in arabic numeration are more complex, but as Kant teaches us to see, the basic principle is the same. Suppose that the problem is to determine the product of twenty-seven and forty-four. One begins by writing the signs for the two numbers in a particular array: namely, one directly beneath the other. Obviously, here again the three levels can be discerned, and here again it is this that enables one to do one's mathematical work. Suppose that one has written '44' beneath '27'. The calculation begins with a reconfiguration at the second level of articulation: the rightmost '4' in '44' is considered instead with the '7' in '27'. Multiplying the two elements in this new whole yields twenty-eight, so an '8' goes under the rightmost column and a '2' above the left. Next one takes the same sign '4' and considers it together with the '2' in '27', and so on in a familiar series of steps to yield, finally, in the last (fifth) row, the product that is wanted. The fifth row is, of course, arrived at by the stepwise addition of the numbers given in the columns at the third and fourth row; it is by reading down that one understands why just those signs appear in the bottom row. But it is by reading across, by conceptualizing the signs in the last row as a numeral, that one knows the answer that is wanted.

Exactly the same point applies in algebra; even in algebra, there is 'a characteristic construction, in which one displays by signs in intuition the concepts, especially of relations of quantities' (Kant, A734/B762). In every case, through the reconfiguration of parts of wholes (made possible, on the one hand, by the fact that those wholes are themselves parts of wholes, and on the other, by the Kantian dichotomy of intuition and concept), one comes in the course of one's reasoning to see something new arise, and thereby to extend one's knowledge. Because the relevant intuitions are pure, rather than empirical, the results are necessary, that is, a priori; and because the whole process is made possible by space and time as the forms of sensibility, the results are obviously and immediately applicable in the natural sciences.

Earlier we distinguished between two very different conceptions of rigor and proof, on the one hand, the intuitive rigor of a picture proof, and on the other, the formal rigor of a calculation or deduction achieved through the essentially mechanical manipulation of signs. Kant effectively combines these two quite different conceptions of rigor and proof in the idea that mathematical practice involves constructions, whether ostensive or symbolic, in pure intuition, and so is able to explain how the judgments of mathematics can be at once necessary, or a priori, and ampliative, substantive extensions of our knowledge. And this works in virtue of the three levels of articulation discernible in each of the systems of signs that Kant considers combined with the fact, made possible by Kant's recognition of two logically different sorts of representations, concepts and intuitions, that collections of those signs can be variously conceived. In such cases one neither merely pictures things nor merely manipulates signs; one's work is neither merely intuitive nor merely formal. Instead, one reasons *in* the system of signs, actualizing, through the course of one's reasoning, the conclusion that is latent in one's starting point.

Unfortunately, this works only because one starts with something that can be exhibited in an intuition—a number, say, or a finite line length. It is not surprising, then, that we find that once intuition had been banished from the practice of mathematics over the course of the nineteenth century, the two notions of rigor, intuitive and formal, came apart again—only this time there could be no question which of the two notions was needed in mathematics. As Einstein famously put it in 1921, 'insofar as mathematical theorems refer to reality, they are not certain, and insofar as they are certain, they do not refer to reality. ... The progress entailed by axiomatics consists in the sharp separation of the logical form and the realistic and intuitive contents.'[22] One can have deductive rigor by focusing on the signs and the rules governing their use—that is, syntax—or one can have meaning and truth by focusing on that for which the signs stand, their semantic values. What one cannot have is both at once, not now that it is concepts rather than intuitions that are at issue.

As Kant helps us to see, objects given in intuitions are thought through concepts, and so can be variously conceived in ways that combine intuitive clarity and deductive rigor. Our problem is that the same obviously cannot be said of concepts themselves. Although it is possible to take a bottom-up view of concepts by appeal to objects that exemplify them, and also possible to take a top-down view of concepts by appeal to inferential relations among them as stipulated in an axiomatization, it is impossible to do both at once. Deductive rigor, which requires fixing in advance the logical relations among one's primitive concepts in axioms and definitions, thus seems to require a kind of formalism, and thereby the loss of the sort of rigor that, if Kant is right, is displayed both in a Euclidean demonstration and in calculations in arithmetic and algebra. This (exclusive) either/or, either (top-down, syntactic) deductive rigor or (bottom-up, semantic) content and meaning, emerged first in geometry, in Pasch and in Hilbert, but it eventually, and inevitably, surfaced in logic as well, and is now the standard, model-theoretic view.[23] It is also the source of the oscillations between formalism and Platonism that have bedeviled the philosophy of mathematics for the last century.

What is needed is an account of mathematical practice that combines deductive rigor with a clear understanding of why and how the conclusion follows from the premises. And for that, so it would seem, following Kant, we need a conception of the written language of mathematics that enables reasoning from concepts that is deductively rigorous but also ampliative, a language that does for concepts and reasoning what, on Kant's reading, the language of arithmetic and algebra does for numbers, functions, and computations. But how is such a conception possible? Have we not shown

---

[22] From his lecture 'Geometrie und Erfahrung'; quoted in Freudenthal (1962: 619).
[23] For some of the history, see Nagel (1939), Goldfarb (1979), and Demopoulos (1994).

that, with the shift over the course of the nineteenth century from (as Kant would put it) reason in its intuitive employment to reason in its discursive employment, the two conceptions of rigor came again to be utterly incompatible? Have we not seen that if mathematics as it has come to be practiced is to be deductively rigorous (hence top-down), then it can have *no* truck with 'meaningful mathematical problems', 'mathematical ideas', or 'clarity' (which seem one and all to be bottom-up)? Fortunately, in philosophy as in mathematics, there is no *ignorabimus*.[24] What is needed is a new, post-Kantian conception of concepts; and Frege shows us how to develop one.[25]

Although not always recognized as such, Kant's distinction between intuitions and concepts is (among other things) a properly logical advance.[26] Ancient logic is a term logic in which no logical distinction is drawn between terms that can be applied only to one thing and terms that can be applied to many. Any individual, Socrates, say, can be called many things (that is, by many names): Socrates, pale, man, snub-nosed, wise, mortal, and so on. In effect, the terms in a classical term logic combine both a 'referential' and a 'predicative' aspect—which is why it is valid in such a logic to infer from the fact that all S is P that some S is P. (If there is nothing to call an S, then there is nothing to be said about the Ss.) Later rationalists and empiricists would emphasize, respectively, the predicative or the referential aspects of terms, or of their cognitive correlates, but it is only with Kant that a clean break is made. Intuitions are referential; they give objects. Concepts are predicative; they are ways the objects given in intuitions can be thought (correctly or incorrectly).[27]

---

[24] The claim, for the case of mathematics, is of course Hilbert's: 'The conviction of the solvability of every mathematical problem is a powerful incentive to the worker. We hear within us the perpetual call: There is the problem. Seek its solution. You can find it by pure reason, for in mathematics there is no *ignorabimus*' (1902); quoted in Detlefson (2005: 278).

[25] It must be emphasized that the conception of language to be outlined here, following Frege, is deeply different from standard conceptions. Here I can only gesture at the reading that is developed in Macbeth (2005).

[26] Thompson (1972–3) makes the point that Kant has a monadic predicate calculus, i.e. the calculus that Russell once described as 'the first serious advance in real logic since the time of the Greeks'—which Russell himself thought was discovered first by Peano, and independently, by Frege (Russell 1914: 50). As Russell saw, the extension of the monadic predicate calculus to the full logic of relations is a merely technical advance.

[27] This new conception of concepts in Kant is also indicated by the fact that Kant is the first to hold that not concepts, but judgments, are the smallest unit of cognitive significance, that concepts are significant only as predicates of possible judgments. (On the Peircean conception, as in Frege, the smallest unit of significance is the inference, because without inference there is no truth.)

From Kant's perspective, ancient term logic rests on a conflation of two logically different sorts of representations. What Frege realized, by the early 1890s, is that this Kantian distinction of two logically different sorts of representations *similarly involves a conflation*, this time of two logically different logical distinctions, that of *Sinn* and *Bedeutung* with that of concept and object. As Frege puts the point, 'it is easy to become unclear...by confounding the division into concepts and objects with the distinction between sense and meaning so that we run together sense and concept on the one hand and meaning and object on the other' (1892–5: 118). Frege himself at first made just this mistake; he confused cognitive significance or *Sinn*, sense, with the notion of a concept, and objective or semantic significance with the notion of an object. As a result, he at first thought, with Kant, that all content and all truth lie in relation to an object. Our quantificational logics, as Tarski has made explicit, are founded on precisely this Kantian thought—which is why we are faced with the dilemma of formalism or Platonism in the philosophy of mathematics. The dilemma is forced on us because we have not yet learned, following Frege, to distinguish between objects and objectivity, on the one hand, and between concepts and 'conceptual' (better: cognitive) significance, on the other. Once having made this distinction between these two different distinctions, we can begin, at least, to understand the nature of a properly logical language *within which* to reason discursively—that is, from concepts alone—and thereby how again to combine intuitive with deductive rigor in the practice of mathematics.[28]

Concepts, on Frege's mature view, are laws of correlation, objects to truth-values in the case of first-level concepts, and lower-level concepts to truth-values in the case of higher-level concepts. A concept is thus something in its own right, something objective that can serve as an argument for a function in a judgment. One can, for example, judge of two concepts that one is subordinate to the other: that is, that the second-level relation of subordination is correctly applied to them. That second-level relation of subordination, similarly, is something objective about which to judge, correctly or incorrectly. It is, for instance, a transitive relation; *subordination* has the property of being transitive. There is, then, for Frege a natural division of 'levels' of knowledge. First, there are facts about the everyday objects of which we have sensory experience. Such facts are one and all a posteriori and

---

[28] By 'intuitive' here I do not mean involving Kantian intuition, but instead that one can see or understand clearly what is proved and why it must be true given one's starting points.

contingent (setting aside instances of laws of logic or of a special science); and in *Begriffsschrift*, Frege's formula language of pure thought, these facts are expressed using object names and first-level concept words.

One level up are facts about first-level concepts: for example, the fact that *cat* is subordinate to *mammal*—that is, that being a cat entails being a mammal (from which it follows that any particular cat is necessarily a mammal). Such a law can be expressed in *Begriffsschrift* either using the conditional stroke and Latin italic letters lending generality of content, or using the conditional stroke together with the concavity and German letter.[29] In the latter case, we have (at least on one function/argument analysis of the sentence) a sign for the second-level relation of subordination, one that is formed from the conditional stroke together with the concavity. To move up a level again, to consideration of second-level concepts such as subordination, is to move from the domain of the special sciences to the domain of the science of logic. The subject matter of logic on Frege's (mature) view is the second-level properties and relations that hold of the first-level concepts that constitute in turn the subject matter of the special sciences—including mathematics if logicism is wrong.

In *Begriffsschrift*, Frege's formula language of pure thought, concept words are given *only* relative to a function/argument analysis of a whole *Begriffsschrift* sentence, and inevitably more than one analysis is possible. Independent of any analysis, a sentence of his logical language expresses only a thought, which is a function of the senses of the primitive signs involved, and designates a truth-value. To determine what such a sentence is about, what the argument is, and for what function, one must provide an analysis, carve the sentence into function and argument, and there will be many ways to do this, as Frege's two-dimensional notation makes especially perspicuous.

Concept words, which are given only relative to an analysis, designate concepts—or at least, they purport to. They also express senses. Indeed, a *Begriffsschrift* expression, which is formed by combining the primitive signs of the language in appropriate ways, most immediately maps or traces a sense; it shows in its composition the sense through which something objective is (or purports to be) grasped. Consider, for example, the concept of continuity (of a function at a point). This concept takes mathematical functions and

---

[29] True accidental generalities can also be expressed these ways in Frege's logic. (Because inferences can be drawn only from acknowledged truths in Frege's logic, this does not introduce any difficulties into the logic.) The basic case, however, is that of a relationship among concepts that is not grounded in contingent facts about objects, but is immediately about concepts. See Macbeth (2005).

points as arguments to yield truth-values as values. But our grasp of that concept is mediated by a sense, one that we can have more or less clearly in mind. By the time Frege was writing, the content of this concept—that is, the sense through which it is grasped—had been clarified, and in 'Boole's Logical Calculus and the Concept Script' (1880/1) Frege shows just how that sense is expressed in a complex two-dimensional array in *Begriffsschrift*. Such an expression, formed from the primitives of *Begriffsschrift* together with some signs from arithmetic, *designates* the concept of continuity; it is a *name* for that concept. But that complex of primitive signs also expresses a sense: that is, the inferentially articulated content that is grasped by anyone who clearly understands what it means for a function to be continuous at a point. Concepts, as Frege understands them, are thus internally inferentially articulated. Such inferential articulation fundamentally contrasts with the sort of external articulation that is provided by an axiomatization on Hilbert's understanding of it—that is, an axiomatization fixing inferential relations between concepts rather than, as is the case on Frege's conception, within concepts.[30]

In a *Begriffsschrift* sentence, then, at least as it is conceived here, three levels of articulation are discernible. First, there are the primitive signs out of which everything is composed; then there are the concept words, the function and argument, that are given relative to an analysis of the sentence; and finally there is the whole sentence, which expresses a thought and designates, or ought to designate, a truth-value, either the True or the False. As should be evident, the primitives of the language so conceived cannot be taken to designate independent of a context of use. Only in the context of a sentence, and relative to an analysis into function and argument, can we speak of the designation of a sub-sentential expression. What one grasps when one grasps the meaning of a primitive of the language, then, is the sense expressed, and thereby the contribution that that primitive makes to the thought expressed by a sentence containing it, and, relative to some assumed analysis in which the primitive occurs as a designating expression, the designation. But that primitive expression can equally well appear as a component of a complex expression that designates something quite different. Frege's concavity, for example, which, taken alone, functions rather like a quantifier, also occurs in a wide range of expressions for other higher-level concepts such as the

---

[30] See Macbeth, forthcoming, for a more extended discussion of these different conceptions of inferential articulation.

second-level relation of subordination, or that of the continuity of a function at a point. Again, it is only relative to a function/argument analysis that sub-sentential expressions of *Begriffsschrift*, whether simple or complex, can be said to designate. (Needless to say, such a conception of language is essentially late; only someone already able to read and write could devise or learn such a language.)

As it is understood here, a *Begriffsschrift* sentence is rather like a Euclidean diagram, in that it can be regarded in various ways, given now one function/argument analysis and now another. A sentence containing Frege's (complex) sign for the concept of continuity can, for instance, be analyzed so as to yield that concept word; but it can also be analyzed in other ways, in ways that effectively cut across the boundaries of this concept word—and it may need to be so analyzed for the purposes of proof. It is precisely because concept words in *Begriffsschrift* are at once wholes made up of primitive parts and themselves parts of larger wholes—namely, sentences—that a *Begriffsschrift* proof can be fruitful, an extension of our knowledge. Given what the concepts involved mean, the senses through which they are given, one comes to see in the course of the proof how aspects of those senses can be figured and refigured to yield something new.[31]

Kant already taught us to see the course of a demonstration in Euclid as realizing the figure that is wanted, and the course of a calculation in arabic numeration as realizing the product (say) that is wanted. Frege, I am suggesting, similarly can teach us to see the course of a proof as realizing the conclusion that is wanted—teach us, that is, to see a proof as a *construction*, just as Peirce suggests we should. So conceived, a proof does not merely establish the truth of the conclusion (assuming the truth of the premises); it shows *how* the conclusion follows from the premises, how the conclusion is contained in the premises 'as plants are contained in their seeds, not as beams are contained in a house' (Frege 1884: §88). Much as one calculates *in* arabic numeration, so one reasons *in Begriffsschrift* in a way that is at once deductively rigorous and intuitively rigorous, in a way that one can follow and understand. And one can do this because *Begriffsschrift* puts a thought before one's eyes. Frege's logical language is in this way an utterly different sort of logical language from any with which we are familiar. As the point might be put, it is not a *mathematical* logic at all; it is not an algebra of thought that reveals valid patterns or structures. It is instead a *philosophical*

---

[31] See Macbeth (2007) for some examples of how this works in practice.

logic within which to express thoughts, and thereby to discover truths. As Kant taught us to read calculations in arithmetic and algebra not as merely mechanical manipulations of signs but as constructions revelatory of truth, so Frege teaches us to read a proof in symbolic logic not as a merely formal, deductively valid derivation but as a fully meaningful inference to a conclusion that is thereby revelatory of truth.

But not all contentful chains of reasoning are revelatory of their conclusions. As Lakatos (1976) shows, the practice of mathematics often proceeds by way of a process of proof and refutation—that is, dialectically in a way that involves both *modus ponens*, inference from acknowledged truths to other truths that are entailed by them, and also *modus tollens*, inference from the acknowledged falsity of some putative conclusion to the falsity of what had mistakenly been taken to be true. But if that is right, then an axiomatization of some domain of knowledge should be seen as providing not so much the foundation of that domain as a vehicle for the discovery of truths. Quite simply, by making one's conceptions explicit in axioms and definitions, one can then test their adequacy 'experimentally', by deriving theorems, just as Peirce suggests. If a manifest falsehood—for example, a contradiction—is derived, then one knows that one's conceptions are faulty, that one has not achieved adequate grasp of some concept, or perhaps is mistaken in thinking that there is any concept there to be grasped at all.

This is, of course, just what happened to Frege. His Basic Law V, which made explicit the notion of a course of values as Frege understood it, was shown by Russell to be flawed. But whereas for Russell (who, by his own admission, wanted certainty the way others want religious faith) that discovery was a disastrous blow to the very foundations of arithmetic, for Frege, a mathematician concerned with understanding, it was a crucial step forward, one that, as Frege (1980 [1902]: 192) writes to Russell, 'may perhaps lead to a great advance in logic, undesirable as it may seem at first'. For it is only through such a discovery that we can recognize the flaws in our understanding, and on that basis formulate better conceptions. In fact, Frege came to think, the notion of a course of values cannot be salvaged; his logicist thesis had been mistaken. But, as Frege was well aware, his logic and the language he devised for it remained intact. What has been suggested here is that it is just such a logic and such a language that are needed if we are to understand the practice of contemporary mathematics, reasoning from concepts alone.

Mathematics has its own proper subject matter, its own concepts and conceptions on the basis of which mathematicians not only reason but also judge, for instance, the 'naturalness' (that is, the inherently mathematical character) of various structures and lines of argument. But if the language that mathematicians use is understood as the tradition has taught, in terms of a fundamental dichotomy of logical form and (empirical) content, of syntax and semantics, then, as we have seen, there is, and can be, no properly mathematical subject matter. Frege long ago developed an alternative conception of language, one that combines deductive rigor with contentfulness, syntax with semantics, and thereby enables reasoning from the contents of concepts—that is, on the basis of their inferentially articulated senses. Such a conception of language is essentially Peircean, and because it is, it enables us to understand just how mathematics can be at once a priori, by reason alone, and also inherently fallible. Because concepts are grasped through senses that may be only imperfectly understood, we can make mistakes, just as Frege did with his Basic Law V; and so too we can correct our mistakes. It is for just this reason that mathematics is rational; it is rational, in Sellars's words (1956: §38), 'not because it has a *foundation* but because it is a self-correcting enterprise which can put *any* claim in jeopardy, though not *all* at once'.[32] Though it cannot be the whole story, this pragmatist conception of language, truth, and logic would thus seem to be an essential ingredient in any intellectually satisfying account of mathematical practice as it emerged in the nineteenth century and continues today.

REFERENCES

Aspray, William, and Kitcher, Philip (eds.) (1988). *History and Philosophy of Modern Mathematics,* Minnesota Studies in the Philosophy of Science, 9. Minneapolis: University of Minnesota Press.

Avigad, Jeremy (2006). 'Methodology and Metaphysics in the Development of Dedekind's Theory of Ideals'. In Ferreiros and Gray (2006), 159–86.

Azzouni, Jody (2006). *Tracking Reason: Proof, Consequence, and Truth.* Oxford: Oxford University Press.

Benacerraf, Paul (1965). 'What Numbers Could Not Be'. *Philosophical Review,* 74: 47–73. Repr. in Benacerraf and Putnam (1983), 272–94.

——(1973). 'Mathematical Truth'. *Journal of Philosophy,* 70: 661–80. Repr. in Benacerraf and Putnam (1983), 403–20.

---

[32] It should be noted that Sellars himself is talking about empirical knowledge rather than mathematical knowledge, but as Frege and Peirce together help us to see, the point generalizes.

_____ (1981). 'Frege: The Last Logicist'. In P. A. French, T. E. Uehling Jr., and H. K. Wettstein (eds.), *The Foundations of Analytic Philosophy*, Midwest Studies in Philosophy, 6, 17–35.

_____ and Putnam, Hilary (eds.) (1983). *Philosophy of Mathematics: Selected Readings*, 2nd edn. Cambridge: Cambridge University Press.

Burge, Tyler (2005). *Truth, Thought, Reason: Essays on Frege*. Oxford: Oxford University Press.

Burgess, John (2004). 'Quine, Analyticity and Philosophy of Mathematics'. *Philosophical Quarterly*, 54: 38–55.

_____ (2005). *Fixing Frege*. Princeton: Princeton University Press.

_____ and Rosen, Gideon (1997). *A Subject with No Object: Strategies for Nominalist Reconstruction of Mathematics*. Oxford: Clarendon Press.

Chihara, Charles (2005). 'Nominalism'. In Shapiro (2005), 483–514.

Coffa, J. Alberto (1991). *The Semantic Tradition from Kant to Carnap: To the Vienna Station*, ed. Linda Wessels. Cambridge: Cambridge University Press.

Corry, Leo (1992). 'Nicholas Bourbaki and the Concept of Mathematical Structure'. *Synthese*, 92: 315–48.

Demopoulos, William (1994). 'Frege, Hilbert, and the Conceptual Structure of Model Theory'. *History and Philosophy of Logic*, 15: 211–25.

Detlefson, Michael (2005). 'Formalism'. In Shapiro (2005), 236–317.

Ewald, William (ed.) (1996). *From Kant to Hilbert: A Source Book in the Foundations of Mathematics*, 2 vols. Oxford: Clarendon Press.

Feferman, Solomon (1998). *In the Light of Logic*. New York: Oxford University Press.

Ferreirós, José, and Gray, Jeremy J. (eds.) (2006). *The Architecture of Modern Mathematics: Essays in History and Philosophy*. Oxford: Oxford University Press.

Field, Hartry (1980). *Science without Numbers*. Princeton: Princeton University Press.

Frege, Gottlob (1880/1). 'Boole's Logical Calculus and the Concept Script'. Repr. in Frege (1979), 9–46.

_____ (1980 [1884]). *The Foundations of Arithmetic*, trans. J. L. Austin. Evanston, IL: Northwestern University Press.

_____ (1892–5). 'Comments on Sense and Meaning'. Repr. in Frege (1979), 118–25.

_____ (1980 [1902]). Frege to Russell, 22 June 1902, in Hans Kaal (trans.), Gottfried Gabriel *et al.* (eds.), *Philosophical and Mathematical Correspondence*, Chicago: University of Chicago Press, 131–3.

_____ (1979). *Posthumous Writings*, trans. Peter Long and Roger White, ed. Hans Hermes, Friedrich Kambartel, and Friedrich Kaulbach. Chicago: University of Chicago Press.

Freudenthal, Hans (1962). 'The Main Trends in the Foundations of Geometry in the 19th Century'. In Ernest Nagel, Patrick Suppes, and Alfred Tarski (eds.), *Logic, Methodology and Philosophy of Science: Proceedings of the 1960 International Congress*, Stanford, CA: Stanford University Press, 613–21.

George, Alexander, and Velleman, Daniel J. (2002). *Philosophies of Mathematics.* Malden, MA: Blackwell.

Giaquinto, M. (2002). *The Search for Certainty: A Philosophical Account of Foundations of Mathematics.* Oxford: Oxford University Press.

Goldfarb, Warren (1979). 'Logic in the Twenties: The Nature of the Quantifier'. *Journal of Symbolic Logic,* 44: 351–68.

Gray, Jeremy (1992). 'The Nineteenth Century Revolution in Mathematical Ontology'. In Donald Gillies (ed.), *Revolutions in Mathematics,* Oxford: Clarendon Press, 226–48.

Grosholz, E., and Breger, H. (eds.) (2000). *The Growth of Mathematical Knowledge.* Dordrecht: Kluwer.

Hellman, Geoffrey (1989). *Mathematics without Numbers: Towards a Modal-Structural Interpretation.* New York: Oxford University Press.

——(2001). 'Three Varieties of Mathematical Structuralism'. *Philosophia Mathematica,* 9: 148–211.

——(2005). 'Structuralism'. In Shapiro (2005), 536–62.

Hempel, Carl G. (1945). 'On the Nature of Mathematical Truth'. *American Mathematical Monthly,* 52: 543–56. Repr. in Benacerraf and Putnam (1983), 377–93.

Jacquette, Dale (ed.) (2002). *Philosophy of Mathematics: An Anthology.* Malden, MA: Blackwell.

Kant, Immanuel (1764). 'Inquiry Concerning the Distinctness of the Principles of Natural Theology and Morality'. Repr. in David Walford with Ralf Meerbote (trans. and eds.), *Theoretical Philosophy, 1755–1770,* Cambridge: Cambridge University Press, 1992, 243–75.

——(1998 [1781/7]). *Critique of Pure Reason,* trans. and ed. Paul Guyer and Allen W. Wood (eds.). Cambridge: Cambridge University Press.

Kitcher, Philip (1983). *The Nature of Mathematical Knowledge.* New York: Oxford University Press.

Lakatos, Imre (1976). *Proofs and Refutations: The Logic of Mathematical Discovery.* Cambridge: Cambridge University Press.

——(1978). 'A Renaissance of Empiricism in the Recent Philosophy of Mathematics'. In John Worrall and Gregory Currie (eds.), *Mathematics, Science and Epistemology,* Cambridge: Cambridge University Press. Repr. in Tymoczko (1986), 29–48.

Lakoff, George, and Núñez, Rafael (2000). *Where Mathematics Comes From: How the Embodied Mind Brings Mathematics into Being.* New York: Basic Books.

Macbeth, Danielle (2004). 'Viète, Descartes, and the Emergence of Modern Mathematics'. *Graduate Faculty Philosophy Journal,* 25: 87–117.

——(2005). *Frege's Logic.* Cambridge, MA: Harvard University Press.

——(2007). 'Striving for Truth in the Practice of Mathematics: Kant and Frege'. In D. Greimann (ed.), *Essays on Frege's Conception of Truth,* Grazer Philosophische Studien, 75, New York: Rodopi, 65–92.

_____ (forthcoming). 'Inference, Meaning, and Truth in Brandom, Sellars, and Frege'. In Bernhard Weiss and Jeremy Wanderer (eds.), *Reading Brandom: Making It Explicit*, London: Routledge.

Maddy, Penelope (2005). 'Three Forms of Naturalism'. In Shapiro (2005), 437–59.

Manders, Kenneth L. (1987). 'Logic and Conceptual Relationships in Mathematics'. In The Paris Logic Group (eds.), *Logic Colloquium '85*, Holland: Elsevier, 193–211.

Nagel Ernest (1935). ' "Impossible Numbers": A Chapter in the History of Modern Logic'. In Department of Philosophy of Columbia University (ed.), *Studies in the History of Ideas*, iii, New York: Columbia University Press. Repr. in Nagel (1979), 166–94.

_____ (1939). 'The Formation of Modern Conceptions of Formal Logic in the Development of Geometry'. *Osiris*, 7. Repr. in Nagel (1979), 195–259.

_____ (1979). *Teleology Revisited and Other Essays in the Philosophy and History of Science*. New York: Columbia University Press.

Parsons, Charles (1980). 'Mathematical Intuition'. *Proceedings of the Aristotelian Society*, 80: 145–68.

_____ (1990). 'The Structuralist View of Mathematical Objects'. *Synthese*, 84: 303–46.

Peirce, Charles Sanders (1931). *Collected Papers of Charles Sanders Peirce*, iii, ed. C. Hartshorne and P. Weiss. Cambridge, MA: Harvard University Press. Referred to as *CP* iii.

_____ (1992). *The Essential Peirce: Selected Philosophical Writings*, i: *1867–1893*, ed. Nathan Houser and Christian Kloesel. Bloomington and Indianapolis: Indiana University Press. Referred to as *EP* i.

_____ (1992). *Reasoning and the Logic of Things: The Cambridge Conference Lectures of 1898*, ed. Kenneth Laine Ketner. Cambridge, MA: Harvard University Press. Referred to as *RLT*.

Putnam, Hilary (1967). 'Mathematics without Foundations'. *Journal of Philosophy*, 64: 5–22. Repr. in Benacceraf and Putnam (1983), 295–311.

_____ (1971). *Philosophy of Logic*. New York: Harper.

_____ (1975). 'What is Mathematical Truth?'. In *Mathematics, Matter, and Method: Philosophical Papers*, i, Cambridge: Cambridge University Press, 60–78. Repr. in Tymoczko (1986), 49–65.

Quine, W. V. O. (1937). 'Truth by Convention'. In Otis H. Lee (ed.), *Philosophical Essays for A. N. Whitehead*, New York: Longmans, Green and Co., Inc. Repr. in Benacerraf and Putnam (1983), 329–54.

_____ (1948). 'On What There Is'. *Review of Metaphysics*, 2: 21–38. Repr. in Quine (1980), 1–19.

_____ (1951). 'Two Dogmas of Empiricism'. *Philosophical Review*, 60: 20–43. Repr. in Quine (1980), 20–46.

_____ (1980). *From a Logical Point of View*, 2nd edn. Cambridge, MA: Harvard University Press.

Resnick, Michael (1997). *Mathematics as a Science of Patterns*. New York: Oxford University Press.

Rota, Gian-Carlo (1997). *Indiscrete Thoughts*, ed. Fabrizio Palombi. Boston: Birkhäuser.

Rotman, Brian (2000). *Mathematics as Sign: Writing, Imagining, Counting*. Stanford, CA: Stanford University Press.

Russell, Bertrand (1914). *Our Knowledge of the External World*. London: George Allen & Unwin.

Sellars, Wilfrid (1956). 'Empiricism and the Philosophy of Mind'. In Herbert Feigl and Michael Scriven (eds.), *The Foundations of Science and the Concepts of Psychology and Psychoanalysis*, Minnesota Studies in the Philosophy of Science, 1, Minneapolis: University of Minnesota Press. Repr. in *Science, Perception and Reality*, London: Routledge & Kegan Paul, 1963, 127–96.

Shapiro, Stewart (1997). *Philosophy of Mathematics: Structure and Ontology*. New York: Oxford University Press.

——— (ed.) (2005). *The Oxford Handbook of Philosophy of Mathematics and Logic*. New York: Oxford University Press.

Stein, Howard (1988). '*Logos*, Logic, and *Logistike*: Some Philosophical Remarks on Nineteenth-Century Transformation of Mathematics'. In Aspray and Kitcher (1988), 238–59.

Tappenden, Jamie (1995*a*). 'Extending Knowledge and "Fruitful Concepts": Fregean Themes in the Foundations of Mathematics'. *Nous*, 29: 427–67.

——— (1995*b*). 'Geometry and Generality in Frege's Philosophy of Arithmetic'. *Synthese*, 102: 319–61.

——— (2006). 'The Riemannian Background to Frege's Philosophy'. In Ferreirós and Gray (2006), 97–132.

Thompson, Manley (1972–3). 'Singular Terms and Intuitions in Kant's Epistemology'. *Review of Metaphysics*, 26: 314–43.

Tymoczko, Thomas (ed.) (1986). *New Directions in the Philosophy of Mathematics*. Boston: Birkhäuser.

van Heijenoort, Jean (ed.) (1967). *From Frege to Gödel: A Source Book in Mathematical Logic, 1879–1931*. Cambridge, MA: Harvard University Press.

Wilson, Mark (1992). 'Frege: The Royal Road from Geometry'. *Nous*, 26: 149–80. Repr. in William Demopoulos (ed.), *Frege's Philosophy of Mathematics*, Cambridge, MA: Harvard University Press, 1995, 108–59.

CHAPTER 23

LIBERAL EQUALITY: WHAT, WHERE, AND WHY

KOK-CHOR TAN

I. THE IDEA OF LIBERAL EQUALITY

IN CONTEMPORARY American philosophy, liberalism, as opposed to libertarianism, or classical liberalism, is understood to have an egalitarian distributive commitment.[1] That is, in addition to the protection of the basic liberties of persons, liberal justice serves also to regulate social and economic inequalities between them. It is with this economic aspect of liberal equality that this chapter is concerned, rather than liberal equality in the more general and abstract sense of equal concern for persons.[2] The term "liberal equality" (and

I am grateful to Cheryl Misak for helpful comments on earlier drafts, and to Samuel Freeman for numerous discussions on this topic.

[1] For one discussion on how libertarianism is distinct from liberalism, see Freeman (2001).

[2] Dworkin (2000), Sen (1992), and Kymlicka (1990) have noted that all plausible political philosophies must begin from some presumption that all persons are entitled to equal concern. Where different conceptions differ is in how each interprets what equal concern entails. For discussions on liberal equality more generally, see Gutmann (1980) and Beitz (1989).

its cognates such as "liberal egalitarianism", etc.) will thus refer specifically to economic and social equality unless otherwise qualified.[3]

Discussions of liberal equality, and also of egalitarian justice more generally, are very much in the mainstream in the current debate. Yet this has not always been so, and it is no exaggeration to say that the philosophical industry on distributive equality was spurred on by the publication in 1971 of John Rawls's *A Theory of Justice* (1971; rev. edn. 1999). For much of the twentieth century, Anglo-American analytic philosophy took the role of philosophy to be that of linguistic and conceptual analysis, and to the extent that moral philosophy is studied by analytic philosophers, it is to clarify the meaning of moral terms such as "good", "right", and so on. Normative questions, such as how to envision a just society, questions that were standard subjects for much of the history of philosophy from the ancients onwards, were regarded as questions falling outside the purview of philosophy. As is so often said, one great influence of *Theory* was that it reversed that trend and revitalized moral and political philosophy within the analytic tradition by showing how substantive questions, such as what are the appropriate principles of justice for a society, could be systematically and rigorously examined. In reviving moral and political philosophy, Rawls consequently set the terms of debate for much of the ensuing analytic discussion on justice and distributive equality. A particular enduring influence of Rawls, that which is of immediate concern here, is that of showing how liberalism can have an egalitarian feature. Given Rawls's impact on the philosophical landscape, one might say that a unique contribution of American philosophy is the systematic advancement of a liberalism that takes distributive equality seriously; or a liberalism that "pays moral tribute to the socialist critique", as Amy Gutmann puts it (Gutmann 1989: 339; quoted in Lukes 1991: 52).

This spurt of interest in egalitarian justice, and in liberal equality in particular, in American philosophy was further fueled by other influential contributions by American philosophers. Ronald Dworkin, whose writings on liberal equality (e.g. 1981*a* and *b*), some reprinted in revised form in *Sovereign Virtue* (2000), is a notable example. Other American contributors to the egalitarian discourse include Elizabeth Anderson, Richard Arneson, Joshua Cohen, Samuel Freeman, Martha Nussbaum (2000, 2006), Thomas Nagel,

---

[3] Hence it is useful, as a convenient shorthand, to refer to the economic aspect of justice as "economic justice", and the aspect of justice dealing with the distribution of political and civil liberties as "political justice", when a distinction between these two "coordinate roles" of justice (as Rawls puts it) is desirable (Rawls 1971; Dworkin 2000: 12; also Beitz 1999*a*).

John Roemer (1996), T. M. Scanlon (1975, 1986, 2003), and Samuel Scheffler among others. From across the Atlantic, analytic philosophers (mainly based in the United Kingdom, but not limited to it) such as G. A. Cohen, David Miller, and Philippe Van Parijs (1995), and economists like Amartya Sen enriched the discussion considerably. Given this influence from abroad, it is perhaps difficult now to identify a distinctively American debate on liberal equality as opposed to a distinctive Anglo-American take on the topic. Still, it is important to notice that many of the defining issues in liberal equality are framed by Rawls's theory, and that the topic of liberal equality is very much a staple topic in American philosophy today.

In addition to the internal discussion among liberal egalitarians about how best to conceptualize the ideal of liberal equality, there is also a lively ongoing external debate between liberal egalitarians and critics. Libertarians like Robert Nozick, specifically responding to Rawls (Nozick 1975; also Narveson 2001), reject liberal equality as too intrusive on individual liberty, on the one side. On the other flank, Marxists reject liberal equality as insufficiently egalitarian (e.g. Nielsen 1985). And more recently, a growing number of commentators are evaluating the prospects of extending liberal egalitarian justice to the international domain. Here the early works of Charles Beitz and Thomas Pogge, themselves beginning from Rawlsian premises, provide the reference point (Beitz 1999*b* [1979]; Pogge 1989).

My focus is on the internal debate; specifically, I will survey three fundamental questions of liberal equality that have received considerable attention in the literature. The first question is the most familiar and well-rehearsed one. It is the question that Amartya Sen has famously posed as "Equality of What?" (Sen 1980), or as Gerald A. Cohen (1989) puts it, what is the "currency" of egalitarian justice? That is, with respect to what should liberal egalitarians be egalitarians about? This is also referred to as the question of *equalisandum*—i.e. the object with which an egalitarian principle is concerned. This is one of the early substantive debates within liberal equality that Rawls's theory spawned.

The second question is: Where is the "site" or locus of egalitarian justice (cf. G. A. Cohen 1997)? For some liberals, egalitarian distributive principles are directed primarily at the background political, social, and economic institutions of society—what Rawls calls the basic structure of society—that determine persons' entitlements. On this view, individuals may do as they wish within the rules of institutions so long as the justness of institutions is preserved. Yet others, like G. A. Cohen (1992, 1997, 2000), reject this institutional focus of justice, holding instead that liberal egalitarian principles should have broader scope, and that in a truly just egalitarian society, personal choices and conduct within the rules of institutions ought to come under some egalitarian requirements as well.

The third question is: Why does equality matter? That is, what is it that morally motivates the concern for distributive justice in a social order, and relatedly, what is the point of a distributive principle? Take two contesting positions in the current literature. Is the motivating concern of distributive egalitarianism that of mitigating or discounting the effects of luck on persons' life prospects generally (Arneson, G. A. Cohen, Dworkin)? Or is the motivating concern of distributive equality more specifically and narrowly that of sustaining the appropriate kinds of relationship between persons who are fellow democratic citizens (Anderson, Scheffler, Freeman)?

To stylize somewhat, we may refer to these questions of liberal equality as the *what*, *where*, and *why* questions. Together they address the fundamentals of liberal equality. Critically surveying these questions, then, can provide one entry point into the current debate on liberal equality.

The what, where, and why questions are, of course, related, in that the answer an egalitarian gives to one will influence how she addresses the other two. But they are nonetheless distinct questions, and a response to one does not generate an immediate and direct response to the other two. For example, as we will see, liberal egalitarians who agree on why equality matters need not agree on where equality matters and/or equality of what. Thus looking at each of these questions separately has the virtue of helping us see more precisely where different liberal egalitarians agree and disagree with each other, thereby allowing for a more perspicuous analysis of the different alternative conceptions of liberal equality. It also allows us to contemplate different combinations of responses to these questions for the purpose of coming up with the most reasonable overall account of liberal equality.[4]

Given Rawls's importance to the contemporary debate on liberal equality, and especially given, as we will see later below, that the debates on the what, where, and why of liberal equality have their genesis as reactions to Rawls's own views on these matters, it will be useful to begin by noting some of the main features of Rawls's theory of justice.

---

[4] While these questions are distinct from, and do not directly address, another important question, the question of *how to distribute* (i.e., what principle of distribution ought to be operational), they do influence how we conceptualize an appropriate distributive principle. But this is a question that is more derivative of how we address the other three questions; at any rate, I will put this matter to one side.

II. Rawls's Justice as Fairness

This is not the place to offer an explication of Rawls's theory that can do justice to its complexity and sophistication. For the present purpose, I will simply mention some central features of Rawls's method and the conclusions that he derives from his method.[5]

Rawls's grand aim in *A Theory of Justice* is to advance a systematic alternative conception of justice to that of utilitarianism, which was then the dominant moral theory in the Anglo-American tradition, and he attempts to do this by recalling the social contract tradition (1971: 11 ff.; 1999: 10 ff.). Under Rawls's deployment of the social contract method, the parties in the initial contracting situation—what Rawls calls the "original position"—are conceived to be symmetrically situated, and free and equal. The question the parties in the original position are asking is this: what are the appropriate principles of justice for regulating the "basic structure" of their society: that is, the fundamental social, economic, and political institutions of society? That the parties are symmetrically placed in the "original position" means that no one can propose principles of justice to his or her advantage during the deliberative process. This fairness condition of the original position is encapsulated by situating the parties behind an imaginary "veil of ignorance" where they have no knowledge of specific contingent facts about themselves, such as their conceptions of the good life, their status and social class, their natural talents, and so on. Thus, in the original position so constructed, no deliberator may, for instance, use her superior social position to compel others to accept her idea of justice; or, to take another example, no party will be able to forward a conception of justice favorable to her particular conception of the good life (since all parties are deprived of information about their social standing and conceptions of the good). The basic idea here in Rawls's social contract methodology is that principles of justice agreed to by parties in an initial position that is fair will also themselves be fair. Hence Rawls refers to his theory of justice as "justice as fairness" (1971: 12; 1999: 11).

Since the original position with the veil of ignorance is a hypothetical construction, each one of us can imagine ourselves as a party to this deliberation about justice. So what principles of justice would we rationally and reasonably commit ourselves to under Rawls's social contract? Rawls reasons that between

---

[5] For recent excellent introductions, see Freeman (2007) and Pogge (2007).

his proposed two principles of justice ("justice as fairness") and plausible conceptions of utilitarian justice, we would prefer his principles of justice to utilitarianism. One formulation of the two principles is as follows:

(a) Each person has the same indefeasible claim to a fully adequate scheme of equal basic liberties, which scheme is compatible with the same scheme of liberties for all.

(b) Social and economic inequalities are to satisfy two conditions: first, they are to be attached to offices and positions open to all under conditions of fair equality of opportunity; and second, they are to be to the greatest benefit of the least advantaged members of society (the difference principle).[6]

The first principle protects the civil and political rights of citizens consistent with the commitments of classical liberalism. It is the second principle, the distributive principle serving to regulate social and economic inequalities, and its celebrated "difference principle", that is directly relevant to the present discussion. The difference principle, to specify, holds that inequalities under a social arrangement are acceptable only if there is no feasible alternative arrangement under which the least advantaged can do better. Together, the two principles mark a departure from classical liberalism by incorporating an egalitarian distributive commitment within the liberal conception of justice.

Rawls's general contribution to political philosophy can thus be appreciated in two parts. One is the social contract methodology that he offers as a systematic alternative to utilitarianism; the second concerns the principles that he proposes under this method. Both the method and the principles have generated much debate and discussion, and continue to be widely influential (Daniels 1975; Freeman 2003). This oft-cited remark of Nozick sums up Rawls's impact neatly: "Political philosophers now must either work within Rawls's theory or explain why not" (1975: 183).

The reasoning process in the original position leading to the two principles is complex and multi-faceted (Rawls 1971: 150 ff.; 1999: 130 ff.; 2001: part 3). It involves two pair-wise comparisons, between the two principles of "justice as fairness" in each case and two different conceptions of utilitarian social justice. Rawls refers to these as the "two fundamental comparisons" (2001: 94). Very briefly, under the first fundamental comparison, the parties in the original position are to choose between justice as fairness and "the principle of average utility". Because the principle of average utility simply aims to maximize

---

[6] The formulation here is from Rawls 2001: 42–3.

average utility without any direct regard for the distribution of utility among persons, rational agents behind the veil of ignorance, not knowing their actual place in society and not wanting to risk all for the sake of possible gain, will decide in accordance with the maximin rule—that is, that of maximizing the worst possible outcome (Rawls 2001: 97–9). Accordingly, they will choose justice as fairness with its distributive commitment over the principle of average utility.

But while maximin reasoning supports justice as fairness over the principle of average utility, it need not support justice as fairness over other plausible conceptions of utilitarian justice. Hence a second fundamental comparison is introduced. Under this second pair-wise comparison, the parties are asked to choose between justice as fairness and the principle of *restricted* utility (Rawls 2001: 120). Since the principle of restricted utility maximizes average utility only above the threshold of a guaranteed basic minimum for all, parties behind the veil of ignorance need not necessarily find it irrational to accept this utilitarian principle. A rational deliberator may accept the risk of adopting such a principle for society given that there is a tolerable limit to how much she can lose out in this gamble. So the maximin rule is quite indecisive here. But considerations of reciprocity, stability, and publicity suggest that justice as fairness, with its distributive egalitarian commitment, would be preferred over the principle of restricted utility (Rawls 2001: 120 ff.). For instance, while it could be rational (or at least not irrational) for a person to want a social order in which average utility is maximized once a guaranteed minimum for all is in place, as under the principle of restricted utility, such an arrangement could allow for inequalities among citizens that offend against the ideal of reciprocity appropriate to a democratic society (Rawls 2001: 124). Thus parties in the original position who see themselves as free and equal members of a democratic society in which the ideal of reciprocity is to be honored will find the principle of restricted utility inferior as a conception of social justice (even if it is not necessarily irrational for a self-interested person to adopt such a principle). Under the second fundamental comparison, it is the parties' assumed reasonableness, rather than rationality, it seems, that is decisive.

So much for a brief background. Three additional points are of immediate relevance to the present discussion, which will be explained more fully below. Rawls takes (i) the *equalisandum* of distributive justice to be what he calls "primary goods"; he takes (ii) the site of distributive justice to be the basic structure of society; and he believes that (iii) equality matters because of the ideal of reciprocity as it is understood in a democratic political society.

III. Equality of What?

Rawls takes what he calls "primary goods" to be the appropriate metric of distributive equality. Primary goods for Rawls are "all-purpose goods" that any rational person needs in order to pursue her conception of the good life (1971: 62, 92). These primary goods include political and civil liberties and free choice of occupation, the powers of prerogatives of offices, income and wealth, and what Rawls calls the social bases of self-respect (Rawls 1971: 62, 92; 2001: 58–9). Of relevance to distributive equality are the primary goods of income and wealth. Rawls's difference principle—which holds that inequalities between persons are acceptable when the worst-off representative individuals benefit most from the inequalities—defines the worst-off by reference to persons' income and wealth combined, and consequently, the metric of equality—that is, the thing the unequal distribution of which the difference principle serves to regulate—is the income and wealth of persons.

Rawls's position on "equality of what" may be characterized as a species of resource egalitarianism, in that what is important for Rawls are the all-purpose means or resources that persons have with which to pursue their various admissible ends in life, whatever these may be. In this regard, Rawls and Dworkin (2000) share the same general position on what the most appropriate metric of equality is. Yet, as we will see below, while both Rawls and Dworkin are resource egalitarians, they hold different views as to what the relevant resources are. But first, let us turn to some criticisms of resource egalitarianism as a whole.

According to Amartya Sen, resource egalitarians like Rawls and Dworkin are working with the wrong "evaluative space" (1980, 1992). For Sen, the proper metric of equality is not resources, like income and wealth, *pace* Rawls, but persons' "capability" to achieve certain human ends or human "functionings". Functionings are the different combinations of "beings and doings" that are constitutive of a flourishing and meaningful human life, which can include such basic elements as being well nourished and living a normal healthy life, to more complex ones such as having self-respect and being able to participate as a productive and participating member of society (1992: 4–5, 39, ch. 3). Focusing on income and wealth as the metric of equality is inadequate if the motivating concern of liberal egalitarians is to secure the freedom of persons to pursue their ends in life. This is because persons differ with respect to their personal ability to transform or convert their income and wealth into all-purpose means with which to pursue their ends. For instance, a disabled person who has an equivalent amount of income and wealth as an able-bodied compatriot, will in fact have less with which to pursue her goals in life, since she will have to use part of her resources to acquire special services and assistance just to get by in ways that the able-bodied person can take for granted (Sen 1992: 22, 27). As he puts it, "what we can or cannot do, can or cannot achieve, depends not just on our incomes but also on the variety of physical and social characteristics that affect our lives and make us what we are" (Sen 1992: 28). Thus, because of the inequalities in the personal capability of persons to actually convert resources into ends or functionings, focusing on income and wealth misses the real object of inequality. Given the differences in persons' actual capability to convert primary goods into ends, Sen (1980) famously remarks that Rawls's commitment to equalizing primary goods amounts to a form of "fetishism". This is an argument that has also been recently developed by Martha Nussbaum (2006) with powerful illustrations from the problem of justice for persons with disabilities. But for the purpose of this survey, I focus on Sen's original challenge.

Sen acknowledges that resource egalitarians like Rawls and Dworkin are correct to reject equality of welfare which would aim to equalize persons' achieved well-being defined in some way. For instance, Dworkin has argued that equality of welfare is prone to the expensive tastes and the offensive tastes objections. Why should a person who has set out deliberately to cultivate an expensive taste, and so who now needs more resources to achieve a comparable level of welfare compared to others, be entitled to more resources (Dworkin 2000: ch. 1; also G. A. Cohen 1989: 912–16)? Equality of welfare also seems absurdly to require the compensating of persons who, because of their objectionable political preferences, find certain progressive social policies a compromise on their personal well-being. A racist, for example, may be less happy than others living in a non-segregated society. Moreover, equality of welfare cannot account for what Sen calls the problem of "entrenched deprivation" (Sen 1992: 55). That is, a person who has lower life expectations because of her disadvantaged background circumstances may be able to achieve a similar level of well-being with fewer resources than another person who is used to more privileges. Equality of welfare will, in this case, allow fewer resources to be assigned to the socially disadvantaged because of her easier to satisfy welfare. But this is, of course, intuitively perverse.

Thus, what is of moral concern is not whether persons actually achieve well-being or certain functionings or ends (which can include well-being), but their freedom with which to achieve well-being or ends. But, according to Sen, while resource egalitarians are right to reject welfare as the response to "equality of what?", they have failed to locate the correct evaluative space of equality. If what is at stake is the freedom of persons to achieve their ends, then what needs to be subject to a distributive ideal is not persons' access to resources but the capability of persons to utilize these resources effectively. The metric of capability rightly targets the "actual freedom" that a person has to pursue her ends or achieve certain functionings, whereas the metric of resources merely addresses persons' "means to freedom" (Sen 1992: 81). The reason for this misallocation on the part of resource egalitarianism, on Sen's diagnosis, is that while Rawls and other resource egalitarians are rightly sensitive to what Sen calls "inter-end" variations among persons (i.e. the differences in persons' conceptions of the good and ends), and hence are rightly resistant to equality of welfare, they overlook "inter-personal" variations (i.e. persons' different capabilities for transforming primary goods into "actual freedoms" to achieve ends), and hence fail to see that resource equality does not do enough (Sen 1992: 85, 87, 26–8).

Rawls's response to Sen's challenge is multi-pronged and addresses different possible interpretations of variations in personal capability (Rawls 2001: 68–176; also Freeman 2006a: 411–21; Daniels 1990). But I will recount only the part of his response that specifically targets Sen's claim that the currency of primary goods cannot account for personal variations in capability due to ill health, disabilities, and the like. Rawls does not deny that in a well-ordered society persons' share of primary goods ought to be adjusted against such severe personal setbacks and lack of capability. But he thinks that the "flexibility" of the notion of primary goods allows for such adjustments (Rawls 2001: 171 ff.). First, primary goods are flexible, in that they are (by nature of the original position reasoning with the veil of ignorance, where particular histories and information and contingencies are left out) left under-specified. What specific entitlements persons have in virtue of their basic rights and liberties that the original position reasoning secures will have to be determined and detailed at a later stage (when the veil of ignorance is lifted) in the quest for justice: namely, what Rawls calls "the legislative stage". It is at this stage that the identified general principles of justice are to be applied against the specificities and details of a particular society. The basic rights and liberties of the disabled *qua* citizens will entitle them to a series of special social and public support services; but since working out what these social entitlements are would require having in hand certain facts and details (about the specific kinds of individual needs and corresponding support and compensation needed), the special rights of the disabled are determined not at the original position (where only general facts are available), but only at the legislative stage, where the principles of justice are implemented for society. The key point here, however, is that there is thus a built-in flexibility as to the content of persons' specific entitlements as specified by the index of primary goods. Moreover, given that the index of primary goods is an index of persons' expectations "over the course of a complete life" (Rawls 2001: 172), a person's actual allocation of primary goods at a given point in time can be adjusted to accommodate differences in needs due to accidents, illnesses, and so on over the normal course of her complete life. This longitudinal allocation of primary goods is another way in which an index of primary goods is believed to be flexible enough to accommodate differences in personal capabilities.

Primary goods are also flexible in another important way: the primary goods of income and wealth need not be defined narrowly as "*personal* income and *private* wealth", but can be more broadly and flexibly understood to include public goods and services (as in public health care, special public provisions of different kinds for the disabled). What this means, then, is that a disabled person's overall income and wealth will include not only her *personal* income and wealth but also the various special social assistance and support that a just society ought to provide for her (Rawls 2001: 172). The language of primary goods can require that a society provide such special assistance to its disabled members if the primary goods of income and wealth are understood in this more expansive social sense. Focusing on income and wealth need not be neglectful of, and disadvantageous to, the disabled if the extra costs of her living a (as close as possible to) normal life are taken account of in this way. Thus Sen's, and also Nussbaum's, well-taken point that disabled persons need more resources just to achieve equivalent functionings as able-bodied persons can be accounted for under resource egalitarianism. If the disabled do receive special social compensation and infrastructural support, focusing on income and wealth as the metric of equality does not necessarily disadvantage them. Again, the crucial point here is that what kind and how much public services to provide for the disabled will have to be determined at the legislative stage, for such policy decisions require information not available at the original position (Freeman 2006a).

So, if Rawlsian primary goods can be adjusted to accommodate the special needs of persons with disabilities (and other cases of special needs), the distinctiveness of Sen's capability approach becomes less obvious. Indeed,

Sen acknowledges that if the index of primary goods has this flexibility, and if interpersonal variations can in fact be accommodated at the legislative stage, as Rawls suggests, then "the force of [Sen's] criticism" is reduced (Sen 1992: 83–4, n. 23).

As mentioned above, equality of welfare is implausible in the eyes of many egalitarian theorists—among other things, on account of the problems of expensive and offensive tastes. But egalitarians such as Arneson who are partial to individual welfare yet cognizant of the problems associated with welfare egalitarianism have proposed that it is the *opportunity* for welfare that is to be the metric of equality (Arneson 1989). Focusing on "opportunity" for welfare escapes the offensive and expensive tastes objections, for here we are not held up by a person's expensive tastes that he has deliberately cultivated or required to make accommodation for a person's offensive taste. Rather, we are interested only in the opportunity sets that are available to persons in their pursuit of welfare, and the aim of distributive justice is to equalize these opportunity sets among persons. A person who has the same opportunity set for welfare will have no grounds for complaint if she finds that upon schooling herself into a finer lifestyle, that opportunity set is no longer adequate for her to achieve her previously felt level of well-being. What is objectionable is when some persons, through no choice of their own, have more limited opportunities for welfare than others. Yet, in spite of taking opportunities to be the metric of equality, the advantage of this position, according to its proponents, is that it does not lose sight of the fact that it is well-being that ultimately matters to persons. G. A. Cohen (1989) has also advanced a similar position, although carefully qualified. For Cohen, it is ultimately persons' "access to advantage" that is the currency of egalitarian justice.[7]

Interposing the notion of "opportunity" as an intermediary, so to speak, between the ideals of equality and welfare seems to successfully sidestep the problems that straight-off welfare egalitarians face. Still, further arguments are needed to see if the metric of opportunity really captures a position that is truly distinct from that of resources. This will have to depend on what the relevant opportunity sets are for opportunity egalitarians, and whether, importantly, there are ways of evaluating comparative worth of opportunity sets that the language of "resources" (under some plausible and

[7] Cohen prefers "access" to "opportunity", because the latter seems to suggest only external and social conditions, whereas the former can include personal abilities as well; and he prefers "advantage", which is a more encompassing notion, to "welfare", because he holds that all that matters for persons is not just welfare, though welfare does matter (1989: 916–17).

appropriate definition of resources) does not cover. For instance, one might think that the kinds of social opportunities that the opportunity egalitarians are concerned with are reducible to income and wealth, especially if the category of income and wealth is construed to include publicly funded services and goods (as discussed above), and hence already accounted for under Rawls's primary goods approach. The task ahead for opportunity egalitarians is to show how the ideal of equality of opportunity picks out a position distinct from resource egalitarianism without reverting back into simple welfare egalitarianism.

From the above, we see that there is room for debate as to what are the relevant resources for resource egalitarianism. Dworkin believes that Rawls's focus on income and wealth is too limited an account of resources. For one, in a similar vein to Sen, he argues that Rawls's difference principle, given its fixation with income and wealth, inadvertently and pervasively penalizes the disabled. Consider the case of a disabled person who through sheer application and determination does better in terms of income and wealth compared to a less ambitious able-bodied person (who is nonetheless still a participating and contributing member of society). By concentrating solely on income and wealth as the relevant resources, and by defining the standing of persons in terms of income and wealth, the difference principle will have the effect of transferring resources from the better-off but disabled person to the worse-off able-bodied person. Yet this seems perverse, for it penalizes, so to speak, the hard-working disabled person to subsidize the less ambitious able-bodied one, when the former is indeed the more unfortunate one (Dworkin 2000: 115–16). But, unlike Sen, Dworkin does not draw the conclusion that we need an alternative to the metric of resources. Instead, he argues that what we need is an alternative understanding of resources to Rawls's primary goods. For Dworkin, resource egalitarians should understand by resources not just income and wealth, *pace* Rawls, but also the various kinds of "personal resources" such as persons' natural endowments, talents, intelligence, and so on (2000: 115–16).[8] Once personal capacities are considered as among the resources to be distributed equally, resource egalitarianism can be sensitized to the differences between personal ability that Rawls's focus on income and wealth allegedly neglects. For this reason, Dworkin also thinks that his account

---

[8] Indeed, one of Dworkin's responses to Sen is that resources understood in this way will take care of the concerns that motivate Sen's capability approach and also Cohen's equality of access to advantage (Dworkin 2000: 299–303).

of resource equality can address Sen's concern about differences in personal capability (Dworkin 2000: ch. 7).[9]

As implied above, part of the force of Dworkin's objection to Rawls presupposes that Rawls's motivation for distributive equality is based on the idea that society ought to mitigate the effects of luck on persons' life prospects (a topic to which we will turn below). Thus, accordingly, the difference principle as construed by Rawls, with its focus on income and wealth, fails to live up to its own motivating goal. This argument has also been further developed by Kymlicka (1990: 78–9). But this particular aspect of the objection need not faze Rawls if he does not subscribe to luck egalitarianism; and, as I will note below, Rawls is not a luck egalitarian in the relevant sense.

Still, even if Rawls does not subscribe to luck egalitarianism as the motivation for why equality matters, it does seem intuitively unfair if a disabled person is deemed to be the more advantaged member of society for the purpose of redistribution simply because she has more income and wealth on account of her perseverance and determination. But Rawls's response to Sen, as discussed above, can be modified to address Dworkin's and Kymlicka's worry. If society provides its disabled members with various appropriate degrees of support, assistance, and exemptions, then these must be factored in as part of the disabled person's overall income and wealth entitlements, as noted earlier. Rawls's scheme need not penalize the ambitious disabled person compared to the less ambitious able-bodied one if the former enjoys publicly provided support on account of her disability in addition to enjoying the rewards of her ambition. Utilizing the index of income and wealth will appear to overlook the problem of disability, and be seemingly unfair to persons with special needs, only if we take income and wealth to consist only of *personal* income and wealth, and not take account of the public and social support that a just society ought to provide for its specially needy citizens.

---

[9] For Dworkin, the right balance between individual choice and circumstance (due to differences in personal ability, etc.) is best worked out through the mechanism of an imaginary insurance market (that operates in an initial condition of background equality). The insurance market will afford persons a choice as to how to handle possible vagaries in the distribution of natural talents, for example. The lower and upper bounds of compensation the average persons would rationally take out, for any potential shortfall on this hypothetical scenario identify the range of social support that persons are entitled to in the actual world (2000: ch. 2). This is a complex theory that I will not get into. The relevant point here is that Dworkin arrives at a distributive principle different from Rawls's in part because he treats talents as resources and because of the way he seeks to "neutralize the effects of differential talents" (2000: 91).

Although "equality of what?" is the best scrutinized of the three questions I am surveying, it is far from being a settled issue, and will continue to engage the attention of egalitarians. I have tried in the above to identify some of the key important points raised in the debate, as well as possible directions for further discussion.

IV. Where Does Equality Matter?

Rawls famously writes that "the primary subject of justice is the basic structure of society, or more exactly, the way in which the major social institutions distribute fundamental rights and duties and determine the division of advantages from social cooperation" (1971: 7; 1999: 6–7). That is, the principles of justice are aimed primarily at the basic social, economic, and political institutions of society, and not at the choices and decisions of individuals within the rules of institutions. On this view of the subject-matter of justice, then, the site of distributive equality is principally the background institutions of society. This means that the commitment to distributive equality is fundamentally a commitment on the part of members of society to order and organize the basic institutions of their society against certain distributive principles. Thus, for Rawls, society's basic institutions are to be structured in such a way that any resulting inequalities in persons' fundamental claims are acceptable only where there is fair equality of opportunity and where there are no alternative feasible institutional arrangements in which the worst-off will benefit more (the difference principle). But this institutional focus also means that persons are not expected to regulate their day-to-day decisions and actions against these egalitarian principles. On the contrary, persons may be left free to pursue ends that are egalitarian in neither motivation nor outcome within the rules of institutions properly regulated by egalitarian principles. As Rawls puts it, "within the framework of background justice set up by the basic structure, individuals and associations may do as they wish insofar as the rules of institutions permit" (2001: 50; also Nagel 1991).

On this institutional egalitarian view, as we may call it, egalitarian justice has a very specific locus—the basic structure, or the background institutions of society, is where equality matters. But why this special and exclusive focus on the basic structure or the background political, social, and economic institutions of society? One reason Rawls gives is that the effects of the basic structure on persons' life chances are profound and pervasive from the start (1971: 7–8; 1999: 7; 2001: 55). The basic structure determines fundamentally persons' basic entitlements and rights, and hence the life prospects of persons living under it. A just society would then want to regulate this background condition to ensure that persons' fundamental entitlements are not improperly influenced by contingencies like their social class, native endowment, "good or ill fortune", and the like (2001: 55).

But the fact that the basic structure affects the lives of persons profoundly and pervasively explains why the basic structure is a *necessary* subject of social justice; it does not show that it is also *sufficient* to focus on it. Now Rawls also says that focusing on the basic structure allows us "to regard distributive justice as a case of background procedural justice", which consequently frees society from having to regulate each and every personal transaction within the rules of institutions (2001: 54). But this does not yet completely justify the limited institutional focus, for one may still ask why it is the case that an ideally just society need not subject personal transactions to the demands of justice, but may instead seek to provide space for non-egalitarian pursuits within just institutional rules.

To fully understand Rawls's reason for this exclusive focus on institutions, we need to turn to his starting assumptions about the role of justice and some of the more specific moral and social assumptions informing his idea of justice. For Rawls, justice is an important social virtue because it defines the appropriate social background conditions against which persons can freely and equally pursue their different ends in life or their conceptions of the good human life (2001: 2–3, 40–1). These personal pursuits include not just asocial private ends but also a range of social ends and commitments like those associated with familial relations, friendship, and other forms of group relations that people normally have. It is because of the value and moral importance of such personal pursuits that society ought to ensure that each and every one is able to pursue his or her conception of the good freely and equally, and not be unfairly disadvantaged. As Rawls puts it, "while justice draws the limits and the good shows the point, justice cannot draw the limit too narrowly" (1993: 174). This remark suggests that justice is important because it defines the boundaries within which people may pursue their own conceptions of the good life, that give value and point to their lives, and that it must do this without being too restrictive of the good.

That social justice identifies the parameters within which persons may pursue their ends but does not determine the ends themselves is in turn due to the presumption that there is a diversity of morally worthy ends or goods that persons can have reasons to value, and that these ends or goods need not be necessarily egalitarian in their motivation or effect. Put another way, not all that is morally good and valuable is reducible to, or subsumable under, a given set of principles of justice, such as Rawls's two principles. More particularly, not all that persons have reasons to value is reducible to, or subsumable under, an egalitarian principle in the sense that the egalitarian ideal constitutes the final and ultimate good. For example, the good of friendship or kinship ties need not be reducible to certain principles of egalitarian justice. Rather, egalitarian justice is just one value among others.

It is this presumption of "moral pluralism" that justifies the institutional approach in Rawls's view (Scheffler 2006; Nagel 1991; Freeman 2006b: ch. 6). Because of this presumption, one relevant question has to be this: how is it possible to reconcile the demands of egalitarian justice, on the one side, and the various moral demands of personal life, on the other? The institutional approach provides one solution to this problem. Taking the principles of justice to be concerned primarily with the basic institutions of society allows for a division of moral labor between the demands of justice, on the one side, and the demands of personal commitments and ends, on the other. The institutional focus thus attempts a reconciliation of these two potentially competing demands in the following way: in the name of justice, persons have the duty to establish and support just institutions; but within the rules of these institutions, persons may freely pursue their ends. They may "do as they wish" insofar as the rules of institutions permit, secure in the knowledge that so long as they pursue their ends within just rules, justice for society is preserved. The institutional focus thus provides a way of balancing the pursuit of egalitarian justice, on the one hand, and personal pursuits, on the other. And it achieves this balance while preserving the dominance of justice—what counts as admissible personal pursuits is given by the rules of institutions as regulated by principles of justice. That is, justice frames admissible personal pursuits, and the basic structure provides one means of framing.

In several influential writings, G. A. Cohen takes exception to this limited focus of social justice (G. A. Cohen 1992, 1997, 2000; also Murphy 1999). Cohen argues that justice should be concerned not only with the background institutions of society but also with the choices of persons within the rules of institutions, with their decisions within the rules of institutions. After all, wouldn't real egalitarians not only want just institutional rules but also be prepared to subject their personal choices and decisions to some egalitarian considerations? A truly egalitarian and just society, for Cohen, thus will not only have just institutions but also exhibit what he calls an "ethos" of justice (and that will be reflected by the decisions of persons in "the thick of daily life" within the rules of just institutions). The institutional approach, according to Cohen, seems to be "an evasion" of the burdens of justice (2000: 4).

Taking Rawls as the representative institutional egalitarian, Cohen draws attention to Rawls's difference principle to substantiate his claim that institutional egalitarianism evades the burdens of justice. The difference principle, to recall, permits inequalities so long as these inequalities are also to the advantage of the worst-off in society. There is thus an incentive provision built into the difference principle: the talented may be specially rewarded if this is what it takes to move them to benefit society. But is this not a case of catering to the acquisitiveness of the talented, wonders Cohen? In a society informed by an egalitarian ethos, the talented would not require the extra incentives in order to be inclined to provide the service, and so the worst-off would stand to benefit even more (since additional resources could be passed on to them instead of giving them to the talented as incentives). To be sure, Cohen accepts that the talented may need some incentives without which they could not "literally" do the job that is asked of them. This would include compensation for additional training and education that they may have to undergo, compensation if the work they are asked to do is indeed especially arduous, and so on; and these are incentives that Rawls also recognizes (Cohen 2000: 127; 1992). But Cohen's objection is that the difference principle allows also for what we may call "extra incentives"—that is, incentives that are asked for and paid out to the talented not because they literally need the extra rewards in order to be able to perform the needed task, but simply because of their "acquisitiveness". And this is a failure of justice, and a failing of the institutional approach's indifference to personal choice and decisions within the rules of institutions.

Cohen presents a very troubling criticism for institutional egalitarians. But perhaps his concern can be assuaged, at least with respect to Rawls's institutional egalitarianism. First, it is plausible, under Rawls's overall scheme, that the extra incentives that the talented can demand and actually receive are reduced drastically in an ideal society in which the difference principle operates in tandem with a principle of equal basic liberties and a principle of fair equality of opportunity. After discounting for discriminations of various sorts that involve violations of persons' basic liberties and inequality in opportunities, one can plausibly believe that the special skills required of certain professions need not be so scarce as to command the kind of market price that they tend to do in our society, with all its various forms of historic and background injustices. So, if the difference principle, with its incentive provision, is understood to be part of a package of principles of justice, and not as an isolated principle, the worry that it can allow acquisitive talented individuals to receive extra incentives over and above that which they need to do the socially beneficial job is perhaps addressed (Daniels 2003; Tan 2004*a*).

Another mitigating consideration is also available to Rawls: it is basic to the institutional view that just institutions can have educative effects on persons, and one can surmise that a society whose institutions live up to Rawlsian principles will be a society characterized by strong mutuality and reciprocity among its members. This, plausibly, would temper the acquisitiveness of the talented—their inculcated sense of solidarity with their fellow citizens can overcome whatever selfish acquisitiveness they would otherwise be prone to have. The fact that executives (just assuming for the sake of discussion that their service does somehow benefit the worst-off in society) in contemporary American society make outlandish demands for compensation, a situation that rightly troubles Cohen, may be due to certain deformations of their character as a result of living in a society with serious unjust background institutions. If there is this institutional causal explanation for personal selfishness, then in correcting for institutional failings, institutional egalitarianism must effectively tackle these problems of personal attitudes rather than be irresponsive to them (J. Cohen 2002).

Thus, the presumption that a just Rawlsian society will ensure equal protection of persons' liberties and fair equality of opportunity, and the presumption of the educative effects of just institutions on persons living under them, may go some way towards tempering the inequalities that the incentive provision in the difference principle can allow. If this is right, then Rawlsian institutional justice need not result in incentives-based inequalities to the degree characteristic of contemporary American life that rightly exercises Cohen and other egalitarians. The inequalities between the talented and the worst-off that an ideal Rawlsian society permits need not be as great as Cohen's criticism implies, Rawls's institutional focus notwithstanding.

Still one may object that the Rawlsian institutional approach allows for certain inequalities that need not exist in a society that is also informed by an egalitarian "ethos". Individuals with an egalitarian ethos will not take advantage of the incentive provision of the difference principle to demand incentives beyond that without which they could not *literally* do the socially beneficial job. After all, if they are true egalitarians, the skilled or talented will see that their worst-off compatriots stand to benefit even more should they, the talented, not make demands for any rewards beyond those that they literally need in order to provide the required services. Thus the institutional approach, in limiting the reach of justice in this way, still permits a residual inequality that would not exist in a society with an ethos of justice. Does this not show, then, that personal choices and attitudes do matter from the point of view of egalitarian justice? And does this not expose a limitation of the view that social justice is concerned only with the justice of institutions but not with personal conduct within the rules of institutions?

To examine this objection better, let us imagine a highly skilled surgeon (who we will assume contributes to societal good) who now wishes to abandon her career in medicine to pursue the arts. She has come to see the life of an artist, even a struggling and comparatively unsuccessful one, to be more valuable to her, given the overall conception of the good life she now has, and she holds this view even though she knows that her contribution to society as an artist will be quite limited. Thus, to remain a surgeon, she will incur a great personal opportunity cost: namely, that of not pursuing a life plan that she now finds more worthwhile and meaningful. Suppose, however, that society can offer her additional monetary compensation that, in her eyes, can offset the opportunity cost to her of practicing medicine. Should the artist/surgeon, if she is a true egalitarian, not require such enticement but be prepared to compromise her pursuits simply out of concern for the worst-off? Should she, were she a true egalitarian, not be willing to forgo her idea of the good without compensation for the sake of the worst-off in her society?

This example, rather than calling the institutional approach into question, affirms the importance of giving persons space within the rules of justice to pursue a meaningful personal life. Looking specifically at the difference principle, and the institutional approach to justice that it expresses, it is on account of the recognition of the importance of the freedom of occupational choices, and the recognition of the diverse valuable ends and conceptions of the good life that persons have, that Rawls provides room for incentives in his principle. A just society will need persons with special skills to perform socially beneficial tasks; but a just society has also to recognize that persons are free to pursue a diversity of ends, including occupational choices, that need not have any egalitarian consequence. Offering incentives to talented persons to take on certain socially useful professions is a legitimate way of re-weighting the opportunity sets available to such persons (Rawls 2001: 78; Williams 1981; Estlund 1998; and Tan 2004*a*). It provides a means to entice persons, like our fictional artist/surgeon, to freely take on or stay in a socially beneficial profession in spite of other independently morally valuable and acceptable alternatives they might have.

It is thus the belief that persons ought to be free to pursue a variety of personal commitments, and that there is a plurality of valuable ends, including things like career and occupational choices as well as other social commitments like familial ones, that motivates the institutional approach. The aim of justice, as said, is to secure the appropriate social conditions in which persons may pursue their various ends and conceptions of the good freely and fairly. As Freeman writes, "The primary reason Rawls builds incentives into the difference principle is not to encourage capitalist self-seeking but to accommodate the plurality of goods and citizens' freedom to determine and pursue their conception of the good" (Freeman 2006*b*: 12; Scheffler 2006). If we accept with Rawls (and many modern moral and political philosophers do) the idea of the plurality of goods—that is, that there are various morally worthy ends and goods that persons may pursue that need not be subsumed under one unified account of what the good is—it is not so clear that allowing individuals appropriate space within the rules of just institutions to pursue their ends and structuring a scheme of incentives to entice persons to take on socially needed roles represents an evasion of the burdens of justice. On the contrary, it serves the point of justice: namely, to ensure that persons are able freely to pursue their different valuable ends. In the end, then, whether the institutional approach is defensible hinges on how we understand the unity or disunity of value and the nature of human moral agency (Nagel 1979; Pogge 2000; cf. Murphy 1999).

The above discussion of incentives assumes that the incentive schemes are offered in a society with more or less just and stable institutions. That is, the issue was whether a just society has to have more than just institutions; and the institutional approach holds that when there are just institutional rules, persons are free to pursue their own ends within these rules. But this relationship between personal pursuits and justice quite clearly changes when there are no just institutions and institutional rules to speak of, or when existing just institutions are under clear and present threat. In such cases, the natural duty that persons have to establish, support, and maintain just institutions may mean that individuals will have to forgo personal pursuits that they would otherwise be free to enjoy under more propitious circumstances. For instance, a society whose basic structure is under threat because of unjustified outside aggression may plausibly conscript its members to contribute in different ways to the just cause of defending society and its basic institutions. Or, to take another case, an outlaw society, whose basic institutions are severely unjust, may be one in which its members can be expected to put personal pursuits on hold while they work towards restoring justice in their society. Finally, to use the above example of the aspiring artist-cum-surgeon, consider a state of medical emergency in which the surgeon's services are urgently needed. Here it would be a strain to say that this artist/surgeon remains within her rights to refuse to serve unless given appropriate incentives. A just person would see in these cases that the urgent need of society—namely, that of securing basic justice—has priority over her own personal ends, and the primacy of justice that defines the terms of acceptable personal conduct will also require certain personal sacrifices when justice itself is under threat.

So the claim that a just society may allow persons freely to pursue ends within the rules of its institutions is a claim that applies within "ideal theory"—that is, where there exist just institutions that are stable and secure, and where there is compliance. Under non-ideal conditions, where these institutions do not exist, or where their existence is under threat, this claim need not hold. For example, in societies marked by severe distributional inequality because of the lack of appropriate institutional commitments, it is harder to say that persons may freely pursue non-egalitarian ends and still profess to be committed egalitarians. Given these existing unjust inequalities, one would expect real egalitarians to be more willing to take on more personal sacrifices for the sake of promoting egalitarian justice in their society. This is where the force of G. A. Cohen's criticism is really felt. But this concern is consistent with the institutional approach to justice, which accepts that there is a primary duty on all persons to support and maintain just egalitarian institutions. It is only when such institutions are antecedently in place that persons may go on to do as they wish within the rules of institutions and be secure in the knowledge that background justice is preserved.[10]

---

[10] In the "General Appendix" of *Rescuing Justice and Equality*, G. A. Cohen (forthcoming) confronts criticisms of his site of justice thesis. I regret that I am unable here to discuss Cohen's responsible and powerful replies to his critics. See also Sypnowich (2006) for further recent discussions on Cohen's contribution to egalitarian theory.

V. Why Does Equality Matter?

Why does distributive equality matter? That is, why should a just social order be committed to some egalitarian distributive principle for the purpose of limiting economic inequalities between persons? One view, which can be broadly called "democratic equality", holds that distributive equality matters because democratic relations among fellow citizens require such a commitment. As Rawls puts it, some distributive principle "is essential to democratic equality once we view society as a fair system of social cooperation between free and equal citizens from one generation to the next" (2001: 133, 6; also Anderson 1999; Scheffler 2003*b*, 2005; Freeman 2006*b*: ch. 4). The argument can be laid out in the following steps: democratic society is conceived as a fair system of social cooperation; a fair system of social cooperation honors, among other things, the ideal of reciprocity; this means that the terms of social cooperation must be those that all participants can be reasonably expected to endorse; accordingly, a social order that admits of distributive inequalities among participants that some can reasonably reject (or that cannot be reasonably justified to them) violates the ideal of reciprocity; thus, a just democratic social order has to limit such inequalities by means of a distributive principle. As Rawls summarizes it, a reason for "being concerned with inequality in domestic society" is to ensure that the gap between rich and poor "not be wider than the criterion of reciprocity allows" (1999*b*: 114; 2001: 49, 124). Scanlon has also provided a study of the different "non-egalitarian" reasons, including reasons associated with the ideal of democracy, for why equality matters (Scanlon 2003; Rawls 2001: 130–2).[11]

An alternative view as to why equality matters is often referred to as luck egalitarianism. On this view, equality matters not because of democratic reciprocity, but more because of the presumption that no one should be worse off simply because of bad luck (Arneson 1989, 2000; G. A. Cohen 1989, 2000; Kymlicka 1990; Sen 1992; Dworkin 2000, 2003). For luck egalitarians, any departure from the benchmark of equal division is acceptable only when it reflects the efforts and choices of persons, and "not the myriad forms of lucky and unlucky circumstances" (G. A. Cohen 2000: 130). Thus, the point of an egalitarian distributive principle on luck egalitarian grounds is to ensure that

---

[11] For parallel views on why equality matters, see also Nagel 1991, 2005; R. Miller 1998; D. Miller 1999; and Blake 2001.

a distributive arrangement tracks as closely as possible people's real choices, while discounting their good or bad luck. As some luck egalitarians put it, a distributive arrangement should be "endowment-insensitive" but "ambition-sensitive" (Dworkin 2000: 89; Kymlicka 1990: 75–6). For convenience, I will refer to this core luck egalitarian ideal as the luck/choice principle.

Understood specifically as accounts of why equality matters, democratic equality and luck egalitarianism hold very different views as to the conditions under which considerations of distributive equality gain traction. For democratic egalitarians, distributive equality is a moral commitment only among persons who share a democratic political order. The value of distributive equality is derived from the more fundamental and general value of democracy. In contrast, for luck egalitarians, distributive commitments may be uncoupled from the idea of democratic reciprocity, and can be of value even among persons who are not fellow democratic citizens so long as their shared social world is one in which persons' entitlements can be affected by various forms of lucky and unlucky circumstancs. The potential substantive difference between luck and democratic egalitarians can be seen in the debate surrounding global justice. There is a tendency for democratic egalitarians to limit distributive equality to the domestic state (Rawls 1999*b*; Freeman 2006*b*: chs. 8 and 9; also R. Miller 1998), and a tendency for luck egalitarians to take distributive equality to have global application (e.g., Pogge 1989; Beitz 1999*b*).[12]

Some commentators read Rawls as a luck egalitarian (Hurley 2005), and indeed many luck egalitarians claim to take their inspiration from Rawls. Others reject this attribution of luck egalitarianism to Rawls (Scheffler 2003*b*, 2005, and Freeman 2006*b*), a reading that I will support below. At any rate, the luck egalitarian position is by now independently subscribed to by many influential egalitarians on account of its immediate intuitiveness: the presumption of initial equality and that persons are to be held responsible for their own choices but not for the vagaries of luck.

Yet, in spite of this initial intuitiveness, luck egalitarianism has come under much criticism in the recent literature. Indeed, these critiques attempt to show

---

[12] This is only a tendency, and the difference only a potential, as I noted, because it is open to democratic egalitarians to support global distributive equality by showing how the ideal of democratic reciprocity also generates global distributive demands. For democratic equality arguments for global distributive justice, see Bertram 2005; see also parallel considerations in Beitz 2001 and Tan 2006. Some commentators have extended luck egalitarian principles to support reparations for past injustices (Pierik 2006), and special language rights (Van Parijs 2003).

that the intuitiveness of luck egalitarianism is only a mirage, that on further scrutiny the luck/choice principle is exposed to be a rather implausible, and even absurd, principle of equality. Consider the following objections.

The first is that luck egalitarianism is a morally implausible if not absurd account of why equality matters. The following considerations are often forwarded as evidence of luck egalitarianism's implausibility. For one, luck egalitarians have to hold that a poor chooser who has squandered everything and who is now in dire straits is not entitled to social assistance (Anderson 1999; Scheffler 2003a, 2003b, 2005). But this is morally counter-intuitive. For another, luck egalitarians will have to be in the absurd business of compensating persons for all of their good and bad luck, including, for example, providing publicly funded plastic surgery for the unlucky ugly person (Anderson 1999: 335). Finally, it is suggested that luck egalitarians have to imply that the person whose life is not going so well because of bad luck has a less worthy life, and so even when luck egalitarians come to the assistance of victims of poor luck, they hold that person in contempt or pity (Anderson 1999: 302 ff.; Wolff 1998: 109–13).

The second objection is that luck egalitarianism misses the whole point of equality. Because of their fixation on mitigating the effects of luck on persons' lives, and so given their fixation on how people relate to their own bad or good luck, luck egalitarians fail properly to appreciate that equality is a social ideal. The point of equality is to regulate the relationships among persons in a social order, and once this point is correctly acknowledged, it will be seen that mitigating the effects of luck on persons' lives is quite beside the point (Anderson 1999: 312–16; Scheffler 2003b: 21–4; 2005). As a symptom of this problem, a further criticism can be raised, which is that luck egalitarianism is an incomplete account of distributive justice. Distributive justice is concerned with the background rules of society that determine persons' entitlements; yet the luck egalitarian principle has only the form of a principle of redress (Freeman 2006b: 132–5).

While there has been much discussion among luck egalitarians concerning the precise place of the luck/choice cut, the proper metric of equality given the luck egalitarian starting premise, and the appropriate distributive pattern, given the interest in discounting the effects of luck on distribution, these discussions are premised on the supposed plausibility and indeed appeal of the basic luck/choice principle (e.g. G. A. Cohen 1989; Dworkin 2000). [13] Yet

---

[13] See also Scanlon 1986 for an important dicussion on the significance of choice.

the objections identified above deny the principle its appeal and plausibility. It is important, then, that these objections be addressed by proponents of luck egalitarianism if the luck egalitarian ideal is even to get off the ground and if the debates among luck egalitarians over how to refine and flesh out their basic position are not to be moot. Below I canvass some responses that may be available to the luck egalitarian against these objections.

Consider, first, the charge that luck egalitarianism is morally implausible because it leaves poor choosers to their dire fates. In response, one might say that this objection commits a category mistake of a sort. The mistake is that it attributes to luck egalitarianism a much wider domain of operation than luck egalitarians should claim or need to claim. The luck/choice principle is not meant to determine moral agents' entitlements across the whole of morality, or even the entire domain of social justice, but is designed to apply only with the sub-domain of distributive justice. The luck/choice principle, rather, is meant to determine how goods or resources (or some other appropriate metric of equality) are to be distributed among persons in an ongoing productive social order beyond that which persons need for living a minimally decent human life. A productive society in which all members' basic needs are met will still have to decide how justly to distribute additional resources among its members, and this is the question of distributive justice. It is with respect to this specific distributive question that the difference between luck and choice becomes salient for luck egalitarians.

Thus the luck/choice principle says nothing about whether or not a person who is about to perish is entitled to urgent social assistance, for the case here is not that of distributive justice but the morally distinct one of basic humanitarian assistance or human decency. In these sorts of cases, a person is entitled to assistance because her humanity demands it, or human decency requires it, or her human rights demand it. Her own past decisions are quite irrelevant here as a matter of moral decision making. The luck/choice principle is simply the wrong principle to apply here, and it is the wrong principle because luck egalitarianism is not a doctrine about morality across the board, but a doctrine of distributive justice specifically. So luck egalitarians can share the intuition of the objection that a person who is floundering is entitled to rescue regardless of her past free choice, but denies that this presents a challenge to luck egalitarians.

The division of moral domains asserted here is neither eccentric nor arbitrary, but is in fact a commonly accepted idea in contemporary moral philosophy. Indeed, more relevantly for the present discussion, it is an idea ascribed to by many democratic egalitarians themselves.[14] Of course, the idea that a person is entitled to rescue because human decency demands it does not mean that she will in fact be rescued. Absolute scarcity may mean that persons do not get what they are in principle entitled to; and in cases where trade-offs need to be made, it is of course plausible that the relevant past decisions of affected persons can play a deciding role in how to allocate scarce resources. Here, we simply have a case in which a person's principled entitlement to basic goods is outweighed by other considerations.[15] My claim above is only to point out that luck egalitarians do not need to say that a person who has chosen poorly and is now in dire straits forfeits any entitlement to social assistance as a matter of principle.

Another consideration against the moral plausibility of luck egalitarianism, as mentioned above, is that it seems that, absurdly, it has to compensate persons for all of their bad luck. But this worry is deflected if luck egalitarianism is understood to have an institutional focus. As we noted earlier, Rawls takes the institutions of society to be the primary subject matter of social justice. In part this is also because he takes natural facts in themselves to be neither just nor unjust. What is just or unjust is "the way the basic structure of society makes use of these natural differences and permits them to affect the social fortune of citizens, their opportunities in life, and the actual terms of cooperation between them" (1999a: 337). On this view, social justice is principally concerned with the basic structure of society—that is, its main political and social institutions—and does not deal directly with natural facts as such.

Luck egalitarians, it seems to me, can and should affirm this clearly circumscribed subject matter of justice, or of where distributive justice matters. For luck egalitarians, what is a concern of justice is the way in which institutions handle natural contingencies, particularly if institutions advantage and disadvantage persons solely on account of their natural fortunes or misfortunes. Thus natural facts in themselves, such as persons' good or bad luck *per se*, are neither just nor unjust on the institutional view of luck egalitarianism. What is just or unjust is how social institutions combine with

---

[14] See, e.g., Nagel's (2005) distinction between duties of humanitarian aid versus duties of distributive justice and Rawls's (1999b) parallel distinction between duties of assistance and duties of distributive justice. More generally, see Nagel's idea of the "fragmentation of value" (Nagel 1979).

[15] This point is addressed not so much to critics of luck egalitarians, who would not, I think, deny this, but to luck egalitarians who might object to my attempt to limit the choice/luck principle to the domain of distributive justice on the grounds that poor choosers may not get some support if a trade-off between them and wise choosers is needed.

these natural facts, specifically whether persons are accorded more or fewer resources or opportunities simply because of certain facts of nature about them. Yet this institutional focus is still a distinctively luck egalitarian one: it is luck egalitarian in that how institutions handle matters of luck is a concern for luck egalitarians. Thus, there is nothing in luck egalitarianism that precludes the institutional approach to justice; and luck egalitarians can certainly take institutions to be the primary subject of justice and retain their distinctive position on why distributive equality matters.

On this institutional view of luck egalitarianism, the claim that luck egalitarians have absurdly to compensate persons for all their natural misfortunes misses its mark. The fact that a person who finds himself ugly and unluckily so (to recall Anderson's example) does not bother the luck egalitarian so long as social institutions in society are not structured such that this person's ugliness is translated into actual social disadvantages for him. If, counterfactually, society is such that ugly persons are indeed disadvantaged (either through deliberate institutional design or because of widespread personal prejudices) with respect to the background institutions of society, then this would rightly exercise the luck egalitarians (and either institutional reforms in the case of unjust institutions or corrective and counteracting institutional measures in the case of widespread personal discrimination will be called for). But not, again, because natural bad luck *per se* poses problems of justice, but because in this case a mere contingency has been handled by institutions in such a way as to generate a real social disadvantage for the unlucky person.

This institutional understanding of luck egalitarianism also provides a decisive response to the allegation that luck egalitarians are disrespectful or contemptuous of the unlucky. Focusing on institutions, the question becomes not how worthy or pitiful a person's life is, but whether the social order is according to this person her fair share. Luck egalitarians are moved to act when the institutions of society are ordered such that some persons obtain a lesser share simply because of some arbitrary facts, not because they think the lives of these persons are poorer, and hence they are to be given charitable hand-outs, but because they have not been given their fair share from the beginning. And this is a mark of respect for persons, rather than of contempt and disrespect.

The institutional focus also grounds a possible response to the second objection, that luck egalitarians have a wrongly asocial account of equality. An institutional approach to justice is by definition concerned with the social background against which individuals interact and relate to each other. Luck egalitarianism is not an asocial alternative to equality, but an interpretation of what social equality is. For luck egalitarians, the ideal of social equality between persons requires that any social order that individuals collectively support is not one in which the distribution of resources tracks the various forms of good and bad luck of individuals, but their ambition and choice. It is this specific understanding of how persons are to relate to each other as equals that generates a distribution commitment for luck egalitarians. Democratic egalitarians may of course reject this interpretation of what social equality entails, but this is different from saying that luck egalitarians don't have a social account of equality.

This concern with background institutions also suggests that it is too hasty to think that luck egalitarianism is only a principle of redress, and not really a principle of distributive justice (cf. Freeman 2006b: 134–5). In virtue of its institutional focus, luck egalitarianism is indeed concerned with how the basic political, social, and economic institutions of society combine to determine persons' fundamental economic entitlements. Its luck/choice principle is not simply a principle of redress, whose basic role is to reassign resources from the lucky to the less lucky against a fixed background institutional order that has determined who owns what, but is a principle whose role it is to determine how that background order should be regulated. Put another way, luck egalitarianism provides a principle for the social order that persons may collectively impose on each other, not just a principle for how persons are to relate to each other within the rules of a given social order.

A further response to the charge that luck egalitarianism is simply about redistribution, and not distributive justice, is available once the specific justificatory purpose of luck egalitarianism is clarified. Luck egalitarianism is meant as a response to the question, "Why does equality matter?". How equality is to matter, what the currency of equality is, and so on, are matters that will have to be further worked out. The objection that luck egalitarianism is an incomplete account of distributive justice because it has only the form of a principle of redress thus mistakenly treats luck egalitarianism as a substantive theory of equality, when it is meant to ground a commitment to equality. In a way, then, this objection commits a category mistake—it treats a grounding principle of equality (that is, a principle designed to explain why equality matters) as a substantive principle of equality (that is, as a principle that explains how the commitment to equality is best to be realized), and then shows how it falls short as a substantive principle. If, on the contrary, the limited justificatory function of luck egalitarianism is clarified, then the fact that it has the appearance of a principle of redress is not a shortcoming, because it does not claim to be a complete and substantive principle of distribution.

It seems to me that understanding this very specific role of luck egalitarianism—that is, that it is meant to motivate the commitment to distributive equality, and does not by itself specify what that commitment entails—provides a tidy way of understanding why Rawls is not a luck egalitarian, common interpretation to the contrary. The view that Rawls is a luck egalitarian is perhaps understandable given Rawls's own allusions to how justice should discount the effects of certain kinds of arbitrary contingencies (e.g. 1971: 15; 2001: 55). Rawls famously notes that distributive shares should not be determined by factors that "are arbitrary from a moral point of view", such as the distribution of natural talents among persons (1971: 63). Indeed, this and similar remarks by Rawls have led some commentators into thinking that Rawls is a luck egalitarian of sorts (Hurley 2005). Yet, as we saw, Rawls has also made statements supporting democratic equality. My account of the limited justificatory role of luck egalitarianism provides a way of reconciling these apparently conflicting remarks, and of showing why Rawls is not strictly a luck egalitarian, his references to the differences to arbitrariness and contingencies notwithstanding. As some of these remarks show, some notion of the difference between choice and circumstance is invoked by Rawls in his working out of the requirements of distributive egalitarianism—that is, in showing how the demand of distributive equality is to be substantively expressed once we accept that we have such a commitment. But the reason why we have such a commitment is not because of the goal of mitigating the effects of luck on persons' life prospects, but because of the ideal of democratic reciprocity. So, to the extent that luck egalitarianism is read more specifically as an account of why equality matters (and not in itself an account of what equality entails), Rawls is not a luck egalitarian, because the luck/choice distinction does not motivate the commitment to equality, even though in working out what equality requires once that commitment is motivated, Rawls has to invoke the luck/choice distinction in some form.

Whether luck egalitarianism remains a viable contender as a response to the question "Why does equality matter?" will depend on how the common objections against the ideal (of which I have discussed only two) can be addressed. This is a rich debate that cuts to the core question as to the moral basis of the commitment to distributive equality. In the above, I have suggested that if luck egalitarianism can be understood to be principally an *institutional* account of *why distributive justice matters*, the objections that it is morally implausible and wrongly asocial can be evaded, and I have tried to indicate how a luck egalitarian position along these lines can be developed.

VI. CONCLUDING REFLECTIONS

The objective of this survey is to offer an overview of some of the interesting and challenging issues in the current discussion on liberal equality, and to note the prominence of these discussions in current American political philosophy. In addition to being important and interesting questions in their own right, distinguishing the questions of equality of what, where the site of equality is, and why equality matters can help us situate the various egalitarian theories on offer with regard to where they agree and disagree. For Rawls, the what, where, and why questions are answered in the following way: primary goods (income and wealth), institutions, and democratic equality, respectively. For Dworkin, the answers are: resources (broadly construed to include personal resources), institutions, and luck egalitarianism. For G. A. Cohen, it is opportunity (more precisely, access to advantage), social ethos in addition to institutions, and luck egalitarianism. For Sen, it is capability, not only institutions, and (on one plausible interpretation) luck egalitarianism. In the process of this survey, I have suggested the possibility of an institutional luck egalitarian view with respect to primary goods.

One area in need of further exploration is whether considerations of liberal equality apply globally. In contemporary political philosophy, the subject of global justice is very much in the forefront. Few commentators seriously deny that the rich countries of the world have some kind of duty of assistance or humanity towards persons affected by severe poverty and its associated ills, natural catastrophes, curable but crippling and fatal diseases, and problems associated with non-functioning social institutions (e.g. Rawls 1999b; Nagel 2005). The interesting issue is whether global justice includes an egalitarian distributive commitment globally; that is, whether inequality among persons of the world as a whole is a concern of justice independently of the problem of poverty and the like. The short and compressed history of contemporary global distributive justice may be described as covering three (inevitably overlapping) stages. In the first stage were attempts by global egalitarians to extend arguments for domestic distributive justice to the global domain. Thus Beitz (1999b [1979]) and Pogge (1989), pioneers of the current debate, saw their task to be that of globalizing Rawlsian arguments for distributive equality. In response, some commentators pointed out that global egalitarianism runs roughshod over national self-determination and other more local commitments of justice. The form of this objection is not so much to reject the principle of global distributive equality as to introduce competing moral considerations and principles of justice to the demands of global distributive justice. So these early responses do not directly reject the principle of global egalitarianism, but present what we may call a "limitation argument" against global egalitarianism (D. Miller 1995, 2000; Jones 1999). The second stage of the debate thus involves examination of national self-determination and other forms of valuable particularist demands, to show how and why national and other particular demands of justice need not limit the demands of global egalitarianism justice (Scheffler 2001; Tan 2004b, 2005; Fabre 2005). The debate in this stage largely assumes the independent plausibility of a global egalitarian principle, and the focus of inquiry is on the supposedly competing principles of justice (nationalistic versus global). But another, more recent, line of argument denies the independent plausibility of global egalitarianism altogether. This constitutes roughly the third stage of the global justice debate. Some commentators, building on Rawls (1999b), have attempted to show how and why an egalitarian distributive commitment is unique to the political society, given the special features of such a society, and hence why considerations of global distributive justice do not even arise (R. Miller 1998; Blake 2001; Nagel 2005; Freeman 2006b: chs. 8 and 9; Sangiovanni 2007). What this position holds in effect, then, is that the move in the first stage of the debate, then of extending egalitarian arguments to the global domain, is a serious misstep due to the failure to appreciate the special quality of the state. The present and third stage of the global justice debate involves reexamining the conditions under which distributive equality matters and whether these conditions in fact do obtain globally as well (Julius 2006; Tan 2006; and Van Parijs 2007). In an important way, the growing interest in the issue of global distributive justice is motivating a thorough and refined examination of the conditions of distributive equality. While the case of global egalitarianism is far from settled, it can be considered progress that the debate is helping to clarify our understanding of why equality matters.

Whether or not there is a case for global distributive equality will depend crucially on how we address the questions of equality of what, where equality matters, and, perhaps most importantly, why equality matters. Still, how we are properly to address these fundamental questions of equality cannot be wholly blind to the fact of new social challenges raised by increasing globalization, where the borders of the political society have become less definitive as proper markers of distinct and unique domains of distributive justice. If, following Dewey's well-known dictum, philosophy is to be concerned "with the problems of men", heightened sensitivity to new pressing global challenges should inform our philosophical analysis of liberal equality, and the idea that discussions of distributive equality can sensibly begin from the presumption of an enclosed nation-state may soon be outmoded.

References

Anderson, E. (1999). 'What is the Point of Equality?'. *Ethics*, 109: 287–337.

Arneson, R. (1989). 'Equality and Equal Opportunity for Welfare'. *Philosophical Studies*, 56: 77–93.

——— (2000). 'Luck Egalitarianism and Prioritarianism'. *Ethics*, 110/2: 339–49.

Beitz, C. (1989). *Political Equality*. Princeton: Princeton University Press.

——— (1999a). 'International Liberalism and Distributive Justice: A Survey of Recent Thought'. *World Politics*, 51: 69–96.

——— (1999b [1979]). *Political Theory and International Relations*, 2nd edn. Princeton: Princeton University Press.

——— (2001). 'Does Global Inequality Matter?'. *Metaphilosophy*, 32/1: 95–112.

Bertram, C. (2005). 'Global Justice, Moral Development, and Democracy'. In Brock and Brighouse (2005), 75–91.

Blake, M. (2001). 'Distributive Justice, State Coercion, and Autonomy'. *Philosophy and Public Affairs*, 30: 257–96.

Brock, G., and Brighouse, H. (eds.) (2005). *The Political Philosophy of Cosmopolitanism*. Cambridge: Cambridge University Press.

Cohen, G. A. (1989). 'On the Currency of Egalitarian Justice'. *Ethics*, 99/4: 906–44.

——— (1992). 'Incentives, Inequality and Community'. In G. B. Peterson (ed.), *The Tanner Lectures on Human Values*, xiii, Salt Lake City, UT: University of Utah Press, 261–329.

——— (1997). 'Where the Action Is: On the Site of Distributive Justice'. *Philosophy and Public Affairs*, 26/1: 3–30.

——— (2000). *If You're an Egalitarian, How Come You're so Rich?* Cambridge, MA: Harvard University Press.

——— (forthcoming). *Rescuing Justice and Equality*. Cambridge, MA: Harvard University Press.

Cohen, J. (2002). 'Taking People As They Are?'. *Philosophy And Public Affairs*, 30/4: 363–86.

Daniels, N. (1975). *Reading Rawls*. New York: Basic Books.

―― (1990). 'Equality of What: Welfare, Resources or Capabilities?'. *Philosophy and Phenomenological Research*, 50: 273–96.

―― (2003). 'Democratic Equality: Rawls's Complex Egalitarianism'. In Freeman (2003), 241–76.

Dworkin, R. (1981*a*). 'What is Equality? Part I: Equality of Welfare'. *Philosophy and Public Affairs*, 10/3: 185–246.

―― (1981*b*). 'What is Equality? Part II: Equality of Resources'. *Philosophy and Public Affairs*, 10/4: 283–345.

―― (2000). *Sovereign Virtue*. Cambridge, MA: Harvard University Press.

―― (2003). 'Equality, Luck, and Hierarchy'. *Philosophy and Public Affairs*, 31/2: 190–8.

Estlund, D. (1998). 'Liberalism, Equality and Fraternity in Cohen's Critique of Rawls'. *Journal of Political Philosophy*, 5: 99–112.

Fabre, C. (2005). 'Global Distributive Justice: An Egalitarian Perspective'. In D. Weinstock (ed.), *Global Justice, Global Institutions*, Calgary: Calgary University Press, 139–64.

Freeman, S. (2001). 'Illiberal Libertarians: Why Libertarianism is Not a Liberal View'. *Philosophy and Public Affairs*, 30/2: 105–52.

―― (ed.) (2003). *The Cambridge Companion to Rawls*. Cambridge: Cambridge University Press.

―― (2006*a*). 'Book Review—Frontiers of Justice: The Capabilities Approach vs. Contractarianism'. *Texas Law Review*, 85/2: 385–430.

―― (2006*b*). *Justice and the Social Contract*. New York: Oxford University Press.

―― (2007). *Rawls*. London: Routledge.

Gutmann, A. (1980). *Liberal Equality*. Cambridge: Cambridge University Press.

―― (1989). 'The Central Role of Rawls's Theory'. *Dissent*, Summer: 338–42.

Hurley, S. (2005). *Justice, Luck and Knowledge*. Cambridge, MA: Harvard University Press.

Jones, C. (1999). *Global Justice: A Cosmopolitan Defense*. Oxford: Oxford University Press.

Julius, A. J. (2006). 'Nagel's Atlas'. *Philosophy and Public Affairs*, 34/4: 176–93.

Kymlicka, W. (1990). *Contemporary Political Philosophy: An Introduction*. Oxford: Oxford University Press.

Lukes, S. (1991). 'Equality and Liberty: Must They Conflict?'. In D. Held (ed.), *Political Theory Today*, Stanford, CA: Stanford University Press, 48–66.

Miller, D. (1995). *On Nationality*. Oxford: Oxford University Press.

―― (1999). *Principles of Social Justice*. Cambridge, MA: Harvard University Press.

―― (2000). *Citizenship and National Identity*. Cambridge: Polity.

Miller, R. (1998). 'Cosmopolitan Respect and Patriotic Concern'. *Philosophy and Public Affairs*, 27/3: 202–24.

Murphy, L. (1999). 'Institutions and the Demands of Justice'. *Philosophy and Public Affairs*, 27/4: 251–91.

Nagel, T. (1979). 'The Fragmentation of Value'. In *Mortal Questions*, Cambridge: Cambridge University Press, 128–41.

——— (1991). *Equality and Partiality*. New York: Oxford University Press.

——— (2005). 'The Problem of Global Justice'. *Philosophy and Public Affairs*, 33/2: 113–47.

Narveson, J. (2001). *The Libertarian Idea*. Peterborough, Ont.: Broadview Press.

Nielsen, K. (1985). *Equality and Liberty: A Defense of Radical Egalitarianism*. Totowa, NJ: Rowman & Allanheld.

Nozick, R. (1975). *Anarchy, State and Utopia*. New York: Basic Books.

Nussbaum, M. (2000). *Women and Social Development*. Cambridge: Cambridge University Press.

——— (2006). *Frontiers of Justice: Disabilities, Nationality, and Species Membership*. Cambridge, MA: Harvard University Press.

Pierik, R. (2006). 'Reparations for Luck Egalitarians'. *Journal of Social Philosophy*, 37/3: 423–40.

Pogge, T. (1989). *Realizing Rawls*. Ithaca, NY: Cornell University Press.

——— (2000). 'On the Site of Distributive Justice: Reflections on Cohen and Murphy'. *Philosophy and Public Affairs*, 29/2: 137–69.

——— (2007). *John Rawls: His Life and Theory of Justice*. Oxford: Oxford University Press.

Rawls, J. (1971). *A Theory of Justice*. Cambridge, MA: Harvard University Press; rev. edn. 1999.

——— (1993). *Political Liberalism*. New York: Columbia University Press.

——— (1999a). 'Kantian Constructivism in Moral Theory'. In *Collected Papers*, ed. S. Freeman, Cambridge, MA: Harvard University Press, 303–58.

——— (1999b). *The Law of Peoples*. Cambridge, MA: Harvard University Press.

——— (2001). *Justice as Fairness*, ed. E. Kelly. Cambridge, MA: Harvard University Press.

Roemer, J. (1996). *Theories of Distributive Justice*. Cambridge, MA: Harvard University Press.

Sangiovanni, A. (2007). 'Global Justice, Reciprocity, and the State'. *Philosophy and Public Affairs*, 35/1: 3–39.

Scanlon, T. M. (1975). 'Rawls's Theory of Justice'. In Daniels (1975), 169–205.

——— (1986). 'The Significance of Choice'. In S. M. McMurrin (ed.), *The Tanner Lectures on Human Values*, Salt Lake City: University of Utah Press, 149–216.

——— (2003). 'The Diversity of Objections to Inequality'. In *The Difficulty of Tolerance*, Cambridge: Cambridge University Press, 202–18.

Scheffler, S. (2001). *Boundaries and Allegiances*. Oxford: Oxford University Press.

——— (2003a). 'Equality as the Virtue of Sovereigns: A Reply to Ronald Dworkin'. *Philosophy and Public Affairs*, 31/2: 199–206.

——— (2003b). 'What is Egalitarianism?'. *Philosophy and Public Affairs*, 31/1: 5–39.

——— (2005). 'Choice, Circumstance, and the Value of Equality'. *Politics. Philosophy and Economics*, 4/1: 5–28.

Scheffler, S. (2006). 'Is the Basic Structure Basic?'. In Sypnowich (2006), 102–29.

Sen, A. (1980). 'Equality of What?'. In S. McMurrin (ed.), *The Tanner Lectures on Human Values*, i, Salt Lake City, UT: University of Utah Press, 353–69.

—— (1992). *Inequality Reexamined*. Cambridge, MA: Harvard University Press.

Sypnowich, C. (ed.) (2006). *The Egalitarian Conscience: Essays in Honor of G. A. Cohen*. Oxford: Oxford University Press.

Tan, K. C. (2004*a*). 'Justice and Personal Pursuits'. *The Journal of Philosophy*, 101/7: 331–62.

—— (2004*b*). *Justice without Borders: Cosmopolitanism, Nationalism and Patriotism*. Cambridge: Cambridge University Press.

—— (2005). 'The Demands of Justice and National Allegiances'. In Brock and Brighouse (2005), 164–79.

—— (2006). 'The Boundary of Justice and the Justice of Boundary: Defending Global Egalitarianism'. *Canadian Journal of Law and Jurisprudence*, 19/9: 319–44.

Van Parijs, P. (1995). *Real Freedom for All*. Oxford: Oxford University Press.

—— (2003). 'Linguistic Justice'. In W. Kymlicka and Alan Patten (eds.), *Language Rights and Political Theory* Oxford: Oxford University Press, 153–68.

—— (2007, forthcoming). 'Global Distributive Justice: A Survey'. In R. Goodin, P. Petitt, and T. Pogge (eds.), *Contemporary Political Philosophy*, Cambridge: Blackwell.

Williams, A. (1998). 'Incentives, Inequality, and Publicity'. *Philosophy and Public Affairs*, 27/3: 225–47.

Wolff, J. (1998). 'Fairness, Respect and the Egalitarian Ethos'. *Philosophy and Public Affairs*, 27/2: 97–122.

CHAPTER 24

LEGAL PHILOSOPHY IN AMERICA

BRIAN H. BIX

To THE EXTENT that there is something distinctive about legal philosophy in America or by Americans (cf. Leiter 1997), it connects to a pragmatic or prescriptive focus, and a fixation on judicial reasoning in general, and constitutional decision making in particular. However, American theorists have also made important contributions to analytical legal philosophy (if mostly thereby furthering projects begun in Britain or continental Europe).

This chapter offers an overview of the major areas and approaches where American theorists have offered significant contributions to legal philosophy. Section I discusses American legal realism; section II looks briefly at the legal process school; section III gives brief overviews of law and economics and the other post-realist critical theories; section IV summarizes the approach of Lon Fuller; section V examines the legal theory of Ronald Dworkin; and section VI summarizes some significant American contributors to schools of thought that originated in Europe, as well as American contributions to the analysis of legal concepts and doctrinal areas.

I. American Legal Realism

At the center spoke of almost all legal philosophy in America is the movement known as "(American) legal realism", the work of a loose group of theorists working in the 1920s, 1930s, and 1940s (Fisher *et al.* 1993). While it may seem unusual to begin the history of American legal philosophy in the twentieth century, for the most part the few American legal theorists writing in the eighteenth and nineteenth centuries were either unimportant followers of European schools or else are remembered mostly for their role in inspiring the legal realists.

Many of the themes (and much of the tone) of the legal realists can be found in the earlier work of Oliver Wendell Holmes Jr. (1841–1935). In *The Common Law*, Holmes wrote:

The life of the law has not been logic: it has been experience. The felt necessities of the time, the prevalent moral and political theories, intuitions of public policy, avowed or unconscious, even the prejudices which judges share with their fellow-men, have had a good deal more to do than the syllogism in determining the rules by which men should be governed.   (Holmes 1881: 5)

In these few sentences one can find (or at least read in) most of the themes for which the American legal realist movement would be remembered.

Roscoe Pound (1870–1964), with the "sociological jurisprudence" of his early work (Pound 1911, 1912), was also an important influence (though Pound would live long enough to become a conservative critic of the legal realists (Pound 1931; Llewellyn 1931)). American legal realism may also be traceable, at least in part, to Rudolf von Jhering (1818–92) and other European theorists of the late nineteenth century (particularly those associated with the "Free Law Movement") (e.g. Fuller 1934: 440 n. 46; Herget and Wallace 1987). A more obvious and more proximate source of influence were the American pragmatist philosophers; in fact, some consider Holmes himself to be an integral part of the pragmatism movement in American philosophy (e.g. Menand 2001), and the pragmatist philosopher John Dewey published two articles on legal topics that contributed significantly to the realist movement (Dewey 1924, 1926). Additionally, there were ongoing exchanges of ideas between the American legal realists and the Scandinavian legal realists (the two movements overlapped both in time and tone, but there were also substantial differences in theme and methodology (e.g. Bix 2006: 257–9)).

In the label "American legal realism", "realism" follows the conventional use of that term—to be worldly, skeptical, or cynical—not the narrow philosophical sense associated with Platonism and other forms of metaphysical realism. This "realism" was made vivid in another image of Holmes's: that we should cut through all the false moralistic language of the lawyers, judges, and legal commentators, by taking on the perspective of "the bad man", who wants to know only what the courts are "likely to do in fact" (Holmes 1897: 460–1). The "bad man" is the client who wants to know which actions will land him in jail or cost him a fine, and which will not; everything else is, to him, superfluous and beside the point.

The main focus of American legal realism was judicial decision making. On that topic, the realists' writings contained a number of themes: that decisions were strongly underdetermined by legal rules, concepts, and precedent (that is, that judges in many or most cases could have, with equal warrant, come out more than one way); that a proper understanding of judicial decision making would show that it was fact-centered (e.g. Frank 1930, 1949); that judges' decisions were often based (consciously or unconsciously) on personal or political biases and constructed from hunches (e.g. Hutcheson 1929); and that express reference to public policy and the social sciences should play a larger role in such decisions (e.g. Cardozo 1921). Feeding into this central focus on adjudication was a critique of judicial reasoning in particular, and legal reasoning in general: that beneath a veneer of scientific and deductive reasoning, legal rules and concepts were in fact often indeterminate and rarely as neutral as they were presented as being. It was the indeterminacy of legal concepts and legal reasoning that, according to the realists, led to the need to explain judicial decisions in other terms (hunches and biases), as well as an opportunity to encourage a different focus for advocacy and judicial reasoning: social sciences and "public policy".

The legal analysis dominant at the time when the legal realists were writing was criticized as "formalistic"; this meant that the argument was presented as if the conclusion followed simply and inexorably from undeniable premises. Once the proper label was found for an object or action ("contract", "property", "trespass", and so on), the legal conclusion soon followed (e.g. F. S. Cohen 1935). The notion that most judicial decisions should or could be deduced from general concepts or general rules, with no attention to real-world conditions or consequences, realist (and proto-realist) critics labeled as "mechanical jurisprudence" (Pound 1908).

An equally distinctive version of formalism had been influential in American legal education. Christopher Columbus Langdell (1826–1906), Dean of the Harvard Law School and originator of the "case method" of teaching law, famously advocated that law was a science, whose principles and doctrines could be "discovered" in cases, much as biologists discover the principles of their science in their laboratories. Langdell tried to derive the law from basic axioms and logical deduction. Real-world consequences and moral evaluations were excluded from this process. In one discussion of whether a proper understanding of contract law entailed the "postal acceptance rule", Langdell's response to the argument that one rule "would produce not only unjust and absurd results" was: "The true answer to this argument is, that it is irrelevant" (Langdell 1880: 20–1).

As noted, the American legal realists' attack on formalism could be divided into two separate criticisms: (1) arguing against the idea that legal concepts and standards were "neutral" or "objective"; and (2) arguing against the idea that general legal concepts or general legal rules could determine the results in particular cases. As to the first criticism, the realists argued that the premises lawyers used were open to question, and that labels and categories hid moral and policy assumptions that should be discussed openly.

As to the second criticism—which Holmes famously summarized by the comment, "General propositions do not decide concrete cases" (*Lochner v. New York*, 198 US 45, 76 (1905) (Holmes, J., dissenting))—the idea is that adjudication can rarely be accurately seen as a mechanical, logical deduction from general premises. At least in difficult cases, there remains a logical gap between the general legal proposition, or the statute couched in general terms, and the result of particular cases. On this analysis, the final conclusion regarding, for example, whether the plaintiff's action was the "proximate cause" of the defendant's injury or not will be based on unstated premises regarding public policy (or perhaps based on unstated biases or prejudices).

One can offer an additional point to the attack as well. Even when one can determine what the law is *and* it is sufficient to decide the case, it may be that the law should be changed. The American legal realists were certainly not the first to subject the law to moral criticism. However, the realists' attack on the scientific pretensions of Langdell's "legal science", and on the notion that law was a self-contained moral-logical system, created an opening for moral (and policy-based) criticism, for the possibility that legislative or judicial reform of the law might be morally (and legally) legitimate. We can see Holmes in two sentences taking much of the power out of the argument from tradition: "It is revolting to have no better reason for a rule of law than that so it was laid down in the time of Henry IV. It is still more revolting if the grounds upon which it was laid down have vanished long since, and the rule simply persists from blind imitation of the past" (Holmes 1897: 469). (For Holmes, a strong believer in judicial restraint (in judges deferring to legislative decisions and following precedent strictly), this was an argument for *legislative* change of old common-law rules. In the hands of some of the later realists, like Benjamin Cardozo (1870–1938), however, the same argument was a justification for *judicial* reform of outdated rules (e.g. Cardozo 1921).)

The American legal realist view of adjudication was that judges often have discretion, and that judicial decisions were often in practice determined by factors other than the legal rules. The realists hoped to move the focus from conceptual analysis to policy-based arguments and fact finding. One can get a sense of realism's view of judges and judging just from the titles of some of its best-known articles: e.g. "Are Judges Human?" (Frank 1931); "What Courts Do in Fact" (Frank 1932); "Transcendental Nonsense and the Functional Approach" (F. S. Cohen 1935); and "The Judgment Intuitive: The Function of the 'Hunch' in Judicial Decision" (Hutcheson 1929).

It is important to note that the claim that general principles in fact *do not* determine the results of particular cases, and the claim that they *cannot* do so, are quite distinct. The first is a statement about causation in the world: why judges decide cases the way they do. The second is an analytical statement about logical possibility, the nature of language, or the nature of rules, the assertion being that one cannot derive in a deductive fashion the result in (some, most, all) legal cases from general principles. The two claims are independent; one can affirm the first without affirming the second (and perhaps vice versa). Both themes were present in the writings of the legal realists, though the realists tended to be significantly more persuasive on the causal (descriptive) claim than on the more ambitious, analytical one. The first theme, at least, has also become embedded in the way in which modern American lawyers and legal academics think about law, and in the way in which law is taught in American law schools. If it was once subversive to think that extra-legal factors influence judicial decisions, it now seems naïve to doubt it. And it is commonplace to assume, at least for relatively important and difficult cases, that strong legal arguments can be found for both sides.

The realists preferred a picture of law as a human product meant to serve social needs, and subject to criticism and reform when it fails to serve those needs, or fails to serve them well. This view now seems so obvious and so much a matter of common sense that it is hard to comprehend how it could once have been controversial. However, it is in contrast to a view of law and legal reasoning as robustly "autonomous" (cf. Bix 2003).

The problem with formalist reasoning, according to the realists, was that it could result in legal doctrines and legal rules that were *too* autonomous—too abstracted from the conditions of life. Felix Cohen described the formalist thinking of his day as "an autonomous system of legal concepts, rules, and arguments . . . independent both of ethics and of such positive sciences as economics or psychology. In effect, it is a special branch of the science of transcendental nonsense" (F. S. Cohen 1935: 821).

What was to fill the conceptual gap left when one's faith in the neutrality and determinacy of legal concepts was undermined? For many of the realists, the answer was social science, the understanding of how people actually behave, and the way in which legal rules reflect or affect behavior. This turn to the social sciences can be seen in a number of places, including "The Brandeis Brief", a legal advocate's brief (named after the prominent lawyer and, later, United States Supreme Court Justice who used it, Louis D. Brandeis) that supplements and supports legal doctrinal argument with extensive sociological research. This faith in the social sciences can also be seen indirectly through the work that many realists did in the President Franklin D. Roosevelt's "New Deal", creating administrative agencies and regulations meant to solve various social problems through the law. The weak point of realist thinking in this area was the tendency towards technocracy, the belief that social-scientific expertise by itself would be sufficient to lead to right results, missing the point that there is always a need for a moral or political structure within which to present (or to do) the empirical work; there could not be "neutral experts" on how society should be organized. This misplaced faith in the possibility of neutral expertise on social matters was to continue through the legal process school (discussed below, in section II), only to be rejected by the various critical approaches to law (discussed briefly, below, in section III) that were to arise in the 1970s and 1980s.

Two other realists warrant special mention: Karl Llewellyn (1893–1962) and Robert Hale (1884–1969). Llewellyn was arguably the leader of the realists, the major advocate for realism (e.g. Llewellyn 1930, 1931; Twining 1985), and its most influential scholar. In his earlier work, Llewellyn argued for the difference between "paper rules" and "real rules"—that we should not too quickly assume that announced "black-letter" legal rules were either accurate predictors of how courts decide cases or reliable summaries of how judges came their decisions (Llewellyn 1930: 438–43, 447–53). He also argued for a greater congruence between legal rules and the social norms accepted by those subject to the law, especially within his specialty, commercial law. For example, Llewellyn argued that if business people see themselves as bound to a commercial transaction under a certain set of facts, the law should usually also treat them as so bound. He was able to put these ideas into practice in his work as a primary author of the Uniform Commercial Code (see, e.g., Wiseman 1987), a set of uniform laws that continues to this day (with some amendments to update and revise the Code) to regulate much of commercial life within the United States.

A more marginal figure in the realist movement, though one who has had disproportionate influence on later critical theory, Robert Hale (1884–1969) brought a sharply political tone to his criticisms of legal reasoning. Hale's most significant argument (1923, 1943) was that conventional legal thought made too much turn on the distinction between "public" and "private" areas of law. Under that conventional view, "public law" is administrative law and constitutional law, where government regulation and coercion is expected and legitimate, while "private law" is the law of contract, property, employment, etc., where the government does not intervene, but leaves private parties to purely consensual interactions under purportedly neutral private law rules. Hale's basic contention was that the ground rules of private transactions (e.g. which forms of persuasion and pressure are acceptable, and which are unacceptable and will justify legal relief) are never neutral, but in fact favor some parties over others (e.g. employers over employees, corporations over consumers), and that coercion is pervasive even in private transactions (e.g. in the State's willingness to enforce certain transactions and punish others). As was perhaps common with many of the arguments by the American legal realists, Hale's critique was built on an insight that was then overstated. Governments are responsible for the baselines they create for private interactions, but the type of responsibility involved is different from that of public-law actions, and the two forms of "intervention" need to be treated differently for the purpose of political and moral evaluation (Leiter 1996: 278–9; 2005: 65; for a general debate on Hale's merits, see B. H. Fried 1998 and Epstein 1999).

In various ways, American legal realism can be seen as the forerunner of various modern critical perspectives on law: law and economics, critical legal studies, critical race theory, and feminist legal theory. The connection is partly indirect: by undermining the confidence in the "science" of law and the ability to deduce unique correct answers from legal principles (as well as questioning the "neutrality" of those legal principles), the realists created a need for new justifications of legal rules and judicial decisions, justifications that would have to come from outside law and legal reasoning, narrowly understood. Thus, the realists' arguments were the starting point for most of the modern "law and" interdisciplinary work in legal scholarship. Additionally, the realists offered a set of arguments that could be used to support claims of pervasive bias (against the poor, against women, or against minorities) in the legal system, tools that would be further developed by later critical theory movements. Finally, the legal realists experimented (with limited success) with methodological approaches that would bear greater fruit from later theorists: for example, empirical investigations regarding the effects of rules, and the application of economic ideas to legal analysis.

II. Focus on Judicial Reasoning

There are a handful of themes that are distinctive to legal philosophy in the United States (though far from universal among American theorists). The first, already mentioned in connection with the American legal realists, is a tendency towards "pragmatism" (understood here broadly as an anti-foundationalist, anti-metaphysical approach, focused on practice and "the bottom line"). A second theme is a focus on judicial reasoning and decision making in general, and constitutional reasoning and decision making in particular. This focus is evident with the realists, but it can also be found in quite different works, like the legal process school of the 1950s and 1960s, the work of Ronald Dworkin (discussed in section V, below), and the recent work within analytical legal philosophy by those known as "inclusive legal positivists" (mentioned below, in section VI).

The legal process school was primarily a response to American legal realism (e.g. Duxbury 1995: 205–99). The legal process school conceded many of the realists' criticisms of the "formalist" judging of that period—for example, that legal materials were frequently indeterminate, and that some extra-legal values or norms would be required to decide many legal disputes; however, the legal process theorists argued that there was nonetheless room for a distinctively *legal* response to disputes. Legal process saw the distinctive legal response as involving understanding the relative strengths and weaknesses of different institutions and decision-making processes ("institutional competence"), and thus being able to determine whether (for example) it would be best to use adjudication, arbitration, agency rule making, or public legislation to resolve a particular dispute (Hart and Sacks 1994). Additionally, legal process offered a picture of adjudication in which courts *had* discretion, but this discretion was bounded by a proper understanding of the judicial role (e.g. Wechsler 1959). The major text of the legal process school was a casebook by Henry M. Hart Jr. (1904–69) and Albert M. Sacks (1920–91), *The Legal Process: Basic Problems in the Making and Application of Law* (Hart and Sacks 1994). The influential basic text of the legal process school was completed in 1958 (the "tentative edition"), and widely circulated, but was not formally published until decades later.

The legal process approach focused on the question of *how* and *by whom* decisions should be made: "What is the best procedure for finding the answer to this sort of question?" and "Which institution would be best placed to resolve a problem of this sort?". The legal process approach combined emphasis on the functions of law with detailed attention to the relative institutional competence of various institutions within the law, and how these institutions interact.

Especially at times when there is pervasive doubt about achieving certainty or consensus in resolving basic social questions (as the American legal realists created doubt in American legal thought), it is understandable that people might prefer to focus on the question of who should decide, and how. There is a sense, however, that, in the way in which the legal process approach developed, questions of process and institutional competence were *over-* emphasized, leading to an indifference to the justice of the results reached and a mistaken and extreme version of judicial restraint (cf. Wechsler 1959; Horwitz 1992: 247–68).

Legal process was an intermediate movement in American jurisprudential thought. As noted, it can be seen as a kind of mainstream response to the challenges raised by American legal realism. In turn, critical legal studies and the other critical theories developed in large part in reaction to legal process's emphasis on "neutral" procedures.

III. LAW REFORM AND CRITICAL THEORY

Pragmatism and a focus on judicial decision making have already been mentioned as major themes in American legal philosophy. A third theme is a tendency to focus on law reform: a preference for prescriptive theory or justice-focused theory, over analytical theory or other non-evaluative investigations into the nature of concepts, practices, and institutions. The theme of a prescriptive or critical focus may be most evident with feminist legal theory, critical race theory, and critical legal studies, but it is also implicit in law and economics.

As American schools of legal thought tend to be grounded less in purely philosophical argument, and more in non-philosophical claims—either political views about how society should be organized or economic theories—only brief overviews of these prescriptive or critical schools of thought will be offered in the present text.

Law and economics is the most influential approach to law in contemporary American legal scholarship, with significant (if markedly less dominant) influence in other countries. This approach calls for the application of economic ideas both basic (incentives/disincentives, Pareto and Kaldor–Hicks efficiency) and more intricate (game theory, public choice theory, social choice theory, bounded rationality, etc.) to legal regulation and legal processes. There are also some distinctive ideas that arose regarding the intersection of law and economics: most significantly, the Coase theory, from Ronald Coase's paper "The Problem of Social Cost" (1960).

In "The Problem of Social Cost", Coase argues against a particular welfare-economics justification for state regulation. Some economists had asserted that businesses that impose costs on third parties ("externalities") through pollution or other nuisances should be forced to "internalize their externalities", through fines, tort law liability, or taxation; for otherwise the businesses in question would be receiving a kind of subsidy, which would lead to an inefficient distribution of goods and services. Coase argued that this view was based on a series of misunderstandings. What is now known as "the Coase Theorem" is in fact an intermediate step in the article's analysis: that in a world without transaction costs, the distribution of legal entitlements (e.g. to pollute or to prevent pollution) would not matter, because the party that valued the right the most could always buy the right from a lower-valuing user, if the higher-valuing user did not have it initially. A further conclusion of Coase's analysis is that, in a world *with* pervasive transaction costs (such as our world), the initial distribution of legal rights *does* often matter, because high transaction costs may prevent a higher-valuing user from buying the right from a lower-valuing user (thus resulting in "inefficiency"). While the welfare economists had suggested that the proper response to externalities was government intervention by way of fines, tort liability, or taxation, Coase shows that private transactions in a world without transaction costs would respond adequately to the problem of externalities, and state regulation would have no effect on the efficiency of the ultimate distribution of entitlements. And, Coase argued, in a world *with* significant transaction costs, government intervention is still unlikely to produce efficient outcomes consistently, as efficient regulation would require a level of knowledge of the parties' costs and alternative uses of resources that would be impractical, if not impossible, to obtain.

Another central text of law and economics is Guido Calabresi and A. D. Melamed's "Property Rules, Liability Rules, and Inalienability: One View of the Cathedral" (1972), in which they analyzed the different legal remedies as offering different sorts of protection for legal entitlements: most prominently, "property rules" (an entitlement may not be violated without the owner's consent; violations will meet with judicial injunctions) and "liability rules" (violations of entitlements are allowed as long as market-value compensation is paid afterwards, through a judicial order of compensation). As the authors point out, a third sort of protection, inalienability rules (not allowing the transfer of an entitlement, even with consent) is also present in some circumstances—for example, not being allowed to sell or transfer one's right to liberty by selling oneself into slavery (Calabresi and Melamed 1972: 1111–15). The analysis of which sort of protective rule is used to protect different entitlements (and which sort would be most "efficient") has proved to be an insightful approach to private wrongs (tort, delict), and the analysis has been extended to many other areas of law.

The most influential figure in the law and economics movement is Richard Posner (1939–), who was an early advocate for the movement, and who continues to be an extraordinarily prolific scholar, applying economic ideas to a wide range of topics (e.g. Posner 2007). In his work, Posner has followed Gary Becker (e.g. Becker 1976) in the view that economic (rational actor model) analysis can be usefully applied even to non-market behavior.

In many of his earlier writings, Posner argued that a theory of wealth maximization served well both as an explanation of the past actions of the common-law courts (explaining why common-law rules of private law were, allegedly, "efficient") and as a theory of justice, justifying how judges and other officials should act (Posner 1981). Neither claim has garnered much support (though the descriptive claim, modified in various ways, continues to have some advocates), and Posner has retreated somewhat from the equation of wealth maximization and justice, though he still claims that it is usually a worthy objective for judges and law makers. (Posner now characterizes his own views as "pragmatist" (e.g. Posner 1990: 454–69), though this follows a modern broad use of "pragmatism", which seems to include a remarkably wide range of theorists and theories.)

Variations on neoclassical economics have also become prominent in American legal scholarship, including game theory (e.g. Baird, Gertner, and Picker 1994), public choice theory (e.g. Farber and Frickey 1991; Stearns 1997), and behavioral economics (e.g. Sunstein 2000). Game theory analyzes social interactions and the effects of legal norms through a version of economic analysis in which some of the rationality assumptions of neoclassical economics are loosened; the approach also emphasizes the strategic interactions of individuals. The best-known "game" is the prisoner's dilemma, which shows how rational pursuit of individual self-interest, where cooperation is called for, can lead to results that are contrary to both individual and collective interests. Public choice theory applies rational actor models to analyze the actions of judges and legislators, where viewing them as acting for their self-interest rather than for the common good seems to have value in both explanation and prediction. Behavioral law and economics attempts to incorporate some of the empirical findings of bounded rationality into descriptive and predictive economic analysis (leading, according to some scholars, to justifications for protective legal rules). Behavioral economics effectively incorporates some of the criticisms of rational actor analysis into economic work. There are other well-known problems with economics at both a descriptive and a prescriptive level (e.g. Nussbaum 1997; Hausman 2006), but none of these critiques have slowed the growing dominance that law and economics holds in American legal thought.

Critical race theory and related ethnic or identity movements (LatCrit theory, critical Asian-American theory, queer theory, etc.) usually focus on concerns relating to a particular oppressed group—their experiences and perceptions within American society and relating to the American legal system—but there is generally no distinctive methodology or philosophical perspective. Among the theoretical views important to work by these schools are ideas about the "social construction" (e.g. Boghossian 2001) of race and the notion of "unconscious racism" (Lawrence 1987).

For feminist legal theory, the *philosophical* content is more salient and distinctive, but the school is best understood as an application (or, more precisely, a series of applications—sometimes overlapping, sometimes conflicting) of different ideas from modern feminist theory to legal regulation and legal processes. Important theoretical notions within this movement include Carol Gilligan's ideas (1982) about an "ethic of care", an approach to moral reasoning offered as an alternative to thinking grounded on individuals, rights and justice, focusing instead on relationships, connection, and dependency. Gilligan argued that this "different voice" of moral analysis is largely associated with women and girls, with more traditional analyses of justice and rights being associated with boys and men. Gilligan's work has been central to the approach of the "cultural" or "difference" branch of feminist legal theory (e.g. West 1997). By contrast, Catharine MacKinnon's very influential feminist critique of law is grounded in a "domination theory" that derives partly from traditional Marxist analysis (e.g. MacKinnon 1987, 1989). For MacKinnon, if there is any "different voice" among women, it has been caused by pervasive, coercive, and violent domination by men.

Critical legal studies (CLS) flourished, briefly and amid constant controversy, in the late 1970s and early 1980s, before fading under institutional attack and internal division. CLS applied to legal studies a panoply of ideas borrowed or modified from a wide range of sources, including American legal realism, neo-Marxist theory, phenomenology, and postmodernism (e.g. Kelman 1987). Among the conclusions common among CLS scholars were that the legal materials frequently did not determine the outcome of cases ("radical legal indeterminacy"), that legal rights often did more long-term harm than good, that the appearance of neutrality and non-intervention in the market and in the family hid pervasive biases and inequalities ("attack on the public–private distinction", a variation of Hale's critique, discussed above, in section I), and a skepticism about the coherence or neutrality of legal reasoning as a purportedly autonomous and valuable form of reasoning (leading to the CLS slogan, "Law is politics").

IV. Lon Fuller

Lon L. Fuller (1902–78) is a bridging figure in American legal philosophy: a sympathetic critic of the American legal realist movement (Fuller 1934), his work strongly influenced the legal process school; and Fuller's procedural natural law theory and critique of legal positivism raised many of the issues and arguments elaborated in somewhat different (and more sophisticated) form by Ronald Dworkin.

Fuller (1958, 1969) argued that law contained an "internal" (or "inner") morality, "requirements" of law making that other and later theorists have discussed under the rubric of "the rule of law". Fuller's "eight principles of legality" (laws should be general; they should be promulgated; retroactive law making should be minimized; laws should be understandable; they should not be contradictory; laws should not require conduct beyond the ability of those affected; laws should remain relatively constant through time; and there should be a congruence between the laws as announced and as applied (Fuller 1969: 33–91)) help portray law as a sort of process, as "the enterprise of subjecting human conduct to the governance of rules" (Fuller 1969: 96). For Fuller, it is an aspect of law that, he claims, legal positivists miss, that one cannot understand "order" without understanding "good order", and that one cannot understand "law" without knowing what it means for law to be (procedurally) good. Fuller also emphasized the "reciprocity" between government and citizens that must be present in a good legal system (Fuller 1969: 39–40).

Fuller argued that his "principles of legality" are aspects of justice, and therefore have moral value, even if they might be compatible, in exceptional regimes, with substantive evil. Fuller took this to be a refutation of the separation that legal positivists advocate between law and morality. Whether his critique is valid, or should be construed as a refutation of legal positivism, remains highly disputed in the literature (e.g. Kramer 1998).

V. Ronald Dworkin

Ronald Dworkin (1931–) is probably the most influential English-language legal theorist of this generation. In his early writings (Dworkin 1977), he challenged a particular version of legal positivism, under which law is seen as being composed entirely of rules and judges have discretion whenever the dispute before them is not covered by existing rules. Dworkin offered an alternative vision of law, in which the resources for resolving disputes "according to law" are more numerous and varied, and the process of determining what the law required in a particular case is more subtle.

Dworkin argued that, along with rules, legal systems also contain principles. Legal principles are moral propositions that are stated in or implied by past official acts (e.g. statutes, judicial decisions, and constitutional provisions).

While rules act in an "all or nothing" way (if a rule applies, it is conclusive, it decides the case), principles can apply to a case without being dispositive. Principles (e.g. "One should not be able to profit from one's own wrong" and "One is held to intend all the foreseeable consequences of one's actions") have "weight" favoring one result; there can be—and often are—principles favoring contrary results on a single legal question.

Dworkin argued for the existence of legal principles (legal principles that are part of the legal system, which judges are bound to apply where appropriate) by reference to legal practice (in the United States and England). Particularly telling for Dworkin's argument are those "landmark" judicial decisions where the outcome appears to be contrary to the relevant precedent, but the court still held that it was following the "real meaning" or "true spirit" of the law; and also more mundane cases, where judges have cited principles as the justification for modifying, creating exceptions in, or overturning legal rules.

Because there are (numerous) principles as well as rules, there will be few if any occasions where the law "runs out" and judges must decide the case without legal guidance—though, at first glance, legal determinacy might seem also to be undermined by the abundance of sometimes contrary material. However, Dworkin had a response to that problem. On his approach, judges consider a variety of theories regarding what the law requires in the area in question, rejecting those which do not adequately "fit" past official actions. Among the theories that adequately "fit", the judge chooses the one that best combines "fit" and moral value, making the law the best it can be. Two tenets of Dworkin's early writings were thus indirectly related: that law contains principles as well as rules, and that for nearly all legal questions there are unique right answers.

In his later work (Dworkin 1985, 1986, 1987, 2006), Dworkin reworked his earlier ideas somewhat, offering what he called "an interpretive approach" to law. In *Law's Empire*, he argued that "legal claims are interpretive judgments and therefore combine backward- and forward-looking elements; they interpret contemporary legal practice as an unfolding narrative" (Dworkin 1986: 225). According to Dworkin, every time a judge is confronted with a legal problem, he or she needs to construct a theory of what the law is. That theory must adequately fit the relevant past governmental actions (legislative enactments and judicial decisions), while making the law the best it can be.

According to Dworkin, both law (as a practice) and legal theory are best understood as processes of "constructive interpretation", interpretation that makes its object the best it can be (in his words, an interpretation that makes it "the best possible example of the form or genre to which it is taken to belong" (Dworkin 1986: 52)). Constructive interpretation is both an imposition of form upon an object being interpreted (in the sense that the form is not immediately apparent in the object) and a derivation of form from it (in the sense that the interpreter is constrained by the object of interpretation, and not free to impose any form the interpreter might choose). Dworkin believes that constructive interpretation is also the proper approach to artistic and literary interpretation, and his writings frequently compare the role of a judge with that of a literary critic (e.g. Dworkin 1985: 158–62).

Constructive interpretation depends upon being able to assign a distinctive value or purpose to the object of interpretation, whether that object is a work of art or a social practice. It is that value or purpose which serves as the criterion for determining whether one interpretation of the object is better or worse than an alternative. For the constructive interpretation of law, Dworkin states that the purpose of law is to constrain or justify the exercise of government power (Dworkin 1986: 93, 109, 127).

The past actions of officials, whether judges deciding cases and giving reasons for their decisions or legislators passing statutes, are the data that legal officials and legal commentators interpret constructively. In making the law, or an area of the law, the best it can be, the criteria Dworkin mentions most often are (as in his earlier work) "fit" and moral value. For some legal questions, the answer may seem easy, because only one theory shows adequate "fit". However, where the law is unsettled or inconsistent, or where the legal question is novel, there will usually be alternative theories with adequate "fit". Among these, some will do better on "fit", others better on moral value. In making comparisons among alternative theories, the relative weighting of "fit" and moral value will itself be an interpretive question, and will vary from one legal area to another (e.g. protecting expectations may be more important regarding estate or property law, while moral value may be more important for civil liberties questions).

Dworkin also writes of "Integrity": the belief that judges should decide cases in a way which makes the law more coherent, preferring interpretations which make the law more like the product of a single moral vision. Dworkin wrote: "Judges who accept the interpretive ideal of integrity decide hard cases by trying to find, in some coherent set of principles about people's rights and duties, the best constructive interpretation of the political structure and legal doctrine of their community" (Dworkin 1986: 255). The interpretation of the law should, to the extent possible (given the relevant interpretive constraints), "express . . . a coherent conception of justice and fairness" (Dworkin 1986: 225). In some ways, the development of an interpretive theory around the concept of "Integrity" can be seen as a somewhat grander, somewhat more sophisticated version of the spirit underlying common-law reasoning: a form of decision making based in part on consistency, though a consistency sensitive to principle, and in part on a belief that past decisions should be seen as rough approximations or intuitions about justice and fairness.

Dworkin's writings (both earlier and later) can be seen as attempts to come to terms with aspects of legal practice that are not easily explained within the context of legal positivism. For example, (1) the fact that participants in the legal system argue over even the most basic aspects of the way the system works (e.g. over the correct way to interpret ambiguous statutes, and over how one should apply constitutional provisions to new legal questions), not just over peripheral matters or the application of rules to borderline cases; (2) even in the hardest of hard cases, lawyers and judges speak as if there were a unique correct answer which the judge has a duty to discover; and (3) in landmark cases, where the law seems on the surface to have changed radically, both judges and commentators often speak of the new rule having "already been present" or the way the law "works itself pure".

A standard response to Dworkin's work (both to his early writings and to the later, interpretive approach) is that judges and legal theorists should not look at law through "rose-colored glasses", making it "the best it can be"; rather, they should describe law "as it is". The key to understanding Dworkin, in particular his later work, is to understand his response to this kind of comment: that there is no simple description of law "as it is"; or, more precisely, that describing law "as it is" necessarily involves an interpretive process, which in turn requires determining what is the best interpretation of past official actions. Law "as it is", law as objective or non-controversial, is only the collection of past official decisions by judges and legislators (which Dworkin refers to as the "pre-interpretive data", which are subject to the process of constructive interpretation). However, even collectively, these individual decisions and actions cannot offer an answer to a current legal question until some order is imposed upon them. That order is the choice, the moral-political choice, between tenable interpretations of those past decisions and actions. If asked, say, "What is the law regarding economic recovery for nervous distress?", it is quite possible that a lawyer will not be able to offer any authoritative source which speaks directly to the specific problem posed; that is, the question may be unsettled in the laws of that jurisdiction. It may be that the lawyer can point to certain statutes that are relevant, and to certain decisions by courts at various levels on related matters, and perhaps even to the writings of commentators suggesting that future decisions on this question come out one way rather than another, but it may be that none of these items directly and conclusively answers the question posed. To get that answer, the lawyer must go through a certain kind of reasoning process, deriving an answer from the various materials. For Dworkin, this is an act of "interpretation".

What of the situations where there do seem to be authoritative legal sources directly on the point? For example, the lawyer might triumphantly announce that the appellate court had rendered a decision on the very issue just a few weeks earlier. Is that the end of the matter? Is there then no need for "interpretation"? Even putting aside possible questions of whether the appellate court decision might be subject to a different interpretation (its language perhaps having been ambiguous), Dworkin might point out that a skilled advocate could still argue, looking at all the relevant past legal decisions, that the appellate court decision was mistaken and should be overturned, or that the decision was too broad and that it will probably be limited later.

The interpretive approach has the advantage of reflecting, and being able to account for, the way that law (or at least certain areas of the law) is regularly subject to change and re-characterization. This strength may also be the approach's weakness: that it emphasizes the possibility of revision too much and the likelihood of settledness too little; and that it celebrates the notion of the great individual judge rethinking whole areas of law and thereby deflecting attention from the important roles of consensus and shared understandings (cf. Cover 1986; Bix 1993: 111–18).

A related challenge has been offered to Dworkin's approach to law: that it is legal theory for (or from the perspective of) judges and adjudication, rather than the full theory of law it purports to be. Making the best theory of law one can from the relevant past legal decisions may be the appropriate prescription if one is a judge within a legal system; however, why would one take the same perspective if one were merely a citizen in the society? From the perspective of the ordinary citizen, there are a number of reasons to think of law in terms of a prediction of how judges (and police officers) will interpret the rules (recall Holmes's "bad man" from section I). Not only is there the desire to avoid legal sanctions, but if law is going to succeed in coordinating behavior, then it is important that different citizens view what the law requires in roughly the same way (e.g. if they all have comparable ideas about what traffic laws or anti-pollution laws require). Arguably, this kind of consensus is unlikely to come about—or at least, less likely to come about—if citizens were to take up Dworkin's interpretive approach to the law.

What is distinctive to Dworkin's approach, and part of what makes it seem suspicious to many other theorists, is the continuity between what would usually be thought to be jurisprudential questions (the nature of law in general or the basic nature of a particular legal system) and what would usually be considered practical or doctrinal legal questions (what the law in this jurisdiction requires on some issue or how a judge should resolve a dispute). Constructive interpretation is Dworkin's response to both kinds of queries, and he has expressly offered that "no firm line divides jurisprudence from adjudication or any other aspect of legal practice" (Dworkin 1987: 14). Most theorists discussing the nature of law would be more hesitant to find implications of their general theories for more particular questions of legal doctrine, finding such implications, if at all, only in rare and highly unusual cases. By contrast, Dworkin argues that one's jurisprudential stance is implied in every legal dispute settled.

For a long time, the idea most closely associated with Dworkin's work in legal theory was the "right answer thesis", the claim that all (or almost all) legal decisions have a unique right answer. While it is interesting to note some of the ways in which the presentation of this view, and attacks on it, have changed over time, there are three themes that persist throughout Dworkin's many discussions of that thesis. The first is that this claim reflects our practice: that even in difficult decisions, judges and lawyers discussing, arguing, and deciding cases act as if, and talk as if, there were a right answer to be found. This reference to practice often elicits responses along the lines that judicial "right answer" rhetoric is just a matter of show or convention, and that judges in more reflective moments endorse a contrary position. A second theme, which has become more prominent in Dworkin's later writings, is that there are right answers to legal questions for the simple reason that judges must reach a result for the questions placed before them, and some answers are better than others. While many other theorists are concerned with distinguishing among judicial decisions, differentiating between those that are based on legal standards and those that are based on extra-legal standards, and between those which apply prior decisions ("apply existing law") and those that make fresh decisions ("make new law"), Dworkin finds such distinctions to be beside the point. He sees no reason not to view every standard that a judge is required to apply as a "legal" standard. Arguments about which aspects of judicial decisions are based on "legal" factors and which on "extra-legal" factors seem to him of little interest. A third theme is that the best way—and perhaps the only way—to prove or disprove the existence of unique right answers in (all) legal cases is to consider individual, difficult cases, and construct an argument that a particular result is the unique, correct one, or to argue that in this case, no one answer is better than the alternatives. There is unlikely to be a global argument establishing or refuting legal determinacy.

General challenges have been raised to the possibility of right answers on Dworkin's approach based on problems of incommensurability (whether one can meaningfully state that one theory is better than another when one alternative is better on one value, e.g. "fit", and the other alternative is better on a different value, e.g. "moral worth") (Bix 1993: 96–106) and demonstrability (that given Dworkin's other premises, Dworkin cannot conclude both that there are unique right answers to all legal questions and that these right answers will not be demonstrable, at least in principle, under optimal conditions) (Moore 1987).

What interests would be served by asserting a "right answer thesis", especially when no one assumes that the right answer will be demonstrable? One point is a psychological/sociological one directed at judges and advocates. If they believed that in difficult cases there was likely to be a unique correct answer, however difficult it might be to discover, and however much competent lawyers might disagree about which answer was the correct answer, their efforts and arguments would be directed at the legal materials: trying to construct an argument for one answer or another being the right one. On the other hand, if it were thought that because of the law running out, or incommensurability problems, or the indeterminacy of language, or whatever, that there were usually no unique right answers for the more difficult legal questions, then the attention of advocates and judges in such cases might turn too quickly (whatever "too quickly" might mean here) to legislative questions of which proposed legal rule would be best. Dworkin would argue that it is better (that it is the better interpretation of our own practices) that courts remain, to the extent possible, "forums of principle", attempting to discover the answers to legal disputes within the existing legal materials.

There is a vast critical literature on Dworkin's jurisprudential work, of which only a small sample of the arguments could be offered here. A broader overview can be found in M. Cohen (1984), Burley (2004), and Hershovitz (2006).

VI. OTHER ANALYTICAL SCHOOLS

American theorists have made substantial contributions elsewhere in analytical legal philosophy, but these contributions have been more in the way of elaborations or modifications of existing traditions: e.g. Robert P. George (1999) and Mark C. Murphy (2006) within the Thomist natural law tradition; Stanley L. Paulson (1980, 1992) and Michael Green (2003) on the work of Hans Kelsen (1992) and his neo-Kantian form of legal positivism; and Jules L. Coleman (2001), Frederick Schauer (1998), David Lyons (1993), Philip Soper (1987), Gerald J. Postema (1982), and Scott Shapiro (1998) on the work of H. L. A. Hart (1994) and his hermeneutic and social-fact-centered form of legal positivism. As to the last group, those elaborating on Hart's legacy, American theorists have been particularly prominent in developing the "inclusive legal positivism" version of Hart's work, which argues that legal systems can contain moral criteria for legal validity, but only if so determined by the system's own conventions (as contrasted with "exclusive legal positivists", who argue that law, by its nature, can never have moral criteria for legal validity, and some natural law theorists, who argue that by the nature of law, legal norms or legal systems must meet certain moral criteria (Bix 1999)).

Within analytical legal philosophy, there is another sub-area in which American theorists have been prominent, an area that sometimes goes under the title "the philosophical foundations of the common law". This area involves the descriptive, interpretive, or prescriptive/justificatory investigation of doctrinal areas of law (e.g. tort law, contract law, property law) or concepts within those areas (e.g. causation, excuse, *mens rea*). While in some ways well established, the theories of doctrinal areas of law remain somewhat unsettled as to the nature of the claims being made (or, perhaps to raise the same point a different way, the criteria for success for such theories). Like much common-law legal argument itself, theories of doctrinal areas tends to sit uneasily between description and prescription—in what some call "rational reconstruction" (and which has some similarity to Ronald Dworkin's "construction interpretation" (Dworkin 1986: 52)).

Some of the American contributions in these areas have come from the application of economic analysis, from within the law and economics movement, discussed in section III (e.g. Posner 2007). Outside that distinctive (and not entirely persuasive) view of these legal concepts and areas (but see Kraus 2007 for a more sympathetic view), there have been substantial works by the likes of Wesley Hohfeld (1913, 1917) and Joel Feinberg (1970) on the nature of rights; Michael Moore on criminal law (e.g. Moore 1998); Jules Coleman on tort law (e.g. Coleman 2001); Charles Fried (1981) and Thomas Scanlon (1990, 2001) on contract law; and Stephen R. Munzer (1990) on property. There are also some theorists who have raised questions about whether there are or should be general and universal theories regarding particular doctrinal areas, or regarding all doctrinal areas—arguing instead for theories more narrowly tied to a certain jurisdiction, or to a sub-category of cases within that jurisdiction (e.g. Bix 2007).

Finally, one should note Brian Leiter's work (e.g. Leiter 2007), which offers a critical view of mainstream analytical legal philosophy. His naturalist critique of conceptual analysis raises doubts about the theories of the nature of law offered by most legal positivists and by a number of other analytical legal philosophers.

CONCLUSION

It is a common experience: jurisprudential scholarly presentations at American law schools are met with questions like, "But what is the bottom line?" and "What normative prescriptions follow from your analysis?". American legal thought has, for some decades, been focused on the questions of legal practice and legal reform, with purely analytical inquiries being both rare and received with suspicion. American legal practice has a substantial tradition of constitutionally based judicial review of legislation, and in its shadow many political questions get transformed into legal questions; for that reason, legal theory in America tends to be converted into theories about judicial decision making. The American legal realists responded to one tradition of judicial decision making with an alternative vision of what judges can and should do; and significant portions of the more recent schools of American legal thought, from legal process to law and economics to the various critical theories, have centered on how judges should decide cases. In some ways, for better and for worse, Ronald Dworkin's work is a culmination of American legal philosophy: Dworkin's theory is functionally a theory of the nature of law, but built primarily from an interpretation of judicial decision making. It thus contains elements of both traditional analytical legal theory and the distinctive practice orientation of American jurisprudence.

References

Baird, Douglas G.; Gertner, Robert H.; and Picker, Randal C. (1994). *Game Theory and the Law*. Cambridge, MA: Harvard University Press.

Becker, Gary S. (1976). *The Economic Approach to Human Behavior*. Chicago: University of Chicago Press.

Bix, Brian (1993). *Law, Language and Legal Determinacy*. Oxford: Clarendon Press.

——— (1999). 'Patrolling the Boundaries: Inclusive Legal Positivism and the Nature of Jurisprudential Debate'. *Canadian Journal of Law and Jurisprudence*, 12: 17–33.

——— (2003). 'Law as an Autonomous Discipline'. In Peter Cane and Mark Tushnet (eds.), *The Oxford Handbook of Legal Studies*, Oxford: Oxford University Press, 975–87.

——— (2006). *Jurisprudence: Theory and Context*, 4th edn. London: Sweet & Maxwell.

——— (2007). 'Some Reflections on Contract Law Theory'. *Problema*, 1: 143–201.

Boghossian, Paul (2001). 'What is Social Constrcuction?'. *Times Literary Supplement*, 23 Feb.: 6–8.

Burley, Justine (ed.) (2004). *Dworkin and his Critics*. Oxford: Blackwell.

Calabresi, Guido, and Melamed, A. D. (1972). 'Property Rules, Liability Rules, and Inalienability: One View of the Cathedral'. *Harvard Law Review*, 85: 1089–128.

Cardozo, Benjamin N. (1921). *The Nature of the Judicial Process*. New Haven: Yale University Press.

Coase, Ronald H. (1960). 'The Problem of Social Cost'. *Journal of Law and Economics*, 3: 1–44.

Cohen, Felix S. (1935). 'Transcendental Nonsense and the Functional Response'. *Columbia Law Review*, 35: 809–49.

Cohen, Marshall (ed.) (1984). *Ronald Dworkin and Contemporary Jurisprudence*. London: Duckworth.

Coleman, Jules L. (2001). *The Practice of Principle: In Defence of a Pragmatist Approach to Legal Theory*. Oxford: Oxford University Press.

Cover, Robert M. (1986). 'Violence and the Word'. *Yale Law Journal*, 95: 1601–29.

Dewey, John (1924). 'Logical Method and the Law'. *Cornell Law Quarterly*, 10: 17–27.

——— (1926). 'The Historic Background of Corporate Legal Personality'. *Yale Law Journal*, 35: 655–73.

Duxbury, Neil (1995). *Patterns of American Jurisprudence*. Oxford: Clarendon Press.

Dworkin, Ronald (1977). *Taking Rights Seriously*, revised edn. Cambridge, MA: Harvard University Press.

——— (1985). *A Matter of Principle*. Cambridge, MA: Harvard University Press.

——— (1986). *Law's Empire*. Cambridge, MA: Harvard University Press.

——— (1987). 'Legal Theory and the Problem of Sense'. In Ruth Gavison (ed.), *Contemporary Legal Philosophy*, Oxford: Oxford University Press, 9–20.

——— (2006). *Justice in Robes*. Cambridge, MA: Harvard University Press.

Epstein, Richard A. (1999). 'The Assault that Failed: The Progressive Critique of Laissez Faire'. *Michigan Law Review*, 97: 1697–721.

Farber, Daniel A., and Frickey, Philip P. (1991). *Law and Public Choice: A Critical Introduction.* Chicago: University of Chicago Press.

Feinberg, Joel (1970). 'The Nature and Value of Rights'. *Journal of Value Inquiry,* 4: 243–51.

Fisher, William; Horwitz, Morton; and Reed, Thomas (eds.) (1993). *American Legal Realism.* New York: Oxford University Press.

Frank, Jerome (1930). *Law and the Modern Mind.* New York: Brentano's.

—— (1931). 'Are Judges Human?', Parts I and II. *University of Pennsylvania Law Review,* 80: 17–53, 233–67.

—— (1932). 'What Courts Do in Fact', Parts I and II. *Illinois Law Review,* 26: 645–66, 761–84.

—— (1949). *Courts on Trial: Myth and Reality in American Justice.* Princeton: Princeton University Press.

Fried, Barbara H. (1998). *The Progressive Assault on Laissez Faire: Robert Hale and the First Law and Economics Movement.* Cambridge, MA: Harvard University Press.

Fried, Charles (1981). *Contract as Promise: A Theory of Contractual Obligation.* Cambridge, MA: Harvard University Press.

Fuller, Lon L. (1934). 'American Legal Realism'. *University of Pennsylvania Law Review,* 82: 429–62.

—— (1958). 'Positivism and Fidelity to Law—A Reply to Professor Hart'. *Harvard Law Review,* 71: 630–72.

—— (1969). *The Morality of Law,* rev. edn. New Haven: Yale University Press.

George, Robert P. (1999). *In Defense of Natural Law.* Oxford: Clarendon Press.

Gilligan, Carol (1982). *In a Different Voice: Psychological Theory and Women's Development.* Cambridge, MA: Harvard University Press.

Green, Michael Steven (2003). 'Hans Kelsen and the Logic of Legal Systems'. *Alabama Law Review,* 54: 365–413.

Hale, Robert L. (1923). 'Coercion and Distribution in a Supposedly Non-Coercive State'. *Political Science Quarterly,* 38: 470–94.

—— (1943). 'Bargaining, Duress, and Economic Liberty'. *Columbia Law Review,* 43: 603–28.

Hart, H. L. A. (1994). *The Concept of Law,* 2nd edn. Oxford: Clarendon Press.

Hart, Henry M. Jr. and Sacks, Albert M. (1994). *The Legal Process: Basic Problems in the Making and Application of Law,* ed. William N. Eskridge Jr. and Philip P. Frickey. Westbury, NY: Foundation Press.

Hausman, David (2006). 'Philosophy of Economics'. In Edward N. Zalter (ed.), *The Stanford Encyclopedia of Philosophy* (Summer 2006 Edition), <http://plato.stanford.edu/archives/sum2006/entries/economics/>.

Herget, James E., and Wallace, Stephen (1987). 'The German Free Law Movement as the Source of American Legal Realism'. *Virginia Law Review,* 73: 399–455.

Hershovitz, Scott (ed.) (2006). *Exploring Law's Empire: The Jurisprudence of Ronald Dworkin.* Oxford: Oxford University Press.

Hohfeld, Wesley Newcomb (1913). 'Some Fundamental Conceptions as Applied in Judicial Reasoning'. *Yale Law Journal*, 23: 16–59.

_____ (1917). 'Fundamental Legal Conceptions as Applied in Judicial Reasoning'. *Yale Law Journal*, 26: 710–70.

Holmes, Oliver Wendell Jr. (1881). *The Common Law*. Boston: Little, Brown, and Co.

_____ (1897). 'The Path of the Law'. *Harvard Law Review*, 10: 457–78.

Horwitz, Morton J. (1992). *The Transformation of American Law 1870–1960: The Crisis of Legal Orthodoxy*. New York: Oxford University Press.

Hutcheson, Joseph C. Jr. (1929). 'The Judgment Intuitive: The Function of the "Hunch" in Judicial Decision'. *Cornell Law Quarterly*, 14: 274–88.

Kelman, Mark (1987). *A Guide to Critical Legal Studies*. Cambridge, MA: Harvard University Press.

Kelsen, Hans (1992). *Introduction to the Problems of Legal Theory*, trans. Bonnie Litschewski Paulson and Stanley L. Paulson. Oxford: Clarendon Press.

Kramer, Matthew H. (1998). 'Scrupulousness without Scruples: A Critique of Lon Fuller and his Defenders'. *Oxford Journal of Legal Studies*, 18: 235–63.

Kraus, Jody (2007). 'Transparency and Determinacy in Common Law Adjudication: A Philosophical Defense of Explanatory Economic Analysis'. *Virginia Law Review*, 93: 287–359.

Langdell, Christopher Columbus (1880). *A Summary of the Law of Contract*, 2nd edn. Boston: Little, Brown, and Co.

Lawrence, Charles R. III (1987). 'The Id, the Ego, and Equal Protection: Reckoning with Unconscious Racism'. *Stanford Law Review*, 39: 317–88.

Leiter, Brian (1996). 'Legal Realism'. In Dennis Patterson (ed.), *A Companion to the Philosophy of Law and Legal Theory*, Oxford: Blackwell, 261–79.

_____ (1997). 'Is There An "American" Jurisprudence?'. *Oxford Journal of Legal Studies*, 17: 367–87.

_____ (2005). 'American Legal Realism'. In Martin Golding and William A. Edmundson (eds.), *The Blackwell Guide to Philosophy of Law and Legal Theory*, Oxford: Blackwell, 50–66.

_____ (2007). *Naturalizing Jurisprudence: Essays on American Legal Realism and Naturalism in Legal Philosophy*. Oxford: Oxford University Press.

Llewellyn, Karl N. (1930). 'A Realistic Jurisprudence—The Next Step'. *Columbia Law Review*, 30: 431–65.

_____ (1931). 'Some Realism about Realism—Responding to Dean Pound'. *Harvard Law Review*, 44: 1222–64.

Lyons, David (1993). *Moral Aspects of Legal Theory: Essays on Law, Justice, and Political Responsibility*. Cambridge: Cambridge University Press.

MacKinnon, Catharine A. (1987). *Feminism Unmodified: Discourses on Life and the Law*. Cambridge, MA: Harvard University Press.

_____ (1989). *Toward a Feminist Theory of the State*. Cambridge, MA: Harvard University Press.

Menand, Louis (2001). *The Metaphysical Club: A Study of Ideas in America*. New York: Farrar, Straus & Giroux.

Moore, Michael S. (1987). 'Metaphysics, Epistemology, and Legal Theory'. *Southern California Law Review*, 60: 453–506.

—— (1998). *Placing Blame: A General Theory of the Common Law*. NewYork: Oxford University Press.

Munzer, Stephen R. (1990). *A Theory of Property*. Cambridge: Cambridge University Press.

Murphy, Mark C. (2006). *Natural Law in Jurisprudence and Politics*. Cambridge: Cambridge University Press.

Nussbaum, Martha C. (1997). 'Flawed Foundations: The Philosophical Critique of (a Particular Type of) Economics'. *University of Chicago Law Review*, 64: 1197–214.

Paulson, Stanley L. (1980). 'Material and Formal Authorisation in Kelsen's Pure Theory'. *Cambridge Law Journal*, 39: 172–93.

—— (1992). 'The Neo-Kantian Dimension of Kelsen's Pure Theory of Law'. *Oxford Journal of Legal Studies*, 12: 311–32.

Posner, Richard (1981). *The Economics of Justice*. Cambridge, MA: Harvard University Press.

—— (1990). *The Problems of Jurisprudence*. Cambridge, MA: Harvard University Press.

—— (2007). *Economic Analysis of Law*, 7th edn. New York: Aspen Publishers.

Postema, Gerald J. (1982). 'Coordination and Convention at the Foundations of Law'. *Journal of Legal Studies*, 11: 165–203.

Pound, Roscoe (1908). 'Mechanical Jurisprudence.' *Columbia Law Review*, 8: 605–23.

—— (1911). 'The Scope and Purpose of a Sociological Jurisprudence, Part I'. *Harvard Law Review*, 24: 591–619.

—— (1912). 'The Scope and Purpose of a Sociological Jurisprudence, Part II'. *Harvard Law Review*, 25: 140–68.

—— (1931). 'The Call for a Realist Jurisprudence'. *Harvard Law Review*, 44: 697–711.

Scanlon, Thomas M. (1990). 'Promises and Practices'. *Philosophy and Public Affairs*, 19: 199–226.

—— (2001). 'Promises and Contracts'. In Peter Benson (ed.), *The Theory of Contract Law: New Essays*, Cambridge: Cambridge University Press, 86–117.

Schauer, Frederick (1998). 'Positivism Through Thick and Thin'. In Brian Bix (ed.), *Analyzing Law: New Essays in Legal Theory*, Oxford: Clarendon Press, 65–78.

Shapiro, Scott (1998). 'On Hart's Way Out'. *Legal Theory*, 4: 469–507.

Soper, Philip (1987). 'Choosing a Legal Theory on Moral Grounds'. In Jules Coleman and E. F. Paul (eds.), *Philosophy and Law*, Oxford: Blackwell, 31–48.

Stearns, Maxwell L. (1997). *Public Choice and Public Law*. Cincinnati: Anderson Publishing Co.

Sunstein, Cass R. (ed.) (2000). *Behavioral Law and Economics*. Cambridge: Cambridge University Press.

Twining, William (1985). *Karl Llewellyn and the Realist Movement*. Norman, OK: University of Oklahoma Press.

Wechsler, Herbert (1959). 'Toward Neutral Principles of Constitutional Law'. *Harvard Law Review*, 73: 1–35.

West, Robin L. (1997). *Caring for Justice*. New York: New York University Press.

Wiseman, Zipporah Batshaw (1987). 'The Limits of Vision: Karl Llewellyn and the Merchant Rules'. *Harvard Law Review*, 100: 465–545.

CHAPTER 25

....

AMERICAN MORAL PHILOSOPHY

....

BRAD HOOKER

THE UNITED STATES was founded by thinkers who mixed natural rights theory with the idea that society is and ought to be based on a social contract. Thomas Jefferson's Declaration of Independence affirms the self-evidence of certain *natural* rights—that is, rights that are justificatorily prior to any human authority or binding agreement. In secure possession of these rights, people would consent to a range of social and political practices and institutions, which would then be justified by that consent.

The pronouncements associated with the founding of the United States expressed the idea that 'all men are created equal'. Admittedly, federal law did not come close to matching those pronouncements until slavery was abolished. Women had to wait even longer before they acquired the legal right to vote. And the *de facto* law in many southern states did not accord with the idea of equal moral status until nearly 200 years after the founding documents were written. The commitment to equal moral status may have taken a long time to pervade American culture, but it has been a shared presupposition of American moral philosophy.

The most important systematic philosophers in North America before the twentieth century were Charles Sanders Peirce (1839–1914), William James

(1842–1910), and John Dewey (1859–1950), though most of Dewey's career and influence fell in the twentieth century. Peirce focused on logic and epistemology, but his general pragmatism influenced James, who ventured into moral philosophy, though this was not one of his central concerns. Dewey was hugely prolific, and his *œuvre* contains three books focused on moral philosophy (*Ethics*, co-authored with James Tufts, 1908, revised 1932; *Human Nature and Conduct*, 1922, and *Theory of Valuation*, 1939). His interest in human psychology, his hostility to dogmatism, and his commitment to instrumentalism and experimentation were deeply influential in American thought in general, and moral and social philosophy in particular. (Perhaps the two most celebrated works in American moral philosophy of this period that were influenced by Dewey were Ralph Barton Perry's *General Theory of Value* (1926) and C. I. Lewis's *A Theory of Knowledge and Valuation* (1949).)

Nevertheless, the giants of early twentieth-century moral philosophy were British, not American. Whereas Dewey was a naturalist in moral metaphysics, an experimentalist in moral epistemology, and a contextualist about what questions need answering, G. E. Moore, H. A. Prichard, W. D. Ross, and C. D. Broad followed Henry Sidgwick in espousing non-naturalism in moral metaphysics and foundationalist intuitionism in moral epistemology.

The non-naturalism served to distinguish basic moral questions—for example, what constitutes goodness and rightness—from empirical and naturalistic questions. Of course most decisions about what to do are rightly sensitive to empirical information. However, whether the property of containing pleasure is the only one that can make a state of affairs good seems utterly different from any empirical or naturalistic question. Likewise, whether the property of producing pleasure is the only one that can make an act right seems utterly different from any empirical or naturalistic question. Since basic questions about the constitution of goodness and rightness are so different from empirical and naturalistic questions, and indeed so different from questions about supernatural commands or will, there came to be what is known as the 'autonomy of ethics'.

But how can we know moral truth if not by studying divine commands or the natural order of the world? Moore took from his teacher Sidgwick the intuitionist idea that some propositions about value and duty are self-evident, at least to someone with a refined sensibility who understands the propositions and contemplates them carefully. A proposition is self-evident if it is intellectually compelling independently of what other propositions might be offered in its support.[1] Foundationalist intuitionism promises to begin with enough self-evident knowledge of evaluative truths for it to be the case that, when we combine this evaluative knowledge with empirical information, we can infer what actions to do, what habits to develop, what policies to support.

However, Sidgwick and many later self-described intuitionists sometimes practised a form of reasoning that must be described as coherentist. They tried to make our intuitions about general principles cohere with our intuitive moral judgements about more specific matters. In this model, no general principle and no specific moral belief are taken as beyond question and possible revision or rejection. Each element is under pressure to fit with all the others. We shall later see the importance of this style of moral reasoning in the thought of John Rawls.

The more immediate reaction to early twentieth-century British intuitionism came from those primarily in Britain who thought intuitionism too dogmatic and non-naturalism too mysterious. But they agreed with the intuitionists that moral judgements did not purport merely to report empirical facts or ascribe natural properties to actions, states of affairs, characters, etc. In the 1930s, under the influence of the Vienna Circle, various British philosophers, including A. J. Ayer and Bertrand Russell, began developing the view that value judgements are not actually reports of facts at all, but rather expressions of emotion or attitudinal stance. Hence was born the doctrine that came to be known as emotivism.

The young American C. L. Stevenson went to study at Cambridge in the early 1930s, as did William Frankena and Richard Brandt. That these three philosophers, each of whom later became a leading figure in twentieth-century American moral philosophy, went to Cambridge at that time testifies to Cambridge's philosophical supremacy while Moore, Broad, and especially Wittgenstein taught there. Wittgenstein was dominant. And Stevenson said he chose to focus on moral philosophy partly because Wittgenstein avoided this area. Anyway, between 1937 and 1944, Stevenson published work that persuaded much of the Anglophone philosophical community to embrace emotivism (Stevenson 1937, 1938, 1944).

Emotivism openly admits that moral dispute might not be rationally resolvable. Two people—for example, Lisa and Tim—might simply differ

---

[1] See Butler (1726); Clarke (1728); Price (1787); Reid (1788); Sidgwick (1874); Moore (1903); Prichard (1912); Rashdall (1929); Broad (1930); Ross (1930, 1939); Carritt (1947); Ewing (1947, 1951); Nagel (1986: ch. 8; 1997: ch. 7); Thomson (1990: 12–20); Dworkin (1996); Audi (1999, 2005).

in their basic moral attitudes. Lisa might try to persuade Tim to revise his moral views on, say, abortion. She might do this by trying to get him to see more vividly the effects on women whose professional and personal lives are disrupted by nausea and tiredness during pregnancy and disrupted much more by the responsibilities of raising an unwanted child. Tim might try to get Lisa to appreciate more vividly just how recognizably human foetuses can be. But there is no philosophical guarantee that, if Lisa and Tim were to agree on all the empirical facts about foetuses, pregnancy, and parenthood, their attitudes to abortion would be the same.

If they really care about persuading one another, however, they might not give up trying to do so. For example, Lisa might try to find other topics about which Tim has moral attitudes that are in tension with his attitude to abortion—for example, killing in self-defence or euthanasia. Yet, no matter how long their discussion goes on, there is no philosophical guarantee that one of them will be able to prove the other mistaken. If they do end up agreeing, this is at least in part because of the contingent, natural fact that, when focused on certain empirical circumstances, they happen to have the same attitude.

Philosophy of language and philosophy of science were dominant from the middle 1930s for the next twenty-five years. During this period, many leading philosophers felt reluctant to venture into normative ethics. It was often said that philosophers have no special expertise in, or insight into, matters of right and wrong. Philosophers could defend views about the nature of moral language and judgement. But if there are no literally true propositions that x is morally required or y is morally wrong, the only moral insight or expertise one could legitimately claim to have is that one has moral attitudes that are based on fuller empirical information or are more consistent.

According to the emotivists, moral disagreement does not entail an error on one or the other side. John Rawls's 1951 'Outline for a Decision Procedure in Ethics' suggested that disagreement does indicate error.[2] The right way to proceed in systematic moral thought, Rawls suggested, is to

1. Think carefully about one's own general moral principles.
2. Think carefully about what one thinks is morally required in this or that specific circumstance.

---

[2] The paper emerged from the doctoral dissertation which Rawls submitted in 1950 to Princeton, where Rawls had also been an undergraduate until serving in the army 1943–5. The utilitarian Walter Stace had not only taught Rawls when Rawls was an undergraduate, but also supervised Rawls's doctoral work.

3. Consider the views of unbiased experts both about general moral principle and about what is morally required in specific circumstances.
4. Try to get all of these into a consistent and coherent whole, which Rawls dubbed 'reflective equilibrium'.

Achieving such a reflective equilibrium between our general principles and our judgements about specific kinds of case turns out to be more difficult than we might expect. Over and over, most people find that their general principles need qualification or supplementation in order to cohere with what certainly seem to be the right judgements about particular cases. The problem is multiplied when we must not only get our own views into a coherent set but also get agreement from others. Nevertheless, the goal Rawls identified is a coherent set of moral views all of which would be agreed to by others who are unbiased and well informed.

This methodological innovation has undoubtedly been the most influential contribution an American has made to contemporary moral philosophy. By the late twentieth century, nearly every important writer on moral philosophy accepted the methodology in practice if not in name. Any general moral principle that is proposed gets 'tested' by seeing whether its implications are plausible. If a principle is found to have implications that seem very wrong, then the question is whether the general principle is nevertheless, on reflection, more plausible than the denial of what follows from it. Very often, general principles are on the losing side of the battle. In effect, they are refuted by their implications.

While Rawls was teaching at Princeton (1950–2), J. O. Urmson spent a year there on leave from Oxford. Rawls won a Fullbright fellowship and spent the 1952–3 academic year at Urmson's college in Oxford. This is important for many reasons. The most immediate was that the distinction between act-utilitarianism and rule-utilitarianism was developing at this time, and Urmson and Rawls were leaders in this. Stephen Toulmin's vaguely rule-utilitarian *An Examination of the Place of Reason in Ethics* had been published in 1950, but Urmson's 1953 'The Interpretation of the Moral Philosophy of J. S. Mill' and Rawls's 1955 'Two Concepts of Rules' came to be seen as the classic early formulations of rule-utilitarianism.

Act-utilitarianism holds that an act is morally right if and only if the act would produce at least as much utility (or, alternatively, *expected* utility) as any other available act. Rule-utilitarianism holds that agents should follow whatever rules would produce the most utility (or expected utility). So formulated, act-utilitarianism and rule-utilitarianism might be compatible. G. E. Moore, for example, had claimed that an act is right if and only if it maximizes the good, and that the *modus operandi* most likely to maximize the good is to follow tried and tested general rules.

But Rawls's rule-utilitarianism seemed to go further than merely claiming that agents ought to follow rules and do their part in certain social institutions and practices. His paper accepted that utility can be used to evaluate rules, institutions, and practices, which is something that act-utilitarians had accepted. But Rawls contended that rules, institutions, and practices selected for their utility then determine what counts as morally right action. So a particular act can be morally right, on this conception, even if that particular act doesn't maximize utility (or expected utility).

The terminology 'act-utilitarianism' and 'rule-utilitarianism' was coined by Richard Brandt in his influential textbook *Ethical Theory* (1959). Together with John Harsanyi (who later shared a Nobel Prize for economics), Brandt became one of the most influential exponents of rule-utilitarianism. (See Harsanyi 1976, 1977, and 1982; see Brandt 1979, 1992.) But, by the time Brandt's textbook was published, utilitarianism was under severe attack for its potential to endorse injustice. Even Rawls was already beginning to set out an anti-utilitarian theory which he called 'justice as fairness' (1958). And many other philosophers were arguing that rule-utilitarianism either doesn't really oppose act-utilitarianism or is incoherent. After Rawls's student David Lyons published *Forms and Limits of Utilitarianism* in 1965, there was growing doubt that any form of utilitarianism is plausible.

What was especially important about Urmson's and Rawls's papers was the proposal that moral thought should have a two-level structure. First, there is a criterion for evaluating rules, institutions, and social practices. Then, the institutions, social practices, and rules deemed acceptable according to that criterion are to be used to determine which acts are right and which wrong. Utility was the criterion that Rawls and others at the time proposed for evaluating rules, institutions, and social practices. But, as Rawls later argued, one could think the multi-level structure for moral thought appropriate even if one thought that the criterion to use in evaluating institutions, practices, and rules is not one focused on utility.

During the 1960s, Rawls's work on political justice took a decidedly contractualist form. His first book, *A Theory of Justice*, did not come out until 1971, but drafts of parts of it had been in wide circulation for years. Indeed, already former students and followers were applying his contractualist scheme to ethics. (See Richards 1971.)

As explained in Rawls's book, one feature of utilitarianism that he found appealing is utilitarianism's promise to provide a principled way of resolving conflict. Utilitarianism, at least in its simplest and most familiar form, promises to resolve possible conflicts among various principles and values by reference to the criterion of maximum utility: what should be done is whatever would maximize utility. Utilitarianism's promise to leave questions of principle resolved contrasts with the messy intractability resulting from a theory with multiple foundational principles that are not lexically ordered. For example, suppose that the two foundational principles of social justice are that utility should be maximized and that equality should be maximized. Or the two principles might be about maximizing equality and maximizing liberty. In any case, there may well be many situations in which one of these foundational principles favours one arrangement and the other principle favours a different arrangement.

Another feature of utilitarianism that Rawls found attractive is its manifest impartiality. This consists in taking benefits or harms to any one individual to be just as important as the same-size benefits or harms to any other individual. While accepting that moral and political justification must be fundamentally impartial, Rawls thought that utilitarianism offered a flawed conception of impartiality. Utilitarianism conceives of impartiality along the lines of a perfectly *impartially benevolent* observer—that is, an observer who cares equally about everyone's welfare. Rawls proposed a different model of impartiality.

In Rawls's model of impartiality, we are to imagine the choice of principles for selecting institutions, practices, and rules being made in a self-interested way *but behind a 'veil of ignorance'*. This veil screens out any self-knowledge that might allow partiality or bias to be activated. Choosers behind the veil of ignorance do not know whether they are themselves rich or poor, untalented or talented, male or female, religious or not, etc. If these choosers do not know which groups they fall into, they will not be biased towards any particular groups. Their choice of principles could not but be utterly unbiased, and thus would be impartial.

Rawls borrowed the idea of the veil of ignorance from Harsanyi. Harsanyi had supposed that, from behind the veil of ignorance, one would know all the general facts about society, such as the sizes of different social groups. He also supposed that, behind the veil where one did not know anything particular about oneself, one had an equal chance of being anyone. Therefore, if one knew that (for example) 95 per cent of the population is able-bodied and 5 per cent disabled, one would assume one had a 95 per cent chance of being one of the able-bodied. When doing a calculation of the expected personal good for oneself of this or that possible social arrangement, one would then factor in these probabilities. Harsanyi concluded that one would choose the principle that institutions, practices, rules, and so on should be selected on the basis of the amount of utility they would produce, since this is the way to maximize expected utility for someone behind the veil of ignorance. So Harsanyi's use of the veil of ignorance led to a rule-utilitarian principle.

Rawls wanted to avoid Harsanyi's rule-utilitarian conclusion. So he proposed that those behind the veil of ignorance should not assume that they have an equal chance of turning out to be anyone, or rather, that those behind the veil should make no assumptions about the probabilities of having this or that characteristic. For all someone behind the veil knows, there might be a very high chance that he or she is poor, disabled, and otherwise disadvantaged. Rawls held that those behind the veil of ignorance should give special attention to the possibility that they themselves turn out to be in the worst-off group, whichever the worst-off group is. If those behind the veil of ignorance give special attention to the possibility that they turn out to be in this group, they will insist that the worst-off group be left as well off as possible.

Utilitarianism accepts that burdens for the worse-off can be compensated for by benefits to the better-off. In contrast, Rawls's contractualism holds that burdens for the worst-off are justified only if no other arrangement would give better prospects to its worst-off (where there is no presumption that the worst-off under one arrangement are also the worst-off under another arrangement). Whereas utilitarianism focuses on average utility, Rawlsian contractualism focuses on the plight of the worst-off. An inegalitarian system might maximize average utility, and this is possible without there being any sort of compensation to those left worst off. Rawlsian contractualism can also accept an inegalitarian system—but only if any other arrangement would leave at least some people even worse off. In this way, Rawlsian contractualism is more egalitarian than utilitarianism is.

Rawlsian contractualism was also seen as more individualistic than utilitarianism. Utilitarianism is straightforwardly collectivist: the good of the many can outweigh the good of the few. Losses to some can be offset by larger benefits to others. Rawlsian contractualism rejects this way of thinking. The contractualist test is: would each individual have sufficient reason to accept such-and-such arrangement?

One formulation of Kant's categorical imperative was 'Treat humanity always as an end-in-itself, never merely as a means'. But what is it to treat people as ends-in-themselves rather than as means? One plausible answer is that it is to treat them as valuable in themselves, not merely as an instrument to something else that is valuable. But if this is how we understand Kant's formulation, we do not get a clear contrast with utilitarianism. For utilitarianism takes people to be valuable in themselves, not merely valuable as instruments to other things.

So let us consider another possible interpretation of 'Treat humanity always as an end-in-itself, never merely as a means'. This interpretation construes treating people as end-in-themselves as treating people in ways to which they either *do consent*, or *would* consent under certain idealized conditions, or at least *could* consent.

Just as forms of utilitarianism proliferated during the 1950s and early 1960s, so forms of contractualism proliferated from the late 1960s, largely but not exclusively in Rawls's wake. Rawls's theory most definitely focused on principles to which he argued everyone *would consent under certain idealized conditions* (namely, from behind a veil of ignorance without knowledge of either one's own personal characteristics or the prevalence of this or that set of characteristics). Many worried that he hadn't specified the right conditions. Others worried that what mattered is not what people would agree to under counterfactual conditions, but what they have actually accepted.

For example, one especially important set of publications in moral philosophy during the 1970s came from Gilbert Harman. In his 1975 paper 'Moral Relativism Defended' and then in his 1977 book *The Nature of Morality*, Harman propounded the view that the best explanation of our moral attitudes is that they evolved out of implicit bargaining between haves and have-nots. He also argued that we should see moral 'oughts' as deriving not from objective moral facts antecedent to human desires but instead from contingent and perhaps variable human desires. When we try to explain why, for instance, observers see moral wrongness in sadistic torture, we need only refer to the observers' beliefs about empirical facts, such as the victim's suffering and the perpetrator's maliciousness, and to the moral attitudes of the observers, such as their moral principles against sadism and torture. What is not necessary for a full and adequate explanation, according to Harman, is reference to real moral truth.

The difficulty of making room for moral truth in a general naturalistic conception of reality continued as a focus of attention for moral philosophers. Proponents of so-called Cornell realism (e.g. Nicholas Sturgeon, Peter Railton, David Boyd, and David Brink) contended that moral truths could indeed pull their weight in naturalistic explanations (e.g. one person's evil character, or someone else's good character, might play a crucial role in the best explanation of certain events). (See Railton 1986; Sturgeon 1988; Boyd 1988; and Brink 1989.) They also contended that moral properties are naturalistic ones. But Sayre-McCord (1988b) countered with the argument that the very idea of the best explanation in natural science can itself depend on evaluative facts, such as the evaluative fact that, where two explanatory theories are equally good at explaining and predicting events, the simpler and more elegant theory is better.

While American moral philosophy has most definitely contributed significantly to the development of thought about the nature of moral properties, its contribution to normative ethics has been greater. As mentioned above, in the middle part of the twentieth century Rawls and some of his students contributed to the development and then the demise of utilitarianism. Many of his former students—for example, Thomas Hill Jr. (1991, 2000, 2002) Onora O'Neill (1989, 1996), Barbara Herman (1996, 2007), and Christine Korsgaard (1996a, 1996b)—went on to argue that suitably refined Kantian moral philosophy is more attractive than other views. This body of work on Kantianism is penetrating, innovative, and undoubtedly registers as one of the high water marks of American moral philosophy. Another former Rawls student, Thomas Nagel, has been one of the leading defenders of the idea of moral objectivity (Nagel 1970, 1979, 1986) as well as an important contributor to the development of moral contractualism (Nagel 1991). Other of Rawls's former students who have written extensively on contractualism are Jean Hampton (1986) and, most influentially, Thomas Scanlon (1998). In fact, Scanlon's book was so long in development and so carefully argued that many philosophers feel that contractualist ethics stands or falls with his treatment.

American normative ethics has had other important streams. One of these has been work on desert by Joel Feinberg (1970a), George Sher (1987), Fred Feldman (1997), and Shelly Kagan (1999). Another has been the work of Feinberg (1970b), Judith Jarvis Thomson (1971, 1990), Robert Nozick (1974), Ronald Dworkin (1977), Alan Gewirth (1978), Carl Wellman (1985), L. Wayne Sumner (1987), and Hillel Steiner (1994) on rights. Yet another has been feminist moral theory, with Carol Gilligan's *In a Different Voice: Psychological Theory and Women's Development* and Nell Noddings's *Care: A Feminine Approach to Ethics and Moral Education* leading the way.[3]

Gilligan and Noddings reacted against the Kantian and Rawlsian emphasis on justice and rules and rights. Gilligan claimed that her empirical studies showed that females tend to think in a more flexible, conflict-avoiding, relationship-preserving ways, which are not inferior to more typically male thinking about justice, rules, and rights. Noddings developed the 'ethics of care', which is focused on one's particular relationships in a way that does not seek impartial justification and is not guided by general principles. (For criticism of feminist ethics, see Hampton 1993 and Driver 2005.)

Feminist ethics is often associated with virtue ethics. The term 'virtue ethics' refers to a family of moral theories sharing the doctrine that right acts are just whatever ones a virtuous person would do. So virtue ethics takes the evaluation of character to be more fundamental than the evaluation of acts. This approach can be traced back through Hume and Aquinas to Aristotle. But it was revived in the twentieth century by Philippa Foot, a British philosopher who worked at UCLA for roughly half of her career, and Alasdair MacIntyre, another British philosopher who worked even longer in the USA.

The proponent of virtue ethics closest to feminist ethics is definitely Michael Slote, starting with his *From Morality to Virtue* (1992) and culminating in his *The Ethics of Care and Empathy* (2007). Slote's 'sentimentalist' account maintains that whether an act is morally right depends on whether it comes from a morally good motive. Slote focuses on universal benevolence or caring, which he takes to be intrinsically morally good.[4]

Benevolence might seem to fit much better as the foundational or core concern of utilitarian ethics than of virtue ethics. Ironically, however, while the virtue ethicist Slote has increasingly taken benevolence to be the foundational virtue, those working in the utilitarian tradition have been moving in the opposite direction. Robert Adams (1976), Derek Parfit (1984), and Peter Railton (1984), for example, have argued that the pattern of concern most likely to maximize the impartial good might be one passionately committed to various more personal projects and particular commitments. In part this is because human beings cannot sustain strict impartiality towards everyone

---

[3] Moral psychology had been a focus of American moral philosophy since James and Dewey. See the first half of Brandt (1979), Part 3 of Rawls (1971), and Sinnott-Armstrong (2006).

[4] Another influential account has been Hurka (2001), which follows G. E. Moore in contending that virtue consists in loving the good and hating the bad, sentiments broader than benevolence.

and at the same time have intense feelings. (For elaboration, see Hooker 2000: 138–41.)

But if a utilitarian or other impartial consequentialist theory allows the agent to have a certain constellation of commitments and passions other than impartial benevolence, what is this theory to say about the morality of the acts that such commitments and passions produce? It certainly seems that, if we have the constellation of commitments and passions that consequentialism licenses, then consequentialism can hardly condemn us for acting as that constellation of commitments and passions mandates. How silly it would be to think people should be blamed—much less punished—for acting on the motivation that they were right to have.

One line of response to this is to say that there is a set of acts that are morally wrong though the agent had precisely the motivation he or she should have had. However, what is the force of 'morally wrong' when predicated of such acts? Wrongness has a particularly tight and intimate connection with blameworthiness. This connection is too tight to be comfortable with the idea that there is a set of acts that are wrong though the people who do those acts are not blameworthy.

Another line of response is the following. Consequentialism or, more specifically, utilitarianism can assess passions, projects, and, more generally, patterns of motivation as good. And it can assess acts as regrettable or fortunate, depending of course on their consequences. But consequentialism and utilitarianism should eschew thinking in terms of 'wrong act'. For while people should be blamed for having the wrong pattern of motivation, they must not be blamed for acting on the right pattern of motivation. (See Railton 1988; for the opposed view, see Norcross 2006.) And, given the tightness of the tie between wrongness and blameworthiness, if people cannot rightly be blamed for acting on the right pattern of motivation, they are not wrong to do so.

But for a moral theory to lose the concept of 'wrong act' is a desperate move. Could punishment be justified where the concept 'wrong act' is lost? Intuitively, people can be *responsible* for their concerns, intentions, and acts, and they can be *blamed* for their concerns, intentions, and acts. They cannot rightly be *punished* for their concerns; however, they can rightly be punished for their intentions and acts—but only if those intentions and acts are wrong! (For a well-developed theory of wrongness and blame, see Gert 2005.)

Interest in the connections between concepts like 'wrong' and 'blameworthy' and ideas of agency and responsibility is mushrooming. Prominent examples are Susan Wolf (1993), R. Jay Wallace (1994), John Martin Fisher and Mark Ravizza (1998), and George Sher (2005).

Connected closely to ideas about responsibility and blame are questions about whether one is more responsible, and to blame, for bad consequences that were part of one's intention (i.e. part of one's aim or one's means to achieve that aim) than one is for bad consequences that were not. A similar question arises about whether one is more responsible for bad consequences that result from what one does than one is for bad consequences that one could have prevented but didn't. These questions have been the focus of prolonged debate in American moral philosophy, with influential contributions from Philippa Foot (1978), Judith Jarvis Thomson (1971, 1990), Charles Fried (1978), James Rachels (1975), Shelly Kagan (1988), Warren Quinn (1989a, 1989b), Jonathan Bennett (1995), Samuel Scheffler (1979, 2004), Frances Kamm (1998, 2000, 2006), and Jeff McMahan (2001).

Such debates return us to questions about people's rights to life, liberty, property, and equal protection by the law. On the one side there is the strain of American consequentialism, which tends to think of all rights in a fairly pragmatic way. While this side has had some forceful and eloquent advocates, it has always been the smaller group. On the other side are those who think at least some rights are so intuitively compelling that any moral theory failing to endorse them is thereby too implausible to accept. For most American moral philosophers, the goal is to find a moral theory that coheres as well as possible with all our considered moral convictions, especially the ones about what it is wrong to do to people without their consent. And most American moral philosophers have concluded that any such theory must be grounded in non-pragmatic considerations, such as the Kantian idea of respect for persons (for a recent example, see Audi 2005), or, more specifically, respect for rational agency (see Sumner 1987 and Griffin 2008).

REFERENCES

Adams, Robert (1976). 'Motive Utilitarianism'. *Journal of Philosophy*, 73: 467–81.
Audi, Robert (1999). 'Self-Evidence'. *Philosophical Perspectives*, 13: 205–28.
_____ (2005). *The Good in the Right*. Princeton: Princeton University Press.
Bennett, Jonathan (1995). *The Act Itself*. New York: Oxford University Press.
Boyd David (1988). 'How to be a Moral Realist'. In Sayre-McCord (1988a).
Brandt, Richard B. (1959). *Ethical Theory*. Englewood Cliffs, NJ: Prentice-Hall.
_____ (1979). *A Theory of the Good and the Right*. Oxford: Clarendon Press.

_____ (1992). *Morality, Utilitarianism, and Rights*, New York: Cambridge University Press.

Brink, David (1989). *Moral Realism and the Foundations of Ethics*. New York: Cambridge University Press.

Broad, C. D. (1930). *Five Types of Ethical Theory*. London: Routledge.

Butler, Joseph (1726). *Fifteen Sermons Preached at the Rolls Chapel*. London.

Carritt, E. F. (1947). *Ethical and Political Thinking*. Oxford: Clarendon Press.

Clarke, Samuel (1728). *A Discourse of Natural Religion*. London.

Dewey, John, (1922). *Human Nature and Conduct*. Repr. in John Dewey, *The Middle Works, 1899–1924*, xiv, ed. J. A. Boydston, Carbondale, IL: Southern Illinois University Press, 1976.

_____ (1939). *Theory of Valuation*. Repr. in *The Later Works, 1925–1953*, xiii, ed. J. A. Boydston, Carbondale, IL: Southern Illinois University Press, 1981.

_____ and Tufts, James (1908). *Ethics*, rev. edn. 1932. Repr. in John Dewey, *The Later Works, 1925–1953*, vii, ed. J. A. Boydston, Carbondale, IL: Southern Illinois University Press, 1981.

Driver, Julia (2005). 'Consequentialism and Feminist Ethics'. *Hypatia*, 20: 183–99.

Dworkin, Ronald (1977). *Taking Rights Seriously*. Cambridge, MA: Harvard University Press.

_____ (1996). 'Objectivity and Truth: You'd Better Believe It'. *Philosophy and Public Affairs*, 25: 87–139.

Ewing, A. C. (1947). *Ethics*. London: Macmillan.

_____ (1951). *The Fundamental Questions of Philosophy*. London: Routledge.

Feinberg, Joel (1970*a*). *Doing and Deserving*. Princeton: Princeton University Press.

_____ (1970*b*). 'The Nature and Value of Rights'. *Journal of Value Inquiry*, 4: 263–7. Repr. in Feinberg, *Rights, Justice, and the Bounds of Liberty*, Princeton: Princeton University Press, 1980, 143–55.

Feldman, Fred (1997). *Utilitarianism, Hedonism, and Desert*. New York: Cambridge University Press.

Fisher, John Martin, and Ravizza, Mark (1998). *Responsibility and Control: A Theory of Moral Responsibility*. New York: Cambridge University Press.

Foot, Philippa (1978). *Virtues and Vices*. Oxford: Blackwell.

Fried, Charles (1978). *Right and Wrong*. Cambridge, MA: Harvard University Press.

Gert, Bernard (2005). *Morality: Its Nature and Justification*. New York: Oxford University Press.

Gewirth, Alan (1978). *Reason and Morality*. Chicago: University of Chicago Press.

Gilligan, Carol (1982). *In a Different Voice: Psychological Theory and Women's Development*. Cambridge, MA: Harvard University Press.

Griffin, James (2008). *On Human Rights*. Oxford: Clarendon Press.

Hampton, Jean (1986). *Hobbes and the Social Contract Tradition*. New York: Cambridge University Press.

_____ (1993). 'Feminist Contractarianism'. In Louise B. Anthony and Charlotte Witt (eds.), *A Mind of One's Own*, Boulder, CO: Westview Press, 227–55.

Harman, Gilbert (1975). 'Moral Relativism Defended'. *Philosophical Review*, 84: 3–22.

———(1977). *The Nature of Morality*. New York: Oxford University Press.

Harsanyi, John (1976). *Essays on Ethics, Social Behaviour and Scientific Explanation*. Dordrecht: Reidel.

———(1977). 'Rule Utilitarianism and Decision Theory'. *Erkenntnis*, 11: 25–53.

———(1982). 'Morality and the Theory of Rational Behaviour'. In A. Sen and B. Williams (eds.), *Utilitarianism and Beyond*, Cambridge: Cambridge University Press, 39–62.

Herman, Barbara (1996). *The Practice of Moral Judgment*. Cambridge, MA: Harvard University Press.

———(2007). *Moral Literacy*. Cambridge, MA: Harvard University Press.

Hill, Thomas Jr. (1991). *Autonomy and Self-Respect*. New York: Cambridge University Press.

———(2000). *Respect, Pluralism, and Justice: Kantian Perspectives*. New York: Oxford University Press.

———(2002). *Human Welfare and Moral Worth: Kantian Perspectives*. New York: Oxford University Press.

Hooker, Brad (2000). *Ideal Code, Real World: A Rule-Consequentialist Theory of Morality*. Oxford: Oxford University Press.

Hurka, Thomas (2001). *Virtue, Vice, and Value*. New York: Oxford University Press.

Kagan, Shelly (1988). *The Limits of Morality*. Oxford: Clarendon Press.

———(1999). 'Equality and Desert'. In Louis Pojman and Owen McLeod (eds.), *What Do We Deserve?*, New York: Oxford University Press, 298–314.

Kamm, Frances (1998). *Morality, Mortality*, i: *Death and Whom To Save From It*. Oxford: Clarendon Press.

———(2000). *Morality, Mortality*, ii: *Rights, Duties, Status*. Oxford: Clarendon Press.

———(2006). *Intricate Ethics: Rights, Responsibilities, and Permissible Harm*. New York: Oxford University Press.

Korsgaard, Christine (1996a). *Creating the Kingdom of Ends*. New York: Cambridge University Press.

———(1996b). *The Sources of Normativity*. New York: Cambridge University Press.

Lewis, C. I. (1949). *A Theory of Knowledge and Valuation*. LaSalle, IL: Open Court.

Lyons, David (1965). *Forms and Limits of Utilitarianism*. Oxford: Clarendon Press.

MacIntyre, Alasdair (1984). *After Virtue*. South Bend, IN: University of Notre Dame Press.

McMahan, Jeff (2001). *The Ethics of Killing*. New York: Oxford University Press.

Moore, G. E. (1903). *Principia Ethica*. Cambridge: Cambridge University Press.

Nagel, Thomas (1970). *The Possibility of Altruism*. Princeton: Princeton University Press.

———(1979). 'The Fragmentation of Value'. In *Mortal Questions*, Cambridge: Cambridge University Press, 128–41.

———(1986). *The View from Nowhere*. New York: Oxford University Press.

———(1991). *Equality and Partiality*. New York: Oxford University Press.

_____ (1997). *The Final Word*. New York: Oxford University Press.

Noddings, Nell (1984). *Care: A Feminine Approach to Ethics and Moral Education*. Berkeley: University of California Press.

Norcross, Alastair (2006). 'The Scalar Approach to Utilitarianism'. In Henry West (ed.), *Blackwell Guide to Mill's Utilitarianism*, Malden, MA: Blackwell Publishers, 217–32.

Nozick, Robert (1974). *Anarchy, State, and Utopia*. New York: Basic Books.

O'Neill, Onora (1989). *Constructions of Reason: Explorations of Kant's Practical Philosophy*. Cambridge: Cambridge University Press.

_____ (1996). *Towards Justice and Virtue*. Cambridge: Cambridge University Press.

Parfit, Derek (1984). *Reasons and Persons*. Oxford: Clarendon Press.

Perry, Ralph Barton (1926). *General Theory of Value*. New York: Longmans.

Price, Richard (1787). *A Review of the Principal Questions of Morals*. London.

Prichard, H. A. (1912). 'Does Moral Philosophy Rest on a Mistake?'. *Mind*, 21: 21–37.

Quinn, Warren (1989a). 'Actions, Intentions, and Consequences: The Doctrine of Double Effect'. *Philosophy and Public Affairs*, 18: 334–51.

_____ (1989b). 'Actions, Intentions, and Consequences: The Doctrine of Doing and Allowing'. *Philosophical Review*, 98: 287–312.

Rachels, James (1975). 'Active and Passive Euthanasia'. *New England Journal of Medicine*, 292: 78–80.

Railton, Peter (1984). 'Alienation, Consequentialism, and the Demands of Morality'. *Philosophy and Public Affairs*, 13: 134–71.

_____ (1986). 'Moral Realism'. *Philosophical Review*, 95: 163–207.

_____ (1988). 'How Thinking about Character and Utilitarianism Might Lead to Rethinking the Character of Utilitarianism'. *Midwest Studies in Philosophy*, 13: 398–416.

Rashdall, Henry (1929). *A Theory of Good and Evil*. Oxford: Clarendon Press.

Rawls, John (1951). 'Outline for a Decision Procedure in Ethics'. *Philosophical Review*, 60: 177–97.

_____ (1955). 'Two Concepts of Rules'. *Philosophical Review*, 64: 3–32.

_____ (1958). 'Justice as Fairness'. *Philosophical Review*, 67: 164–94.

_____ (1971). *A Theory of Justice*. Cambridge, MA: Harvard University Press.

Reid, Thomas (1788). *Essays on the Active Powers of Man*. Edinburgh.

Richards, D. A. J. (1971). *A Theory of Reasons for Action*. Oxford: Clarendon Press.

Ross, W. D. (1930). *The Right and the Good*. Oxford: Clarendon Press.

_____ (1939). *The Foundations of Ethics*. Oxford: Clarendon Press.

Sayre-McCord, Geoffrey (ed.) (1988a). *Essays on Moral Realism*. Ithaca, NY: Cornell University Press.

_____ (1988b). 'Moral Theory and Explanatory Impotence'. In Sayre-McCord (1988a), 256–81.

Scanlon, Thomas (1998). *What We Owe to Each Another*. Cambridge, MA: Harvard University Press.

Scheffler, Samuel (1979). *The Rejection of Consequentialism*. Oxford: Clarendon Press.

Scheffler, Samuel (2004). 'Doing and Allowing'. *Ethics*, 114: 215–39.

Sher, George (1987). *Desert*. Princeton: Princeton University Press.

——— (2005). *In Praise of Blame*. Princeton: Princeton University Press.

Sidgwick, Henry (1874). *Methods of Ethics*. London: Macmillin.

Sinnott-Armstrong, Walter (2006). 'Moral Intuitionism Meets Empirical Psychology'. In Terence Horgan and Mark Timmons (eds.), *Metaethics After Moore*, Oxford: Clarendon Press, 339–65.

Slote, Michael (1992). *From Morality to Virtue*. New York: Oxford University Press.

——— (2007). *The Ethics of Care and Empathy*. New York: Routledge.

Steiner, Hillel (1994). *An Essay on Rights*. Oxford: Blackwell.

Stevenson, C. L. (1937). 'The Emotive Meaning of Ethical Terms'. *Mind*, 46: 14–31.

——— (1938). 'Persuasive Definitions'. *Mind*, 47: 331–50.

——— (1944). *Ethics and Language*. New Haven: Yale University Press.

Sturgeon, Nicholas (1988). 'Moral Explanation'. In Sayre-McCord (1988a), 229–55.

Sumner, L. Wayne (1987). *The Moral Foundations of Rights*. Oxford: Clarendon Press.

Thomson, Judith Jarvis (1971). 'A Defense of Abortion'. *Philosophy and Public Affairs*, 1: 47–66.

——— (1990). *The Realm of Rights*. Cambridge, MA: Harvard University Press.

Toulmin, Stephen (1950). *An Examination of the Place of Reason in Ethics*. Cambridge: Cambridge University Press.

Urmson, J. O. (1953). 'The Interpretation of the Moral Philosophy of J. S. Mill'. *Philosophical Quarterly*, 3: 33–9.

Wallace, R. Jay (1994). *Responsibility and the Moral Sentiments*. Cambridge, MA: Harvard University Press.

Wellman, Carl (1985). *A Theory of Rights*. Totowa, NJ: Rowman & Allanheld.

Wolf, Susan (1993). *Freedom within Reason*. New York: Oxford University Press.

CHAPTER 26

ESSENCES, INTERSECTIONS, AND AMERICAN FEMINISM

ANN GARRY

IN ORDER to capture some of what is interesting and influential in contemporary North American feminist philosophy, I pursue two strategies. In the first half of the essay I offer a very brief historical sketch and characterization of a few fields of feminist philosophy. In the second half, I focus in more detail on a cluster of feminist issues in metaphysics concerning 'essentialism' and 'intersectionality'.

A LITTLE RECENT HISTORY

Contemporary North American feminist philosophy began to flourish in the 1970s.[1] Its political and intellectual roots were in the 'second wave' of feminist

Thanks go to my colleagues Mark Balaguer, Talia Bettcher, Sharon Bishop, David Pitt, and Kayley Vernallis who all responded within days to a plea to comment on a draft of this essay.

[1] Three clarifications: (a) by 'North American feminist philosophy' I mean to include feminist philosophers writing in English in North America from the 1970s onward regardless of their birth

activism that started in the 1960s; but its practitioners also had roots in the various philosophical traditions found in mid-twentieth-century graduate philosophy departments. Philosophers were among the feminists who began to teach, write, and speak about feminist theory at the same time as they were engaged in feminist activism both inside and outside the academy. They were among the creators of Women's Studies programs and were enriched by the interdisciplinary work that occurred there. Across the academic disciplines, as well as outside the academy, the common bond among feminists was not a universally adopted definition, method, or doctrine of feminism, but a shared commitment to end women's oppression and to make the world a better place for all women. Feminist philosophy grew up whenever and wherever feminists needed to make philosophical sense of issues arising in the world, a world that included their classrooms, offices, personal relationships, and even theorizing itself. It was not a simple matter of applying the 'tools of one's philosophical trade' to a new set of issues. The tools themselves needed to be examined for biases and limitations.

Feminist philosophers came to appreciate the extent to which philosophy as a discipline was itself a part of the world that needed changing. Philosophy has traditionally both influenced and reflected the fundamental values of the societies in which it exists; it is one of the cluster of cultural institutions in which human beings live, understand their lives, and, in only some cases, flourish. Neither philosophy nor other cultural institutions such as organized religion, law, and the family have fostered women's flourishing. Feminist philosophers hoped that their work would not only reveal the sexism, androcentrism, and other forms of male bias and misogyny in philosophy, but also produce new philosophy that would encourage women's full personhood and participation in all spheres of life. This is not to say that feminist philosophers agreed on the details, only that they shared the same cluster of motivations.[2]

nation. Most of these women are teaching in the United States and Canada, although there are some Mexican feminists such as María Pía Lara who should be included. (b) By 'feminist philosophers' I refer most frequently to those trained in academic philosophy. However, theorists in other disciplines contribute as well. One of the most influential feminist theorists/philosophers, Catharine MacKinnon, has a background in law and political theory; Patricia Hill Collins is a sociologist; and Carol Gilligan is a psychologist. (c) Although I often refer to feminist philosophers as women (and most are), there are some men who do feminist philosophy. Collections of essays that include a number of male philosophers are May, Strikwerda, and Hopkins (1996) and Digby (1998).

[2] For readers unfamiliar with feminist philosophy, let me note how important it is to take seriously the extent and depth of feminists' philosophical disagreements. For example, debate begins even as one tries to name the field and describe its scope: is it 'feminist philosophy', 'feminism in philosophy',

Traditional philosophers in North America and elsewhere tended to be (at best) somewhat mystified by the need for and nature of feminist philosophy. In spite of all the deep disagreement among traditional philosophers, many believed that philosophy was supposed to be abstract, objective, detached from politics, and concerned with universal human truths, principles, and assumptions. In North America this was most notably exemplified by analytic philosophers. Feminist philosophers, on the other hand, held political values that guided their choice of philosophical topics, theories, and critiques, believed that 'universal' or 'generic' theories were often covertly androcentric or male-biased, found that attention to women's bodies and concrete experiences were worthy of philosophical consideration in ethics and epistemology. Some even thought that philosophy should discuss (gasp!) rape and pornography. Such discussions did not sound like philosophy to many feminists' male colleagues or professors. Feminists, on the other hand, believed that their traditional male professors and colleagues were fleeing as fast as they possibly could from an examination of one of the most important facets of our lives—gender. This was especially shocking, since the 'examined life' is allegedly close to the heart of the profession itself.

I want to take 1975 as a snapshot of what the field of feminist philosophy looked like in North America in the 'early days'. Women philosophers had been writing and teaching feminist material for several years, but little academic feminist philosophy had been published since Simone de Beauvoir's *Le Deuxième Sexe* in 1949. One could read every published work of feminist philosophy—popular or academic—and have plenty of time left over. By popular feminist philosophy I am thinking of works such as Shulamith Firestone's *The Dialectic of Sex* (1970), Kate Millett's *Sexual Politics* (1970), Ti-Grace Atkinson's *Amazon Odyssey* (1974), and Mary Daly's early books on religion and philosophy (1968, 1973). Academic feminist philosophy was far less available. Two special issues of journals on feminist philosophy had appeared, *The Monist* (Mothersill 1973) and *The Philosophical Forum* (Gould and Wartofsky 1973–4); and rare individual articles appeared in philosophical journals: for example, those of Christine Garside in *Dialogue* (1971), Judith

'philosophical feminism', or 'doing philosophy as a feminist'? There is also disagreement about the appropriate way to couch fundamental values: should feminists seek to end oppression, end subordination, or seek a more affirmatively stated goal? Since it would be too disruptive to continue to note this at every turn, just keep in mind that feminist philosophers, on almost every point, are as likely to disagree with each other as are other types of philosophers. Readers should not be misled by the even-handed tone I have attempted to use; this essay represents my 'take' on the field.

Thomson in *Philosophy and Public Affairs* (1971), Alison Jaggar (1974) and Joyce Trebilcot (1975) in *Ethics*, and Susan Haack (1974) and Trudy Govier (1974) in *Philosophy*. Many of the early essays seem very 'tame' by today's standards. Anthologies helped feminism make its way into the classroom. Christine Pierce had an essay in an interdisciplinary anthology (Gornick and Moran 1971). Two anthologies on moral issues edited by pro-feminist men contained several feminist essays (Wasserstrom 1975 and Baker and Elliston 1975). A few anthologies of essays in feminist philosophy were in the pipeline, but none was published until 1977 (English 1977 and Vetterling-Braggin *et al.* 1977).

It was unusual to find feminist papers presented on the programs of the American Philosophical Association or Canadian Philosophical Association. Alison Jaggar (APA, 1972) and Susan Sherwin (CPA, 1975) were, to my knowledge, the first. However, the gates of the primary professional associations were not immediately opened wide. Instead, in the United States feminist talks and papers were given at meetings of the Society for Women in Philosophy (SWIP) at various locations around the country as well as in conjunction with APA meetings. Canadian SWIP was founded in 1976. The vast majority of colleges and universities as yet had no separate feminist philosophy course. If there were any at all, it was literally one course.[3]

CONTEMPORARY CONCERNS OF NORTH AMERICAN FEMINIST PHILOSOPHY

More than three decades later, one short bookshelf of feminist philosophy has turned into rows and rows of library stacks. At most one meager feminist philosophy course on a campus has become a philosophical specialty in which dissertations are written, colleagues are appointed, and courses taught at all levels. Yet to call it a 'specialty' can be misleading. It is more useful to think of feminist philosophy as a set of *approaches* to philosophical questions rather than to consider it a field such as philosophy of language or philosophy of

---

[3] The first course I taught, in spring 1975 at California State University, Los Angeles, included Harriet Taylor Mill and John Stuart Mill, Simone de Beauvoir, Shulamith Firestone, and some essays from the *Philosophical Forum* special feminist issue. Fourteen students enrolled. Today at CSULA, more than 600 students each year enroll in sections of a comparable course.

mind. Feminist philosophers concern themselves with almost every field of philosophy and reshape each field as they reconceptualize its issues.[4] They also use—and transform—a variety of philosophical methods. In North America this includes the typical range of Western philosophical methods: analytic philosophy, pragmatism, phenomenology, critical theory, hermeneutics, and poststructuralism. Although my focus here pays less attention to feminists of either a pragmatic or a continental bent, this is simply a matter of space. All of the methods listed have been influential.[5]

During the decades in which feminist philosophers have been developing their views and engaging with various philosophical traditions, the traditions themselves have changed as well. Today many North American philosophers, both traditional and feminist, find themselves wanting to balance several competing factors in their thinking. On the one hand, they are doing *philosophy*, a normative enterprise, not merely a descriptive one. On the other hand, many are pulled to 'naturalize' philosophy—not to replace philosophy with empirical work, but to recognize the relevance of empirical factors and research in the ways they frame questions as well as determine what counts as a plausible philosophical view. Still others are pulled by the 'postmodern' to examine very closely the deepest traditional philosophical assumptions about the possibility of objective knowledge or of unified selves capable of being stable moral agents and knowers, and so forth.

Feminist philosophers' desires to steer some kind of balanced course are deeply influenced by the factors just mentioned, but also by political and moral motivations. Feminist philosophy, directly or indirectly, supports or contributes to ending the oppression of all women. This is not just a negative task of rooting out sexism, androcentrism, and other forms of male bias in philosophy, but also a positive task of constructing philosophical theories that will support the flourishing of all women as full-fledged human beings. Thus feminists' 'normative' requirements include, for example, a sufficiently

---

[4] Only philosophy of mathematics has to date escaped feminist intervention. A number of anthologies organized by philosophical field give a sense of the range of feminist philosophical fields: e.g. Fricker and Hornsby (2000); Pearsall (1999); Kourany (1998); Jaggar and Young (1998); and Garry and Pearsall (1996). The *Stanford Encyclopedia of Philosophy*, <http://plato.stanford.edu>, also has excellent feminist essays covering a very wide range of topics. Since feminist treatments of logic tend to be omitted from the preceding sources, see Nye (1990) and Falmagne and Hass (2002).

[5] See, e.g., pragmatists Charlene Haddock Seigfried (1993, 1996); Shannon Sullivan (2001); and Sharyn Clough (2003). A wide range of continentally influenced feminists include Sandra Bartky (1990); Iris Marion Young (1990*a*, *b*); Judith Butler (1993, 1999); Nancy Fraser (1989); and Kelly Oliver (1998). Similar authors are collected in Allen and Young (1989); Nicholson (1990); and Cahill and Hansen (2003).

substantive theory of justice to argue against oppression, epistemological theories that can unearth and correct biased empirical studies, androcentric metaphysical claims, and so on. Although normativity is required, feminist philosophy almost always also needs to be 'naturalized' in order for gender, something social, to find a way into the philosophical discussion at all. There is no space for consideration of gender when issues are analyzed solely in abstract and universal terms (e.g. a traditional analysis of "s knows that p").

At the same time as feminist philosophers are motivated to pursue normative, substantive theories, they are also pulled by other forces to be very wary of their dangers. This is not simply because this is 'a postmodern era' full of competing sets of values and standards; it is also a result of various controversies among feminists. From the start of academic feminism in the last third of the twentieth century, and continuing to the present day, there have been controversies among groups of feminists: between lesbians and heterosexual women, among women from dominant white groups and other ethnicities/races, among women of different classes, between able-bodied and less able-bodied women, between transgendered women and nontranswomen, between Western and non-Western women, between women of the developed 'north' and from the less developed 'south', and so on. Women on the less powerful sides of the controversies have objected to the kinds of privileged status given to the more powerful groups' experiences and characteristics and to the overgeneralizing claims that women in the powerful groups make. These kinds of controversies came to be known for a time, collectively and unfortunately, as 'the problem of difference'; however, what is at stake in each controversy varies. I will attend to some of these stakes later in the discussion of essentialism and intersectionality. Feminist philosophers have learned a tremendous amount from these controversies, both philosophically and in terms of politics and morality. Today, even feminist philosophers who are not otherwise inclined toward pluralistic theories or postmodern approaches nevertheless tend to be pluralists, because they recognize the great diversity among women, their experiences, their values, and so on. For the vast majority of feminist philosophers, pluralism does not mean relativism—the need for normative standards precludes a move to relativism. So feminist philosophers wanting to balance normativity and diversity must steer their courses carefully.

In order to get a sense of what concerns feminist philosophers in North America today, I briefly characterize feminist issues in two broad areas of philosophy: (1) ethics, philosophy of law, and social and political philosophy;

and (2) epistemology and philosophy of science. I then turn to a more detailed discussion of one topic in feminist metaphysics. I make no attempt to draw a general contrast between North American feminist philosophy and feminist philosophy in other parts of the world. It would be particularly hard to do this for English-speaking philosophical communities. The important disagreements among feminist philosophers tend not to break out along national or continental lines—as was suggested in the preceding paragraph. This is not to say that national context is trivial, but that it is only one among many factors that go into the concrete location of feminist voices. Nevertheless, in choosing a metaphysical topic to treat in more detail, I settled on essentialism and intersectionality because this cluster of issues illustrates some of the impact that the pluralistic ethnic context of North America has had on feminist philosophy.

ETHICS, PHILOSOPHY OF LAW, AND SOCIAL AND POLITICAL PHILOSOPHY

The fields I want to treat together in this brief section cover an enormous range of issues, but share common features. I find Alison Jaggar's strategy for thinking about feminist approaches to ethics very helpful, and believe that it can be applied to the other fields that explicitly deal with values as well. Jaggar points out that in order to act on a commitment to correct male biases in traditional ethics,

Feminist ethics . . . begins from the convictions that the subordination of women is morally wrong and that the moral experience of women is as worthy of respect as that of men. On the practical level, then, the goals of feminist ethics are the following: first, to articulate moral critiques of actions and practices that perpetuate women's subordination; second, to prescribe morally justifiable ways of resisting such actions and practices; and, third, to envision morally desirable alternatives that will promote women's emancipation. On a theoretical level, the goal of feminist ethics is to develop philosophical accounts of the nature of morality and of the central moral concepts that treat women's moral experience respectfully, though never uncritically.   (Jaggar 2001: 538)

I believe that with the appropriate substitutions of 'legal', 'political', or 'social' for 'moral', Jaggar gives us a useful and open-ended way to think about the concerns of feminist philosophers in these fields. This does not mean that there is a separate sphere for feminist ethics or political philosophy, or that men and women should develop different kinds of moral or social theories. Instead it means that we should assume that any moral, social, or political issue will be a feminist issue in some respect unless we can determine that it has no gendered dimensions.

Moral, political, social, and legal philosophy were among the earliest fields to engage feminist philosophers. Although sometimes people focus on feminists in the 1970s and early 1980s who were hoping to explain the root causes of women's oppression, there was always a rich variety of feminist work being done. Below I list a few of the issues, giving references that merely scratch the surface of the body of feminist literature. Feminist philosophers have

- Critiqued canonical philosophers' views about women, especially their 'virtues', 'character', and 'nature' that rationalized women's subordination (Clark and Lange 1979; Okin 1992).[6]
- Offered analyses and revisions of the cluster of concepts used in these fields: equality, justice, autonomy, oppression, exploitation, freedom, coercion, power, privacy, rights, responsibilities, and so on (A. Allen 1988, 2003; MacKinnon 1989; Young 1990a). For example, autonomy can be thought to be relational or social, not only a characteristic of an isolated individual (Meyers 1989; Friedman 2003).
- Developed proposals and analyses concerning 'applied' issues such as abortion, affirmative action, pornography, sexual assault, marriage, pregnancy discrimination, heterosexism, health care, and atrocity/evil that reflected sophisticated appraisals of both overt and covert sexism and androcentrism in our thinking, our institutions, and our practices (MacKinnon 1987; Sherwin 1992; Calhoun 2000; Brison 2002; Card 2002; Shrage 2003).
- Focused on ways in which women's moral experiences and moral emotions have been overlooked or devalued, and strategies for rectifying this. The most well-known examples here are analyses focusing on an ethics of care or maternal ethics (e.g. Gilligan 1982, 1988; Ruddick 1995; Held 2006), but work has been done from other traditions including lesbian ethics (Hoagland 1988; Card 1995).

---

[6] For detailed work see the volumes in the Pennsylvania State University Press series *Re-reading the Canon*. Individual volumes are entitled *Feminist Interpretations of [Philosopher]*. Philosophers range from Plato to contemporary figures. See, e.g., Freeland (1998) and Lange (2002).

- Called attention to the variety of kinds of moral relationships that people have with each other, including friendship and asymmetrical relations of dependency (Lugones and Spelman 1983; Friedman 1993; Kittay 1999).
- Focused on gendered facets of global issues and the complexities of transnational feminism (Narayan 1997; Jaggar 1998; Schutte 1998; Okin *et al.* 1999; Narayan and Harding 2000; Nussbaum 2000, 2004; Donchin 2004).
- Analyzed a number of methodological issues—e.g. the role of narratives in ethics (Lara 1998; H. L. Nelson 2001; Brison 2002; Walker 2007)—and the biases implicit in various methods of moral justification and the concepts on which they rely—e.g. moral rationality and objectivity, and proposed alternatives to them (Walker 2007, several summarized well in Jaggar 2000).

Feminist philosophers are pursuing a number of paths to do these kinds of work, some of which are not compatible with each other. One cannot identify 'feminist ethics' with any single approach to moral theories or issues, an error sometimes made by identifying feminist ethics with the 'ethics of care'.[7] There is room for multiple approaches. One approach that I would encourage is for feminists to put forth sets of standards or conditions of adequacy that any moral or political theory must meet. In that way we can be sure that such theories are applicable to all human beings and respectful of all individuals' lives and experiences.[8]

---

[7] Nel Noddings used 'feminine' in her title *Caring: A Feminine Approach to Ethics* (1984). The distinction between 'feminine' and 'feminist' ethics has been used to understand differences in focus—e.g., by Alison Jaggar (1989 and later) and Rosemarie Tong (1993).

[8] I have focused more on ethics than on political or legal philosophy in this section. There have been influential (incompatible) theories in the latter fields that I must mention briefly. In political philosophy, feminist theories have sometimes been labeled in terms of the traditional discourses from which they arose: liberal, radical, Marxist, and socialist feminists (socialists do not subsume gender oppression under economic oppression) (Jaggar 1983). Radical feminists are hard to characterize. Loosely speaking, early radical feminists such as Firestone (1970), rooted gender oppression in biology, whereas recent radicals such as MacKinnon root women's oppression in the construction of their sexuality and in the depth and pervasiveness of sexual violence against women. We should note that MacKinnon herself rejects the term 'radical feminism' in favor of 'feminism unmodified' (1987). Women of color have sometimes objected to the widespread and hegemonic use of these categories (see Sandoval 1991, 2000).

Theories in feminist philosophy of law tend to be labeled by whether they propose ideals and remedies in terms of 'sameness' (advocating gender neutrality wherever possible) or 'difference' (advocating various ways in which law can take into account men's and women's different situations) or propose to reject that dichotomy and make the central focus ending male dominance by means of law (respectively, Williams 1982; Littleton 1987; and MacKinnon 1987, 1989). Of course, there are other variations such as pragmatism and intersectional analyses. More attention will be given to the legal theory of intersectionality later (Crenshaw 1989).

EPISTEMOLOGY AND PHILOSOPHY
OF SCIENCE

Feminist philosophers write prolifically in epistemology and philosophy of science. Feminist epistemological concerns were initially developed in the context of philosophy of science and the practices of science; through the decades the fields have shared a set of core concepts and continued to be intertwined. Elizabeth Anderson (2003) characterizes feminist epistemology and philosophy of science as fields that study

> the ways in which gender does and ought to influence our conceptions of knowledge, the knowing subject, and practices of inquiry and justification. It identifies ways in which dominant conceptions and practices of knowledge attribution, acquisition, and justification systematically disadvantage women and other subordinated groups, and strives to reform these conceptions and practices so that they serve the interests of these groups.

The kinds of topics that feminist philosophers address in these areas range from the ways in which gendered inequities have worked to harm both science and women to systematically rethinking methods and concepts of the fields. Just as in ethics and other fields that deal more explicitly and systematically with values, feminists have offered a number of strategies, not all compatible with each other, to produce philosophies of science and theories of knowledge that can promote the interests of subordinated groups and treat them as full-fledged people. These strategies—feminist empiricism, feminist standpoint theory, and feminist postmodernism—were distinguished by Sandra Harding (1986) and have been criticized, slightly modified, and often retained as useful, even if not altogether satisfactory. Each kind of feminist theory transforms the traditional discourse from which it grew and contains a variety of positions within it; some theories cross back and forth among the categories.

Feminist empiricists encompass two different groups: feminist philosophers who begin their work within the post-positivist Anglo-American traditions in epistemology and philosophy of science (e.g. Longino 1990; L. H. Nelson 1990) and women scientists who have been fighting to rid their disciplines of sexism and androcentrism by more strictly and carefully applying the best existing methods of their disciplines. Feminist standpoint theorists draw from Marx's notion that the standpoint of the proletariat is epistemically privileged, but have refined this kind of approach in ways that make it more plausible. Harding, for example (1991, 1993), does not automatically grant epistemic privilege to subordinated people, but advocates starting research and other inquiries from the lives of women and members of other subordinated groups and attending to the social conditions in which knowledge is produced and authorized.[9] Feminist postmodernists use the resources of poststructuralism to critique not only the traditional institutions and concepts of science, philosophy of science, and epistemology, but also the other feminist theories in these fields (Haraway 1991, 1997; Code 2006).[10]

Below are several clusters of fruitful issues that concern feminist epistemologists and philosophers of science.

- Women have been ill served by science, philosophy of science, and epistemology in a number of ways. These fields have excluded them from inquiry, denied them epistemic authority, denigrated allegedly 'feminine' cognitive styles and approaches to research, and produced theories that disadvantaged women—either by representing them explicitly as inferior or deviant or by making women as well as power relations between genders invisible (Keller 1985, 1992; Anderson 2003). Feminists believe that as increasing numbers of women, other subordinated groups, and their political allies enter these fields, both the cognitive content of and social equity in the fields should improve greatly.
- The key concepts used in science, philosophy of science, and epistemology have been rethought: for example, knowledge, knowers, rationality, objectivity, and evidence. Some feminists advocate that knowledge itself is best understood as social, not individual (Longino 1990; L. H. Nelson 1990). Others press for an understanding of individual knowers themselves as social (Code 1995). Still others debate whether traditional ideals of objectivity have any value and delineate alternative conceptions of objectivity (Harding 1991, 1993; Antony 1995; Haslanger 1995, 2002; Lloyd 1995b).
- One of the more important methodological topics concerns the ways in which values and 'biases' enter scientific practice, philosophy of science,

---

[9] See Harding (2004) for a variety of feminist standpoint theories, written by scholars from a number of different disciplines.

[10] It is difficult to decide who is sufficiently 'postmodern' to be placed in the category; this difficulty illustrates the limitations of the categories and the ways in which individual works cross or transcend them. One can see Haraway as both a standpoint theorist and a postmodernist. Code (2006) draws from various traditions in her recent thoroughgoing reconceptualization of epistemology that rests on an ecological model. Thoroughly postmodern philosophers such as Butler (1993, 1999) would not want to have 'a theory of knowledge' at all.

and epistemology. Feminists explore the kinds of values that facilitate rather than block free inquiry, as well as critique androcentric (and hypocritical) notions of value-free inquiry (Longino 1990; Anderson 1995b; Lloyd 1995a), and explore bias as a problem, a paradox, and a resource (Antony 2002; Anderson 2003).

- Critiques have been given of particular uses of science and philosophy of science: for example, Lloyd's (2005) study of evolutionary theory's errors about female orgasm, or Fausto-Sterling's (1992, 2000) work on sexed bodies.
- Philosophers of science and, to a lesser degree, epistemologists have begun to explore the connections between feminist and post-colonial studies (Harding 1998, 2006; Duran 2001).

METAPHYSICS

Although metaphysics has not engaged as large a number of feminist philosophers as the other fields we have discussed, it is nevertheless important to feminists, in part because theories in other areas of philosophy as well as other disciplines rest on metaphysical assumptions. For example, what metaphysical assumptions about 'human nature' are made by theories in ethics, political philosophy, or economics? In addition, academic metaphysics is at least loosely connected to cultural 'world views' or views about reality that play influential roles in people's lives. Although postmodern feminists have sometimes criticized the enterprise of metaphysics itself—whether done by feminist or by traditional philosophers—other feminist philosophers, believing metaphysics to be important, have critiqued the frequent androcentric character and less frequent overt sexism of traditional metaphysics.[11] Sally Haslanger argues that feminists have contributions to make in all the major areas of metaphysics: studies of what is real, of the basic concepts used in understanding ourselves and the world, and of the presuppositions of inquiry (2000a: 108).

Although I believe that Haslanger is correct about the possible scope of feminist contributions to metaphysics, to date many of the metaphysical (and

---

[11] Lloyd (1995b), Witt (1995, 2002), Antony (1998), and Haslanger (2000a) favor doing metaphysics; anti-metaphysical critiques come from Fraser and Nicholson (1990) and Butler (1993, 1999).

anti-metaphysical) issues that have engaged feminists have been related in one way or another to human beings. For example, I mentioned discussions of 'human nature' and human beings above (Nussbaum 1995a, 2000, and Antony 1998, 2000). Feminists have contributed significantly to the discussion of the 'social construction' of 'reality', especially of the categories 'men' and 'women' (e.g. Butler 1993, 1999 and Haslanger 2000b, who offer very different alternatives). We can also ask in what ways feminists think differently from traditional philosophers about the self or personal identity, in particular the self's moral dimensions (Meyers 1997; Brison 2002), or about the 'mind–body' problem, the 'objects of psychology', or the 'problem of other minds' (Overall 1988; Young 1990b; Scheman 1993, 2000).

In order to take a more detailed look at a set of issues in feminist philosophy, I want to consider a cluster of issues that center around 'essentialism'.[12] I have chosen this set of issues in part because it illustrates the complex connections between politics and theory. What has driven the feminist controversy over 'essences' is not so much particular antecedent metaphysical commitments, but an appreciation of the implications that various metaphysical views have for feminist politics and theory as well as for moral behavior. A second factor influencing my choice is that if there is anything that can be called 'characteristically North American' in feminist philosophy/theory, it might be the particular ways in which North American theorists treat the differences among us all. As I noted in the first section of this essay, the necessity of confronting divisions along virtually every axis of privilege and subordination has had a great deal of influence on the positions that feminist philosophers take today.

Linda Martin Alcoff has recently written that the anti-essentialists have 'won the debate' with essentialists, not because essentialists have all changed their positions, but because 'they must now show that their views are not, and were never, truly essentialist' (2006: 152).[13] There is certainly at least a kernel of truth in what Alcoff says. Most feminists today who argue that there are necessary and sufficient conditions for being a woman (e.g. Haslanger 2000b) or who want to talk about the 'metaphysics of sex and gender'

---

[12] Readers hoping for a univocal, neutral definition of 'essentialism' may be disappointed. In feminist contexts someone who claims or assumes that there is either a set of necessary and sufficient conditions for being a woman or a set of experiences that women universally share is likely to be labeled an essentialist. However, this is only the beginning of the story.

[13] A number of facets of my approach in this section (thought not all) are similar to Alcoff's in Alcoff 2006: ch. 6. Because I heard earlier incarnations of her chapter as lectures, it is likely that I have been influenced by Alcoff in ways of which I am no longer aware.

(e.g. Alcoff herself, 2006) believe that their views do not fall prey to earlier 'anti-essentialist' objections. However, there are other feminist proposals that suggest that the debate is not over. Naomi Zack (2005) has proposed a new essentialist view that directly attacks certain kinds of anti-essentialism; and Martha Nussbaum's essentialism remains at the core of her ongoing projects (2000, 2004). I want to discuss these two views briefly in order to see where controversy remains, and to offer a simple way out of it.

First, let us step back to remind ourselves why feminist philosophers are bothered by essences and essentialism. To start with, there is a history of problematic essences attributed to women. It is widely known that many major Western philosophers and other intellectuals had no qualms about characterizing the nature or essence of human beings and of men and women in ways that failed to attribute to women the qualities, capacities, or virtues equal to those of men in the culture of the author. The precise terms vary by time and place, and from the start were overlaid with other hierarchies. Consider Aristotle: men, but not women, have a natural fitness to command, and only free men have a faculty of deliberation that has authority. Free women's faculty of deliberation lacks authority, and slave men and women lack the deliberative faculty itself (1941: *Politics*, 1259^a–1260^b). So free women, slave men, and slave women are hardly on a par with free men with respect to being the essential 'rational animal'. If one were citing Rousseau, Freud, or a contemporary evolutionary psychologist rather than Aristotle, the upshot would be similar. Intellectual support is being provided for cultural views that do not recognize women as full-fledged human beings on a par with men. A hierarchical power structure is left untouched and unexamined. Women's lesser position in the author's culture is justified, explained, or even seen as necessary.

It is no surprise that feminists object to such views—both for the negative content of women's 'nature' or 'essence' and for the fact that such views appear to make women's nature fixed and unchangeable. Before we look at some of the alternatives that have been considered, we should note that it is a mistake to consider all critics of universal claims about women or of women's essence as 'postmodern'. Postmodern feminists are perhaps the most radical 'anti-essentialists', in that they reject the entire way of speaking; for example, Judith Butler (1993, 1999) finds it important to destabilize the category 'woman' (and 'sex' and 'gender').

Nevertheless a variety of other positions exist, each differing somewhat from the others. A few alternatives are listed below.

On the one hand we have:

- Fixed (or natural) essence of women, often explained as necessary and sufficient conditions.

On the other hand, among the alternatives would be:

- Changing characteristics of women over time or place.
- Variable characteristics among women at the same time and place, especially variations by ethnicity/race, sexuality, class, etc.
- Characteristics that are not natural but are socially constructed.
- Rejection of the whole way of speaking that includes essences.

A second set of contrasts focus on *experiences* rather than characteristics of women:

- Women have a set of experiences in common (in virtue of which they are women).

- Experiences of women (or of womanhood) are diverse in all the ways listed above.
- Rejection of the whole way of speaking that looks for common experiences.

Although these alternatives have sometimes been merged or confused by their critics or their proponents, they differ in important ways. Consider examples in the first set of alternatives above. There might be necessary and sufficient conditions for being a woman, but they could be socially constructed rather than natural. Or there might not be necessary and sufficient conditions, but the variations among women's characteristics might be natural rather than socially constructed (though surely many would be socially constructed). And many of the alternatives listed here do not dictate any particular metaphysical view such as realism or anti-realism. Although the alternatives raise different philosophical issues and questions of fact, I suspect that anti-essentialists have sometimes merged the claims because the claims they are attacking about the 'essence of woman' or 'women's universally shared experiences' have had similar kinds of negative real-life consequences. Recall that what is at stake in these discussions is not merely theoretical, but also concerns real-life political and moral human interactions.

The 'stakes' for feminists include at least the following: (a) how best to deal with race and racism as well as heterosexism in both practice and theory; (b) how to develop theories that can accommodate the varieties of women's experiences; (c) how best to explain the grounds for rejecting traditional biological categories of sex (or gender) as inadequate to encompass the full range of women. As we discuss the stakes, it is important to keep in mind a point from the first section of the essay: feminist philosophers want to retain sufficient normativity to ground both their political and their philosophical positions.

In order to appreciate the views of philosophers who firmly believe that we need 'essences' of some kind in order to supply the normativity required to pursue feminist goals, we first need to look briefly at a few anti-essentialist arguments that focus on (a)–(c) above. The concept of 'intersectionality' considers (a) and (b).

Intersectionality is the most widely accepted way in which feminists in North America think about multiple facets of oppression and experience, though it remains controversial. Intersectional analyses hold that oppressions by race, ethnicity, gender, class, and so on, do not act independently of each other in our lives; instead, each is shaped by and works through the others. Intersectionality caught on very quickly among feminist theorists after Kimberlé Crenshaw (1989) introduced it in legal contexts to explain why an analysis in terms of either race alone or sex alone (a 'single-axis' analysis) was inadequate for an explanation of the kind of discrimination that African-American women were suffering under US law. Although Crenshaw originally intended the term to apply to multiple *oppressions* and included only race and gender, because the concept resonated with so many people, it is sometimes used today more broadly to illuminate the ways in which different facets of our social situation interact with and through each other—whether they are 'axes' of privilege or of oppression. This wider kind of intersectional analysis can not only make the point that the oppression experienced by a Latina lesbian living in the USA will not be separable into three isolated oppressions, it can also illuminate the ways in which an axis of privilege would intersect with oppressions on the basis of gender, ethnicity, and sexual orientation in a Latina lesbian from a wealthy family.[14] The different interpretations of intersectionality share key insights: (i) each facet of a person shapes the other facets, so individuals in the same 'social group' will have both similarities and differences with others in the group; (ii) oppression (and privilege) of members of a group will be shaped by and work though individuals' other facets.

Crenshaw (1991) uses examples of different ways in which domestic violence affects African-American women and men. So, for example, although both women and men in the African-American community rally against police mistreatment of African-American men who are batterers, this position sometimes has the negative consequence of leaving unprotected the African-American women being battered. One's interests coincide with those of other group members only up to a point, because of the other facets of oneself that are not shared; group-identity-based commonality is thus partial.

Intersectionality requires that no woman's experience is seen as 'woman's' *simpliciter*. There is no space to take one race or class of women as a paradigm from which others deviate. In this spirit María Lugones (2003) calls upon feminist theorists to be pluralistic from the start.

Although intersectional approaches can incorporate differences of sexual orientation, there are other questions concerning lesbians, intersexuals, and transgendered people that require discussion of reasons to reject a biological essence of women—that is, stake (c) above. The focus here would be not on experiences and oppressions, but on who should 'count' as women, the role of bodies in gendered identity, and the degree to which heterosexuality is central to the definition of woman. Any traditional binary designation of men and women as exhausting the complexity of sexed bodies and gendered identity cannot stand up to the complex reality of the actual bodies and subjectivities of transpeople and intersexuals. No 'biological' set of characteristics can constitute necessary and sufficient conditions for being a woman (Fausto-Sterling 1992, 2000; Hale 1996).[15]

---

[14] Crenshaw's original use of 'intersectionality' did not include oppression on the basis of sexual orientation, age, disability/ability status, or similar factors. However, because the spirit of the concept includes more than oppression by race, class, and gender, I speak of it as encompassing a more open-ended range of oppressions. Because the open-ended list gets shortened as one writes, some intersections are not treated in this essay: e.g. oppression on the basis of disability/gender (see, e.g., Tremain 2005).

[15] My discussion of marking boundaries between women and non-women does not address the question of whether we need to mark the boundaries at all, and if we do not (or, indeed, if we cannot), what the subject of 'feminism' might be.

The other issue in stake (c) is whether heterosexuality is crucial to being a woman. If it is, then lesbians are not women. Although many people, including feminists, have the initial response, 'If lesbians are not women, who is?', Monique Wittig (1992) and others have argued that lesbians are not women.[16] C. Jacob Hale responds to Wittig with a Wittgensteinian analysis. Hale's conclusion (1996) is that some lesbians are women, and some probably are not; but that in any case heterosexuality (or any other single property) is not a necessary condition for being a woman. There is no space to lay out their arguments here. My own view is that the most helpful model to use in thinking of gender that will enable us to deal with the issues in 'stake (c)' is to see gender as a very untidy continuum, rather than focusing on the 'poles' of the continuum as we do now. Only in this way can the realities of the lives of transpeople, intersexuals, and lesbians not be erased or distorted.

FINALLY, TWO ESSENTIALISTS

Let us now turn to two feminist philosophers who believe that anti-essentialist proposals take us down the wrong road and argue that essences are, in fact, needed for feminists to succeed at their goals.[17] Martha Nussbaum and Naomi Zack explicitly want to retain 'essences' (both claiming to avoid typical feminist objections to 'essentialism', as Alcoff leads us to expect). Both of them desire the normativity that they believe derives from universal claims about women, but their projects are different. Nussbaum's project is to ensure that women are treated as fully human. Zack's project is to create inclusive feminism.

[16] Although we cannot pursue the important controversy over the centrality of heterosexuality to the category of woman, let me note an interesting irony. In the 1970s a 'woman-identified woman' was sometimes considered the paradigm feminist (Radicalesbians 1971). Such women need not be lesbians; a 'lesbian continuum' spans lesbians who in fact desire women sexually and other women who simply give women personal and political priority in their lives (Rich 1980). So imagine the surprise of many feminists to read Wittig's (1992) claim that lesbians are not women at all.

[17] There are other feminists who have offered interesting analyses; e.g., both Sally Haslanger and Linda Alcoff claim that women are an 'objective type'. Haslanger explicitly (2000b) speaks of necessary and sufficient conditions for being a woman, conditions that are socially constructed. Haslanger's analysis of woman in terms of social position is similar to MacKinnon's analysis in many ways, but is couched in an analytic philosophical style that makes each facet distinct (see MacKinnon 1989). Alcoff has proposed that women and men differ 'by virtue of their different relationship of possibility to biological reproduction' (2006: 172). I have chosen to discuss Zack because, unlike Haslanger and Alcoff, she explicitly rejects intersectionality.

Nussbaum (1995*b*: 96) believes, with MacKinnon, that 'Being a woman is not yet a way of being a human being'.[18] Nussbaum acknowledges that she is both an 'essentialist' and a 'universalist' as she goes about her project to ensure justice for women. Her strategy is to focus on a common set of capacities and functions that women and men around the earth have. The approach that Amartya Sen and Nussbaum take is well known: they focus on 'central human capabilities' that are not reducible to biology, theology, or metaphysics. Nussbaum argues that her version of essentialism and universalism is compatible with an account of capabilities that is at once normative, tentative, open-ended, a 'continuous sort of experiential and historical truth', and allows that the capacities put forth are 'differently constructed by different societies' (1995*b*: 74). Nussbaum believes that her capacities can account for all the diversity that feminists need in the struggle for worldwide justice for women. Nussbaum is serious about 'essences' in at least the following respect: she takes a very minimal, 'lower-level threshold' of capabilities (such as the need for food and drink, sexual desire, the cognitive capabilities of perceiving, imagining, and thinking (including practical reasoning, humor, and play, and so on)) to be necessary for being human. Although anyone with Wittgensteinian proclivities might worry about the strictness of these conditions, Nussbaum wants to ensure that one can't help including women as human beings.

Nussbaum opposes 'anti-essentialists' who focus on differences either among women or between men and women and seek 'norms defined relatively to a local context and locally held beliefs' (1995*b*: 63). We might call these opponents 'difference' anti-essentialists and 'local norms only' relativists. Neither is a fictional opponent, but the two differ from one another. However, Nussbaum is not opposing 'social construction'. She draws no stark contrast between 'capabilities' and 'social construction'; indeed, she acknowledges that our experiences of our bodies are culturally shaped (1995*b*: 76). Her concern is that without a sharp focus on the common set of capabilities women will continue to be socially constructed right out of the category of human being.

Naomi Zack also advocates a universal characterization of women and opposes anti-essentialist views that focus on differences among women, especially intersectional analyses. Her goal is to put forth an inclusive feminism

---

[18] Nussbaum cites MacKinnon's quotation from Rorty 1991: 231; MacKinnon's recent book, *Are Women Human?* (2006), bears ample witness to her position that women are still not treated as human beings.

suitable for 'universal advocacy for women's interests' (Zack 2005: 1). In contrast to Nussbaum's aim to make certain that women share all the capabilities of men, Zack is trying to capture the necessary and sufficient conditions for being a woman rather than a man: woman's essence. Her most concise statement of the essence of women is this:

All women share the nonsubstantive, relational essence of being assigned to or identifying with the historical, socially constructed, disjunctive category of female birth designees [*F*], biological mothers [*M*], or heterosexual choices of men [*P*]—category FMP. Category FMP captures what women have in common as the imagined but real group that is the logical contrary of the group of men, in human male–female, man–women gender systems.   (2005: 162)[19]

Zack's view is designed to oppose feminist theories and strategies that rely on intersectionality as a way of understanding multiple oppressions as well as similarities and differences among women. Zack believes that intersectional analyses have been bad for women because they lead to fragmentation, intellectual segregation, and lack of empathy. Intersectionality is a problem theoretically because its proponents, Zack believes, maintain that women in different ethnic groups have different genders. Thus both the practical and the theoretical consequences that she believes follow from intersectionality drive Zack to a universalist normative analysis of women. She, like Nussbaum, believes that only this kind of analysis carries sufficient normative weight to deal with injustice and oppression.

Although Nussbaum and Zack share an eagerness to claim the label 'essentialist' for their views and presumably believe that they are 'good', not 'bad', essentialists, can they meet anti-essentialist objections? The answer depends on the objection. Anti-essentialism based on postmodern rejection of this kind of discourse would apply squarely to both Nussbaum and Zack. Neither of them can meet postmodern objections, but they would both consider that a badge of honor! After all, they both believe that the positions of such critics harm crucial feminist projects. To consider other anti-essentialist objections, we must treat Nussbaum and Zack separately.

Nussbaum believes that universal human capabilities allow room for extremely wide variations of experiences and ways in which the experiences are shaped by cultures, so she fights back when she is attacked by

---

[19] I added the letters in italics for clarification. Zack spells out their meaning as follows: F—designated female from birth; M—biological mothers; P—primary sexual choice of [heterosexual] men (Zack 2005: 8).

anti-essentialists who focus on the 'wide varieties of women's experiences'. She believes that she is not inappropriately imposing 'Western' standards and values on women around the earth. There is no meeting of minds, however, because Nussbaum believes that anti-essentialists focus too much on differences, and they believe that Nussbaum focuses on them too little. Beyond that, Nussbaum's concerns do not mesh well with the usual feminist 'stakes' of the anti-essentialism/essentialism controversies: race and racism, how to define women in contrast with men, and so on. One could interpret this either as a partial success—namely, that she has avoided the 'bad' essentialism—or as a failure to engage with central issues. In fairness, however, not all feminists must have similar projects. Having a different project need not imply a desire to escape this set of issues. In addition, recall that Nussbaum's concern is not only with universal capabilities, but also with universal moral standards; the latter are at least as important for retaining her desired level of normativity as the exact character of universal capabilities. Nevertheless, Nussbaum's insistence on claiming the label 'essentialist' is at best misleading opponents to think that she's staking a claim that directly opposes their own.

Unlike Nussbaum, Zack's focus is precisely to engage the anti-essentialists on the intersectionality turf and to ground her analysis in metaphysics. In terms of stakes (a)–(c) that I identified earlier, Zack's analysis is designed to treat all three: racism/heterosexism, the diversity of women's experiences, and the need for a ground to attack a biological essence of women. (a) Her book is clearly motivated by her desire to prevent negative consequences by race. (b) and (c) Her double-layered disjunction, 'assigned to or identifying with F or M or P', is designed to deal with diversity among women and their experiences, as well as to deny that biology is a sole determinant of women. Since Zack wants to end racism and accommodates both the socially constructed character of women and their variety of experiences, there is much agreement between Zack and the anti-essentialists she is criticizing. But methods and metaphysics matter to Zack. My suspicion is that many of Zack's opponents would at best find her 'nonsubstantive, relational' essence to be of little use, either practically or philosophically, even if they understand the motives from which it stems. Of course, Zack is intent on showing the dire political and theoretical consequences of their disregard.[20]

---

[20] Zack has not yet responded in print to critics of *Inclusive Feminism*, her responses to members of a SWIP-sponsored panel on the book during the American Philosophical Association's Pacific Division meeting in March 2005 revealed that she takes her metaphysics quite seriously.

To my mind, the most controversial theoretical consequence of intersectionality concerns the proliferation of genders among women. It not only is controversial in itself, but also lends support to a position that could undermine gender as an analytical category. Zack takes quite literally that intersectionality implies that women of different ethnic groups (and presumably sexual orientations) have different genders. The best-known advocates of intersectionality do not state this, though it can be found in Elizabeth Spelman's similar position.[21] However, I want to argue that intersectionality need not multiply genders for each different ethnicity/race or social class; indeed, it does not make sense for it to do so. Intersectional analyses need gender, class, race/ethnicity to do precisely that—intersect. The individual axes must have some minimal degree of stable meaning for the analysis to work. If every intersection produced a new gender or a new race (or both!), there would be no way to make sense of the ways in which ethnicity affects one's gendered experience. As we noted earlier, those who favor intersectionality tend to favor it because it illuminates the wide varieties of women's experiences across other axes of oppression and enables them to find suitable remedies for multiple oppressions. The 'gender axis' needs to be intelligible across other 'axes', or there is nothing to appeal to in the explanation or remedy. Thus, not only does intersectionality fail to entail a proliferation of genders, its proponents should fight strongly against such a move in order for the theory to retain its power of explanation.

Is there not a simpler way than Zack's to deal with diversity? Yes. Wittgenstein's family-resemblance approach is both simpler and has the virtue of being able to incorporate intersectionality. Substitute 'woman' for 'number' in Wittgenstein's passage below.

And we extend our concept of number as in spinning a thread we twist fibre on fibre. And the *strength of the thread* does not reside in the fact that some one fibre runs through its whole length, but in the overlapping of many fibres. But if someone wished to say: "There is something common to all these constructions—namely the disjunction of all their common properties"—I should reply: Now you are only playing with words. One might as well say: "something runs through the whole thread—namely the continuous overlapping of those fibres". (1958: §67; [my italics])

A family-resemblance analysis of 'women' will accommodate much more simply everything that Zack incorporates into her disjunctive 'essence' of

---

[21] Although Spelman's influential *Inessential Woman* (1988) does not use the term 'intersectionality', her analysis is intersectional in spirit. Spelman accepts plural genders for women. María Lugones also speaks in terms of multiple genders for women (2007).

women—except, of course, her metaphysics. Let's run through it quickly. Women differ at the same time as they have similarities; however, the similarities between some women will not be the same as those between others. This is why Zack starts with a disjunction, 'F or M or P', then adds a further disjunctive layer on top of it—'assigned to or identifies with F or M or P'. One of the factors that has traditionally been used most forcefully to categorize human beings as women is being a mother or at least having the capacity for motherhood. Most women have similar sets of reproductive capacities and physical features. (Hale (1996) notes that the absence of a penis is deemed fairly salient.) But those who don't have these capacities/features will have something else in common with the first group of women. They very likely think of themselves and identify publicly and subjectively as women and are treated as women by others. Even if heterosexuality plays an important role in the creation and maintenance of 'women' as we know them, lesbians are still women because of other characteristics that they share with other women—physical, subjective, social, and so forth.

The next step is to determine whether a family-resemblance analysis can adequately distinguish women from men. It can. We can mark the group of women without having necessary and sufficient conditions for being a woman.[22] To do so, we ask the *purpose* for which we are trying to find boundaries for the group. If a feminist is arguing for equal pay for women or comparable pay for 'women's jobs', she need not care about chromosomes or androgen levels. On the other hand, if a clinical drug trial measures different responses of men and women to a new cholesterol-lowering drug, then hormones and other physical factors matter more than social roles. Even if a critic of a Wittgensteinian approach finds far too much reliance on 'purposes' here, this approach works at least as well as Zack's in any case. Zack, after all, would need to choose which disjunct is most important for a particular context or purpose.

The final question is whether a family-resemblance analysis is consistent with feminists' need for normativity. Again, it is at least as good as Zack's view. Normativity is not just about metaphysics; it requires a moral component as well as something to mark off the category of women. Before we leave the category of women, let us note that not only can family resemblances mark off the category, but nothing about this analysis prevents women from

---

[22] Cressida Heyes (2000), using a Wittgensteinian approach, maintains that feminist practices should ground our categorizations of women. See also Scheman and O'Connor (2002) for a variety of feminist Wittgensteinian analyses.

being an 'objective type'—interpreted by Haslanger (2000*b*) as a type that is not a random or arbitrary collection of things. Both Zack and Wittgenstein get us this far. Of course, neither satisfies the moral and political facets of normativity. This should not surprise us, because metaphysical claims are not usually designed to fulfill the need for moral and political normativity. Such normativity rests instead on feminists' moral and political theories carrying the force needed to argue for justice and other forms of social change.

Concluding Remarks

As we close, let's keep in mind that in spite of the disagreements among feminist philosophers—whether over the value of the concept of intersectionality or in various debates in ethics or philosophy of science—shared motivations and goals underlie their work. They philosophize in a manner that engages with the world, specifically to help improve the lives of women in a way that is anti-racist and anti-heterosexist. As philosophers and as feminists they differ over the most useful theories for doing so. Such engaged philosophy presents great challenges. At any given time one must prioritize an issue to address—whether it is close to home or, increasingly, transnational or global—will it be heterosexist marriage laws in the United States, economic exploitation of men and women in the 'global south', rape of women during civil war, or something else? Yet, while analyzing gender oppression in rape or class exploitation in the global south, one must also attend to the ways in which privilege and oppression along other axes bear on the issues. The point of taking multiple axes of oppression into account is not simply to improve our theories. It is to help improve the lives of our fellow human beings by combating racism and heterosexism, as well as sexism. Social justice and morality require us to do so.

References

Alcoff, Linda Martín (2006). *Visible Identities: Race, Gender, and the Self*. New York: Oxford University Press.

———and Kittay, Eva Feder (eds.) (2006). *The Blackwell Guide to Feminist Philosophy*. Malden, MA: Blackwell.

_____ and Potter, Elizabeth (eds.) (1993). *Feminist Epistemologies*. New York: Routledge.

Allen, Anita L. (1988). *Uneasy Access: Privacy for Women in a Free Society*. Totowa, NJ: Rowman & Littlefield.

_____ (2003). *Why Privacy Isn't Everything: Feminist Reflections on Personal Accountability*. Lanham, MD: Rowman & Littlefield.

Allen, Jeffner, and Young, Iris Marion (1989). *The Thinking Muse: Feminism and Modern French Philosophy*. Bloomington, IN: Indiana University Press.

Anderson, Elizabeth (1995a). 'Feminist Epistemology: An Interpretation and a Defense'. *Hypatia*, 10/3: 50–84.

_____ (1995b). 'Knowledge, Human Interests, and Objectivity in Feminist Epistemology'. *Philosophical Topics*, 23/2: 27–58.

_____ (2003). 'Feminist Epistemology and Philosophy of Science'. In *Stanford Encyclopedia of Philosophy*, <http://plato.stanford.edu>.

Antony, Louise M. (1995). 'Sisters, Please, I'd Rather Do It Myself: A Defense of Individualism in Feminist Epistemology'. *Philosophical Topics*, 23/2: 59–94.

_____ (1998). ' "Human Nature" and Its Role in Feminist Theory'. In Kourany (1998), 63–91.

_____ (2000). 'Natures and Norms'. *Ethics*, 111: 8–36.

_____ (2002). 'Quine as Feminist: The Radical Import of Naturalized Import'. In Antony and Witt (2002), 110–53.

_____ and Witt, Charlotte (eds.) (2002). *A Mind of One's Own: Feminist Essays on Reason and Objectivity*, 2nd edn. Boulder, CO: Westview Press.

Aristotle (1941). *The Basic Works of Aristotle*, ed. Richard McKeon. New York: Random House.

Atkinson, Ti-Grace (1974). *Amazon Odyssey*. New York: Links Books.

Baker, Robert, and Elliston, Frederick (eds.) (1975). *Philosophy and Sex*. Buffalo, NY: Prometheus Books.

Bartky, Sandra (1990). *Femininity and Domination: Studies in the Phenomenology of Oppression*. New York: Routledge.

Beauvoir, Simone de (1949). *Le Deuxième Sexe*. Paris: Gallimard.

Brison, Susan J. (2002). *Aftermath: Violence and the Remaking of a Self*. Princeton: Princeton University Press.

Butler, Judith (1993). *Bodies That Matter: On the Discursive Limits of "Sex"*. New York: Routledge.

_____ (1999). *Gender Trouble: Feminism and the Subversion of Identity*. New York: Routledge.

Cahill, Ann J., and Hansen, Jennifer (eds.) (2003). *Continental Feminism Reader*. Lanham, MD: Rowman & Littlefield Publishers.

Calhoun, Cheshire (2000). *Feminism, the Family, and the Politics of the Closet: Lesbian and Gay Displacement*. New York: Oxford University Press.

Card, Claudia (1991). *Feminist Ethics*. Lawrence, KS: University Press of Kansas.

_____ (1995). *Lesbian Choices*. New York: Columbia University Press.

Card, Claudia (1999). *On Feminist Ethics and Politics*. Lawrence, KS: University Press of Kansas.

——— (2002). *The Atrocity Paradigm: A Theory of Evil*. New York: Oxford University Press.

Clark, Lorenne M. G., and Lange, Lynda (eds.) (1979). *The Sexism of Social and Political Theory: Women and Reproduction from Plato to Nietzsche*. Toronto: University of Toronto Press.

Clough, Sharyn (2003). *Beyond Epistemology: A Pragmatist Approach to Feminist Science Studies*. Lanham, MD: Rowman & Littlefield Publishers.

Code, Lorraine (1995). *Rhetorical Spaces: Essays on Gendered Locations*. New York: Routledge.

——— (2006). *Ecological Thinking: The Politics of Epistemic Location*. New York: Oxford University Press.

Collins, Patricia Hill (2000). *Black Feminist Thought: Knowledge, Consciousness, and the Politics of Empowerment*. New York: Routledge.

Crenshaw, Kimberlé (1989). 'Demarginalizing the Intersection of Race and Sex: A Black Feminist Critique of Antidiscrimination Doctrine, Feminist Theory and Antiracist Politics'. *University of Chicago Legal Forum*, 139–67.

——— (1991). 'Mapping the Margins: Intersectionality, Identity Politics, and Violence against Women of Color'. *Stanford Law Review*, 43/6: 1241–99.

Daly, Mary (1968). *The Church and the Second Sex*. New York: Harper & Row.

——— (1973). *Beyond God the Father: Toward a Philosophy of Women's Liberation*. Boston: Beacon Press.

Digby, Tom (ed.) (1998). *Men Doing Feminism*. New York: Routledge.

Donchin, Anne (2004). 'Converging Concerns: Feminist Bioethics, Development Theory, and Human Rights'. *Signs*, 29/2: 299–324.

Duran, Jane (2001). *Worlds of Knowing: Global Feminist Epistemologies*. New York: Routledge.

English, Jane (ed.) (1977). *Sex Equality*. Englewood Cliffs, NJ: Prentice-Hall.

Falmagne, Rachel Joffe, and Hass, Marjorie (eds.) (2002). *Representing Reason: Feminist Theory and Formal Logic*. Lanham, MD: Rowman & Littlefield.

Fausto-Sterling, Anne (1992). *Myths of Gender: Biological Theories about Women and Men*. New York: Basic Books.

——— (2000). *Sexing the Body: Gender Politics and the Construction of Sexuality*. New York: Basic Books.

Firestone, Shulamith (1970). *The Dialectic of Sex: The Case for Feminist Revolution*. New York: Bantam Books.

Fraser, Nancy (1989). *Unruly Practices: Power, Discourse, and Gender in Contemporary Social Theory*. Minneapolis: University of Minnesota Press.

——— and Nicholson, Linda J. (1990). 'Social Criticism without Philosophy: An Encounter between Feminism and Postmodernism'. In Nicholson (1990), 19–38.

Freeland, Cynthia A. (ed.) (1998). *Feminist Interpretations of Aristotle*. University Park, PA: Pennsylvania State University Press.

Fricker, Miranda, and Hornsby, Jennifer (eds.) (2000). *The Cambridge Companion to Feminism in Philosophy*. New York: Cambridge University Press.

Friedman, Marilyn (1993). *What Are Friends For? Feminist Perspectives on Personal Relationships and Moral Theory*. Ithaca, NY: Cornell University Press.

_____ (2003). *Autonomy, Gender, Politics*. New York: Oxford University Press.

Frye, Marilyn (1983). *The Politics of Reality: Essays in Feminist Theory*. Trumansburg, NY: Crossing Press.

_____ (1992). *Willful Virgin: Essays in Feminism, 1976–1992*. Freedom, CA: Crossing Press.

Garry, Ann (1995). 'A Minimally Decent Philosophical Method? Analytic Philosophy and Feminism'. *Hypatia*, 10/3: 7–30.

_____ and Pearsall, Marilyn (eds.) (1996). *Women, Knowledge, and Reality: Explorations in Feminist Philosophy*, 2nd edn. New York: Routledge.

Garside, Christine (1971). 'Can a Woman Be Good in the Same Way as a Man?'. *Dialogue*, 10/3: 534–44.

Gilligan, Carol (1982). *In a Different Voice: Psychological Theory and Women's Development*. Cambridge, MA: Harvard University Press.

_____ (1988). *Mapping the Moral Domain: A Contribution of Women's Thinking to Psychological Theory and Education*. Cambridge, MA: Harvard University Press.

Gornick, Vivian, and Moran, Barbara K. (eds.) (1971). *Woman in Sexist Society: Studies in Power and Powerlessness*. New York: Basic Books.

Gould, Carol C., and Wartofsky, Marx W. (eds.) (1973–4). *The Philosophical Forum*, 5/1–2.

Govier, Trudy (1974). 'Woman's Place'. *Philosophy*, 49/189: 303–9.

Haack, Susan (1974). 'On the Moral Relevance of Sex'. *Philosophy*, 49/187: 90–5.

Hale, C. Jacob (1996). 'Are Lesbians Women?'. *Hypatia*, 11/2: 94–121.

Haraway, Donna J. (1991). *Simians, Cyborgs, and Women: The Reinvention of Nature*. New York: Routledge.

_____ (1997). *Modest_Witness@Second_Millennium. FemaleMan©_Meets_Onco Mouse™: Feminism and Technoscience*. New York: Routledge.

Harding, Sandra G. (1986). *The Science Question in Feminism*. Ithaca, NY: Cornell University Press.

_____ (1991). *Whose Science? Whose Knowledge? Thinking from Women's Lives*. Ithaca, NY: Cornell University Press.

_____ (1993). 'Rethinking Standpoint Epistemology: What Is "Strong Objectivity"?'. In Alcoff and Potter (1993), 49–82.

_____ (1998). *Is Science Multicultural? Postcolonialisms, Feminisms, and Epistemologies*. Bloomington, IN: Indiana University Press.

_____ (2004). *The Feminist Standpoint Theory Reader: Intellectual and Political Controversies*. New York: Routledge.

_____ (2006). *Science and Social Inequality: Feminist and Postcolonial Issues*. Urbana, IL: University of Illinois Press.

Haslanger, Sally (1995). 'Ontology and Social Construction'. *Philosophical Topics*, 23/2: 95–125.

Haslanger, Sally (2000a). 'Feminism in Metaphysics: Negotiating the Natural'. In Fricker and Hornsby (2000), 107–26.

—— (2000b). 'Gender and Race: (What) Are They? (What) Do We Want Them to Be?'. *Nous*, 34/1: 31–55.

—— (2002). 'On Being Objective and Being Objectified'. In Antony and Witt (2002), 209–53.

Held, Virginia (2006). *The Ethics of Care: Personal, Political, and Global.* New York: Oxford University Press.

Heyes, Cressida J. (2000). *Line Drawings: Defining Women through Feminist Practice.* Ithaca, NY: Cornell University Press.

Hoagland, Sarah Lucia (1988). *Lesbian Ethics: Toward New Value.* Palo Alto, CA: Institute of Lesbian Studies.

Jaggar, Alison M. (1972). 'Four Views of Women's Liberation'. Paper presented at the Western (now Central) Division, American Philosophical Association.

—— (1974). 'On Sexual Equality'. *Ethics*, 84: 275–92.

—— (1983). *Feminist Politics and Human Nature.* Totowa, NJ: Rowman & Allanheld.

—— (1989). 'Feminist Ethics: Some Issues for the Nineties'. *Journal of Social Philosophy*, 20/1–2: 91–107.

—— (1998). 'Globalizing Feminist Ethics'. *Hypatia*, 13/2: 7–31.

—— (2000). 'Feminism in Ethics: Moral Justification'. In Fricker and Hornsby (2000), 225–44.

—— (2001). 'Feminist Ethics'. In Lawrence B. Becker and Charlotte B. Becker (eds.), *Encyclopedia of Ethics*, New York: Routledge, 528–39.

—— and Young, Iris Marion (1998). *A Companion to Feminist Philosophy.* Malden, MA: Blackwell.

Keller, Evelyn Fox (1985). *Reflections on Gender and Science.* New Haven: Yale University Press.

—— (1992). *Secrets of Life, Secrets of Death: Essays on Language, Gender, and Science.* New York: Routledge.

Kittay, Eva Feder (1999). *Love's Labor: Essays on Women, Equality, and Dependency.* New York: Routledge.

Kourany, Janet A. (ed.) (1998). *Philosophy in a Feminist Voice: Critiques and Reconstructions.* Princeton: Princeton University Press.

Lange, Lynda (2002). *Feminist Interpretations of Jean-Jacques Rousseau.* University Park, PA: Pennsylvania State University Press.

Lara, María Pía (1998). *Moral Textures: Feminist Narratives in the Public Sphere.* Berkeley: University of California Press.

Littleton, Christine (1987). 'Reconstructing Sexual Equality? *California Law Review*, 75/4: 1279–1335.

Lloyd, Elisabeth (1995a). 'Feminism as Method: What Scientists Get That Philosophers Don't'. *Philosophical Topics*, 23/2: 189–220.

—— (1995b). 'Objectivity and the Double Standard for Feminist Epistemologies'. *Synthese*, 104: 351–81.

_____ (2005). *The Case of the Female Orgasm: Bias in the Science of Evolution*. Cambridge, MA: Harvard University Press.

Longino, Helen E. (1990). *Science as Social Knowledge: Values and Objectivity in Scientific Inquiry*. Princeton: Princeton University Press.

_____ (2002). *The Fate of Knowledge*. Princeton: Princeton University Press.

Lugones, María (2003). 'The Logic of Pluralist Feminism'. In *Pilgrimages/Peregrinajes: Theorizing Coalition against Multiple Oppressions*, Lanham, MD: Rowman & Littlefield, 65–75.

_____ (2007). 'Heterosexualism and the Colonial/Modern Gender System'. *Hypatia*, 22/1: 186–209.

_____ and Spelman, Elizabeth (1983). 'Have We Got a Theory for You! Feminist Theory, Cultural Imperialism and the Demand for "the Woman's Voice"'. *Women's Studies International Forum* (embedded first issue of *Hypatia*), 6/6: 573–81.

MacKinnon, Catharine A. (1987). *Feminism Unmodified: Discourses on Life and Law*. Cambridge, MA: Harvard University Press.

_____ (1989). *Toward a Feminist Theory of the State*. Cambridge, MA: Harvard University Press.

_____ (2006). *Are Women Human? And Other International Dialogues*. Cambridge, MA: Belknap Press of Harvard University Press.

May, Larry, Strikwerda, Robert A., and Hopkins, Patrick (eds.) (1996). *Rethinking Masculinity: Philosophical Explorations in Light of Feminism*. Lanham, MD: Rowman & Littlefield.

Meyers, Diana T. (1989). *Self, Society, and Personal Choice*. New York: Columbia University Press.

_____ (ed.) (1997). *Feminists Rethink the Self*. Boulder, CO: Westview Press.

Millett, Kate (1970). *Sexual Politics*. Garden City, NY: Doubleday.

Mothersill, Mary (ed.) (1973). *The Monist: Special Issue on Women's Liberation: Ethical, Social and Political Issues*, 57/1.

Narayan, Uma (1997). *Dislocating Cultures: Identities, Traditions, and Third-World Feminism*. New York: Routledge.

_____ and Harding, Sandra (eds.) (2000). *Decentering the Center: Philosophy for a Multicultural, Postcolonial, and Feminist World*. Bloomington, IN: Indiana University Press.

Nelson, Hilde Lindemann (2001). *Damaged Identities, Narrative Repair*. Ithaca, NY: Cornell University Press.

Nelson, Lynn Hankinson (1990). *Who Knows: From Quine to a Feminist Empiricism*. Philadelphia: Temple University Press.

Nicholson, Linda J. (ed.) (1990). *Feminism/Postmodernism*. New York: Routledge.

Noddings, Nel (1984). *Caring: A Feminine Approach to Ethics and Moral Education*. Berkeley: University of California Press.

Nussbaum, Martha C. (1995*a*). 'Aristotle on Human Nature and the Foundations of Ethics'. In J. E. J. Althan and Ross Harrison (eds.), *World, Mind, and Ethics: Essays on the Ethical Philosophy of Bernard Williams*, Cambridge: Cambridge University Press, 86–131.

Nussbaum, Martha C. (1995*b*). 'Human Capabilities, Female Human Beings'. In Martha C. Nussbaum and Jonathan Glover (eds.), *Women, Culture, and Development: A Study of Human Capabilities*, New York: Oxford University Press, 61–104.

Nussbaum, Martha C. (2000). *Women and Human Development: The Capabilities Approach*. New York: Cambridge University Press.

——— (2004). 'Women's Education: A Global Challenge'. *Signs*, 29/2: 325–56.

Nye, Andrea (1990). *Words of Power: A Feminist Reading of the History of Logic*. New York: Routledge.

Okin, Susan Moller (1992). *Women in Western Political Thought*. Princeton: Princeton University Press.

——— Cohen, Joshua, Howard, Matthew, and Nussbaum, Martha C. (eds.) (1999). *Is Multiculturalism Bad for Women?* Princeton: Princeton University Press.

Oliver, Kelly (1998). *Subjectivity without Subjects: From Abject Fathers to Desiring Mothers*. Lanham, MD: Rowman & Littlefield.

Overall, Christine (1988). 'Feminism, Ontology, and "Other Minds"'. In Lorraine Code, Sheila Mullett, and Christine Overall (eds.), *Feminist Perspectives: Philosophical Essays on Method and Morals*, Toronto: University of Toronto Press, 89–106.

Pearsall, Marilyn (ed.) (1999). *Women and Values: Readings in Recent Feminist Philosophy*, 3rd edn. Belmont, CA: Wadsworth.

Radicalesbians (1971). 'The Woman-Identified Woman'. In *Notes from the Third Year: Women's Liberation*, New York: Notes from the Second Year, Inc., 81–4.

Rich, Adrienne (1980). 'Compulsory Heterosexuality and Lesbian Existence'. *Signs*, 5/4: 631–60.

Rorty, Richard (1991). 'Feminism and Pragmatism'. *Michigan Quarterly Review*, 30: 231–58.

Ruddick, Sara (1995). *Maternal Thinking: Toward a Politics of Peace*, with a new preface. Boston: Beacon Press.

Sandoval, Chela (1991). 'U.S Third World Feminism: The Theory and Method of Oppositional Consciousness in the Postmodern World'. *Genders*, 10: 1–24.

——— (2000). *Methodology of the Oppressed*. Minneapolis: University of Minnesota Press.

Scheman, Naomi (1993). *Engenderings: Constructions of Knowledge, Authority, and Privilege*. New York: Routledge.

——— (2000). 'Feminism in Philosophy of Mind: Against Physicalism'. In Fricker and Hornsby (2000), 49–67.

——— and O'Connor, Peg (eds.) (2002). *Feminist Interpretations of Ludwig Wittgenstein*. University Park, PA: Pennsylvania State University Press.

Schutte, Ofelia (1998). 'Cultural Alterity: Cross-Cultural Communication and Feminist Theory in North–South Contexts'. *Hypatia*, 13/2: 53–72.

Seigfried, Charlene Haddock (ed.) (1993). *Hypatia* Special Issue: *Feminism and Pragmatism*, 8/2.

____ (1996). *Pragmatism and Feminism: Reweaving the Social Fabric*. Chicago: University of Chicago Press.

Sherwin, Susan (1975). 'Thriving: An Improvement over Happiness'. Paper presented at the Canadian Philosophical Association.

____ (1992). *No Longer Patient: Feminist Ethics and Health Care*. Philadelphia: Temple University Press.

Shrage, Laurie (2003). *Abortion and Social Responsibility: Depolarizing the Debate*. New York: Oxford University Press.

Spelman, Elizabeth V. (1988). *Inessential Woman: Problems of Exclusion in Feminist Thought*. Boston: Beacon Press.

Stanford Encyclopedia of Philosophy, <http://plato.stanford.edu>.

Sullivan, Shannon (2001). *Living Across and Through Skins: Transactional Bodies, Pragmatism, and Feminism*. Bloomington, IN: Indiana University Press.

Thomson, Judith Jarvis (1971). 'A Defense of Abortion'. *Philosophy and Public Affairs*, 1/1: 47–66.

Tong, Rosemarie (1993). *Feminine and Feminist Ethics*. Belmont, CA: Wadsworth.

Trebilcot, Joyce (1975). 'Sex Roles: The Argument from Nature'. *Ethics*, 85/3: 249–55.

Tremain, Shelley (ed.) (2005). *Foucault and the Government of Disability*. Ann Arbor: University of Michigan Press.

Vetterling-Braggin, Mary, Elliston, Frederick A., and English, Jane (eds.) (1977). *Feminism and Philosophy*. Totowa, NJ: Rowman & Allanheld.

Walker, Margaret Urban (2003). *Moral Contexts*. Lanham, MD: Rowman & Littlefield.

____ (2007). *Moral Understandings: A Feminist Study in Ethics*. New York: Oxford University Press.

Wasserstrom, Richard A. (1975). *Today's Moral Problems*. New York: Macmillan.

Williams, Wendy W. (1982). 'The Equality Crisis: Some Reflections on Culture, Courts and Feminism'. *Women's Rights Law Reporter*, 7/175: 15–34.

Witt, Charlotte (1995). 'Anti-Essentialism in Feminist Theory'. *Philosophical Topics*, 23/2: 321–44.

____ (2002). 'Feminist Metaphysics'. In Antony and Witt (2002), 302–18.

Wittgenstein, Ludwig (1958). *Philosophical Investigations*, 3rd edn., trans. G. E. M. Anscombe. New York: Macmillan.

Wittig, Monique (1992). *The Straight Mind and Other Essays*. Boston: Beacon Press.

Young, Iris Marion (1990a). *Justice and the Politics of Difference*. Princeton: Princeton University Press.

____ (1990b). 'Pregnant Embodiment'. In *Throwing Like a Girl and Other Essays in Feminist Philosophy and Social Theory*, Bloomington, IN: Indiana University Press, 160–74.

Zack, Naomi (2005). *Inclusive Feminism: A Third Wave Theory of Women's Commonality*. Lanham, MD: Rowman & Littlefield.

NAME INDEX

Aboulafia, Mitchell vii, x, 169
Abrams 20
Ackoff, Russell 359
Adams, Robert 588
Addams, Jane 146
Adler, Mortimer 259, 356
Adorno, Theodore 237
Agassiz, Louis 61
Ahmed, Arif viii, x, 290
Aiken, Henry 457, 458
Albritton, Rogers 387, 388, 458, 459
Alcoff, Linda Martin 607, 608, 612
Allan, Edgar 343
Allen 25, 599
Alston, William 473
Ambrose, Alice 383, 384, 390
Anderson, Anthony 456
Anderson, Douglas vii, x, 38, 197, 201, 202,
    258
Anderson, Elizabeth 101, 516, 518, 537, 539,
    604, 605, 606
Anderson, Wallace 5
Angell, James 356
Anscombe, Elizabeth 458
Antony 605, 606, 607
Aquinas, St. Thomas 45, 258, 356, 571, 588
Aristotle 39, 41, 42, 43, 44, 45, 48, 53, 114, 116,
    120, 225, 422, 423, 497, 588, 608
Armstrong, David 232, 386
Arneson, Richard 516, 518, 526, 537
Arnold 358
Arrington, Robert L. xi, 391, 394, 396
Atkinson, Ti-Grace 597
Austin, J. L. 387, 388, 452, 458
Avigad 490
Ayer, A. J. 361, 431, 457, 580
Ayres 236
Azzouni 497, 498,

Baier, Kurt 469
Baird 562
Baker, G. P. 390
Baker, Robert 598
Balaguer, Mark 595
Barnes 366
Bartky, Sandra 599
Baruch, Bernard 254
Bawden, Heath 218
Becker, Gary 561
Beiser 29
Beitz, Charles 515, 516, 517, 538, 545
Bell, E. T. 359
Bellamy, Edward 237
Bellamy, Joseph 15
Belnap, Nuel 404, 424, 426
Benacerraf, Paul 459, 483, 494, 495, 496, 499
Beninger 155
Bennett, Jonathan 590
Bense 24
Bergman, Gustav 454
Bergson, Henri 146, 200, 225
Bergstrom 305
Berkeley, J. 39, 46, 47, 51, 280, 292, 293, 296,
    298
Bernstein, Richard 188, 256, 257
Bertram 538
Bettcher, Talia 595
Biletzki 392
Billings, Elizabeth Storrs 145
Bishop, Sharon 595
Bix, Brian H. ix, x, 551, 552, 556, 568, 570, 571,
    572
Black 384, 385, 391, 459
Blake 537, 546
Blattner, Bill 404
Bloom, Harold 20
Bloor, D. 366

Blumberg, Arthur 352, 355, 359
Blumer, Herbert 146
Boardman 15
Boehm 22
Boghossian, Paul 562
Bohr 216
Boisvert 87, 92
Boltzman, Ludwig 340
Bolzano 490, 491, 492
BonJour, Laurence 273, 299, 311, 404
Boole 46, 507
Bourbaki 496
Bourdieu, Pierre 245, 250
Bouwsma 384, 385, 392
Boyd, David 587
Boyd, Robert 246, 247, 249
Bradley, F. H. 200, 205
Brandeis, Louis D. 556
Brandom, Robert 219, 257, 389, 397, 404, 409,
    410, 411, 412, 413, 417, 418, 422, 423, 424,
    425, 426, 437, 446
Brandt, Richard 469, 580, 583, 588
Breger 497
Brent 131, 199
Bridgman, Percy 347, 359, 360
Brink, David 587
Brison 602, 603, 607
Broad, C. D. 229, 579, 580
Brodbeck, May 361
Brodsky 90
Brooks, David 245, 246, 251
Brouwer 482, 483
Brown, T. Wistar xii
Buckley, William F. 259
Burge, Tyler 67, 459, 472, 499
Burgess, John 459, 462, 483, 495, 496
Burke 92
Burley 570
Butler, Joseph 580
Butler, Judith 599, 605, 606, 607, 608
Butts, Robert 359
Byrne 472

Cahill 599
Calabresi, Guido 561
Caldwell, William 201, 209, 214, 215
Calhoun 602
Camp, Joe 404, 424
Campbell 258, 345

Canfield, Jack 375
Capps, John 256, 259, 260, 261
Card 602
Cardozo, Benjamin 553, 555
Carnap, Rudolf xiii, 216, 219, 291, 293, 294,
    295, 302, 333, 347, 352, 355, 356, 357, 358,
    359, 361, 364, 365, 380, 381, 382, 386, 453,
    454, 456–8, 460–1, 462, 463, 464
Carpenter 24, 25, 28
Carritt 580
Cartwright, Nancy 355, 367
Cartwright, Richard 459
Carus, P. 52, 145, 198, 200, 201, 209, 210, 214,
    215, 347, 348
Caspary 256
Cassirer 386
Castañeda, Hector-Neri 404, 459
Cauchy 490
Cavell, Stanley xi, 20, 32–5, 35, 377, 387, 388,
    393, 458, 473
Chalmers, D. 130
Cherniak 72
Chisholm, Roderick 264, 452
Chomsky, Noam 259, 264, 310, 387, 461
Chubb, Thomas 9
Church, Alonzo 456, 459
Churchland, Paul 404
Churchman 359
Clark 602
Clarke 580
Clendenning 110
Clifford 69, 71
Clough, Sharyn 599
Coase 560, 561
Code xii, 605
Coffa 353, 491, 492
Cohen, F. S. 553, 555, 556
Cohen, G. A. 517, 518, 523, 526, 531, 532, 533,
    536, 537, 539, 545
Cohen, I. B. 342
Cohen, J. 516, 533
Cohen, M. 570
Cohen, Morris R. 127, 350, 351, 358, 359, 451
Cohen, Robert S. 362
Cohen, S. 472
Colden, Cadwallader 342
Coleman, Jules L. 571, 572
Coleridge, Samuel Taylor 20, 21, 30, 343
Collins, Patricia Hill 596

Columbus 191, 554
Commager, H. 88
Conant, James 391, 393, 394, 404, 443
Conforti, J. 15
Conrad, C. 15
Cormier, Harvey 201
Corry 496
Costello 57
Cotter 258
Coughlan, N. 87
Craig, E. 317,
Crary 393, 394
Crenshaw, Kimberle 603, 610, 611
Curtis 161
Curtiss 163

Daly, Mary 597
Daniels 520, 524, 533
Danto, Arthur 473
Darwin, Charles 61, 63, 71, 152, 188, 237, 246, 263, 264, 265, 344, 345, 348, 350
Davidson, Donald viii, xi, xiii, 257, 271, 285, 305, 322, 377, 382, 397, 430–41, 444–7, 464–6
Dayton, Eric 272, 273
De Beauvoir, Simone 597, 598
Dedekind, P. 491
Deleuze, G. 192
Demopoulos 503
Dennett, Daniel xiii, 72, 257, 258, 376, 377, 404, 408
DeRose, K. 472
Derrida, J. 417
Descartes, R. 4, 34, 46, 115, 134, 188, 204, 225, 228, 264, 299, 407, 487, 490
Desmond 224
Detlefson 488, 504
Devitt, M. 68
DeVries, William 404
Dewey, John vii, xi, xiii, 16, 19, 20, 21, 28–32, 33, 34, 35, 40, 51, 53, 55, 56, 57, 58, 87–106, 110, 126, 127, 128, 132, 133, 146, 147, 153, 165, 166, 182, 185, 186, 187, 188, 191, 192, 193, 197, 198, 201, 202, 207, 208, 209, 213, 215, 216, 217, 220, 225, 236, 255, 256, 257, 263, 264, 265, 266, 270, 285, 288, 290, 316, 348, 349, 350, 351, 355, 356, 393, 396, 397, 432, 450, 451, 452, 485, 547, 552, 579, 588
Diamond, Cora 390, 393, 394, 395, 443

Dickstein 256
Digby 596
Diggins, John 90, 258
Dilthey, Wilhelm 146, 162, 177
Donchin 603
Donnellan, Keith 459
Dorfman 236, 240
Dreben, Burton 388, 393, 458
Dretske, F. 472
Dreyfus 421, 422
Driver 588
Duhem, Pierre 340
Dummett, Michael 257, 317, 331, 390, 435
Duran 606
Du Bois vii, 169–73, 176–83
Duxbury 558
Dworkin, Ronald 471, 515, 516, 518, 522, 523, 527, 528, 537, 538, 539, 545, 564–70, 571, 572

Earman 363, 405
Ebersole 386
Edel 90, 91
Edwards, Jonathan vii, xiii, 1–16
Einstein, Albert 149, 229, 259, 351, 353, 455, 503
Eldridge, Michael 256
Eliot, Charles 61, 62
Elliston 598
Elster, Jon 99
Emerson, Ralph Waldo vii, xi, 15, 19–22, 24–8, 31–6, 38, 39, 51, 61, 343
Emmet 190
Engel 194
Enrigues, Frederigo 340
Epstein 557
Estlund 535
Euclid 78, 486, 487, 488, 489, 500, 501, 503, 508
Euler 490
Evans 65, 307, 318, 465
Ewald 483
Ewing 580

Fabre 546
Falmagne 599
Fann 391
Farber 562
Faris, Ellsworth 146
Fausto-Sterling 606, 611

Fechner 200
Feferman, Solomon 456, 483
Feigl, Herbert 352, 355, 358, 359, 361, 365,
    380, 389, 454, 457
Feinberg, Joel 469, 572, 587
Feldman, Fred 587
Ferreiros 490
Fesmire 98, 256, 264
Festenstein, Matthew vii, xi, 87, 90, 101, 103,
    104, 106, 187, 256, 258
Feyerabend, Paul 365, 366
Field, H. 496
Fiering, Norman 5, 6
Fine, Arthur 220
Firestone, Shulamith 597, 598, 603
Firth, Roderick 273, 452, 458
Fisher, Martin 590
Fisher, R. A. 359, 360
Fisher, William 552
Fitch, Frederic B. 231, 463
Flanagan 189
Flower 91
Fodor, Jerry 264, 387, 397, 411, 472
Fogelin 293, 389, 392
Føllesdal 463
Foot, Philippa 377, 454, 458, 459, 588, 590
Forster 390
Foster 465
Foucault, M. 192, 404
Frank, Jerome 553, 555
Frank, Philip 352, 362, 365
Frank, R. 248
Frank, Thomas 236
Frankel 482
Frankena, William 452, 580
Franklin, Benjamin 342
Fraser, Nancy 599, 606
Frede, Michael 459
Freeland 602
Freeman, Samuel 515, 516, 518, 519, 520, 524,
    525, 531, 535, 537, 538, 539, 543, 546
Frege, Gottlob 256, 352, 381, 382, 393, 394,
    449, 450, 453, 455, 482, 484, 491, 498, 499,
    501, 504–10
Freud 185, 236, 237, 608
Freudenthal 503
Frey 244
Fricker 599
Frickey 562

Fried, B. H. 557
Fried, Charles 572, 590
Friedman, Marilyn 602, 603
Friedman, Michael 324, 353, 354, 363, 368,
    380
Frost 358
Frye, Northrop 20
Fuller, Lon 551, 552, 563–4
Fuller, Margaret 38

Gödel 352, 454, 456, 457
Gadamer, Hans-Georg 434
Gale, Richard 60, 73
Galison 367
Gallup 155
Garry, Ann ix, xi, 595, 599
Garside, Christine 597
Garver 390
Gauthier 405
Gaynesford 375, 388
Geach, Peter 469
Gemes, Ken 404, 413
George, Alexander 483
George, Robert P. 571
Gert 589
Gertner 562
Gettier, Edmund 459, 472
Gewirth, Alan 587
Giaquinto 483
Gibbard 472
Gibbons, Alice Howe 62
Giere 367
Gifford 63, 450
Gilligan, Carol 563, 588, 596, 602
Girel 24, 27
Glock, Hans-Johann viii, xi, 311, 375, 382, 391,
    392, 395, 396, 397
Glymour, Clark 366, 405
Godfrey-Smith 94
Goldfarb, W. 393, 395, 503
Goldman, A. 472
Good 256, 259
Goodman, Nelson 257, 356, 358, 364, 452, 458,
    464
Goodman, Russell B. vii, xi, 31, 33, 197, 210
Gornick 598
Gouinlock 90
Gould, Timothy 35
Gould, Carol C. 597

Govier, Trudy 598
Gowans, Christopher 273
Gray 490
Green, Michael 571
Green, Warren x
Greenlee 132
Grice P. 331, 377, 387, 454, 458
Griffin, D. 224
Griffin, J. 590
Grosholz 497
Grover 424
Guelzo, Allen 9, 15
Gunn 258
Gupta 405
Gutmann 515, 516

Haack, Susan 187, 218, 258, 272, 598
Habermas, Jürgen 201, 257, 258
Hacker 379, 380, 385, 390, 394
Hacking, Ian 94, 367
Haeckel, Ernst 348
Hahn 291, 380, 457
Hale, C. Jacob 611, 612, 617
Hale, Robert 556, 557, 563
Hallett 391
Hampshire, Stuart 377, 454, 458
Hampton, Jean 587, 588
Hansen 599
Hanson, N. R. 363
Haraway 605
Hardcastle 360
Harding, Sandra 366, 603, 604, 605, 606
Harman, Gilbert 331, 459, 472, 586
Haroutunian, Joseph 15
Harper R. S. 62
Harsanyi, John 583, 584, 585
Hart, H. L. A. 458, 471, 571
Hart, Henry M. 559
Hart, R. 258
Hartley 47, 546
Hartshorne, Charles 153, 230
Haslanger 605, 606, 607, 612, 618
Hass 599
Hatfield 340, 348
Haugeland, John 404, 422, 423, 424, 425
Hausman C. 16, 258
Hausman D. 562
Hawking 230
Hayes 342

Heath, Joseph viii, xi, 235, 246
Hedge 22
Heereboord 5
Hegel, G. W. F. 28, 39, 41, 47, 48, 49, 50, 51,
    52, 53, 57, 58, 104, 171, 173, 179, 180, 181,
    182, 183, 200, 229, 237, 264, 347, 404, 415,
    419, 426, 444
Heidegger, M. 33, 132, 158, 393, 404, 422, 426,
    430, 431, 432
Held 602
Hellman 496
Helmholtz 491
Hempel, Carl 352, 354, 355, 357, 361, 362, 364,
    365, 367, 386, 431, 454, 455, 460, 485, 486
Henderson 348
Henkin, Leon 456
Herder 171, 172, 177, 178, 179, 182, 183
Herget 552
Haldane 359
Herman 587
Hershovitz 570
Heyes, Cressida 617
Hibbert 63
Hickman 256
Higginbotham 465
Hilbert 455, 482, 483, 503, 504, 507
Hildebrand 90, 256
Hill, Thomas Jr. 587
Hintikka 378, 380, 391, 395
Hitler, A. 216
Hoagland 602
Hobbes, T. 75
Hodges 134
Hodgson 246
Hohfeld, Wesley 572
Holbrook, Clyde 11
Hollinger 351
Holmes, Oliver Wendell 61, 198, 552, 553, 554,
    555, 568
Holt, E. B. 451
Holt, Henry 62
Holton, Gerald 360, 362
Honneth 106
Hook, Sidney 258, 259, 260, 261, 262, 265, 266
Hooker, Brad ix, xii, 578, 589
Hookway, Christopher viii, xii, 269, 286, 287,
    307
Hopkins, Patrick 596
Hopkins, Samuel 15

Hornsby 599
Horwitz 559
Houser 450
Howard, Don 362, 364
Hull, David 367
Hume, David 14, 32, 46, 48, 52, 134, 291, 293, 295, 296, 389, 588
Hurka, Thomas 588
Hurley 538, 544
Husserl, Edmund 129
Hutcheson 3, 14, 553, 555
Hutchins Robert M. 356
Hutchinson, Abigail 2
Hylton 290, 304, 310, 327
Hyman, John xi, 375

Ingersoll, Charles Jared 343
Irzik 363
Ishiguro 378, 393

Jackman, Henry vii, xii, 60, 65, 68, 69, 79
Jacobs, Jane 236
Jacquette 483
Jaggar, Alison 598, 599, 601, 603
James, William vii, xi, xii, xiii, 16, 19, 20, 21, 22, 23, 24–8, 32, 33, 34, 35, 39, 40, 42, 55, 56, 57, 58, 60–84, 91, 110, 113, 115, 117, 127, 128, 131, 146, 152, 158, 160, 169, 171, 172, 173, 174, 175, 176, 177, 179, 180, 181, 182, 185, 186, 187, 192, 193, 197, 198, 199, 200, 201, 202, 205, 206, 207, 208, 209, 210, 211, 212, 213, 214, 215, 216, 218, 219, 225, 257, 258, 263, 269, 270, 271, 276, 285, 290, 320, 343, 348, 349, 356, 396, 397, 450, 452, 458, 473, 485, 578, 579, 588
Jefferson, Thomas 342, 578
Jeffrey, Richard 362, 364, 455, 459
Jesus 8, 10
Jevons, Stanley 46
Jhering, Rudolf von 552
Jones 546
Jordan 74
Joyce, James 160
Julius, A. 546

Köhler, Wolfgang 359
Kagan, Shelly 472, 587, 590
Kaldor 560
Kalhat, Javier 375
Kamm, Frances 590

Kant, I. 15, 21, 32, 33, 39, 41, 43, 47, 48, 49, 50, 51, 53, 110, 112, 130, 131, 132, 134, 136, 219, 264, 271, 274, 279, 281, 282, 283, 287, 288, 331, 380, 389, 390, 404, 409, 426, 435, 440, 451, 452, 483, 484, 486, 488, 489, 490, 491, 492, 493, 494, 499, 500, 501, 502, 503, 504, 505, 508, 509, 571, 586, 587, 588, 590
Kaplan, David 377, 455, 459, 463, 464, 466
Katz, Jerrold 264
Kazmi 463
Keats, John 20, 21, 31
Keller 367, 605
Kelman 563
Kelsen, Hans 571
Kemp, Catherine 169
Kennedy 70
Kerr 138, 139
Ketner 485
Keyser, Cassius 47
Kierkegaard 393
Kim, Jaegwon 439, 440
Kirchhoff 346
Kirk 327, 329, 440
Kitcher, Philip 367, 483, 497
Kittay 603
Klagge 390
Kleene, Stephen 456
Klein, Alex 60, 62, 219
Kloppenberg 186
Klyce, Skudder 91
Kober 385
Kornblith 68
Korsgaard, Christine 96, 587
Kourany 599
Kramer 564
Kraus, E. 225
Kraus, J. 571
Kremer, Michael 404
Kremer, P. 411
Kripke, S. 299, 318, 322, 365, 376, 377, 389, 390, 398, 453, 459, 463, 464, 466–8, 474
Kuhn, Thomas 53, 363, 365, 366, 433, 472
Kukla, Rebecca xii, 405, 417, 418, 424, 426
Kuklick, Bruce 216, 258, 343, 473
Kyburg, Henry 364
Kymlicka 515, 528, 537, 538

Lachs 134, 137, 138, 139
Lackey 376

Lakatos, Imre 366, 497, 509
Lakoff 483
Lalleman, Theo 160
Lambert 488
Lance, Mark viii, xii, 403, 408, 411, 412, 417, 418, 424
Lane 258
Langdell, Christopher Columbus 554
Lange, Marc 404, 425
Lange, Lynda 602
Langer, K. 386
Langford, C. H. 453
Lango, John W. viii, xii, 224, 225, 227, 229, 231
Laplace 25, 54
Lara, María, Pía 596, 603
Larson 465
Laudan, Larry 366
Lawrence 562
Lawson 138, 139
Lazerowitz, Morris 384, 385
Lear 396
Lee, Sang 5, 15
Lehrer, Keith 459
Leibenstein, Harvey 244
Leibniz 48, 129, 230, 307, 490
Leiter, Brian 551, 557, 572
Lemke, Siegland 177
Leonardo 55
Lepore, Ernest 440
Lesniewski 457
Levi, Isaac 219
Lewis, C. I. viii, 132, 134, 215, 217, 219, 257, 269–88, 357, 381, 452, 453, 458, 473
Lewis, David 64, 459, 463, 464, 472, 474
Lippmann, Walter 89, 101
Littleton 603
Llewellyn, Karl 552, 556–7
Lloyd 605, 606
Locke, John 3, 4, 9, 12, 46, 47, 174, 410
Longino, Helen 367, 604, 605, 606
Lovejoy, A. O. 186, 359, 451
Lowe 224
Lowell 379
Lucas 228, 232
Lucretius 128
Ludlow, Peter 465
Ludwig, Kirk 440
Lugones, María 603, 611, 616

Lukasiewicz 457
Lukes 516
Lycan 472
Lyons, David 571, 583

Macbeth, Danielle viii, xii, 404, 412, 482, 487, 490, 499, 504, 506, 507, 508
MacFarlane, John 405
MacGilvray 90, 258
Mach, Ernst 340, 347, 348, 380
MacIntyre, Alasdair 588
MacKinnon, Catharine 563, 596, 602, 603, 612, 613
Maddy 495
Maher 408
Malcolm, Norman 384, 385, 386, 387, 388, 390, 393, 452, 459
Malebranche 5
Malisoff, William 351, 359, 360
Manders 498
Manuel, Frank E. 178, 179
Marcus, Ruth 453, 462, 463
Marcuse, Herbert 259, 366
Margenau, Henry 359, 360
Marion 390
Marsden 2, 3, 6
Marsh, James 28
Marshall 244
Marsoobian 377
Martin, Tony 459
Marx, Karl 170, 185, 235, 236, 237, 240, 248, 249, 258, 259, 362, 517, 563, 603, 604
Maxwell x
May 596
Mayhew, Jonathan 11
McCarthy 254, 255, 393
McCord 587
McCormick 126
McCosh, James 343
McCumber, John 255, 257
McDermott, Gerald 9
McDermott, J. 256
McDermott, M. 332, 333
McDowell, John 377, 378, 388, 389, 390, 397, 404, 412, 420, 422, 423, 424
McFarland 236
McGee 322
McGinn 130
McKeon, Richard 356

McKinsey, Michael 459
McMahan, Jeff 590
Mead, George Herbert vii, 145–66, 174, 182, 236, 356, 396, 397
Mead, Hiram 145
Melamed, A. D. 561
Menand, Louis 190, 198, 199, 208, 217, 255, 258, 348, 356, 552
Menger, Karl 352
Merleau-Ponty 404, 422, 426
Meyers 602, 607
Mill, Harriet Taylor 598
Mill, John Stuart 30, 380, 582, 598
Miller, A. 390
Miller, D. 517, 537, 546
Miller, Perry 3, 15
Miller, R. 537, 538, 546
Millett, Kate 597
Misak, Cheryl viii, xii, 43, 60, 81, 101, 189, 190, 194, 197, 201, 202, 203, 212, 214, 218, 269, 290, 291, 317, 354, 375, 450, 515
Monk 384, 396
Montague, R. 456, 459, 463, 464
Montague, W. P. 359, 382
Moore, A. W. 218, 356
Moore, G. E. 138 , 200, 210, 212, 213, 214, 384, 385, 386, 451, 453, 454, 579, 580, 583, 588
Moore, M.S. 570, 572
Moran, R. 598
More, Henry 4
Morgan, C. Lloyd 146, 151
Morgan, T. H. 359
Morgenbesser 215
Mormann 354
Morris, Charles W. 146, 153, 216, 352, 355, 356, 357, 358, 361
Mothersill 597
Mounce 258
Moyal-Sharrock 391
Muller, H. J. 359
Mumford 90
Munzer, Stephen R. 572
Murphey, J. P. 258, 290
Murphey, L. 531, 535
Murphey, Murray 270, 276, 277, 278, 279
Murphy, Mark C. 571
Murray, 201
Musgrave 366

Núñez 483
Nagel, Ernest 217, 257, 351, 352, 356, 358, 367, 452, 472, 488, 490, 503
Nagel, Thomas 130, 459, 469, 516, 529, 531, 535, 537, 541, 545, 546
Nakhnikian, George 459
Narayan 603
Narveson 517
Nehamas 405
Nelson, H. L. 603, 604, 605
Neurath, Otto 216, 219, 291, 353, 355, 380, 381, 431
Newman, James R. 452
Newman, M. H. A. 321
Newton, Sir Isaac 4, 311, 342
Nicholson 599, 606
Nielsen 517
Nietzsche 98, 348, 430, 431, 433
Noddings, Nell 588, 603
Norcross 589
Nozick, Robert 312, 458, 470, 471, 517, 520, 587
Nussbaum, Martha 516, 523, 525, 562, 603, 607, 608, 612, 613, 614, 615
Nye, A. 599

O'Connor 617
O'Leary-Hawthorne 412
O'Neill, Onora 587
Ockham 45, 46, 47, 135
Okin 602, 603
Oliver, Kelly 599
Oppenheim, F. 16, 119
Oppenheim, Paul 355, 456
Ostwald, Wilhelm 340

Pap, Arthur 361
Pappini, Giovanni 186
Parfit, Derek 588
Parker, Kelly A. vii, xii, 110
Parmenides 41
Parsons 495, 496
Passmore 451
Paulson, Stanley L. 571
Peano 450, 504
Pears, David 378, 458
Pearsall 599
Peirce, C. S. v, vii, viii, xiii, 4, 15, 22, 33, 38–59, 61, 81, 84, 92, 101, 110, 111, 115,

116, 117, 118, 119, 120, 121, 122, 123, 127,
128, 129, 130, 131, 133, 137, 147, 149, 153,
154, 160, 161, 162, 185, 186, 187, 188, 189,
192, 197, 198, 199, 200, 201, 202, 203, 204,
205, 206, 207, 208, 210, 212, 213, 214, 216,
217, 218, 219, 220, 257, 258, 263, 269, 270,
271, 279, 284, 285, 286, 287, 288, 290, 291,
340, 341, 345, 346, 347, 348, 349, 350, 354,
356, 358, 397, 449, 450, 451, 452, 458, 473,
483, 484, 485, 491, 492, 493, 497, 498, 499,
504, 508, 509, 510, 578, 579
Peregrin 411
Perry, R. B. 21, 25, 451, 452, 473, 579
Phelps 260
Philipp 375
Picker 562
Pierce, Christine 598
Pierik 538
Pietroski, Paul 439, 440
Pinkard, T. 405
Pirandello, Luigi 144
Pitt, David 595
Planck, Max 340, 353, 455
Plantinga, Alvin 459, 473
Plato 15, 32, 34, 41, 44, 45, 129, 138, 149, 161,
225, 380, 397, 435, 494, 495, 496, 498, 499,
503, 505, 553, 599, 602
Playfair, John 488
Plotinus 22, 229
Poe, Edgar Allan 343
Pogge, Thomas 517, 519, 535, 538, 545
Poincaré, Henri 340
Pojman 74
Popper, Karl 366
Porter, Noah 343
Posner, Richard 194, 561, 652, 571
Postema, Gerald J. 571
Potter, Andrew xi
Pound, Roscoe 552, 553
Pratt, James 64, 65, 191, 201, 212, 213, 214,
215, 218
Price, Huw 194, 244
Price, R. 580
Prichard, H. A. 579, 580
Prior, Arthur 463
Proops 394
Ptolemy 78
Putnam, Hilary xi, 67, 75, 91, 93, 100, 101, 127,
128, 185, 186, 187, 189, 193, 194, 219, 257,

258, 361, 363, 365, 376, 377, 387, 388, 397,
449, 455, 458, 466, 472, 483, 485, 495, 497
Putnam, R. A. 91
Pyrrho 392

Quine, W. V. O. viii, 201, 219, 229, 257, 265,
266, 269, 271, 284, 285, 288, 290–334, 352,
356, 357, 358, 362, 367, 376, 381, 382, 383,
386, 388, 396, 397, 398, 403, 411, 426, 430,
434, 435, 443, 449, 451, 452, 454, 456, 457,
458, 460–1, 462, 463, 466, 467, 473, 483,
493, 494, 495, 496, 497
Quinn, Warren 590

Rachels, James 590
Railton, Peter 587, 588, 589
Ramberg, Bjørn viii, xiii, 430
Ramsey, Paul 13
Ransdell 41
Raposa 15
Rashdall 580
Ravizza, Mark 590
Rawls, John 257, 264, 403, 458, 468, 469, 470,
471, 516, 517, 518, 519–35, 537, 538, 541,
544, 545, 546, 580, 581, 582, 583, 584, 585,
586, 587, 588
Raz, Joseph 471
Read 393
Reck 145
Reed, Adolph L. 170
Reichenbach, Hans 352, 353, 354, 355, 358,
359, 361, 365, 386, 454, 455, 457, 459
Reid, Thomas 41, 47, 343, 580
Reisch 355, 357, 363
Rescher, N. 228, 405
Resnick 496
Restall 411
Rich 612
Richard 463
Richards, D. A. J. 584
Richards, I. A. 153
Richardson, Alan viii, xiii, 339, 353, 363
Richardson, Henry 89, 90, 103
Richerson, Peter 246, 247, 249
Ricketts 393
Riemann 490
Ring, Merrill 377
Robin 199
Roemer, John 517

Roosevelt, Franklin D. 556
Rorty, Richard v, viii, xi, xiii, 39, 42, 90, 127,
    128, 131, 185, 186, 187, 192, 193, 194, 198,
    199, 201, 202, 214, 216, 218, 256, 258, 263,
    264, 266, 271, 285, 393, 396, 405, 424,
    430–47, 485, 613
Rosenberg, Jay 404
Rosenthal 258
Ross, W. D. 579, 580
Rosser, J. B. 456
Rota 498
Rotman 499
Rouse, Joe 405, 422, 425
Rousseau 104, 179, 211, 608
Royce, Josiah vii, xii, 16, 40, 52, 55, 57, 58, 64,
    84, 110–23, 126, 127, 128, 131, 146, 205,
    215, 269, 270, 348, 452, 473
Ruddick, 602
Rudner, Richard 359
Rush, Benjamin 342
Russell, Bertrand 23, 92, 134, 138, 197, 198,
    200, 210, 211, 212, 214, 215, 216, 225, 226,
    230, 256, 259, 292, 293, 304, 321, 347, 352,
    358, 359, 361, 379, 381, 382, 394, 449, 451,
    453, 454, 457, 482, 483, 504, 509, 580
Russell, Francis 55
Russell, John E. 65
Ryan, Alan 87, 90, 188
Ryder 377
Ryle, Gilbert 458

Saatkamp 128
Sacks, Albert M. 559
Salmon, Wesley 361, 364
Sandoval 603
Sangiovanni 546
Santayana, George vii, xiii, 125–40, 179, 225,
    348, 350, 451
Sarton, George 359
Sartre x
Sass 395
Saul, Jennifer 269
Sayre-McCord 587
Scanlon, T. M. 459, 471, 517, 537, 539, 572, 587
Schauer, Frederick 571
Scheffler, Israel 458
Scheffler, Samuel 472, 517, 518, 531, 535, 537,
    538, 539, 546, 590

Schelling, Friedrich 21, 22, 32, 44, 47, 48, 51,
    52, 54
Schelling, T. C. 248, 343
Scheman 607, 617
Schiller 40, 55, 186, 200, 201, 202, 205, 213
Schilpp, Paul A. 225, 231
Schinz, Albert 87, 202
Schlick, Moritz 291, 293, 317, 352, 353, 354,
    359, 379, 380, 454, 457
Schneider 343
Schor 246
Schroeder 287, 387
Schumpeter, Joseph 243
Schutte 603
Schwyzer 390
Scott, Dana 456
Scotus, Duns 43, 45, 46, 53
Searle, John 257, 264, 377, 387, 469, 472
Sebeok 155
Segal 465
Seibt, Johanna 405
Seigfried, Charlene Haddock 599
Sellars, Wilfrid 82, 257, 271, 272, 361, 363, 377,
    389, 397, 403–26, 434, 435, 436, 451, 455,
    459, 460, 484, 485, 510
Sen, Amartya 515, 517, 522, 523, 524, 525, 526,
    527, 528, 537, 545, 613
Shanker 390
Shapere, Dudley 366
Shapiro 311, 312, 483, 496, 571
Sheffer, Henry 384
Shepard, Thomas 7
Sher, George 587, 590
Sherwin, Susan 598, 602
Shimony, Abner 362
Shoemaker, Sydney 459, 472
Shook 200
Shorey 126
Shrage 602
Sidgwick, Henry 579, 580
Singer, Edgar A. 340, 348, 359
Sinnott-Armstrong 588
Skinner, B. F. 146, 360
Sklar 354
Sleigh, Robert 459
Slote, Michael 588
Sluga 378
Smith, Adam 173, 176, 180

Smith, John E. 2, 7, 15
Smullyan 463
Soames, Scott viii, xiii, 216, 440, 461, 462, 463, 465, 467, 468
Socrates 39, 41, 138, 139, 504
Sommer, Frank Henry 472
Spelman, Elizabeth 603, 616
Spencer, Herbert 25, 237, 348
Spinoza 32, 39, 128, 129, 307
Sprigge 132, 136, 139
Stace, Walter 581
Stadler 340, 352
Stallo, John Bernhard 347
Stalnaker, Robert 459, 460, 463, 464, 467
Stearns 562
Stein, Howard 362, 490
Steiner, Hillel 587
Stern, David 375, 378, 391, 392
Stevens, S. S. 360
Stevenson, C. L. 459, 460, 468, 469, 580
Stewart 47, 343
Stich 72
Stidd 393
Stockbridge 8
Stoddard, Solomon 2, 8
Stout, H. S. 3
Stout, J. 258
Strawson 69, 311, 331, 408
Strikwerda 596
Stroll 391
Strong 65
Stroud, Barry 390
Stuhr 90, 132, 265
Stump 367
Sturgeon, Nicholas 587
Stutzer 244
Suckiel 73, 206
Sullivan, Shannon 599
Summer 590
Sumner, L. Wayne 587
Sunstein 562
Suppe 363
Swedenborg 61
Sypnowich 636

Talisse, Robert B. viii, xiii, 194, 197, 254, 257
Tan, Kok-Chor ix, xiii, 515, 533, 538, 546
Tappenden, J. 490, 498
Tarski, Alfred 352, 358, 381, 382, 454, 456, 457, 460–4, 494, 505

Taylor, John 11, 12
Taylor 405
Tennyson, A. 115
Thalma, Leon E. 160
Thau, M. 472
Thomas, Frederick W. x
Thompson, M. 504
Thomson, Judith Jarvis 580, 587, 590, 598
Thoreau, Henry David 33, 34, 35, 61, 343
Tiles, J.E. 94, 97
Tiller, Glenn vii, xiii, 125, 138
Tilman, R. 236, 237
Tolman, R. C. 359
Tong, Rosemarie 318, 603
Tool, M. 238
Toulmin, Stephen 582
Trammell, R. 222
Trebilcot, Joyce 598
Tremain 611
Truman, H. 254
Tufts, James 91, 579
Twining, W. 556
Tye, M. 472

Uebel, Thomas xiii, 354
Unger, P. 82
Upham, Thomas 343
Urmson, J. O. 377, 454, 458, 582, 583

Van Fraassen, Bas 297, 298, 367, 368, 404, 473
Van Parijs, Philippe 517, 538, 546
Veblen, Thorstein viii, 235–51
Velleman, D. 583
Vernallis, Kayley 595
Vetterling 598
Viète 487
Vlastos, Gregory 455

Wadsworth, T. 11
Waismann 294, 380
Walker, M. 603
Wallace, R. J. 590
Wallace, S. 552
Walton, Kendall 473
Ward, Roger A. vii, xiii, 1, 8, 16
Wartofsky, M. 362, 597
Washington, George 342
Wasserstrom, R. 598
Watson, John B. 146, 147, 161

Watts, Isaac 10
Weber, M. 351
Weber, Michel 224, 228
Wechsler, H. 559
Weed, F. 247
Weierstrass 490
Weiss, Paul 153, 359
Welchman, J. 587
Wellman, Carl 587
West, C. 256, 258
West, R. 563
Westbrook, Robert viii, xiii, 87, 89, 90, 101,
    194, 256, 258
Westman, C. 359
Whewell 46
Whitby, Daniel 9, 10
White, H. 408, 454, 457, 458
White, Morton 15, 87, 90
Whitehead, Alfred North viii, xii, 146, 149,
    150, 224–33, 357, 386, 449, 454, 482
Wiggins, David 257
Wigner, E. 359
Williams, A. 535
Williams, Donald C. 126,
Williams, M. 134, 394, 397
Williams, Wendy W. 604
Wilshire, Bruce 256, 257

Wilson, D. 345
Wilson, Margaret 459
Wilson, Mark 490, 498
Winch 378, 390
Wiseman 557
Witt 606,
Wittgenstein, Ludwig viii, xi, 33, 210, 257, 303,
    318, 362, 363, 375–98, 404, 426, 432, 443,
    453, 458, 459, 580, 612, 616, 617, 618
Wittig, Monique 612
Wolf, Susan 590
Wolff, J. 539
Woolley, H. T. 218
Wordsworth, William 20, 21, 30, 33
Wright, Chauncey 198, 348
Wright, Crispin 257, 311, 328, 390, 483
Wright, Sewell 359
Wundt, Wilhelm 146, 152

Young, Iris Marion 599, 602, 607

Zack, Naomi 608, 612, 613, 614, 615, 616, 617,
    618
Zahar, E. 366
Zamir, Shamoon 173, 174, 179
Zermelo 482, 483
Ziff, Paul 473

SUBJECT INDEX

abduction 42, 43, 47, 122, 204, 346–7, 363
aesthetics 54, 87, 264, 343, 386, 473
analytic/synthetic 411, 412, 490–1
assertion 93, 95, 98, 113–14, 116, 119, 132,
    191, 193, 203, 397, 410, 412, 419, 424,
    555
atomism 48, 134, 230–1, 263, 378, 383

behaviorism 147, 155, 164, 386–7
belief 30, 45–6, 56–8, 60, 68–74, 77, 79–80,
    84, 92–4, 113, 132–8, 145, 147, 154, 183,
    186–194, 199, 203–14, 218–19, 267, 271,
    279, 292–3, 296, 299, 300–1, 304, 309,
    325, 345, 419, 423, 438, 453, 469, 472, 493,
    535, 556, 566–7, 580

capitalism 235, 240, 430, 470,
causation 82, 230–1, 271, 346, 439–40, 464,
    555, 571
Cartesianism 376
categorical 114, 307–9, 313, 586
cognitivism/non-cognitivism 453, 468
Cold War viii, 87, 198–9, 254–5, 257–60, 263,
    266
colonial 606
common sense 9, 45, 47, 64, 65, 66, 82, 83, 114,
    130–1, 132, 204, 251, 388, 451, 453, 556
community 3, 16, 39, 41–2, 49, 53, 57, 59,
    110–11, 115–17, 120, 158, 160, 162, 164,
    166, 189, 193, 198, 218, 242, 249, 262, 264,
    266, 305, 351, 352, 364–5, 390, 403–4,
    438, 451, 474, 566, 580, 611
conceivability 467
consciousness vii, 4, 5, 11, 12, 29, 32, 61, 75,
    114, 130, 132, 133–34, 147–8, 156, 159,
    161, 171, 173–5, 179–82, 205, 276, 278,
    286, 293, 387, 415, 434, 472
conventionalism 390
convergence 43, 81, 84

correspondence theory 25, 62, 65, 187, 202,
    218, 263, 425, 438

deduction 42, 44, 346, 502, 554
deflationism 424
democracy vii, xiii, 31, 32, 70, 87, 91, 100–1,
    102, 104–5, 106, 194, 209, 216, 255, 260,
    261, 262, 266, 445, 537, 538
determinism 10, 69

empiricism 21, 22, 23, 29, 30, 32, 56, 65, 75,
    96, 99, 134, 208, 216–17, 219, 263, 271,
    272, 285, 290, 291, 292–3, 296, 297–8,
    299–300, 317, 330–4, 352, 356, 360, 362,
    367, 380, 381, 389, 420, 455, 457, 473, 604
epistemology v, xi, 29, 33, 52–3, 87, 106, 110,
    166, 204, 208, 226, 264, 270–3, 281, 283,
    290, 298–9, 305, 309, 319, 321, 325, 329,
    331, 333, 349, 353, 378, 386, 403, 420–1,
    430, 433–5, 438–41, 450, 472, 579, 597,
    601, 604–6,
equality ix, 470, 515–18, 520–9, 531–3,
    536–40, 542–7, 584, 602
essence ix, 5, 10, 49, 64, 74, 79, 115, 126, 129,
    130, 132, 133, 134, 136, 137, 138, 180, 346,
    378, 379, 388, 393, 407, 412, 437, 447, 468,
    595, 608–9, 610, 611, 612, 613, 614, 616
essentialism 263, 376, 467, 498, 595, 600, 601,
    607–8, 612–15,
ethics v, vii, xii, 54, 74, 85, 87, 91, 101–2, 104,
    110–11, 166, 173, 194, 206, 209, 217, 259,
    263, 264, 270, 353, 394, 403, 430, 459, 468,
    472, 556, 579, 581–2, 584, 587–8, 597,
    598, 600–4, 618
evolution 29, 32, 39, 40, 42, 44, 48, 50, 51,
    53–5, 72, 79, 163, 188, 199, 208, 235, 236,
    239, 246–7, 263, 273, 303, 312, 314, 341,
    349, 363, 365, 378, 398, 416, 433, 438, 468,
    472, 606, 608

fallibilism/infallibilism 51, 72, 76–7, 81, 84,
    92, 119, 121, 189, 198, 204, 219, 499
feminism ix, 595–8, 600, 603, 611–13, 615
foundationalism 187–9, 192, 219, 263, 272–3,
    281, 412
freedom 1, 9–11, 52, 54, 67, 79, 100, 137,
    164–5, 170, 180, 262, 311, 408, 444, 522,
    534, 534–5, 602

given, the viii, 269, 271–88, 357, 389, 412, 413,
    420, 423, 434, 452, 498, 500
grammar 53, 130, 134, 324, 394

habit 4, 5, 15, 92, 98, 214

idealism vii, 3, 6, 16, 23, 32, 40, 48, 51, 52, 54,
    64, 104, 110–13, 117, 119, 121, 190, 201,
    205, 214, 263, 385, 389, 451, 453
identity 3, 12, 82, 120, 129, 164, 178, 260, 318,
    324, 386, 414, 473, 562, 607, 611
individualism 48
induction 42, 44, 69, 134, 205, 293, 346, 364
inferentialism 409, 411
inquiry vii, xii, 3, 5, 10, 11, 13–16, 30, 40–3,
    45–7, 51–4, 56–7, 65, 68, 72–3, 78, 81–2,
    84, 87–95, 99–106, 111, 117, 120, 189–91,
    193–4, 197, 199, 202–5, 208–9, 217,
    219–20, 240, 259–61, 265, 271, 278, 291,
    295, 300, 312, 340–1, 345, 350, 441–4,
    447, 450, 468, 493, 497–9, 546,
    604–6
intentionality 66, 378, 388
interpretation 8, 12, 16, 34, 83–4, 88–91,
    115–18, 120, 121, 171, 192, 244, 270, 273,
    274, 276–8, 280–3, 297, 306, 319, 321,
    351, 380, 389–90, 393–5, 397, 465, 471,
    494, 543–5, 565–72, 586
intuition 15, 116, 279, 487–91, 502, 505, 540

judgment 2, 48, 73, 95, 97, 99, 112, 134, 159,
    175, 191, 241, 244, 391, 471, 484, 491, 493,
    500, 505, 555
justice xiii, 12, 24, 35, 306, 322–4, 380, 469,
    515–21, 523–7, 529–36, 538–47, 559–64,
    567, 583–4, 588, 600, 602, 613, 618
justification 12, 68–9, 71–2, 74, 188, 194,
    272–4, 281, 292–3, 295–6, 305, 326, 328,
    390, 392, 416, 420, 422–3, 465, 472, 555,
    560, 565, 584, 588, 603–4

knowledge xi, 2, 4, 13, 15, 20, 33, 35, 42, 50, 52,
    67–8, 88, 91–4, 100–1, 103, 107, 112–13,
    115, 117–18, 120–1, 132–6, 138, 140,
    149–50, 166, 187–8, 191, 206–8, 213, 218,
    225–7, 237, 257, 270, 272–4, 276–88, 334,
    340–2, 344, 352–4, 356, 358, 366, 379–80,
    397–8, 415, 417–20, 422, 433, 445–6, 449,
    452–3, 457, 465, 467–70, 472, 483, 486,
    489–93, 497, 499, 501–2, 505, 508–9, 519,
    531, 536, 561, 579–80, 584, 586, 598–9,
    604–5

law x, 6, 22, 53, 74, 158, 164, 178, 240, 244–5,
    251, 309, 311, 351, 364, 415, 439, 458, 468,
    471–2, 506, 509–10, 551–2, 554–72, 578,
    590, 596, 600–1, 603, 610
legal positivism 563–4, 567, 571
liberalism 165, 350, 515–16, 520
logic v, viii, xii, 38–40, 42–3, 45–8, 51, 53–8,
    78, 82, 87–9, 91–2, 94, 111, 114, 116–17,
    121, 123, 137, 150, 153, 164, 186, 191, 197,
    200, 202, 208, 216–19, 221, 225, 256, 264,
    265, 270, 294, 311–12, 319, 332–3,
    339–40, 345–7, 351–5, 357–9, 362, 364,
    366, 378–82, 384, 390, 393–4, 403, 411,
    418, 422, 449–50, 452–3, 455–9, 462–4,
    482–3, 485, 489–96, 498, 503–6, 508–10,
    552, 579, 599
logical empiricism xiii, 216–17, 352, 360, 380
logical positivism 255, 341, 351–64, 366–8,
    377–8, 380, 385, 455

mathematics viii, xii, 29, 42, 114, 123, 219,
    224, 226, 229, 311, 332, 333, 352–3,
    358–9, 376, 383–4, 390, 426, 455–6,
    482–6, 488–507, 509–10, 599
meaning 10, 12, 15, 32, 40, 43, 47, 52–4, 57–8,
    63, 65, 68–9, 76, 78–9, 83, 89, 93, 113,
    119, 137, 149, 151, 153, 159–61, 166,
    170–1, 185, 193–4, 210, 213–14, 217, 257,
    290–2, 302, 304, 308, 309, 316, 317, 320,
    323–6, 328–30, 332–4, 345–6, 351,
    354–5, 370, 376, 378, 380–3, 386–90,
    396–8, 406, 408–14, 434, 450, 453, 455–7,
    460–2, 464–8, 484–5, 487–9, 491–3, 503,
    505, 507, 516, 565, 614, 616
metaphysics viii, xii, 40–1, 43, 49, 54–7, 78,
    84, 87, 106, 110–11, 114–16, 119–20, 122,
    128, 150, 166, 187, 189, 203, 213, 216, 225,

227–32, 264, 270, 283, 343, 346–7, 350,
    353, 354, 362, 378–9, 382, 395, 403,
    417–18, 430–47, 450, 453, 472, 579, 595,
    601, 606–7, 613, 615, 617
morality xii, 8, 11, 14, 91, 102, 158–9, 176,
    207, 213, 265, 344, 416, 499, 540, 564, 586,
    588–9, 600–1, 618

natural kinds 54
naturalism 16, 60, 127, 219, 258–9, 264–6,
    291, 295, 299, 321, 344, 348, 350, 376–7,
    397, 436, 442–3, 451, 453, 466, 483, 495,
    579–80
nominalism 44–5, 47–8, 50–2, 54, 483, 496
normative 42, 54, 60, 70–1, 93, 105, 237,
    241–2, 246, 251, 273, 389, 398, 405–25,
    439, 444, 468–70, 516, 572, 581, 587, 599,
    600, 613–14
norms viii, 71–2, 78, 397, 403, 410, 413, 415,
    417–18, 421, 426, 557–8, 562, 571, 613

objectivity 74, 76–7, 84, 189, 198, 202, 206,
    209, 216, 220, 393, 440, 444–6, 498, 505,
    587, 603, 605

perception 4, 13–15, 26, 46, 56, 65, 83, 94,
    126, 134, 148, 150, 232, 271, 279, 282,
    285–7, 293, 347, 389, 425, 451–2, 562
phenomenology 50, 54, 179–80, 229, 271, 283,
    285–7, 377, 563, 599
pragmaticism 41, 47, 51, 53, 55, 56, 58, 186,
    200, 450
pragmatics 356, 418, 463
pragmatism v, vii, viii, x, xi, xiii, 19, 20, 24,
    27–8, 32, 38–41, 43–7, 51–3, 55–9, 63,
    72, 77, 78, 81, 88–90, 92–3, 104, 110–11,
    113, 115–18, 131, 138, 145–6, 149, 154,
    165–6, 185–6, 188–94, 197–202, 205–10,
    212–20, 236, 254–60, 263–6, 269–71,
    282–3, 291, 344–7, 349–50, 355–6, 358,
    360, 377, 388, 396–7, 403, 413, 418, 426,
    431–2, 437, 442–3, 445–6, 450–1, 473,
    484–6, 552, 558–9, 562, 579, 599, 603
probability 57, 113, 349, 358, 361, 382, 454–5
progress 70, 76, 128, 176, 178, 183, 251, 312,
    363, 365, 426, 441, 444–5, 463, 503, 546
puritanism 1–3, 7, 8, 126

rationalism 11, 116, 118, 263–4
rationality xi, 60, 63, 68–70, 72, 77, 90, 100,
    158–9, 172, 179, 238, 258–9, 365, 367,
    420–2, 433, 521, 560, 562, 603, 605
realism/anti-realism/quasi-realism 40, 43–5,
    47–9, 51, 53–4, 58, 94, 119, 122, 137, 193,
    263, 273, 280, 282–3, 285–7, 347, 350,
    362–3, 367, 451–2, 472, 551–3, 556–9,
    563, 587, 609
reality xi, 2, 3, 5, 11–15, 24, 26, 29, 35, 41, 43,
    47, 49–51, 53–4, 56, 65, 80, 82–3, 88, 94,
    106, 113–15, 118–22, 129, 149, 151–3,
    165, 181, 187, 193–4, 208–9, 224–33, 271,
    280, 282–5, 295, 314–15, 331, 362, 378,
    380–1, 383, 390, 393, 397, 425, 442, 444,
    452, 494, 503, 587, 606–7, 611
reason 15, 48, 50, 127, 351, 582
reasoning 45, 48–9, 51, 74, 96, 122, 207, 210,
    280, 319, 321, 346–7, 387, 395, 483,
    489–93, 496–500, 502, 510, 520, 521, 524,
    551, 553, 556–8, 563, 567–8, 575, 580,
    613
reference 16, 65–8, 93, 99, 104, 119, 149, 156,
    176, 179, 191, 201, 244, 301, 304, 308–9,
    314–16, 318, 323, 367, 383, 396, 406, 435,
    440, 460–3, 466, 467, 517, 522, 553, 565,
    569, 584, 586
relativism 108, 165, 194, 221, 366, 368, 394,
    398, 417, 586, 600
religion 3, 6–8, 15, 26, 32, 79, 80, 87, 111, 137,
    171, 213, 265, 342, 396, 445, 473,
    596–7
representationalism 434
revolution 188, 349, 438, 468
romanticism vii, 19–23, 25, 27–9, 31–3, 35,
    453

science v, viii, xiii, 32, 39, 42–3, 46, 53–4, 57,
    82, 87, 88, 90, 117, 128, 136–7, 171, 186,
    192, 202, 203, 207, 209, 211, 213, 216–17,
    219, 225, 227–9, 231, 240, 257, 259, 265,
    291–2, 294–5, 298–300, 311, 339–68,
    376, 379–82, 387, 391, 393, 396–8, 405,
    422, 425–6, 433, 443, 445, 449–56, 458–9,
    461, 469, 472, 485, 489–90, 492, 494–6,
    506, 554, 556–7, 574, 581, 587, 601,
    604–6, 618

scientism 237, 255, 257, 431,

semantics 83, 265, 328, 354, 356, 361, 364,
    381–2, 389, 391, 410–11, 424–5, 440, 455,
    461–5, 467, 494

skepticism/skeptic 30, 52, 78, 81, 126, 129,
    132–6, 138–9, 165, 187–90, 192–3,
    198–9, 210, 231, 366, 384–7, 457, 472,
    563

social construction 562, 607, 613

syntax 355–7, 364, 381, 394, 449, 458, 463,
    496, 503

technology 366

theology 3, 8, 13, 15, 16, 202, 230, 264, 344–5,
    499, 613

transcendental 33, 84, 111, 115, 121, 132–3,
    173–4, 202, 205, 213, 264, 555–6

truth xii, 4, 6, 11, 33, 39, 40, 42, 43, 45, 47–8,
    51, 53–8, 63–6, 68, 70–84, 101, 111–15,
    117, 119–23, 126, 129–30, 132, 136–9,
    149, 185, 187, 189–94, 197–206, 208–13,
    215–16, 218, 220, 228, 257, 263, 299, 300,
    307, 312, 318–19, 321, 326, 328, 331–4,
    345, 348, 354, 357, 379, 382–3, 387, 393,
    396, 410, 420–1, 424–5, 430, 435–9, 444,
    450–1, 453–4, 456–7, 460–7, 469, 484–5,
    487–8, 491, 493–4, 498, 503–10, 586–7,
    597, 607, 613

universals 230–2, 347

utility 236, 243, 396–7, 470, 520–1, 583–5

verificationism xii, 217, 291, 301, 328, 330,
    380, 387, 473